NUMISMATIC STUDIES

34

WEALTH AND WARFARE
The Archaeology of Money in Ancient Syria

Frédérique Duyrat

NUMISMATIC STUDIES

34

THE AMERICAN NUMISMATIC SOCIETY
NEW YORK
2016

ISSN 0517-404x
ISBN 978-0-89722-346-1

Library of Congress Cataloging-in-Publication Data

Names: Duyrat, Frãedãerique, author.
Title: Wealth and warfare : the archaeology of money in ancient Syria /
Frãedãerique Duyrat.
Description: New York : The American Numismatic Society, 2016. | Series:
Numismatic studies ; 34 | Includes bibliographical references and index.
Identifiers: LCCN 2016034512 | ISBN 9780897223461 (alkaline paper)
Subjects: LCSH: Coin hoards—Syria. | Syria—Antiquities. | Excavations
(Archaeology)—Syria. | Coins, Ancient—Syria. | Coins, Greek—Syria. |
Coins, Roman—Syria. | Money—Syria—History—To 1500. |
Wealth—Syria—History—To 1500. | Military history, Ancient.
Classification: LCC CJ277.S95 D78 2016 | DDC 737.495691—dc23
LC record available at https://lccn.loc.gov/2016034512

Printed in Canada

For Jérôme,
with whom nothing is impossible

"Se méfier des intellectuelles."
(Beware of intellectual women.)

C. Grimaud, *Futurs époux*, Paris, 1920
Part 3: Marriage, Chap. 3: Choice of Fiancée

Contents

List of Figures

Chapter 4: Before Alexander

Chapter 5: Alexander and the Successors (333–280 BC)

Chapter 6: The Two Syrias

Chapter 7: From Kings to Cities

List of Maps

List of Tables

Acknowledgements

(Rendering unto Caesar what is Caesar's)

This page of traditional acknowledgments is relatively short, and so inversely proportional to my gratitude for the colleagues and friends who have supported me throughout the effort of writing this book. Thomas Faucher, Julien Olivier, Alexandros Tzamalis, Oliver Hoover, Arthur Houghton, Catharine Lorber, Gabriella Bijovsky, Donald Ariel, and Haim Gitler updated me with always rare and valuable information on the constantly shifting data I was studying. François de Callataÿ has, as usual, displayed unequaled bibliographic generosity. Arnaud Suspène, my colleague at the University of Orléans, takes the prize for fellowship and tenacity in all our joint enterprises, past and still to come. Aurore Le Nestour has been a sure and lively guide who revealed to me the wealth of possibilities in the world of libraries. Olivier and Paule Picard always expressed complete confidence in me, making me want to carry on.

Thomas Faucher merits special mention. The cartographic material accompanying this volume would not exist without him, and this study would have lost a large part of its interest. He was never grudging with his time when it came to helping me with his computer expertise. I hope he will find this a token of my thanks for his adaptability, availability, and friendship.

Alain Bresson and Andrew Meadows encouraged me to delve more deeply into the issue of currency flows, which has now become the subject of a section in this volume. In economic history, I have benefited from the vast learning and open-mindedness of François Velde, Patrice Baubeau, and Jérôme Jambu. Although scholars in very different fields, they agreed to look at questions of economic history in antiquity that I brought to them, and they often guided me through the modern and contemporary bibliography. Andrew Meadows labored particularly to improve the manuscript and to see it through the publication process: an attentive and critical editor, he also generously shared the latest knowledge he had about the hoards I was studying. All errors, however, remain my responsibility.

I thank the American Numismatic Society for having accepted this book for publication, Bill Higgins for having agreed to translate this sometimes very technical prose with praiseworthy patience and numismatic interest (his translations of French literature appear with the initials WEH), and Andrew Reinhard for the patience and care he took while preparing the edition of this book.

I unfairly leave unnamed numerous colleagues and friends whose energy and ideas I have often borrowed. They know, however, that I do not forget them.

Last but not least, I could never have made the long march that the writing of this book represents without the unfailing support, confidence, and cooperation of Jérôme.

Frédérique Duyrat
Bibliothèque nationale de France, Paris

Preface[1]

I finished writing this book at the end of 2010 and submitted it to the Sorbonne on December 18th. The same day, people started to protest against the Tunisian government in Sidi Bouzid. Three weeks later,[2] Zine el-Abidine Ben Ali, president of the country for 25 years, had to flee Tunisia. Soon after, a revolutionary wave known as the Arab Spring touched all the Arab countries. In March 2011, the movement reached Syria. Non-violent protesters gathered in all the main cities of the country asking for more democracy and justice. During the following months, military operations in response to the protests gradually turned the movement into an armed revolution. By the end of the year, the Free Syrian Army was fighting the governmental forces, and Syria had entered a state of civil war.

Modern Syria is the core of this study, but understood in a broad sense, the "Syria" of the book's title also includes the territory of the neighboring states: Jordan, Lebanon, and Israel, as well as the margins of Turkey with the region of Iskenderun and the Turkish-Syrian border. None of those countries was as affected as Syria by the Arab Spring and the following events. At the beginning of 2012, a new protagonist entered the Syrian civil war: the al-Nusra Front.[3] Initially supported by the organization called The Islamic State of Iraq, the two organizations merged in April 2013 creating the Islamic State of Iraq and Al-Sham (ISIS or Daesh, the latter being the acronym of the name in Arabic).[4] Since then, Syria has been the theater of one of the most barbarous wars of recent centuries, characterized by war crimes and persecution of civilians.[5]

1. This preface largely relies on online newspapers and Wikipedia articles for the summary of the five last years. Most of the events mentioned are recent and have not yet benefitted from a synthesis by historians with the necessary distance. Data are scattered in the media.

2. 14th January 2011.

3. Jabhat al-Nuṣrah li-Ahli ash-Shām: The Support Front for the People of Al-Sham. http://en.wikipedia.org/wiki/Al-Nusra_Front. Accessed 8 November 2015.

4. Also called Islamic State of Iraq and the Levant (ISIL).

5. https://en.wikipedia.org/wiki/Islamic_State_of_Iraq_and_the_Levant. Accessed 8 November 2015.

Beyond the human aspect of this conflict, one of the distinctive features of the presence of ISIS in Syria is the treatment of cultural heritage. It takes two different forms. The most obvious is the systematic destruction of cultural heritage recently called "cultural cleansing" by UNESCO's Director-General Irina Bokova.[6] The list of the museums and archaeological sites destroyed, largely publicized by ISIS' propaganda, increases constantly.[7] The purpose is clear: to destroy the cultural heritage of any kind of "non-orthodox" culture, whether pre-Islamic, Christian, Muslim, or any other. Northern Iraq and Eastern Syria have been severely damaged since the beginning of this campaign in 2014.

But there is a second aspect to the "cultural strategy" of ISIS. This group is completely different from all the preceding forms of international terrorist organizations since it is only marginally dependent on foreign funding and possesses now an impressive war chest. While conquering the north of Iraq and the east of Syria, they also took control of oil and gas fields, as well as crop production areas (wheat and barley). Looting banks, drugs- and arms-trafficking, ransoming hostages, creating taxes, or extorting the eight million people living under their control and using false charities complete their revenue. The traffic of antiquities is also an essential resource for the group.[8] The resource represented by looting and illegal traffic of antiquities has been estimated at around $200 million per year, and may represent the second largest source of income for ISIS.[9] Specific attention appears to be devoted by ISIS to the administration of looting archaeological sites, as emphasized by Dr. Amr Al-Azm of Shawnee State University, Ohio:

> Islamic State or ISIS did not start the looting. They came across a pre-existing situation and institutionalized it," he says. "At first there was a casual arrangement to loot whereby ISIS applied an obscure Islamic tax of 20 per cent payable to the "State Treasury" but since the beginning of 2015 this has been formalized. You now have to have a licence issued by an "archaeological administration" office with punishments if you are caught digging an area where you are not allowed.[10]

The organization of more methodic looting is part of the process of trying to look like an organized state. During the summer of 2015, another event related to numismatics was part of

6. http://www.reuters.com/video/2014/11/02/iraqs-heritage-needs-protection-from-isl?videoId=3467-81460. Accessed 8 November 2015.

7. https://en.wikipedia.org/wiki/Destruction_of_cultural_heritage_by_ISIL. Accessed 8 November 2015.

8. Satellite imagery of looted, famous Syrian sites are available on the website of the American Association for the Advancement of Science. http://www.aaas.org/page/ancient-history-modern-destruction-assessing-status-syria-s-tentative-world-heritage-sites-7#Dura-Europos. Accessed 15 November 2015.

9. Oil may account for $800 million a year, http://www.newsweek.com/2014/11/14/how-does-isis-fund-its-reign-terror-282607.html. Accessed 14 November 2015. On the difficulty of evaluating these resources, see Interpol website: http://www.interpol.int/Crime-areas/Works-of-art/Frequently-asked-questions.

10. Interviewed by the Financial Times, 29 June 2015. http://www.ft.com/cms/s/0/fbecb8a2-09df-11e5-a6a8-00144feabdc0.html#axzz3rUbLLoX. Accessed 14 November 2015. See also references in Casana 2015, p. 149. Confirmed by an enquiry of journalist Simon Cox, BBC Radio 4, broadcast on Sunday, February 22, 2015: http://www.bbc.co.uk/programmes/b052j57v.

the same process. ISIS announced that it had restored the gold dinar as its official coinage, with subdivisions in silver—dirhams—and copper—fulus. The reverse of the one dinar coin is a world map, symbol of the appetite for conquest of ISIS. One mint was dismantled by the Turkish authorities in Turkey, in the region of Gaziantep. Contrary to the claim of ISIS, it seems that one part of the coins seized were in fact only gold plated.[11]

The pretention of developing a state organization remains only an appearance in many areas. Moreover, the chaos caused by this multiparty war is beneficial to different groups of looters. A recent study by Casana based on satellite images shows that all areas in the war zones are looted, whatever the political authority: the Kurdish People's Protection Unit (YPG), the Assad regime, the Syrian opposition, or ISIS.[12] According to this enquiry, areas under ISIS and the Assad regime's control have been pillaged using heavy machinery to dig the archaeological sites when other looters still use manual methods. However, the number of sites damaged would appear to be higher in areas under YPG and the Syrian opposition control, probably due to a phenomenon of "weakest centralised authority."[13] Of 15,000 sites in Syria, Casana estimates that 3,000 may have been looted during the last three or four years.

This pillaging directly feeds the antiquities market in Europe, Asia, and the United States. It is extremely difficult to identify objects coming from looting. If they have never been catalogued by a museum or in archaeological records, they have no established provenance. The sand or earth remaining on those artifacts is often the only sign of a recent archaeological discovery.[14] Coins are even more difficult to trace to their source. Mass-produced in large numbers and often circulating over wide areas, they have an intrinsic value when struck in precious metal, as well as an artistic and historical interest. Moreover, they can be easily found with basic metal detectors. They are mentioned in the red list of cultural objects published by the International council of museums (ICOM).[15] However, although an endangered category, not a single coin is shown on, for instance, the Interpol list of most wanted works of art.[16] Alerts regarding the looting of coins are extremely rare, although coins are often found in illegal commerce,[17]

11. Jambu 2015, with references to online data.

12. Casana 2015, table p. 151. Apamea was systematically looted, block by block, with heavy machinery and numerous workers, during the occupation by a Syrian government garrison between 2012 and 2013 (p. 150). Two-thirds of the site may have been looted, Gill 2015, p. 74. A similar situation is depicted in Ebla, Casana 2015, p. 151.

13. Casana 2015, p. 150.

14. Gill 2015 and http://www.bbc.co.uk/programmes/b052j57v.

15. http://icom.museum/resources/red-lists-database/red-list/syria/.

16. http://www.interpol.int/fr/Crime-areas/Works-of-art/Posters. It is interesting to observe that, among the numerous groups devoted to the protection of cultural heritage against looting and illegal traffic, no numismatist is a member of the board. See for instance: The Association for Research into Crimes against Art (ARCA), http://www.artcrimeresearch.org/our-people/; http://traffickingculture.org/people/, an association that "unites a diverse group of experts in the global fight against cultural racketeering: the illicit trade in antiquities by organized criminals and terrorist organizations"; or among the associates of the private company Art Recovery International http://artrecovery.com/About.

17. One alert concerning coins supposedly pillaged in Syria and sold on Facebook was posted on Twitter and relayed by globalvoice.org in June 2015, https://fr.globalvoices.org/2015/06/05/186876/.

or in military raids.[18] If the documents photographed by the Association for the Protection of Syrian Archaeology are authentic, it is noticeable that the licences for looting granted by ISIS to individuals cover "collecting antiquities and buried money."[19] Moreover, the looters' interest in numismatics has been emphasized by the discovery, in June 2015, of an ISIS cache containing weapons and a book with articles on numismatics.[20] As noticed by Wartenberg, it is an academic book probably stolen from a museum library, and it contains useful numismatic overviews on coinage issued in Syria from the 5th cent. BC to Byzantine times.[21] One of the main problems is that coins circulated, sometimes widely, sometimes only locally. It is very difficult to reach conclusions about their findspot when they have no archaeological context. Wartenberg devoted an article to the examination of three Syrian coinages, trying to determine the impact of the state of war in the country.[22] The answer remains rather uncertain. For the rare radiate issues of Zenobia and Vabalathus Augustus struck in Antioch, there has been a marked increase of items available for sale since 2012. But for the wreathed tetradrachms of Western Asia Minor that mostly circulated in Syria, it can be suggested that the generally increased number of coins available in commerce came from Syria, but it cannot be proven.

Coins are difficult to track, it is true. Issued in their millions, standardized, often bearing a high intrinsic value or at least a significant market value, they are among those small valuable objects that smugglers like to carry through borders.[23] However, the principles to improve the protection of cultural heritage are already well known. They have been promulgated in the 1970 UNESCO convention and start with "Inventories, export certificates, monitoring trade, imposition of penal or administrative sanctions, educational campaigns, etc." More precisely, article 5 states that each country must have national services: "establishing and keeping up to date, on the basis of a national inventory of protected property, a list of important public and private cultural property whose export would constitute an appreciable impoverishment of the national cultural heritage."[24] Scientific knowledge of the objects is fundamental to determine where they come from. It is very difficult to provide an up-to-date list of national coin collections, especially in countries with important archaeological resources. The French national collection or that of the American Numismatic Society, which contain very few coins from excavations, consist of more than 600,000 objects each. In a country like Syria, almost 100% of the coins come from excavations, legal or not. Their number is impossible to evaluate, and the

18. An example occurred in May 2015 when a US army operation against an ISIS leader led to the discovery of numerous artifacts. "More than half the items are coins made of gold, silver, and bronze". http://eca.state.gov/cultural-heritage-center/iraq-cultural-heritage-initiative/isil-leaders-loot.

19. http://apsa2011.com/apsanew/al-rikaz-department-of-isis-licenses-excavation-works-in-exchange-for-monetary-percentage/. Accessed 15 November 2015.

20. https://twitter.com/hasavrat/status/606138513428516864 relayed by Sam Hardy on his blog: https://conflictantiquities.wordpress.com/2015/06/04/ypg-confiscated-a-numismatic-book-from-turkish-islamic-state-fighters-in-syria-do-you-recognise-it/.

21. http://www.anspocketchange.org/isis-numismatics-and-conflict-antiquities/.

22. https://www.academia.edu/16306945/Collecting_Coins_and_the_Conflict_in_Syria.

23. http://www.bbc.co.uk/programmes/b052j57v and Gill 2015, p. 74.

24. http://www.unesco.org/new/fr/culture/themes/illicit-trafficking-of-cultural-property/1970-convention/.

number of potential new discoveries could be several millions. This sheer quantity means that any attempt to obtain an overview of coins in Syrian collections is hopeless.

However, if a description by object seems impossible today in Syria, while it is so common in all the major collections in the world,[25] other approaches are possible. Coins are issued by mints whose output can be evaluated as long as we possess a die study. Coins circulate, and their circulation can relatively safely be reconstructed, either through finds in archaeological context or through hoards. Coins in commerce or in museum collections have often lost their provenance. But as they are mass-produced objects, the missing data can partially be reconstructed. The aim of this book is precisely to establish the limits of what we can learn from coin circulation, to compare the data from commerce to the data from legal excavations, to try to understand the chronological evolution of coin circulation and how much political events or warfare affect it, to evaluate what coin finds tell us of the wealth and poverty of the people who collected them. But the method developed in this book would have no value without a critical examination of the source itself. One chapter has been devoted to how the contemporary history of the countries within the scope of this study has influenced the documentation. The recent history of this area has already consequences on the market: Syrian coins are scattered through sales all over the world. But this book determines more precisely than ever what circulated in the ancient Near East and can provide the patterns by which to evaluate the loss suffered by the Cultural Heritage of this region. If not at the level of the coin, at least at the level of the issue, the mint, or the number of hoards. It is a study of the ancient history of Syria (5th–1st cent. BC), based on a collection of evidence that ended when the current Syrian events were on the verge of beginning. However, it seeks to contribute to the knowledge of the Syrian Cultural heritage, with the hope it will be returned to its people one day.

Paris, November 16, 2015

25. For instance the ANS, http://numismatics.org/search/; Berlin Münzkabinett, http://ww2.smb.museum/ikmk/; London British Museum, http://www.britishmuseum.org/research/collection_online/search.aspx; Paris BnF, http://catalogue.bnf.fr/ and http://gallica.bnf.fr/.

Introduction

This work has its origins in my doctoral dissertation.[1] Seeking to map out the long lists of hoards where coins from Aradus appeared, I had to overcome obstacles I never imagined. First, I had to locate these hoards, sometimes found in villages of the Near East requiring maps in Arabic to pinpoint. Some, probably as a result of a mistake in their name, resisted my efforts, like the "Akken" Hoard (*CH* 2.95, **213**). Mapping requires computer abilities I do not have. At the French Institute of Near Eastern Archaeology I benefited from the unstinting collaboration of graphics specialist Sophie Vattéoni. While working on these hoards, I noticed that, in number at least, cartographic studies were rare—almost nonexistent for Syria—and that no overall study existed for the Near East. Pioneers in this field, Josette and Alain Elayi only provided maps without relief, drawn by hand, and limited to the circulation of Phoenician coins from the Persian period.[2] So I conceived the idea for this study, which assembles all the data that I have been able to gather on the hoards and archaeological excavations between the Mediterranean and the Euphrates, the foothills of the Taurus and Gaza, from the first deposits of the Achaemenid era to the end of the first century BC. Systematic collection of data stopped in 2010, the year I presented this study at the Sorbonne. The methodology, the merging and comparison of data, the conclusions that can be drawn, and the remaining margin of imprecision or error will have to be tested over a long time before achieving validation.

The maps in *Arados hellénistique* were the result of manual checking through printed maps, especially the 1:50,000 maps of the Free French Forces of the Levant. Technology having advanced a great deal since then, hoards and sites studied in the present volume have benefitted from a global reference system based on their geographical coordinates. As with my dissertation, I have enjoyed the help of a graphics specialist, in this case Thomas Faucher, a post-doctoral fellow in the research program NOMISMA, dedicated to the mapping of Greek hoards. During the last several years, the interest of Greek numismatists has, indeed, focused a great deal on these issues of mapping coin circulation. In addition to the NOMISMA program under the

1. Duyrat 2005a.
2. Elayi, Elayi 1993a.

direction of Marie-Christine Marcellesi at the Sorbonne (Paris 4), the American Numismatic Society has begun to provide, through the collaborative website nomisma.org, an interactive and evolving cartography of the hoards in the *Inventory of Greek Coin Hoards*.

In this favorable context, the effort offered here seeks to extend to a regional study the methods I employed for understanding the circulation of Aradian coin issues. The latter illustrate the city's choices, whether production of coins with an extensive orbit of circulation but without civic identity, such as Alexanders and pseudo-Ephesian drachms; or local tetradrachms for regional circulation, clearly struck with local types; or abundant production of bronzes which flow into the regional economy in proportions that elude us, largely because of the poor preserved sample[3] and the small amount of information archaeologists provide us about their coin finds. This situation is not peculiar to Aradus. Die-studies of bronze always produce poor ratios of specimens to dies, for two principal reasons. The first is that the copper-tin alloy is less ductile than silver or gold. Dies, therefore, were used up relatively quickly and probably broke often. Moreover, bronze coins are little hoarded, compared to silver and gold, with some exceptions. So they generally turn up in isolation, unprotected and very corroded. Less desirable, they were probably hoarded in proportions far inferior to their issued volumes, whereas gold and silver benefited from the reverse phenomenon. The die-to-specimen ratio of bronze thus combines two weak traits. One is inherent: to arrive at any given number of output, bronze required more dies when compared with coins in precious metal. The other is accidental: vis-à-vis original production, we possess proportionally less bronze than gold or silver.[4]

Bronze remains the poor relation in Hellenistic Syrian numismatics: there are few publications and few large catalogues devoted to it. There can be no question here of filling in this gap, but rather of trying to exploit the data collected in this volume's two catalogues where, very unequally, gold, silver, and bronze appear. A change of scale means that methods must also evolve to adapt to scrappy material, whose chronology is not always well established. This study will therefore propose some new options along the way.

Interest in hoards is nothing new. The first learned study of a recognized hoard is usually dated to 1765: the work of Joseph Pellerin, a passionate collector who gathered and catalogued some 35,500 Greek coins.[5] Pellerin's presentation is amazingly precise and highlights the man's learned qualities.[6] He establishes the hoard's provenance with a good deal of precision based on the statements of the individual who sold it to an agent in Latakia and then disappeared. Next,

3. Die frequency indices are often below 3 for bronze.

4. A recent paper by Gândilă 2009 emphasizes the strong and apparently reliable representation of bronze coins of the Byzantine period in public collections. But to reach the impressive coin-per-die ratio obtained by Picard for Thasos (sometimes 12:1!), a full corpus and die-study remain the only solution. Picard 2015, pp. 159–160.

5. Babelon 1901, p. 176. The French Royal Cabinet bought this entire collection: Sarmant 1994, pp. 136–39. I have kept Pellerin's publication as the first learned study of a hoard since it concerns a Syrian hoard, but Kinns 1990 has shown that the oldest article—25 pages—devoted to a hoard is, in fact, the work of G. S. Bayer, from 1729, concerning a group of coins of Erythrae. Still, he himself never calls this ensemble a hoard.

6. Pellerin 1765, pp. 104–40.

Figure 0.1. Tetradrachm of Myrina broken and scored. Latakia hoard (*IGCH* 1544, **184**; BnF, Paris, fonds général 747).

he describes the coins' physical appearance: they arrived in Paris without having been truly cleaned. The specimens that can be located today in the collection of the Cabinet des Médailles in Paris[7] carry the traces of clumsy cleaning that left the metal deeply scored (Fig. 0.1).[8] Pellerin notes that "these coins…number more than a hundred," without further specification. The rest of the description concentrates especially on the rarity of the coins. There is no list, as there would be today; but there is discussion of each item thought to be interesting, with a historical commentary wherever possible. He comments on mints, periods, monograms, varieties, royal portraits, and the history of kingdoms and cities, the dating of the lot, all with an erudition and keenness that compel admiration. Philip Kinns forcefully stresses the novelty of Pellerin's investigation, who with this article opens the portals of modern numismatics: provenance, container, number of specimens, their physical condition; all were studied in detail. Three plates illustrate the chief coins, and their original mints are identified with considerable insight, including the Alexanders (Figs. 0.2–0.4).[9] "Almost Pellerin's first question was: 'When was the hoard buried?', and both the answer he gave and the terms in which he presented it remain essentially valid today. For here we have the concept of burial date for the first time."[10] Likewise, Pellerin is the first to consider the hoard as an archaeological ensemble that, in his opinion, might be evidence of a merchant's voyage.[11] Even if the hypothesis is false—it is based on the provenances of Alexanders of Asia Minor that in fact abound in Syria—the approach he inaugurates still remains that of all those who deal with hoards.

Pellerin's interest, however, is limited to novel items: "After having spoken of the coin of Mithridates and those of Alexander, coming from the deposit discovered near Latakia, there is little left to say about the coins of the other kings found there: they contain nothing not known,"[12] except for a tetradrachm of Antiochus II. This is a result of the typical eighteenth-

7. The Pellerin Collection was integrated into the general holdings of the Cabinet des Médailles without keeping any separate labeling. Finding any specimens requires particularly close examination and the use of engravings in the *Recueil* (Pellerin 1765, see Figs. 0.2–0.4).

8. See the example of the tetradrachms of Alabanda and Alabanda as Antioch, *fonds général* 1 and 2.

9. See also Fig. 1.1.

10. Kinns 1990, p. 107.

11. Pellerin 1765, p. 110.

12. "Après avoir parlé de la médaille de Mithridate et de celles d'Alexandre, provenant du dépôt découvert près de Latakié, il reste peu de choses à dire concernant les médailles des autres rois qui s'y sont trouvées: elles ne contiennent rien qui ne soit connu." Pellerin 1765, p. 133.

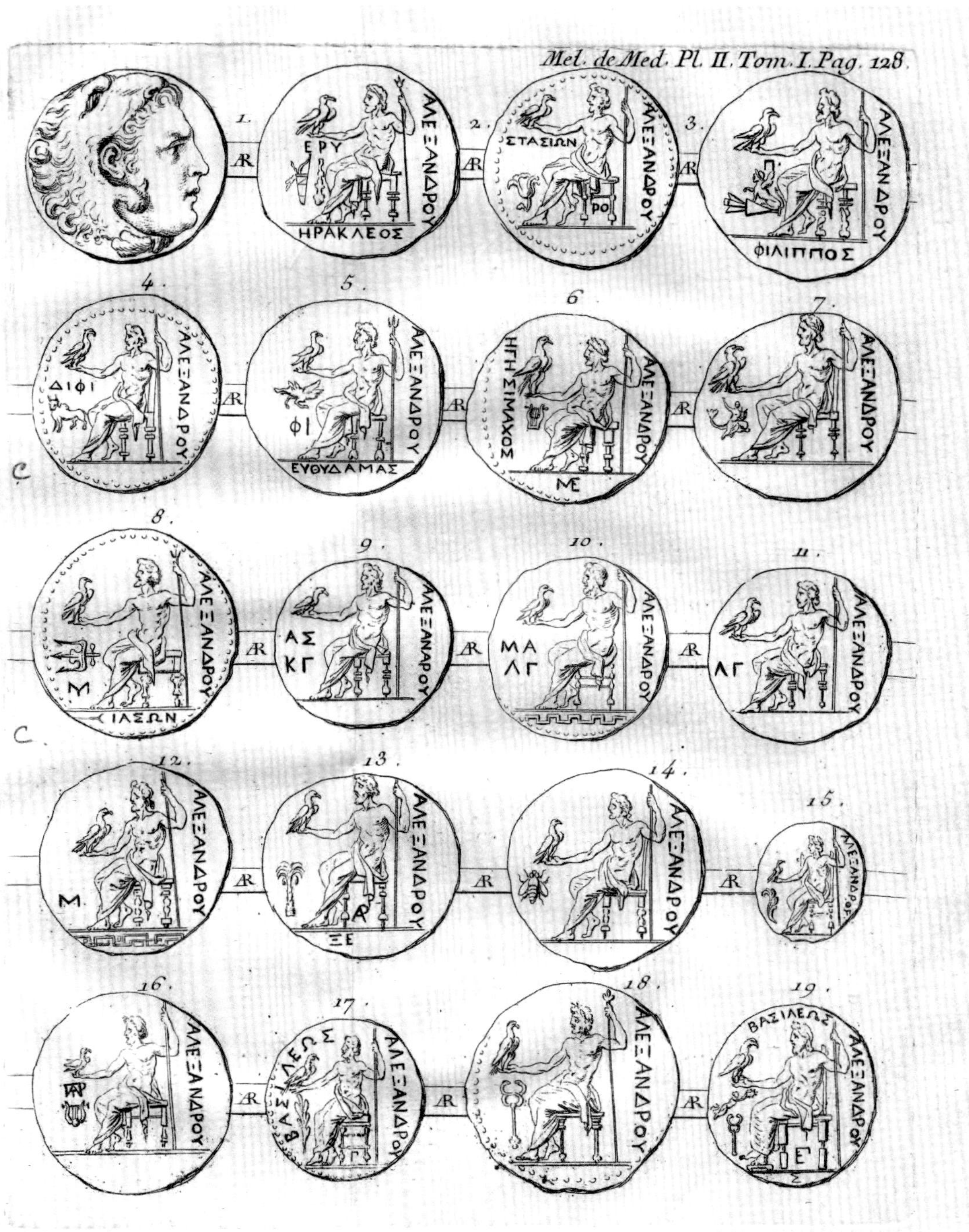

Figure 0.2. Pellerin 1765, pl. 2 illustrating the Latakia hoard.

Figure 0.3. Pellerin 1765, pl. 3 illustrating the Latakia hoard.

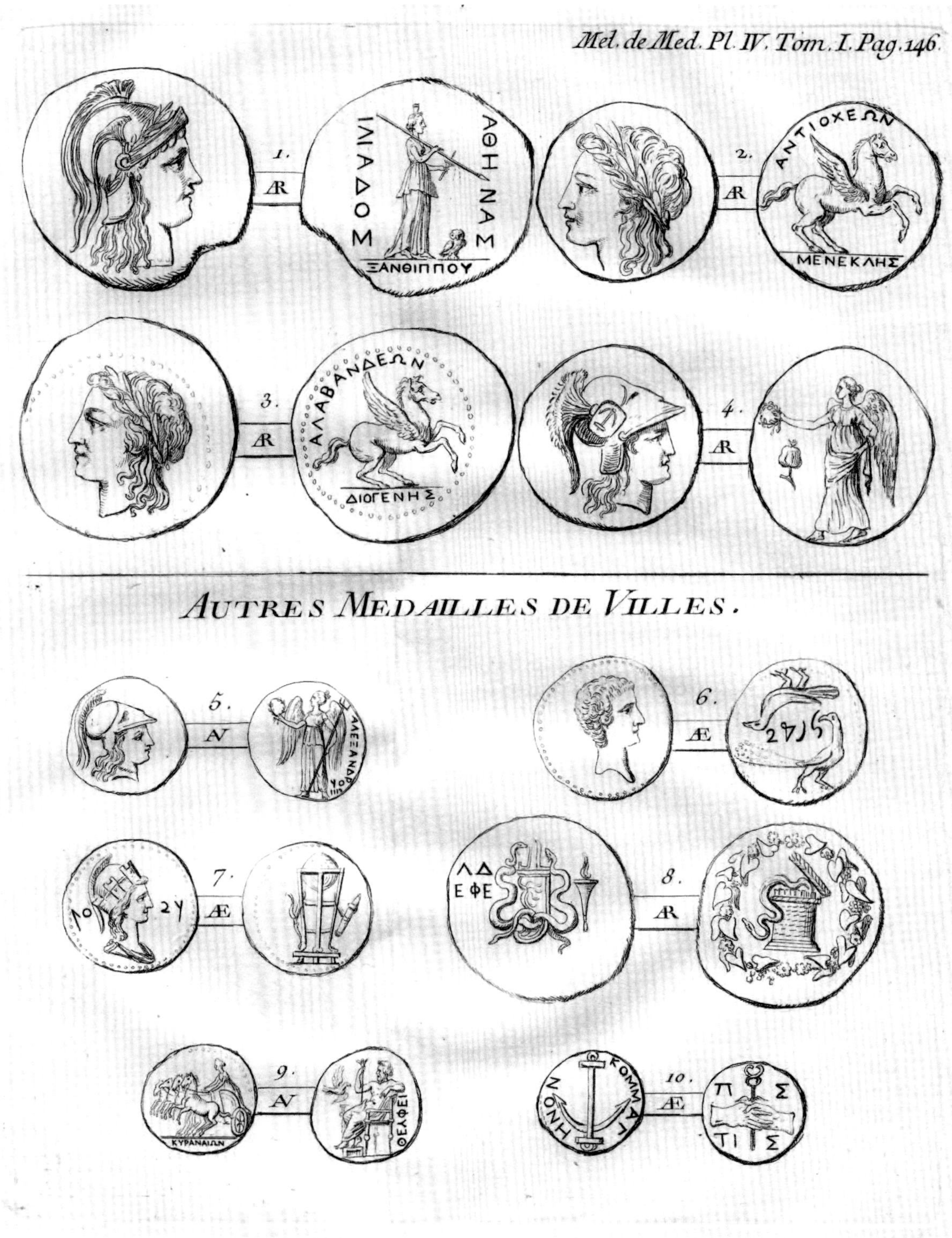

Figure 0.4. Pellerin 1765, pl. 4 illustrating the Latakia hoard.

century collector's attitude, seeking to fill in the gaps in already known series, not to accumulate specimens. But the foundations had been laid: Pellerin posed the big questions for which we still seek the answers when studying hoards. It was not until the nineteenth century, however, that this approach became typical and habitual.[13]

It was the study of Roman Republican hoards in Italy that subsequently advanced the knowledge of this type of material. Bartolomeo Borghesi played a major role in this area, emphasizing the presence of wear, the need to avoid overly schematic analysis of these ensembles, and the idea of relative dating of hoards. Yet he never formalized his thinking on hoards, and all his learning is scattered, mostly in his correspondence.[14]

Despite the age of these first scholarly studies, systematic recording of hoards really only began in the twentieth century. The study of hoards' find dates is, from this point of view, rather enlightening. If one goes by the inventory of Sydney Noe published in 1937, only 20 discoveries predate 1800 (14 from the 18th century), out of a total of 1,186 assembled hoards.[15] Beginning in the twentieth century and especially after the foundational efforts of Edward Newell,[16] the study of hoards has become one of the fundamental approaches to the study of Greek coinage. At the same time, the development of archaeological excavation has contributed new information on the circulation of small change. The complexity of this material and its sheer quantity has not allowed a global approach to coin circulation throughout the Greek world. The study offered here is limited to one region, Achaemenid and Hellenistic Syria, but it is based on the largest quantity of material possible, coming from hoards and excavations, matched with critical reflection on these sources and on what the historian may expect from them. By offering this methodological attempt, one may hope to improve our general mastery of this material. Perhaps it will not prove a vain hope, to arrive, one day, region-by-region, at a view of the entirety of coin circulation in the Greek world.

1. DEFINITIONS

1.1. Currency Circulation

The definition of currency circulation generally found in economics textbooks applies only to a totally monetized economy, an economy in which all payments are made in physical or virtual coin. Ancient economies used very varied means of payment, whether in the form of coinage or not, and practices differed by regions and periods, leading to the co-existence of very diverse customs, sometimes in the same city.[17] To hope to define the place of coinage in exchanges and its geographic and chronological development with the least imprecision possible, it is therefore

13. Eckhel 1792, pp. lxxxi–lxxxii, contributes nothing new.
14. Borghesi 1862–1872; Crawford 1990 provides a brief and useful summary.
15. Noe 1937, pp. 352–53.
16. Especially the publication of the Demanhur hoard between 1911 and 1923.
17. Cf., e.g., Cahill 2002, pp. 265–73.

necessary to take into account hoards and coins from excavations or chance finds, to analyze their spatial and temporal evolution, and to compare these results with what written and archaeological sources tell us about centers of power, places and practices of commerce, historical occurrences, such as wars, which influence monetary production, and the habits of users. The physical material studied has itself a relative value: since it depends upon the degree of monetization, the extent of the owner's wealth, the availability and scarcity of precious metals, a hoard of coins does not represent the same worth to all people in all places. The definition of coinage, its role in any given society's exchanges at any given time would, ideally, have to be considered in order to give a precise image of reality.

The project, so defined, is particularly ambitious given the extent and variety of the data that it seeks to encompass. Within the limits of this study—the work of several years—it was not realistic to treat all these aspects, some of which in fact elude us permanently. The establishment of the database and its handling have required investigations and an effort that are still not complete and probably never will be: information never ceases to accrue. Some new hoards were added in June 2010, thanks to the manuscript of *Coin Hoards* X that Andrew Meadows sent me prior to its publication. In July 2010, digging among the rich files of the American Numismatic Society turned up two new lots previously noted by Arnold Spaer,[18] and I owe to the kindness of Oliver Hoover the references for one last hoard published in the excavation report from Mt. Garizim that had escaped my notice.[19] In contrast, the hoards from Mt. Carmel and Megadim cited in the thesis of Julien Olivier, defended in 2012, have been added to the corpus (**299**, **324**). Pierre-Marie Blanc (Institut Français du Proche-Orient) alerted me in May, 2010, to an eighth hoard consisting of 252 coins, including 127 tetradrachms and 125 coins of smaller size, apparently all of Alexander and his successors, that was found on the banks of the Euphrates, near Qalat Najem. In October, J. and A.-G. Elayi submitted to the *Revue Numismatique* an article dealing with "Un nouveau trésor de monnaie d'Arwad du IVe s. av. J.-C." that consisted of 83 silver coins, 78 of which come from that mint.[20] Gaëlle Thévenin and Thomas Bauzou are preparing the publication of a hoard of at least 1,216 tetradrachms and drachms with owl types found in Rafah (Gaza Strip, near the Egyptian border) in January 2010. Finally, the authors of the collection of Ptolemaic hoards (*Egyptian Hoards* I) sent me their articles in advance of publication.[21] Such a shifting corpus required forsaking all hope of its definitive closure. So I simply stopped as of 2010. Primary emphasis is on the method of interpreting the large number of assembled numismatic data, their assessment, and the basic conclusions that can be drawn from them. Accordingly, the reader will be able to fault the commentary for being a trifle dry and more keyed to exploiting the corpus than the secondary literature. This effort is meant to open up future perspectives of more in-depth study.

18. Message from A. Meadows, July 22, 2010.
19. It therefore does not appear in the catalogue: Magen 2008, p. 221.
20. It has the number 84 if one follows the continuous numbering of their corpus, Elayi, Elayi 1993a.
21. Keen 2016; Lorber 2016; Meadows forthcoming 2016a–f; Olivier, Meadows 2016.

1.2. Hoard and Treasure

The French word for "hoard," *trésor*, comes from the Latin *thesaurus*, itself borrowed from the ancient Greek θησαυρός (*thēsauros*).[22] The *Digest* defines it thus: "Thesaurus est vetus quaedam depositio pecuniae, cuius non extat memoria, ut iam dominum non habeat" (*thesaurus*: an old deposit of money, long forgotten, so that it no longer has an owner).[23] The general dispositions of the *French Code Civil* concerning property law state that "un trésor est un ancien dépôt de richesse, dont on n'a pas conservé le souvenir, et qui de ce fait n'a pas de propriétaire" (art. 716).[24] The value of the find is not an issue in this legal understanding, directly drawn from Roman law, which only takes into account the hidden character of the group in question and the absence of any verifiable owner. Moreover, it distinguishes two ways of safeguarding a hoard: hide it or bury it.[25] In fact, the jurisprudence cited in the Code only mentions precious objects: "ancient coins" with a value on the antiquities market, gold coins, and ingots. English employs two distinct words: *hoard*, which stresses the idea of accumulation, of a reserve;[26] and *treasure* (derived from the French *trésor*) that instead connotes value, precious character, riches kept in a safe place. Absence of ownership is also one of the defining criteria, which, just as in the *Code Civil*, comes from Roman law. English sharpens meaning with the usage *treasure trove*, which implies the find's lack of ownership. The *Oxford English Dictionary* defines as *treasure*, "wealth or riches stored or accumulated, esp. in the form of precious metals; gold or silver coin; hence in general, money, riches, wealth. Usually collective, without article or plural." It continues, in an extended sense: "anything valued and preserved as precious."[27] The expression *treasure-trove*, deriving from the French *trésor trouvé*, designates "anything of the nature of treasure which anyone finds; *spec.* in *English Law*: Treasure (gold or silver, money, plate, or bullion) found hidden in the ground or other place, the owner of which is unknown."[28] French also employs the words *dépôt*[29] and *trouvaille*,[30] which, however, do not apply only to coin hoards. It was only in

22. The word, in the sense of place where one deposits offerings or riches, is not attested in Greek before Herodotus 1.14; 2.150; and, to evoke the silver buried in the soil of Laurion (θησαυρός χθονός, *thēsauros khthonos*) in Aeschylus, *Persians* 238. Cf. Hill 1936, p. 1.

23. *Digest* 41.1.31.1, cited by Hill 1936, p. 5. Hill devotes a section of his book to the way Roman law regulates the question of hoard ownership (pp. 5–47).

24. "A hoard is everything hidden or buried for which there is no legal claimant, and which is discovered by pure chance" The formulation is a little different, but the definition is the same in the Napoleonic Code of 1804.

25. Thus, a decree of the first civil chamber of the French Cour de Cassation dated November 19, 2002, (*Bulletin des arrêts. Chambres civiles* 9 [Nov. 2002], no. 279) mentions the discovery of gold ingots and gold and silver coins in a gas stove. This find is not considered a *trésor* since the owners of the stove are also the owners of its contents: "ces biens, dont les consorts Delor justifiaient être propriétaires, ne pouvaient constituer un trésor" (these goods, of which the partners Delor substantiated their ownership, could not possibly constitute a hoard).

26. *Oxford English Dictionary* (Oxford, 1989), s.v. Hoard: "An accumulation or collection of anything valuable hidden away or laid by for preservation or future use; a stock, store, esp. of money, a treasure."

27. *OED*, s.v. Treasure. "By the English law treasure must be 'hidden in the soil or in buildings,'" Hill 1936, p. 8.

28. *OED*, s.v. Treasure-trove.

29. Pellerin 1765, p. 104, entitles his study of the hoard of Latakia "Médailles provenant d'un dépôt trouvé en Syrie," and he systematically uses this word throughout. The index of the works of Borghesi 1864 under the word "trésors" refers to "dépôts de médailles."

30. Thus the indexes of the *Revue Numismatique* published in 1908 and 1915 refer, for the word *trésors*, to "trouvailles."

the 20th century that trésor definitively became the standard usage in French, like "hoard" in English.[31]

John Kleeberg proposes the following definition in the introduction to *Numismatic Finds of the Americas*: "Two or more coins or other valuable objects, removed from circulation and intentionally concealed, usually with the purpose of eventual recovery, but not recovered by the original owner, and not recovered until a substantial period of time has passed, typically a decade or more."[32] The issue of how long abandonment lasted obviously never arises for antiquity. But the number of coins is a problem: can a single coin be considered a hoard, especially if it is in gold?[33] The entire problem comes down to knowing whether the coin was simply lost, provided it is not found in a container that clearly indicates the intent to protect it. Nowhere in the documentation I have consulted does this hypothetical case arise. Yet, a deposit from the excavation of Hama consists of a bronze of Antiochus VIII "found beneath limestone lion 6B600," in House II and inventoried as Hoard 1.[34] It seems difficult to call this a hoard; it is not at all certain that the coin was placed in that spot intentionally. It is a bronze of Antiochus VIII (125–96 BC), whereas the limestone lion apparently dates from the period 30 BC–100 AD. In general, the authors of the Hama excavation publications have tended to consider as hoards what are probably fortuitous coinage groups. The editors of *IGCH*, in any event, have not deigned to recognize them in their publication.[35]

Should the presence of a container itself be part of the definition of a hoard? The question arises in several instances. An extreme example is the hoard of Seleuceia Pieria, found during American excavations on the site (*IGCH* 1526, **138**). Dorothy Waage notes in her introduction: "All of the coins are chance finds; no hoard was found in the course of the excavations (the ten Ptolemaic tetradrachms, one of Antigonus Monophthalmus, and one of Demetrius Poloiorcetes [*sic*] were found together but not in a container)."[36] This is manifestly mistaken, since the catalogue specifies that the 12 tetradrachms were found together. The extreme rarity of isolated coins in precious metal guarantees that this is a hoard. The absence of a preserved container is not surprising, as will become clear: it happens frequently. So one must conclude, with John Melville Jones: "Sometimes coins are found in association with one another, but there is no sign of any container. They must have been hidden in a chink in a wall or in some other crevice, buried in the mud floor or placed in some wrapping that has completely disappeared in the course

31. Since English and French are the principal languages for Syrian hoard publications, I have not extended my inquiry to other languages. Note, however, that Spanish distinguishes "hoard," tesoro, from "find," *hallazgo*: Alfaro Asins et al. 2009, s.v. *Tesoro* ("Conjunto de monedas reunidas voluntariamente, ocultadas o perdidas en un momento determinado y nunca recuperadas por su proprietario [collection of coins purposely gathered, hidden or lost at a particular time, and never reclaimed by its owner]) and Hallazgo, which the dictionary does not really define, presenting, instead, what is a typology of coinage finds.

32. Kleeberg 2009, p. 1.

33. The dictionary edited by Amandry 2001, s.v. "trésor," also stresses the importance of the metal in defining as a hoard a group of just two coins.

34. Thomsen 1986, p. 63.

35. Cf. the entry on the Hama excavations in Chapter Two (**14**).

36. Waage 1952, p. vii.

of time. Even in such circumstances, if coins appear to have been brought together and hidden, we may call them a hoard."[37]

Coins without container may constitute a hoard, but within what limits? At Balatah-Shechem, 1 drachm and 12 bronze coins dating from the end of the fourth to the third centuries BC were found in the same Hellenistic house, but there is no further elaboration on the circumstances of discovery.[38] Were they scattered or clustered? Do they form a hoard or not? The area was closed, sealed. Are we to conclude that the inhabitants left their coinage spread out in a relatively circumscribed space, that occasional losses occurred over a three hundred year period? But bronze's longevity in circulation leads the numismatist to wonder: it is not impossible that bronzes of different periods were collected at the same moment, for other examples of this exist. In this particular instance, the vagueness of the published archaeological data does not permit us to settle the matter.

The normal vocabulary of modern numismatics only retains the word *hoard* as strictly descriptive, unlike *treasure*, which, with its connotation of riches, easily arouses fanciful notions. In French, context introduces this nuance. The accepted meaning of the word trésor in Emile Littré's *Dictionnaire de la langue française* solely focuses on "*trésor*" conceived of as a "heap of gold, silver or other precious objects" ("amas d'or, d'argent ou d'autres objets précieux").[39] Modern and contemporary literature echoes this definition very vividly. Robert Louis Stevenson's *Treasure Island* is one of the most famous examples of this quest for a hidden fortune, as is the miraculous hoard of the Abbé Faria in Alexandre Dumas' *The Count of Monte Cristo*. Kleeberg's chosen cover illustration for his publication of American hoards is taken from a comic book version of this story.[40] It shows Edmond Dantès in front of a coffer brimming with gold coins, ingots, and jewels, his hands full of coins pouring through his fingers. An insert states, "he forced the casket open." A bubble tells what the character is thinking: "An unaccountable, unheard of treasure! Now I can return to life. Now I shall have rank, influence and power at my command. Now I can revenge myself on the men who condemned me to a fate worse than death." The image is all the more intriguing because Dumas, on the contrary, does not disclose the thoughts of his hero, who remains silent and upset in the face of his discovery: "un autre se fût précipité, eût poussé des exclamations de joie; Dantès s'arrêta, pâlit, douta".[41] The American comic book restores a much more popular idea of discovering a hoard that will enable the hero to avenge his fate.

Descriptions of misers are also instructive, with their archetypal manias and passion for gold. Take the case of Honoré de Balzac's père Grandet, whose example Georges Le Rider liked to cite in his seminars. He provides us with a lesson in how to build a hoard: "Le matin, monsieur

37. Melville Jones 1998, s.v. "Hoards and finds."

38. Sellers 1962, pp. 88–89.

39. Littré, *Dictionnaire de la langue française*, Paris, 1874, s.v. "*trésor*."

40. Kleeberg 2009.

41. A. Dumas, *Le comte de Monte Cristo*, Pléiade ed., Paris, 1981, p. 252 ("anybody else would have rushed about, would have cried out for joy; Dantès stood still, grew pale, disbelieved"—WEH).

Grandet, suivant sa coutume pour les jours mémorables de la naissance et de la fête d'Eugénie, était venu la surprendre au lit, et lui avait solennellement offert son présent paternel, consistant, depuis treize années, en une curieuse pièce d'or. . .les pièces d'or qu'elle récoltait au premier jour de l'an et à la fête de son père, lui composaient un petit revenu de cent écus environ que Grandet aimait à lui voir entasser. N'était-ce pas mettre son argent d'une caisse dans une autre…?"[42] Eugénie Grandet saves those gold coins in a purse stuffed into a piece of her bedroom furniture. But the ground remains the hiding-place of choice. Jean de La Fontaine describes "the Miser who lost his hoard" thus: "Il avoit dans la terre une somme enfouie/…. Il y fit tant de tours qu'un fossoyeur le vit, /Se douta du dépôt, l'enleva sans rien dire."[43] A few strokes sketch the practices that, eventually, lead to establishing deposits of riches liable to transformation into hoards if their owners hide them and die without having transferred them. Yves-Marie Bercé's study of hoards in modern times is thus replete with examples of domestic caches, under the ground, the flooring, or in the walls of houses, generally in contexts connected to a time of war or currency reform.[44] A special issue of the journal *Historia*, aimed at the general public, entitled "Treasure Hunts," includes some extraordinary stories of pirates and island treasure hunting and the finds that enriched their discoverers.[45]

One could multiply the examples, so much does the idea of hoards feed the human imagination, even today. Bercé has written what he himself describes as a "cultural history of the economy" in a work devoted to hoards from the sixteenth century to our own time.[46] The three principal themes running through his book are the loss of valuables, which thus become hoards; the treasure hunt, including the magical aspects of these finds; and the ownership of these discoveries. Such a work can avail itself of literary and legal evidence that are totally lost, if they ever existed, for Greek antiquity and particularly for Achaemenid and Hellenistic Syria. So it will probably not be possible to write a similar "cultural history of the economy" of Achaemenid and Hellenistic Syria. Instead, a detailed study of hoards will allow us to gain an idea of the fortune they represent, or not, and to try to achieve some tangible sense of the reasons for their loss and to restore them to their context.

42. Honoré de Balzac, *Eugénie Grandet*, 1833, La comédie humaine III, Pléiade ed., Paris, 1976, p. 1045 ("In the morning, Monsieur Grandet, following his custom for those memorable days, Eugénie's birthday and her patron saint's feast, came to surprise her in bed, and solemnly offered up to her his paternal present, for thirteen years now an intriguing gold coin. . . .The gold coins she collected on New Year's Day and on her father's patron saint's day amounted to a little income of nearly 100 écus that Grandet adored seeing pile up for her. Was it not putting his own money from one box into another?"—WEH).

43. *Fables* 20.4. ("He had in the ground a buried sum. He visited it so often, a gravedigger saw him. A hoard! he suspected, and silently filched it."—WEH).

44. Bercé 2004, chap. 1.

45. *Historia* 370 bis (1977).

46. Bercé 2004, p. 9.

2. NUMISMATIC SOURCES

2.1. Inventories of Hoards

Noe in 1925 was the first to undertake as complete an inventory as possible of known hoards or of those, yet unpublished, that he had studied in the Athens Museum and in Constantinople, and also including those he was aware of and were going to be published.[47] Accordingly, this first collection goes far beyond the title of "Bibliography" he gave to it. The second edition, in 1937, gathers nearly twice as many hoards (1,186 vs. 629), alphabetically arranged, still using the same format: place and date of discovery, presumed date of burial, succinct description of the content.

In 1967, the International Numismatic Commission established a team charged with preparing a new inventory: the *Inventory of Greek Coin Hoards* assembles 2,387 hoards and corrects Noe's publication. Indeed, some coin assemblages Noe accepted as hoards were shown not to be so or to belong to several distinct groups. Moreover, *IGCH* does not recognize finds of "non-numismatic" objects, lots containing only imitations, or finds later than 30 BC.[48] It deletes 255 of Noe's entries in all. Classification this time is geographic, in awareness of coherent spheres of circulation, and chronological within each of these geographical regions. Descriptions are a little more detailed and followed by a bibliography. The introduction, by Margaret Thompson, Otto Mørkholm, and Colin Kraay, recalls the conditions in which hoards are usually brought to light: "Deposits are found and rapidly dispersed within and without the country of origin with the result that parts of a single hoard may trickle into private and public collections over a number of years under diverse labels of provenance and date of discovery."[49] The editors' work chiefly consisted in reassembling portions of the same hoard that arrived on the market with conflicting information. Arriving at a perfect reconstitution is impossible, and this incomplete aspect of the corpus is the primary characteristic to remember whenever a study depends on this type of material.

The usefulness of a regular inventory of hoards led to the publication of the series of *Coin Hoards* by the Royal Numismatic Society in London.[50] The first volume, which appeared in 1975, announced its objectives: to inventory hoards that entered public collections or were seen on the market, and to pair this inventory with an up-to-date bibliography. The project originally foresaw yearly publication, but since the 1980's the scope and difficulty of the enterprise have led to a more irregular pace of separate volumes, while each issue of the *Numismatic Chronicle* provides an incomplete account annually. The classification criteria are different from those of Noe and *IGCH*: all hoards are inventoried and published in chronological order of their burial,

47. "Descriptions of hoards in the Museums of Athens and Constantinople have been included even though they have not been published, and despite that there is no immediate prospect of their publication," Noe 1925, p. 8.

48. Thompson, Mørkholm, Kraay 1973, p. vii.

49. Ibid., p. viii.

50. At the same time, the Bibliothèque nationale de France undertook the publication of the series *Trésors monétaires* that inventories finds made on French soil. The first volume dates from 1979.

Table 0.1. Greek hoards in *Coin Hoards*

	Total	Greek Hoards, 6th–1st cent. BC	Syrian Hoards, 6th–1st cent. BC
CH 1, 1975	436	147	9
CH 2, 1976	578	180	9
CH 3, 1977	510	114	6
CH 4, 1978	523	79	7
CH 5, 1980	410	57	2
CH 6, 1981	509	91	6
CH 7, 1985	735	148	13
CH 8, 1994	604	550	64
CH 9, 2002	744	731	92
CH 10, 2010	471	471	36
Total	**5,520**	**2,568**	**244**

from the mid-fifth century BC to the eighteenth century AD, and from Europe to China. This practice changed with the eighth volume, published nine years after the seventh. This dealt with only Greek hoards (sixth century BC to second century AD), to the exclusion of provincial and Roman coins, since the unpublished material was too abundant to maintain the procedures established in the previous volumes. Volumes 9 and 10 are thus exclusively devoted to Greek coins and broken down in geographic regions, like *IGCH*.

The first volume aroused such interest that it encouraged intense international cooperation, with numerous numismatists inventorying hoards they knew of and alerting editors to them. Volume 3 of *Coin Hoards*, which appeared in 1977, was the first composed with computer assistance. The *Coin Hoards* series also has another novel aspect: in each volume, more remarkable hoards are published initially with very brief, descriptive articles, but with much more substantial articles in the last two issues. Table 0.1 gives the numbers for hoards inventoried in *Coin Hoards*. These figures are not those of unpublished hoards, for certain of them were already known; but they have been completed, corrected, or have simply benefited from new publications. So it often occurs that a single hoard has several entries. Moreover, the editors of the earlier volumes of *Coin Hoards* sometimes listed collections of hoards under a single number. That is the case with Henri Seyrig's *Trésors du Levant*, listed, with two exceptions, in *CH* 1.75, and the *Trésors de monnaies phéniciennes* of J. and A.-G. Elayi (*CH* 8.587). They are listed again, this time with a separate entry, in *Coin Hoards* 9. Despite these approximations, the following table gives a useful order of magnitude for the number of Greek hoards listed in the inventories currently available. The column for Syrian hoards takes into account only their first publication and thus gives the actual number of new hoards that *Coin Hoards* has brought to our awareness.[51]

The four major inventories of hoards give the following totals (Table 0.2):

Table 0.2. Place of Syria in hoard inventories

	Total	**Classical and Hellenistic Syria**
Noe 1925	629 (18 uncertain)	16
Noe 1937	1,186	39
IGCH 1973	2,387	154[52]
CH 1–10 1975–2010	5,520	244

IGCH incorporates all the hoards in Noe 1937 that survived criticism, and the latter work itself included all the lots present in Noe 1925. Each time the number of inventoried hoards doubled. The total of those appearing in *Coin Hoards* 1–10 is also nearly double the total of *IGCH*. The increase in the number of Syrian hoards seems less imposing in *Coin Hoards*, but the fact that this column does not contain duplicate entries, unlike the "Total" column, partially tempers this impression. The progression in the number of hoards inventoried supports the reliability of this source. For example, in 1902, Rouvier cites only four hoards to confirm the provenance of some Sidonian double staters: Tell el-Mellaha (*IGCH* 1499, **49**), Jdita (*IGCH* 1517, **92**), Beithir (*IGCH* 1489, **18**), Qasr Naba (*IGCH* 1506, **85**).[53] Currently, the catalogue of the present work takes account of 14 hoards attesting the circulation of these large denominations just for Syria.[54]

2.2. Regional Studies Based on Hoards

Hoard inventories form important databases, but they do not provide any commentary on the material assembled. Some authors have individually offered thoughts derived from hoards. Adrien Blanchet in 1900 was the first to venture a systematic historical approach founded on hoards. He was concerned with the Germanic invasions in Gaul. His work gathers 868 hoards, very briefly described, and proposes a breakdown by reigns and French administrative regions.[55] It contains no map; but the table by regions shows that those covering the massifs

51. This column only takes into account the hoards that had not previously been inventoried. Those already known through *IGCH* are not counted; those with two entry numbers in *CH* are recorded in the first volume where they appear.

52. The Dura Europos hoard (*IGCH* 1770, **212**) has been added to the count in Thompson, Mørkholm, Kraay 1973, p. 201.

53. Rouvier 1902, pp. 255–59.

54. **15**, **17**, **18**, **19**, **23**, **41**, **49**, **60**, **68**, **73**, **85**, **92**, **99**, **107**.

55. Blanchet 1900, pp. 50–51.

of the Ardennes and the Vosges revealed only a few finds, in contrast to their neighbors, and thus enables a reconstruction of the invaders' progress responsible for this concentration of buried wealth. Blanchet also tried to relate the hoards and the different periods of war Gaul experienced, stressing the heavy burial activity from AD 255–280 and the contemporaneous construction of ramparts in numerous cities. This first study presents a logical methodology that takes account of the spatial and chronological spread of burials and seeks to relate them with what other sources inform us about the region's history. The linkage, surely a little too neat, with military episodes also occupies a large part of the same author's lectures at the Collège de France published in 1936.[56] Other authors naturally followed Blanchet's method in the succeeding decades.

It is not practical to present here all the regional studies of ancient hoards that have been published, because they are rather numerous, if one considers the whole of the Mediterranean basin. I include only a few examples dealing with the Balkans.[57] Evgeni Paunov and Ilya Prokopov have assembled 132 hoards containing Roman Republican *denarii* found in Bulgaria, only 32 of which had benefited from an individual study.[58] Denarii actually circulate in the region from the mid-1st century BC, intermingled with other currencies from the region (coins of Thasos) and from Illyria, and constitute half of the hoards, a fact the authors connect with military payments. The relatively succinct commentary also offers some pages on the geography of the hoarding. Despite the brevity of the analysis, this publication stresses the relationship between the penetration of foreign coinage and periods of war. Prokopov's labors on Thasian tetradrachms led him to include on one map 334 reported hoards.[59] Shortly afterwards, Picard mapped out 136 hoards of coins with Thasian types, thus demonstrating that the burials occurred far away, in the interior of Thracian territory, whereas the coins were probably struck by Rome to pay for operations against the Thracians.[60] Picard concluded that they were war booty. They are evidence for the participation of certain peoples in the war against Rome, while others, Roman allies, did not hoard them. The frequent presence of these coins north of the Danube seems to indicate that the peoples of this area participated in combat, even though literary texts rarely mention them.[61]

The connection between hoarding and wars is also at the heart of the collaborative effort directed by Cécile Morrison, Vladislav Popovic, and Vujadin Ivanisevic, devoted to Byzantine hoards in the Balkans and Asia Minor.[62] Their work is distant, geographically and chronologically, from mine, but to my knowledge it is the only one to offer a methodology and a commen-

56. Blanchet 1936, pp. 30–32 for Syria.
57. I reserve Touratsoglou 1998 for further treatment later in this volume.
58. Paunov, Prokopov 2002.
59. Prokopov 2006, p. 335.
60. Picard 2008.
61. Picard 2008, p. 482 rejects the separation between the genuinely Thasian tetradrachms and imitations proposed by Prokopov 2006.
62. Morrison, Popovic, Ivanisevic 2006.

tary developed and derived from the gathered material. That material is especially abundant: 368 hoards from the 6th and 7th centuries AD, presented in a systematic and detailed manner. A number of them are unpublished and represent long years of work for an entire team of scholars from several countries of the region concerned (Balkans and Asia Minor). This collaboration has allowed them to create detailed files for each hoard, in the manner of *Coin Hoards*, and particularly to offer a general commentary that includes an initial geographical presentation of the area. This is indispensable because some of the burials are associated with conflicts and thus to the routes armies used to circulate. The administrative system and the coin issues of the 6th and 7th centuries benefit from chapters that illuminate the historical and numismatic context in which the burials occurred. Connections between invasions and hoarding can then be highlighted, notably with the help of maps, as well as regional peculiarities. Such an approach seems exemplary to me. My goal, as one person working alone, is not to give an equally complete account for Achaemenid and Hellenistic Syria on material of the scope presented in this book. On the other hand, it is possible to propose some avenues of study that it will be appropriate to explore in the future.

To return to the East, some publications of hoard groups have given rise to historical analyses. Daniel Schlumberger was a pioneering figure in demonstrating that Greek coinage was better represented in Achaemenid Empire hoards than the coinage of the Great King. This affirmation originates with the discovery in Kabul in 1933 of a hoard (*IGCH* 1830) containing 64 Greek coins and only 8 Persian *sigloi*. To test whether this proportion could be verified, Schlumberger gathered 59 other hoards from the ancient Achaemenid Empire.[63] They led him to conclude that "the silver coinage of the Great King has only a very secondary place in the circulation of the empire."[64]

Paul Naster devoted an article to the same period, based on the 29 hoards he could assemble, but limited to Phoenician coinages before Alexander.[65] The composition of these finds establishes the primacy of Sidon, followed by Tyre, ahead of Aradus and Byblos, as well as the absence of these coins west of Cilicia. His article is the occasion for a discussion of the attributions of these coins that remain in dispute. As in the preceding studies, the geographical and chronological approach to hoards clarifies questions concerning coin diffusion. J. and A.-G. Elayi have taken on this subject in an exhaustive way by compiling an inventory of hoards of Phoenician coins, updated by various articles since their work's first appearance in 1993.[66]

More modestly, Leo Kadman deals with currency circulation in Palestine, based on several hoards.[67] He emphasizes the substantial increase in coins known from hoards in Palestine since Noe's publication in 1937, all periods combined (Table 0.3).

63. He made, in fact, a selection from Noe 1937, rounded out by some unpublished finds.

64. "la monnaie d'argent du Roi ne tient dans la circulation de l'empire qu'une place très accessoire." Schlumberger 1953, p. 12.

65. Naster 1967, p. 4.

66. Elayi, Elayi 1996, 1999, 2003a, 2003b, 2009a.

67. Kadman 1967.

Table 0.3. Increase in hoard numbers between 1937 and 1967 in Palestine

	Hoards	**Silver Coins**	**Bronze Coins**
Noe 1937	18	700	1,800
Kadman 1967	70	8,000	13,000

In this account, he enumerates only 2 hoards of Alexander and Alexander's immediate successors, 4 of Ptolemaic coins, and 5 of Seleucid coins; but he recognizes that these figures ignore hoards dispersed illegally.[68] He also calls attention to the importance of Tyrian shekels in the coin circulation of Hellenistic Palestine. The rest of his article deals with later periods.

More recently, Seyrig brought together 48 Hellenistic hoards. He introduces them as follows: "Most of the hoards this book presents were observed in the course of the years we spent in the Orient, whether in Lebanon, where we resided, or during trips to Syria and Turkey. We have added to them some hoards of similar type, already published in whole or in part, but which cry out to be so again. The reader must never lose sight of the fact that our hoards were recorded in commerce and so do not come with the guarantees that lend credence to hoards discovered in a scientifically conducted excavation."[69]

In general, hoards are studied much more individually, or by types of coinages and by region. But, to my knowledge, a full-scale geographic presentation based upon a systematic critique of this type of source has never been attempted. And yet the overwhelming majority of coins in precious metal currently in private and public collections come from hoards. A sizeable number of them therefore elude our knowledge. Nonetheless, known hoards provide considerable material. Panos Iossif has given an example in a statistical study of the typology of Seleucid coins, "Quantifying Seleucid Religion through Coins: Is It Possible to Calculate 'Iconography' and 'Religion'?" He estimates the frequency of appearances of Zeus and Apollo on Seleucid coins based on a sample of 7 gold octadrachms, 55 staters, 9,969 tetradrachms, 732 silver fractions, mostly drachms, and 1,305 bronzes, this imposing array furnished by 259 hoards.[70] The catalogue of the present volume gathers 47,821 coins from 355 hoards,[71] all metals included, taking account only of specimens actually seen by editors, not of assumed totals. This is only a rough figure, since most hoards were seen briefly, in the trade; but it is certainly a minimum: numerous finds have never been inventoried. Probably the vast majority of our coins in precious metal come from hoards. Better knowledge of the latter allows us partially to restore its archaeological dimension to a material that is otherwise chiefly an object in a display case.

68. Ibid., pp. 314–15.

69. "La plupart des trésors que présente ce livre ont été observés au cours des années que nous avons passées en Orient, soit au Liban où nous résidions, soit au cours de voyages en Syrie et en Turquie. Nous leur avons adjoint quelques trésors du même genre, déjà publiés en tout ou en partie, mais qui demandaient à l'être de nouveau. Le lecteur ne devra jamais perdre de vue que nos trésors ont été recensés dans le commerce et n'offrent par là même, aucune des garanties qui accréditent les trésors découverts dans une fouilles scientifiquement conduite." Seyrig 1973, p. 7.

70. Iossif 2011a.

71. Five were rejected: **51**, **213**, **245**, **359**, **360**.

2.3. Excavation Coins

By "excavation coins" I mean only isolated finds. Hoards found in an authorized, archaeological context are presented with other hoards. Excavation coins, just for the Hellenistic period, represent a firm total of 13,976 coins.[72] They provide an indispensable counterweight to hoards for understanding currency circulation. Bronzes were indeed little hoarded, save in special circumstances. On the other hand, silver and gold coins are only rarely discovered in isolation. From this point of view, the example of coins from the Athenian agora is quite illuminating: of the 14,604 in Kroll's inventory, two were in gold, one in electrum, 177 in silver,[73] of which 129 are Athenian out of the 10,909 Classical and Hellenistic period coins from the city found on the site. These figures represent less than 2% of the total, even though the monetization of exchange was undoubtedly much more advanced in Athens than in Syria. Both sources of information, excavation coins and hoards, therefore complement our understanding of how the circulation of gold, silver, and bronze intersect. Moreover, a large percentage of hoards are known only through the coin trade, and so lack context. Archaeological publication of coins thus permits us to recover a portion of the scientific data that is lost for a large part of our material.

There is no bibliographical tool equivalent to the *Inventory of Greek Coin Hoards* or *Coin Hoards* for Syrian excavation coins.[74] The best to be found is the systematic inventory of coins by Israeli archaeologists, whose resources are discussed in chapter three. Kevin Butcher attempted a comparative study of results from the excavation of the souks of Beirut with other digs in the region.[75] But he limited it to certain sites whose results could shed light on his conclusions selectively. Another of his articles compared finds from the Orontes valley in the same way, but only between the 1st century BC and the second century AD.[76] A comparative article by Haim Gitler presents, in 39 graphs, the fruit of research on eight sites in Jerusalem and at Masada from the third century BC until the Arab Conquest (640 AD). It proves very difficult to use because there is no commentary.[77]

Paradoxically, despite the good scientific conditions surrounding their discovery, it becomes clear that coins found in an archaeological context are no easier to study than those that come to us through the antiquities market.

Isolated coins found outside an excavation context are difficult to assess, although they occasionally provide very important information. The coins gathered by Seyrig during his long stay

72. The 58 sites presented in the catalogue revealed an array of 49,355 coins from all periods together.

73. 3 Lysimachi, 9 Alexanders, 2 Philip III, 3 Demetrius Poliorcetes, 1 Euboean League, 16 Histiaea, 129 Athens, 5 Aegina, 1 Corinth, 1 Achaean League, 1 Elis, 1 Siphnos, 4 Rhodes, 1 Ptolemy VI. Kroll 1993, conspectus, pp. xvii–xxvi.

74. This type of tool ought to be developed with publications. One could cite, for France, the *Dictionnaire des monnaies découvertes en Gaule méditerranéenne (530–27 av. notre ère)* by Michel Feugère and Michel Py. It presents the coins by typology, but closes with a thick topographical index detailing the finds on each site. The ground covered represents about a fourth of the French national territory.

75. Butcher 2001–2002, pp. 51–58.

76. Butcher 2002.

77. Gitler 1996b.

in the Near East are proof of this. He was able to describe how some of his coins came into his hands, devoid of any archaeological context, thus: "Some inhabitants of Tyre enhance their livelihood by rinsing and sieving the sand of the shore to find small bits of gold debris, washed up by the sea on the slopes where the ancient city lies. This industriousness naturally turns up more copper and lead than precious metal, and often one finds in the hands of these washers assortments of coins and seals, the majority of which the sea's salinity has unfortunately corroded."[78]

3. PARAMETERS OF THIS STUDY

The editors of *IGCH* have already defined the scope of this study: "The region here designated 'the Levant' comprises ancient Syria, Coele Syria, the coastal districts of Phoenicia and Palestine down to the Egyptian border, and the Transjordan area."[79] This region does not have any political, geographic, or even numismatic coherence since it groups together zones with different weight standards. It represents a collection of peoples and cities that belonged to the satrapy of Transeuphratene under the Achaemenids and that the Seleucids and Ptolemies then divided up. It is a region defined partially by default. It is distinct from Mesopotamia and Egypt with their different geographic and historical features, and it is separated from Asia Minor by the Taurus mountain range, not an obstacle to coin circulation but still a physical border with the Levant. In 1763, Pellerin was already noting "most ancient authors who spoke of Syria gave it varying borders. It would take too long to rehearse here their opinions on this matter. . . . One will follow those who have given it the largest extent, namely, from north to south, from the Taurus and Amanus Mountains to Egypt, and from west to east, as far as the Euphrates and the Arabian Desert." The four principal subdivisions of Syria for him are Commagene, Seleucis, Phoenicia, and Palestine.[80] One could debate endlessly the appositeness of the region's name. In the introduction to his book, *Le dossier syrien des archives de Zénon de Caunos (261–252)*, Xavier Durand recognizes that "it is not easy to define with a single word the region to which these documents refer us. We have kept two from among other possibilities. The most traditional is the word 'Palestine,' the most convenient and the least precise. If we take the word 'Palestine' in its most recent historical sense, that of the British Mandate (1917–1948), we will have to add almost all of Lebanon, the southern part of Syria (the Damascus and Hauran regions), and a part of present-day Jordan. The most precise word would be 'Syria.' This is the name that the Zenon papyri prefer over the official name of the province, 'Syria and Phoenicia.'"[81] When all is

78. "Quelques habitants de Tyr aident à leur subsistance en lavant et tamisant le sable du rivage pour y trouver de petits débris d'or, arrachés par la mer aux pentes qui portent la ville antique. Cette industrie rapporte, naturellement, plus de cuivre et de plomb que de métal précieux, et l'on trouve souvent chez ces laveurs des lots de monnaies et de bulles, dont la plupart sont malheureusement corrodées par le sel marin". Seyrig 1951, p. 225.

79. Thomson, Mørkholm, Kraay 1973, p. 200.

80. "la plupart des anciens auteurs qui ont parlé de la Syrie, lui ont donné des limites différentes. Il seroit trop long de rapporter ici leurs opinions à cet égard [...]. On s'en tiendra à ceux qui lui ont donné le plus d'étendue ; savoir, du nord au sud, depuis les monts *Taurus* et *Amanus* jusqu'à l'Egypte, et de l'ouest à l'est jusqu'à l'Euphrate et à l'Arabie déserte." Pellerin 1763, pp. 177–78.

81. "il n'est pas facile de définir d'un seul mot la région à laquelle nous renvoient ces documents. Nous en avons retenu deux parmi d'autres possibles. Le plus traditionnel est le mot 'Palestine', le plus commode et le moins précis.

said and done, the name "Syria" is not the worst, granting that in its ancient sense the eastern frontiers of these regions are quite fluid. To set the Euphrates as a limit is doubtless not appropriate, if one follows the definitions of Syria given above; but this choice of the Euphrates is in fact partly theoretical because ancient monetary circulation is limited to the region *IGCH* calls "the Levant", that is, a large strip along the Mediterranean whose contours I have had occasion to define elsewhere.[82]

These geographic contours involve juggling with the current borders, which are meaningless for archaeological material and do not prevent it from circulating on a regional scale. Yet these borders are politically meaningful, and archaeology is an instrument of general policy in mutually hostile countries seeking their own national identity. *De facto*, moving from one national territory to another entails noticeable variations in the documentation: there are huge disparities in the density of material, the amount of illicitly found coins, and the scientific handling of data and their diffusion, all of which have to be evaluated before undertaking any study.

The Hellenistic period is the heart of this work. But it would not have been possible to understand the peculiarities of this era numismatically without putting them in perspective, without presenting the material that preceded it. The Hellenistic period offers interesting perspectives. The profound changes linked to the Macedonian Conquest, the division of the region between the Seleucids and Ptolemies in the third century, the Seleucid portraits changing with every reign, the widespread practice of dating coinage, and the abundant production provide excellent chronological and geographical indicators that allow us to hope for fruitful intersections with other types of sources.

To make the material more accessible, the catalogue data have been mapped out as much as possible. There are many ways to put data on a map. The ideal would be summary maps from which one could see at a glance all the data available for a given period. The sheer amount of material made this option difficult to realize. So I have preferred to provide the simplest maps, the most basic possible: by reigns and civic mints. Obtaining complete information on a period will thus require comparing several maps. But this way of operating permitted recording all hoards with known locations. That is the other difficulty cartography poses: a significant number of the hoards are known to us without a definite findspot. It was not possible to locate them, and so the maps only partially reflect the database. The following table (Table 0.4) gives an idea of the variations in data between the hoard densities indicated on some maps and what the catalogue reveals for a given coinage. From 40% to more than a half of the data has been lost, meaning that the maps only partially illustrate the reality, which the hoards themselves reflect only in a partial way.

Si nous prenons le mot 'Palestine' en son sens historique le plus récent, celui du Mandat Britannique (1917–1948), il faut y ajouter la quasi-totalité du Liban, la partie méridionale de la Syrie (Damascène et Hauran) et une partie de la Jordanie d'aujourd'hui. Le plus précis serait celui de 'Syrie'. C'est le nom que les papyrus de Zénon emploient de préférence au nom officiel de la province de 'Syrie et Phénicie'." Durand 2003, p. 11.

82. Duyrat 2004.

Table 0.4. Rates of loss by map[83]

Issuing Authority	Total Hoards	Located Hoards	Unlocated Hoards
Classical and Hellenistic Athens and imitations	47	28	19 (40.4%)
Antiochus III	26	12	14 (53.8%)
Antiochus VII	43	25	18 (41.9%)

Within the parameters of the present volume, discussing the physical material has assumed major importance. But the task is still not finished. For example, it would be helpful to clarify usage of the names of denominations. In many older publications, Greek names are employed to denote fractions produced on local standards. Updating identifications with the help of the latest catalogues, where possible, would also be required. Thus, Ptolemaic bronzes are generally classified by reign, following the practice of Svoronos' catalogue, which has not been superseded.[84] Now Picard, in his study of excavation coins from Alexandria, shows that the major reform of 261 BC and the several others that follow have nothing to do with regnal changes. At the present time, however, it is not possible to correct these attributions, and it is necessary to accept these coinage classifications knowing all the while they are obsolete. Quite conveniently, however, Ptolemaic bronze coinage completely disappears from excavations after the Fifth Syrian War, won by Antiochus III. Since Svoronos' classifications for the first three reigns are the most secure, statistical treatment of the material remains reasonably trustworthy. The same question arises with the Seleucids, often classified following Newell when we now possess an updated standard catalogue.[85] In addition, our knowledge of certain coinages has progressed rapidly, their study undergoing a thorough reexamination. One of the most telling examples is the coinage of Samaria. A first catalogue, published by Meshorer and Qedar in 1991, was followed, in 1999, by a second, totally revised and containing twice as many varieties. Revising old identifications is a considerable undertaking, one not possible within the limits of this book. Archaeological publications and hoard publications, one might add, do not always provide sufficient data to facilitate such revision, which will necessarily impede updating at least some of the material.

Datings proposed by hoard editors are not discussed here. Their accuracy is certainly a relative matter, often accompanied by cautionary formulae: *circa*, about, around, before or after such and such a date are the most common. The level of precision increases with time since a fair number of Syrian coinages of the Hellenistic period bear dates and provide a reliable *terminus post quem* for dating hoards.

83. Percentages are of unlocated hoards vs. total hoards.
84. Svoronos 1904–1908.
85. Houghton, Lorber 2002; Houghton, Lorber, Hoover 2008. In these two catalogues, the authors have published a chapter revising attributions of Seleucid coins from hoards. My corpus integrates these revisions.

Achieving standardization of data and refinement of methodology have therefore been the primary goal for determining whether it was possible to draw reliable conclusions from a corpus of this type. The project is organized around two catalogues—hoards and excavations—followed by a methodological chapter. Four chronological chapters sketch in broad strokes the state of coin circulation in Syria before Alexander's arrival, during the conquest and the era of the Successors, down to the third, second, and first centuries BC. Two final chapters open up several lines of approach to the material. Each section highlights certain themes that appeared especially interesting, without exhausting the subject or the bibliography. Hoards, coinage in general, touch on numerous aspects of the civilization that produced them. Thus, the essential bibliography for confronting the questions raised often transcends the purview of numismatics, strictly considered, and takes on encyclopedic proportions. I have merely stressed some themes and foresworn any attempt to treat all the avenues of research the assembled material opens.

A comparative approach with the rather more advanced studies of Roman historians would be profitable. That is something for the future. The catalogue I offer here is thus open-ended; time will continue to enrich and improve it. In its current form, halted in 2010, it makes possible a first survey, the laying down of some methodological bases, the teasing out of a few of the many themes that this material suggests. This structure, once established, will enable us, through criticism and support, to lay out the limits and the knowledge we hope to acquire from this material.

Chapter 1

Hoards

1. Introduction to the Catalogue

The catalogue canvasses the different corpora and studies of published hoards currently available. Various collections likely to deal with Syrian hoards from the Persian or Hellenistic periods have been systematically consulted. The bibliographies of S. P. Noe,[1] the Inventory of Greek Coin Hoards, and Volumes 1–10 of *Coin Hoards* are its foundation.[2] Supplementing these collections are works that bring together hoards assembled according to various criteria: the *Trésors du Levant* by H. Seyrig (1973); the huge survey (1993) of J. and A.-G. Elayi, *Trésors de monnaies phéniciennes et circulation monétaire (Ve–IVe siècles av. J.-C.)*, along with a number of their articles;[3] the synthesis of M. J. Price on *The Coinage in the Name of Alexander the Great and Philip Arrhideus* (1991); and Seleucid Coins by A. Houghton, C. Lorber, and O. Hoover (2008). Some articles dealing with coin circulation in the Near East also list hoards. Thus, in 1939, Rostovsteff published "Some Remarks on the Monetary and Commercial Policy of the Seleucids and Attalids" in *Anatolian Studies Presented to William Hepburn Buckler*. This article posed certain key questions about coin circulation, using hoards as evidence. The International Numismatic Convention held in Jerusalem in 1963 (its proceedings were published in 1967) was the setting for two papers on hoards that provided useful lists: P. Naster dwelt on "Le développement des monnayages phéniciens avant Alexandre." More important, L. Kadman, in "The Monetary Development of Palestine in the Light of Coin Hoards," presented seventy hoards found in Palestine, dating from the fourth century BC to the beginning of the seventh century AD. They were the basis for his description of the nature of the coinages used in this region by period. His table displaying the hoards often differs, however, from their original publications, and it required a thorough double-checking.

1. Noe 1925 and Noe 1937.

2. I am particularly grateful to Andrew Meadows of the American Numismatic Society for having sent me a copy of *Coin Hoards*, Vol. 10, in April 2010, a few months prior to its publication.

3. Elayi, Elayi 1996; Elayi, Elayi 2003b; Elayi, Elayi 2009a.

After this trawling it was necessary to read all the scholarly literature devoted to each hoard in order to reconstruct as far as possible its origin, composition, and interpretation. This bibliography is quite highly extensive and varied, ranging from mere mentions to entire works dealing with particularly noteworthy groups. Publication places greatly complicate such research, a certain number of articles appearing in non-numismatic journals or in journals difficult to come by. Laying hands on some of these items occasionally turned into a veritable treasure hunt, and certain titles eluded me to the end; hence their absence here.

To complete the search, I have also consulted the rich Archives bequeathed by Henri Seyrig to the Département des Monnaies, Médailles et Antiques of the Bibliothèque nationale de France. Some lovely trouvailles have resulted: the Amrith hoard 1955 (**284**), unpublished, which appears in the catalogue below; some other finds, non-Hellenistic; not to mention clarifications about the circumstances of discovery and the content of certain hoards (Khirbet Qumran, **357**, for example).

Unpublished hoards or those requiring a new edition have been cited in as much detail as possible. The Jablah (**175**), Paris 1991 (**338**), and Khirbet Qumran (**357**) groups require fuller publication. I possess photos of the first two, and the third is so important that it will be necessary to compile a thick dossier of publications before being able to present it satisfactorily. The current work is not the place for such an in-depth study, and the presentation of these groups remains relatively summary.

Hoards of uncertain origin presented a problem. The catalogue retains those for which a Syrian provenance is very probable owing to their content or what little information we do have. Thus, hoards consisting of imitations of Antiochus VII struck in Cappadocia have been omitted unless their editors explicitly noted them as Syrian. *Seleucid Coins* 2 has assembled a substantial list of hoards seen in the coin trade.[4] Of unknown provenance, some are considerable in size. Two, though quite interesting, have still not been included here. The so-called "Seleucus I hoard" (*CH* 10.265) probably comes from Asia Minor where it was buried, arguably c. 281 BC. The second, called the "Seleucus III hoard" (*CH* 10.272), is of uncertain origin. It is a huge hoard, reconstituted from seven lots gathering at least 6,500 coins, probably more. Considering the uncertainty of its provenance and its size, I have preferred not to add it to the catalogue and thereby create a massive discrepancy with the other finds. Syrian or not, it is quite unusual and would lead to a similar distortion of the same kind as Demanhur in fourth-century BC Egypt.[5]

In total, the catalogue contains 360 listings, the Syria hoard (*CH* 9.449), consisting of two lots with very different dates, entered as numbers **88** and **260**. Two collections originally presented as hoards have been shown not to be such (**245**, **360**). Various scholars had already spotted them in their examinations. These pseudo-hoards have been eliminated from the statistics contained later in this study, as has the Lebanon (?) or Dinar (?) hoard (*CH* 8.143, **51**), which is probably a hoard of Asia Minor. The Akken hoard (*CH* 2.95, **213**) also poses too many problems

4. *SC* 2, 2, pp. 140–55.
5. See Duyrat 2005b.

of location and chronology to be included.[6] The Nablus hoard (*IGCH* 1629, **359**) could be made up of two different lots dating to the first century BC and the first century AD. The excluded groups appear with the designation [rejected hoard] in the catalogue. Statistics are therefore based upon 355 items.

Hoards are presented taking into account the most recent publications or those closest to the actual discovery (archeologists, collectors examining the group at a coin dealer's). References to Noe[7] are given more out of a desire to be exhaustive, since his descriptions regularly prove incomplete or erroneous when compared to investigations undertaken on the material directly. Still, it has seemed necessary to go as far back as possible in order to find the origins of each hoard and reduce errors. Noe's inventory, moreover, was the most complete available in 1937, and so it enables us to gauge the progress in our documentation over seventy years.

The catalogue's format follows practices in use for almost a century. By the time he published his first *Bibliography of Greek Coin Hoards* in New York, in 1925, Noe had already established the criteria that subsequently endured: mention of the site and date of discovery, presumed date of burial, brief description. The authors of the *Inventory of Greek Coin Hoards* followed this practice, as did those of the different volumes of *Coin Hoards*. Noe chose an alphabetical classification by name of site, which suited his undertaking, a bibliography of hoards. *IGCH* and *CH* generally preferred a classification by larger regions and a chronological presentation within each. The catalogue of Syrian hoards provided here follows a chronological order; classification by sub-regions did not seem appropriate, since it would have scattered important data. Historical analysis will restore the regional realities that are not evident in the catalogue.

Hoards are listed by the modern name of the locality where they were reportedly found, possibly followed by its ancient name. Next mentioned are the references in *IGCH*, *CH*, and Noe 1937, when they exist, as well as the supposed date of discovery. This decision clearly burdens the reference system, but it is necessary. Indeed, certain finds have been discovered in several lots or have undergone republication. These data have, in each instance, been assigned a new number in *CH*, thereby permitting easy assessment of the different stages in our information about a single hoard. On the other hand, the 48 hoards in Seyrig's *Trésors du Levant anciens et nouveaux* and the 75 of J. and A.-G. Elayi's *Trésors de monnaies phéniciennes et circulation monétaire (V–IVeme s. av. J.-C.)* were initially listed under only one number: *CH* 1.75 and *CH* 9.587, respectively.

Regularizing the format is no easy matter, beginning with the names of the locales where the coins were discovered. The problem of spelling Arab names is impossible to standardize definitively, since it involves a choice between proper transliteration, a complicated procedure for the uninitiated, and each editor's practice according to his national conventions. This was

6. Cf. below, p. 130.
7. Noe 1937.

already the case in 1925[8] and since even those favoring Arabic transliteration have been unable to reach complete agreement, I have decided to preserve the most current transliteration, even if it is not the most "correct."

The hoard's site and date of discovery are sometimes only approximate. Since an important part of our information comes from the antiquities market, where these finds are dispersed, the precise origin of lots tends to get lost. Their contents occasionally allow deduction of a provenance, but this does not replace exact knowledge of it.[9] One of the most classic examples of re-attribution, outside of Syria, is the "Armenak hoard" (Cilicia), which in fact was probably found in northern Phrygia, according to Thompson's detailed study.[10] The date of discovery is often, in fact, the date of appearance on the market, with the date of actual discovery unknown. The catalogue provides numerous examples of this situation.

I have tried to give the current state of our knowledge at the start of each hoard's entry. Whenever possible, the heading "Contents" points out the number of coins actually studied by editors, out of the originally supposed number. When a hoard was discovered in an excavation, this information is also provided. At the end of each entry, the "Disposition" of the hoard is specified, which will obviously be very temporary in the case of a dealer advertising a group for sale.

The variety of coinages represented made a standardized format difficult. For each hoard, the coins from the Persian period are followed by those of the Hellenistic Age, beginning with Alexander and the Successors; then come dynastic coinages and civic issues. Ideally, these ought to have been listed in the geographical order usual in Greek numismatics.[11] This is not the case here, where the original editor's order has been maintained for now. Nor has it been possible to revise completely the identifications editors have proposed; some are old and do not adhere to the most recent classifications. Three identifications, in particular, are problematical:

1. Coins of Philistia. Gitler and Tal have settled the ongoing debate over the coins Mildenberg called "Philisto-Arabian,"[12] but which others have called by different names. Considering the coins to be the production of mints in Philistia—the region of Ashdod, Ascalon, and Gaza—Gitler and Tal call them simply Philistine.[13] I have adopted this appellation, without, however, examining the coins further.

2. The mint of Tyre under Alexander. Newell thought that Alexander shut down the mint after his siege of the city and that a new mint opened at Ake.[14] Lemaire has carefully shown that this hypothesis is highly implausible and that it is almost certainly the Tyre mint that struck the

8. Noe 1925, p. 2.
9. Cf. Chap. 8, which deals with hoards of uncertain origin.
10. Thompson 1986.
11. Cf. the discussion below on this issue, p. 214–216.
12. Mildenberg 1995 and 1997.
13. Gitler, Tal 2006, pp. 31–36.
14. Newell 1923a, p. 134.

long series of tetradrachms of Alexander attributed in English-speaking scholarship to Ake.[15] But this article, written in French, has not registered much among English language numismatists. Price did counter it energetically, while Le Rider briefly defended it in his review of Price's book on the coinage in the name of Alexander. That is where the debate stands.[16] My catalogue lists these coins under the two names: Ake/Tyre.

3. The contested attribution of coins between John Hyrcanus I and II. Coins in the name of *YHWHNN* were first divided between Hyrcanus I and II. Meshorer, however, attributed them all to Hyrcanus II, but before the results of the excavation of Mt. Garizim revealed that they predate 113–111 BC and so must belong to the reign of John Hyrcanus I.[17] The attributions of the publications of the excavated coins have been accepted here without revision, in the absence of any opportunity to examine the coins.

As for reliable reattributions, it is insufficient just to replace one authority's name with another's. It is first necessary to verify the material, at least minimally, something that is for the most part impossible. That is why, with the exception of the first two examples given above, attributions are maintained as is.[18] In the same vein, it would have been necessary to revise the names given to denominations: a number of older publications call "obols" or "staters" coins of the Persian period that have no connection to the Greek system. The obsolete nature of some of the collected data inevitably entails some margin of error in the conclusions drawn from the material.

The Seleucids used the Attic-Alexandrine standard, with few exceptions.[19] All the silver hoards of the Hellenistic period belong to this standard, except in Coele Syria, where the Ptolemaic standard prevailed under the Ptolemies and where Antiochus III maintained it after his conquest in 202–198 BC. The Seleucids strike coins there on this standard from the middle of the second century.[20] Hoards containing coins on the Ptolemaic standard are indicated as "AR Ptolemaic."

The burial dates provided are misleadingly precise: they should generally be understood as *post quem*.

15. Lemaire 1976, esp. p. 17.

16. Price 1979 and 1991a, pp. 405–407; Le Rider 1992b, p. 222. Cf. also Le Rider 2007, pp. 126 ff., for his latest views on this issue, in English translation.

17. Meshorer 2001, pp. 25–26, for a recent summary.

18. When a hoard has been dated differently by successive authors, the different dates proposed are noted.

19. Under Seleucus I, the Babylon mint issued silver staters representing Baal on the obverse and a lion on the reverse, as well as fractions with the same types. *SC* 1.1, pp. 43–45. The standard on which these coins were struck is unclear.

20. Le Rider 1995.

2. Catalogue

ABBREVIATIONS USED

AE	Bronze
AR	Silver
AV	Gold
Didr.	Didrachm(s)
Diob.	Diobol(s)
Dr.	Drachm(s)
Frag(s).	Fragment(s)
Hemiob.	Hemiobol(s)
Ob.	Obol(s)
St.	Stater(s)
Tetr.	Tetradrachm(s)
Tetrob.	Tetrobol(s)
Demetrius II (1)	Demetrius II (First Reign)
Demetrius II (2)	Demetrius II (Second Reign)
SE	Seleucid Era

Bibliographical references, with rare exceptions that refer to the General Bibliography, are not abbreviated, in order to make catalogue consultation easier. They are listed in their chronological order of publication.

2.1. HOARD OF THE SIXTH CENTURY

1. Ras Shamra. *IGCH* 1478 = Noe 851. April 1936

Burial: 525–520
Contents: 39 AR and 2 frags. of a st., some fused, pot hoard from the centre of a hearth
Coins studied: 39/154+

Salamis, Cyprus: 6
Stageira, Macedonia: 4
Abdera: 1
Thraco-Macedonian mints: 28
Pieces of unworked silver

The staters were in the process of being melted down (two fragments preserve the shape of the crucible's base); this was interrupted, and the group was hastily buried. Judging by the weight of both melted pieces and intact coins, Schaeffer 1939 estimates the original number of coins was at least 154. The group was discovered in a part of the site much disturbed by clandestine diggers, who had not reached as far as the archaeological level where the pot was buried, at the foot of the acropolis northeast of Ugarit.

Kraay 1956, p. 48, notes the absence of Athenian tetradrachms ("It might be argued that this represents a single consignment, brought direct perhaps by a Thasian trader, in which, therefore, no Athenian coins are to be expected") and he cites the mention of a temple of Thasian Heracles at Tyre (Herodotus 2.44). He proposes a burial date c. 525–520 BC.

Cf. the Antilebanon hoard that also contained some coins in the process of being melted down (*CH* 6.4 = *CH* 8.45, **8**).

Disposition: 21 in Paris, 18? in Damascus according to *IGCH*

Bibliography:

Schaeffer, C. F. A. "Une trouvaille de monnaies archaïques grecques à Ras Shamra," in *Mélanges syriens offerts à M. René Dussaud*, Paris, 1939, pp. 461–487.
Schlumberger, D. *L'argent grec dans l'empire achéménide*, Paris, 1953, p. 10, no. 21.
Kraay, C. M. "The Archaic owls of Athens: classification and chronology," *Numismatic Chronicle* (1956), pp. 43–68.

2.2. HOARDS OF THE FIFTH CENTURY

2. Marash, ancient Antioch in the Taurus, Commagene. *IGCH* 1484. 1898

Burial: 5th cent. BC
Contents: 100 AR

Athens: tetr.

Disposition: Istanbul?

Bibliography:

"Marash—Athenian Coins," *American Journal of Archaeology* (1899), p. 251.
Schlumberger, D. *L'argent grec dans l'empire achéménide*, Paris, 1953, p. 8, no. 8.

3. Vicinity of Gaza. *CH* 8.29. 1983

Burial: 5th cent. BC
Contents: 16 AR, pot hoard

Philistia: 14 ob.
Athens: 2 tetr.

Disposition: Commerce

4. Jablah. *IGCH* 1479 = Noe 605. 1929

Burial: 500–490
Contents: 16+ AR

Acanthus: 4 tetr.
Athens: 12 tetr.

Schlumberger 1953, p. 9, n. 3, describes the circumstances of the find, based on information from Seyrig: "During 1929, some anepigraphic tetradrachms of Acanthus, coming from the region of Latakia, appeared on the Beirut market; at the end of the same year, some Athenian tetradrachms also appeared, Archaic in type, without a laurel on the helmet, from the region of Jablah (Gabala), south of Latakia. Certain Beirut dealers affirmed that the coins were from one and the same find, and the fact that the coins are contemporaneous lends credence to their assertions."[21] Schlumberger's account numbers the Athenian tetradrachms at "about 14."

Desneux 1949, pp. 66–67, puts two tetradrachms of this hoard in his classification of Acanthian tetradrachms: Seyrig sent him photographs, specifying in the accompanying letter that the coins were associated with Athenian tetradrachms struck with a head of Athena and a helmet without laurel, "without being able to vouch unequivocally for the unity of the find, although it seems to me quite probable"[22] (cited by Desneux 1949, p. 67, n. 1).

Disposition: New York 7 (Athens 6, perhaps also 1 tetr. of Acanthus). Information from H. Seyrig

Bibliography:
Desneux, J. "Les tétradrachmes d'Akanthos," *Revue belge de numismatique* 95 (1949), pp. 5–122, nos. 41–41bis, pl. XXXVII.
Schlumberger, D. *L'argent grec dans l'empire achéménide*, Paris, 1953, p. 9, no. 19.
H. Seyrig Archives, Bibliothèque nationale de France, dossier 386: photographs of casts of the Athenian tetradrachms from this hoard.

5. Region of Seleuceia. *IGCH* 1480 = Noe 55. Before 1898

Burial: 500–480
Contents: AR

Acanthus: tetr.?
Mende: tetr.?
Getas, King of the Edones: 2 octadrachms?

Babelon 1907 specifies that this "small find" comes from the mountain between Antioch and Latakia. Svoronos 1918–1919, p. 43, cites correspondence sent by Rouvier in Beirut to Babelon as a source for the provenance. He attributes the two specimens in the Paris collection to the Ichnae (Babelon 1907, no. 1459) and to Getas, king of the Edones (Babelon 1907, no. 1458, incorrectly cited as 1457).

Disposition: Paris 2

21. "Dans le courant de l'année 1929, apparurent sur le marché de Beyrouth des tétradrachmes anépigraphes d'Acanthe provenant de la région de Lattaquié ; puis à la fin de cette même année, des tétradrachmes d'Athènes, de type archaïque sans laurier sur le casque, provenant de la région de Djéblé (Gabala), au sud de Lattaquieh. Certains marchands de Beyrouth assurent qu'il s'agit d'une seule et même trouvaille, et leurs dires paraissent confirmés par le fait que ces monnaies sont contemporaines."

22. "sans pouvoir affirmer l'unité de la trouvaille d'une manière absolument formelle, bien qu'elle me paraisse très probable."

Bibliography:
Babelon, E. *Traité des monnaies grecques et romaines*, Paris, 1907, II, 1, nos. 1458–1459.
Svoronos, J.-N. "L'hellénisme primitif de la Macédoine prouvé par la numismatique," *Journal international d'archéologie numismatique* 19 (1918–1919), pp. 1–262, pl. IV, 6 and 4. (correcting E. Babelon)
Schlumberger, D. *L'argent grec dans l'empire achéménide*, Paris, 1953, p. 9, no. 15.

6. Latakia. *CH* 6.5. 1979

Burial: 480
Contents: 25+ AR
Coins studied: 6/25+

Acanthus: 2 tetr.
Athens: 2 tetr.
Aegina: 1 st.
Phaselis: 1 st.

This hoard is described as coming from a different source from *CH* 6.4 (**8**), to which it does not belong.

Disposition: Dispersed

7. Syria. *CH* 7.12. 1978/9

Burial: 480
Contents: 8+ AR, ingots and cut coins

Athens: 1 tetr.
Thasos: 1 st.
Orescii: 1 st.
Neapolis, Macedonia: 1 st.
Thraco-Macedonian: 1 st. (Obv. Griffin standing r., 13.96 g)
Samos: 1 tetr. cut
Naxos: 1 st.
Salamis, Cyprus: 1 st.
20+ kg of ingots and of cut coins, perhaps a decadr. of Athens

CH 7 relates this group to *CH* 6.4 and 6.5, but the description does not fit with either of those two hoards. The three groups are accordingly presented separately.

8. Antilebanon. *CH* 6.4 = *CH* 8.45. 1978

Burial: 475
Contents: 66 AR and ingots

Abdera: 2 octadr.
Thasos: 1 st.
Macedonia, uncert.: 1 tetr., 1 st.
Aegae, Macedonia: 1 st.
Aineia: 1 tetrob.
Acanthus: 3 tetr.
Terone: 1 tetr.
Carystos: 1 tetr., 1 didr.
Athens: 17 tetr.
Aegina: 9 st.
Carthaia: 1 st.
Naxos: 1 st.
Sinope: 1 dr.
Ephesus: 1 dr.

Teos: 1 st.
Chios: 4 didr.
Samos: 1 tetr.
Achaemenid dynasty, Sardis: 1/6th siglos, 3 sigloi
Lycia, uncert. dynast: 2 st.
Phaselis: 6 st.
Paphos: 1 st.
Salamis: 1 st.
Cyrene: 1 tetr.
Uncert.: 2 cut pieces
Unworked silver: c. 20 kg

Several findspots have been indicated for this deposit: Homs, Latakia, and somewhere in the Antilebanon. The uncoined metal weighs 20 kg in total and is in the form of "bars," cut pieces (*Hackstücken*) and cast pieces (*Gussabfälle*). The last are studied in the article cited below because they represent in part the result of the coins' melting (cf. pl. 17 o, the original types being unidentifiable). The coins have widely varied provenances, reminiscent of those in the Jordan hoard (*IGCH* 1482, **13**): northern Greece 17% (*IGCH* 1482, **13**: 11.5%), central Greece 3%, Athens 26% (*IGCH* 1482, **13**: 27.5%), Aegina 13.5%, Cyclades 3%, Asia Minor and Cyprus 33% (*IGCH* 1482 **13**: 33%), Cyrenaica 1.5%, uncertain 3%.

Disposition: Commerce, several pieces in the British Museum

Bibliography:
Hurter, S. and E. Paszthory. "Archaischer Silberfund aus dem Antilibanon," in A. Houghton, S. Hurter, P. Erhart Mottahedeh, and J. Ayer Scott (eds.) *Festschrift für Leo Mildenberg*, Wetteren, 1984, pp. 111–125, pls. 14–17.

9. Near East. *CH* 7.16. 1980

Burial: 475
Contents: 5 AR and fragments

Neapolis, Macedonia: 1 frag. st.
Thasos: 1 st.
Naxos: 1 frag. st.
Samos: 1 frag. tetr.
Salamis, Evelthon: 1 st.

These coins were presented to the Ashmolean Museum in Oxford in the autumn of 1980, with the sole indication that they came from the Near East, but not Egypt. They all belong to varieties known in the Asyut hoard, with the exception of the stater from Neapolis. This mint's activity seems to have been early and short-lived, which explains the absence of its output in later hoards.

Disposition: Ashmolean Museum, Oxford

Bibliography:
Kraay, C. M. "Near East, 1980," *CH* 7 (1985), pp. 38–39.

10. Moshav Dalton, 8 km west of Hazor. *CH* 8.587 = *CH* 9.346. 1971

Burial: 450–400?
Contents: AR

Tyre: 44 shekels?

This hoard is known only through a brief mention in Foerster 1971. Elayi, Elayi 2003, based on private correspondence with Foerster, specify that the lot consists of 44 coins.

Disposition: Unknown

Bibliography:
Foerster, G. *Hadashot Archeologiot* 40 (1971), p. 2.
Elayi, Elayi 1993a, p. 240, no. 52.
Elayi J. and A.-G. Elayi. "Nouveaux trésors de monnaies phéniciennes (*CH* IX)," *Transeuphratène* 26 (2003), p. 106.

11. Byblos. *CH* 8.587 = *CH* 9.356. 1933–1938

Burial: 450
Contents: 13 AR, in a bronze box, authorized excavation, found with some silver flans cut up, and one, in gold, intact; also with some casting residues, jewels and silver toiletry accessories, some fragmentary.

Byblos: 9 st., 1 fraction (Sphinx/double lotus)
Tyre: 1 st. (Dolphin/Owl)
Lycia: 1 st. (Lion/Trisceles)
Achaemenid dynasty, Sardis: 1 siglos (type 3)

Elayi, Elayi 2003, pp. 87–88, reprising Dunand's description, state that the hoard was found enclosed in a bronze box shaped like an anepigraphic Egyptian cartouche (pl. Ic).

Bibliography:
Dunand, M. *Fouilles de Byblos* II, *1933–1938*, Paris, 1954, pp. 67–69, nos. 7113–7123, figs. 44–45.
Elayi, Elayi 1993a, pp. 87–90, no. 10, pl. Ic.
Elayi J. and A.-G. Elayi. "Nouveaux trésors de monnaies phéniciennes (*CH* IX)," *Transeuphratène* 26 (2003), p. 106.

12. Northern Syria. *IGCH* 1481 = *CH* 8.587 = *CH* 9.357. 1953

Burial: 450
Contents: 4+ AR

Byblos: 3 shekels
Achaemenid dynasty, Sardis: 1 siglos

According to Elayi, Elayi 2003, this small hoard might be the oldest that we know of containing Phoenician coins. Jenkins 1959 states clearly: "The provenance of our stater, as of several others which now exist, is not known: there may well have been a small hoard" (p. 41). A specimen previously published in Newell 1926, p. 9, and discovered in the port of Byblos with fractional denominations makes the attribution certain.

Disposition: New York 1 (Byblos), London 1 (Byblos)

Bibliography:
Newell, E. T. *Some Unpublished Coins of Eastern Dynasts*. ANS NNM 30, 1926.
Jenkins, G. K. "Recent acquisitions of Greek coins by the British Museum," *Numismatic Chronicle* (1959), pp. 23–45, no. 21.

Elayi, Elayi 1993a, pp. 115–116, no. 17, pl. 18.
Elayi J. and A.-G. Elayi. "Nouveaux trésors de monnaies phéniciennes (*CH* IX)," *Transeuphratène* 26 (2003), p. 106.

13. Region of Bostra, Hauran, Jordan, called "Jordan" or "Jordanian" Hoard. *IGCH* 1482 = *CH* 9.355. 1967

Burial: 445
Contents: 113 AR, ingots, fragments, jewelry, plated coin

Messina: 1 st.
Acanthus: 3 frags. of tetr.
Aegae: 1 frag. of a st.
Bisaltae: 2 frags. of octadr.
Lete: 2 frags. of a st.
Macedonian tribes: 2 frags.
Alexander I of Macedon: 1 octadr.
Abdera: 1 frag. of tetr.
Thasos: 1 frag. of tetr.
Corcyra: 1 st.
Athens: 11 coins and 20 frags., including 1 Wappenmünzen ob. with wheel, 1 frag. of a decadr., 1 dr.
Aegina: 2 frags. of a st.
Corinth: 1 st.
Elis: 1 dr.
Delos: 1 frag. of a st.
Clazomenae: 1 frag. of a st.
Ephesus: 1 dr.
Miletus: 5 diob.
Chios: 2 frags. of a didr.
Caria: 1 AR (1.79 g)
Lycia: 1 st., 1 diob., 1 frag. of a st.
Phaselis: 1 st., 1 frag. of a st.
Baalmelek of Citium: 1 st., 4 frags. of a st.
Idalion: 3 frags. of a st., 1 tetrob.
Lapethus: 1 frag. of a st.
Paphos: 2 frags. of a st., 1 tetrob., 1 frag. of a tetrob.
Salamis: 2 frags. of a st., 1 ob.; Evelthon: 1 frag. of a st., 1 ob.
Cyprus: 1 frag., 1 st.
Tyre: 1 double shekel
Gaza: 1 dr. (intrusion?)
Achaemenid dynasty, Sardis: 1 siglos
Uncert. mints: 3 fractions (Heads of bulls confronted/Head of bull 1,14 g; Female head/Incuse square 1.72 g); 6 frags.
Unidentified: 15 frags.
10 little frags. of silver (51.01 g)
32 pieces of jewelry (beads, elements of bracelets and necklaces, earrings) and frags. of silver

This hoard was probably discovered in the early months of 1967 on the border between Syria and Jordan, in the Hauran. It was acquired in one principal lot containing jewelry, and in two other, smaller lots. It seems complete, with the exception of two beautifully made Archaic Athenian tetradrachms that Kraay, Moorey 1968 could not examine. It also contains a Wappenmünze and only one double shekel of Tyre, despite the latter mint's proximity. The authors conclude, on the basis of the hoard's evidence, that the shekel belongs to the first series from Tyre, to be dated a little before the mid-fifth century (p. 191). The coin from Gaza does not have the same patina as the others and could be an intrusion. The breakdown of origins is similar to that of the Zagazig hoard (Egypt, *IGCH* 1645, 84 coins vs. 89 identified in the Jordan hoard): Thraco-Macedonian region: 13/Zagazig 23; Athens 31/34; Asia Minor 15/12; Cyprus 21/1. The large representation of Cypriot coins in the Jordan hoard could stem from privileged ties with Syria, since the island's coins did not circulate towards Egypt. Thraco-Macedonian coins are common in Syrian hoards of this period. Some are more than a quarter-century old and have been cut several times. The Athenian coins, numerous, as was to be expected in this period, belong to quite varied series: Kraay, Moorey 1968, pp. 207–208, note the presence of a Wappenmünze fraction, of a halved decadrachm, of 27 tetradrachms from before 480, versus seven after that date, four of which must have shown up just before the burial, given their unworn appearance. Production of the years 480 450 BC consequently seems to have been weaker than in the preceding period. The virtual absence of Aeginetan coins, which were struck in abundance at the end of the sixth century, is surely a sign of deliberate exclusion or chance according to Kraay and Moorey (p. 208). In fact coins of this mint are rare in Syria (**6:** 1 st.; **8:** 9 st.; **15:** 1 st.; **17:** 8 st. and 3 frags.).

Mattingly 1986 connects this hoard with Cimon's last campaign (450/49 BC), on Cyprus, and approves of Kraay's proposed dating, c. 445 BC, as do Elayi, Elayi 1993a, p. 241 ("around 450 or a little after").
Starr 1970 uses this hoard to establish his dating of Athenian tetradrachms: it does not contain a specimen from the standardized series, which would therefore be later, Starr's Group V ceasing to be struck c. 449 (p. 63); in contrast, "pre-Persian" tetradrachms are as frequent here as those from the time of the Persian Wars (p. 81). He observes that at this time tetradrachms far from dominate in Levantine circulation (p. 85, a rapid overview of the hoard, p. 88). Kagan 1987, p. 22, emphasises the circularity in the argument for dating this series, but he does not contest Kraay's dating of the early Athenian tetradrachms.

We must stress that the majority of the coins are broken. Their association with fragments of both ingots and jewelry argues for use as weighed metal (*Hacksilber*), not as a hoard of denominated coinage.

Disposition: Oxford, Ashmolean Museum 82 and jewelry.

Bibliography:
Kraay, C. M. and P. R. S. Moorey. "Two fifth century hoards from the Near East," *Revue numismatique* (1968), pp. 181–210, pls. 19–23.
Starr, C. G. *Athenian Coinage, 480–449* B.C., Oxford, 1970.
Kagan, J. "The Decadrachm Hoard: Chronology and Consequences," in I. Carradice (ed.) *Coinage and Administration in the Athenian and Persian Empires*, Oxford, 1987, pp. 21–28.
Mattingly, H. B., "The Jordan Hoard (*IGCH* 1482) and Kimon's last campaign," in I. Carradice (ed.) *Proceedings of the 10th International Congress of Numismatics, London, September 1986*, Wetteren, 1989, pp. 59–64.
Elayi, Elayi 1993a, pp. 240–241, no. 53.
Mattingly, H. B., "A new light on the early silver coinage of Teos," *Revue suisse de numismatique* 73 (1994), p. 8.
Elayi, J. and A.-G. Elayi. "Nouveaux trésors de monnaies phéniciennes (*CH* IX)," *Transeuphratène* 26 (2003), pp. 105–117.

14. Ramallah. *CH* 8.59, pl. V 21–23

Burial: 430
Contents: 76+ AR

Athens: tetr.

Disposition: Commerce

15. Northern Syria. *CH* 1.14 = *CH* 8.587 = *CH* 9.363. 1974

Burial: 425
Contents: 16+ AR

Aradus: 1 third st. (Ichthyomorphic deity/Galley); 1 sixth (Ichthyomorphic deity/Galley); 1 twelfth (Ichthyomorphic deity/Prow)
Sidon: 1 double shekel (Galley/Chariot); 1 half-shekel (Galley/Archer between two ibex protomai, Bes); 7 sixteenths (Galley/ Archer between two ibex protomai, Bes)
Getas, King of the Edones: 1 octadr.
Acanthus: 1 tetr.
Aegina: 1 st.
Achaemenid dynasty, Sardis: 1 siglos (Type II)

Nicolet studied this hoard at the Cabinet des Médailles in Paris, where it had been brought on Oct. 16, 1974. The edition of Elayi, Elayi 1993a is based on her notes. The latter distinguish Greek coins, struck in the first half of the fifth century, from Phoenician coins dating from the third quarter of the same century.

Bibliography:
Elayi, Elayi 1993a, pp. 149–151, no. 29.
Elayi, J. and A.-G. Elayi. "Nouveaux trésors de monnaies phéniciennes (*CH* IX)," *Transeuphratène* 26 (2003), p. 107.

16. Region of Jbeil? Uncertain date.

Burial: after 425
Contents: 54 AR, 3 ingots AR

Byblos: 24 shekels, 4 third st. or quarters, 3 fractions (0.68 g, 0.72 g, 0.63 g)
Tyre: 3 shekels, 4 quarters, 1 sixteenth
Sidon: 4 half-shekels, 1 sixteenth
Athens: 3 tetr.
Citium: 1 AR
Lycia: 1 AR
Uncert.: 5 AR
Ingots: 3 AR

Elayi, Elayi 2009 write that they take their description of this hoard from Seyrig's Archives. The authors make some additions: two fractions from Citium and from Lycia. I have not been able to locate this hoard in the Seyrig Archives kept at the Bibliothèque nationale de France.

Disposition: Beirut Museum

Bibliography:
Elayi, J. and A.-G. Elayi. "Nouveau trésor de Byblos d'après les archives de H. Seyrig (TLXXXIII)," *Transeuphratène* 38 (2009), pp. 65–76.

17. Massyaf (formerly called Lebanon Hoard or Syrian Hoard). *IGCH* 1483 = *CH* 8.587 = *CH* 9.362. 1961

Burial: 425–420 Kraay, Moorey[23]
Contents: 104 AR, including coins that have been cut, clipped or plated, jewelry and fragments of jewelry

Acragas: 1 frag. tetr.
Syracuse: 1 frag. tetr.
Acanthus: 1 frag. tetr.
Bisaltae: 1 frag. octadr.
Macedonian tribe: 1 frag. octadr.
Thasos: 1 frag. st.
Eretria: 1 frag. tetr.
Athens: 14 tetr., 19 frags., 2 dr. including 1 plated? (1.52 g)
Aegina: 8 st., 3 frags.
Melos: 2 st.
Thera: 1 st.
Tenedos: 1 didr.
Chios: 1 didr.
Cnidus: 1 dr.
Citium, ʿAzbaal: 2 frags. st.
Salamis: 2 st.
Sidon: 1 double shekel (intrusion?), 2 frags.; 6 half-shekels, 2 frags.; 3 sixteenths
Tyre: 2 shekels, 2 frags.; 1 quarter shekel

23. A. Meadows points out to me that the absence of Cilician coins from the hoard suggests that we should probably reject the lower date (c. 425–400) proposed by Elayi, Elayi 1993a and 2003b.

Achaemenid dynasty, Sardis: 1 siglos
Unidentified and frags.: 17
Frags. of un-coined silver: 4
Jewelry: 2 silver spirals for hair (?), silver frag.

Kraay, Moorey 1968, p. 210, note that the hoard was initially called the "Lebanon hoard" because it was exported from that country to Western Europe. Information on its precise provenance, in fact, points to Massyaf, in northern Syria. Among the fragments of non-monetary metal, a chiseled metal disk weighing 7.08 g could be a coin flan, to judge from the photograph (102, pl. 27). The breakdown of mints differs greatly from the Bostra hoard (*IGCH* 1482, **13**): Athenian coins: 35; Aeginetan 11; Phoenician 16. Thraco-Macedonians are only marginally present, Athenian coins are still numerous but belong to later series, and the larger share of Phoenician output counterbalances the weak representation of Cypriot mints. The double shekel from Sidon is much later than the other coins: it can hardly be dated before 380, and so would be an intrusion. Elayi, Elayi 1993a, p. 244, revise the coin's dating to the reign of Ba'alshillem II (407/2–372/68 BC), so the gap between it and the rest of the hoard would be no more than 20 years or so. The issues represented in this hoard stretch over more than a century; the burial would date from the last quarter of the fifth century. Elayi, Elayi 1993a, p. 245, also note the absence of coins from Aradus, a mint that was in theory active at the time of burial, which occurred in proximity to the territory this city dominated. Perhaps the fact that Aradian production consisted essentially of small denominations explains the absence.

Starr 1970, p. 85, emphasizes the presence of standardized Athenian tetradrachms, which make their appearance in the Near East between the burial of the Bostra hoard c. 445 BC (*IGCH* 1482, **13**) and the burial of the Massyaf hoard c. 430 BC, in his opinion (brief description, p. 88). Still calling the Massyaf hoard the "Lebanon hoard," Starr writes, p. 85: "The great wave of standardized Athenian coinage was spilling by this point out into the Near East, and drew with it scattered examples of earlier groups; I should be inclined to put the bulk of the hoard at about 430 BC, though a few later coins appeared in it."

Cahn 1970 publishes the drachm from Cnidus in the collection of the Bibliothèque nationale de France (no. 32, 2). Kraay, *Numismatic Chronicle* (1964), p. 20, cites this hoard because it contains rare fifth-century staters from Melos. Two other hoards he mentions were discovered on Melos itself. The same author, in *Journal of Hellenic Studies* 84 (1964), p. 78, notes that the presence of Sicilian fractions in eastern hoards is exceptional.

My description of the Phoenician coins follows Elayi, Elayi 1993a.

Disposition: Paris 97 (fig. 4.1), Beirut 5, private collections 2

Bibliography:
Kraay, C. M., "The Melos hoard of 1907 re-examined," *Numismatic Chronicle* (1964), pp. 1–20.
_______. "Hoards, small change and the origine of coinage," *Journal of Hellenic Studies* 84 (1964), pp. 76–91.
Kraay, C. M. and P. R. S. Moorey. "Two fifth century hoards from the Near East," *Revue numismatique* (1968), pp. 210–231, pls. 24–28
Starr, C. G. *Athenian Coinage, 480–449* B.C., Oxford, 1970.
Cahn, H. A. *Knidos. Die Münzen des sechsten und des fünften Jahrhunderts v. Chr.*, Berlin, 1970.
Elayi, Elayi 1993a, pp. 241–245, no. 54.
Elayi, J. and A.-G. Elayi. "Nouveaux trésors de monnaies phéniciennes (*CH* IX)," *Transeuphratène* 26 (2003), p. 107.

18. Beithir, 22 km northeast of Saida. *IGCH* 1489 = *CH* 8.587 = *CH* 9.366 = *CH* 10.216 = Noe 134. 1901

Burial: 407–368 (*CH* 9.366); 370 (*IGCH*); after 368 (Elayi, Elayi 2003)
Contents: 510+ AR, overstrikes
Coins studied: 179/510

Sidon: 170+ or 177+ double-shekels ,
Athens: 2+ or 9+ tetr. facing eye

Rouvier 1901 and 1902, pp. 256–58, states that this hoard was discovered at the beginning of 1901 in the Chouf Mountains, in the valley of the Nahr el-Awaleh (the ancient Bostrenus). Of the original 510 coins, only 179 were brought to Beirut; villagers melted the rest on the site. Rouvier examined all that had been preserved and acquired 11 for his personal collection. His two publications contradict each other: in 1901, he states that the find contained 9 Athenian owls and 170 double staters; in 1902, he counts but 2 owls versus 177 coins from Sidon. In 1901, p. 372, he notes ten or so specimens overstruck on earlier Sidonian coins.

Disposition: London 5; American Numismatic Society 11; Archaeological Institute, Jerusalem 1.

Bibliography:
Rouvier, J. "Note sur une trouvaille de doubles statères des rois phéniciens de Sidon," *Bulletin archéologique du comité des travaux historiques et scientifiques* (1901), pp. 371–373.
_______. "Les rois phéniciens de Sidon d'après leurs monnaies sous la dynastie achéménide," *Revue numismatique* (1902), pp. 243–260.
Schlumberger, D. *L'argent grec dans l'empire achéménide*, Paris, 1953, p. 9, no. 16.
Naster, P. "Le développement des monnayages phéniciens avant Alexandre," in A. Kindler (ed.) *International Numismatic Convention, Jerusalem, 27–31 December 1963. The Patterns of Monetary Development in Phoenicia and Palestine in Antiquity*, Tel Aviv, 1967, pp. 4 and 10, no. 1.
Elayi, Elayi 1993a, pp. 128–133, no. 21, pls. 18–19.
Elayi, J. and A.-G. Elayi. "Quelques compléments à l'étude du trésor sidonien de Beithir TXXI," *Bulletin de la Société française de numismatique* 58/2 (2003), pp. 33–35.
_______. "Nouveaux trésors de monnaies phéniciennes (*CH* IX)," *Transeuphratène* 26 (2003), p. 107.

19. Near East. *CH* 8.587 = *CH* 9.367. 1984

Burial: 407–367; before 372 (Elayi, Elayi 2003)
Contents: 50+
Coins studied: 6/50+

Sidon: 6 double-shekels (Galley/Chariot)

Data on this lot were collected from dealers in California. Elayi, Elayi 1993a attribute the six specimens studied to Ba'alshillem II (407/2–372/68 BC), the entire hoard comprising coins with the same types.

Disposition: Commerce

Bibliography:
Elayi, Elayi 1993a, pp. 152–153, no. 31, pls. 25–26.
Elayi, J., and A.-G. Elayi. "Nouveaux trésors de monnaies phéniciennes (*CH* IX)," *Transeuphratène* 26 (2003), p. 108.

20. Aleppo, ancient Beroea, Cyrrhestica. *IGCH* 1490 = *CH* 8.587 = *CH* 9.360 = Noe 28. Before 1866

Burial: end of the 5th cent. BC?
Contents: AR, pot hoard

Athens, imitations: fractions
Tyre: sixteenths (God on hippocamp/Owl)
Sidon: twenty-fourths (Galley in front of city walls/Archer)

This hoard is known only through a note of Brandis 1886. The fractions imitating Athenian types are drachms and/or obols with Aramaic inscriptions (*LBLB*) and the initials of Athens in Greek. "The specimens of this type located in the Turin Museum were found at Aleppo in a container together with sixteenth-staters from Phoenicia (bearded man on a seahorse) (owl with whip and scepter) and with twenty-fourths displaying iconography of the Great King (King as archer) (tower and wall)."[24]

Disposition: Turin?

Bibliography:
Brandis, J. *Das Münz-Mass- und Gewichtswesen in Vorderasien bis auf Alexander den Grossen*, Berlin, 1886, pp. 378–379, n. 3.
Schlumberger, D. *L'argent grec dans l'empire achéménide*, Paris, 1953, p. 9, no. 14.
Naster, P. "Le développement des monnayages phéniciens avant Alexandre," in A. Kindler (ed.) *International Numismatic Convention, Jerusalem, 27–31 December 1963. The Patterns of Monetary Development in Phoenicia and Palestine in Antiquity*, Tel Aviv, 1967, p. 6, no. 11.
Elayi, Elayi 1993a, pp. 245–246, no. 55.
Elayi, J. and A.-G. Elayi. "Nouveaux trésors de monnaies phéniciennes (*CH* IX)," *Transeuphratène* 26 (2003), p. 107.

2.3. HOARDS OF THE FOURTH CENTURY

21. Phoenicia. *CH* 10.218 = *CH* 10.219. 1998

Burial: 400
Contents: 16 AR, pot hoard

Athens and imitations: 12
Aradus: 4

This hoard was found in central Phoenicia among pottery fragments. J. and A.-G. Elayi saw all the coins but could photograph only 11.

Disposition: Commerce

Bibliography:
Elayi, J. and A.-G. Elayi. "Nouveau trésor de monnaies aradiennes, athéniennes and/or pseudo-athéniennes," *Transeuphratène* 18 (1999), pp. 75–84.
_______. "Nouveaux trésors de monnaies phéniciennes (*CH* IX)," *Transeuphratène* 26 (2003), p. 115.
Flament, C. *Le monnayage en argent d'Athènes de l'époque archaïque à l'époque hellénistique (c. 450 – c. 40 av. J.-C.)*, Louvain-la-Neuve, 2007, p. 206.

22. Ascalon. *CH* 8.587 = *CH* 9.369. 1989

Burial: 4th cent. BC

24. Brandis 1886: "Die im Turiner Museum befindlichen Exemplare dieser Sorte sind mit Sechszehntelstatern aus Phönikien (bärtiger Mann aus Seepferd)(Eule mit Peitsche und Scepter) und Vierundzwandzigsteln mit grossköniglichem Wappen (König als Bogenschütz)(Thurm und Mauer) zusammen in einem Gefäss in Aleppo gefunden worden." Elayi, Elayi 1993a found no trace of them in the numismatic museum in Turin.

Contents: 31 AR, in excavation

Imitations of Athenian coins: 31 ob.

These obols were gathered in a linen sack and were discovered in the Ascalon excavations conducted by L. E. Stager. The obverse depicts the head of Athena, helmeted, facing left, the reverse an owl, the legend AΘE, crescent moon and olive shoot. Gitler has distinguished five groups on the basis of the reverse dies, a single die having served to strike 21 obols, while several obverse dies are known for the same coins, which is unusual. The small number of die pairs represented recalls the Samaria hoard (Meshorer, Qedar 1991, **50**). These obols are characteristic of the coinage circulating in the southern Levant in the fourth century BC. They imitate Athenian tetradrachms, and not the fractions of that coinage. The Ascalon mint probably struck these small denominations, the grouping of dies showing that the coins did not circulate enough to be included with the production of other die pairs. Burial must have occurred rather soon after minting. This hoard ought to be excluded from the catalogue of Elayi, Elayi 1993a because it does not contain any Phoenician coins, contrary to what the sole mention of this hoard at the time of its publication led one to understand.

This hoard can be compared to that from the region of Hebron (*CH* 9.484, **132**).

Disposition: Ascalon

Bibliography:
Elayi, Elayi 1993a, p. 207, no. 45.
Gitler, H. "New fourth-century B.C. coins from Ascalon," *Numismatic Chronicle* 156 (1996), pp. 1–9, pls. 1–4.
Elayi, J. and A.-G. Elayi. "Nouveaux trésors de monnaies phéniciennes (*CH* IX)," *Transeuphratène* 26 (2003), p. 108.

23. Beirut. *CH* 8.587 = *CH* 9.372. 1982–1983

Burial: 4th cent. BC
Contents: 200 AR
Coins studied: 1/200+

Sidon, double-shekels : 1+ Ba'alshillem II (407/2–372/68)

The single specimen examined in Elayi, Elayi 1993a comes from a sale catalogue; it is the dealer who stated that the original lot contained around 200 coins, of which a hundred or so appeared on the California market.

Disposition: Commerce, 1 Kovacs F.L., San Matteo, California, 6, 13 Nov. 1985, no. 163.

Bibliography:
Elayi, Elayi 1993a, pp. 127–128, no. 19.
Elayi, J. and A.-G. Elayi. "Nouveaux trésors de monnaies phéniciennes (*CH* IX)," *Transeuphratène* 26 (2003), p. 108.

24. Near East. *CH* 7.28. 1966

Burial: 4th cent. BC
Contents: 12 or 2 x 6 AR?

Achaemenid dynasty, Sardis: 12 sigloi

The auction catalogue does not specify the provenance of these two lots of six Persian sigloi, the second "from a similar hoard" without further clarification. Lot 210 is, however, noteworthy, because all of its coins "have ancient counterstamps," which appears not to be the case with lot 211.

Disposition: Commerce, New York

Bibliography:
H. M. F. Schulman, 14 June 1967, lots 210–211.

25. Phoenicia or Palestine. *IGCH* 1505. 1965 or before

Burial: 4th cent. BC
Contents: 60+ AR

Athens: tetr. (with countermarks and cuts)

Disposition: Dispersed. Information from Y. Meshorer

26. Tel Michal. *CH* 10.226. 1996

Burial: 4th cent. BC
Contents: 11 AR
In excavation

Athens: 11 tetr.

These tetradrachms were not found in a container, but the excavators still considered this a hoard. The coins were apparently struck with ore from Laurion and so are not imitations, according to the metallurgical analyses of Gitler, Ponting, Tal 2009.

Bibliography:
Ariel, D. T., in A. Gorzalczany and Y. Rand (eds.) "Tel Michal," *Hadashot Arkheologiyot - Excavations and Surveys in Israel* 109 (1999), pp. 49–50.
________. "Coins from Tel Mikhal (Tel Michal)," *'Atiqot* 52 (2006), pp. 71–88.
Gitler, H., M. Ponting, and O. Tal. "Athenian tetradrachms from Tel Mikhal (Israel): a metallurgical perspective," *American Journal of Numismatics* 21 (2009), pp. 29–49.

27. Unknown Findspot. *CH* 8.587 = *CH* 9.399. 1983

Burial: 400–350
Contents: 24 AR

Aradus: 24 third st. (Bearded head/Galley; *M'*)

The sale catalogue in which this hoard appeared had only one, group photograph, which does permit identification of the coins as thirds of shekels. They showed unequal wear, according to the sale catalogue.

Bibliography:
J-L. Malter, *Collectors' Journal of Ancient Art* 4 (15 jan. 1983), inside back-cover.
Elayi, Elayi 1993a, pp. 67–69, no. 7.

Elayi, J. and A.-G. Elayi. "Nouveaux trésors de monnaies phéniciennes (*CH* IX)," *Transeuphratène* 26 (2003), p. 110.

28. Byblos. *CH* 8.587 = *CH* 9.373. March, 1983

Burial: 400–333
Contents: 1,600+ AR

Byblos shekels
The Lebanese press reported the discovery of this hoard of 1,600 coins, and Hakimian 1987, p. 201, noted it, the hoard having been entrusted to the Department of Antiquities. Elayi, Elayi 1993a, pp. 107–108, add that it sparked the manufacture of counterfeits that rapidly came on to the market and were tracked by the Counterfeit Report and the Bulletin on Counterfeits, "which seems to indicate that not all the coins were recovered by the Department of Antiquities in Beirut."[25] These coins arrived on the antiquities market at the same time as hoard no. 14 of Elayi, Elayi 1993a (*CH* 9.374, **29**), and the contents could no longer be differentiated. Hoard no. 15 of Elayi, Elayi 1993a (*CH* 9.439, **72**) is perhaps a part of the present hoard. The kings represented are 'Addirmilk, 'Ozbaal, and 'Aynel, whose reigns span the entire fourth century.

Disposition: Beirut 1,600?, commerce 1+

Bibliography:
Hakimian, S. "Une archéologie parallèle: les découvertes clandestines et fortuites au Liban," *Berytus* 35 (1987), pp. 199–209.
Elayi, Elayi 1993a, pp. 92–115, no. 13, pls. 5–17.
Elayi, J. and A.-G. Elayi. "Nouveaux trésors de monnaies phéniciennes (*CH* VIII)," *Transeuphratène* 11 (1996), pp. 95–114, pp. 98–99.
_______. "Nouveaux trésors de monnaies phéniciennes (*CH* IX)," *Transeuphratène* 26 (2003), p. 108.

29. Byblos. *CH* 8.587 = *CH* 9.374. 1984–1985

Burial: 400–333
Contents: AR

Byblos: shekels and fractions

In 1987, Naster, p. 48, introduced this find as follows: "another hoard discovered in 1983 by a student with a metal detector [...] within the lower part of a wall cleared away during the excavation"; " Monsieur P. Bordreuil saw to it that the coins arrived at the Museum of Beirut."[26] Later, Tabet noted this hoard without detailing its content: "an important, clandestine find of Giblite staters, of which numerous fractions were brought to light some five years ago right within the ancient city of Byblos."[27] It contained at least one stater of 'Azbaal, which this collector acquired.

These coins came on to the antiquities market at the same time as hoard no. 13 of Elayi, Elayi 1993a (*CH* 9.373, **28**), and the contents could no longer be differentiated. Hoard no. 15 of Elayi, Elayi 1993a (*CH* 9.439, **72**)

25. "ce qui semble indiquer que la totalité des pièces n'ont pas été récupérées par la Direction des Antiquités de Beyrouth."

26. "autre trésor découvert en 1983 par un étudiant avec un détecteur de métaux [...] à l'intérieur de la partie inférieure d'un mur déblayé lors des fouilles"; "M. P. Bordreuil a fait en sorte que les pièces arrivent au Musée de Beyrouth.»

27. "une importante trouvaille clandestine de statères giblites dont un très grand nombre de fractions a été mis au jour il y a quelque cinq ans dans l'enceinte même de l'ancienne ville de Byblos."

is perhaps a part of the present hoard. The kings represented are ʿAddirmilk, ʿOzbaal, and ʿAynel, whose reigns span the entire fourth century.

Disposition: Dispersed.

Bibliography:
Naster, P., "Trésors de monnaies de Byblos du IVe. av. J.-C. trouvés à Byblos," in T. Hackens and G. Moucharte (eds.) *Numismatique et histoire économique phéniciennes et puniques, Studia Phoenicia* 9, Louvain, 1987, pp. 41–50, pl. 10.
Tabet, N., in P. Bordreuil and E. Gubel (eds.) "Bulletin d'antiquités archéologiques du Levant inédites ou méconnues V," *Syria* 67 (1990), pp. 483–520, pp. 504–505.
Elayi, Elayi 1993a, pp. 92–115, no. 14, pls. 5–17.
Elayi, J. and A.-G. Elayi. "Nouveaux trésors de monnaies phéniciennes (*CH* IX)," *Transeuphratène* 26 (2003), p. 108.

30. Unknown Findspot. *CH* 8.587 = *CH* 9.383. 1985/1986

Burial: 400–333 (Elayi, Elayi 2003)
Contents: several hundreds AR
Coins studied: 1/several hundreds

Sidon: 1 division (Galley/King fighting a lion)

Doyen 1987 states that he examined several hundreds of specimens from this find at different London dealers in September, 1987.

Disposition: Dispersed. Charleville-Mézières 1.

Bibliography:
Doyen, J.-M. Musées de Charleville-Mézières. *Catalogue des monnaies antiques, monnaies du monde celtique et des cités grecques*, Paris, 1987, p. 65, no. 92, pl. 6.
Elayi, Elayi 1993a, p. 153, no. 32.
Elayi, J. and A.-G. Elayi. "Nouveaux trésors de monnaies phéniciennes (*CH* IX)," *Transeuphratène* 26 (2003), p. 109.

31. Region of Arwad. *CH* 8.123 and 8.587 = *CH* 9.386. 1983

Burial: 390–350
Contents: 27 AR and fragments, three figurines and a pair of silver earrings, a bronze arrowhead, seven terracotta statuettes

Aradus: 23 thirds of shekels (Bearded head/Galley)
Byblos: 1 shekel, 1 cut shekel
Thasos: 1 fragment of a st.
Athens: 1 tetr.

Accompanying the coins were three silver figurines of lions walking, a pair of earrings in the same metal, a bronze arrowhead, four broken figurines in terracotta of the "Persian Rider" type, two broken "plaques of Astarte," and a fragment of a male figurine. The coins are in very poor condition, and "they must have been out of circulation when the owner of the hoard collected them" (Elayi, Elayi 1993a, p. 41).[28]

28. "devaient être démonétisées lorsque le propriétaire du trésor les a rassemblées."

Disposition: Commerce London

Bibliography:
Elayi, J. and A.-G. Elayi. "Trésor d'époque perse de la région d'Arwad," *Revue numismatique* (1990), pp. 7–16, pls. 1–2.
Elayi, Elayi 1993a, no. 2.
_______. "Nouveaux trésors de monnaies phéniciennes (*CH* VIII)," *Transeuphratène* 11 (1996), pp. 95–114, p. 99.
_______. "Nouveaux trésors de monnaies phéniciennes (*CH* IX)," *Transeuphratène* 26 (2003), p. 109.

32. Syria. *IGCH* 1485. 1932

Burial: 380 (Schlumberger); end of the 5th cent. BC (Elayi, Elayi)
Contents: 7 AR

Aradus: 2 thirds of a shekel (BMC 3 and 7)
Sidon: 1 sixteenths of a shekel (BMC 15)
Philistia: 1 dr. (Bearded head/Owl, 3.96 g), 3 ob. (Gorgon/Flower in an incuse square; two struck from the same pair of dies. 0.84 g, 0.69 g, 0.68 g)

This hoard is described in the Seyrig Archives at the Bibliothèque nationale de France (dossier 208), with this comment: "Origin unknown. In the bazaar of Aleppo. September, 1932."[29] Once again, a hoard of very low weight. Elayi, Elayi 1993a suggest a parallel between a Philistine type with rosette and some Tyrian fractions with a similar reverse (Elayi, Elayi 1991b).

Disposition: unknown

Bibliography:
Schlumberger, D. *L'argent grec dans l'empire achéménide*, Paris, 1953, p. 9, note 1.
Elayi, Elayi 1993a, pp. 246–248, no. 57.
H. Seyrig Archives, Bibliothèque nationale de France, dossier 208.

33. Al Mina. *IGCH* 1486 = *CH* 8.587 = *CH* 9.395 = Noe 39. 1936

Burial: 375
Contents: 55 AR, in a silver purse, in excavation

Aradus: 51 (1 fraction ("ob.") BMC 45 ff., Bearded head/Galley, c. 0.80 g; 48 "eighth ob." BMC 76–78, Bearded head/Turtle; 2 "sixteenths" Bearded head/Turtle)
Sidon: 4 (3 sixteenths Galley/King fighting a lion, 1 thirty-second Galley/Archer)

This hoard, like the two others Woolley found during the excavations of 1936, comes from level III, which the excavators dated between c. 420 and 375 BC. It was enclosed in a silver container 6.7 cm high and 2.5 cm in diameter, with a lid and rings for hanging (Woolley 1938, p. 166). Elayi, Elayi 1993a, p. 62, observe that the object's small diameter would preclude storing large-sized coins, Athenian tetradrachms, Sidonian double shekels or Tyrian shekels. *IGCH* and *CH* 9.395, following Woolley 1938 and Robinson 1937, count only 54 AR. Elayi, Elayi 1993a, p. 64, list three Sidonian sixteenths of a shekel, instead of two, clarifying that Robinson made a mistake, because Woolley's photographs, published in 1936, show 55 coins, including three sixteenth

29. "Origine inconnue. Dans le bazar d'Alep. Septembre 1932."

shekels that are in the collection of the Ashmolean Museum. If so, Woolley 1938 repeats the mistake of Robinson 1937.

Distinguishing one-eigth "obols" (c. 0.1 g) from one-sixteenths (c. 0.05 g) is practically impossible; Elayi, Elayi 1993a further dispute the use of the word "obol."

Elayi and Elayi (1996) believe they can fill out this hoard with coins that appeared on the market in 1986–1987 (*CH* 8.144, **34**).

Disposition: London 20 (bought on 11th June, 1937); Oxford, Ashmolean Museum 8

Bibliography:
Robinson, E. S. G. "Coins from the excavations at Al-Mina (1936)," *Numismatic Chronicle* (1937), pp. 182–196.
Woolley, C. L. "Excavations at al Mina, Sueidia I. The archaeological report," *Journal of Hellenic Studies* 58 (1938), pp. 1–30; "The excavations at al Mina, Sueidia II," *Journal of Hellenic Studies* 58 (1938), pp. 133–170.
Schlumberger, D. *L'argent grec dans l'empire achéménide*, Paris, 1953, p. 10, no. 22.
Naster, P. "Le développement des monnayages phéniciens avant Alexandre," in A. Kindler (ed.) *International Numismatic Convention, Jerusalem, 27–31 December 1963. The Patterns of Monetary Development in Phoenicia and Palestine in Antiquity*, Tel Aviv, 1967, pp. 6, 10, no. 12.
Elayi, Elayi 1993a, pp. 62–67, no. 6, pl. 5.
_______. "Nouveaux trésors de monnaies phéniciennes (*CH* VIII)," *Transeuphratène* 11 (1996), pp. 95–114, pp. 99–101.
_______. "Nouveaux trésors de monnaies phéniciennes (*CH* IX)," *Transeuphratène* 26 (2003), p. 109.

34. Al Mina? *CH* 8.144, pl. XVIII, 21–30. 1986–1987

Burial: c. 375 (Elayi, Elayi 1996) or c. 340.
Contents: 14+ AR

Aradus: 14 fractions (Male head/Turtle), between 0.04 and 0.10 g

Elayi, Elayi 1996 suggest that this is a part of the famous purse of tiny fractions found at Al-Mina in 1936 (*IGCH* 1486, **33**). If so, the burial date would be c. 375 BC.

Disposition: Commerce

Bibliography:
Elayi, J. and A.-G. Elayi. "Nouveaux trésors de monnaies phéniciennes (*CH* VIII)," *Transeuphratène* 11 (1996), pp. 95–114, pp. 99–101.

35. Phoenicia or Palestine. *IGCH* 1491 = *CH* 8.587 = *CH* 9.398

Burial: 375
Contents: 8 AR

Athens: 1 tetr. (5th cent. BC)
Sidon: 3 sixteenths (Galley/King confronting a lion)
Philistia: 4 AR

Elayi, Elayi 1993a were able to enhance the information in *IGCH* thanks to data provided by Dan Barag. The authors date the Sidonian fractions to the reign of Ba'alshillem II (407/2–372/68 BC, on their chronology).

Disposition: Jerusalem, Hebrew University, 6 + 2 stolen in 1948. Seen by Mørkholm.

Bibliography:
Elayi, Elayi 1993a, pp. 206–207, no. 44, pl. 33.
Elayi, J. and A.-G. Elayi. "Nouveaux trésors de monnaies phéniciennes (*CH* IX)," *Transeuphratène* 26 (2003), p. 110.

36. Al Mina. *IGCH* 1487 = *CH* 8.587 = *CH* 9.396. 1936

Burial: 375
Contents: 25 AR, pot hoard, in excavation

Athens and imitations: 18 tetr.
Aradus: 7 fractions (BMC 4 ff.: Bearded head/Galley, c. 0.80 g)

This hoard comes from a house containing a large quantity of ceramics in different shapes, often inspired by Greek models. The structure's floors were destroyed, and thus it is impossible to say whether the coins were found on the floor or buried beneath. "Since the coins are of the early part of the fourth century they must on internal evidence be assigned to our Level 3" (Woolley 1938, p. 142), a level that is itself dated to the first part of the fourth century by another hoard of similar composition (*IGCH* 1488, **37**).

Wooley 1938, pp. 141–42, writes that "in room 7 there was found a vase of plain drab clay, type L3, ht. 0.15 m, containing a hoard of 35 Attic silver coins." This is an erroneous description stemming from Robinson 1937, which counts a total of 35 coins but describes only 25. On p. 186, n. 1, Robinson observes that casts of these coins are in the British Museum. He judges that 6 tetradrachms (four are illustrated, pl. IX, 1–4) are authentic Athenian issues, "and twelve of such crudeness that it is difficult to regard all, and impossible to regard some [e.g., pl. IX, 5–8], as genuine Athenian coins." The execution of the crescent is clumsy on the reverse of the illustrated specimen, pl. IX, 7, and is missing on that of pl. IX, 8. *CH* 9.396 states: "One of the Aradian obols and seven of the Athenian imitations not located in Elayi, Elayi 1993a are in fact in the British Museum."

Disposition: 8 London, British Museum; 3 Oxford

Bibliography:
Robinson, E. S. G. "Coins from the excavations at Al-Mina (1936)," *Numismatic Chronicle* (1937), pp. 182–196, pl. IX, 1–8.
Woolley, C. L. "Excavations at al Mina, Sueidia I. The archaeological report, *Journal of Hellenic Studies* 58 (1938), pp. 1–30; "The excavations at al Mina, Sueidia II," *Journal of Hellenic Studies* 58 (1938), pp. 133–170.
Schlumberger, D. *L'argent grec dans l'empire achéménide*, Paris, 1953, p. 10, no. 23.
Naster, P. "Le développement des monnayages phéniciens avant Alexandre," in A. Kindler (ed.) *International Numismatic Convention, Jerusalem, 27–31 December 1963. The Patterns of Monetary Development in Phoenicia and Palestine in Antiquity*, Tel Aviv, 1967, no. 13.
Elayi, Elayi 1993a, pp. 198–200, no. 40, pl. 32.
Elayi, J. and A.-G. Elayi. "Nouveaux trésors de monnaies phéniciennes (*CH* IX)," *Transeuphratène* 26 (2003), p. 109.

37. Al Mina. *IGCH* 1488 = *CH* 8.587 = *CH* 9.397. 1936

Burial: 375
Contents: 43 AR including some plated coins, jewelry, in excavation

Athens and imitations: 26 tetr.
Aradus: 6 fractions (BMC 45 ff.: Bearded head/Galley, c. 0.80 g)
Sidon: 9 sixteenths of a shekel (Galley/King fighting a lion)
Uncert.: 1 fraction (Four-pronged trident/Wreath? in an incuse square); 1 fraction (Bearded head laureate/Head in lion-scalp headdress?)

According to the description of Woolley 1938, different from one page to the next, this hoard was found with some ingots of silver (p. 13), or lead (p. 140), and pieces of jewelry, intact (gold and electrum necklace, p. 25, fig. 9; silver pin hung on a silver chain) or broken, in a house Woolley suggested belonged to a silversmith. He adds, p. 140: "the coins date the building to the first quarter of the fourth century." Pottery also dates the occupation of this level between 430 and 375 BC, Woolley 1938, p. 24, n. 354.

The description of Robinson 1937, pp. 186–87, differs: "This second hoard comprised a gold necklace, a silver bracelet, and 43 coins." Among the Athenian tetradrachms, Robinson (p. 187) notes three plated coins, as was one of the Sidonian fractions (p. 190); pp. 188–89, the majority of the tetradrachms had chisel or stamp marks (the letters yod, E; incised circle, circle with two horizontal bars), sometimes both.

Disposition: London

Bibliography:
Robinson, E. S. G. "Coins from the excavations at Al-Mina (1936)," *Numismatic Chronicle* (1937), pp. 182–196, pl. IX, 9–14.
Woolley, C. L. "Excavations at al Mina, Sueidia I. The archaeological report," *Journal of Hellenic Studies* 58 (1938), pp. 1–30; "The excavations at al Mina, Sueidia II," *Journal of Hellenic Studies* 58 (1938), pp. 133–170.
Schlumberger, D. *L'argent grec dans l'empire achéménide*, Paris, 1953, p. 10, no. 24.
Naster, P. "Le développement des monnayages phéniciens avant Alexandre," in A. Kindler (ed.) *International Numismatic Convention, Jerusalem, 27–31 December 1963. The Patterns of Monetary Development in Phoenicia and Palestine in Antiquity*, Tel Aviv, 1967, no. 14.
Elayi, Elayi 1993a, pp. 200–201, no. 41.
Elayi, J. and A.-G. Elayi. "Nouveaux trésors de monnaies phéniciennes (*CH* IX)," *Transeuphratène* 26 (2003), p. 110.

38. Palestine? *IGCH* 1492 = *CH* 8.587 = *CH* 9.400. 1943

Burial: 371–354; 365–352 (Elayi, Elayi 1993a)
Contents: 8+ AR

Sidon: 1 thirty-second (Galley/Archer); 4 sixteenths (Galley/King fighting a lion)
Tyre: 1 thirty-second (Animal head/Dolphin)
Athens, imitations: 2 ob.

Elayi, Elayi 1993a set forth a revised publication of a part of this hoard, following a description of A. Spaer, owner of these fractions bought in December, 1943, in Jerusalem. The Sidonian sixteenths date from the reign of 'Abd'ashtart I, which Elayi, Elayi 1993a place between c. 371/67 and 357/54 BC.

Disposition: A. Spaer, Jerusalem

Bibliography:
Naster, P. "Le développement des monnayages phéniciens avant Alexandre," in A. Kindler (ed.) *International Numismatic Convention, Jerusalem, 27–31 December 1963. The Patterns of Monetary Development in Phoenicia and Palestine in Antiquity*, Tel Aviv, 1967, p. 5, no. 9.

Kadman, L., "The monetary development of Palestine in the light of coin hoards," in A. Kindler (ed.) *International Numismatic Convention, Jerusalem, 27–31 December 1963. The Patterns of Monetary Development in Phoenicia and Palestine in Antiquity*, Tel Aviv, 1967, no. 2?: 12 AR Sidon.
Elayi, Elayi 1993a, pp. 147–148, no. 27.
Elayi, J. and A.-G. Elayi. "Nouveaux trésors de monnaies phéniciennes (*CH* IX)," *Transeuphratène* 26 (2003), p. 110.

39. Saida. *CH* 8.98. 1983

Burial: 370 BC; end of the 5th cent. BC (Elayi, Elayi 1996)
Contents: 36+ AR

Sidon: 36+ shekels

Elayi, Elayi 1996 judge that the dating is much too low and that the hoard belongs, rather, to the end of the fifth century BC.

Disposition: Dispersed

Bibliography:
Betlyon, J. W., "A new chronology for the pre-Alexandrine coinage of Sidon," *American Numismatic Society. Museum Notes* 21 (1976), p. 21, no. 15.
Elayi, J. and A.-G. Elayi. "Nouveaux trésors de monnaies phéniciennes (*CH* VIII)," *Transeuphratène* 11 (1996), pp. 95–114, p. 109, no. 76.

40. Beach south of Beirut. *IGCH* 1500 = *CH* 8.587 = *CH* 9.404. Autumn, 1966

Burial: 368–333 BC
Contents: 27 AR including plated coins, 6 AE

Sicyon: 1 AR
Cyzicus: 2 AR
Erythrae: 1 AR
Miletus: 1 AR
Samos: 1 AR
Citium: 1 AR
Aradus: 2 AR (1 Ichthyomorphic deity/Galley)
Byblos: 5 AR (3 Galley/Lion attacking a bull)
Sidon: 7 AR (1 Galley/Archer; 1 Galley/Archer between two ibex protomes, Bes; 5 Galley/King fighting a lion)
Tyre: 5 AR, 1 AR plated, 6 AE (1 AR and 1 AE Winged hippocamp, dolphin/Owl; 1 AR Winged hippocamp/Owl; 4 AR and 5 AE Dolphin/Owl)

A stroller along the beach between Beirut and Tyre unearthed this group of fractions. Sheridan notes that a coin of Tyre is plated (no. 11) and that the coins are generally worn and in poor condition. He adds, "it is probable that the plating was done in an official mint, inasmuch as it does not seem practical to counterfeit such small pieces profitably" (p. 1128) and that the British Museum possesses several of these plated coins. The Byblos coins, four of which were broken, underwent spectrometric analysis that showed they were 4.5% copper and 95% silver. The variety of denominations led Sheridan to conclude that a ship passenger assembled this hoard as he travelled from the Propontis to Byblos via the ports of Asia Minor and Cyprus.

Elayi, Elayi 1993a sharpen the description of 23 Phoenician coins, with 3 remaining uncertain. One may add that the hoard consists entirely of fractions. The heaviest is a Cyzicene of 1.17 g (forepart of a boar, tuna/lion's head). The 27 silver coins (including the plated coin) weigh in toto 16.65 g., or less than one Attic tetradrachm.

For comparison, cf. *CH* 9.548, **294**.

Disposition: Private collection

Bibliography:

Sheridan, W. W., "From Cyzicus to Tyre: numismatic evidence of an ancient ship's trip, circa 400 B.C.," *The Numismatist* (August 1971), pp. 1127–1133, one pl. p. 1129.

Elayi, Elayi 1993a, pp. 201–206, no. 43.

Elayi, J. and A.-G. Elayi. "Nouveaux trésors de monnaies phéniciennes (*CH* IX)," *Transeuphratène* 26 (2003), p. 110.

41. Lebanon. *CH* 2.39 = *CH* 8.587 = *CH* 9.406. 1970

Burial: 365–350
Contents: 50+ AR

Sidon: 50 double-shekels (1+ BMC 29)

Disposition: Dispersed.

Bibliography:

Elayi, Elayi 1993a, p. 139, no. 25.

Elayi, J. and A.-G. Elayi. "Nouveaux trésors de monnaies phéniciennes (*CH* IX)," *Transeuphratène* 26 (2003), p. 110.

42. Jablah. *CH* 8.587 = *CH* 9.405. 1983

Burial: 365–333
Contents: 100+ AR
Coins studied: 90/100

Aradus: 89 thirds of a shekel (Bearded head/Galley M')
Sidon: 1 sixteenths of a shekel? (Galley/Man confronting a lion, 0.80 g)

The one-third shekel, no. 51 in the catalogue of Elayi, Elayi 1993a, is overstruck on a coin with hippocamp, probably from Aradus, whose type appears on the obverse. 53 coins are countermarked, generally on the obverse; 6 have graffiti. All are worn and appear to have circulated for a long time. The group weighs less than 400 g and is described by Elayi, Elayi 1993a, p. 60 as "a rather modest hoard." The fraction from Sidon would be witness to the port activity of Gabala, other coins of Sidon being known in northern Phoenicia.[30]

Disposition: Stockholm 1; Private collection, Germany 89

Bibliography:

Elayi, Elayi 1993a, pp. 44–60, no. 4, pls. 2–4, figs. 15–16.

30. Elayi, Elayi 2004b, pp. 86–87.

Elayi, J. and A.-G. Elayi. "Nouveaux trésors de monnaies phéniciennes (*CH* IX)," *Transeuphratène* 26 (2003), p. 110.

43. Unknown Findspot, southern Asia Minor probably. *CH* 9.416. 1984–1985

Burial: Middle of the 4th cent. BC
Contents: 81+ fractions AR
Coins studied: 54/81+ AR

Protomes of bulls facing each other/Protome of bull: 1
Great King/Facing head: 2
Great King/Bearded male head: 2
Bearded male head/Great King: 1
Protomes of lions back-to-back/Head of Baal: 3
Female figure kneeling/Kneeling Archer: 3
Head of Hermes/Head of lion: 2
Lion scalp/Head of Pan: 4
Spearhead/Bearded head: 1
Head of ram/Facing head: 2
Head of Athena/Pegasus protome: 1
Great King/Head of Athena: 2
Kneeling archer/Winged animal: 2
Boar forepart/Female head: 4
Ares/Head of lion: 5
Head in crown/Incuse reverse: 1
Head in crown/Pellet: 1
Facing head of Apollo/Head: 2
Hermes/Heracles: 1
Facing head/Sphinx: 2
Facing head veiled/Head of Ares: 2
Bull forepart/Beardless head: 2
Bearded head facing/Bearded head facing: 1
Beardless head/T: 1
Gorgoneion/Siren: 3
Head of Hermes/Lion walking: 1
Janiform female head/Bird-deity: 1

These fractions were placed on sale in lots and may have been accompanied by bronze coins, although this is not certain. The highly degraded character of some of the specimens thwarted thorough description. Four very similar lots (A–D) probably come from the same hoard; a fifth is more doubtful (E): it contained a rather large number of novel items compared to the other lots. Troxell, Kagan 1989 remove them from their description, which presents all of lots A and B and a selection of lots C, D, and E.

All these fractions are hemiobols or tetartemoria. Identification and dating are very difficult. The incuse squares suggest striking in the fifth century; some coins could come from Celenderis, Nagidos under the satrap Pharnabazus, Cilicia (Tarsus), and Caria in the fourth century. These fractions were certainly used in local transactions; elsewhere bronze coins would have been preferred. They are probably local issues, with or without satrapal authorization.

Disposition: Dispersed in five lots. Private collections. Nos. 26 and 27: American Numismatic Society.

Bibliography:
Troxell, H. A. and I. H. Kagan. "Cilicians and their neighbours in miniature," in G. Le Rider, K. Jenkins, N. Waggoner, and U. Westermark (eds.) *Kraay-Mørkholm Essays. Numismatic Studies in Memory of C. M. Kraay and O. Mørkholm*, Louvain, 1989, pp. 275–290, pls. 63–64.

44. Byblos. *CH* 8.120, pl. IX, 1–16. 1986

Burial: 350
Contents: 12+ AR

Byblos: 1 eighth; 11+ sixteenths (8 rev. Sphinx, 1 Seated lion, 1 Falcon, 1 Head of lion)

This small group may have belonged to a more important hoard, according to *CH*. Elayi, Elayi 1996 see here a part of the hoards published under numbers 13–15 in Elayi, Elayi 1993a (**28**, **29**, **72**).

Disposition: Commerce

Bibliography:
Elayi, J. and A.-G. Elayi. "Nouveaux trésors de monnaies phéniciennes (*CH* VIII)," *Transeuphratène* 11 (1996), pp. 95–114, p. 99.

45. Near East. *CH* 8.199. 1985

Burial: 350
Contents: 25+ tetr. AR

Athens and imitations (Memphis)

Disposition: Commerce. Coin World, 4 Dec. 1985, p. 12.

46. Near East. *CH* 8.126, pl. IX, 17–20; pl. X, 1–5. 1951

Burial: 350
Contents: 19 AR, 2 ingots

Athens: 16 tetr.
Athenian imitations: 2 dr., 2 tetr. (Memphis)
Achaemenid dynasty, Sardis: 1 siglos (?)
Ingots: 2

Disposition: Commerce

47. Beirut. *CH* 8.118. 1983 or before

Burial: c. 350
Contents: 400 AR

Byblos st.

Elayi, Elayi 1996 question the findspot because coins from Byblos did not circulate outside the city's territory. The discovery date of this group leads them to connect it with hoard no. 13 in Elayi, Elayi 1993a (*CH* 9.373, **28**), of which about 100 specimens were able to be examined on the London market.

Disposition: Commerce

Bibliography:
Elayi, J. and A.-G. Elayi. "Nouveaux trésors de monnaies phéniciennes (*CH* VIII)," *Transeuphratène* 11 (1996), pp. 95–114, pp. 98–99.

48. Unknown Findspot. *CH* 8.129. Before 1993

Burial: 350–330
Contents: AR

Aradus

Elayi, Elayi 1996 assume that the dating of the hoard in *CH* implies the presence of tetradrachms of Alexander. This is not necessarily so, since those coins remain exceptional in hoards prior to the 320s.

Disposition: Commerce.

Bibliography:
Elayi, J. and A.-G. Elayi. "Nouveaux trésors de monnaies phéniciennes (*CH* VIII)," *Transeuphratène* 11 (1996), pp. 95–114, pp. 109–110, no. 77.

49. Tell el-Mellaha, some kilometers south of Beirut. *IGCH* 1499 = *CH* 8.587 = *CH* 9.419. c. 1886

Burial: 345–333
Contents: 60–70 AR

Sidon: double-shekels, Galley/Chariot (Tennes, Evagoras II, ʿAbdashtart II, Mazaios)

Rouvier 1902, p. 255, specifies that this hoard was discovered "in the remains of ancient buildings buried in the sand, by the seaside, a few kilometers south of Beirut, between the Ghadir and Choueifat rivers, at Tell el-Mellaha."[31] Rouvier 1896, p. 389, uses this hoard as one of the arguments for locating here the ancient Laodiceia in Canaan and the earlier Phoenician city on the same site, the modern city being, in his opinion, built on the site of the Roman city. The excavations of the city-center of Beirut have definitively rendered this hypothesis obsolete.

Rouvier acquired some specimens. Newell notes that he did, too, but his files do not permit us to recognize them in the ANS collection.

Disposition: Dispersed.

Bibliography:
Rouvier, J. "Une métropole phénicienne oubliée. Laodicée, métropole de Canaan," *Revue numismatique* (1896), pp. 377–396.
_______. "Les rois phéniciens de Sidon d'après leurs monnaies sous la dynastie achéménide," *Revue numismatique* (1902), pp. 243–260.
Naster, P. "Le développement des monnayages phéniciens avant Alexandre," in A. Kindler (ed.) *International Numismatic Convention, Jerusalem, 27–31 December 1963. The Patterns of Monetary Development in Phoenicia and Palestine in Antiquity*, Tel Aviv, 1967, pp. 5, 10, 19, no. 6.
Elayi, Elayi 1993a, p. 128, no. 20.
Elayi, J. and A.-G. Elayi. "Nouveaux trésors de monnaies phéniciennes (*CH* IX)," *Transeuphratène* 26 (2003), p. 111.
Absent from Noe and Schlumberger.

50. Samaria. *CH* 8.587 = *CH* 9.413. Before 1990 (back cover picture)

Burial: 345 Meshorer, Qedar; 355 Elayi, Elayi
Contents: 326 AR and fragments, some plated, 6 AE pot hoard, with some beads and fragments of jewelry

Aradus 11: 5 AR fractions from 0.50 to 0.94 g (Bearded head/Galley); 1 plated and 5 AE (Ichthyomorphic deity/Galley)

31. "dans les restes d'anciennes constructions enfouies sous le sable, au bord de la mer, à quelques kilomètres au sud de Beyrouth, entre le Nahr Ghadir et le Nahr Choueifat, à Tell el-Mellaha."

Sidon 43 AR: 34 sixteenths of which 1 plated and 6 thirty-seconds Galley/King confronting a lion; 1 quarter Galley/Chariot; 1 AE Bearded head with headdress/Galley; 1 frag. of a siglos plated
Tyre 32 AR: sixteenths and thirty-seconds? Winged hippocamp/Owl
Samaria: 182
Athens, imitations: 66 fractions

These coins were gathered in a terracotta pyxis of local manufacture. The date and conditions of discovery are unknown.

Elayi, Elayi 1993a, revisiting the inventory of Meshorer, Qedar 1991, count 7 bronze coins, a specimen from Sidon, said to be plated in the earlier publication, being, in fact, a known type of bronze. Elayi and Elayi think as well that 16 coins attributed to Samaria are actually imitations of Athenian coins, and they revise the totals for the hoard accordingly: 82 Athenian imitations and 166 "from Philistia, some attributable to Samaria," because they dispute the idea of Meshorer, Qedar 1991 that all 166 derive from the latter mint (p. 228). The description given above borrows the nomenclature of Elayi, Elayi 1993a, which seems preferable to the "obols" and fractions of obols used by Meshorer, Qedar 1991.

Disposition: Private collection, United States.

Bibliography:
Meshorer, Y. and S. Qedar. *The Coinage of Samaria in the Fourth Century B.C.*, Jerusalem, 1991.
Elayi, Elayi 1993a, pp. 218–231, no. 49.
Elayi, J. and A.-G. Elayi. "Nouveaux trésors de monnaies phéniciennes (*CH* IX)," *Transeuphratène* 26 (2003), p. 111.

51. Lebanon? Dinar Hoard? *CH* 8.143, pls. XIV–XVIII = *CH* 9.422. 1985 [rejected hoard]

Burial: 340

Contents: 150+ AR

Achaemenid dynasty, Sardis: sigloi, many countermarked, 66 King with bow and spear (Type III); 93 King with bow and dagger (Type IV)

Carradice 1998 publishes a die-study based on a catalogue of 424 Persian sigloi preserved in the museums of Fethiye (the Dinar hoard, *CH* 8.27) and Afyon (these could also come from the Dinar hoard because they were bought in the same area within ten years of that hoard's discovery and display the same characteristics, cf. especially comparative table 4, p. 81). The coins are identified on the basis of already known specimens in the Lebanon hoard, sigloi from which appear in the die-classification. Carradice, p. 78, stresses the common features of the Lebanon and Dinar hoards; and recalling the former's uncertain provenance (known only from a mention in *CH*), he suggests the possibility of its actually belonging to the Dinar hoard.

The latter hypothesis seems to me highly plausible: Persian sigloi are relatively rare in Syrian hoards, always just a few items, generally mixed in among other coinages, mostly in fifth-century hoards. The Lebanon hoard therefore appears very atypical, but is much less so in an Asia Minor context.

Disposition: Commerce

Bibliography:
Carradice, I. "The Dinar hoard of Persian sigloi," in R. Ashton and S. Hurter (eds.) *Studies in Greek Numismatics in Memory of M. J. Price*, London, 1998, pp. 65–81, pls. 17–20.

52. Sebastiye (ancient Samaria). *CH* 7.40. May, 1970

Burial: 340
Content: 2+ AR plated

Samaria: 2 obols, helmeted head right/horse right, *YRB'* (0.48 g);[32] beardless head wearing tiara and diadem r. (satrapal cap)/head wearing cap r. (0.68 g)

Spaer acquired these two coins at Sebastiye, the dealer indicating a local provenance. Pronounced oxidation had tightly fused them after they were plated, and the copper underneath showed through at several points. The obverse of the second obol shows an individual wearing a Persian tiara that often appears on Greek coins from Ionia to Cyprus. Perhaps these are issues of a Samarian governor named Jeroboam, or of a Samaritan high priest.

Disposition: collection A. Spaer

Bibliography:
Spaer, A. "More about Jeroboam," *Israel Numismatic Journal* 4 (1980), pp. 2–3, pl. 1.

53. Qasr Naba, between Zahle and Baalbek. *IGCH* 1493 = *CH* 8.587 = *CH* 9.425. Between 1929 and 1967

Burial: 340–333
Contents: 30 AR

Byblos: 1 sixteenth (Galley/Lion attacking a bull)
Sidon 28: 4 sixteenths (Galley/Archer); 1 half-shekel? (Galley/Lion attacking a bull); 4 sixteenths (Galley/Archer between two ibex protomai, Bes); 19 sixteenths (Galley/Lion attacking a bull)
Philistia: 1 dr. (Female head/Bes)

The Seyrig Archives (Bibliothèque nationale de France, dossier 209) indicate that this hoard was discovered in alluvial deposits after the swelling of the torrent at Qasr Naba; no discovery date is indicated. Elayi, Elayi 1993a recall that scholar's residence of many years in Beirut (1929–1967), during which he came to know about this find. Once again, the hoard consists only of fractions buried at the end of the Persian period, according to Elayi, Elayi, p. 139.

Disposition: Dispersed. Information from H. Seyrig.

Bibliography:
Elayi, Elayi 1993a, pp. 137–139, no. 24.
Elayi, J. and A.-G. Elayi. "Nouveaux trésors de monnaies phéniciennes (*CH* IX)," *Transeuphratène* 26 (2003), p. 111.

54. Near East. *CH* 10.253

Burial: 340–330
Contents: 76 and 2 coin-shaped dumps AR

Athens: 48 tetr. (63%)
Athens, imitations: 28 tetr. Including Egyptian imitations (Sabaces) (37%)

32. Meshorer, Qedar 1999, no. 42.

This group's provenance and discovery date are unknown. It shows similarities with the Iraq 1973 hoard (*CH* 1.78 = 2.49 = 3.22 = 7.188 = 10.248) and the Syria 1989 hoard (*CH* 8.158, **76**), which supports the idea that this is indeed a hoard, but perhaps an incomplete one. Discovery is rumored to have occurred on the west coast of Arabia, but the presence of Egyptian and Levantine imitations, the test-marks on the coins, and the two coin-shaped dumps imply a Near-Eastern origin instead. The absence of Alexander coins or coins from Phoenicia warrants dating the burial before 330. no. 51 is struck in the name of Sabaces and so would be the first example of this type found outside of Egypt.

Disposition: New York, American Numismatic Society (nos. 59, 71, 77 and 78 (2 dumps))

Bibliography:
van Alfen, P. "A new Athenian 'owl' and bullion hoard from the Near East," *American Journal of Numismatics* 16–17 (2004–2005), pp. 47–62, pls. 6–16.

55. Tell Abu Hawam, near Haifa (ancient Shiqmona). *IGCH* 1502 = *CH* 8.587 = *CH* 9.426 = Noe 1039. August 15, 1930

Burial: 337
Contents: 109+ AR, pot hoard discovered accidentally on the tell, in the foundations of a building.

Tyre: 14 shekels (Phoenician weight) (BMC 11 ff.); 95 st. (Attic weight) (BMC 25 ff., to year 33), same types: God on winged hippocamp/Owl

Lambert 1931 explains that the hoard was situated a meter beneath the surface of the tell, near fragments of an earthen jug that still bore traces of silver oxidation. The Department of Antiquities obtained 64 coins, while "a further batch of 47 coins, believed to complete the hoard, was sold on the same day to a Haifa antiquities dealer by an unknown individual, probably to be identified with the laborer who found the coins in the first instance and who afterwards left the work and disappeared" (p. 10). Hamilton's 1933 excavation report does not mention this hoard; Hamilton 1934, p. 3, suggests that "its presence proves nothing as to the date of the wall except that this cannot have been built after the cache." Stern 1968 proposes a new dating of the site's level II, based on this hoard. Indeed, he sees it as the sole dependable item for dating, even though Hamilton 1934 had dismissed it. This group is interesting because it contains Tyrian coins on two different standards but pre-dating the Macedonian conquest. This hoard ought to be compared with those of Wadi Daliyeh (*IGCH* 1503, **87**) and Tell el-Fukhar (*IGCH* 1501, **84**), which are from the same period and of similar composition. Pseudo-Scylax makes Shiqmona a Tyrian city, and Stern 1968, p. 217, n. 19, suggests that the devastation that befell Tyre in 332 is reflected in this region.

Elayi, Elayi 1993a, pp. 183–84, note the absence of the uninscribed Tyrian series expected between staters of Phoenician and Attic weight: the hoard being probably incomplete, it would be imprudent to draw any conclusions about the chronology of Tyrian coinages. They also think judge that it is not possible to connect the burial of this hoard with the Macedonian conquest: the latest coin, on their reckoning, comes from 337, and there is no other information suggesting a later burial. One might add that the hoard was placed under a wall foundation, which is not all that typical of an emergency situation.

Disposition: Jerusalem, Rockefeller Museum

Bibliography:
Lambert, C. "A hoard of Phoenician coins," *Quarterly of the Department of Antiquities in Palestine* 1 (1931), pp. 10–20, pl. 19.
Regling, K. *Zeitschrift für Numismatik* (1931), p. 137, offers a brief review of Lambert 1931.
Hamilton, R. W. "Tell Abu Hawam," *Quarterly of the Department of Antiquities in Palestine* 3 (1933), pp. 74–80, for the levels concerned: pp. 78–79.

_______. "Excavations at Tell Abu Hawam," *Quarterly of the Department of Antiquities in Palestine* 4 (1934), pp. 1–69.
Cross, F. M. "The discovery of the Samaria papyri," *The Biblical Archaeologist* 26/4 (1963), pp. 110–121.
Kadman, L. "The monetary development of Palestine in the light of coin hoards," in A. Kindler (ed.) *International Numismatic Convention, Jerusalem, 27–31 December 1963. The Patterns of Monetary Development in Phoenicia and Palestine in Antiquity*, Tel Aviv, 1967, no. 3.
Naster, P. "Le développement des monnayages phéniciens avant Alexandre," in A. Kindler (ed.) *International Numismatic Convention, Jerusalem, 27–31 December 1963. The Patterns of Monetary Development in Phoenicia and Palestine in Antiquity*, Tel Aviv, 1967, pp. 6, 14–17, no. 10.
Stern, E. "The dating of stratum II at Tell Abu Hawam," *Israel Exploration Journal* 18 (1968), pp. 213–219, pp. 215–219 on this hoard.
Elayi, Elayi 1993a, pp. 170–185, no. 35, pls. 27–32.
Elayi, J. and A.-G. Elayi. "Nouveaux trésors de monnaies phéniciennes (*CH* IX)," *Transeuphratène* 26 (2003), p. 111.

56. Vicinity of Tripoli, Lebanon. *IGCH* 1495 = *CH* 8.587 = *CH* 9.427. 1937

Burial: 337–333
Contents: 114 AR

Aradus: 5 st. (Bearded head/Galley M'G, BMC 66–68); 61 "tetrob." (thirds of shekels?); 48 "ob." (sixteenths?)

Disposition: Dispersed. Information from E. S. G. Robinson

Bibliography:
Elayi, Elayi 1993a, pp. 43–44, no. 3.
Elayi, J. and A.-G. Elayi. "Nouveaux trésors de monnaies phéniciennes (*CH* IX)," *Transeuphratène* 26 (2003), p. 111.

57. Eastern Turkey or Syria. *CH* 8.152, pl. XX, 6–7

Burial: 335
Contents: 100+ AR

Athens, imitations: 2 tetr. with Aramaic letter on the cheek.

Disposition: Commerce

58. Damascus. *CH* 8.587 = *CH* 9.428. February, 1959

Burial: 335
Contents: 12+ AR

Tyre: 'Ozmilk 12 shekels (Attic weight) (years 8–15), God on winged hippocamp/Owl

Disposition: Commerce. Information from H. Seyrig.

Bibliography:
Elayi, Elayi 1993a, pp. 189–191, no. 38.

Elayi, J. and A.-G. Elayi. "Nouveaux trésors de monnaies phéniciennes (*CH* IX)," *Transeuphratène* 26 (2003), p. 112.

59. Vicinity of Gaza. *CH* 8.587 = *CH* 9.429. 1985–1990

Burial: 335
Contents: 50+ AR

Tyre: ʿOzmilk 50 shekels (years 9–15)

The dates indicated on the coins correspond to the years c. 341–c. 335 BC, according to the chronology of Elayi, Elayi 1993a. Thus burial would not be connected with the arrival of Alexander's army. This hoard could be a part of *CH* 9.431 (**61**), if one of the given locations is mistaken.

Disposition: Commerce

Bibliography:
Elayi, Elayi 1993a, pp. 185–186, no. 36.
Elayi, J. and A.-G. Elayi. "Nouveaux trésors de monnaies phéniciennes (*CH* IX)," *Transeuphratène* 26 (2003), p. 112.

60. Saida. *CH* 8.587 = *CH* 9.430. 1959

Burial: 335; c. 332 (Elayi, Elayi 1993a)
Contents: 20 AR

Sidon, double-shekels : Tennes 10; ʿAbdʾashtart II 10

This hoard is only known through the Seyrig Archives (Bibliothèque nationale de France, dossier 237.III), who apparently examined it in November, 1959, at a dealer's in Beirut, where a broker from Saida had brought them. The latest specimen is dated to year 10 of the reign of ʿAynel, that is, 335 BC on the chronology of Elayi and Elayi. The specimens are well preserved.

Disposition: Dispersed

Bibliography:
Elayi, Elayi 1993a, pp. 126–127, no. 18.
Elayi, J. and A.-G. Elayi. "Nouveaux trésors de monnaies phéniciennes (*CH* IX)," *Transeuphratène* 26 (2003), p. 112.

61. Unknown Findspot. *CH* 8.587 = *CH* 9.431. 1987

Burial: 335
Contents: 6+ AR

Tyre: ʿOzmilk 6 shekels (Attic weight) (years 10–15), God on winged hippocamp/Owl

This hoard might belong to *CH* 9.429 (**59**).

Disposition: Commerce

Bibliography:
Elayi, Elayi 1993a, pp. 191–192, no. 39, pl. 32.
Elayi, J. and A.-G. Elayi. "Nouveaux trésors de monnaies phéniciennes (*CH* IX)," *Transeuphratène* 26 (2003), p. 112.

62. Northern Galilee. *CH* 8.149, pl. XVIII, 31–44; pl. XIX, 1–31; pl. XX, 1–5. 1983

Burial: 335
Contents: 50 AR

Tyre: 50 st. (Bearded god on hippocamp/Owl, flail and sceptre)

This could be the hoard inventoried by Elayi, Elayi 1993a, no. 36: Gaza, 1985–1990 (*CH* 9.429, **59**), if one of the locations is mistaken.

Disposition: Commerce

Bibliography:
Elayi, J. and A.-G. Elayi. "Nouveaux trésors de monnaies phéniciennes (*CH* VIII)," *Transeuphratène* 11 (1996), pp. 95–114, pp. 101–108.

63. Phoenicia. *CH* 8.154, pl. XX, 8–10. 1985

Burial: 335; c. 339 (Elayi, Elayi)
Contents: 3+ AR

Sidon: 1 Mazaios year 16 = 347/6 BC (c. 339 BC according to Elayi, Elayi 1996); 1 ʿAbdashtart III year 3 = 340/339 BC (368/365 BC according to Elayi, Elayi
Tyre: 1 shekel undated

Disposition: Commerce

Bibliography:
Elayi, J. and A.-G. Elayi. "Nouveaux trésors de monnaies phéniciennes (*CH* VIII)," *Transeuphratène* 11 (1996), pp. 95–114, pp. 110–111, no. 78.

64. Phoenicia. *CH* 8.156, pl. XX, 11–12. 1988

Burial: 335; before 333 (Elayi, Elayi)
Contents: 12+ AR

Tyre: 2 shekels; 10 fractions

Disposition: Commerce

Bibliography:
Elayi, J. and A.-G. Elayi. "Nouveaux trésors de monnaies phéniciennes (*CH* VIII)," *Transeuphratène* 11 (1996), pp. 95–114, pp. 111–112, no. 79.

65. Near East, Jbeil? *CH* 9.432 = *CH* 10.243. 1992

Burial: 335–330 (*CH* 10); 339–335 (Elayi, Elayi 1992)
Contents: 394 AR
Coins studied: 93 + 4 (Ronde 2002)/394

Byblos: 92 + 4 sixteenth st. (Galley l., winged hippocamp/Lion attacking a bull)
Sidon: 1 fraction (Galley/Individual fighting a lion), *MZ* (Mazaios), year 10

Elayi and Elayi published 93 coins of this hoard and were able to identify the other 301 despite the absence of cleaning. Ronde 2003 publishes four supplementary coins. The find belonged to a private collector at the time of publication. All the coins are fractions; all the coins of Byblos have the same types. The specimen from Sidon is dated probably between 339 and 335 BC. It weighs 0.83 g. The modal weight of the Byblos specimens, cleaned, is 0.68 g (mean weight: 0.72 g), uncleaned, 0.83 g (mean: 0.80 g). The hoard's total weight is 307.52 g. It belongs to the category of hoards of 100 to 500 grams, the most common, according to the catalogue of Elayi, Elayi 1993a, p. 327. This is the ninth coin deposit of Byblos these authors have inventoried, the eight previous showing that the coins of this mint circulated little outside the city's territory. For this reason Elayi, Elayi 1993a suggest that this hoard was discovered in the region of Jbeil. The vast majority of the coins date from the reign of 'Aynel, probably the middle thereof, judging by the classification Elayi and Elayi adopt, between 339 and 335 BC, and so with no connection to the Macedonian conquest.

Disposition: Private collection

Bibliography:
Elayi, J. and A.-G. "Nouveau trésor de monnaies de Byblos (1992)," *Revue belge de numismatique* 139 (1993), pp. 17–30, pls. I–IV.
Ronde, A. "Etude sommaire de trois 'trésors' proche-orientaux de provenance incertaine," *Bulletin de la Société française de numismatique* 57/4 (avril 2002), pp. 57–62.
_______. "Compléments et rectificatifs à l'article du Bulletin d'avril 2002 sur trois trésors proche-orientaux," *Bulletin de la Société française de numismatique* 58/4 (avril 2003), p. 64.
Elayi, J. and A.-G. Elayi. "Nouveaux trésors de monnaies phéniciennes (*CH* IX)," *Transeuphratène* 26 (2003), pp. 112 and 116–117.

66. South of the Aradian Peraea. *CH* 8.81 = *CH* 8.587 = *CH* 9.368 September, 1983

Burial: 334
Contents: 187 AR
Coins studied: 26/187

Aradus: 25+ shekels (Bearded head/Galley); 161 further shekels quickly examined
Athens: 1 tetr.

The 161 uncleaned coins of this hoard that could not be studied seem to be shekels from Aradus, according to Elayi, Elayi 1986. Some of them had circulated a great deal.

Elayi, Elayi 1993a clarify that this hoard was discovered during construction work on the mainland a little to the south of Arwad. It was enclosed in a pot that could not be studied. Only 26 coins could be examined following excessive cleaning; the rest received a rapid survey. The burial date rests on the numbers on the Aradian shekels marked with the letters *M'G* (possibly the initial of Gerashtart, last known king of Arwad), year 6 being the last year represented in the hoard.

Disposition: Private collection

Bibliography:
Elayi, J. and A.-G. Elayi "A treasure of coins from Arwad," *The Journal of the Ancient Near Eastern Society* 18 (1986), pp. 3–24, pls. I–VI.
Elayi, Elayi 1993a, no. 1.
_______. "Nouveaux trésors de monnaies phéniciennes (*CH* VIII)," *Transeuphratène* 11 (1996), pp. 95–114, p. 98.
_______. "Nouveaux trésors de monnaies phéniciennes (*CH* IX)," *Transeuphratène* 26 (2003), p. 108.

67. Safed (ancient Seph), Galilee. *CH* 8.587 = *CH* 9.433. 1965

Burial: 334
Contents: c. 160 AR
Coins studied: 130/160 AR

Tyre: ʿOzmilk 130 shekels (Attic weight) (years 1–16), all of the type god riding winged hippocamp/Owl

The Seyrig Archives (Bibliothèque nationale de France, dossier 237.II) indicate that this hoard was brought on to the Beirut market by a man from Safed in the spring of 1965; 115 shekels are described, the find containing at least 160 coins. A letter from H. C. Lindgren to Seyrig notes 15 additional specimens seen at a Beirut dealer's. Year 16 of ʿOzmilk would correspond to 334 BC, and "the hoard might have been buried c. 334, since we see no reason to connect this burial at any cost to the arrival of Alexander's armies"[33] (Elayi, Elayi 1993a, p. 188).

Disposition: Dispersed. Information from H. Seyrig and H.C. Lindgren.

Bibliography:
Elayi, Elayi 1993a, pp. 187–189, no. 37.
Elayi, J. and A.-G. Elayi. "Nouveaux trésors de monnaies phéniciennes (*CH* IX)," *Transeuphratène* 26 (2003), p. 112.

68. Near East. *CH* 10.244. Before 2006 (c. 1986?)

Burial: 334–330
Contents: 475 AR

Sinope: 3 dr.
Amisos: 1 dr. (imitation?)
Asia Minor, Persian royal mint: 5 tetr.
Mausolus, Caria: 1 tetr.
Aspendus: 2 st.
Tarsus, Mazaios: 11 st.
Issus, Mazaios: 1 shekel
Sidon, Mazaios: 5 double-shekels
Tyre: 7 shekels
Athens, imitations: 30 tetr.
Athens: 49 tetr. + 360 tetr. Pi-style

33. "le trésor pourrait avoir été enfoui vers 334, car nous ne voyons pas de raison de lier à tout prix cet enfouissement à l'arrivée des armées d'Alexandre."

This group of coins arrived at the American Numismatic Society between 2006 and 2008 in three lots said to come from the same hoard. No precise provenance could be given; the hoard is thought to originate in northern Syria. It was allegedly discovered around twenty years prior to its entering the collection of the ANS. More than 90% of the coins are Athenian "owls." They belong to groups whose striking stretched from the end of the fifth century to the end of the fourth. 75% are in the Pi style.

The geographic breakdown of the coins shows that they were collected after the 350s. The absence of Alexander tetradrachms suggests burial before 330 BC. The similarity to the Syria 1989 hoard (**76**) is obvious. Perhaps they are two parts of the same ensemble or two distinct hoards reflecting the state of currency circulation at the time. The mints represented roughly follow the route taken by the Macedonians at the time of the conquest. The die connection between two imitation Athenian tetradrachms of Artaxerxes III Ochus struck in Egypt argues in favor of a satrapal hoard meant for a payment and transported to Syria. There is no guarantee that this had anything to do with Alexander's campaign. It might, however, be evidence of the upheavals in coin circulation owing to the period's troubled political conditions. One might add that the complete absence of Alexander tetradrachms argues for a burial date earlier than the 320s.

Disposition: American Numismatic Society, New York

Bibliography:
Anderson, L. and P. van Alfen. "A fourth century BCE hoard from the Near East," *American Journal of Numismatics* 20 (2008), pp. 155–198, pls. 47–58.

69. Byblos. *IGCH* 1496 = *CH* 8.587 = *CH* 9.435 = Noe 175. 1931

Burial: 333
Contents: 217 or 218 AR, including plated coins, pot hoard, in excavation

Byblos: ʿOzbaal 139 shekels, ʾAddirmilk 30 shekels, ʿAynel 49 shekels

This vase, actually a small jug of local type, 22 cm high,[34] was found between the tell of Byblos and the sea, near another that contained coins of Sidon and tetradrachms of Alexander and Philip (*IGCH* 1515, **107**). They are sometimes confused (Noe 175, Seyrig Archives [Bibliothèque nationale de France, dossier 210]), although they form two separate lots. Different editors have, however, emphasized the physical proximity of the two containers and the high probability that they had the same owner. Hoard formation having lasted throughout almost the entire fourth century, Elayi, Elayi 1993a, p. 87, propose seeing here "a reserve successively augmented by several individuals, like a family endeavor, for example."[35] One might add that 7 shekels of Byblos were found between the two hoards and may come from them. Unlike the coins contained in the vases, they were very damaged by their time in the ground.

Noe 1937 makes clear that his information comes from a letter of Seyrig, director of the Antiquities Service, dated June 18, 1931. Elayi, Lemaire 2009, pp. 77–78, state that they worked from notes Donceel took at the Beirut Museum in 1964, Seyrig's notes stored at the Bibliothèque nationale de France, and photos of casts kept at the Israeli Department of Antiquities and Museums. The hoard totals 217 coins according to Dunand and the Seyrig Archives, but the reconstitution by Elayi, Lemaire 2009 comes to 218.

Dunand 1939, p. 407, no. 6091–6307, mentions in passing the existence of plated specimens with a lead core but without identifying the coins concerned.

Disposition: Beirut Museum

34. Elayi, Lemaire 2009, p. 90.
35. "une réserve alimentée successivement par plusieurs individus, de type familial par exemple."

Bibliography:
Dunand, M. *Fouilles de Byblos* I, *1926–1932*, Paris, 1939, pp. 407–409, nos. 6091–6307, pl. 171 and xci– xcii.
Naster, P. "Le développement des monnayages phéniciens avant Alexandre," in A. Kindler (ed.) *International Numismatic Convention, Jerusalem, 27–31 December 1963. The Patterns of Monetary Development in Phoenicia and Palestine in Antiquity*, Tel Aviv, 1967, pp. 5, 12–13, no. 2.
Naster, P. "Trésors de monnaies de Byblos du IVe. av. J.-C. trouvés à Byblos," in T. Hackens and G. Moucharte (eds.) *Numismatique et histoire économique phéniciennes et puniques, Studia Phoenicia* 9, Louvain, 1987, pp. 41–50, pl. 10.
Elayi, Elayi 1993a, pp. 83–87, no. 9.
Elayi, J. and A.-G. Elayi. "Nouveaux trésors de monnaies phéniciennes (*CH* IX)," *Transeuphratène* 26 (2003), p. 112.
Elayi J. and A. Lemaire. "Le trésor de Byblos TIX," *Transeuphratène* 38 (2009), pp. 77–98, pls. IX–XI.

70. Byblos. *CH* 8.587 = *CH* 9.437. 1933–1938

Burial: 333
Contents: 10 + 58 AR

Lot A: Byblos 10 st. 'Ozbaal (Galley/Lion attacking a bull)
Lot B: Byblos 58 st. 'Ozbaal, 'Addirmilk, 'Aynel (Galley/Lion attacking a bull)
+ 1 shekel of Byblos discovered several meters away from lots A and B.

Naster 1987, p. 48, was the first to reconstitute these two groups, followed by Elayi, Elayi 1993a, in the wake of Dunand's rather imprecise descriptions. The coins were found in the same excavation zone, apparently in two, undispersed lots, with the exception of one last shekel found in the neighboring excavation zone.

Disposition: Unknown.

Bibliography:
Dunand, M. *Fouilles de Byblos* II, 2, *1933–1938*, Paris, 1958, p. 833, nos. 16399–16408 and 16409–16467.
Naster, P. "Trésors de monnaies de Byblos du IVe s. av. J.-C. trouvés à Byblos," in T. Hackens and G. Moucharte (eds.) *Numismatique et histoire économique phéniciennes et puniques, Studia Phoenicia* 9, Louvain, 1987, pp. 41–50, pl. 10.
Elayi, Elayi 1993a, pp. 90–91, no. 11.
Elayi, J. and A.-G. Elayi. "Nouveaux trésors de monnaies phéniciennes (*CH* IX)," *Transeuphratène* 26 (2003), p. 113.

71. Byblos *CH* 8.587 = *CH* 9.438. 1957

Burial: 333
Contents: 439 AR

Byblos: 438 shekels, of which 135 'Ozbaal, 31 'Addirmilk, 35 'Aynel (Galley/Lion attacking a bull) studied by Dunand. The other coins were of the same reigns.
Tyre: 1 shekel (Dolphin/Owl)

Naster 1987, p. 48, counts 438 coins in this hoard: he does not mention the Tyrian shekel in his summary description on p. 43. Chéhab 1977 does mention this coin, attributing it to the "Third Byblos hoard." Although the Byblos hoard studied here is Dunand's fourth discovery, published by Naster 1987, Elayi, Elayi 1993a think that the shekel belongs to this group, not the third.

The Tyrian shekel is clearly older than the coins from Byblos: it dates from the end of the third quarter of the fifth century, according to Elayi, Elayi 1993a, p. 92, whereas the Byblos coins run the gamut of the fourth century. Elayi and Elayi date the find to the end of the Persian period.

Disposition: Beirut Museum

Bibliography:
Chéhab, M. *Monnaies gréco-romaines et phéniciennes du Musée national*, Paris, 1977, p. 54, no. 2709, pl. 53, 1.
Naster, P. "Trésors de monnaies de Byblos du IVe s. av. J.-C. trouvés à Byblos," in T. Hackens and G. Moucharte (eds.) *Numismatique et histoire économique phéniciennes et puniques, Studia Phoenicia* 9, Louvain, 1987, pp. 41–50, pl. 10.
Elayi, Elayi 1993a, pp. 91–92, no. 12.
Elayi, J. and A.-G. Elayi. "Nouveaux trésors de monnaies phéniciennes (*CH* IX)," *Transeuphratène* 26 (2003), p. 113.

72. Byblos. *CH* 8.587 = *CH* 9.439. 1988

Burial: 333
Contents: AR

Byblos: shekels (Galley/Lion attacking a bull)

This group came on the market in 1988 and is perhaps a part of hoards 13 (*CH* 9.373, **28**) or 14 (*CH* 9.374, **29**) inventoried in Elayi, Elayi 1993a. The latest coins are fourth-century, before 333 BC.

Disposition: Commerce

Bibliography:
Elayi, Elayi 1993a, pp. 92–115, no. 15, pl. 17.
Elayi, J. and A.-G. Elayi. "Nouveaux trésors de monnaies phéniciennes (*CH* IX)," *Transeuphratène* 26 (2003), p. 108.

73. Palestine. *IGCH* 1498 = *CH* 8.587 = *CH* 9.442. 1963

Burial: 333
Contents: c. 30 AR
Coins studied: 2/30

Sidon: double-shekels ('Abd'ashtart I and Mazaios)

Two double shekels of Mazday (years 2 and 18) entered Spaer's collection. Elayi, Elayi 1993a are struck by the absence of coins of kings of Sidon contemporary with the rule of Mazday over their city and wonder if the double shekels attributed to 'Abd'ashtart I are not in fact of 'Abd'ashtart II. They date the burial to the end of the Persian period.

Disposition: Spaer Collection 2. Information from Y. Meshorer and A. Spaer

Bibliography:
Elayi, Elayi 1993a, pp. 148–149, no. 28, pl. 25.

Elayi, J. and A.-G. Elayi. "Nouveaux trésors de monnaies phéniciennes (*CH* IX)," *Transeuphratène* 26 (2003), p. 113.

74. Phoenicia. *IGCH* 1497 = *CH* 8.587 = *CH* 9.443 = *CH* 10.257. 1946 or before

Burial: 333 or before; before 335 (Elayi, Elayi 1993a)
Contents: 15+ AR

Byblos: ʿOzbaal 6 shekels (Galley and hippocamp/Lion); ʿAddirmilk 2 shekels (same types); ʿAynel 4 shekels (same types); uncert. 3 shekels

Elayi, Elayi 1993a emphasize the absence of coins of ʿOzbaal, but this observation is no longer justified if 10 new coins published by Meadows 2006 are indeed part of this hoard. The hoard's provenance could be the region of Byblos, since the coins of that mint did not circulate widely.

Meadows 2006 digs back to the notes in Robinson's hoard diary, which seem to be the basis for the entry in *IGCH*. Three coins entered the British Museum, the first in 1946, which modifies the lot's discovery date. Moreover, 10 other coins with the same types acquired by a British soldier in the Near East during the Second World War were shown to the British Museum in 2006. Meadows suggests they come from the same find, and his is the catalogue reproduced here. Two obverse dies connect the shekels of ʿOzbaal.

Disposition: Information from E.S.G. Robinson. London 3, Private collection 10.

Bibliography:
Elayi, Elayi 1993a, pp. 114–115, no. 16.
Meadows, A. R. "Coin hoards 2005 – More from the 'Phoenicia' hoard (*IGCH* 1497)," *Numismatic Chronicle* 166 (2006), pp. 381–382, pls. 72–73.
Elayi, J. and A.-G. Elayi. "Nouveaux trésors de monnaies phéniciennes (*CH* IX)," *Transeuphratène* 26 (2003), p. 113.

75. Unknown Findspot. *CH* 8.587 = *CH* 9.444. 1988

Burial: 333?
Contents: 8 AR

Aradus: 8 shekels (Bearded head/Galley, mʾ sometimes followed by a number up to 4+)

The coins are photographed as a group in the sale catalogue from which they are known, with only one coin face discernible.

Bibliography:
Malter, J. L. Collectors' Journal of Ancient Art 6 1/2 (winter/spring, 1988), H 11–12.
Elayi, Elayi 1993a, pp. 69–70, no. 8.

76. Syria, 100 km east of Aleppo. *CH* 8.158. 1989

Burial: 333
Contents: 164 AR

Sinope, Pontus: 4
Cyzicus: 1

Ephesus: 1
Persian Satrap: 1 Archer/horseman
Tarsus: 1 Datames; 5 Mazaios
Hierapolis-Bambyce: 2 Abdhadad; 2 Abyati; 1 Baal seated, *B'L DGN*/Seated lion, *YM*
Tyre: 4 (to year 12 = 338/7 BC)
Athens: Price 124, van Alfen 91
Athens, imitations: according to Price, Memphis 10; Sabaces 8. Van Alfen adds 33 imitations (11 pi-style, 12 frontal eye, 10 illegible)

Price 1993 studied these coins and clearly thought they were a hoard. It reveals new Athenian "owl" imitations in the name of Artaxerxes III Ochus, some already known issues, others in a very different style (nos. 152–153) or with new inscriptions (nos. 154–156): *zayin*, *het*, and *kaph* (magistrate?) that recall some specimens in the Paris collection (Le Rider 1961, p. 13, no. 7). Three Egyptian signs associated with the pharaoh appear (?) on no. 156 beneath the Aramaic letters *ayin* and *samek*. This coin forms a connection with those of the satrap Sabaces inscribed in Aramaic. A coin of Mazaios struck in Hierapolis with Tarsian types bears an unpublished legend: *B'L DGN*, "Baal, the giver of grain" (no. 18). Its weight, 8.16 g, comes close to a Babylonian shekel.

Almost all these coins show chisel marks. None postdates Alexander's arrival, according to Price. Elayi, Elayi 1993a mention a coin of Tyre and one of Aradus bearing chisel marks. Price had sent them copies of the photographs of these coins, but he himself does not mention any Aradian specimen in his publication of the hoard in 1993. I have retained his description.

Van Alfen 2002 studies the numerous countermarks on these coins: they appear on 14% of the "owls" (pl. p. 5) and seem to be typical of Levantine or Egyptian imitations. 64% of the Athenian coins are authentic, and 36% are imitations, according to his identifications (versus 87%/13% in Price). The article then offers an overview of pre-Alexander coinages in Egypt.

Disposition: Commerce London

Bibliography:
Price, M. "More from Memphis and the Syria hoard," in M. Price, A. Burnett, and R. Bland (eds.) *Essays in Honour of Robert Carson and Kenneth Jenkins*, London, 1993, pp. 31–35, pls. 9–10.
van Alfen P., "The 'owls'" from the 1989 Syria hoard, with a review of pre-Macedonian coinage in Egypt," *American Journal of Numismatics* 14 (2002), pp. 1–58.
_______. "A new Athenian "owl" and bullion hoard from the Near East," *American Journal of Numismatics* 16–17 (2004–2005), p. 48.
Elayi, Elayi 1993a, p. 246, no. 56.

77. Nablus. *IGCH* 1504 = *CH* 9.440. 1968

Burial: 333/2
Contents: 965+ AR, including plated coins, jewelry

Sinope: 2 dr.
Amisos: 1 frag. of dr.
Athens, imitations: 206+ tetr. and fractions
Cilicia: fractions
Cyprus: fractions
Byblos: 1 sixteenth? (Galley/Lion attacking a bull)
Sidon: 102 sixteenths, 25 thirty-seconds (Galley/King confronting a lion)
Sidon?: 3 sixteenths, 1 thirty-second (Galley/King confronting a lion)
Tyre: 95 shekels (God on hippocamp, Dolphin/Owl), 73 twenty-fourths (Hippocamp/Owl), including a plated coin

Tyre: 4 twenty-fourths (Hippocamp/Owl)
Philistia: 60+ fractions

Elayi, Elayi 1993a reconstituted this hoard from data provided by Silvia Hurter on the specimens in the Spaer collection and those acquired by public collections. Meshorer, Qedar 1991, p. 40 and catalogue, publish 51 specimens. In the present state of our knowledge, imitation fractions of Athenian coins form the majority of the hoard. A Tyrian fraction of 0.29 g is plated (no. 258 in the catalogue of Elayi, Elayi 1993a).

Disposition: A. Spaer, Jerusalem 263+; New York 20 fractions; London 13; Oxford 13; Copenhagen 14. Paris? (cité par Elayi, Elayi 1993a, p. 232); Sternberg F., Zürich, 20–21 nov. 1989, no. 137.

Bibliography:
Annual Report of the American Numismatic Society for the Period Ending September 30, 1969, New York, 1969, p. 10.
Meshorer, Y. and S. Qedar. *The Coinage of Samaria in the Fourth Century B.C.*, Jerusalem, 1991.
Elayi, Elayi 1993a, pp. 231–239, no. 51, pl. 34.
Elayi, J. and A.-G. Elayi. "Nouveaux trésors de monnaies phéniciennes (*CH* IX)," *Transeuphratène* 26 (2003), p. 113.

78. Nablus. *CH* 9.441. Before 1890

Burial: 333–330
Contents: 17+ AR

Athens and imitations (not distinguished in the publication): 17 tetr.

This group comes from the collection of H. Gillman, American consul at Jerusalem from 1886 to 1891. At least eight of these coins are encrusted with yellowish earth. The collector's notes indicate that all coins come from around Nablus and were bought on four occasions between June 11, 1890, and March 3, 1891. The first lot, bought in Jerusalem, belonged to a group found in a pot containing, notably, Greek (one of Joppa?) and Venetian coins (8, c. 1890). The lot may also have contained Athenian drachms. Traces of earth are discernible on the coins of each group. Despite Gillman's care in describing the provenance of these coins, the hoard's original composition is difficult to determine. These specimens seem authentic, although the collector acquired several modern counterfeits. The die-axes are similar to those of authentic Athenian tetradrachms (240–270°). Most belong to Bingen's types pi IV and V.

Disposition: Kelsey Museum, Ann Arbor

Bibliography:
Visonà, P. "A Hoard of 4th Century Athenian Tetradrachms from Nablus," *Numismatica e antichità classiche* 27 (1998), pp. 141–149, pls. 1–2.

79. Latakia. *IGCH* 1494 = *CH* 8.587 = *CH* 9.414 = Noe 605a. 1936

Burial: 333–325?
Contents: 169 AR, pot hoard
Coins studied: 5/169 AR
Aradus: 23 shekels (1 at the American Numismatic Society, Bearded head/Galley, *M'G* 3, 10.22 g); 146 fractions (4 at the American Numismatic Society, Bearded head/Galley *M'*, third shekel)

The hoard is known only through mentions in Noe 1937 and *IGCH*.

Disposition: New York 5 (1 shekel; 4 third shekels). Notes at the American Numismatic Society

Bibliography:
Elayi, Elayi 1993a, pp. 61–62, no. 5, pl. 5.
Elayi, J. and A.-G. Elayi. "Nouveaux trésors de monnaies phéniciennes (*CH* IX)," *Transeuphratène* 26 (2003), p. 111.

80. Abu Shusheh, Judaea (the "Gezer" Hoard). *IGCH* 1507 = *CH* 8.587 = *CH* 9.434 = Noe 429. 1930

Burial: 333–320
Contents: 114+ AR, including plated coins, 10 AE

Athens, imitations: 25 or 42 (Elayi, Elayi 1993a) AR
Sidon: 29 AR; 7 AE (1 sixteenth Galley and fortifications/Archer; 2 thirty-seconds and 2 AE Galley/Archer; 14 sixteenths Galley/King confronting a lion, including 1 plated; 5 AE galley/chariot. Possibly also part of the hoard: 12 sixteenths Galley/King confronting a lion)
Sidon or Philistia: 1 AR (Galley/Archer: Newell 1938, no. 22); 1 AE (Horseman/Archer)
Tyre: 3 AR (1 god on winged hippocamp, dolphin/Owl, 2.63 g plated; 2 Hippocamp/Owl, 0.76 g and 0.48 g); 1 AR Tyre (Dolphin/Head of lion)
Philistia: 29 or 37 AR Elayi, Elayi 1993a; 14 in Newell 1938, several Athenian imitations
Alexander III: 2 AE
Alexander, imitation: 1 AR

The Department of Antiquities of Palestine acquired 71 coins, mostly fractions, when they came up for sale in small lots in Jerusalem and Jaffa (five coins), according to Lambert 1932. Data provided by the Jerusalem dealer indicate Abu Shusheh and Yebnah, near Gezer, as the provenance. These coins form a coherent ensemble and were covered with a thin layer of dark corrosion, supporting the hypothesis that this is a hoard. Some Philistine coins were in excellent, almost mint condition.

Newell 1938 notes that other specimens with the same characteristics were offered for sale in Europe at almost the same time. He includes them in his inventory (nos. 20, 25, 27, 29, 30, 31).

Kraay 1978 wonders whether this is actually a hoard or merely a collection of coins gathered on the same site. He details the identification and description of the 12 Philistine coins kept in Jerusalem.

Gitler 1996 states that 16 specimens from this hoard were acquired by the Palestine Archeological Museum (hoard 7, card 4) in February, 1933, from Dr. A. Reifenberg of the Hebrew University in Jerusalem, who had previously bought them from a Jaffa dealer, F. Salahi.

Elayi, Elayi 1993a consider that 24 Athenian and imitation, 13 Sidonian, and 10 Philistine coins in the Rockefeller Museum could belong to this same find. They also examined the museum's 71 specimens originally published by Lambert 1932 and the six specimens at the American Numismatic Society, for a total of 124 coins. nos. 10 and 39 were plated (0.72 g; 2.63 g). The 34 Phoenician coins in their catalogue weigh 25.67 g of silver (two coins are plated). Elayi, Elayi 1993a, p. 216, recall the existence of Sidonian possessions on the neighboring coast (Jaffa most notably), which could explain the presence of bronzes from this mint.

The present description includes the additions of Elayi, Elayi 1993a. The highly composite character of this hoard is noteworthy, in that it comprises pre-Alexander coinage as well as Alexanders, imitation tetradrachms and fractions, and mixes bronze and silver, an uncommon occurrence.

Disposition: Jerusalem, Rockefeller Museum 71; Cahn 14 October 1931, nos. 574–578 (= Newell 1938, nos. 20, 27, 29–31); Cahn 27 February 1933, no. 398 (Newell 1938, no. 25); New York 6 (coins published by Newell 1938)

Bibliography:
Lambert, C. "Egypto-Arabian, Phoenician, and other coins of the fourth century B.C. found in Palestine," *Quarterly of the Department of Antiquities in Palestine* 2 (1932), pp. 1–10, 2 pls.
Newell, E. T. *Miscellanea Numismatica: Cyrene to India*, ANS NNM 82 (1938), pp. 47–58, pls. III–IV, nos. 20–35.
Schlumberger, D. *L'argent grec dans l'empire achéménide*, Paris, 1953, p. 9, no. 17.
Kadman, L. "The monetary development of Palestine in the light of coin hoards," in A. Kindler (ed.) *International Numismatic Convention, Jerusalem, 27–31 December 1963. The Patterns of Monetary Development in Phoenicia and Palestine in Antiquity*, Tel Aviv, 1967, no. 1.
Naster, P. "Le développement des monnayages phéniciens avant Alexandre," in A. Kindler (ed.) *International Numismatic Convention, Jerusalem, 27–31 December 1963. The Patterns of Monetary Development in Phoenicia and Palestine in Antiquity*, Tel Aviv, 1967, pp. 5, 18–20, no. 7.
Kraay, C. M. "Some notes on the Abu Shusheh hoard," *Israel Exploration Journal* 28 (1978), pp. 190–192, pls. 29–30.
Lemaire, A. "Les trésors d'Abu Shusheh et le monnayage d'Ashdod avant Alexandre," *Revue numismatique* (1990), pp. 257–263.
Elayi, Elayi 1993a, pp. 209–216, no. 47, pls. 33–34.
Gitler, H. "New fourth-century B.C. coins from Ascalon," *Numismatic Chronicle* 156 (1996), p. 8, n. 41.
Elayi, J. and A.-G. Elayi. "Nouveaux trésors de monnaies phéniciennes (*CH* IX)," *Transeuphratène* 26 (2003), p. 112.

81. Tel Gamma. 1970

Burial: 333–302/1, in excavation
Contents: 5 AR

Yehud: 4 (Meshorer 2001 nos. 22 and 24); 1 Frag.

This small group was found on the surface of the site at Tel Gamma in spring, 1970. These coins belong to the last series struck prior to Ptolemy I's conquest of the region in 302/1 BC.

Bibliography:
Rahmani, L. Y. "Silver coins of the 4th century B.C. from Tel Gamma," *Israel Exploration Journal* 21 (1971), pp. 158–160.
Meshorer, Y. *Ancient Jewish Coinage* I, New York, 1982, p. 17.
Meshorer, Y. *A Treasure of Jewish Coins*, Jerusalem, 2001.
Gitler, H. and C. Lorber. "A new chronology for the Ptolemaic Yehud coinage," *American Journal of Numismatics* 18 (2006), pp. 1–41, no. 1.

82. Near Jerusalem. Before 1982.

Burial: 333–302/1
Contents: 3 AR

Judée: 3 (Meshorer 2001 nos. 9, 22b, 22e)

According to Meshorer 1982, p. 17, these coins were found fused together by corrosion. They are on the Persian and Attic standards (cf. Ronen 1998), which shows that the change of standard did not affect the choice of those who hoarded this small group (Gitler, Lorber 2006, p. 6).

Bibliography:
Meshorer, Y. *Ancient Jewish Coinage* I, New York, 1982.
_______. *A Treasure of Jewish Coins*, Jerusalem, 2001, p. 199, no. 22e.
Gitler, H. and C. Lorber. "A new chronology for the Ptolemaic Yehud coinage," *American Journal of Numismatics* 18 (2006), pp. 1–41, no. 2.

83. Near East. *CH* 9.456. 1992

Burial: 333–300
Contents: 36 AR

Athens: 8 tetr.
Athens, imitations: 28 tetr.

This hoard was studied in a private collection. 28 of the 36 tetradrachms show cuts, even as many as four per coin. Seven bear small countermarks of nine different types.

Disposition: Private collection

Bibliography:
Elayi, J. and A.-G. Elayi. "Un nouveau trésor de tétradrachmes athéniens," *Revue numismatique* (1994), pp. 26–33, pls. 1–3.

84. Tell el-Fukhar (ancient Ake). *IGCH* 1501 = *CH* 9.382. 1962

Burial: 332 (Kindler), before 333 (Elayi, Elayi)
Contents: 25 AR, in excavation

Tyre: twenty-fourth st. (BMC 23–24, most dated)

At the beginning of the 1960s, numerous coins were gleaned from the surface of Tell el-Fukhar, the ancient Ake, whence this hoard of 25 Tyrian fractions. Most are dated. Their types are a winged hippocamp on the obverse and an owl with crook and flail on the reverse (Kindler 1967).

Stern 1968, pp. 216–17, connects this hoard to those of Wadi Daliyeh (*IGCH* 1503, **87**) and Tell Abu Hawam (*IGCH* 1502, **55**).

The hoard weighs 14.88 g.

Disposition: Tel Aviv, Kadman Museum.

Bibliography:
Kindler, A. "The mint of Tyre – The major source of silver coin in ancient Palestine," *Eretz Israel* 8 (1967), pp. 318–324, pl. 46,5 (in Hebrew, English summary, p. 79).
Kadman, L. "The monetary development of Palestine in the light of coin hoards," in A. Kindler (ed.) *International Numismatic Convention, Jerusalem, 27–31 December 1963. The Patterns of Monetary Development in Phoenicia and Palestine in Antiquity*, Tel Aviv, 1967, no. 4.
Stern, E. "The dating of stratum II at Tell Abu Hawam," *Israel Exploration Journal* 18 (1968), pp. 213–219.
Elayi, Elayi 1993a, pp. 163–168, no. 33, pls. 26.
Elayi, J. and A.-G. Elayi. "Nouveaux trésors de monnaies phéniciennes (*CH* IX)," *Transeuphratène* 26 (2003), p. 109.

85. Qasr Naba, between Zahle and Baalbek. *IGCH* 1506 = *CH* 8.587 = *CH* 9.445 = Noe 846. 1902

Burial: 332 (Naster 1967), 330–325 (Price 1991a)
Contents: 40+ AR

Byblos: 2 sixteenths (Galley/Lion attacking a bull)
Sidon 35: 9 sixteenths (Galley/Merlon); 6 sixteenths (Galley/Archer); 1 thirty-second (Galley/Bes); 4 sixteenths (Galley/Archer between incuse protomai of ibexes, Bes); 5 sixteenths (Galley/King fighting a lion); 1 double-shekel (Galley/Chariot); 8 double-shekels (Evagoras II to Mazaios); 1 sixteenth (Galley/King fighting a lion) Sidon?
Tyre: 1 sixteenth (Dolphin/Owl)
Alexander III: 1 tetr. Babylon (Price 3581); 1 ob. Sidon (Price 3476)

Rouvier 1902, pp. 258–59, first described this hoard, consisting of numerous fractions. It was discovered at the beginning of 1902, in a village between Baalbek and Zahle, 15 km from Jdita. Rouvier gives the fractions Greek names (tritemoria, etc.), making identification of these denominations difficult. The description here reprises that of Elayi, Elayi 1993a, who address the find's curious composition, which extends from the mid-fifth century to the time of Alexander the Great, something rather unexpected with fractions.

Disposition: Dispersed. Formerly Rouvier collection: 32

Bibliography:
Rouvier, J. "Les rois phéniciens de Sidon d'après leurs monnaies sous la dynastie achéménide," *Revue numismatique* (1902), pp. 243–260.
Schlumberger, D. *L'argent grec dans l'empire achéménide*, Paris, 1953, p. 10, no. 20.
Naster, P. "Le développement des monnayages phéniciens avant Alexandre," in A. Kindler (ed.) *International Numismatic Convention, Jerusalem, 27–31 December 1963. The Patterns of Monetary Development in Phoenicia and Palestine in Antiquity*, Tel Aviv, 1967, pp. 5, 10, no. 5.
Price, M. J. *The Coinage in the Name of Alexander the Great and Philip Arrhideus*, London, 1991, p. 50.
Elayi, Elayi 1993a, pp. 133–137, no. 23.
Elayi, J. and A.-G. Elayi. "Nouveaux trésors de monnaies phéniciennes (*CH* IX)," *Transeuphratène* 26 (2003), p. 113.

86. Aradus. *CH* 9.446. 1999

Burial: 330?
Contents: Many AR

Aradus: st. and tetrob. (BMC 36 ff.)

Disposition: Commerce

Bibliography:
Elayi, J. and A.-G. Elayi. "Nouveaux trésors de monnaies phéniciennes (*CH* IX)," *Transeuphratène* 26 (2003), p. 115.

87. Wadi Daliyeh, 14 km north of Jericho, 12 km west of the Jordan River. *IGCH* 1503 = *CH* 8.587 = *CH* 9.451. 1962

Burial: 330

Contents: 9+ AR
Athens: 1 tetr.
Athens, imitations: 1 fraction
Tarsus: 1 st. Mazaios
Sidon: 1 fraction (Galley/King confronting a lion, 0.50 g)
Tyre: 5 shekels (to ʿOzmilk, year 15)

Cross 1963 relates the discovery of the papyri from Samaria by Bedouin in 1962 in a craggy region north of Jericho. The Bedouin sold the first fragments, before controlled excavation began in the winter of 1962/63. The latter unearthed individual skeletal remains of both sexes and all ages, numerous sherds and pots, jewels, 126 terracotta seals with Persian or Attic motifs, two inscribed, and shreds of clothing and additional papyri, all written in Samaria and administrative in nature (sale or conveyance of slaves, real estate transactions, divorces). The latest papyrus is precisely dated March 18, 335 BC (pp. 113 and 115); the oldest goes back to the years 375–365. The presence of the skeletons and associated physical objects may be connected with the reprisals Alexander ordered against the Samaritans for their assassination of Andromachus, his handpicked governor left in charge of the region (Josephus, *Antiquities of the Jews* 11.297–345; Curtius 4.8.9–10). This reconstruction of events is the basis for the burial of the hoard or its mere abandonment (for is this actually a hoard?) c. 330 BC.

Some coins were purchased along with the papyri, seals, and jewels from Wadi Daliyeh, and Cross believes that this is the likely provenance (p. 116). However, he only describes three coins: an Athenian tetradrachm, a stater of Mazday from Cilicia, and several Tyrian shekels marked with the letter *ain* (ʿOzmilk). The last are key, because they are of Attic weight and dated as late as "year 15." Cross 1963, p. 118, recalls that Alexander did not introduce the Attic standard into Phoenicia and suggests that these coins are probably earlier than the Macedonian conquest.

Stern 1968, pp. 216–17, connects these coins to the hoards of Tell Abu Hawam (*IGCH* 1502, **55**) and Tell el-Fukhar (*IGCH* 1501, **84**) by their context. One might add that the context of the Balatah deposits (*IGCH* 1584, **125**; 1588, **169**) is also similar.

According to the chronology of Elayi, Elayi 1993a, the shekels of ʿOzmilk from Tyre, year 15, correspond to 335 BC and to the last known date on the Wadi papyri. The coins from Philistia are quite difficult to date.

Disposition: Palestine Archaeological Museum, Jerusalem 3.

Bibliography:
Cross, F. M. "The discovery of the Samaria papyri," *The Biblical Archaeologist* 26/4 (1963), pp. 110–121.
Stern, E. "The dating of stratum II at Tell Abu Hawam," *Israel Exploration Journal* 18 (1968), pp. 213–219.
Lapp, P. W. and N. L. Lapp. *Discoveries in the Wâdi ed-Dâliyeh*, AASOR 41, Cambridge (Mass.), 1974, p. 57, no. 21.
Elayi, Elayi 1993a, pp. 216–218, no. 48.
Elayi, J. and A.-G. Elayi. "Nouveaux trésors de monnaies phéniciennes (*CH* IX)," *Transeuphratène* 26 (2003), p. 114.
Letter from H. Seyrig to F. M. Cross giving his point of view, H. Seyrig Archives, Bibliothèque nationale de France, dossier 342.VI.

88. Syria. *CH* 8.587 = *CH* 9.449. 1988

Burial: (a) 330; (b) 2nd cent. BC.
Contents: 30 AR

(a) 4th century (**88**)
Aradus: 1 shekel
Tyre: 1 shekel
Alexander III: 5 tetr.

(b) 2nd century (**260**)
Demetrius I: 2 tetr., 1 dr.
Demetrius II: 1 tetr.
Antiochus VII: 1 tetr.
Alexander II: 1 tetr.
Athens, New Style: 17 tetr.

Elayi, Elayi 1993a were able to study this hoard in the hands of a dealer in Baniyas in 1988. Although in possession of photographs of all the coins, they describe and publish only the two Phoenician shekels. The chronological heterogeneity of the group as a whole leads them to conclude that the specimens probably constitute two hoards, one, fourth century, consisting of Phoenician coins and Alexanders (**88**), the other of Seleucid and Athenian coins dating from the second century (**260**).

Disposition: Commerce

Bibliography:
Elayi, Elayi 1993a, pp. 248–249, no. 58, pl. 34.

89. Vicinity of Gaza. *CH* 8.587 = *CH* 9.448. 1975

Burial: 330–300
Contents: several hundred AR
Coins studied: 10+/several hundred

Aradus: fractions
Sidon: 6 sixteenths (Galley/King confronting a lion), Baʿalshillem II and Mazaios
Sidon or Philistia: 3 sixteenths (Galley/King confronting a lion)
Tyre: 1 sixteenth (Hippocamp/Owl)
Philistia

Post-Alexander lion-staters of Babylon.

Qedar and Lemaire pointed out this hoard to Elayi and Elayi. Only Phoenician coins are described, all fractions.

Disposition: Commerce

Bibliography:
Elayi, Elayi 1993a, pp. 208–209, no. 46, pl. 33.
Elayi, J. and A.-G. Elayi. "Nouveaux trésors de monnaies phéniciennes (*CH* IX)," *Transeuphratène* 26 (2003), p. 114.

90. Lebanon. *CH* 8.172. 1985

Burial: 325/4
Contents: 25 tetr. AR
Alexander III: 5 Amphipolis, 1 Lampsacus, 1 Side, 1 Tarsus, 1 Amathus, 1 Salamis, 5 Aradus, 5 Myriandros, 5 Babylon.

Disposition: Commerce

91. Tel Michal. *CH* 10.256. 1977–1980

Burial: end of the 4th cent. BC, after 325–320?
Contents: 5 tetr. AR, in excavation

Alexander III: Kindler 1989 nos. 21–22 (2 tetr. Aradus); 23 (1 tetr. Ake/Tyre = year 23); 20, 24 (2 tetr. Babylon)

Kindler 1989, p. 320, indicates the existence of this hoard found in an excavation, without specifying the nature of the container, if there was any, or commenting on the find. The fact that it consists only of Alexanders would indicate, in my opinion, burial after 325–320 BC, the time when this type of currency becomes dominant in Syrian hoards.

Disposition: Unknown.

Bibliography:
Kindler, A. "Numismatic report," Z. Herzog et al. (eds) *Excavations at Tel Michal, Israel*, Tel Aviv, 1989, pp. 320–329 and 443.
Ariel, D. T. "Coins from Tel Mikhal (Tel Michal)," *'Atiqot* 52 (2006), pp. 71–88, p. 80 for the date.

92. Jdita, near ancient Chalcis, Coele Syria and Phoenicia. *IGCH* 1517 = *CH* 8.587 = *CH* 9.455 = Noe 512. 1894

Burial: 325–300
Contents: c. 400 AR

Sidon: c. 200 double-shekels (Galley/Chariot)
Alexander III: c. 200 (numerous examples bearing the legends and monograms of Ake/Tyre according to J. Rouvier)

Rouvier 1902, pp. 255–56, was the first to publish this hoard, discovered in 1894. He observes that nearly half of the roughly 400 silver coins are Alexanders.

Disposition: Dispersed

Bibliography:
Rouvier, J. "Les rois phéniciens de Sidon d'après leurs monnaies sous la dynastie achéménide," *Revue numismatique* (1902), pp. 243–260.
Schlumberger, D. *L'argent grec dans l'empire achéménide*, Paris, 1953, p. 9, no. 18.
Naster, P. "Le développement des monnayages phéniciens avant Alexandre," in A. Kindler (ed.) *International Numismatic Convention, Jerusalem, 27–31 December 1963. The Patterns of Monetary Development in Phoenicia and Palestine in Antiquity*, Tel Aviv, 1967, pp. 5, 10, no. 4.
Elayi, Elayi 1993a, p. 133, no. 22.
Elayi, J. and A.-G. Elayi. "Nouveaux trésors de monnaies phéniciennes (*CH* IX)," *Transeuphratène* 26 (2003), p. 114.

93. Saida. *IGCH* 1508 = *CH* 8.190 = Noe 881, 882, 884. 1829, 1852, 1863

Burial: 323–320
Contents: 7,200+ AV in three groups

Philip II: Westermark: 6+ st. (2 Pella, 4 Amphipolis). *IGCH*: 302+
Alexander III: Westermark: 17+ st. (2 Amphipolis, 2 Salamis, 1 Citium, 1 Lampsacus, 2 Miletus, 3 Sardis, 5 Sidon, 1 uncert.). *IGCH*: 6,000+ st. and some double-st., many Sidon to year 10 and Ake/Tyre to year 24
Ptolemy I: 1+ st. (intrusion?)
Kios: Westermark: 10+ st.; 8 in Le Rider 1963
Panticapaeum: 1+
Pergamum: 2+ st. or 4+ st.
Rhodes: 3+
Salamis in Cyprus, Pnytagoras: 2.

IGCH cites Müller 1855, whose description, however, seems different from those of other authors mentioning this hoard. He specifies that, in 1854, "this pot was discovered in an ancient aqueduct outside the city and comprised 1,837 gold coins of Alexander the Great and Philip II."[36] All the other sources mention gardens and three pots containing more than 3,000 coins that came to light in 1852. This information was obtained from a Monsieur Caillol, in charge of classifying the hoard at Constantinople, and from a Monsieur Lavoix of the Cabinet des Médailles in Paris.

Waddington 1865 publishes the most complete description, edited by a Monsieur Pérétié, chancellor of the French consulate general in Beirut. The find comes from a garden called "Diuddar," south of the city, "at a distance of three or four meters from where the sarcophagus of Eshmounazar was found" (p. 3). The first find (1829) was made without any publicity and probably was mostly melted down on site. In 1852, three lead vases were discovered, each containing 1,200 coins. The discoverers were imprisoned and mistreated until they gave up 1,800 coins, which were immediately dispatched to Istanbul. "The entirety of the find rose to more than three thousand coins, among which there is agreement in saying that it might have had nearly three thousand staters of Alexander, some double staters of the same king, and two or three hundred staters of Philip II."[37] Also included were one stater of Philippi and two from Cius. In 1863, three new vases of different shape were discovered in the same spot. Two contained only Alexander staters; some rare foreign coins appeared in the third (Cius, Rhodes, King Pnytagoras, and Panticapaeum). Further investigations of the area did not unearth any more coins. The stater of Ptolemy I is described, p. 14, "juvenile head, beardless and horned, draped in an elephant skin, facing right. R[everse], galley prow (stater on Attic standard)."[38] Acquired by Monsieur Pérétié from a Turkish officer long posted at Saida, it is now in the collection of the Cabinet des Médailles of the Bibliothèque nationale de France. According to Westermark 1979–1980, the lots of 1852 and 1863 probably contained around 7,200 gold coins. She sought out the specimens that could still be located in public collections and published photos. She notes that Waddington believed the stater of Ptolemy I came from the hoard because it had been acquired from a garrison officer at Saida before 1860 and because it recalls certain Alexanders in its obverse type. This latter argument is not tenable: the stater probably dates from c. 314/310 BC and seems late in comparison to what is known of the hoard. Regling 1931 and Le Rider 1963, p. 34, have settled the burial date, thanks to dated staters from Sidon and Ake/Tyre.

Lot 2 (1852)
Huber 1867, pp. 2–4, was a collector who, during a stay in Egypt, acquired 20 Alexanders probably belonging to the lot of 1852, although he dates it 1856.

Sharp 1870 quotes the narrative of an American missionary in Syria and Palestine, W. M. Thomson, *The Land and the Book*, pp. 194 ff. Some workers in a garden made the discovery "about three years ago" (the pas-

36. "ce pot fut découvert dans un ancien aqueduc hors de la ville et se composait de 1837 pièces en or d'Alexandre le Grand et de Philippe II."

37. "La totalité de la trouvaille s'élevait à plus de trois mille pièces, parmi lesquelles on s'accorde à dire qu'il pouvait y avoir près de trois mille statères d'Alexandre, quelques doubles statères du même roi, et deux à trois cents statères de Philippe II."

38. "tête jeune, imberbe et cornue, coiffée d'une peau d'éléphant et tournée à droite, R. Proue de galère (statère de poids attique)."

sage is dated February, 1857), and they tried to hide it in several "copper" pots. News finally made its way to the city governor, who succeeded in getting his hands on two pots containing 2,000 to 3,000 gold coins. The French consul reckoned the total of the find at nearly 8,000 coins. Thomson was enough of a numismatist to observe that the hoard essentially consisted of staters of Philip II and Alexander, and he proposed a burial date during the latter's reign or immediately after. He saw it as a royal hoard hidden by an officer after Alexander's death, since he assumed that no citizen of Sidon could have assembled such a fortune.

Lot 3 (1863)
Weckbecker 1865, Austrian consul general in Beirut, also published a description: he personally had 1,531 staters in his hand. Regling 1931, p. 34, cites the 1863 Saida discovery in his inventory of hoards containing gold coins of Panticapaeum: one stater of Panticapaeum "together with about 3,600 Alexander staters and some from Rhodes, Cius and Pnytagoras of Salamis."

Rouvier 1899, p. 380, mentions the presence of a large number of staters from Ake/Tyre dated years 23 and 24, that is, 309 and 308 BC. He cites Weckbecker but refers to Waddington 1865.

Le Rider 1963, p. 38, uses this hoard to clarify the dating of gold staters of Cius from the 340s to c. 320 BC.

Six 1890, pp. 198–99, identifies two gold coins from the Saida hoard as staters of Pergamum (Head of Heracles r., wearing a lion skin/Fighting Athena facing; Waddington 1865, p. 13, noted one of them). He mentions a specimen in the Paris collection (Luynes 2493). Wroth 1895, p. 99, no. 18, repeats this identification. Marcellesi 2012 and Callataÿ 2012 elaborate further on these rare coins.

Newell 1916 uses this hoard to revise the dating of Alexanders struck at Sidon and Ake/Tyre. *IGCH* notes: "The burial date is problematical, the exact composition of the hd. being uncertain. It is not clear from the account in the *Revue numismatique* that all non-Alexanders really belong and there is the possibility of adulteration in the Alexander record. As Newell points out, the absence of issues of Philip III and the brilliant condition of the Ake and Sidon coins of 324 BC suggest a burial of about that date. One Alexander of Babylon (Sotheby 252) was, however, struck after Philip's death; it may be intrusive. A detailed analysis of the hd. has been prepared by U. Westermark."

Disposition: Istanbul 1800+ 430 (fused or unidentifiable); Vienna 5 Philips, 16 Alexanders (gift of the sultan in 1856); London 3; Cambridge 1; Paris 8; Brussels 1; Berlin 3; Sotheby June 1862 (C.W. Huber collection), 243–63; Dupré 23 April 1867, 317 (Pnytagoras); Sotheby 19 February 1868, 343 (Kios); New York 1?; Stockholm 2

Bibliography:

Müller, L. *Numismatique d'Alexandre le Grand*, Copenhagen, 1855, p. 300, n. 62.

Waddington, W. H. "Trouvailles de Saida et de Marmara," *Revue numismatique* 1865, pp. 3–28, pls. 1–2 (drawings) = Mélanges de numismatique, Paris, 1867, pp. 33–60.

Weckbecker, C. "Fund von Alexander-Stateren zu Saida 1863," *Wiener numismatische Monatshefte* (1865), pp. 5–11.

Sharp, S. "Find of coins near Sidon," *Numismatic Chronicle* (1865), pp. 179–180.

Huber, C. W. "Zur alten Numismatik Aegyptens II," *Wiener numismatische Monatshefte* (1867), pp. 1–30.

Sharp, S. "The Treasure-Trove at Sidon," *American Journal of Numismatics* 4 (1870), pp. 76–78.

Six, J. P. "Monnaies grecques inédites et incertaines," *Numismatic Chronicle* (1890), pp. 185–259, pl. XVII, 19.

Rouvier, J. "L'ère d'Alexandre le Grand en Phénicie aux IVe et IIIe siècles avant J.-C.," *Revue des études grecques* 12 (1899), pp. 362–381.

Waddington, W. H., E. Babelon, and T. Reinach. *Recueil général des monnaies grecques d'Asie Mineure*, I.2, Paris, 1904, p. 310 (coins of Kios).

Newell, E. T. *The Dated Alexander Coinage of Sidon and Ake*, New Haven, 1916, pp. 57–60.

Regling, K. "Die griechische Goldschatz von Prinkipo," *Zeitschrift für Numismatik* 41 (1931), pp. 1–46.

Le Rider, G. *Deux trésors de monnaies grecques de la Propontide (IVe siècle av. J.-C.)*, Paris, 1963, pp. 33–36.

Westermark, U. "Notes on the Saida hoard (*IGCH* 1508)," *Nordisk Numismatik Årsskrift* (1979/1980), pp. 22–35, 3 pls.
Price, M. J. *The Coinage in the Name of Alexander the Great and Philip Arrhideus*, London, 1991, pp. 48–49.
Callataÿ, F. (de), "Les statères de Pergame et les réquisitions d'Alexandre le Grand: l'apport d'un nouveau trésor ('Statères de Pergame 2004')," *Revue numismatique* (2012), pp. 179–196.
Marcellesi, M.-C. *Pergame, de la fin du Ve au début du Ier siècle avant J.-C. Pratiques monétaires et histoire*, Pisa, 2012, pp. 46–47.

94. Near East. *CH* 8.189 = *CH* 9.460. 1993

Burial: c. 322
Contents: 1,412+ dr. AR

Alexander III: 1,412 lifetime and posthumous drachms: Amphipolis 17; Macedonia? 4; Lampsacus 268; Abydos 160; Magnesia 21; Miletus 755; Sardis 170; Aradus 4; Illegible 13

A first lot of around 400 drachms belonging to this hoard was dispersed on the New York market early in 1993. Three others, composed, respectively, of around 800, 85, and 50 coins, subsequently appeared in other American cities. The ensemble forms a very homogeneous group, surely complete, with only issues in the name of Alexander present. The mints of Asia Minor account for the bulk, Miletus alone representing 53% of the deposit. Such composition does not rule out locating the find elsewhere than the Anatolian coast: these kinds of coins flooded the market from the end of the fourth century. That is why the authors of the publication have prudently preferred to maintain the appellation "Near East." The drachms of Aradus are the only ones struck with the legend ΑΛΕΞΑΝΔΡΟΥ ΒΑΣΙΛΕΩΣ. It is also the only Phoenician mint represented in the hoard. The coins' quality justifies proposing a rather early burial date, probably c. 322 BC. This collection is critical for dating the activity of Alexander's mints in Asia Minor. It demonstrates that Colophon and Teos, since their coins are absent, did not begin production prior to 322 BC. Magnesia, Abydos, and Miletus are represented by their first series, which enables us to put their first issues c. 325 BC. Only Lampsacus and Sardis could have begun issuing Alexander drachms before then, but Le Rider is inclined to date the beginnings of these two mints c. 325 BC as well (Le Rider 1998a, p. 54).

Disposition: Dispersed

Bibliography:
Hersh, C. A. and H. A. Troxell. "A 1993 hoard of Alexander drachms from the Near East," *American Journal of Numismatics* 5–6 (1993/1994), pp. 13–43.
Le Rider, G. "Alexander in Asia Minor," in A. Burnett, U. Wartenberg, and R. Witschonke (eds.) *Coins of Macedonia and Rome: Essays in Honour of C. Hersh*, London, 1998, pp. 49–57.

95. Syria or Lebanon. *CH* 8.185 = *CH* 9.465. Before 1991

Burial: 320
Contents: 250 AR?
Coins studied: 171/250
Alexander tetr.: Amphipolis 33; Lampsacus 2; Side 3; Tarsus 9; Salamis 7; Citium 8; Myriandros 13; Aradus: 20; Byblos 2; Tyre 2; Damascus 2; Babylon 30; imitations 4; uncert. 36

These Alexanders appeared in commerce in Jerusalem in April, 1991, and *CH* 8 notes their provenance as Syria or Lebanon, as well as their discovery in 1990. R. Deutsch, the owner of the 4 imitation Alexanders, estimates that the original find had c. 250 items. Davesne, Lemaire 1996, p. 52, dismiss the Palestinian origin indicated at the time of the hoard's sale (Samu'a), since correspondents in Jerusalem, Jaffa, and London did not confirm it. So this hoard poses the question of how antiquities circulate in the region: it would conceivably have traveled from Syria, Lebanon, even southern Turkey (p. 58), to be sold in Jerusalem. The absence of coins in the name of Philip III justifies a date of c. 320 BC.

Disposition: Commerce, Jerusalem

Bibliography:
Davesne, A. and A. Lemaire. "Trésors hellénistiques du Proche-Orient," *Revue numismatique* (1996), pp. 51–76, no. 1, pls. 4–9.

96. Near East. *CH* 5.26, fig. 2. 1978

Burial: 320
Contents: 15+ tetr. AR

Alexander III: 1 Amathus; 6 Citium; 1 Ake/Tyre (year 28); 4 Byblos; 1 Babylon
Philip III: 1 Aradus; 1 Babylon (Aramaic graffiti, fig. 2, 5)

This group probably came from a larger hoard.

Disposition: Commerce

97. Region of Akko? *IGCH* 1509 = *CH* 8.587 = *CH* 9.461. 1966

Burial: 320
Contents: 1+ AR, c. 60 AE
Coins studied: 1 AR, 40 AE

Tyre: 1 AR fraction (Hippocamp/Owl), 22 AE (Dolphin/Head of lion facing)
Alexander III: 18 AE Tyre

This hoard is exceptional because it contains Phoenician bronzes that are rarely hoarded and because it mixes them with Alexander bronzes still little known today, revealing their joint circulation.

Disposition: Copenhagen 1; Israel Museum 22 AE Tyre, 18 AE Alexander.

Bibliography:
Elayi, Elayi 1993a, pp. 168–170, no. 34, pl. 27.
Elayi, J. and A.-G. Elayi. "Une série de petits bronzes d'Alexandre frappés à Tyr," *Revue numismatique* (1998), pp. 107–117.
_______. "Nouveaux trésors de monnaies phéniciennes (*CH* IX)," *Transeuphratène* 26 (2003), p. 114.

98. Region of Hebron or Gaza. *CH* 8.150? = *CH* 9.468. Before 1987

Burial: 320–270
Contents: 34+ AR

Athenian imitation: 1 ob.
Baal/Lion: 33 ob. and hemiob.

CH 8.150 (Gaza) states 34 AR but describes 56:
"Athens: 1 ob. (local imitation)
Baal seated/Lion: 1 st.; 33 hemiob. (possibly minted locally); 21 hemiob. (with spear head symbol above)."

Total weight of the 34 specimens, according to Spaer: 11.41 g. The imitation Athenian fraction is a frequent occurrence in the region. The fractions of Babylonian lion-staters are also common, but some might have been struck locally with moulded dies (obverses), which would explain the sloppiness of the types. Lion-staters and Athenian tetradrachms continue to be struck after the Macedonian conquest, making dating difficult. Spaer observes that no publication even notes fractions of Babylonian lion-staters. If Babylon did not strike any, their presence in Levantine hoards would be an argument for attributing them to coastal mints.

Disposition: Commerce Jerusalem

Bibliography:
Spaer, A. "Two hoards of minor silver," in A. Burnett, U. Wartenberg, and R. Witschonke (eds.) *Coins of Macedonia and Rome: Essays in Honour of C. Hersh*, London, 1998, pp. 104–107, pls. 6–7.

99. Khirbet el-Kerak, 7 km south of Lake Tiberias, Galilee. *IGCH* 1510 = *CH* 8.587 = *CH* 9.462. 1936

Burial: Baramki: 319; *CH* 9.462: 320; Price: 323–320
Contents: 118+ AR, pot hoard

Sidon: 64 double-shekels (Evagoras II 22; ʿAbdashtart II 14; Mazaios 9; uncert. 19)
Tyre: 1 shekel (Bearded god on winged hippocamp/Owl)
Alexander III: 40 tetr. lifetime or early posthumous; Amphipolis 7; Sicyon 1; Side 1; Tarsus 4; Citium 1; Myriandros 2; Damascus 1; Aradus 2; Sidon 3; Ake/Tyre 4; Babylon 13; incertain mint: 1
Philip III: 13 tetr. Babylon

According to Baramki 1945, the coins, sold on the Tiberias market, were all covered with a thin, purplish oxidation. The Palestinian Department of Antiquities acquired 64 double shekels of Sidon, one Tyrian shekel, 40 Alexander tetradrachms, and 13 of Philip III. This would represent only a small portion of the find, which seems to have been quite voluminous. The Sidonian specimens are very worn and seem to have circulated heavily, unlike the Alexander and Philip tetradrachms, which are in good condition.

Elayi, Elayi 1993a, pp. 146–47, stress the interest in this association of pre-Alexander and Alexander coins. It is witness to the brief period when these coins circulated together, during the 320s.

Disposition: Commerce, Tiberias. Jerusalem, Rockefeller Museum 118.

Bibliography:
Baramki, J. "Coin hoards from Palestine II," *Quarterly of the Department of Antiquities in Palestine* 11 (1945), pp. 86–90.
Naster, P. "Le développement des monnayages phéniciens avant Alexandre," in A. Kindler (ed.) *International Numismatic Convention, Jerusalem, 27–31 December 1963. The Patterns of Monetary Development in Phoenicia and Palestine in Antiquity*, Tel Aviv, 1967, no. 8.
Kadman, L. "The monetary development of Palestine in the light of coin hoards," in A. Kindler (ed.) *International Numismatic Convention, Jerusalem, 27–31 December 1963. The Patterns of Monetary Development in Phoenicia and Palestine in Antiquity*, Tel Aviv, 1967, no. 5: does not mention the didr. of Tyre.

Price, M. J. *The Coinage in the Name of Alexander the Great and Philip Arrhideus*, London, 1991, p. 51.
Elayi, Elayi 1993a, pp. 139–147, no. 26, pls. 20–25.
Elayi, J. and A.-G. Elayi. “Nouveaux trésors de monnaies phéniciennes (*CH* IX),” *Transeuphratène* 26 (2003), p. 114.

100. Sfire, 25 km southwest of Aleppo, Cyrrhestica. *IGCH* 1511. 1932

Burial: After 318
Contents: 84 AR

Alexander III: tetr. lifetime and early posthumous, Amphipolis 1 (Newell 1923, 579); Tarsus 2 (Newell 1923, 2096); Citium 1 (Newell 1923, 2619); Myriandros 4 (2 Newell 1923, 2744; 1 Newell 1923, 2796; 1 Newell 1923, 2864); Aradus 11 (3 Newell 1923, 3380; 1 Newell 1923, 3439; 6 Newell 1923, 3467; 1? illegible date); Byblos 16 (Newell 1923, Newell 1923, 3587, Newell 1923, 3624); Sidon 5 (1 Newell 1923, 3753; 2 Newell 1923, 3755; 1 Newell 1923, 3757; 1 Newell 1923, 3762); Ake/Tyre 3 (Newell 1923, 3945, Newell 1923, 3961?, illegible date); Babylon 33 (2 Newell 1923, 4058; 1 Newell 1923, 4117; 1 Newell 1923, 4192; 2 Newell 1923, 4325; 1 Newell 1923, 4425; 1 Newell 1923, 4448; 1 Newell 1923, 4454; 1 Newell 1923, 4456; 1 Newell 1923, 4458; 1 Newell 1923, 4466; 11 Newell 1923, 4479; 9 Newell 1923, 4526); Alexandria 2 (Newell 1923, 4614); Uncert. mints 4 (2 Newell 1912, 251; 1 ibid. delta, theta, epsilon; 1 ibid. delta iota)
Barbarous imitations 2

This hoard's composition is known through the Seyrig Archives (Bibliothèque nationale de France, dossier 211), which state: “find made in spring, 1932, and dispersed in the bazaars.” The coins are identified by the equivalent specimen numbers in the Demanhur hoard, shown in the itemization above.

This hoard of 84 tetradrachms of Alexander was probably buried a little after 318 BC.

Disposition: Dispersed. Information from H. Seyrig. Notes at the American Numismatic Society

Bibliography:
Archive of the American Numismatic Society.
Newell, E. T. *Reattributions of certain tetradrachms of Alexander the Great*, New York 1912.
________. *Alexander Hoards, Demanhur, 1905*. ANS NNM 19, New York, 1923.

101. Lebanon. *CH* 8.207. 1987

Burial: 315
Contents: c. 50 AR, of which 1 plated.

Alexander III: 3 Babylon (1 plated), 3 Ake/Tyre, 1 Sidon, 2 Tarsus
Philip III: 1 Aradus

Disposition: Commerce

102. Hammaman, Syria. *CH* 3.24. 1912 or before

Burial: 315

Alexander III: tetr. (SNG Ashmolean 3012, 3063, 3096, 3100)

103. Phoenicia. *IGCH* 1513. 1968 or before

Burial: 315
Contents: 15 tetr. AR

Alexander III, 9 tetr. lifetime or posthumous: Amphipolis 4, Side 1, Babylon 3, barbarous imitation 1
Philip III: Myriandros 1; Babylon 5

Disposition: Private collections, casts at the American Numismatic Society

104. Baalbek, Beqaa Valley. *IGCH* 1512. 1885

Burial: c. 315 or c. 305
Contents: 21 tetr. AR

Alexander III: Amphipolis 9; Citium 1; Aradus 2; Byblos 2; Babylon 7
Philip III: Babylon 1

This hoard, now dispersed, originally included several hundred coins, according to C. Lagergren, a Swedish diplomat, who bought 22 specimens, all with types of Alexander, on October 22, 1885. It presumably came from the environs of Baalbek where Lagergren was residing at the time of discovery. Just these tetradrachms are preserved in Stockholm. According to Schwabacher, they were buried c. 315 BC. Thompson inclines more to 305 BC (*IGCH*). Since this lot is only a small part of the original find, dating remains conjectural.

Disposition: Stockholm

Bibliography:
Schwabacher, W. "An unrecorded Alexander hoard from Baalbek," *Nordisk Numismatik Årsskrift* (1963), pp. 5–12.

105. Tel Tsippor, 10 km west of Beth Guvrin, Judaea. *IGCH* 1514. 1960

Burial: 311
Contents: 63 AR, in a jug, in excavation

Alexander III: 58 tetr. lifetime and early posthumous; Amphipolis 6; Pella 1; Tarsus 1; Aradus 2; Byblos 3; Sidon 4; Ake/Tyre 8; Babylon 30; Ecbatana 1; Uncert. mints 2
Philip III: 1 tetr. Sidon
Local Imitations of Athens: 4 dr.

This hoard was discovered in a jug during the excavation of Tel Tsippor in 1960: the coins had been inserted into the container through a hole pierced in its side. It consisted of 59 tetradrachms and four drachms bearing numerous graffiti, including Nabataean names. Burial was c. 311 BC, according to Rahmani.

Disposition: Jerusalem, Department of Antiquities

Bibliography:
Rahmani, L. Y. "A hoard of Alexander coins from Tel Tsippor," *Schweizer Münzblätter* 16/64 (nov. 1966), pp. 129–145, with pl.
Kadman, L. "The monetary development of Palestine in the light of coin hoards," in A. Kindler (ed.) *Inter-*

national Numismatic Convention, Jerusalem, 27–31 December 1963. The Patterns of Monetary Development in Phoenicia and Palestine in Antiquity, Tel Aviv, 1967, no. 6 (erroneously indicates 69 coins).
Price, M. J. *The Coinage in the Name of Alexander the Great and Philip Arrhideus*, London, 1991, p. 56.

106. Byblos. *CH* 2.54. 1971

Burial: 310
Contents: 22+ AR

Alexander III 20: 1 Tarsus; 13 Byblos; 4 Sidon; 2 Babylon
Philip III: 1 Byblos; 1 Babylon

Disposition: Commerce. Information from P. Girardi

107. Byblos. *IGCH* 1515 = *CH* 8.587 = *CH* 9.436. 1931

Burial: 309/8 (Le Rider 196); 308/7 (Bellinger 1950–1951); 333(*CH* 9.436)
Contents: 141 AR. Ptolemaic and Attic weight, imitation? Pot hoard in bronze vessel, in excavation.

Sidon: 2 double-shekels (Tennes, year 5 and illegible)
Alexander III: 121 tetr. lifetime and early posthumous: Amphipolis 8 (H. Seyrig 7); Phaselis or Side 3; Tarsus 2; Myriandros 2; Aradus 4; Byblos 7; Berytus 19 (H. Seyrig 20); Sidon 6; Ake/Tyre 24; Babylon 41; Ecbatana 1; Alexandria 2 (H. Seyrig 3); uncertain 2
Philip III: 16 tetr., Aradus 3; Babylon 9; Susa 2; uncertain 2 (including, according to H. Seyrig, a barbarous imitation)
Ptolemy as satrap: 1 tetr. Sidon

The find of these 141 silver coins, enclosed in a broken bronze vase, occurred in 1931, during the controlled excavation of Byblos directed by Dunand. The pot containing the hoard was situated near that of *IGCH* 1496 (**69**), which consisted of Phoenician coins. Several Sidonian shekels were scattered on the ground and may have fallen from either of these vases. The physical proximity of the two containers leads one to suspect that they belonged to the same owner.

Bellinger gives a total of 141 coins but describes only 140 (omitting the tetradrachm of Ptolemy I); the Seyrig Archives (Bibliothèque nationale de France, dossier 210) inventory 122 tetradrachms of Alexander the Great.

Bellinger 1950–1951 observes that this collection, buried 10 years after that of Demanhur (c. 318/7 BC, *IGCH* 1664), provides a rather different glimpse into currency circulation. In Demanhur, Amphipolis is by far the premier mint by production. After Alexander's death, the eastern mints pick up the task and augment their output. According to Bellinger, this phenomenon is connected with the division of Alexander's empire into rival kingdoms, with monetary circulation suffering the consequences. Local mints thereupon met needs by replacing the currency that previously Macedonia had largely provided. Burial was presumably later than 309/8 BC, because issues of Ake/Tyre dated from the following years are absent from the hoard (Bellinger 1950/1951, p. 47).

Naster 1987 sees burial here in two periods, the owner putting aside coins that were in the process of being removed from circulation first, then those of Alexander.

Bibliography:
Dunand, M. *Fouilles de Byblos* I. *1926–1932*, Paris, 1939, pp. 409–412, nos. 6309–6449.
Bellinger, A. R. "An Alexander hoard from Byblos," *Berytus* 10 (1950/1951), pp. 37–49.

Naster, P. "Le développement des monnayages phéniciens avant Alexandre," A. Kindler (ed.) *International Numismatic Convention, Jerusalem, 27–31 December 1963. The Patterns of Monetary Development in Phoenicia and Palestine in Antiquity*, Tel Aviv, 1967, pp. 3–24.
Price, M. J. *The Coinage in the Name of Alexander the Great and Philip Arrhideus*, London, 1991, p. 56.
Elayi, Elayi 1993a, p. 201 no. 42.
Elayi, J. and A.-G. Elayi. "Nouveaux trésors de monnaies phéniciennes (*CH* IX)," *Transeuphratène* 26 (2003), p. 112.

108. Aleppo, ancient Beroea, Cyrrhestica. *IGCH* 1516 = Noe 29. 1892?

Burial: c. 305
Contents: 3,000+ tetr. and dr. AR
Coins studied: 973/3,000+

Alexander III 881: 148 Macedonia ("Amphipolis"); 2 Aegeae (?); 24 "Pella"; 10 Amphipolis; 2 Corinth; 1 Greece; 4 tetr., 9 dr. Lampsacus; 2 tetr., 2 dr. Abydos; 1 dr. "Teos"; 10 dr. "Colophon"; 1 tetr., 4 dr. Magnesia; 3 tetr., 2 dr. Miletus (or Caunus); 37 tetr., 4 dr. Sardis; 1 tetr., 1 dr. uncert. Western Asia Minor; 37 Side; 25 Tarsus; 5 uncert. Southern Asia Minor; 1 Paphos; 6 Amathus; 23 Citium; 12 tetr., 1 dr. Salamis; 15 Myriandros; 21 Damascus; 42 Aradus; 33 Byblos; 2 Berytus; 33 Sidon; 82 Ake/Tyre; 12 uncert. of Syria or Phoenicia; 3 Carrhae (?); 245 Babylon; 1 imitation of Babylon; 2 satrapal mint of Babylon; 4 Susa; 8 uncert.

Philip III 78: 1 dr. Abydos; 1 dr. Sardis; 1 dr. uncert. Western Asia Minor; 8 Salamis; 1 Myriandros; 1 "Marathus"; 5 Sidon; 7 uncert. mint 6A Babylonia; 31 Babylon; 12 satrapal mint of Babylon; 9 Susa; 1 Ecbatana?
Egypt, Early Hellenistic: 14

Newell 1923, p. 10; 1916, p. 58, indicates that the discovery of this hoard occurred in 1892 near Aleppo, according to a manuscript kept in the Coin Cabinet of Vienna (also mentioned in the correspondence of Seyrig preserved in the Cabinet des Médailles of the Bibliothèque nationale de France). Out of the 3,000 silver coins dispersed, two lots are preserved: around 800 tetradrachms in Istanbul and 270 in Vienna. Newell 1923, p. 10, n. 2, assumed that the two lots' proximity made them a single hoard whose precise provenance cannot be determined. Price 1991a adds that the coins attributed to Callatis by *IGCH* cannot come from that mint.

Lorber was able to consult the manuscript in the American Numismatic Society and is preparing to publish a complete description of the hoard.[39] Hers is the list printed here. Of the 857 coins seized by the Turkish authorities, only 710 are clearly identified in Newell's list as coming from the Aleppo hoard, the rest having possibly been included in the collection without mention.

Disposition: 710 Istanbul; 270 Vienna

Bibliography:
Newell, E. T. *The Dated Alexander Coinage of Sidon and Ake*, New Haven, 1916, p. 58.
_______. *Tyrus Rediviva*, New York, 1923, p. 10.
Price, M. J. *The Coinage in the Name of Alexander the Great and Philip Arrhideus*, London, 1991, p. 56.

Voetter, O. A manuscript account of find in Vienna Cabinet. Transcript of this MS by E. T. Newell at American Numismatic Society (949 spec.).
Lorber, C.. "The Aleppo hoard, 1893 (*IGCH* 1516)," in T. Faucher, A. Meadows, and C. Lorber (eds.) *Egyptian Hoards I, Ptolemaic Hoards*, Cairo, 2016.

109. Jericho. *CH* 8.215. 1991

Burial: 305

39. I would like to thank her warmly for allowing me to see the working version of this article.

Contents: 12 AR

Alexander III: 1 Ake/Tyre, 6 Babylon, 1 uncert.
Philip III: 1 Aradus, 1 Marathus, 1 barbarous imitation

This group should be compared to *IGCH* 1514 (**105**) and 1520 (**117**), which also reflect the circulation of Alexanders in the region at the end of the fourth century. The coins are not noticeably worn but are strangely associated with an imitation of very poor quality (the photo shows advanced corrosion, leading to the supposition that the metal is of low quality). Price, p. 25, emphasizes: "Equally important is the presence of the contemporary imitation (no. 12), produced with a particularly crude technique. It is perhaps surprising that anyone should place such a piece in a hoard with 11 perfectly good coins."

Disposition: Commerce

Bibliography:
Price, M. J. "A hoard of tetradrachms from Jericho," *Israel Numismatic Journal* 11 (1990), pp. 24–25, pl. 4.

110. Near East. *CH* 8.216

Burial: 305–300
Contents: 68 tetr. AR

Alexander III: 7 Macedonia (to Price 445), 25 Babylon (to group MI 11), 1 Ecbatana (Price 3889), Ake/Tyre (Price 3298), Tyre (Price 3529)

Disposition: Commerce

111. Ascalon. *CH* 8.220. 1990

Burial: 305–290
Contents: 19 AR and a silver bracelet[40]

Alexander III: tetr. 1 Salamis (Price 3139e); 3 Byblos (Price 3426d); 1 Sidon (Price 3474c); 1 Aradus (Price 3309b); 1 Berytus? (Price 3415); 1 Ake/Tyre (Price 3267–3302); 1 Macedonia (Price 129a); 1 Amphipolis (Price 432a); 2 Sardis (Price 2664a); 2 Ake/Tyre (Price 3279, 3301 or 3302); 3 Tyre (Price 3547, 3548a, 3550); 1 uncertain
Philip III: 1 tetr. Aradus (Price P148)

This hoard has had only one publication, Stager 1991, pp. 29–30, photo, p. 31, in a journal meant for the general public. It dates the burial "shortly before the destruction of about 300 BC," the floors of the building having collapsed on the level under which the group was buried (pp. 29–30). This hoard helps determine that the city's destruction is later than the Macedonian invasion. The establishment of Ptolemaic domination might have occasioned this devastation.

Disposition: Israel Museum?

Bibliography:
Stager, L. E. "Why were hundreds of dogs buried at Ashkelon?," *Biblical Archaeology Review* 17/3 (May–June 1991), pp. 27–42.

40. *CH* provides in error a total of 18 tetradrachms.

112. Ramallah. *CH* 10.224

Burial: Before 302/1
Contents: 8 AR

Yehud series: 7 ob.
Ascalon: 1 ob.

This hoard (all the coins bear the same traces of dirt), bought in commerce, contained 8 coins of the same denomination. It shows that the coinage of Philistia circulated in the mountains to the north of the Achaemenid province of Judah at the same time as the Yehud coins. The Yehud coins seem rather clustered, whereas those known from two other hoards stretch over longer periods. This is an important contribution, in view of the very few hoards known for this type of coinage:
Yehud Series: cf. Gitler, Lorber 2006
Philistine Series: *CH* 9.369, **22**; *IGCH* 1507, **80**; *CH* 8.150, **98**.
Samarian Series: *IGCH* 1504, **77**; *CH* 9.413, **50**.
Three obols share the same obverse die, supporting the idea that this is a hoard.

Disposition: Israel Museum 8

Bibliography:
Gitler, H. "A hoard of Persian Yehud coins from the environs of Ramallah," *Numisma* 250 (2006), pp. 319–324.
Gitler, H. and C. Lorber. "A new chronology for the Ptolemaic Yehud coinage," *American Journal of Numismatics* 18 (2006), pp. 1–41, no. 5.
Meshorer, Y. *A Treasure of Jewish Coins*, Jerusalem, 2001.

113. Region of Nablus? Gaza? *CH* 9.453. Before 1970

Burial: end of the 4th cent. BC
Contents: 7+ AR

Philistia/Samaria: 1
Alexander III: Sidon: 1 ob.; 1 hemiob. (Price 3476; 3478)
Uncert: 4 hemiob.

One of the hemiobols of Alexander might bear an *ain* and have been struck at Gaza, suggesting a need to revisit the hoard's provenance.
Total weight: 2.44 g.

Disposition: Commerce Jerusalem

Bibliography:
Spaer, A. "Two hoards of minor silver," in A. Burnett, U. Wartenberg, and R. Witschonke (eds.) *Coins of Macedonia and Rome: Essays in Honour of C. Hersh*, London, 1998, pp. 104–107, pls. 6–7.

114. Samaria. *CH* 10.237

Burial: end of the 4th cent. BC

Contents: *Hacksilber*, frags. of coins

32 pieces of *Hacksilber*
Athens: 5 frags. of tetr., including one plated

Donated to the Israel Museum in 1999, it is impossible to know whether this hoard is complete or not.

Bibliography:
Gitler, H. "A *Hacksilber* and cut Athenian tetradrachm hoard from the environs of Samaria: late fourth century BCE," *Israel Numismatic Research* 1 (2006), pp. 5–14, pls. 1–2.

115. Unknown Findspot. *CH* 9.457. 1996

Burial: end of the 4th cent. BC
Contents: 14 AR

Alexander III: Ake/Tyre 1 (Price 3254)
Athens, imitations: 6
Lion staters 7: Mazaios 1, without legend 1, gamma 4, pentagram 1

Disposition: Commerce

2.4. HOARDS OF THE THIRD CENTURY

116. Beirut. *IGCH* 1518 = Noe 133. 1900

Burial: 300
Contents: 1,000 AV, AE, pot hoard

Philip II
Alexander III

This large find is known only through a note in the *Blätter für Münzfreunde*: "Beirut. A pot turned up in excavations, containing around 1,000 coins, mostly bronze, but also gold, of Alexander the Great and his father, Philip."[41]

Bibliography:
"Münzfunde," *Blätter für Münzfreunde* 8/9 (1900), p. 137.

117. Galilee, near Tarshiha, c. 20 km northwest of Akko. *IGCH* 1520. 1964

Burial: 300
Contents: 40+ AR
Coins studied: 35/40

41. "Beirut. Bei Ausschachtungsarbeiten traf man auf ein Fässchen, das ungefähr 1 000 Münzen, meist Bronze, aber auch Gold, von Alexander dem Grossen und seinem Vater Philipp enthielt."

Alexander III: Amphipolis 1, Side 1, Citium 2, Salamis 1, Sidon 1 (year 4 = 306/5), Tyre 3, Ake/Tyre 25 (undated, years 20, 23, 31, 32, 35, 36, 37, 38, 9, 11 = 304/3, uncert.), Babylon 1

In 1964, there were rumors that an Arab farmer had discovered an important hoard of Alexander tetradrachms in the vicinity of the village of Tarshiha, but police intervention removed all trace of the discovery. A few months later, a lot of 39 to 41 tetradrachms said to come from this hoard was put up for sale in Tel Aviv. Their appearance made such a surmise plausible. Some other isolated coins of the same appearance went on sale in Haifa and Akko during the same time. No other information could be gathered. Neither leading European dealers nor public collections had any knowledge of the sale of specimens from this hoard. Spaer concludes that the find was surely less important than had been supposed, recalling that hoards of this type in the region normally contain a few dozen coins. His list may contain some specimens that did not originally belong to the hoard, whose reconstitution was difficult.

No. 35, uncertain for Spaer, is identified by the authors of *IGCH* as a tetradrachm of Salamis on Cyprus (Newell 1927, p. 19, no. 2).

Disposition: Private collections, Israel

Bibliography:
Spaer, A. "A hoard of Alexander tetradrachms from Galilee," *Israel Numismatic Journal* 3 (1965–1966), pp. 1–7, pls. I–III.

118. Saida. *IGCH* 1521. Before 1954

Burial: 300
Contents: 23+ AR, pot hoard.

Chersonesus, Thrace: 17 hemidr.
Amisos: 6 dr. and hemidr.

This group was found at the entrance to the city of Sidon. The notice in *IGCH* states that "among the rubbings were a dr. of Rhodes and a tetrob. of Histiaea. As both seem to be 2nd cent. BC, they are presumably intrusive."

Disposition: Dispersed

119. Beirut. *IGCH* 1519. 1964

Burial: c. 300
Contents: 27 AR

Alexander III: 19 tetr. lifetime and early posthumous, Amphipolis 4; Sidon 1; Babylon 11; Alexandria 1; Aradus 1; Berytus 1
Philip III: 7 tetr. uncert. mints.
Seleucus I: 1 tetr.

This group of more than 27 silver coins was probably withdrawn from circulation c. 300.

Disposition: Dispersed. Information from Münzen und Medaillen, Bâle

120. Aleppo, ancient Beroea, Cyrrhestica. *CH* 8.231. 1983

Burial: c. 300
Contents: 9 AR, plated coins

Alexander III (first Seleucids): 7 tetr.; 2 tetr. plated (same obv. die)

Disposition: Commerce

121. Syria? *IGCH* 1522. 1964

Burial: 300–280
Contents: c. 40 AR

Seleucus I: lion stater, Babylon (*SC* 1, 88,2)

Disposition: Dispersed. Information from Y. Meshorer

122. Region of Antakya. *CH* 8.250 = *CH* 10.263. 1992

Burial: 295
Contents: 200+ tetr. AR
Coins studied: 32/200+

Alexander III: 2 Macedonia; 1 Sardis; 1 Salamis, Cyprus; 8 Carrhae; 2 Ake/Tyr; 13 Babylon; 1 Ecbatana
Philip III: 2 Babylon
Seleucus I: 2 Seleuceia on the Tigris

All but three of these coins with Alexander types are posthumous. They are classified here, as is traditional, by legend; but Houghton, Lorber 2002 emphasize that the majority of the tetradrachms in the name of Alexander date from the reign of Seleucus I: 7 + 1 Carrhae, 13 Babylon, 1 Ecbatana. The dating remains that of Kritt 1997. Note that this hoard is mentioned again in *CH* 10 without reference to the earlier mention in *CH* 8 and with some minor differences.

Disposition: Durmaz collection, Ankara

Bibliography:
Arslan, M. and M. J. Price. "A hoard from the Durmaz collection from the region of Antakya," *CH* 8 (1994), pp. 80–81, pls. 30,37–31,1.
Kritt, B. *The Early Seleucid Mint of Susa*, Lancaster, 1997, p. 97.
Houghton, Lorber 2002, p. 96.

123. Aleppo, ancient Beroea, Cyrrhestica. *IGCH* 1524. 1933

Burial: 290–280
Contents: 92 AR

Alexander III: 58 tetr. lifetime; 12 tetr. with anchor
Philip III: 4 tetr.

Demetrius Poliorcetes : 1 tetr. (Poseidon standing)
Seleucus I: 11 tetr. Alexander type; 1 tetr. head of Heracles/Zeus Nikephoros; 5 tetr. chariot pulled by elephants

Seyrig did not personally see these coins: his description comes from H. Bachellier, a collector in Aleppo and owner of the hoard (Seyrig Archives, Bibliothèque nationale de France, dossier 214). The latter, in a letter preserved in the Seyrig Archives, indicates that the coins were very dirty and oxidized when he got them, and covered in a coating "as thick as wax, but with a dark bluish color, scratchable but infernally sticky."[42] He specifies the nature of the symbols on the Alexanders: dolphin, relay torch, Athena, prow, lituus, wreath, caduceus, bee, and monograms; the tetradrachms of Philip III also have monograms, a prow, or a thunderbolt.

Disposition: Dispersed. Information from H. Seyrig

Bibliography:
Houghton, Lorber 2002, p. 97.

124. Near East. *CH* 8.255. 1983?

Burial: 285
Contents: 81 AR

Alexander III: 66 dr.: 9 Sardis, 6 Miletus, 6 Lampsacus, 3 Abydos, 11 Colophon, 31 Magnesia
Philip III: 10 dr.
Lysimachus : 3 dr.
Seleucus I: 1 hemidr.
Pergamum: 1 ob.

Disposition: Commerce, London

125. Balatah (ancient Shechem). *IGCH* 1584. 1956

Burial: 285. Ptolemaic bronze
Contents: 15 AE, in excavation

Ptolemy I: 15 AE

The discovery of these coins occurred during the excavations of Shechem that brought to light Bronze Age remains but also a Hellenistic settlement around the east gate. Wright 1957, p. 32, mentions the facts briefly on the last page of his article: during the excavation of this gate dated to the Bronze Age, "a hoard of 15 copper coins of Ptolemy I of Egypt, dating between 305 and 285 BC, was found in the footing of the Hellenistic tower just outside the gate." There are no further details.

Disposition: unknown

Bibliography:
Wright, G. E. et al. "Shechem, the navel of the land," *The Biblical Archaeologist* 20/1 (1957), pp. 2–32.
Kadman, L. "The monetary development of Palestine in the light of coin hoards," in A. Kindler (ed.) *International Numismatic Convention, Jerusalem, 27–31 December 1963. The Patterns of Monetary Development in Phoenicia and Palestine in Antiquity*, Tel Aviv, 1967, no. 10.

42. "grasse comme de la cire, mais d'une couleur noire bleuâtre, se rayant à l'ongle mais adhérente en diable."

126. Phoenicia. *CH* 9.483. 1997

Burial: c. 285–280
Contents: 800+ tetr. AR

Alexander III: Pella; Amphipolis; Sardis; Side; Tarsus; Uncert. Asia Minor; Citium; Salamis; Myriandros; Ake/Tyre (100+); Aradus; Byblos; Marathus; Sidon; Uncert. Phoenicia or Syria; Babylon (100+); Babylonia; Susa; Ecbatana; Memphis; Uncert. East
Philip III: Salamis; Aradus; Sidon; Babylon; Susa; Uncert. East
Demetrius Poliorcetes : 1 tetr. (Tyre)
Seleucus I: Carrhae; Seleuceia on the Tigris ; Ecbatana

Hersh was able to examine this hoard that was dispersed in several lots on the London and American markets in 1997. Apparently it was discovered in Phoenicia at beginning of the same year. It contained mostly tetradrachms in the name and types of Alexander, often posthumous, as well as dozens of Alexanders in the name of Seleucus I (Seleuceia on the Tigris, Ecbatana, Carrhae) and a tetradrachm from Tyre in the name of Demetrius Poliorcetes in very good condition. This last coin is the basis for Hersh's proposed dating. In his article on *Tyrus Rediviva*, he states that he inspected more than 100 tetradrachms attributed by Newell and Price to Tyre, even though these series are generally scarce; he acquired 18 of them (Hersh 1997, p. 43).

Disposition: Dispersed; several examples in the C. Hersh collection.

Bibliography:
Hersh, C. A. "The Phoenicia 1997 hoard of Alexander-type tetradrachms," *American Journal of Numismatics* 10 (1998), pp. 37–40.
_______. "*Tyrus Rediviva* reconsidered," *American Journal of Numismatics* 10 (1998), pp. 41–59, pls. 6–9.
Houghton, Lorber 2002, p. 97.

127. Latakia. *IGCH* 1523. 1940

Burial: 284 or after
Contents: 9 tetr. AR

Alexander III: 1 Tyre; 2 Babylon
Seleucus I: 4 Seleuceia on the Tigris; 2 Susa

The Seyrig Archives (Bibliothèque nationale de France, dossier 213) describe this lot as follows: "coins found in the environs of Latakia. No patina; yellowish traces in the incuse. May, 1940"; and, again, on another page: "small lot of 9 Attic tetradrachms, seen at Latakia…, clearly of common origin." Newell only knew the tetradrachm of Seleucus I struck at Susa (Newell 1941 325 A, p. 23) from the mould that Seyrig sent him (which is absent from the plates in his volume). Dating is from Kritt 1997.

Disposition: Dispersed

Bibliography:
Newell, E. T. *The Coinage of the Western Seleucid Mints from Seleucus I to Antiochus III*, New York, 1941.
Kritt, B., *The Early Seleucid Mint of Susa*, Lancaster, 1997, p. 78.
Houghton, Lorber 2002, p. 97.

128. Near East. *CH* 7.66. 1981

Burial: 280
Contents: 8+ tetr. AR

Alexander III: 1 Pella
Demetrius Poliorcetes : 1 Amphipolis; 1 Pella; 1 Ephesus; 1 Tarsus; 1 Salamis
Seleucus I: 2 Susa

Disposition: Commerce. British Museum files.

Bibliography:
Houghton, Lorber 2002, p. 98.

129. Syria? *IGCH* 1525. 1966

Burial: 280
Contents: 17 AR

Seleucus I: 17 dr. Seleuceia on the Tigris

Disposition: Dispersed. Information from Münzen und Medaillen, Bâle

Bibliography:
Houghton, Lorber 2002, p. 97.

130. Unknown Findspot. *CH* 9.485. Before 1991

Burial: 275–270
Contents: 252+ AE, pot hoard

Ptolemy I and II: 3 modules (Alexander diademed and horned; Alexander in elephant scalp headdress; Zeus)

These bronzes appeared in commerce in Jerusalem, in April, 1991, along with the pot in which they were discovered. Fathers J.-B. Humbert and J.-M. de Tarragon have studied and photographed all but 66 of them.

Disposition: Commerce in Jerusalem

Bibliography:
Davesne, A. and A. Lemaire. "Trésors hellénistiques du Proche-Orient," *Revue numismatique* (1996), pp. 51–76, no. 4, pls. 12–13.

131. Sikka, southwest of Hebron. *CH* 8.279. 1990

Burial: 265. Ptolemaic bronze
Contents: 250 AE, pot hoard

Ptolemy II (Sv. 356, 360, 363)

Disposition: Commerce

132. Region of Hebron. *CH* 9.484. 1999

Burial: after 261
Contents: 25 AR

Yehud, ob.: 6 *AJC* I Yehud 2; 1 *AJC* I Yehud 9; 1 *AJC* I Yehud 9b; 2 *AJC* I Yehud 12a; 2 *AJC* I Yehud 16; 2 *AJC* addendum I; 10 *AJC* I Yehud 17b
Ptolemy I: 1 tetr. Alexandria (Sv. 267)

Gitler inspected this hoard. The coins carry the same traces of dirt and so were probably discovered together. Additionally, the oldest coins are more worn than the most recent, and more than 60% of the coins were struck with the same dies (Gitler, Lorber 2006, p. 27).

Disposition: Ashkelon

Bibliography:
Meshorer, Y., *Ancient Jewish Coinage* I, New York, 1982, p. 17.
_______. *A Treasure of Jewish Coins*, Jerusalem, 2001.
Gitler, H. and C. Lorber. "A new chronology for the Ptolemaic Yehud coinage," *American Journal of Numismatics* 18 (2006), pp. 1–41, no. 3.

133. Unknown Findspot. Before 1982

Burial: after 261/0
Contents: AR

Judaea: quarter obols, types Ptolemy I/Eagle, *YHDH* (Meshorer 2001 no. 32; Gitler, Lorber 2006, no. 16)

Meshorer 1982, p. 17, does not specify the number of coins found. Apparently they were stuck together, since he does state they were separated in his presence. They belong to the most common group of Ptolemaic coins of Judah, type 16 of Gitler, Lorber 2006, representing nearly 60% of all the coins with Ptolemaic types struck in Judah. They were issued between 261/0 BC, the date of Ptolemy II's reform, and 241/0 BC, the date of the closing of the Jerusalem mint; but they may have circulated longer (Gitler, Lorber 2006, pp. 12–16).

Bibliography:
Meshorer, Y. *Ancient Jewish Coinage* I, New York, 1982.
_______. *A Treasure of Jewish Coins*, Jerusalem, 2001.
Gitler, H. and C. Lorber. "A new chronology for the Ptolemaic Yehud coinage," *American Journal of Numismatics* 18 (2006), pp. 1–41, no. 4.

134. Unknown Findspot. *CH* 9.488. Before 1985

Burial: 260–230
Contents: 31+ AR

Alexander dr.: Lampsacus 3; Abydos 5; Colophon 14; Magnesia on the Maeander 2; Miletus 2; Sardis 4; Uncert.

These 31 drachms were bought on the Jerusalem market between 1980 and 1985 with no provenance indicated. Based on when they were struck, burial could have occurred between 290 and 280 BC; but since the drachms had circulated a great deal, the authors thought it prudent to lower the date.

Disposition: Private collection, Paris

Bibliography:
Davesne, A. and A. Lemaire. "Trésors hellénistiques du Proche-Orient," *Revue numismatique* (1996), pp. 51–76, no. 2, pl. 10.

135. Hüseyinli, near Antakya. *CH* 9.489. 1986

Burial: 259/8
Contents: 58 AV Ptolemaic, 1 AE Seleucid

Ptolemy I and II: 14 trichrysa Alexandria
Ptolemy II: 29 trichrysa Tyre; 6 trichrysa Sidon; 9 trichrysa Cyprus
Antiochus I: 1 AE Antioch

A bulldozer unearthed this lot of gold coins and one bronze by chance in a field in the commune of Hüseyinli köyü, 9 km west of Antakya. The next day, the local authorities successfully reassembled the part of the find that the three discoverers had divided up, as well as the remainder, which still lay buried. Davesne, Yenisoğancı 1992 classify the coins by mint, not by reign. The latest coins are dated between 264/3 BC (actually 266/5 BC, Tyre and Sidon, but the coins are worn) and 258/7 BC. The hoard was buried at the time of the Second Syrian War, still poorly researched. But we do know that Ptolemy II struck coinage at Tarsus in 261/0 BC, indicating he had wrested that city from the Seleucids. Accordingly, the Hüseyinli hoard leads one to think Ptolemaic forces had penetrated deep into Seleucis, probably to be repulsed by Antiochus II from 260/59 to 259/8 BC.

Disposition: Antakya

Bibliography:
Davesne, A. and V. Yenisoğancı. "Les Ptolémées en Séleucide: le trésor d'Hüseyinli," *Revue numismatique* (1992), pp. 23–36.
Davesne, A. "La seconde guerre de Syrie (ca. 261–255 avant J.-C.) et les témoignages numismatiques," in M. Amandry and S. Hurter (eds.) *Travaux de numismatique grecque offerts à G. Le Rider*, London, pp. 123–134.
Houghton, Lorber 2002, p. 98.

136. Nuba, Hebron. *CH* 2.69, fig. 9. 1975

Burial: 255–200
Contents: 8 AR, Attic and Ptolemaic weight

Alexander III: 1 Tarsus (intrusion?)
Ptolemy II: 7 tetr. (Sv. 658 (3); 732 (3); 733)

Disposition: Dispersed

137. Near East. *CH* 5.35. 1978?

Burial: 250
Contents: Several AV
Alexander III: st.
Seleucids: st.

Disposition: Commerce

138. Seleuceia Pieria. *IGCH* 1526. 1932–1939

Burial: c. 250
Contents: 12 AR Attic and Ptolemaic, in excavation

Alexander III of Antigonus Monophthalmus: 1 tetr. Antigoneia on the Orontes
Demetrius Poliorcetes : 1 tetr.
Ptolemy I: 1 tetr. Alexandria
Ptolemy II: 3 tetr. Alexandria, 1 tetr. Tyre, 1 tetr. Sidon, 1 tetr. Joppa, 1 tetr. Gaza
Ptolemy I or II: 2 tetr.

This group is assuredly a hoard, even though Waage 1952, p. vii, did not recognize it as such, explaining: "All of the coins are chance finds; no hoard was found in the course of the excavations (the ten Ptolemaic tetradrachms, one of Antigonus Monophthalmus, and one of Demetrius Poloiorcetes (*sic*) were found together but not in a container)." She elaborates, p. 74: "This coin [the Alexander, no. 788] was found with one tetradrachm of Demetrius Poliorcetes (no. 789 below) and ten of Ptolemies I and II (no. 963–965, 969–974 below) in Seleuceia Pieria. It has been deposited in the Museum at Antioch." No interpretation or dating is offered. Further investigation of the text does not provide any identification of the discovery's context; none of these coins is illustrated.

Disposition: Antakya Museum

Bibliography:
Waage, D. B. *Antioch on the Orontes, IV 2, Greek, Roman, Byzantine and Crusaders' Coins*, Princeton, 1952.

139. Region of Hebron. *CH* 4.40. 1977

Burial: Mid-3rd cent.
Contents: 5+ AR Ptolemaic

Ptolemy I: 1 tetr. (Sv. 229)
Ptolemy II: 2 tetr. (Sv. 365); 1 tetr. Tyre (Sv. 650); 1 tetr. (Sv. 693 var. monogram MA)

Disposition: Commerce

140. Bab, ancient Batnae, between Beroea and Hierapolis. Cyrrhestica. *IGCH* 1534. 1944

Burial: c. 250–200
Contents: 1,080+ dr. AR
Coins studied: 345/1,080+

Alexander III 152: Lampsacus 31; Abydos 33; Colophon 32; Teos 8; Miletus 10; Magnesia 16; Sardis 3; Tenedos? 1; Chios 1; Aradus 1; Euboea? 6; Pamphylia 5; Ephesus 1; Uncert. mints 4
Philip III 36 dr.: Lampsacus 8; Abydos 1; Teos 1; Colophon 16; Magnesia 5; Miletus 1; Sardis 3; Pamphylia? 1
Demetrius Poliorcetes : 6 dr. Miletus
Lysimachus 29 dr.: Lampsacus 5; Abydos 3; Teos 1; Colophon 6; Magnesia 1; Mytilene 1; Ephesus 9; Lysimachia 1; Thrace (?) 1; Uncert. mint 1
Seleucus I: 1 dr. Uncert. mint
Antiochus I: 1 dr. Seleuceia on the Tigris

This hoard, consisting of 1,080 silver drachms, is partially preserved at Yale (209 coins) and in the Seyrig collection (14). The Yale specimens were bought on the Damascus market in 1944, where Seyrig examined 136 other coins from the same find. Of the 345 coins that could be inventoried, 315 come from Asia Minor mints, seven of which are particularly well represented: Colophon, Lampsacus, Abydos, Miletus, Magnesia, Teos, and Sardis. With the exception of Teos, these are major mints at the end of the fourth century and the beginning of the third. The latest coin is that of Antiochus I (c. 274–270 BC). The coins are generally quite worn, the majority being struck at the end of the fourth century or the start of the third. Seleucid issues are quite poorly represented, with only two examples. These peculiarities are attributable to the considerable volume of drachms struck by the Asia Minor mints under Alexander's successors. They flooded the market during the following century, permitting Thompson, Bellinger 1955, p. 45, to conclude: "for the present, therefore, we may assume that this hoard is not far from typical of those buried in the second half of the third century," the date of burial lying probably between 250–200 BC.

Disposition: Yale 209; formerly H. Seyrig collection 14, of which one is in Paris, BnF

Bibliography:
Thompson, M. and A. R. Bellinger. "Greek coins in the Yale Collection, IV: a hoard of Alexander drachms," *Yale Classical Studies* 14 (1955), pp. 3–45.
Houghton, Lorber 2002, p. 98.

141. Amman. *CH* 7.77. 1979

Burial: 249
Contents: 29 AR Ptolemaic

Ptolemy I: 5 tetr. Alexandria
Ptolemy II: 4 tetr. Alexandria; 7 tetr. Sidon; 8 tetr. Tyr; 2 tetr. Ake-Ptolemais; 3 tetr. Joppa

Disposition: Amman

142. Beth-Shan (ancient Nysa-Scythopolis). *IGCH* 1585 = Noe 148. 1921–1923.

Burial: 246
Contents: 20+ AR Ptolemaic

Ptolemy I: 1 tetr.
Ptolemy I or II: 1 tetr.
Ptolemy II: 18 tetr.

These coins were collected in a pot found beneath a Byzantine level. Classification is after Svoronos.

Disposition: Philadelphia, University Museum

Bibliography:
Fitzgerald, G. M. *Beth-Shan Excavations 1921–1923. The Arab and Byzantine Levels*, Philadelphia, 1931, pp. 33, 51, pls. XLI, XXXIII, 25 (pot).
Kadman, L. "The monetary development of Palestine in the light of coin hoards," in A. Kindler (ed.) *International Numismatic Convention, Jerusalem, 27–31 December 1963. The Patterns of Monetary Development in Phoenicia and Palestine in Antiquity*, Tel Aviv, 1967, no. 9.

143. Syria? *IGCH* 1527. Before 1917

Burial: 245
Contents: 13+ AR

Antiochus I: 12 tetr. Seleuceia on the Tigris
Antiochus II: 1 tetr. Seleuceia on the Tigris, *ESM* 189

Disposition: Istanbul. Seen by O. Mørkholm

Bibliography:
Houghton, Lorber 2002, p. 98.

144. Saida. *IGCH* 1586 = *CH* 1.75. 1949

Burial: after 245/4
Contents: 67+ AR Ptolemaic

Ptolemy I: 7 tetr. Alexandria
Ptolemy II: 10 tetr. Alexandria, 7 tetr. Tyre, 8 tetr. Sidon, 2 tetr. Ake-Ptolemais, 1 tetr. Joppa
Ptolemy II or III: 2 tetr. Ephesus
Ptolemy III: 2 tetr. Alexandria, Joppa

Seyrig's notes, preserved in the Bibliothèque nationale de France, show that he saw this hoard in November, 1949, when it had just been discovered "in the vicinity of ancient Sidon" (H. Seyrig Archives, Bibliothèque nationale de France, dossier 6.I.b. = dossier 273). Two tetradrachms of Ptolemy I were countermarked in Byzantium.

Disposition: Dispersed

Bibliography:
Seyrig 1973, no. 40.

145. Tell Sukas, Seleucis. *IGCH* 1528. 1958

Burial: Before 243/2
Contents: 10 AR, pot hoard, in excavation

Alexander III: 3 tetr., 2 posthumous dr. Aradus (undated)
Antigonus Gonatas: 1 tetr.
Lysimachus : 2 tetr.
Antiochus I: 1 tetr. Seleuceia on the Tigris
Antiochus II: 1 tetr. Antioch

Riis announced the find of "a small hoard of 10 silver coins in the bottom of a jug, hidden beneath the floor in a corner of one of the houses…."[43] Seyrig thought this find was deposited before 243/2 BC because the tetradrachms of Aradus it contains are not dated. This mint is quite near, and the hoard probably would have

43. "un petit trésor de 10 monnaies d'argent dans un fond de cruche, caché sous le sol dans un coin d'une des maisons […]."

dated specimens if it were later than 243/2 BC, the time when Aradus begins to note the year of issue on its coins. The three Aradian coins are in excellent condition.

Bibliography:
Riis, P. J. "L'activité de la mission archéologique danoise sur la côte phénicienne en 1958," *Annales archéologiques arabes syriennes* 8–9 (1958/1959), pp. 107–132, pp. 125–126. The commentary on the hoard is by H. Seyrig.
Houghton, Lorber 2002, p. 98.

146. Tel Michal. 1977–1980

Burial: after 241
Contents: 5 AR Ptolemaic, in excavation

Ptolemy II: Kindler 1989 no. 91 (Sidon, 256 BC), 92 (Joppa, 249 BC), 93 (Gaza, 248 BC)
Ptolemy III: Kindler 1989 no. 102 (Sidon, 242 BC), 103 (Joppa, 241 BC)

Kindler 1989, p. 320, notes the existence of this hoard found in excavation, without indicating the nature of the container, if there was one, or commenting on the find.

Bibliography:
Kindler, A. "Numismatic report," in Z. Herzog et al. (eds.) *Excavations at Tel Michal, Israel*, Tel Aviv, 1989, pp. 320–329 and 443.

147. 'Iraq al-Amir, Jordan. *CH* 9.497 = *CH* 10.268. 1993

Burial: 240–235
Contents: 1,229+ AR Ptolemaic, plated coins
Coins studied: 914/1,229+ AR

Ptolemy I: 15 tetr. Alexandria
Ptolemy II 695 tetr.: 55 Alexandria, 31 Gaza, 48 Joppa, 88 Ake-Ptolemais, 177 Tyre, 197 Sidon, 3 Paphos, 11 Salamis (ou Citium), 30 Citium (ou Salamis), 55 Cyprus uncert.
Ptolemy III 134 tetr.: 2 Alexandria, 5 Gaza, 24 Joppa, 20 Ake-Ptolemais, 39 Tyre, 44 Sidon
Uncert. 70: 27 illegible + 5 Alexandria, 10 Joppa, 1 Ake-Ptolemais, 16 Tyre, 11 Sidon

This hoard's discovery is known through an article of Augé that recounts how these coins came to light by chance, during ditch digging. The Jordanian press reported the discovery, and dealers attributed to this hoard coins that were put on sale in Europe and the U. S. in subsequent months. Keen retraces the route of the different lots for which he could obtain photographs. The description above is based on his article, which estimates the hoard amounts to at least 1,229 coins; a group is to be added that was sold by Münzen und Medaillen in Basel, in 1993. 560 of these coins, which could not be examined, were excluded from Keen's article. Thus the hoard might have reached a total of around 1,800 coins. Augé himself saw two additional tetradrachms in Amman (Ptolemy I, Alexandria; Ptolemy II, Tyre) that he did not include in his catalogue, which is limited to the collection of the Amman Archeological Museum. Several of these coins have countermarks, graffiti, and punch marks. The inclusion of coins seen in the trade lowers the burial date slightly in comparison with what the lot preserved in Amman suggests (c. 243/2 BC, according to Augé).

Disposition: Archaeological Museum, Amman 315.

Bibliography:
Augé, C. "Note sur le trésor de monnaies ptolémaïques de 'Iraq al-Amir (Jordanie)," *Annual of the Department of Antiquities of Jordan* 45 (2001), pp. 483–485.
Keen, P. "The Iraq al-Amir Hoard, 1993 (*CH* IX.497)," in T. Faucher, A. Meadows, and C. Lorber (eds.) *Egyptian Hoards I, Ptolemaic Hoards*, Cairo, 2016.

148. Homs. *IGCH* 1529 = Noe 487. 1927

Burial: 230
Contents: 50+ AR

Lysimachus 39: Amphipolis 3, Pella 2, Lysimachia 1, Cyzicus? 2, Lampsacus 5, Smyrna 2, Pergamum 1, Sestos 1, Sardis 3, Magnesia 4, Cius 3, Parion 1, Calchedon 1, uncert. 10
Eumenes I: 1 tetr. (Westermark obv. 3)
Attalus I: 1 tetr. (Westermark obv. 62)
Antiochus I: 5 tetr. Seleuceia on the Tigris
Antiochus II: 1 tetr. Tarsus; 1 tetr. Antioch, 2 tetr. Uncert. mint in Mesopotamia (?)

According to Newell 1938, p. 76, n. 108, and the Seyrig Archives (Bibliothèque nationale de France, dossier 216), "in 1927, an antiquities dealer in Beirut, Roupen Edjadzian, showed E. T. Newell the rubbings of a small hoard discovered, it appears, in the region of Homs." Seyrig stresses the absence, strange for a Syrian hoard, of Alexanders and coins of Seleucus II. Perhaps a sorting had occurred. The list Margaret Thompson sent to him mentions only 29 coins. The Seleucid tetradrachms Newell 1941, no. 980z, 1136, 1138d, 1307g come from this hoard and entered Newell's collection.

Disposition: New York 31 (25 Lysimachus, 2 Attalid, 4 Antiochus II)

Bibliography:
Newell, E. T. *The Coinage of the Eastern Seleucid Mints from Seleucus I to Antiochus III*, New York, 1938.
Rostovtzeff, M. I. "Some remarks on the monetary and commercial policy of the Seleucids and Attalids," in W. M. Calder and J. Keil (eds.) *Anatolian Studies Presented to William Hepburn Buckler*, Manchester, 1939, pp. 277–298, p. 285, no. 1.
Newell E.T., *The Coinage of the Western Seleucid Mints from Seleucus I to Antiochus III*, New York, 1941.
Houghton, Lorber 2002, p. 99.

149. Syria? *IGCH* 1531. 1962

Burial: 225–220
Contents: 15+ AR, 14 tetr., 1 dr.

Demetrius Poliorcetes : 1 tetr. Pella; 1 dr. Chalcis
Antigonus Doson: 1 tetr. Corinth
Attalus I: 3 tetr. (Westermark obv. 30, 68, 94)
Antiochus II: 2 tetr. Phocaea; 1 tetr. Sardis; 1 tetr. Tarsus; 1 tetr. Seleuceia on the Tigris ; 1 tetr. ΔΕΛ mint (Sôter)
Seleucus II: 1 tetr. Sardis; 1 tetr. ΔΕΛ mint
Antiochus Hierax: 1 tetr. Alexandria Troas

Neither the exact content nor the findspot of this discovery are known (Boehringer 1972 mentions Syria). The tetradrachms of Antigonus Doson and Antiochus Hierax show little wear, almost mint condition. Houghton, Lorber 2002 review identifications of the Seleucid coins. *IGCH* mistakenly adds a drachm of Seleucus II.

Disposition: Münzen und Medaillen, Basel, 25, 17 November 1962, no. 443; Winterthur: casts and 1 drachm of Demetrius Poliorcetes.

Bibliography:
Boehringer, C. *Zur Chronologie mittelhellenistischer Münzserien, 220–160 v. Chr.*, Berlin, 1972, pp. 153–154, pls. 23–24.
Houghton, Lorber 2002, p. 99.

150. Jordan. *CH* 8.320. 1987

Burial: 225
Contents: 9+ AR Ptolemaic

Ptolemy I: 2 tetr. Alexandria
Ptolemy II: 2 tetr. Sidon, 1 tetr. Tyre, 1 tetr. Ake-Ptolemais, 1 tetr. Joppa
Ptolemy III: 1 tetr. Tyre, 1 tetr. Gaza

A letter from A. Spaer to M. J. Price preserved at the American Numismatic Society describes this hoard, stressing the coins' advanced wear. They are noticeable for their yellow patina. They apparently do not come from the Syria 1981 hoard (**168**) but from another collection with similar characteristics.

Disposition: Commerce, information from A. Spaer

Bibliography:
Meadows, A. R. "Jordan 1987 (*CH* 8.320)," in T. Faucher, A. Meadows, C.C. Lorber (eds.) *Egyptian Hoards I, Ptolemaic Hoards*, Cairo, 2016c.

151. Northeast Syria. *CH* 8.319

Burial: 225
Contents: 11 AR

Athens: 11 tetr. 3rd cent. BC.

Disposition: Commerce

152. Asia Minor or Northern Syria. *CH* 1.74. 1970

Burial: 220–215, then 200
Contents: 149 AR

Alexander III: 1 tetr. Miletus; 1 tetr. Pergamum; 1 tetr. uncert.
Lysimachus : 1 dr. Magnesia on the Maeander; 1 tetr. Pergamum; 1 tetr. Lampsacus; 2 tetr. Chalcedon; 2 tetr. Byzantium; 2 tetr. Sestos; 2 tetr. Lysimachia; 2 tetr. Ainos; 1 tetr. Amphipolis; 2 tetr. uncert.
Demetrius Poliorcetes : 1 tetr. Salamis, Cyprus (intrusion?); 3 tetr. Amphipolis; 1 tetr. Pella
Antigonus Gonatas: 12 tetr. Pella
Antiochus I: 3 tetr. Seleuceia on the Tigris
Antiochus II: 1 tetr. Sardis; 2 tetr. Antioch; 7 tetr. Seleuceia on the Tigris
Seleucus II: 1 tetr. Ilion; 15 tetr. Sardis; 2 tetr. Tarsus; 12 tetr. Antioch; 5 tetr. Apamea? (ΔΕΛ mint); 6 tetr. Nisibis; 3 tetr. Seleuceia on the Tigris ; 1 tetr. Hecatompylos? (Alexandria in Aria/Artacoana); 21 tetr. uncert.
Antiochus Hierax: 2 tetr. Alexandria Troas; 1 tetr. Parion

Seleucus III: 6 tetr. Tarsus; 10 tetr. Antioch; 2 tetr. Simyra; 1 tetr. Seleuceia on the Tigris
Antiochus III: 1 tetr. Seleuceia on the Calycadnus; 1 tetr. Laodiceia ad Mare; 1 tetr. Antioch; 1 uncert.
Philetairos: 6 tetr. Pergamum
Sinope: 1 tetr.
Perge: 1 tetr.

CH 1.74 and Houghton, Lorber 2002, p. 85, mistakenly indicate a total of 148 coins, neglecting the supplementary number for a Lysimachus from Ainos in Seyrig's catalogue, 1973 (52 bis). Seyrig specifies that he reconstituted this hoard, which went on sale simultaneously in Germany, Switzerland, and the United States in 1970. He failed to identify 25 specimens, for the most part coins of Seleucus II. Houghton, Lorber 2002 propose some new attributions for the Seleucid coins, but their catalogue of 114 coins does not correspond to the 105 tetradrachms of this dynasty Seyrig identified, whose catalogue is repeated here. The identifications will have to be reviewed. I have confined myself to placing a question mark on those attributions of Seyrig that the classifications of Seleucid Coins render obsolete.

Disposition: Paris BnF 40.

Bibliography:
Seyrig 1973, no. 1.
Houghton, Lorber 2002, pp. 85–86.

153. Syria. *CH* 8.323. 1985

Burial: 220
Contents: 3 AR Ptolemaic

Ptolemy II: 2 Tyre
Ptolemy III: 1 Ake-Ptolemais

Disposition: Commerce

154. Tartus, Northern Phoenicia. *IGCH* 1530 = *CH* 1.75. 1940

Burial: after 220?
Contents: 15+ AR

Alexander III 9 tetr.: Amphipolis 3; Cyme 1; Rhodes 1; Aradus 1; Sidon 1; Uncert. mints 2
Demetrius Poliorcetes : 1 tetr.
Antiochus I: 1 tetr. Tarsus
Antiochus II: 1 tetr. Seleuceia on the Tigris ; 1 tetr. Alexandria in Aria/Artacoana
Seleucus II: 1 tetr. uncert. Commagene or Cappadocia; 1 tetr. Alexandria in Aria/Artacoana

This small or partial hoard comprised 15 tetradrachms in poor condition, dispersed today. Seyrig examined it in the "bazaar of Tartus" (H. Seyrig Archives, Bibliothèque nationale de France, dossier 240). Dating is difficult, perhaps after 200, according to Seyrig 1973, p. 22, "but the absence of any coin of Antiochus III, twenty or twenty-five years after his accession (223), is strange.... In fact, the exact date of a hoard such as this, varied and small, must remain a matter for caution."[44] Le Rider 1986, p. 14, considers, however, that burial most probably is later than 220 BC.

44. "mais l'absence de toute pièce d'Antiochos III, vingt ou vingt-cinq ans après son avènement (223), forme un paradoxe [...]. En réalité, la date exacte d'un trésor comme celui-ci, à la fois disparate et exigu, reste sujette à caution."

Bibliography:
Seyrig 1973, no. 2.
Le Rider, G. "Les alexandres d'argent en Asie Mineure et dans l'Orient séleucide au IIIe siècle avant J.-C. Remarques sur le système monétaire des Séleucides et des Ptolémées," *Journal des Savants* (janvier–septembre 1986), pp. 5–51.
Houghton, Lorber 2002, p. 99.

155. Tel Michal. 1977–1980

Burial: after 220–179
Contents: 5 AE, in excavation

Philip V of Macedon: Kindler 1989, nos. 112–116 (Macedonian shield/Helmet)

Kindler 1989, p. 320, notes the existence of this hoard found in excavations, without specifying the nature of the container, if there was one, or commenting on the find.

Bibliography:
Kindler, A. "Numismatic report," in Z. Herzog et al. (eds.) *Excavations at Tel Michal, Israel*, Tel Aviv, 1989, pp. 320–329 and 443.

156. Region of Hebron, Israel. *CH* 8.304, pl. XXXVII, 1–4. 1991

Burial: after 219/8
Contents: 115+ AR Ptolemaic

Ptolemy I 26: 19 Alexandria, 3 Cyprus uncert. mint 9, 4 Cyprus uncert. mint 10.
Ptolemy II 75: 5 Alexandria, 2 Cyprus uncert. mint 9, 2 Cyprus uncert. mint 10, 3 Cyprus uncert. mint 19, 1 Cyprus uncert. mint 20, 2 uncert. Cilicia or Syro-Phoenicia, 1 Palestine uncert. mint 25, 23 Sidon, 20 Tyre, 9 Ake-Ptolemais, 4 Joppa, 2 Gaza, 1 illegible.
Ptolemy III 9: 1 Ptolemais-Lebedos, 2 Tyre, 3 Sidon, 3 Ake-Ptolemais
Ptolemy IV 5: 1 Alexandria, 4 uncert. Syro-Phoenicia

Meadows re-examines this hoard in light of the Spaer correspondence, available at the American Numismatic Society, and its similarities with the Khan el-Abde hoard (*IGCH* 1597, **255**), which leads him to lower the burial date by a good 20 years.[45]

Disposition: Commerce, information from A. Spaer.

Bibliography:
Meadows, A. R. "Hebron Area, Israel, 1991 (*CH* 8.304)," in T. Faucher, A. Meadows, and C. Lorber (eds.) *Egyptian Hoards I, Ptolemaic Hoards*, Cairo, 2016b.

157. Damour, 20 km south of Beirut. *IGCH* 1589 = *CH* 1.75. 1949

Burial: vers 218/7
Contents: 4 AR Ptolemaic

45. The classification follows the catalogue of Ptolemaic coins by Lorber (Lorber forthcoming).

Ptolemy IV: 1 Alexandria, 1 Ascalon, 1 Tyre, 1 Sidon

Seyrig was present when a peasant from Damour brought this hoard to Beirut (H. Seyrig Archives, Bibliothèque nationale de France dossier 6.I.b = dossier 274).

Disposition: Dispersed

Bibliography:
Seyrig 1973, no. 41.

158. Tel Michal. *CH* 7.85 = *CH* 8.307 = *CH* 9.498. 1977

Burial: after 214/3
Contents: 47 AR Ptolemaic, pot hoard, in excavation

Ptolemy I: 10 tetr.
Ptolemy II: 30 tetr. (Sidon, Tyre, Joppa, Gaza and "uncertain era" (2))
Ptolemy III: 7 tetr. (Tyre, Ake-Ptolemais, Joppa, Gaza and uncertain (2))

This hoard was discovered during the 1977 excavations at Tel Michal, 10 km north of Tel Aviv. The 47 Ptolemaic tetradrachms were buried in a vase from the Persian-Hellenistic stratum. Kindler dates the burial c. 240 BC, during the Third Syrian War when Ptolemy III invaded Seleucis. He suggests that the two tetradrachms "of uncertain era" pose a problem since they apparently date, according to the calendar of Aradus, from 212/11 BC (year 48) and 211/10 BC (year 49). The date for the ensemble's withdrawal from circulation might have to be lowered by 30 years. It would then be later than the reign of Ptolemy III, the last king represented in the hoard. Kindler thinks this hypothesis doubtful and prefers to maintain his original dating. He considers that economic reasons would have motivated the burial, since the region lies outside the zone of military operations. Silver's increasing scarcity and the upsurge in bronze in the Ptolemaic realm would have been contributing factors. Mørkholm 1980, pp. 4–7, has reviewed the hoard's dating. Mørkholm indeed has demonstrated that a Ptolemaic coin from Gaza (no. 36 of Kindler's catalogue) dates from the twenty-third year of Ptolemy III's reign, not Ptolemy II's, that is, 225/4 BC. The growing scarcity of silver strikings with these classic types between 242/1 and 220 BC would explain the absence of coins of Ptolemy IV. Thus, Mørkholm finds Kindler's argument against attribution of tetradrachms "of uncertain era" to Aradus untenable. Those present in the hoard, dated 212/11 and 211/10 BC, lower the burial date to c. 210 BC.

Lorber 2007, pp. 110–11, supports the hypothesis that the coins "of uncertain era" are dated according to what Hazzard 1995 calls "the Soter era." The tetradrachms in question would then be from the years 215/4 and 214/3 BC, with burial immediately afterwards. I follow her conclusions.

Bibliography:
Kindler, A. "A Ptolemaic Coin Hoard from Tel Michal," *Journal of the Tel Aviv University Institute of Archaeology* 5 (1978), pp. 159–169.
Mørkholm, O. "A groupe of Ptolemaic coins from Phoenicia and Palestine," *Israel Numismatic Journal* 4 (1980), pp. 4–7, pls. 1–2.
Kindler, A. "Numismatic report," Z. Herzog et al. (eds) *Excavations at Tel Michal, Israel*, Tel Aviv, 1989, pp. 320–329 and 443.
Lorber, C. "The Ptolemaic era coinage revisited," *Numismatic Chronicle* 167 (2007), pp. 105–117.

159. Lebanon. *CH* 8.332, pls. XLI, 19–23; XLII, 1–3. 1983

Burial: 210
Contents: 8 AR Ptolemaic

Ptolemy I: 1 tetr. Alexandria, 3 tetr. Tyre (years 21, 30, 32), 1 tetr. Sidon (year 29), 1 Ake-Ptolemais? (Γ between legs), 2 "uncertain era" (years 48 and 49, Mørkholm 1975–1976, p. 25)

It is possible that this group forms a parcel of no. **168**. This will be suggested by Meadows.

Disposition: Commerce

Bibliography:
Meadows, A. "The 'Syria' 1981 Hoard (*CH* 7.90; 8.306; 8.311; 8.332; 8.344)," in T. Faucher, A. Meadows, and C. Lorber (eds.) *Egyptian Hoards I, Ptolemaic Hoards*, Cairo, 2016a.

160. Syria. *IGCH* 1533 = *CH* 1.75. January, 1960

Burial: 210
Contents: 18 tetr. AR

Alexander III: 2 Pergamum; 1 Mytilene; 1 Chios; 1 uncert.
Lysimachus : 1 Byzantium; 1 Kios; 1 uncert.
Antigonus Gonatas: 1
Antigonus Doson: 1
Antiochus II: 1 uncert.; 1 Seleuceia on the Tigris
Seleucus II: 2 Antioch; 1 ΔΕΛ mint
Seleucus III: 1 Seleuceia on the Tigris
Antiochus III: 1 Tarsus; 1 Antioch

This could be a part of *IGCH* 1535 (**162**).

Disposition: Dispersed

Bibliography:
Seyrig 1973, no. 3.
Houghton, Lorber 2002, p. 100.

161. Homs. *IGCH* 1532 = Noe 488. 1934

Burial: 210
Contents: 60 AR, pot hoard

Alexander III: 1 posthumous tetr., Chios
Lysimachus 34 tetr.: Amphipolis 3, Pella 1, Mytilene 1, Lampsacus 10, Sestos 1, Ephesus 1, Magnesia 3, Parion 1, Byzantium 4, Cius 3, uncert. 5, imitations 1
Eumenes I: 1 tetr. (Westermark obv. 18)
Attalus I: 7 tetr. (Westermark obv. 38, 79, 95, 102 [2], 118)
Antiochus I: 1 tetr. Sardis; 4 tetr. Seleuceia on the Tigris
Antiochus II: 1 tetr. uncert.; 5 tetr. Seleuceia on the Tigris
Interregnum: 1 tetr. ΔΕΛ mint (Sôter)
Seleucus III: 2 tetr. Antioch
Antiochus III: 2 tetr. Antioch; 1 tetr. Laodiceia ad Mare (?)

Newell 1938, p. 76, n. 109: "The hoard was purchased intact, together with the vase in which it was found.... The hoard was buried late in the reign of Antiochus III." Rostovtzeff 1939, p. 285, shares the same view about the date, "a little later-time before the death of Antiochus III." The Seleucid tetradrachms Newell 1938, nos. 178k, 220a and Newell 1941, nos. 1024a, 1029ee, 1049d, 1051l, 1142d, 1144z, 1374d come from this hoard and are listed in his collection.

Disposition: New York 43 (1 Alexander, 28 Lysimachus, 5 Attalids, 9 Seleucids)

Bibliography:
Newell, E. T. *The Coinage of the Eastern Seleucid Mints from Seleucus I to Antiochus III,* New York, 1938.
Rostovtzeff, M. I. "Some remarks on the monetary and commercial policy of the Seleucids and Attalids," in W. M. Calder and J. Keil (eds.) *Anatolian Studies Presented to William Hepburn Buckler*, Manchester, 1939, pp. 277–298, p. 285, no. 2.
Newell, E. T. *The Coinage of the Western Seleucid Mints from Seleucus I to Antiochus III*, New York, 1941.
Westermark, U. *Das Bildnis des Philetairos von Pergamon. Corpus der Münzprägung*, Stockholm, 1961, pp. 14, 17.
Houghton, Lorber 2002, pp. 99–100.

162. Syria. *IGCH* 1535. 1959

Burial: 210
Contents: 250+ tetr. AR
Coins studied: 35 by Boehringer

Alexander III: 8 late tetr., Mytilene 1, Assos 1, Cyme 1, Phocaea (?) 1, Magnesia on the Maeander 1, Miletus 1, Aspendus 1 (year 1), Perge 1 (year 13)
Antigonus Doson: 3 tetr.
Lysimachus : 4 (+1) tetr., Amphipolis 1, Magnesia on the Maeander 1, Parion (?) 1, incertain 1 (+1)
Cavaros: (1 tetr., before 218)
Eumenes I: 1 tetr., Westermark obv. 2
Attalus I: 3 tetr., Westermark obv. 71, 103B, 112 var.
Pergamum, uncert. kings: (3 tetr.)
Antiochus I: 1 tetr. Sardis; 2 tetr. Seleuceia on the Tigris
Antiochus II: 1 tetr. Lysimachia; 2 tetr. Seleuceia on the Tigris
Interregnum: 1 tetr. ΔΕΛ mint (Sôter)
Seleucus II: 2 tetr. Sardis; 1 tetr. Antioch
Antiochus Hierax: 1 tetr. Parion; 1 tetr. Teos (?); 1 tetr. uncert.
Seleucus III: 1 tetr. Antioch; 1 tetr. uncert.
Antiochus III: 2 tetr. Antioch; 1 tetr. Nisibis; 1 uncert. Persis; 11 uncert.

Boehringer specifies that this hoard was discovered before January 10, 1960, in Syria. 32 specimens were sold by Münzen und Medaillen, Basel, in January, 1960, except for the three tetradrachms of Antigonus Doson, which were sold in April. All these coins show similar oxidation. Other specimens were included with them that could have been part of the original hoard comprising around 250 coins. These uncertain specimens are added in parentheses, and Boehringer generally does not provide details on the mints concerned. He dates the burial to the last years of the third century, but the date remains fluid owing to the disappearance of the core of the find. Houghton, Lorber 2002 proposes placing the burial c. 210 BC, based on the portraits of Antiochus III, which come from the start of his reign (c. 223–210).

This might be the same hoard as *IGCH* 1533 (**160**).

Disposition: Münzen und Medaillen, Basel, FPL 202 (August 1960), nos. 9–11; Kricheldorf 2 Nov. 1960, no. 82.

Bibliography:
Boehringer, C. *Zur Chronologie mittelhellenistischer Münzserien, 220–160 v. Chr.*, Berlin, 1972, pp. 158–161, pls. 27–29 (35 ex.).
Price, M. J. *The Coinage in the Name of Alexander the Great and Philip Arrhideus*, London, 1991, p. 61.
Houghton, Lorber 2002, pp. 100–101.

2.5. Hoards of the Second Century

163. Citadel of Afamya (ancient Apamea), Syria. *CH* 8.360. May, 1986

Burial: 200–100
Contents: 1,160 tetr. AR Ptolemaic, pot hoard

Demetrius II: 1,160 Tyre (Eagle on reverse)

Disposition: Commerce

Bibliography:
Houghton, Lorber, Hoover 2008, p. 96.

164. Syria. *CH* 8.339. Before 1991

Burial: 200
Contents: 36 AR Ptolemaic

Ptolemy I: 1 Sv. 247; 1 Sv. 250; 1 Sv. 252?; 2 Sv. 255; 3 Sv. 256; 2 Sv. 259
Ptolemy II: 1 Sv. 339; 1 Sv. 353?; 1 Sv. 354; 1 Sv. 354?; 1 Sv. 362; 1 Sv. 365; 1 Sv. 368; 2 Sv. 548; 1 Sv. 559; Tyre: 4 Sv. 644; 1 Sv. 647; 1 Sv. 649; 1 Sv. 686; Sidon: 7 Sv. 713; Ake-Ptolemais: 1 Sv. 780.
Ptolemy III: 1 Sv. 1027

Spaer saw this hoard or partial hoard of tetradrachms on the market in 1991. The coins shared an identical patina. Spaer and the authors of *CH* 8 likened the hoard to the Syria 1981 hoard, *CH* 7.90 (**168**). The latter contained Ptolemaic tetradrachms down to Ptolemy V and gold octadrachms, some of which were recognized as modern counterfeits. These points do not justify connecting the two lots with certainty, and I have preferred to leave them separate.

Disposition: Commerce. Correspondence of A. Spaer at the ANS.

165. Idna, 12 km west of Hebron. *IGCH* 1587. 1967

Burial: 200
Contents: 25 AE Ptolemaic

Ptolemy II to Ptolemy IV

Disposition: Dispersed. Information from Y. Meshorer

166. Oylum Höyüğü, Cyrrhestica. *CH* 9.501. 1989

Burial: 200–195 (Özgen, Davesne); 203/2 (Houghton, Lorber)
Contents: 134 AR: 59 tetr., 75 dr., in excavation, pot hoard

Alexander III 79: Mesembria 1 tetr.; Heraclea 1 tetr.; Parion 2 tetr.; Lampsacus 17 dr.; Abydos 4 dr.; Assos 1 tetr.; Mytilene 2 tetr.; Phocaea 1 tetr.; Colophon 13 dr.; Magnesia 5 dr.; Miletus 2 dr.; Chios 1 tetr., 2 dr.; Mylasa 1 dr.; Sardis 6 dr.; Western Asia Minor 5 dr.; Termessos 1 tetr.; Perge 1 tetr. (201/0 according to Boehringer); Aspendus: 2 tetr.; Side 1 dr.; Marathus 1 dr.; uncert. 9 dr.
Antigonus Doson: 2 tetr.
Lysimachus 15: Amphipolis 1 tetr.; Byzantium 2 tetr.; Chalcedon 2 tetr.; Cius 3 tetr.; Lysimachia 1 dr.; Lampsacus 2 tetr., 1 dr.; Alexandria Troas 1 tetr.; Pergamum 1 tetr.; Colophon 1 dr.; Magnesia 2 dr.; Uncert. 3 tetr.
Antiochus I: 3 tetr. Seleuceia on the Tigris
Antiochus II: 1 tetr. Ephesus or Miletus; 1 tetr. Antioch; 1 tetr. Uncert. Mesopotamia; 1 tetr. Seleuceia on the Tigris
Interregnum: 1 tetr. ΔΕΛ mint (Sôter)
Antiochus Hierax: 1 tetr. Parion
Seleucus III: 2 tetr. Antioch; 1 tetr. Seleuceia on the Tigris
Antiochus III: 1 tetr. Tarsus; 7 tetr. Antioch; 4 tetr. ΔΕΛ mint; 1 tetr. Laodiceia ad Mare (?); 1 dr. Nisibis (?); 1 tetr. Seleuceia on the Tigris
Antiochus II or III: uncert. 1 tetr.
Philetairos: Gr. V 1 tetr.; Gr. VI: 1 tetr.
Side: 1 tetr.
Ephesus: 3 dr.

The excavations that uncovered this hoard were focused on the Bronze Age. Some Hellenistic walls came to light during an exploration of the vicinity. A jug in a room corner revealed 134 Hellenistic silver coins. None of the latest coins is clearly dated. Houghton, Lorber 2002 propose a tentative dating for the hoard higher than Özgen, Davesne 1994, stressing that this hoard brings into question the low chronology proposed by Boehringer for the Alexanders of Perge.

Kinns 1999 details the Ephesian drachms.

Disposition: Gaziantep Archaeological Museum

Bibliography:
Özgen, E. and A. Davesne. "Le trésor de Oylum Höyüğü," in M. Amandry and G. Le Rider, *Trésors et circulation monétaire en Anatolie antique*, Paris, 1994, pp. 45–49, pls. III–VIII.
Kinns, P. "The Attic weight drachms of Ephesus: a preliminary study in the light of recent hoards," *Numismatic Chronicle* 159 (1999), pp. 47–97, pp. 50–51, no. 1.
Le Rider, G. *Antioche de Syrie sous les Séleucides. Corpus des monnaies d'or et d'argent I. De Seleucos I à Antiochos V (c. 301–161)*, Paris, 1999, pp. 157–158.
Houghton, Lorber 2002, pp. 101–102.

167. Idlib. *IGCH* 1543. 1959

Burial: 200–180
Contents: 1,400 AR: c. 600 tetr.; 800 dr.

Alexander III: numerous posthumous dr.

Lysimachus
Cavaros of Thrace
Seleucids, including Antiochus III
Marathus

Disposition: Dispersed. Information from an *IGCH* correspondent in Beirut.

168. Syria. *CH* 7.90 = *CH* 8.306, pls. XXXVII 5–17; XXXVIII 1–12 = *CH* 8.311 = *CH* 8.344. 1981

Burial: Shortly after october 199
Contents: 941 AR + uncert. number of AV

Ptolemy I 301: 252 Alexandria, 2 uncert. mint 7, 16 Cyprus uncert. mint 9, 30 Cyprus uncert. mint 10, 1 Tyre
Ptolemy I or II: 7
Ptolemy II 431: 12 Alexandria, 21 Cyprus uncert. mint 9, 10 Cyprus uncert. mint 10, 4 Cyprus uncert. mint 19, 7 Cyprus uncert. mint 20, 2 Cyprus uncert., 1 Cyprus illegible, 176 Tyre, 134 Sidon, 35 Ake-Ptolemais, 23 Joppa, 4 Gaza, 1 Ake-Ptolemais or Joppa, 1 imitation Ake-Ptolemais (uncert. mint 23)
Ptolemy III 24: 2 Alexandria, 1 Ainos, 1 uncert. Asia Minor mint 26, 1? uncert. Asia Minor mint 27, 2? Ephesus, 1 uncert. Asia Minor mint 30, 5 Tyre, 8 Sidon, 1 Ake-Ptolemais, 2 Joppa
Ptolemy IV 31: 12 Alexandria, 1 Tyre, 1 Ake-Ptolemais, 1 uncert. 36, 1 uncert. Phoenicia + "reign of Ptolemy IV": 5 uncert. Syro-Phoenician, 10 "uncertain era."
Ptolemy V 147: 10 with portrait of Ptolemy IV (8 uncert., 1 Tyre, 1 Sidon); 73 with portrait of Ptolemy V (46 main series, 4 Dor, 4 Tripolis, 12 Sidon, 3 Berytus, 3 Tyre, 1? Ake-Ptolemais); 31 parallel emissions (9 Alexandria, 22 uncert. Phoenicia); 33 traditional type (dated: 6 uncert. Phoenicia, 1 Joppa; not dated: 25 Alexandria, 1 uncert.)

This hoard has been connected to *CH* 8.339 (**164**), but the descriptions of the two lots do not warrant identifying one, single hoard with certainty. On the other hand, thanks especially to the correspondence of Arnold Spaer with M. J. Price, Meadows has been able to reconstitute the history of several lots offered in the market.[46] This large ensemble was buried during the Fifth Syrian War, perhaps in the Golan region or nearby, and may have been related to the upheavals occasioned by the battle of Panion and the Ptolemaic defeat. It is possible that **159** also forms part of this hoard.

Disposition: Commerce. Notes and photographs at the British Museum

Bibliography:
Meadows, A. R. "The 'Syria' 1981 Hoard (*CH* 7.90; 8.306; 8.311; 8.344)," in T. Faucher, A. Meadows, and C. Lorber (eds.) *Egyptian Hoards I, Ptolemaic Hoards*, Cairo, 2016a.

169. Balatah (ancient Shechem). *IGCH* 1588. 1960

Burial: after 199/8
Contents: 35 tetr. AR pot hoard, in excavation

Ptolemy II: 4 Alexandria, 2 Tyre, 1 Sidon, 2 Ake-Ptolemais, 10 uncert. Coele Syria
Ptolemy III: 1 Sidon
Ptolemy IV or V: 3 Coele Syria or Cyprus
Ptolemy V: 8 Alexandria, 4 Coele Syria

46. The classification is according to Lorber's corpus of Ptolemaic coins (Lorber forthcoming).

While the 1960 excavation did not uncover any Seleucid bronze, it did reveal numerous Ptolemaic specimens that characterize Level II. A small jar buried beneath a floor was found nearby, containing 35 Ptolemaic tetradrachms (Campbell 1960, p. 104, fig. 2). "The mouth of the jug was clogged with a plug of earth" (Sellers 1960, p. 89). Kadman 1967 adds 25 bronzes divided amongst Ptolemy I, II, III, and IV, but his figures do not tally correctly. Sellers 1962 does not mention any bronze in his description of the discovery. Thus, I have not taken them into account. In a thesis on the gold and silver coinage of the Ptolemies in the second century, Olivier has carefully re-examined this hoard and has clarified its composition. The present description and dating are based on this revision.

Disposition: Unknown

Bibliography:
Campbell, E. F. "Excavations at Shechem, 1960," *The Biblical Archaeologist* 23/4 (1960), pp. 102–110, fig. 2.
Sellers, O. R. "Coins of the 1960 excavations at Shechem," *The Biblical Archaeologist* 25/3 (1962), pp. 87–96, fig. 10–12.
Kadman, L. "The monetary development of Palestine in the light of coin hoards," A. Kindler (ed.) *International Numismatic Convention, Jerusalem, 27–31 December 1963. The Patterns of Monetary Development in Phoenicia and Palestine in Antiquity*, Tel Aviv, 1967, no. 7.
Olivier, J. *Archè et chrèmata en Egypte au IIe s. avant J.-C. (204–81 av. J.-C.). Etude de numismatique et d'histoire*, Etudes Alexandrines, Alexandria, forthcoming.

170. Aleppo, ancient Beroea, Cyrrhestica. *IGCH* 1539 = Noe 30. 1896

Burial: 190
Contents: 150+ tetr. AR

Alexander III: late tetr. (several of Rhodes)
Antigonus Monophthalmus: tetr.
Demetrius Poliorcetes: tetr.
Antigonus Gonatas: tetr.
Lysimachus: tetr.
Antiochus I: tetr.
Antiochus II: tetr.
Seleucus II: tetr.
Antiochus Hierax: tetr.
Seleucus III: tetr.
Antiochus III: tetr.
Prusias I: tetr.
Attalus I: tetr.
Eumenes II: tetr.
Side: tetr.

Rouvier 1900, pp. 42–43, n. 2, indicates that this hoard was found "at K…, north of Aleppo," during agricultural work. He had almost all the specimens in his possession (without mentioning the number) and selected the 150 most handsome, which entered his collection. He provides a list of the rulers represented, beginning with "Antigonus, king of Asia (306–301 BC)," and Attalus II. Burial occurred between 150 and 137 BC at the latest. Seyrig (H. Seyrig Archives, Bibliothèque nationale de France, dossier 218) suggests that the coins then attributed to Attalus II belong, in fact, to Attalus I (241–197 BC). Westermark 1961, p. 15, makes clear that the hoard's latest coins, apart from the Attalids, are those of Antiochus III and Prusias I of Bithynia.
Disposition: Formerly in the J. Rouvier collection

Bibliography:
Rouvier, J. "Le monnayage alexandrin d'Arados," *Revue numismatique* (1900), pp. 36–151.
Regling K., "Hellenistische Münzschatz aus Babylon," *Zeitschrift für Numismatik* (1928), pp. 92–132, p. 94 for this hoard, summarises the notes of J. Rouvier.
Westermark U., *Das Bildnis des Philetairos von Pergamon. Corpus der Münzprägung*, Stockholm, 1961, pp. 15–16.

171. Kosseir, Seleucis, near Antakya. *IGCH* 1537. 1949

Burial: c. 190/189
Contents: 82+ AR
Coins studied: 40/82+

Alexander III: 21 late tetr.: Mesembria 2; Assos 2; Chios 1; Colophon 1; Miletus 1; Rhodes 2; Phaselis 4 (to year 24); Perge 3 (to year 20); Aspendus 3; Aradus 1 (year 69); Uncertain mint 1
Lysimachus : 1 lifetime tetr. Lampsacus; 4 posthumous tetr. Ainos, Chalcedon, Tenedos, Uncert.
Antiochus III: 1 tetr. Sardis; 1 tetr. Antioch; 1 tetr. ΔI mint (c. 202 BC); 1 tetr. Seleuceia on the Tigris
Prusias I: 1 tetr.
Side: 9 tetr.

Seyrig was able to see only 40 of the more than 82 tetradrachms announced by his informants. Nine are today in the Museum of Antakya. The tetradrachm of Aradus dated 191/0 BC is in very good condition. The latest tetradrachm from Pamphylia is from 192/1 BC. Based on the beginnings of Pamphylian eras established by Boehringer 1972, p. 62, the latest dates represented in the hoard are, respectively: Perge, year 20 = 200/199 BC; Phaselis, year 24 = 195/4 BC; Aspendus, year 19 = 192/1 BC. Following Boehringer's dating, Seyrig inclines to a burial around the time of the battle of Magnesia or a little after. He also observes that the massive presence of Pamphylian tetradrachms is to be expected: it was a time when they dominated circulation in southern Asia Minor and Syria. Writing on the topic of this abundant production, he speaks of "a veritable export industry in their coinage"[47] (Seyrig 1973, p. 35). This breaks off with the defeat of Antiochus III at Magnesia.

Disposition: Antakya Museum 9

Bibliography:
Seyrig 1973, no. 7.
Houghton, Lorber 2002, p. 103.
Meadows, A. R. "The eras of Pamphylia and the Seleucid invasions of Asia Minor," *American Journal of Numismatics* 21 (2009), pp. 51–88.

172. Latakia. *IGCH* 1536. 1946

Burial: c. 190
Contents: 34 AR

Alexander III, 17 posthumous tetr.: Odessos 1; Chios 3; Miletus 1; Rhodes 6; Phaselis 1 (year 10); Aradus 5 (years 59 (2), 61 (3))
Antigonus Doson: 2 tetr.
Seleucus I: 1 tetr. Seleuceia on the Tigris
Seleucus II: 1 tetr. ΔEΛ mint

47. "une vraie industrie de leur monnaie pour l'exportation."

Antiochus III: 2 tetr. ΔI mint (c. 202 BC); 4 tetr. Edessa (? c. 213)
Alabanda as Antioch: 1 tetr.
Side: 6 tetr.

This hoard was found during excavation work in the rue de France, Latakia. Seyrig examined 32 tetradrachms that constitute only a part of the find. Two additional tetradrachms (Seleucus I and Alabanda as Antioch) are included based upon an oral description given to Seyrig. The rest of the hoard is dispersed. Burial is later than 199/8 BC, based on the date of the most recent tetradrachms from Aradus. Four Rhodian tetradrachms carry the full name of the mint official. This is a rather late feature. The Chian tetradrachm corroborates this observation. Seyrig thought the coins were retired from circulation c. 190 BC.

Disposition: Dispersed

Bibliography:
Seyrig 1973, no. 6.
Price, M. J. *The Coinage in the Name of Alexander the Great and Philip Arrhideus*, London, 1991, p. 62.
Houghton, Lorber 2002, p. 102.

173. Dniye, near Safita, Northern Phoenicia. *IGCH* 1538. 1952

Burial: c. 190
Contents: 41 AR Attic and Ptolemaic

Alexander III, 3 early posthumous tetr.: Amphipolis 2; Uncertain mint 1; 2 early posthumous dr. : Lampsacus, Colophon; 12 late tetr.: Mytilene 1; Clazomenae 1; Phaselis 1 (year 26); Aradus 9 (years 18, 30, 35, 41 (5), 42)
Lysimachus : 1 lifetime tetr. Alexandria Troas; 1 posthumous tetr. Cyzicus
Antiochus II: 1 tetr. Alexandria Troas; 1 tetr. Seleuceia on the Tigris
Antiochus Hierax: 1 tetr. Lampsacus; 1 tetr. Alexandria Troas
Aradus: 1 tetrob. (year 20)
Ptolemy I: 4 tetr.
Ptolemy II: 12 tetr., including 2 Tyre, 1 Sidon, 4 Cyprus (?)
Ptolemy III: 1 tetr.

This hoard of 41 tetradrachms was sold at Beirut (at least partly at Poladian's, on December 12, 1952, according to Seyrig's Archives, Bibliothèque nationale de France, dossier 242) and is perhaps incomplete. Withdrawal from circulation can be estimated at c. 190 BC, based on a tetradrachm of Phaselis dated 193 (?) BC. Strangely, the latest tetradrachm of Aradus is clearly earlier (218 BC), even though "Dniye was certainly part of the Aradian Peraea, and one might have expected the tetradrachms of Aradus to constitute the most recent part of the hoard"[48] (Seyrig 1973, p. 29). So the hoard could have been gathered in several stages. The Ptolemaic coins do not extend beyond the third quarter of the third century, thus forming another separate group.

Disposition: Dispersed

Bibliography:
Seyrig 1973, no. 5.
Price, M. J. *The Coinage in the Name of Alexander the Great and Philip Arrhideus*, London, 1991, p. 62.
Houghton, Lorber 2002, p. 103.

48. "Dniyé […] faisait certainement partie de la pérée aradienne, et l'on pourrait donc s'attendre à ce que les tétradrachmes d'Arados fassent la partie la plus moderne du trésor."

174. Syria, perhaps the Aradian Peraea. *CH* 2.81 = *CH* 10.289. 1971

Burial: c. 190
Contents: 90 AR Attic and Ptolemaic

Alexander III, 40 posthumous tetr.: Megalopolis 1; Sinope 1; Heraclea Pontica 1; Pergamum 1; Miletus 2; Chios 3; Samos 2; Rhodes 4; Phaselis 5; Aspendus 3; Perge 6; Aradus 5 (61, 64, 65 (3)); Gerrha 3; Uncert. mints 3
Antigonus Doson: 1 tetr.
Philip V: 1 tetr.
Antiochus I: 1 tetr. Pergamum (Alexander type); 1 tetr. Seleuceia on the Tigris
Antiochus II: 1 tetr. Seleuceia on the Tigris
Antiochus Hierax: 1 tetr. Parion; 1 tetr. Lampsacus; 1 tetr. Alexandria Troas
Antiochus III: 1 tetr. uncert. Phrygia; 2 tetr. Soli in Cilicia; 1 tetr. Tarsus; 1 tetr. Laodiceia ad Mare (?); 2 tetr. ΔI mint; 2 tetr. Edessa (?); 1 tetr. uncert. mint Mesopotamia; 1 tetr. Uncert.
Ptolemy II: 1 tetr. Alexandria; 1 tetr. Sidon
Ptolemy IV: 1 tetr. Alexandria
Ptolemy V: 2 tetr. Alexandria
Ephesus: 3 dr.
Alabanda: 1 tetr.
Side: 22 tetr.

The find spot of this hoard is not clearly located. It arrived on the market in 1971, with no provenance indicated. Le Rider dates its withdrawal from circulation c. 190 BC. "If one supposes, based on the five Ptolemies, that the discovery occurred near the borders of Phoenicia and Coele Syria, one might then imagine a spot situated in the Aradian Peraea or relatively near its boundaries"[49] (Le Rider 1998b, p. 96).

Disposition: Commerce.

Bibliography:
Le Rider, G. "Un trésor de monnaies d'argent trouvé en Syrie en 1971 (*CH* II 81)," *Hommage à Ernest Will.* Syria 75 (1998), pp. 89–96.
Houghton, Lorber 2002, pp. 102–103.
Meadows, A. R. "The eras of Pamphylia and the Seleucid invasions of Asia Minor," *American Journal of Numismatics* 21 (2009), pp. 53–56.

175. Jablah, quarter of Msaitbe, Syria. 2005

Burial: after 190/189
Contents: 53 AE

Aradus: 26 AE
Aradus or Carne: 17 AE
Aradus, Carne, Gabala or Simyra? 10 AE
Disposition: Depot of the Directorate General of Antiquities of Jablah, Syria.

49. "Ayant supposé grâce au cinq ptolémées que la découverte avait été faite à proximité des frontières de la Phénicie et de la Cœlé-Syrie, on pourrait songer à un endroit situé dans l'ancienne pérée des Aradiens ou relativement proche de ses confins."

Bibliography:
Unpublished hoard, see the presentation infra, pp. 194–196.

176. Baiyada, near Safita, Northern Phoenicia. *IGCH* 1541. 1949

Burial: c. 180–175
Contents: 11 tetr. AR

Alexander III: Aradus 1 (year 61); Temnos 1 (intrusive?); Ephesus 1; Rhodes 3; Phaselis 2; Aspendus 2; Messene 1

This small hoard, scattered today, surely contained rather more than the 11 tetradrachms that could be catalogued. Seyrig notes that the coin from Temnos is probably a modern intrusion: its date of c. 160 BC does not accord with his proposed hoard dating, between 180 and 175 BC, based upon the date of the tetradrachm from Phaselis and the absence of anchor countermarks.

Disposition: Dispersed

Bibliography:
Seyrig 1973, no. 10.
Price, M. J. *The Coinage in the Name of Alexander the Great and Philip Arrhideus*, London, 1991, p. 63.

177. Beqaa Valley. *CH* 10.295. 1995

Burial: After 175–170; 170–160 (*CH* 10); 187/6? (Elayi)
Contents: 40+ tetr. AR
Coins studied: 6/40+

Posthumous Alexanders: Mytilene (1), Temnos (3), Phaselis (1) + 31
Side: 1 autonomous tetr. + 3

The hoard's publication is ambiguous. It states, that the hoard consisted of about "40 silver tetradrachms with types of Alexander" and that the roughly 34 tetradrachms dispersed on the market were "tetradrachms with types of Alexander, among which were three from Side" (p. 11). Yet the Side specimen published is an autonomous civic issue with the types of helmeted head of Athena/Walking Nike, holding a wreath. Elayi 1991 stresses that the lot seems to have consisted solely of foreign coins, like the Tell Kotchek hoard, for example (*IGCH* 1773, **198**), which is not exceptional in Seleucid Syria. The dating proposed by Elayi for the hoard follows the chronology of Alexanders that Price adopted in his catalogue, p. 352: the latest specimen of Phaselis is from 187/6 BC. It is a tetradrachm of year 32 i.e. before 185/4 BC according to Meadows 2009, p. 69, revised by Meadows 2013, p. 142 n. 54. But the tetradrachms from Phaselis and Side are countermarked with an anchor which postpones the burial to after c. 175–170 BC. Furthermore, Lorber 2010 completely revised the date of the Temnos Alexanders. Price 1686 is now dated before 162 BC, Price 1676 shortly before 151/0 BC.

Disposition: Commerce

Bibliography:
Elayi, J. "Un trésor de tétradrachmes aux types d'Alexandre trouvé dans la Beqa," in M. Amandry and S. Hurter (eds.) *Travaux de numismatique grecque offerts à G. Le Rider*, London, 1999, pp. 135–138, pl. 11.

178. Tel Michal. 1977–1980

Burial: after 175–164
Contents: 4 AE, in excavation

Antiochus IV: 4 AE Kindler 1989 no. 123 (Seleuceia on the Tigris), 129, 131, 135 (Ake-Ptolemais)

Kindler 1989, p. 320, notes the existence of this hoard, found in excavation, without indicating the nature of the container, if it existed, or commenting on the find.

Bibliography:
Kindler, A. "Numismatic report," Z. Herzog et al. (eds) *Excavations at Tel Michal, Israel* , Tel Aviv, 1989, pp. 320–329 and 443.

179. Unknown Findspot. *CH* 9.541. Before 1980

Burial: 175–150 and 120–100
Contents: 10+ tetr. AR

Alexander III: Perge 4
Antiochus VIII: 5 Ake-Ptolemais
Side: 1

A Parisian collector acquired this hoard in Jerusalem in the 1980s. The coins of Perge and Side all carry the anchor countermark, which is generally dated to 175–170 BC. The dating of these civic issues does not accord with that of the tetradrachms of Antiochus VIII (121/0–114/3 BC), and it may be necessary to entertain the possibility of two separate hoards.

Disposition: Private collection, Paris.

Bibliography:
Davesne, A. and A. Lemaire. "Trésors hellénistiques du Proche-Orient," *Revue numismatique* (1996), pp. 51–76, no. 3, pl. 11.
Houghton, Lorber, Hoover 2008, p. 113.

180. Syria. *CH* 2.83. 1971

Burial: 175
Contents: 9+ AR

Antiochus III: 1 tetr. Antioch
Seleucus IV: 7 tetr. Antioch; 1 tetr. Damascus (?)

Disposition: Dispersed, photos in Copenhagen

Bibliography:
Houghton, Lorber 2002, p. 103.
Houghton, Lorber, Hoover 2008, p. 87.

181. Lebanon. *CH* 9.507. 1989

Burial: 175?
Contents: 105 tetr. AR+

Lysimachus 15: Amphipolis 1; Pella 1; Ainos 1; Byzantium 1; Chalcedon 1; Lysimachia 1; Lampsacus 3; Sestos 1; Alexandria Troas 1; Cius 1; Uncert. 3
Philetairos: 4 tetr. (gr. III–VI)
Antiochus I: 3 Seleuceia on the Tigris
Antiochus II: 1 Antioch; 4 Seleuceia on the Tigris
Antiochus Hierax: 1 Alexandria Troas
Seleucus III: 1 Antioch
Antiochus III: 1 Soli in Cilicia; 2 Tarsus; 20 Antioch; 5 Damascus (?); 2 Edessa (?); 1 Nisibis; 1 Seleuceia on the Tigris ; 1 Susa; 1 Uncert.
Seleucus IV: 1 Cilician mint; 9 Antioch; 5 Damascus (?); 26 Ake-Ptolemais

These coins were dispersed on the London market in 1989. The hoard produced 26 tetradrachms of Seleucus IV struck at Ptolemais, of which only eight had been previously recorded. They were issued between c. 180 and 175 BC, and clearly had circulated very little. The absence of Alexanders leads one to suppose that this hoard is incomplete.

Disposition: Commerce, London

Bibliography:
Le Rider, G. "Séleucos IV à Ptolemais. Le trésor du Liban 1989," *Revue numismatique* (1992), pp. 37–45.
Houghton, Lorber 2002, pp. 103–104.
Houghton, Lorber, Hoover 2008, p. 102.

182. Jericho (?). *CH* 8.412. 1991.

Burial: c. 170/169
Contents: 16+ AR Ptolemaic + 32 AR "uncertain era"

Ptolemy II: 1 tetr. Ake-Ptolemais
Ptolemy III or IV: 1 tetr. Ake-Ptolemais (imit.)
Ptolemy VI: 2 tetr. Alexandria
"Uncertain Era": 12 tetr., years 73–91

Olivier, Meadows identify 32 tetradrachms of uncertain era down to year 92 in commerce between 1991 and 1997. They may belong with the Jericho hoard, and they would lower the burial date by one year. The authors emphasize the unworn state of the tetradrachms "of uncertain era" from the years 90 and 91. Burial may have been contemporary with the Sixth Syrian War.

Disposition: Commerce, Information from A. Spaer

Bibliography:
Olivier, J. and A. R. Meadows. "Jericho area, c. 1991 (*CH* 8.412)," in T. Faucher, A. Meadows, and C. Lorber (eds.) *Egyptian Hoards I, Ptolemaic Hoards*, Cairo, 2016.

183. Syria. *CH* 1.77. Before 1960

Burial: 170–160
Contents: 142+ AR

Alexander III: 103 Alabanda (to year 6); 1 Myrina; 1 Chios; 7 Phaselis (to year 26); 4 Perge (to year 32); 12 Aspendus (to year 26); 14 Temnos

Numerous countermarks, with anchor or bust of Helios facing.

Disposition: Commerce

Bibliography:
Kleiner, F. Forthcoming, Athens

184. Latakia. *IGCH* 1544 = Noe 603. 1759 (Fig. 1.1)

Burial: 169
Contents: 100+ AR, in an urn
Coins studied: 95/100+

Alexander III: 6 lifetime tetr.: Amphipolis 3; Tarsus 1; Myriandros 1; Damascus 1; 39 late tetr.: Corinth 1; Argos 1; Assos 1; Myrina 2; Cyme 1; Mytilene 1; Methymna 1; Pergamum? 1; Erythrae 2; Clazomenae 1; Colophon 1; Miletus 1; Magnesia on the Maeander 2; Chios 9; Mylasa 1; Antioch on the Maeander? 1; Rhodes 6; Perge 1; Aspendus 1; Aradus 1 (year 65); Uncert. mints 3; 3 dr.: Euboea?, Lampsacus, Magnesia on the Maeander
Lysimachus : 3 tetr.
Mithridates III of Pontus: 2 tetr.
Confederation of Athena Ilias: 1 tetr.
Alabanda: 5 tetr.
Side: 2 tetr.
Seleucus I–Antiochus III: 15 tetr.
Antiochus (son of Seleucus IV): 1 tetr. Antioch
Antiochus IV: 6 tetr. Antioch; 1 tetr. Seleuceia (?); 2 uncert.
Aradus: 12 dr.

Pellerin 1765, p. 2, describes this famous hoard as follows: "a deposit discovered in Syria, judged to have occurred in the reign of Antiochus IV, around 170 BC."[50] The coins had a black coating and blistering, the result, perhaps, of a fire on their burial site (p. 106). They were discovered in the environs of Latakia in 1759. The man who purchased the hoard from its discoverer in Latakia itself brought it to Pellerin. Thus it seems it was complete. Seyrig 1973, p. 54, dates the burial c. 170 BC. Mattingly 1990, pp. 67–78, and 1993, pp. 85–86, has questioned this chronology, preferring a lower date, c. 160, because of the hoard's similarities with that of Babylon (*IGCH* 1774), whose burial is confidently dated to 156/5 BC. Boehringer 1972, p. 70, favors burial c. 164 BC. Le Rider 1991, p. 208, is not averse to this lowering of the date. He observes that if the hoard had been buried c. 170 BC, the 12 Aradian drachms would have had to belong to the first or second year of their issue, "because the issue of Aradian drachms began in 171/0." I objected, in 2005, "that Laodiceia is very close to Aradian territory, at the northern boundary of its Peraea. Moreover, the first issues of drachms were abundant; and if they were related to preparations for war against Egypt, it would not be surprising that they rapidly circulated on the coast, especially towards the big Seleucid ports that must have been highly active

50. "un dépôt découvert en Syrie, qu'on juge y avoir été fait sous le règne d'Antiochos IV, environ cent soixante et dix ans avant l'ère chrétienne."

Figure 1.1. Part of the Latakia hoard (*IGCH* 1544, **184**; BnF, Paris)

at this time. Finally, the issue 'of indeterminate year', if indeed that corresponds to 172/1, increases the odds of finding twelve Aradian drachms in the vicinity of Laodiceia in 170"[51] (Duyrat 2005a, p. 164). Houghton, Lorber, Hoover 2008, p. 87, propose burial c. 169 BC.

Two coins (Aspendus and Side) are countermarked with an anchor.

Disposition: BnF, Paris

Bibliography:

Pellerin, J. *Mélange de diverses médailles pour servir de supplément aux recueils des médailles de rois et de villes qui ont été imprimés en 1762 et 1763*, t. 1, Paris, 1765, pp. 104–140.
Regling, K. "Hellenistische Münzschatz aus Babylon," *Zeitschrift für Numismatik* (1928), p. 94, no. 1.
Rostovtzeff, M. "Some remarks on the monetary and commercial policy of the Seleucids and Attalids," W. M. Calder, J. Keil (eds.) *Anatolian Studies Presented to William Hepburn Buckler*, Manchester, 1939, p. 292, no. 4.
Seyrig 1973, no. 11.
Le Rider, G. "Ephèse et Arados au IIe siècle avant notre ère," *Numismatica e antichità classiche* 20 (1991), p. 208.
Price, M. J. *The Coinage in the Name of Alexander the Great and Philip Arrhideus*, London, 1991, p. 63.
Duyrat, F. *Arados hellénistique. Étude historique et monétaire*, Beirut, 2005, pp. 148–149.
Houghton, Lorber, Hoover 2008, p. 87.

51. "que Laodicée est très proche du territoire d'Arados, à la limite nord de la pérée. En outre les premières émissions de drachmes ont été abondantes et si elles sont bien en rapport avec les préparatifs de guerre contre l'Égypte, il ne serait pas surprenant qu'elles aient rapidement circulé sur la côte, particulièrement vers les grands ports séleucides qui devaient être en pleine activité à ce moment. Enfin l'émission de l'année indéterminée, si elle correspond bien à 172/1 avant notre ère, augmente les chances de trouver douze drachmes aradiennes aux environs de Laodicée en 170."

185. Kishon River, near Haifa. *IGCH* 1590. 1958

Burial: 169
Contents: 100+ AE, found during the dredging of the river.

Antiochus IV: Ake-Ptolemais

Disposition: A. Spaer Jerusalem 12. Information from A. Spaer

Bibliography:
Houghton, Lorber, Hoover 2008, p. 102.

186. Unknown Findspot. *CH* 10.297. 2004

Burial: 169?
Contents: 16 AR

Alexander III: Babylon
Antiochus III: 1 tetr. Nisibis (?)
Seleucus IV: 1 tetr. Damascus (? wreath)
Antiochus IV: 6 tetr. Antioch; 2 tetr. Ake-Ptolemais

Disposition: Commerce

Bibliography:
Houghton, Lorber, Hoover 2008, p. 151.

187. Amrith (ancient Marathus). *IGCH* 1545 = Noe 650. 1893–1894

Burial: 168 or later
Contents: AE

Aradus: Head of Tyche/Tyche standing[52] (years 85–70? There is perhaps a mistake in Seyrig's article. The expected dates would be 85–90 rather than 85–70.); Head of Tyche/Poseidon seated on a prow[53] (years 85–89)
Marathus: Hermes/Eponymous hero[54] (years 85–91)

Rouvier indicates that the find occurred in the region of Amrith during the winter of 1893/4. The coins discovered were of exceptional quality, and he acquired some for his own collection. The burial date is after year 91 on the Aradian era, which Marathus also employed, that is, 169/8 BC.
Disposition: formerly in the Rouvier collection.

Bibliography:
Rouvier, J. "L'ère de Marathus de Phénicie," *Journal Asiatique* (novembre–décembre 1898), pp. 368–369
Seyrig, H. "Monnaies hellénistiques 12. Questions aradiennes," *Revue numismatique* (1964), p. 47.

52. Duyrat 2005a, p. 55, series 4.
53. Duyrat 2005a, pp. 66–67, series 7.
54. Duyrat 2002a, pp. 31–32, series 7.

188. Lebanon. *CH* 9.510. 1997

Burial: 165
Contents: 91 AR, plated coins

Lot A: Aradus: 38 dr. (years 89 (14), 90 (8), 91 (2))
Ephesus: 11 dr. with bee (1 plated according to *CH*).
Lot B: Aradus: 31 dr. (years 89 (8), 90 (8), 91 (13), 93 (1), 1 plated)
Ephesus: 11 dr. with bee (including 1 plated)

These two lots were dispersed on the London market in 1997. They surely form a single hoard because the years match and the Aradian drachms of the two groups were struck from the same dies. The hoard's burial was c. 165 BC. Its composition is in part the basis for Kinns' new chronology for Ephesian drachms.

Disposition: Commerce, London

Bibliography:
Kinns, P. "The Attic weight drachms of Ephesus: a preliminary study in the light of recent hoards," *Numismatic Chronicle* 159 (1999), pp. 47–97, nos. 4 and 5, pp. 60–72, pls. 11–14.

189. Aleppo? *IGCH* 1546 = *CH* 1.75 = Noe 31. 1931

Burial: 165
Contents: 37+ tetr. AR

Alexander III: 1 Myrina; 2 Phaselis; 5 Perge; 10 Aspendus
Antiochus IV: 6 Antioch; 1 Ake-Ptolemais
Side: 12

Seyrig clearly states that he examined 26 tetradrachms of this hoard in the hands of a collector in Aleppo in 1931, while another 11 were sent to Newell; the composition of the two lots was similar. This is only a part of the original find, whose provenance is unknown. Seyrig donated the four specimens at Yale (Alexanders of Aspendus, Phaselis, and an uncertain mint, plus a tetradrachm of Side), according to Rostovtzeff 1939. The tetradrachms of Antiochus IV were in very good condition, unlike the others, which had circulated a great deal. The coins carry numerous countermarks with anchor or bust of Helios.

Disposition: New York 11 (3 Alexanders, 4 Antiochus IV, 4 Side; front cover picture); Yale 4

Bibliography:
Rostovtzeff, M. I. "Some remarks on the monetary and commercial policy of the Seleucids and Attalids," in W. M. Calder and J. Keil (eds.) *Anatolian Studies Presented to William Hepburn Buckler*, Manchester, 1939, pp. 277–298, pp. 290, 291, no. 1.
Seyrig 1973, no. 12.
Houghton, Lorber, Hoover 2008, p. 88.
Seyrig, H. "Antiquités syriennes 67. Monnaies contremarquées en Syrie," *Syria* 35 (1958), pp. 187–197, p. 195 = *Antiquités syriennes* 6, Paris, 1966, p. 9, note 4.

190. Khan Cheikhoun, north of Hama, or Gaziantep. *IGCH* 1547 = *CH* 1.75. 1940

Burial: 165 (*IGCH*) or c. 151/0 (Lorber 2010)
Contents: 103+ tetr. AR

Alexander III: 1 Heraclea Pontica; 1 Cyme; 1 Myrina; 2 Temnos; 1 Mytilene; 3 Alabanda; 18 Phaselis; 25 Aspendus; 28 Perge; 1 uncert.
Side: 22

A considerable number of tetradrachms appeared on the Beirut market during the autumn of 1940. Rumor had it that they came from Khan Cheikhoun, but one of Seyrig's informants stated that they had been discovered in the region of Ain Tab-Gaziantep. The 103 items Seyrig examined were all "covered with a thin and dry oxidation, brown with greenish spots, exposing the white metal in places. All also showed the signs of a lengthy oxidation"[55] (H. Seyrig Archives, Bibliothèque nationale de France, dossier 250). The content is quite similar to the hoards of Ain Tab 1951 (**242**) and Aleppo 1931 (**189**). This could be a case of several lots forming one and the same hoard. Most of the coins from Phaselis, Aspendus, Perge, and Side have countermarks: head of Helios facing and anchor. Lorber suggests a lower dating of this hoard based on her examination of the Alexanders of Temnos.

Disposition: Dispersed

Bibliography:
Seyrig 1973, no. 14, pl. 23.
Price, M. J. *The Coinage in the Name of Alexander the Great and Philip Arrhideus*, London, 1991, p. 63.
Lorber, C. "Commerce ('Demetrius I' hoard), 2003 (*CH* 10.301)," *Coin Hoards* 10, New York, 2010, pp. 153–172.

191. Qal'at el-Moudiq, region of Apamea. *CH* 10.298. Before 1996

Burial: 165
Contents: 45 tetr. AR, plated coins

Lysimachus : 2
Seleucus I: 1 Susa, plated
Antiochus II: 3 Seleuceia on the Tigris
Antiochus Hierax: 1 Lampsacus
Antiochus III: 1 Soli; 3 Antioch; 1 Damascus (?); 2 Edessa (?); 1 Seleuceia on the Tigris ; 1 Susa
Seleucus IV: 1 Cilician mint; 6 Antioch; 3 Damascus (?)
Antiochus, son of Seleucus IV: 1 Antioch
Antiochus IV: 12 Antioch; 5 Ake-Ptolemais
Eumenes I: 1 Pergamum

Disposition: Dispersed

Bibliography:
Elayi J., Elayi A.-G., "Un nouveau trésor de monnaies séleucides de la région d'Apamée de Syrie," *Bulletin du Cercle d'études numismatiques* 41/2 (mai–août 2004), pp. 43–62, ill.
Houghton, Lorber, Hoover 2008, p. 87

55. "couvertes d'une oxydation mince et sèche, brune à taches verdâtres, laissant voir par endroits le métal blanc. Toutes aussi portaient les traces d'une longue oxydation."

192. Near Bethlehem. *CH* 8.432. 1984

Burial: c. 165
Contents: 10 AR Ptolemaic

Ptolemy V: 1 Salamis (Sv. 1332 var.)
Ptolemy VI: 3 Alexandria (Sv. 1489); 4 Paphos (2 Sv. 1390, 1 Sv. 1431, 1 Sv. 1432)
Ptolemy uncert.: 1 tetr., 1 didr.

Disposition: Commerce, information from A. Spaer

Bibliography:
Meadows, A. R. "Bethlehem area, 1984 (*CH* 8. 432)," in T. Faucher, A. Meadows, and C. Lorber (eds.) *Egyptian Hoards I, Ptolemaic Hoards*, Cairo, 2016d.

193. Maʿaret en-Numan, northern Syria. *CH* 6.37 = *CH* 7.98 = *CH* 8.433 = *CH* 9.511. 1980

Burial: 162
Contents: 536+ AR Attic and Ptolemaic

Alexander III: 263 posthumous tetr.: Argos 1; Pella 1; Samothrace 1; Heraclea Pontica 1; Alexandria Troas 3; Assos 3; Myrina 6; Cyme 4; Temnos 10; Methymna 1; Mytilene 6; Pergamum 2; Chios 10; Miletus 10; Smyrna 1; Ephesus 1; Teos 1; Mylasa 2; Alabanda 1; Western Asia Minor 1; Rhodes 2; Phaselis 57; Perge 63; Aspendus 71; Uncertain Pamphylian mint 1; Aradus 1 (year 65); Uncert. mints 2
Lysimachus : 24 posthumous tetr.
Antiochus I: 1 tetr. Seleuceia on the Tigris ; 1 tetr. uncert.
Antiochus II: 2 tetr. Seleuceia on the Tigris
Seleucus III: 1 tetr. Antioch
Antiochus III 22: 5 tetr., 5 dr. Antioch; 1 tetr. ΔΕΛ mint; 9 dr. Apamea (?); 1 tetr. uncert. (Carrhae?); 1 tetr. Edessa (?)
Seleucus IV: 6 tetr., 1 dr. Antioch; 2 tetr. Damascus (?); 1 tetr. Ake-Ptolemais
Antiochus, son of Seleucus IV: 1 tetr., 2 dr. Antioch; 1 tetr. Antioch in Persis (?)
Antiochus IV 87: 5 tetr. Tarsus; 45 tetr., 6 dr. Antioch; 1 tetr. Seleuceia Pieria; 30 tetr. Ake-Ptolemais
Antiochus V: 1 tetr. Tarsus; 29/30 tetr. Antioch; 11 tetr. Ake-Ptolemais
Prusias II: 1 tetr.
Attalids: 7 tetr.
Ptolemy II or III: 1 tetr.
Pergamum: 1 tetr.
Mytilene: 1 tetr.
Cos: 1 tetr.
Side: 38 tetr.
Ephesus: 21 dr.
Aradus: 8 dr.

The 536 coins Mattingly published are only a part of the original hoard. The present description of the Seleucid coins repeats the identifications of Houghton, Lorber, Hoover 2008. Mattingly 1993 places the burial date c. 162. The principal features for him are:

1. The massive presence of Seleucid coins and especially posthumous Alexanders (48.6% of the hoard), essentially from the Pamphylian mints. Coins struck in Syria constitute only a third of the hoard: 170 Seleucids and eight from Aradus.

2. The Alexanders from Pamphylia and the autonomous tetradrachms of Side are almost all countermarked with an anchor (more than 97% of the Pamphylian Alexanders are countermarked, Metcalf 1994, p. 52).

Kinns 1999 notes the freshness of the drachms of Ephesus and their Aradian imitations.

Cf. *CH* 9.491 (**360**): contaminated by this hoard.

Bibliography:
Mattingly, H. B. "The beginning of the Athenian new style silver coinage," *Numismatic Chronicle* (1990), pp. 67–78, p. 71.
Le Rider, G. "Ephesus and Aradus au IIe siècle avant notre ère," *Numismatica e antichità classiche* 20 (1991), pp. 193–212, p. 200.
Price, M. J. *The Coinage in the Name of Alexander the Great and Philip Arrhideus*, London, 1991, p. 64.
Mattingly, H. B. "The Ma'aret en-Numan hoard, 1980," in M. Price, A. Burnett, and R. Bland (eds.) *Essays in Honour of R. Carson and K. Jenkins*, London, 1993, pp. 69–86.
Metcalf, W. E. "A late second century hoard of posthumous Alexandres," *Revue suisse de numismatique* 73 (1994), pp. 19–53, pls. 1–3.
Kinns, P. "The Attic weight drachms of Ephesus: a preliminary study in the light of recent hoards," *Numismatic Chronicle* 159 (1999), pp. 47–97, no. 3 pp. 55–58.
Houghton, Lorber 2002, p. 104.
Houghton, Lorber, Hoover 2008, p. 88.

194. Syria. *IGCH* 1540

Burial: years 160? 140?
Contents: 3 AR

Alexander III, late tetr.: Alabanda 2, Heraclea Latmos (?) 1

This hoard does not appear in the Seyrig Archives kept in the Bibliothèque nationale de France. Its description must be treated with caution: just one "Heraclea" struck Alexanders according to Price, Heraclea Pontica. The identification of this mint rests on stylistic criteria, most of the varieties of which are known from the Mektepini hoard (*IGCH* 1410; Price 1991a, p. 202). Another hypothesis would regard coins attributed to Ionian Heraclea as autonomous tetradrachms. In both cases, the lot's dating must be revised: the Alexanders of Alabanda were struck between the end of the 170s and the end of the 160s, whereas autonomous tetradrachms of Ionian Heraclea date to the 140s.

Disposition: Dispersed. Information from H. Seyrig

195. Southern Palestine. *CH* 4.58. 1977

Burial: Late 160s
Contents: 15+ AR Ptolemaic

Ptolemy VI: 1 tetr. Salamis (Sv. 1393 var., year 7); 3 tetr. Alexandria (Sv. 1489)

Spaer clearly states that the coins seen commercially are rather worn. Yet those whose photographs he sent to the American Numismatic Society are in good condition, leading Meadows to date the hoard to the late 160s.

Disposition: Commerce, information from A. Spaer

Bibliography:
Meadows, A. R. "Southern Palestine, 1977 (*CH* 4.58)," in T. Faucher, A. Meadows, and C. Lorber (eds.) *Egyptian Hoards I, Ptolemaic Hoards*, Cairo, 2016e.

196. Syria. *CH* 8.434, pls. LIV, 30 – LIX, 3. 1990

Burial: 160
Contents: 65 AR

Alexander III: 1 Myrina (Price 1659)
Lysimachus : 7 (including 2 late issues of Byzantium; 1 late issue of Tenedos)
Antiochus I: 2 tetr. Seleuceia on the Tigris
Antiochus II: 1 tetr. Seleuceia on the Tigris
Antiochus III: 1 tetr. Damascus (?); 1 tetr. Edessa (?)
Seleucus IV: 1 tetr. Damascus (?)
Antiochus, son of Seleucus IV: 1 tetr. Antioch
Antiochus IV: 15 tetr. Antioch; 15 tetr. Ake-Ptolemais
Antiochus V: 10 tetr. Antioch; 1 tetr. Ake-Ptolemais
Demetrius I: 1 tetr. Soli in Cilicia
Attalides: 8 (7 Westermark group VII)

The identifications of Seleucid coins are those of Houghton, Lorber, Hoover 2008. The authors of *CH* note "an important group confirming the post-190 date for group VII of the Attalid coinage." The entire hoard is illustrated in the *CH* plates.

Disposition: Commerce

Bibliography:
Houghton, Lorber 2002, pp. 104–105.
Houghton, Lorber, Hoover 2008, p. 90.
Meadows, A. R. "The closed currency system of the Attalid kingdom," in P. Thonemann (ed.) *Attalid Asia Minor. Money, International Relations, and the State*, Oxford, 2013, pp. 149–205, at p. 167.

197. Near East. *CH* 4.55, fig. 7. 1977

Burial: 160
Contents: 5+ AR

Antiochus IV: 1 tetr. Antioch
Alexandria Troas: 2 tetr. (year 168 = 163 BC)
Ilion: 1 tetr. (Athenocles)
Samos: 1 tetr. (Zeus/Statue of Hera)

Disposition: Commerce, British Museum 2
Bibliography:
Price, M. J. *Illustrated London News* (Sept. 1977), p. 69 (*non vidi*).
Houghton, Lorber, Hoover 2008, p. 89.

198. Tell Kotchek, Upper Mesopotamia. *IGCH* 1773 = *CH* 1.75. 1952

Burial: 160 (*IGCH*) or after 150–c. 142 (Lorber 2010)
Contents: 604 AR

Alexander III: 1 Alexandria Troas; 3 Assos; 5 Cyme; 5 Myrina; 197 Temnos; 4 Mytilene; 2 Chios; 342 Alabanda; 15 Phaselis; 7 Perge; 20 Aspendus
Side: 3

Dealers in Aleppo combined this hoard with the Kessab hoard. Seyrig separated the two hoards in his publication, but his notes on the Kessab hoard (H. Seyrig Archives, Bibliothèque nationale de France, dossier 265) enable us to follow how the lots were divided up among the different merchants.

98.63% of the hoard's Pamphylian tetradrachms have countermarks (anchor, turreted head of Tyche, grape cluster), according to the calculations of Metcalf 1994, p. 52. One group may be added to this hoard according to Seyrig's notes (dossier 230).

Bibliography:
Seyrig 1973, no. 15.
Metcalf, W. E. "A late second century hoard of posthumous Alexandres," *Revue suisse de numismatique* 73 (1994), pp. 19–53, pls. 1–3.
Lorber, C. "Commerce ('Demetrius I' hoard), 2003 (*CH* 10.301)," *Coin Hoards* 10, New York, 2010, pp. 153–172, at p. 155.

199. Northern Syria. *IGCH* 1548 = Noe 1033. 1912

Burial: 160

Alexander III: posthumous tetr. (Miletus: monogram and stern)
Lysimachus : tetr.
Antiochus IV: tetr.
Antiochus V: tetr. 164/162
Miletus: 1 tetr.

Regling 1928 notes this hoard in passing, identifying its source: "According to a brief report in a letter to us from a dealer in Aleppo."[56]

Disposition: Dispersed

Bibliography:
Regling, K. "Hellenistische Münzschatz aus Babylon," *Zeitschrift für Numismatik* (1928), pp. 92–132, p. 94 for this hoard.
Rostovtzeff, M. I. "Some remarks on the monetary and commercial policy of the Seleucids and Attalids," in W. M. Calder and J. Keil (eds.) *Anatolian Studies Presented to William Hepburn Buckler*, Manchester, 1939, pp. 277–298, p. 290.
Houghton, Lorber, Hoover 2008, p. 89.

200. Phoenicia. *CH* 1.79. 1971

Burial: c. 155

56. "Nach brieflicher Nachricht eines Händlers aus Aleppo an uns."

Contents: 22 AR

Aradus: 22 dr. (years 88 (?) to 103)

The hoard's burial is dated c. 155 BC. Although its findspot is not known, the fact that it contained only Aradian drachms warrants the suggestion that it was buried in the Aradian Peraea or nearby.

Disposition: Dispersed, informations au British Museum

Bibliography:
Hill, G. F. *Catalogue of the Greek Coins in the British Museum. Phoenicia*, London, 1910, nos. 147–160.

201. ʿArab el-Mulk, Paltos. *IGCH* 1552 = *CH* 1.75 = *CH* 9.513. 1940

Burial: after 152/1
Contents: 28+ AR

Antiochus III: 1 dr. Apamea
Ephesus: 13 dr. with bee
Aradus: 14 dr. (years 90, 91, 95, 97, 98, 99, 100, 102, 106, 107).

This hoard of drachms, now dispersed, was discovered in the ancient Peraea of Aradus, at ʿArab el-Mulk, Classical Paltos. It contained 28 coins and seems incomplete. The latest drachm of Aradus is from 153/2 BC. Seyrig proposes dating the burial after 152/1 BC because we do not know the hoard in its entirety. The drachm of Antiochus III has been attributed to different mints. The identification here is from Houghton, Lorber 2002.

Disposition: Dispersed
Bibliography:
Seyrig, H. "Monnaies hellénistiques 12. Questions aradiennes," *Revue numismatique* (1964), pp. 7–67, pp. 47–50.
Seyrig 1973, no. 17.
Kinns, P. "The Attic weight drachms of Ephesus: a preliminary study in the light of recent hoards," *Numismatic Chronicle* 159 (1999), pp. 47–97, no. 6 pp. 72–75.
Houghton, Lorber 2002, p. 105.

202. Unknown Findspot, the "Demetrius I Hoard." *CH* 10.301. 2003

Burial: 151/0
Contents: 535, of which 532 AR and 3 AV
Alexander III 194: 1 tetr. Assos; 8 tetr. Cyme; 8 tetr. Myrina; 92 tetr. Temnos; 1 tetr. Methymna; 8 tetr. Mytilene; 1 tetr. Magnesia on the Maeander; 26 tetr. Miletus; 1 tetr. Priene; 12 tetr. Chios; 1 tetr. Samos; 9 tetr. Alabanda; 1 tetr. Euromos; 1 tetr. Mylasa; 1 tetr. Rhodes; 3 tetr. uncert. Asia Minor; 6 tetr. Phaselis; 1 tetr. Phaselis (?); 10 tetr. Aspendus; 3 tetr. Perge
Lysimachus 25: 5 tetr. Byzantium, 6 tetr. Chalcedon, 2 tetr. Cyzicus, 6 tetr. Lampsacus, 5 tetr. Abydos, 1 tetr. uncert.

Antiochus III: 1 tetr. ΔI mint (Damascus?)
Seleucus IV: 1 tetr. Antioch
Antiochus IV 52: 42 tetr. Antioch; 9 tetr. Ake-Ptolemais; 1 tetr. uncert.
Antiochus V: 13 tetr. Antioch
Demetrius I: 2 st. AV Cilicia or Northern Syria; 1 tetr. Soli; 1 tetr. Mallos; 1 tetr. uncert. Cilicia; 11 tetr., 1 octadr. AV Antioch
Bithynia: 1 tetr. Prusias I
Cappadocia: 1 tetr. Orophernes
Athens: 105 tetr. New Style
Parion: 3 tetr.
Ilion: 4 tetr.
Tenedos: 2 tetr.
Cyme: 1 tetr.
Myrina: 13 tetr.
Clazomenae: 1 tetr.
Ephesus: 1 dr.
Miletus: 7 tetr.
Alabanda: 1 tetr.
Cos: 1 tetr.
Phaselis: 1 tetr.
Side: 10 tetr.
Aradus: 80 dr. (171/0–156/5 BC)

Lorber was able to examine the pictures of a portion of this hoard in the summer of 2003 before it was dispersed in lots. The coins were not cleaned. Lorber catalogues 535 items, three more than mentioned in her introduction. The latest coins are those of Demetrius I, dated 152/1 BC on the Seleucid Era, and the New Style tetradrachms, from 151/0 BC, according to the chronology of Mattingly, "The Beginning of the Athenian New Style Silver Coinage," *Numismatic Chronicle* 150 (1990), pp. 67–78. This agreement highlights the rapidity with which the New Style tetradrachms circulated and confirms Mattingly's proposed dating. Comparison with other hoards also warrants revisiting the chronology of the Alexanders from Temnos and the wreathed tetradrachms of the cities of Asia Minor. The precise dating for the burial leads to the conclusion that the mints not represented in the hoard were probably not yet striking wreathed tetradrachms in 151/0 BC. However, unless the hoard is not completely representative of contemporary circulation, this hypothesis contradicts the view lately favored by several scholars who see the wreathed tetradrachms as the way the Attalids supported Alexander I Balas against Demetrius I during the campaign of 150 BC. In any case, the 151/0 BC date does invite the association of this hoard with Alexander I Balas' invasion of Syria. The presence of some coins of Demetrius I, struck to finance resistance to that attack, is particularly interesting because these coins, two issues of which were previously unknown, are in a pale gold that contrasts with the other inventoried issues. Some other rare issues must also be mentioned: the tetradrachms of Orophernes, from Paros, from Clazomenae, etc.

The latest drachm from Aradus is from 156/5 BC, although this mint continued regularly striking this denomination until 152/1 BC. Lorber concludes that "apparently this lot doesn't reflect the regular entry of Aradian drachms into the Syrian economy, but rather a payment made in 156/5 BC or shortly after, which remained intact, or partially intact, after its receipt" (p. 158).

Disposition: Dispersed

Bibliography:
Lorber, C. "Commerce ("Demetrius I" hoard), 2003 (*CH* 10.301)," *Coin Hoards* 10, New York, 2010, pp. 153–172.

203. Near East. *CH* 7.100. 1965–1966

Burial: mid-2nd cent.
Contents: 19 tetr., 1 dr. AR+

Alexander III: 6 tetr. Amphipolis (Schulman 229–234); 1 tetr. Temnos (Price 1686, Schulman 227); 1 tetr. Aradus (Price 3316, Schulman 228); 11 tetr. and 1 dr. uncert. (including probably 1 tetr. Alabanda Price 2456, Schulman 245)
Philip III: 1 tetr. Babylon (Price P181, Schulman 243)

The coins are poorly described in the sale catalogue; hence the great number of uncertain attributions and their difficulty: they are assured for only the three photographed coins. The references here are to Price 1991a.

Disposition: Commerce, New York

Bibliography:
H. M. F. Schulman, 9 December 1966, nos. 227–247.

204. Lebanon. *CH* 4.60

Burial: c. 150
Contents: 4 AR Ptolemaic

"Uncertain Era": 4 didr. (years 105, 106, 107 and 109)

The rest of this hoard is lost.

Bibliography:
Mørkholm, O. "The Ptolemaic 'coins of uncertain era,'" *Nordisk Numismatik Årsskrift* (1975/1976), pp. 23–58, p. 49.

205. Northern Syria. *CH* 1.82. 1974

Burial: 150
Contents: 18 AR

Antiochus IV: 4
Antiochus V: 13
Demetrius I: 1

Disposition: Commerce

206. Syria? *IGCH* 1551. 1937

Burial: 150
Contents: 28+ tetr. AR

Demetrius I: 18 Antioch (to 162 BC), 1 uncert. mint.

Disposition: Istanbul

207. Antakya. *IGCH* 1553. 1959

Burial: 150
Contents: 4 AV, 28 AR

Demetrius I: 3 octadr., 1 AV hemistater Antioch; 28 tetr. uncert. mint.

Disposition: Boston 2, Dewing collection 1. Information from H. Seyrig

Bibliography:
Comstock, M. and C. Vermeule. *Greek Coins, 1950 to 1963, Boston Museum of Fine Arts*. Boston, 1964, nos. 277, 279.
Houghton, Lorber, Hoover 2008, p. 90.

208. Latakia. *IGCH* 1561 = *CH* 1.75. 1950

Burial: 150–145?
Contents: 10+ tetr. AR

Alexander III: 1 Myrina; 2 Temnos; 3 Alabanda; 1 Miletus
Lysimachus : 1 Heraclea Pontica; 1 Lampsacus
Alexander I Balas: 1 Antioch (fleur de coin; intrusive?)

"Find brought from Latakia; the coins of which begin to appear on the Beirut market, March 20, 1950"[57] (H. Seyrig Archives, Bibliothèque nationale de France, dossier 252). Seyrig 1973, p. 71, specifies that the dark, uniform patina of these coins guarantees a common provenance.

Disposition: Dispersed

Bibliography:
Seyrig 1973, no. 16.
Houghton, Lorber, Hoover 2008, p. 90.

209. Akkar. *IGCH* 1559 = *CH* 1.75. 1956

Burial: 150–145; after 150–143/2 (Lorber 2010)
Contents: 70 tetr. AR

Alexander III: 37 Temnos; 1 Alabanda; 1 Miletus
Alexander I Balas: 1 Antioch
Myrina: 13
Cyme: 5
Aegae: 2
Smyrna: 2
Heraclea Latmos: 2
Magnesia on the Maeander: 5
Syros: 1

Seyrig saw these coins on the Beirut market, at several dealers, and "trustworthy informants vouched for their provenance."[58] The civic issues are in very good condition, unlike the rest (H. Seyrig Archives, Bibliothèque nationale de France, dossier 254). Seyrig suggests they may belong to the Ghonsle hoard (**210**).

Disposition: Dispersed

57. "Trouvaille apportée de Latakié dont les pièces commencent à apparaître sur le marché de Beyrouth le 20 mars 1950."
58. "attestée par des informateurs dignes de foi."

Bibliography:
Seyrig 1973, no. 18.
Houghton, Lorber, Hoover 2008, p. 90–91.

210. Ghonsle, east of Baniyas. *IGCH* 1560 = *CH* 1.75. 1955

Burial: 150–145; after 148/7 (Lorber 2010)
Contents: 17 tetr. and 4 dr. AR

Demetrius I: 1 tetr., 2 dr. Antioch
Alexander I Balas: 2 dr. Antioch
Myrina: 7 tetr.
Cyme: 4 tetr.
Smyrna: 3 tetr.
Magnesia on the Maeander: 2 tetr.

The Seyrig Archives show that, according to his informants, some Alexanders also belonged to the find (Bibliothèque nationale de France, dossier 255). Seyrig suggests seeing here a portion of the Akkar hoard (**209**).

Disposition: Dispersed

Bibliography:
Seyrig 1973, no. 19.
Houghton, Lorber, Hoover 2008, p. 91.

211. El-Aweiniye, northeast of Tartus. *IGCH* 1550 = *CH* 1.75. 1941

Burial: 150–140
Contents: 78+ tetr. AR and jewelry (?)

Aegae: 19
Cyme: 42
Myrina: 15
Magnesia on the Maeander: 2

According to the Seyrig Archives (Bibliothèque nationale de France, dossier 258), some peasants discovered this hoard, which was then released on to the market over several years. The coins are in excellent condition and apparently had not circulated. Seyrig believed that he saw nearly the entire hoard. In a letter to a Mr. Vollenweider, he denied its connection with a jewelry collection subsequently acquired by the Oriental Institute in Chicago: the same individual did bring the two groups to Beirut and assert their identical origin, but the tetradrachms had hardly circulated and date from the mid-second century, whereas the jewelry included an intaglio with a portrait of Antony, making a single hoard highly unlikely.
Disposition: SNG von Aulock 5, 1594–1595, 1636, 1638–1639, 1663; SNG von Aulock 6, 2042.

Bibliography:
Seyrig 1973, no. 22.

212. Dura Europos. *IGCH* 1770 = Noe 354. 1934

Burial: 150–130 (Le Rider), 160s (Holt and Wright)
Contents: 207 AE, in excavation, pot hoard

Antiochus III 207: 1 Seleuceia on the Tigris ; 203 Antioch; 1 Tyr; 1 Susa (according to Le Rider, contra Mithridates I, Bactria according to Bellinger)

This hoard was found in the course of authorized excavations, on December 3, 1934. The coins of Antiochus III form a compact group, chronologically removed from the specimen of Mithridates I. Nonetheless, Bellinger 1949, p. 179, notes that this fits nicely with the actual facts of circulation, as coins from excavations define them: "The great frequency of the halves among the chance finds in every context down to and including Roman imperial layers shows what large numbers of them must have circulated at Dura. There is nothing surprising in this, for evidently they were the favorite denomination at Antioch too, to judge from the excavations. We may take it for granted that they were still current by the middle of the 2nd century, and date the burial of the hoard from 150 to 130 BC."

Le Rider 1965 attributes to Susa under Antiochus III a bronze that Bellinger 1949 attributed to Bactria under Mithridates I. Holt and Wright 2010 devoted an article to the same coin. It confirms Le Rider's identification on the basis of a new item and suggests a higher deposit date for the hoard, during the 160s.

Bibliography:
Bellinger, A. R. *The Excavations at Dura-Europos conducted by Yale University and the French Academy of Inscriptions and Letters, Final Report, VI, The Coins*, New Haven, 1949, hoard 13, pp. 178–179.
Le Rider, G. *Suse sous les Séleucides et les Parthes*, Paris, 1965, p. 58, no. 43.
Holt, W. C. and N. L. Wright. "A New Seleucid Bronze Coin and Dura Hoard 13 Revisitred", *Israel Numismatic Research* 5 (2010), pp. 59–66.

213. Akken, Lebanon. *CH* 2.95. 1974–1975 [rejected hoard]

Burial: c. 150–125
Contents: 400 AR

Aradus: approximately 400 silver coins

This hoard was seen in the Beirut trade and poses some problems: *CH* 2 locates it in Lebanon, which rules out it's being a find in the region of Akko, for the site of Akken cannot be located in Lebanon.... Moreover, *CH* 2 only indicates that it contained around 400 silver coins without specifying the denomination or the issuing mint. A reference to the index under "Aradus" leads one to suppose that the hoard could be autonomous tetradrachms, the only silver coinage struck in large quantities and hoarded in such proportions during the last third of the 2nd century. This hoard must be treated with the greatest caution: the tetradrachms of series VII do not start being issued until 138 BC, and the date of withdrawal from circulation cannot go back further. The information in *CH* 2 is entirely insufficient for making any use of this hoard.[59]

214. Baarin, 15 km southeast of Massyaf. *IGCH* 1567 = *CH* 1.75. 1955

Burial: 150 or 111/0
Contents: 19 tetr., 2 dr. AR

59. Duyrat 2005a, pp. 168–69.

Demetrius I: 10 tetr., 1 dr. Antioch
Antiochus IX: 1 Sidon year 202
Eucratides of Bactria: 1
Myrina: 1
Cyme: 5
Smyrna: 2

The specimen of Antiochus IX seems very late (111/0 BC) but possesses the same patina as the other specimens, which are earlier than 150 BC. A note of Seyrig (H. Seyrig Archives, Bibliothèque nationale de France, dossier 263) clearly states that the peasant who brought him this lot assured him that all the coins had been found together.

Disposition: Dispersed

Bibliography:
Seyrig 1973, no. 28.
Houghton, Lorber, Hoover 2008, pp. 102–103.

215. Syria? *IGCH* 1554. Before 1917

Burial: 148
Contents: 17 AR

Antiochus IV: 1 tetr. Antioch
Demetrius I: 12 tetr. Antioch
Alexander I Balas: 4 tetr. Antioch (year 164)

Disposition: Istanbul. Seen by Mørkholm

Bibliography:
Houghton, Lorber, Hoover 2008, p. 91.

216. Madaba, Jordan. *IGCH* 1592. 1919

Burial: after 146/5
Contents: 6+ AR Ptolemaic

Ptolemy I: 1 tetr.
Ptolemy II: 1 tetr.
Ptolemy IV: 1 tetr. (Mørkholm 1975–1976, no. 31)[60]
Ptolemy V: 2 tetr.
Ptolemy VI: 1 tetr.

This small hoard contained 6 Ptolemaic silver tetradrachms, now in the British Museum. The authors of *IGCH* date the burial after 146 BC.

Disposition: London 6

60. This coin is in fact an "uncertain era" issue of year 55.

Bibliography:
Jenkins, G. K. "The monetary system in the early Hellenistic period with special regard to the economic policy of the Ptolemaic kings," in A. Kindler (ed.) *International Numismatic Convention, Jerusalem, 27–31 December 1963. The Patterns of Monetary Development in Phoenicia and Palestine in Antiquity*, Tel Aviv, 1967, pp. 53–74, p. 69, note 26.

217. Northern Syria, called the "Caiffa Hoard." *IGCH* 1556 = *CH* 1.75 = Noe 475. Around 1905

Burial: 146/5; or after 150–143/2 (Lorber 2010)
Contents: 38+ tetr. AR

Alexander III: 6 Temnos
Demetrius I: 1 Antioch
Alexander I Balas: 1 Antioch
Demetrius II (1): 1 Antioch
Myrina: 12
Cyme: 14
Magnesia on the Maeander: 3

Tourneur 1906 describes the hoard's discovery as follows: "While digging the foundations for their church, the Carmelite fathers of the Belgian mission in Caïffa (Syria) found a hoard of thirty-eight tetradrachms from Aeolis and Ionia with three coins of Syrian kings intermingled."[61] He then describes the coins just as they are known from the sale catalogue in Brussels, two months later, December 12, 1906, Dupriez Auction 90, nos. 1–38, which does not elaborate on the conditions of discovery ("coins coming from the Caïffa find [Syria]"). Blanchet 1907, p. 111, relates the conditions of discovery with the same words as Tourneur. Regling 1928 provides a list of the hoard without further commentary. He indicates "Haiffa (Caiffa) on the Gulf of Akka" as the provenance. Noe 1937, no. 475, identifies this hoard under the title "Haiffa, Syria, 1906." Seyrig 1973 prefers to think of Caiffa as merely the hoard's last known stop on its way to sale in Belgium: the coins it contains are on the Attic standard, unusual, since Haifa is in the Ptolemaic standard zone. *IGCH* follows Seyrig. One should bear in mind, however, that Haifa is a port, which might explain the presence of coins locally unusable but to be expected in the hands of a royal agent or a merchant dealing with northern Syria. For other hoards of Attic standard coins in the Ptolemaic zone: Lebanon, *CH* 4.60, **204**, c. 150 BC; Sea of Galilee, *CH* 8.458, **219**, c. 145 BC.

Disposition: Dupriez, 90, 12 déc. 1906, nos. 1–38, pls. 1–2.

Bibliography:
Tourneur, V. "La trouvaille de Caiffa," *Gazette numismatique de Bruxelles* 11/1 (octobre 1906), p. 18.
Blanchet, A. "Chronique," *Revue numismatique* (1907), pp. 111–121.
Regling, K. "Hellenistische Münzschatz aus Babylon," *Zeitschrift für Numismatik* (1928), pp. 92–132, pp. 94–95 for this hoard.
Rostovtzeff, M. I. "Some remarks on the monetary and commercial policy of the Seleucids and Attalids," in W. M. Calder and J. Keil (eds.) *Anatolian Studies Presented to William Hepburn Buckler*, Manchester, 1939, pp. 277–298, p. 290.
Thompson, M. "Athens again," *Numismatic Chronicle* (1962), p. 312.
Seyrig 1973, no. 20.
Houghton, Lorber, Hoover 2008, p. 92.

61. "En creusant les fondations de leur église, les PP. Carmes de la mission belge de Caïffa (Syrie) ont trouvé un trésor de trente-huit tétradrachmes d'Aeolide et d'Ionie auxquels se trouvaient mélangées trois pièces des rois de Syrie."

218. Yatta, Region of Hebron. *CH* 9.531. 1978/9

Burial: 146
Contents: 10 AR Ptolemaic

"Uncertain era": 4 didr. (years 105? (2), 107 (1), 109 (1))
Ptolemy VI: 1 tetr. Paphos 161/0 (Sv. 1433)
Alexander I Balas: 1 tetr. Laodiceia in Phoenicia/Berytus (year 163), 4 tetr. Sidon (year 166)

The village of Yatta is located 10 km from Hebron, on the West Bank. This hoard of 10 coins on the Ptolemaic standard was discovered during the winter of 1978–1979. It seems complete. Spaer considers that the coins were removed from circulation c. 143/2 BC, like the Dura hoard. He bases his argument on the Sidonian tetradrachms of Alexander I Balas dated to 166 on the Seleucid Era. Houghton, Lorber, Hoover 2008 suggest placing the burial closer to the latter date, in 147/6 BC, to connect it with the Syrian campaign of Ptolemy VI in the summer of 146. Meadows suggests that this hoard could be part of the Hebron 1979 hoard (*CH* 7.109, **236**).

Disposition: Commerce

Bibliography:
Spaer, A. "More on the 'Ptolemaic' Coins of Aradus," in G. Le Rider, K. Jenkins, N. Waggoner, and U. Westermark (eds.) *Kraay-Mørkholm Essays. Numismatic Studies in Memory of C. M. Kraay and O. Mørkholm*, Louvain, 1989, pp. 267–273, pl. 62.
Houghton, Lorber, Hoover 2008, p. 103.
Meadows, A. R. "Hebron Area, 1979 (*CH* 7.109), Hebron, 1980 (*CH* 7.111), Yatta 1978–9 (*CH* 9.531) and Yatta, 1981," in T. Faucher, A. Meadows, C. Lorber (eds.) *Egyptian Hoards I, Ptolemaic Hoards*, Cairo, 2016b.

219. Sea of Galilee. *CH* 8.458

Burial: c. 145
Contents: 64 AR

Antiochus IV: 63
Demetrius I: 1

Houghton, Lorber, Hoover 2008 note that the hoard content does not support the burial date proposed by *CH* (c. 145 BC). The reign of Demetrius I (162–150 BC) provides a terminus post quem; nothing more precise is possible in the absence of data about the content.

Disposition: Commerce

Bibliography:
Houghton, Lorber, Hoover 2008, p. 104.

220. Tyre. *IGCH* 1591. 1955

Burial: 145
Contents: 20+ AR Ptolemaic
Alexander I Balas: 1 tetr. Laodiceia in Phoenicia/Berytus (year 163)

Demetrius II (1): 1 tetr. Sidon; 1 tetr. Tyre (year 167)
"Uncertain era": 17 didr. (years 110 (1), 112 (2), 113 (2), 114 (3), 115 (6), 116 (1), 2 illegible)

This hoard contained at least three tetradrachms and 17 didrachms on the Ptolemaic standard. Hazzard 1975 attributes two tetradrachms to Alexander I Balas, based on notes Seyrig sent him, *contra* Seyrig 1973 and *IGCH*. Seyrig considered that burial must have occurred under Demetrius II (145–139 BC). If the didrachms are dated according to the Aradian Era, the latest is from year 116, or 143/2 BC. That would coincide nicely with the first reign of Demetrius II. Hazzard 1975, pp. 59–60, associates the burial of this group of coins with the campaign of Ptolemy VI in Syria, in 148/7–145/4 BC. This monarch would presumably have brought with him on his campaign the money needed for his war expenses, as he had done in 169 (Diodorus 30.16). Hazzard 1975 suggests a burial connected with the war's final year: "The appearance of some six Ptolemaic hoards at various sites in Coele Syria suggests that the hoarders, presumably men associated with the Ptolemaic occupation, did not have the time or opportunity to retrieve their savings" (p. 63). In this particular instance, his interpretation supposes an origin of uncertain period, earlier than that on the Aradus calendar. Houghton, Lorber, Hoover 2008 suggest burial c. 145 BC, connected to the campaign of Ptolemy VI.

Disposition: Dispersed. Rubbings in Copenhagen.

Bibliography:
Seyrig 1973, no. 42, according to whom this hoard was discovered in 1955 and not in 1954 as indicated in *IGCH*.
Hazzard, R. A. "The Tyre hoard of 1955: *IGCH* 1591," *Cornucopiae* 3/4 (1975), pp. 57–63.
Houghton, Lorber, Hoover 2008, p. 103.

221. Dura, Region of Hebron. *CH* 3.59 = *CH* 9.529. 1976

Burial: 145
Contents: 87 AR Ptolemaic

"Uncertain era": 60 didr. (years 101 (12), 102 (2?), 104 (5), 105 (10), 106 (3), 107 (7), 109 (13), 110 (1), 111 (2), 113 (1), 114 (1), 115 (2), 117 (1))
Alexander I Balas: 16 tetr. Laodiceia in Phoenicia/Berytus; 3 tetr., 1 didr. Sidon; 4 tetr., 1 didr. Tyre
Demetrius II (1): 1 tetr. Laodiceia in Phoenicia/Berytus (year 167); 1 tetr. Tyre (year 167)

This hoard of 87 silver coins on the Ptolemaic standard was discovered near the village of Dura, 7 km southwest of Hebron on the West Bank, in the spring of 1975 (?). Spaer deems it complete. It does not contain any coin of Demetrius II from 146 to 143 BC, years contemporary with the last didrachms of Aradus (?), whose year 117 corresponds to 143/2 BC. Mørkholm 1975/1976, p. 268, found that the didrachms of years 110 to 117 were not all that numerous. Spaer dates the hoard's burial c. 143/2 BC and connects it to the endemic warfare between Seleucids and Ptolemies during this time, coincident with the rise of Hasmonean power in the region. Houghton, Lorber, Hoover 2008 prefer the dating according to the Soter Era proposed by Hazzard: the latest didrachm "of uncertain era" would be from 147/6 BC, which would allow linking this hoard to Ptolemy VI's campaign.

Disposition: Commerce

Bibliography:
Spaer, A. "More on the 'Ptolemaic' Coins of Aradus," in G. Le Rider, K. Jenkins, N. Waggoner, and U. Westermark (eds.) *Kraay-Mørkholm Essays. Numismatic Studies in Memory of C. M. Kraay and O. Mørkholm*, Louvain, 1989, pp. 267–273, pls. 58–61.
Houghton, Lorber, Hoover 2008, pp. 103–104.

222. Lebanon. *CH* 8.459. 1985?

Burial: 145
Contents: 25 AR Attic and Ptolemaic

Macedonia, First Region: 1
Antiochus IV:?
Demetrius I: 8
Alexander I Balas: 2 Attic, 6 Ptolemaic
Ptolemaic: 4
Myrina: 4
Athens New Style: several?

Disposition: Commerce

Bibliography:
Houghton, Lorber, Hoover 2008, p. 104.

223. Syria. *CH* 8.456. 1984

Burial: 145
Contents: 39+ AR Ptolemaic, from a larger hoard of Seleucid coins

Alexander I Balas: 21+ Tyre (down to 167 SE); 11+ Sidon (down to 166 SE); 5 Laodiceia in Phoenicia/Berytus (down to 167 SE)
Demetrius II (1): 2 Tyre (year 167 SE)

Disposition: Commerce

Bibliography:
Houghton, Lorber, Hoover 2008, p. 92.

224. Northern Syria. *IGCH* 1555. 1906

Burial: 145
Contents: 150+ tetr. AR
Coins studied: 54/150+

Seleucus II: 1 ΔΕΛ mint
Antiochus III: 1 Edessa (?)
Seleucus IV: 3 Antioch, 1 Damascus (?)
Antiochus IV: 7 Antioch; 1 Ake-Ptolemais
Antiochus V: 2 Antioch
Demetrius I: 11 Antioch
Alexander I Balas: 22 Antioch
Demetrius II (1): 4 Antioch; 1 Seleuceia on the Tigris.

IGCH observes that "according to the information available the bulk of the hd. consisted of coins of Demetrius I and Alexander I Bala, about 60 pieces of each king." The identifications are those of Houghton, Lorber, Hoover 2008.

Disposition: Copenhagen 8; Paris 2

Bibliography:
Houghton, Lorber, Hoover 2008, pp. 91–92.

225. Teffaha, east of Tartus. *IGCH* 1557 = *CH* 1.75. 1954

Burial: after 145/4 or after 150–143/2 (Lorber 2010)
Contents: 30 tetr. AR

Alexander III: 15 Temnos; 2 Alabanda; 1 Aspendus
Alexander I Balas: 1 Antioch
Demetrius II (1): 1 Antioch
Myrina: 4
Cyme: 6

Disposition: Dispersed

Bibliography:
Seyrig 1973, no. 21.
Houghton, Lorber, Hoover 2008, p. 91.

226. Region of Hebron. April, 2004

Burial: after 145/4
Contents: 50 tetr. AR Ptolemaic

Ptolemy VI 34: 15 Paphos, 7 Citium, 12 Salamis
Alexander I Balas 14: Berytus, Sidon, Tyre, Ake-Ptolemais
Demetrius II (1): 1 Berytus, 1 Tyre

Barag was shown this hoard in April, 2004. All the coins were covered with a thick, hard, dark grey crust. Two coins of Ake-Ptolemais are of unpublished date (149/8, 148/7 BC). The latest coin dates from 145/4 BC. A comparison with six contemporary hoards of similar content and the presence of die-links with the Paphos hoard (*CH* 4.68) led Barag to conclude that "this coinage was the normal silver currency in circulation in Phoenicia and Coele Syria during the first half of the second century until c. 145 BCE" (p. 36). Unlike other similar hoards, this one does not contain didrachms "of uncertain era." At the time of publication, negotiations were under way to place it in a public collection.

Bibliography:
Barag, D. "Ptolemaic silver currency of Cyprus in Seleucid Phoenicia and Coele Syria," *Israel Numismatic Journal* 16 (2007–2008), pp. 28–56.

227. Unknown Findspot. *CH* 8.467, pls. 62–63 = *CH* 9.526. 1986

Burial: 145 or 125?
Contents: 61 AR Attic and Ptolemaic

1) Attic standard:
Demetrius I: 5 tetr., 16 dr. Antioch

Alexander I Balas: 1 tetr., 12 dr. Antioch
Demetrius II (1):[62] 1 dr. Antioch (intrusive?); 3 tetr. Tyre
Ephesus: 15 dr. with bee
Aradus: 6 dr. (5 illustrated, dated years 90, 91 (2), 104, 106)
2) Ptolemaic standard:
Alexander I Balas: 2 tetr. Berytus.

This hoard was seen in trade and inventoried in *CH* 8. It contained 61 silver coins. The authors of *CH* date burial c. 125 BC, but Kinns 1999, p. 74, suggests that the coin from the second reign of Demetrius II, which is the basis for this dating, can be "admitted to be intrusive, and in fact a burial date of c. 145 BC is much more likely." The latest drachm of Aradus dates from 154/3 BC, representing a sharp gap with the Seleucid coins, and supports Kinns' opinion. With the Seleucid coins coming from Phoenicia or Antioch, the principal mint at this time, one assumes the hoard was buried in the coastal area. The presence of Ephesian and Aradian drachms reinforces this hypothesis. *CH* 9.526 takes account of Kinns' argument, unlike Houghton, Lorber, Hoover 2008, who maintain the dating c. 125 BC.

Disposition: Commerce

Bibliography:
Kinns, P. "The Attic weight drachms of Ephesus: a preliminary study in the light of recent hoards," *Numismatic Chronicle* 159 (1999), pp. 47–97, no. 7 pp. 74–75.
Houghton, Lorber, Hoover 2008, p. 95.

228. Gaziantep. *CH* 9.527 = *CH* 10.308. 1994

Burial: 143
Contents: 1,916 AR

Alexander III: 1 Alexandria Troas; 2 Assos; 1 Aegae; 15 Cyme; 12 Myrina; 86 Temnos; 1 Methymna; 14 Mytilene; 1 Colophon; 1 Miletus; 1 Phocaea; 7 Chios; 110 Alabanda; 1 Antioch on the Maeander; 1 Nisyros; 21 Phaselis; 6 Uncert. Pamphylian mints; 44 Aspendus; 14 Perge; 1 Byblos
Demetrius Poliorcetes : 1
Perseus: 1
Macedonia, First Region: 1
Lysimachus (posthumous): 2 Byzantium; 2 Calchedon; 1 Abydos; 1 Tenedos
Athens, New Style: 197
Prusias II: 9
Cyzicus: 1
Parion: 1
Alexandria Troas: 1
Ilion: 2
Aegae: 51
Cyme: 287
Myrina: 383
Clazomenae: 1
Magnesia on the Maeander: 119
Miletus: 1
Smyrna: 44

62. Kinns assigns this coin to the second reign of Demetrius. In this listing I follow the identification proposed in *SC*.

Alabanda: 4
Side: 23
Seleucus I (intrusive): 1 Seleuceia Pieria; 1 Seleuceia on the Tigris ; 1 uncert.
Seleucus IV: 3 Antioch; 1 Ake-Ptolemais; 2 Damascus
Antiochus IV: 23 Antioch; 2 Ake-Ptolemais
Antiochus V: 15 Antioch; 1 Ake-Ptolemais
Demetrius I: 3 Tarsus; 2 Soli in Cilicia: 3 uncert. (Cilicia?); 17 uncert. (Cilicia or northern Syria); 112 Antioch; 6 uncert. (Mesopotamia)
Alexander I Balas: 104 Antioch; 1 Antioch?; 2 Seleuceia Pieria; 2 Ake-Ptolemais; 1 barbarous imitation
Interregnum: 8
Demetrius II: 1 Seleuceia on the Calycadnus; 4 Soli in Cilicia; 2 Mallos; 11 Mopsus; 4 uncert. (Mopsus?); 2 uncert.; 41 Antioch; 1 Sidon
Antiochus VI: 1 Mallos; 40 Antioch; 25 Apamea

This hoard was seen in four lots, first at the museum of Gaziantep, then in the trade in London, Beirut, and the U.S., in 1994. The latest tetradrachms are New Style Athenian stephanephoroi dated July–September 143 BC, according to the low chronology generally accepted for this currency. The latest Seleucid coin is dated year 169 of the royal period, and no coin of 170 (the year beginning in October, 143 BC) appears among the 1,916 coins studied. The tight synchronicity between the latest Seleucid and Athenian tetradrachms allows Meadows, Houghton 1994 to suggest a burial almost immediately following the issue of these coins, perhaps the autumn of 143. The brief description in the inventory in *CH* and the catalogue in Meadows, Houghton 1994 do not agree (the former omits an Alexander of Assos and another from Methymna).

Disposition: Dispersed

Bibliographie
Augé, C., A. Davesne, and R. Ergeç. "Le début des tétradrachmes d'Athènes du 'nouveau style': un trésor trouvé près de Gaziantep en 1994," *Anatolia Antiqua* 5 (1994), pp. 44–82.
Houghton, Lorber, Hoover 2008, p. 81.
Meadows, A. R. and A. Houghton. "The Gaziantep hoard, 1994 (*CH* 9.527; 10.308)," *CH* 10, pp. 173–223.

229. Cheikh Miskin (Hauran). *CH* 1.86. 1967

Burial: 143/2
Contents: 197 AR Ptolemaic: 185 tetr. and 12 didr.

Alexander I Balas: 146 tetr., 11 didr., 1 dr. Tyre
Demetrius II (1): 35 tetr., 3 didr. Tyr; 1 tetr. Sidon

Disposition: A. Medawar collection, Beirut

Bibliography:
Seyrig 1973, no. 43.
Houghton, Lorber, Hoover 2008, pp. 104–105.

230. Tyre. *IGCH* 1596 = *CH* 10.309 = Noe 1143. 1935

Burial: 143/2

Contents: 85 AE, Tyre
Demetrius I: 21 denomination A, 3 denomination B
Alexander I Balas: 1 denomination D
Demetrius II (1): 25 denomination B; 17 denomination D
Illegible: 18

In May, 1935, a peasant from the region of Tyre informed Newell of this hoard's discovery. Eighteen coins were too damaged to be legible. The remaining 67, cleaned by electrolysis, proved to be already well worn when they were withdrawn from circulation. The flans are beveled, 40 of the 67 bronzes having the obverse on the smaller side of the flan, the others on the larger. The absence of any bronze of Antiochus VII leads one to suppose that burial was contemporary with Tryphon's usurpation and the struggles that convulsed Phoenicia at that time. Tryphon apparently did not occupy Tyre, but the situation may have driven the owner (a peasant?) of this tiny hoard to hide his nest egg. Houghton, Lorber, Hoover 2008 connect this lot of bronzes with the Cheikh Miskin hoard (*CH* 1.86, **229**): "Both hoards may have been lost in the conflict between Tryphon and Jonathan Apphus."

Disposition: New York 29

Bibliography:
Newell, E. T. *The Seleucid Coinage of Tyre*, ANS NNM 73 (1936), pp. 22–26.
Houghton, Lorber, Hoover 2008, p. 105.

231. Kırıkhan, Hatay province. *CH* 1.87A = *CH* 2.90 = *CH* 10.310. 1972

Burial: after 143/2
Contents: 5,000+ AR
Coins studied: 1,104/5,000+

Alexander III 9 tetr.: 1 Cyme, 2 Temnos, 1 Methymna, 2 Alabanda
Athens, New Style: 3 tetr.
Syros: 3+ tetr.
Prusias II: 1 tetr.
Myrina: 87 + 61 tetr.
Cyme: 261 + 182 tetr.
Aegae: 6 + 2 tetr.
Smyrna: 10 + 4 tetr.
Lebedos: 35 + 4 tetr.
Magnesia on the Maeander: 269 + 94 tetr.
Heraclea Latmos: 21 + 22 tetr.
Alabanda: 4 tetr.
Demetrius I: 4 tetr.
Alexander I Balas: 6 tetr.
Alexander I Balas and Cleopatra Thea: 1 tetr.
Demetrius II: 4 tetr.
Antiochus VI: 11 tetr.

Seyrig 1973, no. 23, initially announced this hoard as the "Cilicia hoard." He had seen 450 specimens from it at different dealers in Switzerland, Brussels, and Paris. At the time, the hoard was said to contain at least 1,000 items. Later, after several other lots were inventoried, the original total was estimated at more than 5,000. There is a narrative, by E. Levante, of the discovery in the archives of the American Numismatic Society.[63] It makes clear that the find consisted of both tetradrachms and drachms. A shepherd from the village of Baghras, district of Kırıkhan, made the discovery, and it cost him his life: the coins fell into the stream from whose banks he was watering his flock. The list offered here replicates the most recent description in *Coin Hoards* 10. Seyrig's dating is still viable despite numerous additions: the latest coins are those of Antiochus VI dated to the year 170 on the Seleucid Era, 143/2 BC (*CH* 10, p. 185).

63. I am grateful to A. Meadows for sending me this information. See Annexe 2 for the transcription of the account of the discovery.

Disposition: Antakya Museum 79; Sofia 372

Bibliography:
Anonymous. "A hoard of test-cut Athenian tetradrachms," *Journal of Numismatic Fine Arts* 4 (1975), p. 30.
Seyrig 1973, no. 23.
Houghton, Lorber, Hoover 2008, pp. 81–82.

232. Ras Baalbek, Beqaa Valley. *IGCH* 1593. 1957

Burial: after 143/2
Contents: 45 AR Attic and Ptolemaic

1) Attic standard
Demetrius I: 9 tetr. Antioch
Alexander I Balas: 1 tetr. uncert. mint, Northern Syria
Demetrius II (1): 1 tetr. Antioch
Athens, New Style: 2 tetr.
Myrina: 1 tetr.
Cyme: 3 tetr.
Aegae: 1 tetr.
Smyrna: 1 tetr.
Magnesia: 8 tetr.

2) Ptolemaic standard
Demetrius II (1): 1 didr. Sidon
"Uncertain era": 17 didr. (years 115 (1), 116 (15), 117 (1))

According to Seyrig's notes (H. Seyrig Archives, Bibliothèque nationale de France, dossier 259), he saw a portion of the find and obtained good quality rubbings of the rest. All coins were well preserved, with the exception of the more worn Athenian pieces.

This hoard of 45 silver coins, on the Attic and Ptolemaic standards, was buried about 50 km north of Baalbek, in the Beqaa Valley, probably a little after 143/2 BC. Seyrig 1973 notes that the mixture of standards suits the findspot well, close to the ancient frontier between Seleucis and Coele Syria, where the Ptolemaic standard prevails. The same observation holds for the Dniye (**173**) and Khan el-Abde (**255**) hoards.

Disposition: Dispersed

Bibliography:
Seyrig 1973, no. 24.
Houghton, Lorber, Hoover 2008, p. 92.

233. Hauran (?). *CH* 8.463. 1979 or 1980

Burial: 142/1
Contents: 18 tetr. AR Ptolemaic

Alexander I Balas: 4 Tyre
Demetrius II (1): 2 Sidon; 9 Tyre
Antiochus VI: 3 Ake-Ptolemais

These tetradrachms discovered in the Hauran in unknown circumstances form a homogeneous group issued between 151/0 and 142/1 BC.

Disposition: Private collection

Bibliography:
Le Rider, G. "Un trésor de monnaies Séleucides trouvé dans le Hauran en 1979 ou 1980: Antiochos VI à Ptolemais," in A. Houghton, S. Hurter, P. Erhart Mottahedeh, and J. Ayer Scott (eds.) *Festschrift für Leo Mildenberg*, Wetteren, 1984, pp. 165–169, pl. 25.
Houghton, Lorber, Hoover 2008, p. 105.

234. Southeastern Turkey. *CH* 3.60 = *CH* 4.64. 1976

Burial: 142
Contents: 750 AR

Antiochus III–Antiochus IV: c. 100
Antiochus IV posthumous: 2 dr.
Demetrius I: 300 of which 39+ dr. Antioch; 1 tetr. uncert. mint, Mesopotamia
Alexander I Balas: 150, including 13+ dr. Antioch
Demetrius II (1): 250+, including 1 dr. Antioch; 2 dr. Seleuceia Pieria (?), 1 dr. Syria or Phoenicia
Antiochus VI: 200+, including 6 dr. Antioch; 3 dr. Apamea; 4 dr. Antioch or Apamea; tetr. uncert. mints

Disposition: Commerce

Bibliography:
Houghton, Lorber, Hoover 2008, p. 93.

235. Aleppo? *IGCH* 1562 = *CH* 1.75. Before 1930

Burial: after 142/1–139/8
Contents: 34+ AR

Antigonus Doson: 5
Prusias I of Bithynia: 4
Myrina: 1
Cyme: 4
Lebedos: 4
Magnesia on the Maeander: 2
Heraclea Latmos: 12
Alabanda: 2

Newell 1938 points out that the three coins preserved in New York were brought from Damascus at the start of 1931. They were covered with a thin, dark violet layer of corrosion, with spots of verdigris. Despite extensive correspondence, Newell regrettably failed to determine where the rest of the hoard was located or whence it came. A countermark with Tryphon helmet (142/1–139/8 BC) appears on the coins of Lebedos and Heracleia, providing a chronological terminus.

The Seyrig Archives (Bibliothèque nationale de France, dossier 260) provide some enlightenment: "To believe my informants, the 1930 date would only be when the hoard appeared on the market: it was presumably discovered a number of years before, and had been in the possession of an antiquities dealer in Aleppo for some time."[64] Rostovsteff 1939 repeats this information. Houghton, Lorber, Hoover 2008 add, without clarification: "The inclusion of the royal coins is doubtful."

Disposition: New York 3 (Heraclea 2, Lebedos 1); Seyrig 2 (Alabanda)

Bibliography:
Seyrig 1973, no. 25.
Newell, E. T. *Miscellanea Numismatica: Cyrene to India*, ANS NNM 82 (1938), pp. 21–24, nos. 10–12, pls. I–II.
Rostovtzeff, M. I. "Some remarks on the monetary and commercial policy of the Seleucids and Attalids," in W. M. Calder and J. Keil (eds.) *Anatolian Studies Presented to William Hepburn Buckler*, Manchester, 1939, pp. 277–298, p. 291, no. 2 = pp. 292–293, no. 6.
Houghton, Lorber, Hoover 2008, pp. 93–94.

236. Hebron. *CH* 7.109. 1979

Burial: 140
Contents: 45 AR Attic and Ptolemaic

Lot 1
Alexander I Balas: 1 tetr. Berytus (year 163); 2 tetr. Sidon (years 163, 166); 4 tetr. Tyre (years 165, 166, 167)
Demetrius II (1): 8 tetr. Sidon (years 169, 171, 172)
Antiochus VI: 1 tetr. Ake-Ptolemais (year 169)
Tryphon: 1 tetr. Ake-Ptolemais (year 1)
Lot 2
Ptolemy VI: 5 tetr. Salamis (years 9, 18, 21, 29, 34); 1 didr. Alexandria (undated)
Ptolemy VIII: 1 tetr. Citium (year 26)
"Uncertain era": 21 didr. (years 101 (10), 105 (2), 106 (1), 107 (2), 109 (3), 111 (1), 114 (1), 115 (1))

The brief mention in *Coin Hoards* indicates that this hoard was seen in trade in two lots. It might be part of another hoard discovered at Hebron (*CH* 7.111, **268**), which would lower the burial date to 125 BC. Meadows gives the most accurate description based on correspondence between A. Spaer, A. Houghton, and M. Price. He suggests that this lot could be part of the Yatta 1978/9 hoard (*CH* 9.531, **218**).

Disposition: Commerce

Bibliography:
Houghton, Lorber, Hoover 2008, p. 106.
Meadows, A. R. "Hebron Area, 1979 (*CH* 7.109), Hebron, 1980 (*CH* 7.111), Yatta 1978–9 (*CH* 9.531) and Yatta, 1981," in T. Faucher, A. Meadows, and C. Lorber (eds.) *Egyptian Hoards I, Ptolemaic Hoards*, Cairo, 2016b.

237. Syria. *CH* 8.462, pls. LX 26–32 – LXII 1–10. 1989

Burial: 140
Contents: 3 AV, 40 AR

2 AV octadr. Arsinoe II; 1 AV tetr. Berenice II; 19 tetr.; 21 didr. "Uncertain era" (to year 116)

Disposition: Commerce

64. "A en croire mes informateurs, la date de 1930 ne serait que celle où le trésor est apparu sur le marché : il aurait été découvert bien des années auparavant, et serait resté longtemps dans la possession d'un antiquaire d'Alep."

Bibliography:
Olivier, J. "Syrie 1989 (*CH* 8.462): deux trésors en un?", in T. Faucher, A. Meadows, and C. Lorber (eds.) *Egyptian Hoards* I, *Ptolemaic Hoards*. Cairo 2016, pp. 140–136.

238. Antakya. *IGCH* 1558. 1962

Burial: 140
Contents: 10+ AR

Antiochus VI: tetr. Antioch

Disposition: Dispersed. Information from A. Spaer

239. Saida. *IGCH* 1594 = Noe 883. 1862 or 1863

Burial: 140
Contents: 70 AR Ptolemaic

Alexander I Balas: 1 tetr. Berytus (year 163); Sidon, Tyre
Demetrius II (1): Sidon, Tyre

Weckbecker 1865, p. 97, announces this hoard, found at Saida at the same time as the enormous hoard of gold coins discovered in the same city between 1829 and 1863. Only the tetradrachm of Alexander I Balas struck at Berytus is clearly identified.

Disposition: Dispersed

Bibliography:
Weckbecker, C. "Aus Syrien," *Wiener numismatische Monatshefte* (1865), pp. 97–103.
Houghton, Lorber, Hoover 2008, p. 105.

240. Palestine. *IGCH* 1595. Before 1945

Burial: 140
Contents: 2+ AR Ptolemaic

Alexander I Balas: 1 tetr. Tyre (year 163)
Antiochus VI: 1 tetr. Ake-Ptolemais (year 169)

Disposition: Jerusalem (Hebrew University) 2

Bibliography:
Ben-Dor, S. "Two new Seleucid coins," *Qedem* 2 (1945), (*non vidi*).
Brett, A. B. "Seleucid coins of Ake-Ptolemais in Phoenicia, Seleucus IV to Tryphon," *American Numismatic Society. Museum Notes* 1 (1945), pp. 27–28, no. 21, pl. X, 21: illustrates the coin of Antiochus VI.
Houghton, Lorber, Hoover 2008, p. 106.

241. Region of Hama (ancient Epiphaneia). *CH* 10.312. 2001

Burial: 140 (Elayi, Elayi); 138–111 (*CH* 10)
Contents: 29 AR

Demetrius I: 1 tetr. Soli in Cilicia; 19 tetr. Antioch
Demetrius II (1): 9 tetr. Seleuceia on the Tigris

The absence of coins of Alexander I Balas could be owing to the hoard's incomplete character, but Elayi, Elayi 2002 believe that we have the entire hoard.

Bibliography:
Elayi J. and A.-G. Elayi. "Un trésor de monnaies séleucides de la région de Hama," *Revue numismatique* (2002), pp. 93–102, pls. V–VIII.
Houghton, Lorber, Hoover 2008, p. 93.

242. Ain Tab, present day Gaziantep, Commagene. *IGCH* 1542 = *CH* 9.528 = Noe 24. 1920/1

Burial: 140–120 (Metcalf) or c. 151/0 (Lorber).
Contents: c. 200 AR
Coins studied: 107/200 AR

Alexander III 107 tetr.: Temnos 1; Mytilene 1; Miletus 1; Colophon 1; Chios 1; Alabanda 1; Phaselis 18 (to year 26); Aspendus 48 (to year 28); Perge 33 (to year 33); Aradus 1 (62 = 198/7); uncert. 1

Metcalf 1998, based on notes of Newell, has revised the inventory of Seyrig 1973, no. 13. Newell acquired around 80 coins belonging to the hoard from a dealer named Aziz Khayat (for $3 to $5 per coin). Noe 24 and Rostovsteff 1939, p. 291, reckon Newell's acquisitions at 96 tetradrachms. Another lot arrived in the U. S., where T. L. Elder acquired it in New York. These coins were sold (Elder, March 17–18, 1922, lots 1172–1179), but the casts are still preserved at the American Numismatic Society. Some of these specimens then entered the collection of the ANS. Finally, three specimens went on sale at Spink, January, 1925, nos. 10, 25, 97; Newell bought two others from a certain Ezadjian. The catalogue published by Seyrig is based upon a list Thompson sent him that derives from Newell's hoard notebooks preserved at the ANS.

Metcalf 1998 recalls the different proposed burial dates, between 185 and 160 BC. The advanced wear of the hoard's coins argues in favor of long circulation: they are more worn than the specimens of the Susiana hoard (Le Rider 1965, pp. 248–49), which was buried at the start of the first century BC. Almost all bear countermarks with anchor or head of Helios, leading Metcalf, p. 66, to conclude: "A date [of burial] in the 130s or 120s, or even later, cannot be ruled out."

Lorber suggests a burial c. 151/0 BC on the basis of her revised dating of the Temnos Alexanders.

Disposition: American Numismatic Society New York c. 80 (casts and rubbings of around 20 tetr. or more in the files of the American Numismatic Society). Dispersed.

Bibliography:
Rostovtzeff, M. I. "Some remarks on the monetary and commercial policy of the Seleucids and Attalids," in W. M. Calder and J. Keil (eds.) *Anatolian Studies Presented to William Hepburn Buckler*, Manchester, 1939, pp. 277–298, pp. 290, 291–292, pl. 10.
Seyrig 1973, no. 13
Metcalf, W. E. "A late second century hoard of posthumous Alexanders," *Revue suisse de numismatique* 73 (1994), pp. 19–53, pls. 1–3.

Metcalf, W. E. "The Ain Tab Hoard (*IGCH* 1542)," in A. Burnett, U. Wartenberg, and R. Witschonke (eds.) *Coins of Macedonia and Rome: Essays in Honour of C. Hersh*, London, 1998, pp. 59–66.
Lorber, C. "Commerce ('Demetrius I' hoard), 2003 (*CH* 10.301)," *CH* 10, New York, 2010, pp. 153–172, at p. 155.

243. Unknown Findspot. *CH* 10.311. Before 1997

Burial: 130s
Contents: 128 AR

Demetrius I: 73 tetr. Antioch
Antiochus VII: 53 tetr. Antioch; 1 or 2 tetr. uncertain western mint

This group could only be part of a larger hoard.

Disposition: Dispersed. Seen at the British Museum in 1997

Bibliography:
Houghton, Lorber, Hoover 2008, pp. 152–153.

244. Vicinity of Saida (?). *CH* 10.313. 1993

Burial: 136/5
Contents: 5+ AR

Antiochus VII: 5+ Sidon (years 175–177)

Disposition: Seen by A. Houghton at Spink in January 1994.

Bibliography:
Houghton, Lorber, Hoover 2008, p. 106.

245. Near Antioch. Before 1997 [rejected hoard]

Burial: c. 135
Contents: 1,000+ AR

Seleucids, from Antiochus II to Antiochus VII, especially of Demetrius I and his successors
Non Seleucid coins
Athens, New Style: 145, between 156/5 and 137/6 BC
Athens, New Style, imitations: 4 overstruck on tetr. of Myrina

Hoover, McDonald 1999–2000 only publish the New Style tetradrachms of this lot, and, of particular interest, their 4 imitations, previously unattested prior to this group's appearance on the market. They are overstrikes made with imitation dies on tetradrachms of Myrina (Aeolis). The spread-flan tetradrachms of Myrina basically circulated in the Seleucid Empire only until the mid-130s. According to the authors, the influx of tetradrachms of Myrina, but also of Cyme and Magnesia, would have coincided with the few years when Eumenes II and then Attalus II financially supported Alexander I Balas, who was assassinated in 145. In fact, they suggest these coinages could be the subsidies the Attalids provided Balas, and would probably have ceased being sent to Syria after his death. During the years 140–130 BC, they note, Athenian New Style tetradrachms take over Syrian circulation, rapidly replacing earlier foreign coinages, including that of Myrina. They suggests that the illegal attempt, only modestly successful, to transform tetradrachms of Myrina into New Style tetradrachms illustrates the demonetizing of the former in favor of the latter.

This group has not been the object of more extensive study because it probably consists of several hoards difficult to distinguish from one another; a portion of the coins, catalogued in the files of the British Museum, appeared on the market in 1997. These were coins of Demetrius I (Antioch, down to 151/0 BC), New Style tetradrachms (down to 139/8 BC), and others, of Antiochus VII (Antioch, c. 135 BC). The find's lack of homogeneity immediately suggests several hoards, conceivably two: one with the tetradrachms of Demetrius I, the other with those of Athens and Antiochus VII? Another group of coins of Antiochus VII (down to 131/0 BC) and earlier Seleucid rulers went on sale in the middle of 1997 in the U. S. Apparently it came from the region of Antioch or northern Syria, but it belonged to a different hoard from the coins recorded at the British Museum.[65] This particular instance is a good illustration of how difficult reconstituting hoards can be.

Disposition: Commerce

Bibliography:
Hoover, O. and D. MacDonald. "Syrian imitations of New Style tetradrachms struck over Myrina," *Berytus* (1999–2000), pp. 109–117.

246. Ramallah Region. *CH* 8.464. Early 1992

Burial: 135
Contents: 29 AR

Alexander I Balas: 1 didr. Sidon (year 162, intrusive?)
Antiochus VII, 28 Tyre: 10 tetr. (year 174); 1 dr. (year 175); 10 tetr. (year 176); 2 didr. (year 177)

Disposition: Commerce

Bibliography:
Houghton, Lorber, Hoover 2008, pp. 106–107.

247. Lebanon. *CH* 9.532. 1997

Burial: 133
Contents: 26 dr. AR, plated coins

Antiochus IV: 1 dr. Antioch
Alexander I Balas: 1 dr. Antioch
Antiochus VII: 1 dr. Antioch
Ephesus: 15 dr. with bee
Aradus: 8 dr. (years 89 (1), 90 (2), 91 (2), 104 (1), 2 plated)

This hoard was seen in London in 1997. The Seleucid drachms lower the group's dating to c. 130 BC; but Kinns considers them an intrusion, since the latest Aradian drachm is from 156/5 BC. Houghton, Lorber, Hoover 2008, pp. 151–52, refute this argument: an unpublished hoard of indeterminate provenance also contains Seleucid coins and Aradian drachms that clearly remained in circulation for a relatively long time.
Disposition: Commerce London

65. Houghton relayed this information to me in a communication dated July 22, 2010.

Bibliography:
Kinns, P. "The Attic weight drachms of Ephesus: a preliminary study in the light of recent hoards," *Numismatic Chronicle* 159 (1999), pp. 47–97, no. 8, pp. 75–77.
Houghton, Lorber, Hoover 2008, p. 107.

248. Unknown Findspot. *CH* 8.465

Burial: 133
Contents: 8 AR

Antiochus VII, Tyre: 2 didr. (135 BC); 3 didr. (134 BC): 3 didr. (133 BC)

Disposition: Commerce

Bibliography:
Houghton, Lorber, Hoover 2008, p. 107.

249. Syria? *IGCH* 1549. Before 1964

Burial: after 133/2 BC
Contents: 15 AR

Athens: tetr. New Style (to Thompson 165/4 BC, i.e., 133/2 BC according to Boehringer 1972, p. 201.)

Disposition: Private collection, Beirut. Noted by Mørkholm.

Bibliography:
Boehringer, C. *Zur Chronologie mittelhellenistischer Münzserien, 220–160 v. Chr.*, Berlin, 1972.

250. Syria or Southern Anatolia. 1999

Burial: 131/0
Contents: 150+ tetr. AR

Antiochus V: 8–10 tetr. Antioch
Demetrius I: 20+ tetr. Antioch; 1 tetr. Seleuceia on the Tigris
Alexander I Balas: tetr.
Demetrius II (1): tetr.
Antiochus VI: tetr.
Antiochus VII: 100+ tetr. Antioch; 4+ tetr. Tyre (including years 181 and 182)

Disposition: Commerce. Information from A. Houghton.

Bibliography:
Houghton, Lorber, Hoover 2008, p. 94.

251. Hebron. *CH* 3.61. 1976

Burial: 131
Contents: 124 AR

Antiochus VII, Tyre: 7 didr. (year 176); 52 tetr., 12 didr. (year 177); 14 tetr., 4 didr. (year 178); 9 tetr., 1 didr. (year 179); 12 tetr., 2 didr. (year 180); 11 tetr. (year 181)

Disposition: Commerce

Bibliography:
Houghton, Lorber, Hoover 2008, p. 107.

252. Syria. *CH* 10.314. 1997

Burial: 130
Contents: 173+ tetr. AR

Demetrius II (1): 1 barbarous imitation (western prototype)
Antiochus VII: 1 Tarsus royal mint (?); 1 Tarsus royal mint; 163 Antioch; 2 uncert. (Seleuceia on the Tigris ?); 2 uncert mint. 101; 1 uncert. mint 102; 1 uncert.; 1 Cappadocia (intrusion?)

The rapid inventorying of this hoard, seen in the trade, did not permit Houghton to make definite identifications. The Cappadocian tetradrachm of Antiochus VII seems intrusive to him.

Disposition: Commerce. Information from A. Houghton

Bibliography:
Houghton, Lorber, Hoover 2008, pp. 94–95.

253. Eastern Anatolia? *CH* 9.517. Before 1991

Burial: 130–120
Contents: 379+ AR

Alexander III, 366 tetr.: Parion 1; Assos 1; Cyme 23; Myrina 12; Temnos 39; Methymna 1; Mytilene 7; Chios 1; Alabanda 34; Halicarnassus 1; Nisyros 1; Phaselis 68; Aspendus 118; Magydos 4; Perge 44; uncert. 11
Side: 13 tetr.

299 Alexanders were brought for study to the American Numismatic Society in August, 1991. Their owner indicated that they belonged to a much larger hoard, a part of which (80 tetradrachms) was to be sold in the autumn in Germany (Lanz, 58, November 21, 1991). The content of the two lots confirms that this was indeed a hoard. The tetradrachms were photographed, weighed, and subjected to die-study. No information could be obtained about provenance, which has to be deduced from the content, with all the usual caveats that entails. This is one of the largest hoards of the period, and it provides new insight into circulation during this era. The Alexanders of Phaselis, Aspendus, and Perge are frequently countermarked, as in other contemporary hoards ('Ain Tab [*IGCH* 1542, **242**], Ma'aret en-Numan [*CH* 9.511, **193**]). These countermarks depict the head of Helios, an anchor, a quiver ("cistophoric" countermark), a head of Tyche, or a grape cluster. Metcalf carefully studied them, using them to propose a relative chronology for comparable hoards. The Aleppo (*IGCH* 1546, **189**), 'Ain Tab (*IGCH* 1542, **242**), Khan Cheikhoun (*IGCH* 1547, **190**), Ma'aret en-Numan (*CH* 9.511, **193**), Latakia (*IGCH* 1544, **184**), and Tell Kotchek (*IGCH* 1773, **198**) hoards were all buried between 170 and 150 BC, and they essentially contained Alexanders and tetradrachms of Side. The chronology of the countermarks provides the relative dating of the hoards. The weights of the countermarked and non-countermarked coins in the hoards, whether eastern Anatolian or from Ma'aret en-Numan, reveal no appreciable differences. The

countermarks, therefore, provide an official stamp of approval for the worth of these tetradrachms (Mørkholm 1984, p. 108; Le Rider 1986, p. 34); they appear on more than 90% of the Pamphylian coins in hoards similar to this one (90.43%). Dating remains completely relative because this lot and those like it do not contain any other way to ascertain date other than by the nature and wear of the coins.

Disposition: Commerce

Bibliography:
Metcalf, W. E. "A late second century hoard of posthumous Alexanders," *Revue suisse de numismatique* 73 (1994), pp. 19–53, pls. 1–3.

254. Tyre. *CH* 9.533. 1987

Burial: 129/8
Contents: 109 AR

Antiochus VII, Tyre: 74 tetr. (137/6–130/129 BC), 1 didr. (132/1 BC)
Demetrius II (2), Tyre: 34 tetr. (130/129–129/8 BC)

These coins were sold with Tyre as their provenance. No other information is available.

Disposition: Commerce

Bibliography:
Lorber, C. "The Tyre, 1987 hoard of Seleucid silver (*CH* 9.533)," in A. Meadows and U. Wartenberg (eds.) *Coin Hoards* 9. London, 2002, pp. 253–255.
Houghton, Lorber, Hoover 2008, pp. 108–109.

255. Khan el-Abde, Phoenicia. *IGCH* 1597. 1938

Burial: after 129/8?
Contents: 118+ tetr. AR Attic and Ptolemaic

1) Attic standard:
Tryphon: 16 Antioch; 4 uncert.
Antiochus VII: 1 Tyre

2) Ptolemaic standard:
Tryphon: 13 Ake-Ptolemais
Antiochus VII: 1 Sidon, 2 Tyre
Ptolemy II: 66 (including 5 "Uncertain era": 4 undated, 1 year 51)
Ptolemy III: 1
Ptolemy IV: 14

This collection of at least 118 silver coins was discovered about 15 km north of Tripoli, near the ancient city of Orthosia, in April, 1938. The description of Seleucid material reprises the identifications of Houghton, Lorber, Hoover 2008. According to Seyrig, these items do not really form a hoard; they were scattered on the ground where they were found during earth moving works. He suggests the following explanation for the situation: "As the ruins of ancient Orthosia lie in the immediate vicinity of Khan el-Abde, it seems probable that the original hoard, or hoards, were connected with that town, and that the coins, in the course of time, had been washed down by the waters" (no. 77 to 81 of Seyrig; Mørkholm 1975/1976, p. 49). A hoard was probably gathered at the beginning of the reign of Ptolemy III, the coins of Ptolemy IV forming a lot distinct from the first, according to Seyrig. The Tryphon tetradrachms and those of Antiochus VII are in good condition and so circulated little. They seem to constitute a third group. Three different hoards might be at issue here, perhaps a temple's incremental deposits. Tryphon, as he fled from Mt. Carmel to Apamea, passed by Orthosia in his last year of rule. The coins of this very year are well represented in this lot. Were they particularly abundant at Orthosia because of the usurper's passage, a possibility Seyrig entertains? The latest tetradrachm is of Antiochus VII (139–129 BC). Some other coins are probably still buried in the ground and could occasion further revision of the chronology.

Disposition: New York 2 Tryphon (Ake-Ptolemais)

Bibliography:
Seyrig, H. *Notes on Syrian Coins*, ANS NNM 119, New York, 1950, pp. 1–7.
Mørkholm, O. "The Ptolemaic 'coins of uncertain era,'" *Nordisk Numismatik Årsskrift* (1975–1976), pp. 23–58.
Houghton, Lorber, Hoover 2008, p. 94.

256. Latakia. *IGCH* 1563 = *CH* 1.75. 1948

Burial: c. 128/7
Contents: 10 tetr. AR

Antiochus VII: 2 Damascus
Demetrius II (2): 5 Antioch; 1 Sidon; 2 Ake-Ptolemais

Disposition: Commerce, Beirut

Bibliography:
Seyrig 1973, no. 27.
Houghton, Lorber, Hoover 2008, p. 95.

257. Samaria. *CH* 9.534. 1999

Burial: 128/7
Contents: 15+ AR

Antiochus VII: 7 tetr. and didr. (years 177–183)
Demetrius II (2): 8 (years 183–185)

Disposition: Commerce, Israel

Bibliography:
Houghton, Lorber, Hoover 2008, p. 109.

258. Golan. *IGCH* 1600 = *CH* 1.75. 1932

Burial: 128/7–126/5 (autonomy of Tyre)
Contents: 7 AR Ptolemaic, plated coins - forgeries

Antiochus VII: Newell, Tyre 141, 145
Demetrius II (2): Newell, Tyre 167

"A thin sheet of silver, still solid but blistered in spots, covered a grayish metal, not so dense,"[66] according to Seyrig 1973, p. 116. Seyrig had the occasion to study these coins in the Damascus bazaar in March, 1932, where a resident of Quneitra had brought them.

Disposition: Beirut Museum (information from the H. Seyrig Archives, Bibliothèque nationale de France, dossier 275)

Bibliography:
Seyrig 1973, no. 44.
Houghton, Lorber, Hoover 2008, p. 109.

259. Region of Hebron. July, 2004

Burial: after 128/7, vers 111/0?
Contents: 11 AR Ptolemaic

Ptolemy VI and VIII: 1 tetr. Salamis (164/3 BC)
Ptolemy VI: 1 didr. Alexandria
Antiochus VII: 1 tetr. Tyre (136/5 BC); 3 didr. Tyre (134/3 BC, 133/2 BC, uncert.)
Demetrius II: 1 tetr. (128/7 BC), 4 didr. (130/129 BC, 129/8 BC, 128/7 BC, uncert.)

Barag 2007–2008 examined this hoard in July, 2004. It was discovered south of Hebron. The latest didrachm is from 128/7 BC, so burial is later. The coins' advanced wear leads Barag to suggest a dating c. 111/0 BC or a little after, when Hyrcanus I conquered Idumaea.

Disposition: Dispersed

Bibliography:
Barag D., "Ptolemaic silver currency of Cyprus in Seleucid Phoenicia and Coele Syria," *Israel Numismatic Journal* 16 (2007–2008), pp. 53–55.

260. Syria. *CH* 8.587 = *CH* 9.449. 1988

Burial: after 128
Contents: 30 AR

(a) 4th century (**88**)
Aradus: 1 shekel
Tyre: 1 shekel
Alexander III: 5 tetr.

(b) 2nd century (**260**)
Demetrius I: 2 tetr., 1 dr.
Demetrius II: 1 tetr.

66. "Une mince feuille d'argent, encore solide mais boursouflée par endroits, couvrait un métal grisâtre, peu compact."

Antiochus VII: 1 tetr.
Alexander II: 1 tetr.
Athens, New Style: 17 tetr.

Elayi, Elayi 1993a describe and publish only the two Phoenician coins (the authors studied the hoard, in the hands of a dealer in Baniyas, in 1988). The chronological heterogeneity of these two lots leads them to conclude that they probably constitute two hoards, one consisting of Phoenician coins and Alexanders of the fourth century (**88**), the second of the Seleucid and Athenian coins of the second century presented here. One might add that the presence of tetradrachms of Alexander II helps to narrow the burial date, which has to be either contemporary with or later than his reign (128–123 BC).

Bibliography:
Elayi, Elayi 1993a, no. 58, pp. 248–249.
Elayi, J. and A.-G. Elayi. "Nouveaux trésors de monnaies phéniciennes (*CH* IX)," *Transeuphratène* 26 (2003), p. 114.

261. Tyre. *IGCH* 1598. 1966

Burial: 127/6
Contents: 14 AR Ptolemaic

Alexander I Balas: 1 tetr. Tyre
Antiochus VII: 2 tetr. Tyre
Demetrius II (2): 6 tetr.; 5 didr. Tyre (to year 186 SE = 127/6 BC)

This hoard was seen on the Beirut market on April 5, 1996. A workman found it in the region of Tyre. Fischer proposes a dating based on the classifications of Rogers, "The Second and Third Seleucid Coinage of Tyre," ANS NNM 34 (1927). Houghton, Lorber, Hoover 2008 push back the date by a year, compared to Fischer 1968. The content is reminiscent of *IGCH* 1599 (**262**), which was dispersed several weeks later in Beirut.

Disposition: Commerce

Bibliography:
Fischer, T. "Zwei Münzschätze aus der Zeit des Seleukiden Demetrios II. vergraben um 126/5 (?) v. Chr.," *Schweizer Münzblätter* 18/70 (mai 1968), pp. 51–52.
Houghton, Lorber, Hoover 2008, p. 109.

262. Phoenicia. *IGCH* 1599. 1966

Burial: 127/6
Contents: 30 AR Ptolemaic
Coins studied: 5/30

Demetrius II (2): 1 tetr. Tarsus; 1 tetr. Antioch; 3 tetr. Damascus

This lot appeared on the Beirut market on June 6, 1966. Fischer connects it with the final episode in the struggle between Demetrius II and Alexander I, the former having finally met his death at Tyre. Houghton, Lorber, Hoover 2008 push back the date by a year, compared to Fischer. The content is similar to *IGCH* 1598 (**261**), which was dispersed in Beirut several weeks earlier.

Disposition: Commerce

Bibliography:
Fischer, T. "Zwei Münzschätze aus der Zeit des Seleukiden Demetrios II. vergraben um 126/5 (?) v. Chr.," *Schweizer Münzblätter* 18/70 (mai 1968), pp. 51–52.
Houghton, Lorber, Hoover 2008, p. 109.

263. South of Jerusalem. *CH* 8.469. Early 1991

Burial: 126/5
Contents: 450+ AR

Antiochus VII, Tyre: 11 tetr. (year 177 SE); 3 tetr., 1 didr. (year 178 SE); 2 tetr. (year 179 SE); 7 tetr. (year 180 SE); 3 tetr. (year 181 SE); 3 tetr. (year 182 SE); 1 tetr., 1 didr. (year 183 SE)
Demetrius II (2), Tyre: 1 tetr. (year 183 SE); 5 tetr. (year 184 SE); 34 tetr., 1 didr. (year 185 SE); 4 tetr. (year 186 SE); 6 tetr. (year 187 SE)

Disposition: Commerce, Jerusalem

Bibliography:
Houghton, Lorber, Hoover 2008, pp. 110–111.

264. Bethlehem, Hebron Region. *IGCH* 1603. 1971

Burial: 126/5
Contents: 51+ tetr. AR Ptolemaic

Antiochus VII: 20 Tyre
Demetrius II (2): 31 Tyre (down to 126/5 BC)

Disposition: unknown. Information from A. Spaer

Bibliography:
Houghton, Lorber, Hoover 2008, p. 110.

265. Beth Ummar. *CH* 10.315. 2001

Burial: 126/5
Contents: 50 tetr. and didr. AR Ptolemaic

Antiochus VII: 20 tetr., 1 didr. Tyre (136/5–130/129 BC)
Demetrius II (2): 27 tetr., 2 didr. Tyre (130/129–127/6 BC)

This lot was catalogued in the trade in Israel, in February, 2001. It is not certain that it is complete. The burial date, probably 126/5 BC, would support relating this hoard to the conflict between Demetrius II and John Hyrcanus I.

Disposition: Dispersed

Bibliography:
Meadows, A. R. "Beth Ummar, Israel, 2001 (*CH* 10.315)," *Coin Hoards* 10, New York, 2010, pp. 225–226.

266. Capernaum. *IGCH* 1602 = *CH* 1.75. 1957

Burial: after 126/5
Contents: 300 tetr. and didr. AR Ptolemaic, 60 gold coins with eagle (?) disappeared, in a jar. One silver statuette of a bearded, naked man on three-footed base
Coins studied: 70 tetr. and 8 didr. (2 didr. are not identified in the list)/300

Demetrius II (1): 1 tetr. Tyre
Antiochus VII: 25 tetr., 5 didr. Tyre
Demetrius II (2): 44 tetr., 3 didr. Tyre

A Damascus dealer brought these coins to Beirut in February, 1957. He claimed to have obtained them from a Syrian officer whose soldiers were digging near Capernaum. The gold coins were thought to carry an eagle on the reverse and to be the size of a didrachm, but they and the statuette have never been seen. The latest year represented is contemporary with the death of Demetrius II and the autonomy of Tyre.

Disposition: Dispersed

Bibliography:
Seyrig 1973, no. 45.
Houghton, Lorber, Hoover 2008, p. 110.

267. Nablus. *IGCH* 1601 = *CH* 8.587 = *CH* 9.539 = Noe 727. 1891

Burial: 125
Contents: approx. 400 AR Ptolemaic
Coins studied: 36/400+

Sidon: 3 double-shekels (intrusive?)
Antiochus VII: 14+ tetr. (years 176–183 SE), 1+ didr. (year 179 SE) Tyre
Demetrius II (2): 11+ tetr. (years 183–187 SE), 4 didr. (years 183–186 SE), 1 dr. Tyre
Tyre: 1 tetr. (year 21); 1 didr. (year 18)
Ptolemy II: 1 tetr. Tyre
Ptolemaic: 2 tetr.

Hamburger 1892, p. 329, note 1, is the first mention of this hoard, when his auction house sold some specimens in June, 1892 (Hamburger, sale Dr. G. J. Suhm, June 13, 1892, no. 2105–2114). The coins were discovered in the vicinity of ancient Shechem, and were "apparently buried in the year when John Hyrcanus (187 Seleuc.) captured this city, and consisted mostly of Tyrian tetradrachms and fractions of Antiochus VII and Demetrius II."[67] The Hamburger 1892 sale provides the following details: 14 tetradrachms, 1 didrachm of Tyre, Antiochus VII; 11 tetradrachms, 4 didrachms, 1 drachm of Tyre, Demetrius II; 1 tetradrachm and 1 didrachm, both autonomous Tyrian issues; 3 Ptolemaic tetradrachms (1 Tyrian, 2?); 3 "Persian" octadrachms. I have retained this description. Other lists vary considerably:

67. "augenscheinlich im Jahr der Einnahme dieser Stadt durch Joh. Hyrcan (187 Seleuc.) vergraben, bestand in seinem weitausgrössten Theil aus Tyrer Tetradrachmen und Fraktionen von Antiochus VII. und Demetrius II."

Noe 1937: 1 tetradrachm, 1 didrachm, autonomous issues of Tyre; 14 Tyrian tetradrachms, 1 Tyrian didrachm, Antiochus VII; 11 tetradrachms, 4 didrachms, 1 drachm, all Tyrian, Demetrius II; 1 Tyrian tetradrachm, Ptolemy II; 2 Ptolemaic tetradrachms; 3 Sidonian octadrachms.

Kadman 1967: 14 Antiochus VII, 16 Demetrius II, 3 others, all Seleucid, 370 Tyrian shekels ("until AD").

Later authors (Noe 1937, Kadman 1967, *IGCH*) consider the double shekels of Sidon to be an intrusion. Elayi, Elayi 1993a, p. 231, stress the hoard's disparate chronological character. The latter authors think that since Sidonian double shekels were struck until c. 333 BC, they should not be removed too hastily.

Disposition: Hamburger, 13 juin 1892, nos. 2105–2114.

Bibliography:

Hamburger L., "Die Silber-Münzprägungen während des letzten Aufstandes der Israëliten gegen Rom," *Zeitschrift für Numismatik* (1892), pp. 241–348.
Kadman L., "The monetary development of Palestine in the light of coin hoards," in A. Kindler (ed.) *International Numismatic Convention, Jerusalem, 27–31 December 1963. The Patterns of Monetary Development in Phoenicia and Palestine in Antiquity*, Tel Aviv, 1967, no. 15.
Elayi, Elayi 1993a, p. 231, no. 50.
Elayi, J. and A.-G. Elayi. "Nouveaux trésors de monnaies phéniciennes (*CH* IX)," *Transeuphratène* 26 (2003), p. 115.
Houghton, Lorber, Hoover 2008, p. 111.

268. Hebron. *CH* 7.111. 1980

Burial: 125
Contents: 6 tetr. AR + 1? Ptolemaic

Antiochus VII: 1 Tyre
Demetrius II (2): 5 Tyre (years 159 (2), 167, 171, 186 SE)

Ptolemy VI: 1 Salamis (year 28) was seen with this lot

According to the editors of *Coin Hoards*, this hoard may be a part of *CH* 7.109 (**236**), which contained coins of Ptolemy VI (Salamis) and Ptolemy VIII. But Meadows mentions a letter from A. Spaer, 19 July 1981, with a list of four Ptolemaic weight tetradrachms found at Yatta:

Demetrius II (1): 2 Tyre
Demetrius II (2): 1 Tyre
Ptolemy VI: 1 Alexandria

He questions whether it could be a part of the Hebron 1980 hoard.

Disposition: Commerce

Bibliography:

Houghton, Lorber, Hoover 2008, p. 110.
Meadows, A. R. "Hebron Area, 1979 (*CH* 7.109), Hebron, 1980 (*CH* 7.111), Yatta 1978–9 (*CH* 9.531) and Yatta, 1981," in T. Faucher, A. Meadows, and C. Lorber (eds.) *Egyptian Hoards I, Ptolemaic Hoards*, Cairo, 2016b.

269. Israel. *CH* 4.65, fig. 8. 1977

Burial: 125
Contents: 5 AR

Antiochus VII: 2 tetr. Tyre (years 136/5, 131/0 BC)
Demetrius II (2): 2 tetr. Tyre (years 130/129, 127/6 BC)
Ascalon: 1 hemidr.

Disposition: Commerce

Bibliography:
Houghton, Lorber, Hoover 2008, p. 111.

270. Antakya? *IGCH* 1564. 1963

Burial: 125
Contents: 6+ AE

Alexander II Zebinas: 6 Antioch

Disposition: Dispersed. Information from A. Spaer

271. Unknown Findspot. *CH* 8.468

Burial: 125
Contents: 45 AR Ptolemaic

Antiochus VII: 21 tetr., 5 didr. Tyre
Demetrius II (2): 9 tetr., 1 didr.
Tyre: 9 tetr.

Disposition: Commerce

Bibliography:
Houghton, Lorber, Hoover 2008, p. 111.

272. Antakya. *IGCH* 1565. 1932–1939

Burial: 125–120
Contents: 5 AE, in excavation

Alexander II Zebinas: 5 AE Antioch (Alexander II radiate/Double cornucopia)

Waage 1952 observes that "the following coins were found in the same spot," without being certain that this is, strictly speaking, a hoard.

Disposition: Antakya?

Bibliography:
Waage, D. B. *Antioch on the Orontes, IV 2, Greek, Roman, Byzantine and Crusaders' Coins*, Princeton, 1952, p. 19, nos. 201, 203, 204, 205.

273. Coastal Syria or Northern Lebanon. *CH* 10.318. 2000

Burial: 123/2
Contents: 9 tetr. AR

Alexander II Zebinas: 3 Antioch; 5 Damascus (years 189, 190 SE); 1 uncert. Northern Syria

Bibliography:
Houghton, Lorber, Hoover 2008, p. 96.
Elayi, J. and A.-G. Elayi. "Un nouveau trésor de tétradrachmes d'Alexandre II Zébina," *Annotazioni numismatiche* 43 (2001), pp. 999–1004, ill.

274. Vicinity of Gaza. *CH* 8.470. 1983

Burial: 122
Contents: 6 AR, found in the sea

Cleopatra and Antiochus VIII: Ascalon 2 tetr.; 4 didr.

Disposition: Commerce

275. Northern Israel. *CH* 10.319. 2002

Burial: 121/0
Contents: 329 AE

Ptolemy I: 3 Alexandria
Ptolemy II: 2 Alexandria; 4 Tyre
Antiochus III: 2 Tyre; 69 Ake-Ptolemais
Seleucus IV: 4 Antioch
Antiochus IV: 2 Antioch or Ake-Ptolemais; 162 Ake-Ptolemais; 2 Samaria (?)
Demetrius I: 4 Antioch; 31 Ake-Ptolemais
Antiochus IV or Demetrius I: 16 Ake-Ptolemais
Alexander I Balas: 2 Tyre (of which 1 of 147/6 BC); 3 Marisa; 1 uncert.
Demetrius II (1): 1 Tyre (145/4 BC)
Antiochus VII: 5 Antioch (of which 1 of 133/2 BC); 1 Ascalon
Alexander II Zebinas: 3 Antioch
Antiochus VIII and Cleopatra Thea: 1 Antioch
Cos: 1
Side: 3 (late 3rd cent. BC)
Aradus: 3 (including one of 126/5 BC)
Ake-Ptolemais: 4

Hoover saw this hoard in commerce in America during the summer of 2002.[68] Israel is the provenance, more probably the north of the country since nearly 85% of the coins are from the Ake-Ptolemais mint, in addi-

68. My description follows the catalogue of Hoover 2010, not the inventory listing of *CH*, which is inaccurate.

tion to some specimens from Antioch and Tyre; southern mints are poorly represented. Such a breakdown accords with what excavations in the region have discovered. The latest coin is of Antiochus VIII and Cleopatra Thea. The date is illegible, but their joint reign only lasted from 123 to 121 BC, when Antiochus had his mother assassinated. Since coins of his sole reign are absent, it is probable that the lot was withdrawn from circulation c. 121 BC. The presence of Ptolemaic coins, although surprising, does not seem to be an intrusion: they are similar in size to the other coins and are marked with an identical brown-green patina. Although some other hoards (*IGCH* 1571, **305**; *CH* 9.546, **291**) have also revealed some Ptolemaic bronzes later than 200, this does not invalidate the theory of Houghton, Lorber 2002 that Antiochus III banned this coinage; but it does nuance their argument: surely the Ptolemaic bronzes were not retired from circulation all at once but only disappeared little by little.

The coin of Aradus dated 126/5 BC (no. 316) is unknown to Duyrat 2005a.

Disposition: seen in commerce by O. Hoover.

Bibliography:
Houghton, Lorber, Hoover 2008, p. 108.
Hoover, O.. "Northern Israel Hoard, 2002 (*CH* 10.319)," *Coin Hoards* 10, New York, 2010, pp. 227–241.

276. Thalalaia, near Zahle. *IGCH* 1604 = *CH* 1.75. 1952

Burial: after 121/0
Contents: 24 tetr. AR Ptolemaic

Antiochus VII: 8 tetr. Tyre (years 176, 177, 181, 182 SE)
Demetrius II (2): 6 tetr. Tyre (years 183, 185, 186 SE)
Tyre: 10 tetr. (years 3, 4, 5)

Seyrig 1973 counts only 20 coins for this, the so-called "Zahle" hoard, acquired in that city by a Beirut antiquities dealer in 1952: Antiochus VII: 5; Demetrius II: 7; autonomous of Tyre: 8 (no date, years 3, 4, 5, 6). The description in *IGCH* is noticeably different and is based on rubbings preserved in the American Numismatic Society. It is impossible to unravel the hoard's exact content. The description above follows *IGCH*.

Disposition: rubbings at the American Numismatic Society

Bibliography:
Seyrig 1973, no. 46.
Houghton, Lorber, Hoover 2008, p. 111.

277. Tartus (ancient Antaradus). *CH* 8.471, pls. LXIII 37 – LXVII 1–6. = *CH* 10.322. 1987

Burial: 120
Contents: 200 tetr. AR Attic and Ptolemaic
Coins studied: 148/200

Alexander III: 1 Temnos; 93 other posthumous
Athens: 6 (Thompson 65–72, 94–101, 101, 110, 158–169, 184–201, 247–265)
Clazomenae: 1
Mytilene: 1
Smyrna: 2

Byzantium: 1
Alexander I Balas: 2 Antioch; 3 Ake-Ptolemais with Cleopatra Thea
Demetrius II (1): 1 Mopsus
Tryphon: 8 Antioch
Antiochus VII: 3 unknown Cilician mint; 4 Mallos; 1 uncert.
Demetrius II (2): 5 Antioch; 3 Damascus; 5 Sidon (Attic weight); 1 Tyre (Attic weight)
Alexander II Zebinas: 4 Antioch
Cleopatra Thea and Antiochus VIII: 1 Ake-Ptolemais
Diodotus I, Bactria: 1

Houghton, Lorber, Hoover 2008 state that some modern forgeries of rare Seleucid coins were mixed in with this hoard. Their description should accordingly correct the one provided in *CH*.

Disposition: Commerce

Bibliography:
Price, M. J. *The Coinage in the Name of Alexander the Great and Philip Arrhideus*, Zurich/London, 1991, p. 64.
Houghton, Lorber, Hoover 2008, p. 96.

278. Waqqas, near Pella, Jordan. *CH* 8.472. 1982

Burial: 120
Contents: 90 AR

Antiochus VIII: 90 tetr. Ake-Ptolemais (Attic weight)

Disposition: Dispersed

Bibliography:
Houghton, Lorber, Hoover 2008, p. 112.

279. Bassit, Syria. *CH* 8.476 = *CH* 10.326. 1978

Burial: after 118
Contents: 10 tetr. AR rolled in a sheet of lead, in excavation

Alexander III: 6 Temnos; 3 Alabanda
Antiochus VIII (1): 1 Damascus (119/8)

These 10 tetradrachms were wrapped in lead foil and found 10 cm above the remains of a Hellenistic wall. The contents are no surprise, Alexanders of the cities of Asia Minor being quite common in second-century Syria. Le Rider recalls the similar content of the Tell Kotchek hoard (*IGCH* 1773, **198**). The single Seleucid tetradrachm seems to have been added to make an even 10 coins.

Disposition: Aleppo Museum?

Bibliography:
Le Rider, G. "Un trésor de Bassit (1978)," *Bulletin de correspondance hellénique* 107 (1983), pp. 451–456.
Price, M. J. *The Coinage in the Name of Alexander the Great and Philip Arrhideus*, London, 1991, p. 64.
Houghton, Lorber, Hoover 2008, p. 97.

280. Baalbek Area? *CH* 8.479. 1979

Burial: 113/2
Contents: 76+ AR

Antiochus VII: 2 tetr. Antioch; 6 tetr. Tyre ("to 120")
Demetrius II (2): 2 tetr. Antioch; 1 tetr. Damascus (year 186 SE); 1 tetr. Sidon (year 185 SE); 1 tetr. Ake-Ptolemais (year 185 SE)
Cleopatra Thea and Antiochus VIII: 4 tetr. Antioch; 1 tetr. Damascus; 7 tetr. Ake-Ptolemais
Antiochus VIII: 8 tetr. Antioch; 7 tetr. Damascus (to 197 SE = 116/5 BC); 5 tetr. Sidon (to 200 SE = 113/2 BC?); 20 tetr. Ake-Ptolemais (to 198/200 SE = 115/113 BC)
[Antiochus IX: 1 tetr. Sidon (year 200 SE = 113/2 BC)?]
Tyre: 11 tetr. (to year 14 = 113/2 BC)

A much later Tyrian shekel seen in the lot is apparently an intrusion. The tetradrachm of Antiochus VIII struck at Sidon in 200 BC was previously unknown. Houghton, Lorber, Hoover 2008 surmise that this identification is mistaken and that the coin probably belongs to Antiochus IX.

Disposition: Commerce in Europe

Bibliography:
Houghton, Lorber, Hoover 2008, p. 112.

281. Haifa, Israel. *IGCH* 1605 = *CH* 3.63 = *CH* 8.477. 1969

Burial: 113/2
Contents: 400+ AR, in the sea
Coins studied: 57/400+

Alexander II Zebinas: 1 tetr. Antioch
Antiochus VIII: 14 + 8 tetr. Antioch (121/0 – spring/summer 113 BC); 11 + 3 tetr. Damascus (120/119 – 113 BC); 2 + 2 tetr. Sidon; 2 + 1 tetr. Ake-Ptolemais
Antiochus IX Cyzicene: 2 + 2 tetr. Ake-Ptolemais; 4 + 5 tetr. Sidon (113/2 BC)

Ringel 1974, p. 42, recounts how, in August, 1969, a fisherman who specialized in underwater hoard hunting brought up "a considerable number of Seleucid tetradrachms." The coins lay submerged in a vase, around 50 m offshore, south of Haifa, at Khirbeth Kefar Samir. In his article Ringel was able to bring together the 36 specimens that the Haifa Municipal Museum of Ancient Art and the Maritime Museum acquired or that were photographed in commerce. All were covered with very dark oxidation and were well preserved. Based on information Ringel collected, all the dispersed coins belonged to the reigns of Antiochus VIII, Antiochus IX and, for one or two coins, Alexander II Zebinas. A New Style tetradrachm of Athens also belonged to the lot. The dates are closely clustered, from 118/7 to 113/2 BC. Burial is contemporary with the fratricidal strife between Antiochus VIII and IX, when the latter successfully exerted his control over southern Syria and the Palestinian coast. Loss of the hoard may be tied to a capsizing, shipwrecks abounding on this coast.

In 1978, Spaer published a complementary list of 21 coins of this hoard and estimates the original find numbered around 400. Their appearance is identical to Ringel 1974's description: the mints are the same, and the latest date is also 113/2 BC. I have included them in the list here, after the specimens Ringel described.
All the hoard's coins are on the Attic weight standard.

Disposition: Municipal Museum of Ancient Art, Haifa 26; Maritime Museum of Haifa 2; Private collections, commerce (notably Eidelstein and Holland, Haifa, 10 Nov. 1975, nos. 19–22).

Bibliography:
Ringel, J. "Un trésor de tétradrachmes séleucides retirés de la mer à Haïfa (Israël)," *Revue numismatique* (1974), pp. 42–48, pl. 2.
Spaer, A. "Le trésor séleucide de la mer de Haïfa: complément," *Revue numismatique* 20 (1978), pp. 43–45, pls. 1–2.
Houghton, Lorber, Hoover 2008, pp. 112–113.

282. Lebanon or Syria. *CH* 6.39. 1979

Burial: 113/2
Contents: 100+ AR Attic and Ptolemaic
Coins studied: 18/100+

Demetrius II (2): 3+ tetr.
Antiochus VIII and Cleopatra Thea: 3+ tetr.
Antiochus VIII: 6+ tetr.
Antiochus IX: 1 tetr. Sidon (year 200 SE = 113/2 BC) Attic weight
Tyre: 4 tetr. (to year 14 = 113/2 BC); 1 half-shekel (year 13 = 114/3 BC)

Disposition: Dispersed

Bibliography:
Houghton, Lorber, Hoover 2008, p. 112.

283. Amrith (ancient Marathus). *IGCH* 1566. 1947

Burial: 112/1
Contents: 27 AE

Aradus: 12 (Tyche/Poseidon seated on a prow, 2 year 129, 3 year 130, 6 year 148, 1 uncert.)
Marathus: 15 (Zeus/Two cornucopiae, years 131, 141, 142, 148)

Seyrig 1964 does not indicate how he came to study this small hoard. He details some mint marks and dates, which do not exactly coincide with those in *IGCH*. The description above follows Seyrig, who did handle the hoard.

Disposition: Dispersed

Bibliography:
Seyrig, H. "Monnaies hellénistiques 12. Questions aradiennes," *Revue numismatique* (1964), pp. 7–67, pp. 46–47.

284. Amrith (ancient Marathus). 1955

Burial: after 112/1
Contents: 50 AE

Aradus: 27 (Head of Tyche/Poseidon seated on a prow, between years 126? and 148); 1 (Zeus/Athena on a prow, year 136)
Marathus: 22 (Head of Zeus/Double cornucopia, between years 131 and 142)

Unpublished hoard, discussed below, pp. 197–200.

Disposition: probably dispersed.

Bibliography:
H. Seyrig Archives, Bibliothèque nationale de France, dossier 227 "Amrit 1955."

285. Maresha (ancient Marisa). *CH* 9.544. Summer, 1989

Burial: 112
Contents: 25 AR, in excavation, pot hoard

Cleopatra Thea and Antiochus VIII: 1 tetr. Ascalon
Antiochus VIII (1): 23 tetr. Ascalon (121/0–113 BC)
Antiochus IX: 1 tetr. Ascalon (113/2 BC)

Marisa is located 38 km southwest of Jerusalem. In 259 BC, the Zenon papyri show it to be a Ptolemaic administrative seat; an epitaph in the vast Hellenistic necropolis also points to the existence of a Sidonian colony. Marisa was probably an administrative center in the third and second centuries, until John Hyrca-nus I (108/7 BC) destroyed it. The hoard came to light in a residential area south of the acropolis, under the floor of a room in a Hellenistic building that, judging by the ceramic evidence, was abandoned at the end of the second century BC. The coins were contained in a jug 15 cm tall, of a type common in Marisa. They were fused together, and some were severely corroded.

Disposition: Israel

Bibliography:
Barkay, R. "The Marisa hoard of Seleucid tetradrachms minted in Ascalon," *Israel Numismatic Journal* 12 (1992–1993), pp. 21–26, pls. 3–5.
Houghton, Lorber, Hoover 2008, p. 113.

286. Homs. *CH* 9.545. 1987

Burial: 112
Contents: 19 tetr. AR
Coins studied: 9/19 AR

Antiochus VII: 1 Antioch; 1 Damascus
Alexander II Zebinas: 1 Antioch
Antiochus VIII and Cleopatra Thea: 2 Ake-Ptolemais
Antiochus VIII: 1 Antioch 2nd reign (spring/summer 112/1–111/0 BC); 1 Ake-Ptolemais
Antiochus IX: 1 Antioch 1st reign (spring/summer 113–spring/summer 112 BC); 1 uncert. mint

This group was discovered in the Lebanese part of the Homs Gap, according to information gathered by Elayi and Elayi. The 10 other coins, sold in Australia, seem to have been of the same kings and of Demetrius II (2).

Houghton, Lorber, Hoover 2008 date the burial precisely to 112 BC, thanks to the tetradrachm of Antiochus IX struck at Antioch that is closely connected by control marks to bronzes bearing dates on the Seleucid Era.

Disposition: Dispersed

Bibliography:
Elayi, J. and A.-G. Elayi. "Un trésor de monnaies séleucides de la trouée de Homs," R. Martini, N. Vismara (eds.). *Ermanno A. Arslan Studia Dicata, Glaux*, Milan, 1991, pp. 157–162, pls. xxxviii–xxxix.
Houghton, Lorber, Hoover 2008, p. 97.

287. Palestine. *IGCH* 1606. 1970

Burial: 110/9
Contents: 92 AE

Antiochus III–IV: 6
Ake-Ptolemais: 56 (127/6–110/9 BC)
Uncert., probably Ake-Ptolemais: 25
Tyre: 1
Hasmoneans: 3
Rome: 1 (3rd cent., intrusion)

Disposition: Dispersed

Bibliography:
Kindler, *AHHI* 4.3 (1970), pp. 41–6, illus. (in Hebrew, *non vidi*)
Houghton, Lorber 2002, p. 105.
Houghton, Lorber, Hoover 2008, p. 113.

288. Kessab. *IGCH* 1568 = *CH* 1.75. 1952

Burial: after 105/4
Contents: 392 tetr. AR

Demetrius I: 1 Antioch
Demetrius II (1): 1 Seleuceia on the Calycadnus; 1 Seleuceia Pieria or Laodiceia ad Mare
Antiochus VII: 7 + 1 (?) Tarsus; 1 Mallos; 72 Antioch; 1 Seleuceia Pieria (?); 17 Damascus; 6 Tyre; 2 Seleuceia on the Tigris ; 4 uncert.; 2 Cappadocia
Demetrius II (2): 3 Tarsus; 21 Antioch; 4 Damascus; 1 Ake-Ptolemais
Alexander II Zebinas: 47 Antioch; 12 Damascus; 8 uncert.
Cleopatra Thea: 1 Ake-Ptolemais
Cleopatra Thea and Antiochus VIII: 4 Antioch; 2 Damascus; 10 Ake-Ptolemais
Antiochus VIII: 8 Antioch; 19 Damascus; 5 Sidon; 70 Ake-Ptolemais
Antiochus IX: 2 Antioch; 2 Sidon; 2 uncert. Cilicia
Phraates II: 1 Susa
Seleuceia Pieria: 12
Athens: 41

In notes of Seyrig (H. Seyrig Archives, Bibliothèque nationale de France, dossier 265), this hoard is alternately named "Kessab 1952" or "so-called Idlib find." On November 19, 1952, Seyrig writes that, according to Tigran

Sarrafian, two hoards were sold on the market in 1952. The first, in late spring, with a northwest Syrian provenance, consisted of coins from Athens, Seleuceia, and some Seleucids described above here. The second allegedly came from the Euphrates region and contained Alexanders. Another dealer asserted that it was all the same find, but Seyrig notes "in that case, the pseudo-Alexanders are a glaring anachronism."[69] In an exceptional way, probably owing to the hoard's size, Seyrig took notes naming the dealers where he observed these tetradrachms: Ali, Homs, October, 1952 (from Idlib and Azzaz, Athens and Alexanders), coins then brought by Ali to Beirut, November, 1952 (Alexanders and Seleucids), and by him to the dealer Bustros, February, 1953 (Alexanders, Athens, Seleuceia, Seleucids) and June 10, 1953 (Athens, Alexanders, Seleucids, Phraates); Poladian, Beirut, October, 1952 (northern Syria, Alexanders, Seleucids), then February, 1953 (Alexanders), April, 1953 (Alexanders); Bustros (?), Beirut, June, 1952 (from the vicinity of Aleppo, Alexanders, Seleucids), November 1952 (Athens, Seleucids), April 1953 (Alexanders, Athens, Seleucids), May 7, 1953 (Athens), February 17, 1954 (Seleucids), March 21, 1954 (Seleucids); Gabriel, Beirut, November, 1952 (Athens, Alexanders, Seleucids), coins then brought by Gabriel to Bustros, December, 1952 (Alexanders); Joseph Zeitoun, March, 1953 (Alexanders, Athens, Seleucids); M. Satl, April 26, 1954 (Seleucids), May 4, 1954 (Alexanders). All in all, he lists 19 lots combining two hoards put on the market between June, 1952, and May, 1954.

This burial probably occurred in the context of the war between Antiochus VIII and Antiochus IX. Thompson 1961, pp. 475–77; Thompson 1962, pp. 311–12; Lewis 1962, p. 279, all use this hoard in their debate over the dating of New Style tetradrachms.

Disposition: Dispersed

Bibliography:
Seyrig 1973, no. 30.
Houghton, Lorber, Hoover 2008, pp. 97–99.

289. Samaria Region. Before 1991

Burial: Before 103
Contents: c. 900 AE

Seleucids: AE of the 2nd cent. BC
Hasmoneans, including a large assortment of coins of Yehohanan

Barag 1991, p. 106, n. 2, states that the Institute of Archaeology of the Hebrew University of Jerusalem acquired this unpublished hoard. It does not contain any coin of Alexander Jannaeus (103–76 BC). Moreover, excavation of the Samaritan settlement on Mt. Garizim, destroyed by John Hyrcanus I c. 110 BC, has also revealed a large number of bronzes of Yehohanan accompanied by coins of the Seleucids and Phoenician cities, all dated to the second century BC. Consequently, all the issues in the name of Yehohanan were struck under John Hyrcanus I (135–104 BC), who was the first Hasmonean to strike coinage.

Disposition: The Institute of Archaeology of the Hebrew University of Jerusalem

Bibliography:
Barag, D. "Jewish coins in Hellenistic and Roman times," in T. Hackens et al. (eds.) *A Survey of Numismatic Research, 1985–1990*, I, Bruxelles, 1991, pp. 106–108.

290. Palestine. *IGCH* 1630 = Noe 788. 1930

Burial: 2nd–1st cent.

69. "dans ce cas-là, les pseudo-alexandres font un anachronisme éclatant."

Contents: 86+ AR

Antiochus VII: tetr. Tyre
Demetrius II: tetr. Tyre
Tyre: tetr.

The editors of *IGCH* compare this lot to *IGCH* 1629 (**359**), but their dating must be corrected.

Disposition: Dispersed. Photographs at the American Numismatic Society according to *IGCH*, but not found by Houghton, Lorber, Hoover 2008, p. 117.

Bibliography:
Kadman, L. "The monetary development of Palestine in the light of coin hoards," in A. Kindler (ed.) *International Numismatic Convention, Jerusalem, 27–31 December 1963. The Patterns of Monetary Development in Phoenicia and Palestine in Antiquity*, Tel Aviv, 1967, no. 13.
Houghton, Lorber, Hoover 2008, p. 117.

291. Israel. *CH* 9.546. 1997

Burial: end of 2nd–1st cent. BC
Contents: 2 AE, 1 lead weight

Demetrius II (1): 1 uncert.
Ptolemy II: 1

Disposition: Israel Museum, Jerusalem.

Bibliography:
Kushnir-Stein, A. and H. Gitler. "On some inscribed lead weights from Palestine," *Numismatica e antichità classiche* 28 (1999), pp. 221–234, hoard pp. 225–229, pl. 3.
Houghton, Lorber, Hoover 2008, p. 114.

2.6. HOARDS OF THE FIRST CENTURY

292. Rafah (ancient Rafiah), Gaza Strip. *IGCH* 1609 = *CH* 9.550. Summer, 1968

Burial: beginning of the 1st cent.
Contents: 52 tetr. and didr. AR Ptolemaic

Alexander II Zebinas: 1 tetr. Ascalon
Cleopatra Thea and Antiochus VIII: 2 tetr., 3 didr. Ascalon
Antiochus VIII: 38 tetr. (9 dated 121/0–113 BC; 29 dated 112–103 BC), 3 didr. Ascalon
Antiochus IX: 2 tetr. Ascalon (113/2 BC)
Ascalon: 3 tetr. (2 year 6; 1 year 36)

A part of this hoard, found in the dunes east of Rafah, appeared on the antiquities market of Jerusalem. Another group arrived in Amman and was then transferred to Beirut. The coins appear burnt, and cleaning damaged them. The latest coin (year 36 = 72/1 BC) does not, perhaps, belong to the hoard (specimen sold in Beirut). It illustrates the transition between royal strikings and autonomous issues at Ascalon. Spaer remarks that there does not seem to have been a break between these two productions, although no coin dated from the years 1 to 5 of the autonomous series is known. From 104/3 to 97/6 BC, the typology remains that of the royal issues (Portrait of Antiochus VIII/Eagle on a thunderbolt), the legend on the reverse replaced by the autonomous titulature and dating of Ascalon. After that sovereign's departure from the scene, his portrait was apparently maintained for 95/4 and 93/2, and perhaps even in 78/7 BC. Antiochus IX, or perhaps X (who in theory struck coins only at Antioch), might be represented on the tetradrachms of year 12 (91/0 BC).

Disposition: Collection Spaer, Private collection Beirut, the remainder is dispersed.

Bibliography:
Spaer, A. "Ascalon: from royal mint to autonomy," in A. Houghton, S. Hurter, P. Erhart Mottahedeh, and J. Ayer Scott (eds.) *Festschrift für Leo Mildenberg*, Wetteren, 1984, pp. 229–239, pls. 35–37.
Houghton, Lorber, Hoover 2008, pp. 114–115.

293. Kurnub, near Beersheba, Idumaea. *IGCH* 1631. 1966

Burial: beginning of the 1st cent.
Contents: 70–80 AR

Tyre, tetr.

Disposition: Private collections Jerusalem. Information from Y. Meshorer

294. Ascalon. *CH* 9.548. 1988

Burial: 100
Contents: 1 AR, 46 AE + 1 AE, in excavation

Antiochus III: 1 AE Sardis
Antiochus VII: 1 AE Antioch
Uncert. Seleucid king: 1 AE Tyre
Ptolemy IX/X: 1 AE Paphos
Teos: 1 AE
Samos: 16 AE, 1 diob. AR (1.33 g) + 1 AE
Cos: 5 AE
Cnidus: 1 AE
Rhodes: 12 AE
Lycian League: 5 AE
Side: 1 AE
Tyre: 1 AE

These coins were found during excavation of a house from the end of the Hellenistic period, under a floor. They were so stuck together that Gitler, Kahanov 2002 suppose that they were enclosed in a purse or "a small container." Twelve other bronzes were discovered under the same floor. Only four are legible: one bronze of Samos, which may have belonged to the hoard (and numbered as such, 6a), and three others from the Ascalon mint dated from the reigns of Antiochus IV, second century BC, and Nero, the latter certainly an intrusion.

The latest coin is the Ptolemaic, though it is one of the least well preserved. The large amount of lead in the alloy explains this. Houghton, Lorber, Hoover 2008 attribute to Antiochus III a bronze of Sardis that the original publication assigned to Antiochus Hierax.

This is an unusual hoard: bronzes of western Asia Minor struck from the fourth to the second centuries rarely reached the Levant, as Israeli excavations notably attest. The variety of the cities represented and the rarity of certain issues (Teos, no. 1, and Cnidus, no. 24) lead one to suppose that this was a collection made during a journey. These cities "are all located along a known, natural and logical seafaring route and in all of them remnants of ancient harbours can be traced" (Gitler, Kahanov 2002, p. 265). This statement is based on different sources, including the voyages of St. Paul, which enable reconstruction of ancient routes. These coins were struck between the fourth and the beginning of the first centuries, while they were probably collected all at the same time, implying that bronzes of different periods circulated together.

For comparison, cf. the hoard from south of Beirut, *IGCH* 1500, **40**, and the Megadim hoard, **298**.

Bibliography:
Gitler, H. and Y. Kahanov. "The Ascalon 1988 Hoard (*CH* 9. 548). A periplous to Ascalon in the late Hellenistic period?," in A. Meadows and U. Wartenberg (eds.) *Coin Hoards* 9. Greek Hoards, Royal Numismatic Society, London, 2002, pp. 259–268, pl. 53.
Houghton, Lorber, Hoover 2008, p. 114.

295. "Kefir." *IGCH* 1569 = Noe 543. 1910

Burial: 100
Contents: 17+ AR

Tyre: tetr. (Years 5–25)

IGCH advises: "There is a Kefer in Syria c. 15 km N of Idlib, but more probably 'Kefir' represents Arab Kafr, Kefr, etc. (village) used in countless composite place names all over the area."

Disposition: Istanbul. Seen by Regling

296. Jericho. *IGCH* 1607. 1965–1966

Burial: 100
Contents: 200+ AR Attic (1 ex.) and Ptolemaic, pot hoard
Coins studied: 109/200+

Antiochus VII, Tyre: 44 tetr. and 3 didr.
Demetrius II (2), Tyre: 52 tetr., 1 didr.
Cleopatra Thea and Antiochus VIII: 1 tetr. Ascalon
Antiochus VIII: 2 tetr. + 1 tetr. Attic weight Ake-Ptolemais; 2 tetr. Ascalon
Tyre: 3 tetr. (to year 24 = 103/2 BC) + 2 tetr. (Jordan)

In 1966, a hoard of Seleucid coins said to come from Jordan was offered on the Jerusalem market. A conversation with the seller elicited that it was discovered in December, 1965, or January, 1966, during the laying of foundations for a house north of modern Jericho, 500 m south of Ain es-Sultan and the ancient city. The coins were gathered in a sturdy jar, since lost. Out of the 200 tetradrachms and several didrachms in the find, Spaer saw only 65. 44 others arrived at the Jordanian Department of Antiquities (19 tetradrachms and 1 didrachm, Antiochus VII [Tyre]; 21 tetradrachms, Demetrius II (2) [Tyre]; 2 tetradrachms, autonomous of Tyre; 1 tetradrachm, Antiochus VIII [Ascalon]). The rest were dispersed. The unity of the two lots entitles one to think they are representative of the entire hoard. The coins were covered with a thick layer of oxide and were stuck together. The chronology of the coins runs between 177 of the Seleucid Era (136/5 BC) and year 24 of Tyre (103/2 BC). The burial date could be related to the expeditions of Alexander Jannaeus beyond the Jordan at the start of his reign (Josephus, *Antiquites of the Jews* 13.13.3).

Disposition: Amman 44; A. Spaer Jerusalem 65.

Bibliography:
Spaer, A. "A hoard from Jericho," *Numismatic Chronicle* (1970), pp. 23–28, pls. I–III.
Houghton, Lorber, Hoover 2008, p. 114.

297. Hebron. *IGCH* 1608. 1967

Burial: 100
Contents: 4+ Pb

Alexander Jannaeus

Disposition: Information from Y. Meshorer

298. Megadim, Coast of Mt. Carmel, near Haifa. 1962

Burial: 100
Contents: 7 AE, in excavation

Lycian League: 1
Antiochus V: Tyre
Antiochus VII: Antioch
Ptolemy VIII, IX and/or X: 2 Paphos

Gitler, Kahanov 1992, pp. 264–65, cite this hoard. These few coins were discovered in a Rhodian amphora that was part of the cargo on a ship sunk off of Megadim, on the coast of Mt. Carmel. They were mingled in with other metal objects destined for the foundry.

Disposition: Information from D. T. Ariel who will publish these coins.

Bibliography:
Misch-Brandl, O. and E. Galili. "Finds from the Hellenistic period," in *From the Depths of the Sea: Cargoes and Ancient Wrecks from the Carmel Coast*, Israel Museum Catalogue no. 263, Jerusalem, summer 1985, pp. 12–13.
Parker, A. J. *Ancient Shipwrecks of the Mediterranean and the Roman Provinces*, Oxford, 1992, BAR International Series 580, p. 273, no. 689.
Gitler, H. and Y. Kahanov. "The Ascalon 1988 Hoard (*CH* 9. 548). A periplous to Ascalon in the late Hellenistic period?," in A. Meadows and U. Wartenberg (eds.) *Coin Hoards* 9. Greek Hoards, Royal Numismatic Society, London, 2002, pp. 259–268, pl. 53.

299. Megadim, Coast of Mt. Carmel, near Haifa. 1983

Burial: after 100/99
Contents: 19 tetr. AR

Ptolemy VIII: 1 Salamis, 2 Citium
Ptolemy IX: 1 Alexandria
Ptolemy X: 2 Alexandria
2nd cent. BC?: 13 uncert.

This hoard, like the preceding, was discovered in the sea, near Moshav Megadim, on the coast of Mt. Carmel, by a team from the Underwater Exploration Society of Israel; but it could not be brought to the surface until 1983. It was dispersed; the coins, as a result of their long submersion, were very damaged, often to the point of making identifications impossible. The present description reprises that of Olivier (forthcoming).

Disposition: Israel Antiquities Authority

Bibliography:
Syon, D., C. Lorber, andE. Galili. "Underwater Ptolemaic Coin Hoards from Megadim," *'Atiqot* 74 (2013), p. 1–8.
Olivier, J. *Archè et chrèmata en Egypte au IIe s. avant J.-C. (204–81 av. J.-C.). Etude de numismatique et d'histoire*, Etudes Alexandrines, Alexandria, forthcoming.

300. Golan. *IGCH* 1613. 1940

Burial: 100–75
Contents: 40 AE

Antiochus VII: 1 Jerusalem
Antiochus VIII: 1 Antioch
Sidon? (crude style): 1
Tyre: 25 year 28 = 99/8 BC (BMC 251)
Judah Aristobulus: 2 (BMC 3)
Alexander Jannaeus: 1 (BMC 30)
Uncert. Hasmonean (illegible): 9

These coins were seen in Damascus in 1940, in the hands of a collector who had just acquired them from a peasant who came from the south (H. Seyrig Archives, Bibliothèque nationale de France, dossier 224). Seyrig supposes a southern Golan provenance, near Lake Tiberias. The Tyrian coins are the most recent. The presence of coins from Tyre and Sidon is natural in this area, with which these two large ports maintained frequent relations.

Disposition: Dispersed

Bibliography:
Seyrig, H. "Monnaies grecques des fouilles de Doura et d'Antioche," *Revue numismatique* (1958), pp. 175–176.
Houghton, Lorber, Hoover 2008, p. 115.

301. Tripoli. *IGCH* 1619 = Noe 1130. 1884–1885

Burial: 100–50
Contents: 520 AR
Coins studied: 110/520

Demetrius II (2): 5 tetr.
Alexander II Zebinas: 36 tetr.
Antiochus VIII and Cleopatra Thea: 1 tetr.
Antiochus VIII: 20 tetr.
Antiochus IX: 1 tetr.
Aradus: 27 tetr. (autonomous, years 162–198 = 98/7–62/1 BC)
Tripolis: 20 tetr.

IGCH describes only 110 out of the 520 silver tetradrachms in this hoard. The American Numismatic Society now has in its collection the tetradrachms that once belonged to Rouvier, but information provided by Newell does not specify which specimens come from this hoard. Six 1886, p. 231, n.1, is the first to mention it, but he indicates only that it was discovered in the vicinity of Beirut; he does not elaborate on the content, even though he had the hoard in his possession. Noe 1937 gives some numbers for the Seleucids, citing Six 1886 and Rouvier 1898 as sources. The coins of Antiochus IX allow us to date the burial between 100 and 50 BC. Assembling the collection took place in either two or three phases according to Callataÿ: first, the group of Seleucid tetradrachms (c. 130–c. 95 BC), next the group from Tripolis (c. 102/93 BC), finally that from Aradus (c. 97–c. 61 BC).

Bibliography:
Six, J.-P. "L'ère de Tripolis," *Annuaire de la société française de numismatique et d'archéologie* 10 (1886), pp. 229–234
Houghton, Lorber, Hoover 2008, p. 116.
Rouvier, J. "L'ère de Marathus de Phénicie," *Journal Asiatique* (novembre–décembre 1898), pp. 361–406, p. 13.
Callataÿ, F. (de). "Les tétradrachmes hellénistiques de Tripolis," *Numismatica e antichità classiche* 22 (1993), pp. 111–123, p. 121.

302. Damascus. *IGCH* 1620. 1940

Burial: 100–50
Contents: 68 AE

Antiochus VII: 1 Jerusalem
Antiochus (uncertain): 1
Tyre: 25 (BMC 251)
Sidon: 1 (BMC 91)
Judah Aristobulus: 2 (BMC 1 ff.)
Alexander Jannaeus: 1 (BMC 30 f.)
Hasmoneans: 9 uncert.
Uncertain: 28

Seyrig's notes (H. Seyrig Archives, Bibliothèque nationale de France, dossier 225) do not say much: "Presumed origin: Damascus. March, 1940," followed by the description that appears in *IGCH*.

Disposition: Dispersed. Information from H. Seyrig

Bibliography:
Houghton, Lorber, Hoover 2008, p. 116.

303. North-Central Syria. *CH* 10.337. 2004

Burial: Beginning of the 1st cent.
Contents: 47+ AR

Cappadocia: 47 imitations of Antiochus VII

This hoard was part of a study in which Lorber and Houghton show that a large number of tetradrachms of Antiochus VII are, in fact, Cappadocian imitations. They stress the close relations between the two kingdoms, evident in these coins. The article takes account of other hoards containing this type of currency, several of which could come from eastern Syria, eastern Anatolia, or northern Mesopotamia. They are not included in this catalogue.

Disposition: Dispersed.

Bibliography:
Lorber, C.. and A. Houghton. "Cappadocian tetradrachms in the name of Antiochus VII," *Numismatic Chronicle* 166 (2006), pp. 49–98.

304. Antakya. *IGCH* 1570. Before 1960

Burial: 95
Contents: 8 AR

Antiochus VIII: 7 tetr. Antioch, 1 tetr. Ake-Ptolemais

Disposition: Istanbul. Seen by O. Mørkholm.

305. Kessab. *IGCH* 1571. 1947

Burial: 95
Contents: 22 AE

Antiochus IV: 1 Ake-Ptolemais
Tryphon: 1 Antioch
Antiochus VII: 4 Antioch
Demetrius II (2) 6: Antioch, Damascus
Antiochus VIII and Cleopatra Thea: 1 Ake-Ptolemais
Antiochus VIII: 2 Antioch 1st reign (121/0–spring/summer 112 BC)
Antiochus IX: 1 Antioch 1st reign (spring/summer 113–spring/summer 112 BC)
Ptolemy III: 1 Tyre (Sv. 711); 2 Ake (Sv. 1060)
Aradus: 1 (BMC 104 ff.)
Byblos: 2 (BMC 18, 5,06 g, 19 mm; Tyche/Harpocrates standing holding a cornucopia and his r. in his mouth, 2.70 g, 15 mm)

According to the Seyrig Archives (Bibliothèque nationale de France, dossier 221), this hoard was discovered at Kessab and brought to Beirut in 1947. The find is clearly stated to be "of quite uniform patina, and composed of coins that had circulated a great deal."[70] There are two descriptions of the hoard in Seyrig's archives, and the second attributes its uncertain coinage to Byblos, the identification reported here. The presence of civic issues made Seyrig doubt the hoard's actual provenance, which he was inclined to attribute to Phoenicia instead. He adds, however, that "the find belongs to a category where the coins, spread out over a long period, probably represent the currency of second choice, perhaps partly removed from circulation, but which must still have been current in the country's remoter regions. One will observe that the latest coins are not the most numerous there, as they would be in cities where the velocity of exchange is higher."[71] One might add, as well, that the presence of Ptolemaic bronzes is unusual in northern Syria and could be related to Ptolemaic occupation of several coastal cities between 246 and 219 BC.

Disposition: Dispersed. Information from H. Seyrig

Bibliography:
Houghton, Lorber, Hoover 2008, p. 99.

306. Phoenicia. 2011?

Burial: 95/4
Contents: 9 AR

Ptolemy IX: 4 Alexandria
Ptolemy X: 5 Alexandria

Olivier describes and dates this small hoard, sold on eBay. He connects it with the Gaza Strip hoard (*CH* 4.69, **307**).

Disposition: Commerce

Bibliography:
Olivier, J. *Archè et chrèmata en Egypte au IIe s. avant J.-C. (204–81 av. J.-C.). Etude de numismatique et d'histoire*, Etudes Alexandrines, Alexandria, forthcoming.

307. Gaza Strip. *CH* 4.69. 1977

Burial: 94
Contents: 19+ AR

Ptolemy IX: 4 tetr.
Ptolemy X and Cleopatra III: 8 tetr. (years 12/9 (6); 13/10; 16/13)
Ptolemy X: 7 tetr. (years 18, 20 (3); 21 (3))

Disposition: Commerce

70. "d'une patine bien uniforme, et composée de pièces ayant beaucoup circulé."

71. "la trouvaille appartient à une catégorie où les monnaies, échelonnées sur une longue période, représentent probablement le numéraire de second choix, peut-être démonétisé en partie, qui devait avoir cours dans les cantons écartés du pays. On remarquera que les monnaies les plus récentes n'y sont pas les plus nombreuses, comme elles le seraient dans les villes où la circulation monétaire est active."

Bibliography:
Meadows, A. "Gaza Strip, 1977 (*CH* 4.69)", in T. Faucher, A. Meadows, and C. Lorber (eds.) *Egyptian Hoards* I, *Ptolemaic Hoards*. Cairo 2016, pp. 235–236.

308. Yahmour. *IGCH* 1572. 1956

Burial: after 89/8
Contents: 75+ AR

Aradus: 75 autonomous tetr. (years 122 (2), 128, 129 (2), 130 (2), 131 (5), 132 (3), 133 (2), 137, 138 (2), 139, 140, 148, 149, 151 (2), 152, 160, 161 (3) 162 (3), 163 (16), 164 (10), 165 (5), 166 (3), 167 (2), 168 (3), 169, 171 = 89/8 BC)

Yahmour is a small locality situated inland on the mainland, just south of Aradus. The burial of the hoard, which was perhaps more voluminous, is after 89/8 BC. The Aradian years 160 to 171 constitute two-thirds of the lot. This is owing to Aradus' abundant coin production during this time.

Disposition: Dispersed

Bibliography:
Seyrig 1973, no. 31.

309. Kamishliyye, Syria. *CH* 8.515. 1980

Burial: after 88/7?
Contents: AR

Antiochus XI
Demetrius III
Philip I Philadelphus

Disposition: Commerce

Bibliography:
Houghton, Lorber, Hoover 2008, p. 99.

310. Palestine. *IGCH* 1610. Before 1941

Burial: after 86/5
Contents: 34 AR

Antiochus VII: 1 tetr. Cappadocian posthumous
Antiochus VIII: 1 tetr. Ake-Ptolemais
Aradus: 32 tetr. autonomous

The latest Aradian tetradrachm is from year 173 (87/6 BC). That of Antiochus VIII allows us to put the burial after 86/5 BC. This hoard marks the southern limit for the circulation of autonomous Aradian tetradrachms. It may also indicate a focus of this circulation towards the Nabataean caravans that terminated in Palestine (Rey-Coquais 1974, p. 185). Houghton, Lorber, Hoover 2008 consider that the two Seleucid tetradrachms are probably an intrusion. That of Antiochus VII belongs to a series since attributed to a Cappadocian mint and would be posthumous (104–102 BC).

Disposition: A. Spaer, Jerusalem. Information from A. Spaer.

Bibliography:
Houghton, Lorber, Hoover 2008, p. 115.

311. Lebanon. *CH* 8.511. 1987

Burial: 85
Contents: 37+ AR Ptolemaic

Seleucids, Phoenician mints: 9+ (to Antiochus IX, Sidon 200 SE; 2 Demetrius III Damascus 225 SE)
Sidon: 4 shekels, 1 half-shekel
Tyre: 13 tetr., 7 didr.

Disposition: Commerce

Bibliography:
Houghton, Lorber, Hoover 2008, p. 115.

312. Jaffa. *IGCH* 1611. September, 1949

Burial: 85
Contents: 851 AE and several fragments that represent 4–6 additional coins, in excavation.

Alexander Jannaeus: all of the same type, except one:
850 AE: Star surrounded by a circle, imitative legend in Hebrew/Anchor surrounded by a circle; ΒΑΣΙΛΕΩΣ ΑΛΕΞΑΝΔΡΟΥ. Certain coins are struck only on the obverse or the reverse or bear illegible types. Two modules: 9–11 mm (225 ex.), 6–9 mm (625 ex.).
1 AE: Hebrew legend in a laurel wreath/Double cornucopia, fillets, poppy between the two horns; dotted border.

This large hoard provided Kindler the occasion to survey the types, legends, manufacturing techniques, and the mint that issued these bronzes. The coins are generally thought to be imitations of originals from the Jerusalem mint. They are common in the Jaffa region, as the content of private collections in Benyamina, Heftzibah, and Hadera shows. In contrast, the Jerusalem hoard *IGCH* 1623 (**342**) contains only six of these imitations, a proportion similar to that in a private collection known to Kindler gathered in the region of Jerusalem (only 1% of the bronzes of Alexander Jannaeus are imitations). Since Jaffa was the sole port active in the area at the time of Alexander Jannaeus, it is logical to attribute to him the production of these coins meant for the local population, a production that surely lasted a long time, in view of the numerous dies employed. The dating of the originals is problematical (90–85?); the imitations must be contemporary.

Disposition: Jerusalem, Department of Antiquities

Bibliography:
Kindler, A. "The Jaffa hoard of Alexander Jannaeus' coins," *Israel Exploration Journal* 4 (1954), pp. 170–185 (= *Recent Studies and Discoveries on Ancient Jewish and Syrian Coins*, Jerusalem, 1954, pp. 34–49).
Kadman, L. "The monetary development of Palestine in the light of coin hoards," in A. Kindler (ed.) *International Numismatic Convention, Jerusalem, 27–31 December 1963. The Patterns of Monetary Development in Phoenicia and Palestine in Antiquity*, Tel Aviv, 1967, no. 20. 850 AE only.

313. Tartus (ancient Antaradus). *IGCH* 1574. 1968

Burial: after 83/2
Contents: 28 AR+

Aradus: 24 autonomous tetr. (years 132, 163, 164, 165 (3), 166, 167 (4), 168 (5), 169, 171 (2), 172, 173 (5), 174, 177 = 83/2 BC)
Tyre: 1 tetr. (year 33 = 94/3 BC)

Seyrig noted this hoard, which he saw in Beirut where a broker from Tartus had brought it. Thirty-one years separate the specimen of year 132 (128/7 BC) from the one immediately following it, which bears the date 163 (97/6 BC). From 163 to 177 (83/2 BC), the years are represented nearly without a break. The Tyrian tetradrachm from year 33 (94/3 BC) is on the Ptolemaic standard. The latest Aradian tetradrachm establishes a burial date after 83/2 BC.

Disposition: Dispersed

Bibliography:
Seyrig 1973, no. 33.

314. Akkar. *IGCH* 1583 = *CH* 1.75 = *CH* 10.348. 1951

Burial: Before 76/5 (Houghton, Lorber, Hoover 2008); after 33/2 (H. Seyrig).
Contents: 16 tetr. AR, marble head (?)

Seleucus VI: 2 Antioch
Antiochus X: 9 Antioch
Philip Philadelphus: 1 Tarsus (?); 3 Antioch
Phraates IV: 1 Seleuceia on the Tigris (year 280 = 33/2 BC)

The coins are oxidized in a similar manner (green on the surface, red beneath), guaranteeing the find's unity. Nonetheless, Houghton, Lorber, Hoover 2008 doubt this because the Parthian coin is late (33/2 BC) compared to the others. In his notes, Seyrig (H. Seyrig Archives, Bibliothèque nationale de France, dossier 271) adds that "a small female head in white marble seems to have been discovered with these coins,"[72] which he describes (height: 6.8 cm).

Disposition: Dispersed

Bibliography:
Seyrig 1973, no. 37.
Houghton, Lorber, Hoover 2008, p. 101.

315. Aleppo, ancient Beroea, Cyrrhestica. *IGCH* 1575 = *CH* 1.75. 1940

Burial: 76/5?
Contents: 20+ tetr. AR

Philip I Philadelphus: 20 Antioch

72. "avec ces monnaies aurait été découverte une petite tête féminine de marbre blanc."

These coins were seen by H. Seyrig with a merchant in Homs, who stated that they had been discovered in the town of Aleppo.

Disposition: Commerce, Homs

Bibliography:
Seyrig 1973, no. 32.
Houghton, Lorber, Hoover 2008, p. 100.

316. Seleuceia Pieria. *IGCH* 1573. 1932–1939

Burial: 76/5?
Contents: 4 AE, in excavation. Cores of plated coins?

Philip I Philadelphus: Antioch 4 tetr. (bronze only)

These four bronzes were discovered together under a mosaic. They show no trace of silvering, although they are probably plated tetradrachms. Houghton, Lorber, Hoover 2008 consider they are contemporary with their silver prototypes and lowers Waage 1952's proposed dating.

Disposition: Antakya?

Bibliography:
Waage, D. B. *Antioch on the Orontes, IV 2, Greek, Roman, Byzantine and Crusaders' Coins*, Princeton, 1952, p. 23, nos. 246–249.
Houghton, Lorber, Hoover 2008, p. 100.

317. Syria. *CH* 10.345. Early 1980

Burial: 76/5?
Contents: 53+ tetr. AR

Philip I Philadelphus: 1 Tarsus (?); 52 Antioch

P. Girardi, who lived in Aleppo, brought these coins to Houghton's attention.

Disposition: Commerce

Bibliography:
Houghton, Lorber, Hoover 2008, p. 100.

318. Unknown Findspot. *CH* 10.346. 1991

Burial: 76/5
Contents: 16 tetr. AR

16 AR
Philip I Philadelphus: 12 Antioch; 4 uncert.

Disposition: Commerce

Bibliography:
Houghton, Lorber, Hoover 2008, p. 154.

319. Unknown Findspot. *CH* 10.347. 2003

Burial: 76/5
Contents: 10 tetr. AR

16 AR
Philip I Philadelphus: 10 uncert.

Disposition: Gorny & Mosch 126, 14 Oct. 2003, lot 3066.

Bibliography:
Houghton, Lorber, Hoover 2008, p. 155.

320. Damascus. *CH* 2.121. 1968

Burial: 75?
Contents: 5+ AE

Aretas III of Nabataea: 5+ AE

These coins appeared on the Jerusalem market in 1968, the seller indicating that they were from a more important hoard found in the Damascus region. Their uniform patina confirmed a common origin.

Disposition: Jerusalem, A. Spaer, E. Groswirth, M. Rosenberger collections

Bibliography:
Meshorer, Y. Nabataean Coins, Jerusalem, 1975, p. 15.

321. El-Jib (ancient Gibeon), Judaea. *IGCH* 1612. 1956

Burial: 75
Contents: 23 AE, in excavation

Alexander Jannaeus (103–76 BC)

Pritchard 1962 indicates that these coins were buried directly beneath the floor in the corner of a room. No detailed description; coins photographed in a pile.

Disposition: unknown

Bibliography:
Pritchard, J. M. *Gibeon, Where the Sun Stood Still*, Princeton, 1962, pp. 76–77, fig. 40.
Kadman, L. "The monetary development of Palestine in the light of coin hoards," in A. Kindler (ed.) *International Numismatic Convention, Jerusalem, 27–31 December 1963. The Patterns of Monetary Development in Phoenicia and Palestine in Antiquity*, Tel Aviv, 1967, no. 21.

322. Samaria. *IGCH* 1614 = *CH* 7.110 = Noe 901. 1910

Burial: 74
Contents: 1 AR, 22 AE, in excavation

Antiochus VII: 1 tetr. Tyre, 131/0 BC (no. 3652)
Tyre: 22 AE, dated from 94 to 74 BC (no. 3653–3674)

Reisner et al. 1924 describes how this hoard was discovered in the midst of excavations, wrapped in a rag, beneath the floor of a room in a house from the last period of the pre-Herodian city. The coins were stuck together from corrosion. The Tyrian bronzes constitute more than half of those found during the excavation.

Bibliography:
Reisner, G. A., C. S. Fisher, and D. G. Lyon. *Harvard Excavations at Samaria 1908–1910*, Cambridge, 1924, 1, pp. 52, 253, 261, 264.
Kadman, L. "The monetary development of Palestine in the light of coin hoards," in A. Kindler (ed.) *International Numismatic Convention, Jerusalem, 27–31 December 1963. The Patterns of Monetary Development in Phoenicia and Palestine in Antiquity*, Tel Aviv, 1967, no. 11, counts one more silver coin than the excavation publication.
Houghton, Lorber, Hoover 2008, p. 116.

323. Coele Syria? *CH* 10.349. c. 1988

Burial: 72
Contents: 244 AE, 1 Pb

Seleucus III or Antiochus III: 1 Antioch
Antiochus III: 1 Ecbatana; 1 uncert.
Antiochus IV: 1 Tyr; 1 Ake-Ptolemais; 1 Ake-Ptolemais?
Antiochus V?: 1 Tyre (161/0 BC)
Demetrius I: 1 Tyre
Demetrius II (1): 5 Tyre
Antiochus VII: 1 Antioch
Demetrius II (2): 1 Damascus, 1 Sidon
Antiochus VIII: 1 Antioch; 22 Ake-Ptolemais?
Demetrius III: 1 Seleuceia Pieria; 93 Damascus
Antiochus XII: 66 Damascus
Cleopatra Selene and Antiochus XIII: 1 Damascus (c. 80–72?)
Philip V of Macedon: 1
Ptolemy II or III: 1 Tyre
Aretas III of Nabataea: 1 Damascus
Alexander Jannaeus: 1 Jerusalem
Ituraeans: Ptolemaios son of Mennaios, 1 Chalcis
Antioch: 3
Ake-Ptolemais: 7
Sidon: 27
Uncertain: 2 AE
Uncertain: 1 Pb

This hoard was sold at C. J. Martin Coins, Ltd., in London on December 22, 1988. The container was apparently of organic material, perhaps leather. 200 coins are Seleucid issues, mostly from Damascus (66.12% of the total), followed by Tyre (14.05%), suggesting that the provenance is Coele Syria, probably the region between Damascus, Ake-Ptolemais, and Tyre. 80% of the coins are of Demetrius III and Antiochus XII, 11.5% of Antiochus VIII; other reigns are only marginally represented. This concentration led Wright to wonder whether the absence of the cadet branch of the Seleucids (i.e., descendants of Antiochus IV) does not result from the selective withdrawal of their issues on the orders of the major branch: "It appears from the hoard evidence that during this period, in what was to be the closing phase of the Seleucid kingdom, concepts of succession and legitimacy drove the authorities to prevent the circulation of issues produced by rival Seleukid kings" (p. 263). Iossif 2011b, p. 454, challenges this notion.

One of the Tyrian bronzes seems to be a posthumous issue of Antiochus V: the reading of the date is apparently certain. This is a unique coin. That of Cleopatra Selene and Antiochus XIII, very rare, dates from the period between the occupations of Damascus by Aretas III of Nabataea in 82 and by Tigranes in 72.

The lead coinage bears types related to Ptolemaic types. It could be an instance of an issue struck out of necessity during Ptolemy X's march on Damascus in 103–101 BC, as Hoover 2008 has recently proposed.

Disposition: C. Pitchfork collection, Australia

Bibliography:

Wright, N. L. "A late Seleukid bronze hoard, c. 1988 (*CH* 10.349)," *CH* 10, New York, 2010, pp. 245–264.

324. Coast of Mt. Carmel. 1994

Burial: 72/1
Contents: 1,755+ AR, in excavation

Ptolemy IX or X: 14 tetr. Alexandria
Cleopatra III and Ptolemy X: 89 tetr. Alexandria.
Cleopatra III and Ptolemy X or Ptolemy X alone: 3 tetr. Alexandria.
Ptolemy X: 402 tetr. Alexandria
Ptolemy IX: 19 tetr. Alexandria
Ptolemy XII: 848 tetr. Alexandria
Cleopatra III and Ptolemy X–Ptolemy XII (to 72/1 BC): 380 tetr. Alexandria

The Israel Antiquities Authority discovered this hoard of exceptional size along the shores of Mt. Carmel. 1,755 coins could be studied, while a block of coins, fused together, weighing 23 kg, was kept for exhibition. Each reign is represented by a large number of specimens. The burial date must be related to the campaigns of Tigranes and his presence in Ptolemais.

Galili contributes the following details: "A preliminary assessment, based upon the latest coin identified, suggests that the hoard and the wreckage event can be dated to about 63 BCE. Additional artifacts recovered from the site and probably originated from the same shipwreck are: two lead stocks and a lead assembly piece, all three are of wooden anchors, bronze nails, lead sheathing fragments, a lead brazier, a lead salvage ring and several sounding leads. Judging by the distribution of the artifacts on the sea bottom (at water depth 3–4 m, some 80–130 m offshore), it seems that the sailing ship drifted ashore during a storm, grounded and was wrecked by the shore breakers" (Galili and Sharvit 1999; Galili personal communication 2013).

Disposition: Israel Antiquities Authority

Bibliography:

Galili, E. and J. Sharvit. "Haifa, Underwater Surveys," *Hadashot Arkheologiot. Excavations and Surveys in Israel*, 110 (1999), p. 17.
Olivier, J. *Archè et chrèmata en Egypte au IIe s. avant J.-C. (204–81 av. J.-C.). Etude de numismatique et d'histoire*, Etudes Alexandrines, Alexandria, forthcoming.

325. Hama (ancient Epiphaneia). *IGCH* 1576. 1937

Burial: 70
Contents: 5 AR, in excavation

Aradus: 5 autonomous tetr. (92/1 BC, 87/6 BC (2), 73/2 BC (2))

Disposition: Copenhagen

Bibliography:
Thomsen, R. "The Graeco-Roman coins" in A. Papanicolaou-Christensen, R. Thomsen, and G. Ploug (eds.) *Hama, fouilles et recherches de la fondation Carlsberg, 1931–1938*, III.3, *The Graeco-Roman Objects of Clay, the Coins and the Necropolis*, Copenhagen, 1986, p. 63.

326. Israel. *CH* 8.522. Before 1992

Burial: 70
Contents: c. 4,000 AE

Hasmoneans: *prutot*

The sale catalogue describes the find thus: "hoard of approximately 4,000 Jewish AE *Prutah*: includes small AE leptons and *prutah* of various issuers." Some were cleaned, others still had incrustations.

Disposition: Commerce, New York

Bibliography:
Superior Galleries, New York, 11–12 Dec. 1992, lot 2236

327. Tiberias, Galilee. *IGCH* 1615. 1967

Burial: 70
Contents: 200 AE

Alexander Jannaeus

Disposition: Dispersed. Information from Y. Meshorer.

328. Mardine? Upper Mesopotamia. *CH* 1.75. 1952

Burial: Vers 70–57?
Contents: 88 AR+

Seleucus VI: 1 tetr.
Antiochus X: 1 tetr.
Philip Philadelphus: 30 tetr.
Mithridates II: 19 dr.
Artabanus II: 14 dr.
Sinatruces: 8 dr.
Phraates III: 15 dr.

The lot does not contain any tetradrachms of Tigranes, which is surprising, but perhaps they were removed from the hoard to be sold separately. Such coins are highly sought after by Armenian collectors. In his notes preserved in the Bibliothèque nationale de France (dossier 268), Seyrig states that he saw this find "at Petro Hanazoglou's in Constantinople, November, 1952."

Disposition: Commerce, Istanbul

Bibliography:
Seyrig 1973, no. 34

329. Syria. *IGCH* 1577. 1968

Burial: 69
Contents: 25+ AR

Tigranes I: tetr. Antioch

Disposition: Dispersed. Information from Münzen und Medaillen, Bâle

330. Unknown Findspot. *CH* 10.350. 2007

Burial: 64
Contents: 127 tetr. AR

Philip I Philadelphus: 76 Antioch; 50 Antioch or another mint
Antiochus XIII: 1 tetr.

Disposition: Dispersed, U.S. market

Bibliography:
Houghton, Lorber, Hoover 2008, p. 155.

331. Ascalon. *IGCH* 1616. 1927

Burial: 62
Contents: 24 AR

Antiochus VII: 2 tetr. Tyre (years 174, 182)
Ascalon: 6 tetr. (years 31–41)

Disposition: Unknown. Information from E. S. G. Robinson

332. Nahr Ibrahim. *IGCH* 1618 = Noe 725. 1874

Burial: after 61/0
Contents: 150+ AR

Aradus: more than 150 autonomous tetr.

In this hoard, discovered 25 km north of Beirut, the latest tetradrachm is dated to Aradian year 199, leading one to suppose burial occurred after 61/0 BC. The oldest coins are few in number, most dating from the years 160–199.

Disposition: H. C. Reichhardt: more than 150

Bibliography:
Reichhardt, H. C. "Miscellen. Münzen aradischer Tetradrachmen," *Numismatische Zeitschrift* (1876), p. 385.

333. Lebanon. *CH* 8.527. 1984

Burial: after 61/0
Contents: 23+ AR

Aradus: 23 autonomous tetr. (years 167 to 199 = 61/0 BC)
The hoard's precise findspot is unknown. Burial occurred after 61/0 BC, based on the date of the latest tetradrachm. The group is homogeneous, with the same characteristics as finds made in the Aradian Peraea: it contains tetradrachms of this city exclusively, with under one hundred items. These observations lead one to suppose that it was buried close to the area controlled by Aradus.

334. Palestine *IGCH* 1617. 1942

Burial: after 61
Contents: 30+ AR
Coins studied: 15/30+

Antiochus VII: 1+ tetr. Tyre (year 181)
Demetrius II (2): 4+ tetr. Tyre (years 184, 186)
Tyre: 10 tetr. (years 45–64)

According to Spaer (*IGCH*), the hoard contained at least 15 additional tetradrachms of Antiochus VII and Demetrius II struck at Tyre. Kadman 1967, citing the same source, attributes 10 tetradrachms to Antiochus VII and 10 others to Demetrius II.

Disposition: A. Spaer collection, Jerusalem 14. Information from A. Spaer.

Bibliography:
Kadman, L. "The monetary development of Palestine in the light of coin hoards," in A. Kindler (ed.) *International Numismatic Convention, Jerusalem, 27–31 December 1963. The Patterns of Monetary Development in Phoenicia and Palestine in Antiquity*, Tel Aviv, 1967, no. 14.
Houghton, Lorber, Hoover 2008, p. 116.

335. Aleppo, ancient Beroea, Cyrrhestica. *IGCH* 1578 = *CH* 1.75. 1950

Burial: 55
Contents: 22+ AR

Philip I Philadelphus: 1 Antioch
Roman imitations of Philip I Philadelphus: 21 Antioch

The monogram "AB" is that of the governor Aulus Gabinius (57–55 BC), according to Seyrig 1973.

Disposition: Dispersed

Bibliography:
Seyrig 1973, no. 35.
Houghton, Lorber, Hoover 2008, p. 100.
RPC 1, 4124, p. 610, hoard no. 1.

336. Beirut. *IGCH* 1621 = *CH* 1.75. 1950

Burial: after 54/3
Contents: 34+ AR Ptolemaic

Tyre: 34 tetr. (years 3, 27, 31, 40, 45, 49, 51, 58, 59, 61, 63, 64, 65, 67, 68, 70, 71, 73)

The Seyrig Archives (Bibliothèque nationale de France, dossier 6.I.b) specify the precise findspot as the quarter of Achrafiyeh. There was word of some other coins in the same hoard, but Seyrig never saw them.

Disposition: Dispersed

Bibliography:
Seyrig 1973, no. 47.

337. Hama (ancient Epiphaneia). *IGCH* 1580. 1937

Burial: after 53/2
Contents: 51 AE, in excavation

Antioch: 49 (to 53/2 BC)
Uncert.: 2

These bronzes were discovered near a wall north of house II, in an apparently open space (Ploug 1985, p. 21). Most of the dates are illegible because they were off flan or had disappeared through oxidation. Dating is on two systems: the Seleucid Era and that of Pompey, which began in 66 BC.

Disposition: Copenhagen

Bibliography:
Thomsen, R. "The Graeco-Roman coins" in A. Papanicolaou-Christensen, R. Thomsen, and G. Ploug (eds.) *Hama, fouilles et recherches de la fondation Carlsberg, 1931–1938*, III.3, *The Graeco-Roman Objects of Clay, the Coins and the Necropolis*, Copenhagen, 1986, p. 63.
Ploug, G. (ed.), *Hama, fouilles et recherches de la fondation Carlsberg, 1931–1938*, III.1, *The Graeco-Roman Town*, Copenhagen, 1985.

338. Unknown Findspot (Aradian Peraea?). Before 1991

Burial: after 51/0
Contents: 197+ AR

Lot A: Paris 1991
Aradus: 115 tetr. (years 124, 165, 166, 167, 168 (5), 169, 172, 173 (8), 174 (3), 176 (2), 177 (3), 178 (6), 179, 181 (2), 182, 183, 184 (4), 185 (7), 187 (2), 188 (4), 192 (3), 193 (7), 194 (3), 195 (5), 196 (22), 197 (5), 199 (5), 200 = 60/59 BC).

Lot B: New York, December 1994
Aradus: 80 tetr. (years 130, 160, 162, 163, 165, 166 (2), 167, 168 (5), 173 (5), 174 (3), 176, 177 (6), 178 (2), 179 (4), 180, 181 (8), 182, 183 (3), 184 (3), 185 (2), 187, 188 (3), 192 (5), 193 (4), 194 (2), 195, 196 (3), 197 (4), 198 (2), 199 (2), 201 = 59/8 BC).
Laodiceia ad Mare: 2 tetr., year 30 (52/1) and year 31 (51/0)[73].

These two lots are discussed below, pp. 200–206.

Disposition: Commerce; Paris, BnF 12

Bibliography:
Duyrat, F. *Arados hellénistique. Étude historique et monétaire*, BAH 173, Beirut, 2005, p. 170.

339. Syria. *CH* 1.103. 1970/1

Burial: mid-1st cent. BC

Hundreds of Seleucid tetr. to Philip

Disposition: Dispersed

340. Syria. *CH* 6.50 = *CH* 8.531. No date

Burial: c. 50
Contents: 200+ AR
Coins studied: 21/200

Aradus: 3 autonomous tetr. (years 143, 162, 179 = 81/0 BC)
Laodiceia ad Mare: 18 tetr. (years 14, 15, 17, 18, 20, 23, 25, 26 = 56/5 BC)

This large hoard consisted of 200 tetradrachms at least, only 21 of which are described in *IGCH*. The latest of the Aradian group are dated year 179 (81/0 BC), and the latest from Laodiceia ad Mare is year 26 (56/5 BC), placing burial around 50 BC.

Disposition: British Museum 6

Bibliography:
Mørkholm O., "The autonomous tetradrachms of Laodiceia ad Mare," *American Numismatic Society Museum Notes* 28 (1983), pp. 89–107, p. 98. This hoard was first published in *CH* 6.50, but without the Aradian tetradrachm.

341. Syria. *IGCH* 1579. 1951

Burial: 50
Contents: 179 AR

Ariarathes V: 163 dr.
Ariarathes VI: 6 dr.

73. These coins correspond to the variants 18a and 19a in the catalogue of Mørkholm 1983a, p. 104.

Ariarathes VII: 6 dr.
Ariarathes IX: 2 dr. (series II)
Ariobarzanes I: 1 dr.
Ariobarzanes II: I dr.

Disposition: Dispersed. Information from files at the American Numismatic Society

342. Mt. Ophel, Jerusalem. *IGCH* 1623 = Noe 714. 1926

Burial: 50
Contents: 319 AE, in excavation
Alexander Jannaeus: 303
John Hyrcanus II: 4
Uncertain (probably John Hyrcanus II): 4
Illegible: 8

Lambert attributed Numbers 1–4, marked with an A, to John Hyrcanus I, but they have been reattributed to John Hyrcanus II. Kadman 1967, following Lambert 1927, counts 79 bronzes of John Hyrcanus II and 240 of Alexander Jannaeus.

Disposition: Jerusalem, Department of Antiquities

Bibliography:
Crowfoot, J. W. and G. M. Fitzgerald. *Excavations in the Tyropoeon Valley, Palestine Exploration Fund Annual*, Jerusalem, 1927, pp. 104–105.
Lambert, C. "A hoard of Jewish bronze coins from Ophel," *Palestine Exploration Quarterly* 1927, pp. 184–188 (*non vidi*).
Kadman, L. "The monetary development of Palestine in the light of coin hoards," in A. Kindler (ed.) *International Numismatic Convention, Jerusalem, 27–31 December 1963. The Patterns of Monetary Development in Phoenicia and Palestine in Antiquity*, Tel Aviv, 1967, no. 18.

343. Gaza Region. *IGCH* 1627. 1940

Burial: 50–30
Contents: 400 AR

Ascalon: tetr. (including 1 with portrait of Cleopatra VII; years 21, 25, 33, 34, 40, 41)

Disposition: A. Spaer, Jerusalem 6; private collections, Jerusalem 6; private collections, Tel Aviv 20. Information from A. Spaer

344. Safed (ancient Seph), Galilee. *IGCH* 1622 = Noe 879. Before 1877

Burial: 49
Contents: 6+ AR

Ascalon: 6 tetr. (to year 55 = 49 BC)

Saulcy 1874–1877, in a note discussing unpublished coins of Ascalon in his collection, alludes rather obliquely to this hoard. Concerning item 6, dated to year 41: "I owe the possession of this beautiful coin to the friendship of Monsieur Pérétié. It comes, as far as he knows, from the large find of coins of the Ptolemies made some years ago in the vicinity of Safed, in Galilee"[74] (p. 126). The tetradrachm of Cleopatra VII, year 55, item 7, also comes from this hoard (p. 127). BMC Palestine, nos. 18–20, states clearly that these specimens (two of Ascalon with portrait of 'Ptolemy XV', one with Cleopatra VII's: pl. XII, 1–3, dated years 41, 50, and 55) come from this same hoard and the collections of Pérétié and Saulcy. Noe 1937 points out two specimens in Athens, based upon Svoronos 1904–1908, pl. 63, 9–13, and IV, pl. D, 25. Kadman 1967 provides no details on the contents.

Disposition: London 3 (BMC pl. XII 1–3); Athens 2 (Svoronos 1904–1908, III, pl. 63, 9–13; IV, pl. D, 25)

Bibliography:
Saulcy, F. (de). "Note sur quelques monnaies inédites d'Ascalon," *Revue numismatique* (1874–1877), pp. 124–135.
Svoronos, J.-N. *Τα νομίσματα του κράτους των Πτολεμαίων* 4 vol., Athens, 1904–1908.
Kadman, L. "The monetary development of Palestine in the light of coin hoards," in A. Kindler (ed.) *International Numismatic Convention, Jerusalem, 27–31 December 1963. The Patterns of Monetary Development in Phoenicia and Palestine in Antiquity*, Tel Aviv, 1967, no. 8.

345. Syria. *CH* 10.358. 1991

Burial: 47/6 or after
Contents: 5 tetr. AR

Philip I Philadelphus: 1 uncert. Cilicia; 3 Antioch
Roman imitation of Philip I Philadelphus: 1 Antioch

Houghton saw this hoard in the trade.

Disposition: Commerce

Bibliography:
Houghton, Lorber, Hoover 2008, p. 100.

346. Beth Sahur, near Bethlehem. *IGCH* 1624. 1946

Burial: 47–45
Contents: 63 AE

John Hyrcanus II

Meshorer proposed the burial date. He shows that archaeological discoveries of this sort do not justify saying whether John Hyrcanus I struck coinage. Kadman 1967, following Sukenik 1947, attributes 26 bronzes to John Hyrcanus I and 37 to Alexander Jannaeus.

Disposition: Jerusalem, Hebrew University.

Bibliography:
Kadman, L. "The monetary development of Palestine in the light of coin hoards," in A. Kindler (ed.) *International Numismatic Convention, Jerusalem, 27–31 December 1963. The Patterns of Monetary Development in*

74. "Je dois la possession de cette belle monnaie à l'amitié de M. Pérétié. Elle provient, à ce qu'il croit, de la grande trouvaille de monnaies des Ptolémées, faite il y a quelques années, dans les environs de Safed, en Galilée."

Phoenicia and Palestine in Antiquity, Tel Aviv, 1967, no. 19.
Meshorer, Y. *Jewish Coins at the Second Temple Period*, Tel Aviv, 1967, pp. 50–52.
Sukenik E. L., "A hoard of coins of John Hyrcanus," *Jewish Quarterly Review* 27 (1947), pp. 281–282 (*non vidi*).

347. Syria (Latakia/Laodiceia) or Northern Phoenicia (Arwad/Aradus). *IGCH* 1581 = *CH* 3.78 = Noe 604 and 871. 1922

Burial: after 45
Contents: 123 AR + 27 AR
Aradus: more than 34 autonomous tetr. (the latest is 199 (61/0 BC))
Tyre: more than 10 tetr.
Seleuceia Pieria: more than 9 tetr.
Laodiceia ad Mare: more than 70 tetr.

The inventory of *IGCH* is supplemented by *CH* 3.78:
Aradus: 7 autonomous tetr. (to 186 = 74/3 BC)
Tyre: 10 tetr. (to 86 BC)
Seleuceia Pieria: 10 tetr. (to year 22)

This hoard's findspot is very difficult to pinpoint. A third hypothesis proposes an origin in the region of Aleppo. Noe 1937 probably lists the same find under two different entries (Noe 871 is said to have contained more than 200 tetradrachms of Aradus, Seleucis, and Tyre). These possibilities lie within the Aradian sphere of influence. This hoard contained more than the 123 coins inventoried in *IGCH* and supplemented in *Coin Hoards*. The latest tetradrachm of Laodiceia establishes a burial date after 45 BC, that is, a time when Phoenicia and Syria were joined to form a Roman province. In fact, nos. 47 and 48 in the British Museum carry the legend ΙΟΥΛΙΕΩΝ ΤΩΝ ΚΑΙ ΛΑΟΔΙΚΕΩΝ, and no. 47 is dated with the letter Γ (3), which has been connected to Caesar's passage through the region in 47 and the inauguration of his era at Antioch in autumn, 49 BC. The cities acquired an important autonomy in the first half of the 1st century, encouraging the multiplication of tetradrachm issues with municipal types. As can be seen in this hoard, the circulation of municipal coins endures to the end of the first century despite Roman domination. This explains how coins of Aradus are commingled with those of the large neighboring cities in a hoard nonetheless buried when Aradus was no longer issuing its last tetradrachms, save in small quantities.

Hill 1925 describes the specimens acquired by the British Museum: four dated tetradrachms of Laodiceia.

Disposition: New York 61 (Laodiceia 16, Seleuceia 9, Aradus 31, Tyre 5) and rubbings of other coins; London 4 (Laodiceia)

Bibliography:
Hill, G. F. "Greek coins acquired by the British Museum in 1924," *Numismatic Chronicle* 1925, pp. 14–17, nos. 45–48.

348. Tartus (ancient Antaradus). *IGCH* 1582. 1952

Burial: after 44/3
Contents: 18+ AR

Aradus: 16 autonomous tetr. (years 139, 162, 165, 166 (2), 168 (3), 171, 173 (2), 174, 181, 184, 216 and one illegible date)
Laodiceia ad Mare: 2 tetr.

Seyrig saw this hoard in 1952, in the hands of a broker from Tartus. From years 139 to 184, 14 tetradrachms of Aradus form a homogeneous group. That of 216 stands apart from the rest and belongs to the rare coins, later than 200, inventoried in the present catalogue. The oldest tetradrachm of Laodiceia is dated to 51 BC. The second is dated year 2 of the Caesarian Era, that is, 47/6 BC. (Seyrig 1964, p. 40, n. 2). But it is the latest tetradrachm of Aradus that shows burial occurred after 44/3 BC.

Disposition: Dispersed

Bibliography:
Seyrig, H. "Monnaies hellénistiques 12. Questions aradiennes," *Revue numismatique* (1964), pp. 7–67.
Seyrig 1973, no. 36.

349. Jericho. *CH* 2.128. 1973

Burial: 40 BC or after
Contents: 20 AE

Antigonus Mattathias 20 AE:
13 double cornucopia and inscription in paleo-Hebrew "Mattathias the Great Priest and the Counsel of the Jews"/Ivy wreath, ΑΝΤΙΓΟΝΟΥ ΒΑΣΙΛΕΩΣ
7 Cornucopiae, inscription/Ivy wreath, ΒΑΣ ΑΝΤΙ-ΓΟΝΟΥ

Netzer 1973 announces this discovery, made amidst a rescue dig undertaken on the site of Herod's palace in Jericho during the winter of 1973, on the north hill, near the reservoir. This reservoir seems to have served as a ritual pool around which some buildings have been excavated. It is hard to date the complex with ceramic evidence, but it was probably in active use between the first century BC and the first century AD. The coins were discovered west of the pool. Meshorer 2004 gives details on this hoard, suggesting, p. 289, a comparison with a similar hoard found in Jerusalem (**352**).

Bibliography:
Netzer, E. "Jericho," *Israel Exploration Journal* 23 (1973), p. 260.
_______. *Qadmoniot* 7/1–2 (1974), p. 31: photograph of coins in piles (in Hebrew).
Meshorer, Y. "The coins," in E. Netzer and R. Laureys-Chachy (eds.) *Hasmonean and Herodian Palaces at Jericho: Final Reports of the 1973–1987 Excavations.* II. *Stratigraphy and Architecture*, Jerusalem, 2004, pp. 289–312, hoard p. 299, nos. 579–598 and pl. IX.

350. Jerusalem, Temple Mount, outside the East Wall. *IGCH* 1625. 1968

Burial: 40
Contents: 19 AE

John Hyrcanus II: 19 AE (*BMC* John Hyrcanus I 2 (4), 15 (8), 34 (5), 48 (2))

Disposition: Jerusalem (?)

Bibliography:
Kindler, AHHI 3.1 (1968), pp. 1–8, illus. (in Hebrew, *non vidi*).

351. Palestine. *IGCH* 1626. 1942

Burial: 40
Contents: 43+ AR Ptolemaic

Cleopatra VII: tetr. Alexandria (years 10–12, Sv. 1824–26)

Disposition: A. Spaer, Jerusalem 3 (one of each date). Information from A. Spaer

352. Jerusalem, Jewish Quarter. Year Unknown

Burial: after 40
Contents: 31 AE, 1 flan

Antigonus Mattathias: 31 AE
1 flan (no. U13, in Meshorer 1982, p. 157)

Avigad 1983, p. 74, notes that the Hasmonean buildings have largely disappeared, probably demolished during the time of the Herods. Only cisterns, pools, and baths hewn in the rock, along with material from the Hasmonean era that has been found, provide evidence for the period. Still, several vestiges of Hasmonean buildings are located in sector "A." Some Ptolemaic coins of the third century and Seleucids of the second as well as Hasmonean bronzes, have been discovered in context (with no further details, p. 75). Nor is the hoard itself described in detail: "We also uncovered a hoard of 23 coins of Mattathias Antigonus, last of the Hasmonean kings (40–37 BC), which bear similar legends: 'of King Antigonus' in Greek, and 'Mattathias the High Priest and the hever of the Jews' in archaizing Hebrew" (p. 75). This figure is mistaken: the photo on p. 76 shows 31 coins.

Shiloh and Ariel 1990, p. 115, note that Avigad described as a coin a coin flan intermingled with the find's 31 bronzes. It is clearly discernible in the photo.
Similar hoard: *CH* 2.128 (**349**).

Bibliography:
Netzer, E. *Qadmoniot* 7/1–2 (1974), p. 31 (in Hebrew): picture of the coins in a pile.
Avigad, N. *Discovering Jerusalem*, Jerusalem, 1983, p. 75–77.
Meshorer, Y. *Ancient Jewish Coinage* I, New York, 1982.
Shiloh, Y. and D. T. Ariel (eds.) "Coins, flans, and moulds," *Excavations at the City of David 1978–1985. 2. Imported Stamped Amphora, Handles, Coins, Worked Bone and Ivory, and Glass*, Jerusalem, 1990, pp. 99–118.

353. Kırıkhan, Hatay province. *CH* 9.579. Before 1994

Burial: 38/7
Contents: 3,000+ AR, plated coins
Coins studied: 31/3,000+

Alexander I Balas: 1 dr. Antioch
Ariarathes IV of Cappadocia: 4 dr. (1 plated)
Ariarathes VI: 1 dr. (1 plated)
Ariobarzanes I: 22 dr. (2 plated)
Ariobarzanes II: 2
Ariarathes X: 1

These coins come from the region of Kayseri, the ancient Caesarea in Cappadocia. The oldest dates from 188 BC, the most recent from 38/7 BC. Other hoards of Cappadocian drachms present a range of about 100 years.

Disposition: Private collection Kırıkhan

Bibliography:
Saraç, L. and A. Davesne. "Un lot de drachmes cappadociennes à Kırıkhan (Hatay)," in M. Amandry and G. Le Rider (eds.) *Trésors et circulation monétaire en Anatolie antique*, Paris, 1994, pp. 61–64, pl. IX.
Houghton, Lorber, Hoover 2008, p. 101.

354. 'Ein Feshkha. *CH* 10.361. 2001

Burial: 37
Contents: 8 AE, in excavation

Antigonus Mattathias: 8 Jerusalem

Bibliography:
Bijovsky, G. "A hoard of coins of Mattathias Antigonus from 'Ein Feshkha," *Israel Exploration Journal* 54/1 (2004), pp. 75–76.

355. Jerusalem, Mt. Scopus. *IGCH* 1628. 1944

Burial: after 29
Contents: 11 AR

Demetrius II (1): 2 tetr. Tyre (142/1, 130–129 BC)
Tyre: 9 tetr. (42/1–30/29 BC)

Disposition: Hebrew University, Jerusalem

Bibliography:
Sukenik, *Dinaburg Anniversary Volume*, Jerusalem, 1949, pp. 102–103 (*non vidi*).
Houghton, Lorber, Hoover 2008, p. 117.

356. Syria. *CH* 6.52. 1978

Burial: 25
Contents: 62 AR

Phraates IV: 62 tetr.

Disposition: Commerce, American Numismatic Society 3

357. Khirbet Qumran. March 21, 1955

Burial: 8 BC
Contents: 561 AR, in excavation

Antiochus VII: 28 tetr., 32 didr. Tyre
Demetrius II: 24 tetr., 18 didr. Tyre
Tyre: 312 tetr., 136 didr.
Uncert.: 5 didr.
Roman denarii: 6

Seyrig's 1955 description of the hoard (H. Seyrig Archives, Bibliothèque nationale de France, dossier 232) has this note in his own hand in the margin: "Qumran Hoard. Inventory of the three lots I personally made in Jerusalem, May, 1955."[75] He carefully describes the three lots, especially lot A, which remained in Jerusalem, and which has never been the object of a proper study. The coins on his reckoning break down as follows:

Lot A: 222 coins, tetradrachms, didrachms, and denarii
Lot B: 186 coins, tetradrachms and didrachms
Lot C: 153 coins, tetradrachms and didrachms

The circumstances of the discovery of the hoard(s) stored in three different pots in the same space remain unclear (Lönnqvist, Lönnqvist 2002, pp. 144–45). Father Roland de Vaux never elaborated, and his description differs slightly from Seyrig's notes. Given the paucity of data surrounding the circumstances of the find, it is worthwhile to cite de Vaux at length (1973, pp. 34–35):

> A further and important piece of evidence from the coin finds must also be taken into account. In addition to the coins which we are about to enumerate we discovered in loc. 120 a hoard of 561 pieces of silver preserved in three pots containing respectively 223, 185, and 153 pieces [cf. *Revue biblique*, LXIII (1956), p. 567–8]. Two of these vessels are of a type which is foreign to those found at Qumran. They are small pots with large mouths and without handles, completely filled with coins, and with their mouths closed with a stopper of palm fibre. By contrast the third vessel was one of the juglets in common use at Khirbet Qumran, and, since its neck was too narrow for the pieces of silver to be dropped in through it, they were inserted by means of a hole which either already existed or which was specially made in the belly of the vessel. These three pots were buried beneath the level of Period II and above that of Period Ib. An analysis of the hoard, therefore, can provide one piece of evidence by which the two periods can be chronologically distinguished. Each of these three collections is identical in composition, and the treasure can be considered as comprising a single hoard. With a few exceptions it includes only Tyrian coins, and these are almost exclusively tetradrachmae. Certain pieces go back to the last monarchs of the Seleucid dynasty, but the majority belong to the autonomous currency of Tyre, and the period when this was in use begins in 126 BC. The later one proceeds in the period the more frequently all the various issues are represented, and the larger the number of new types. The most recent coin in the hoard is a tetradrachm from the year 118 of Tyre (9/8 BC) and several earlier pieces have been countermarked in the same year. But this date provides only a terminus post quem for the burial of the hoard, because in the currency of Tyre, a relative lacuna in the issues of new coins follows after the year 118, and it is not until the year 126 (1 BC/AD 1) that new issues reappear in any quantity. Now in a hoard as representative as this the new issues would certainly have been included had it been amassed after that date. The treasure was therefore buried between 9/8 BC and 1 BC/AD 1. As for its origin, two hypotheses may be put forward: either it was hidden in the ruins during the time when the site was abandoned, between Periods Ib and II, or else it was brought in and put in a safe place at the beginning of period II. If the first hypothesis is correct, then this would imply that the building remained in a ruined condition at least up to 9/8 BC If the second is correct then this would mean that the building had been reoccupied, or was in process of being so, in 1. BC/AD 1 at the latest."

75. "Trésor de Qumrân. Inventaire des trois lots, établi à Jérusalem par moi, mai 1955."

Curiously, the Seyrig Archives mention the date of 1954 on the folder containing the description. They also show his correspondence with Father de Vaux about the discovery, as well as Seyrig's initial thoughts about it. Additionally, Father de Vaux cites one of his letters in 1959, p. 27, n. 1, in 1973, p. 35, n. 1: Seyrig provided him with the burial date of the hoard.

According to Lönnqvist, Lönnqvist 2002, Roland de Vaux, the site's excavator, combined the contents of the three lots in 1955, prior to separating them again. During the 1960s, one lot remained in Jerusalem (A), while the other two (B and C) were removed to Amman (Jordan Archaeological Museum). 58 specimens are currently missing from these last two lots, whether lost or given away. Some contamination from the Roman period seems to have confused the exact content of the three lots discovered on site.

Lönnqvist, Lönnqvist 2006 emphasize the choice of containers: three vases, two of which are of a type otherwise unknown at Qumran. Moreover, 9% of the coins from Lot C are worn or damaged, ruling out any idea of a hoard collected over time, which would put a premium on samples in good condition. Common dies connect several coins in this same lot, highly improbable for coins withdrawn from circulation over time. The existence of worn specimens of debased weight, which were strictly forbidden in paying the Temple tax, argues against the notion that this might be a hoard intended to pay that religious obligation.

Meshorer 2003–2006 revises de Vaux 1973's late dating. The hoard's last Tyrian shekels date from 9/8 BC, whereas we know today that the mint also struck these coins in subsequent years. So burial should be placed c. 8 BC.[76] On this basis, Meshorer offers the following chronology: the site was reoccupied after the earthquake of 31 BC, then abandoned for an unknown reason after 8 BC, remaining so for about a decade. This hypothesis contradicts the excavator's, who imagined abandonment between 31 and the reign of Archelaus (4 BC to 6 AD) (Lönnqvist, Lönnqvist 2006, p. 122). Cf. the entry on the archaeological site (**28**) in chapter 2. Lönnqvist 2007 is a monograph devoted entirely to this hoard, based on what was previously published and on the lots preserved in Amman with descriptive files. This reconstitution is doubtful, especially because it includes 10 denarii down to Caracalla, when Seyrig's original description mentioned only 6, which warranted limiting burial between 9 and 1 BC.

The complex history of this hoard has led me to forego presenting it in detail within the framework of the present work. It merits its own, subsequent study.

Disposition: Lot A, Jerusalem (?), lots B and C: 351 Jordan Archaeological Museum, Amman (Lönnqvist 2007, p. 5), but it is more than the 339 coins (186 + 153) counted by Seyrig in his notes.

Bibliography:
Vaux, R. (de). "Fouilles de Khirbet Qumrân. Rapport préliminaire sur les 3e, 4e et 5e campagnes. V. Les monnaies et les dates d'occupation," *Revue biblique* 63 (1956), pp. 567–569.
_______. *Archaeology and the Dead Sea Scrolls*, London, 1973, p. 34.
Sharabani, M. "Monnaies de Qumran au Musée Rockefeller de Jérusalem," *Revue biblique* 87 (1980), pp. 274–284, pls. III–IV. lot A
Humbert, J.-B., A. Chambon, and R. de Vaux. *Fouilles de Khirbet Qumran et de Ain Feschkha*, I, Göttingen, 1994, p. 330.
Lönnqvist, K. and M. Lönnqvist. *Archaeology of the Hidden Qumran. The New Paradigm*, Helsinki, 2002.
_______. "The numismatic chronology of Qumran: fact and fiction," *Numismatic Chronicle* 166 (2006), pp. 121–166, especially pp. 138–140.
Meshorer, Y. "The coins from Qumran," *Israel Numismatic Journal* 15 (2003–2006), pp. 19–23.
Lönnqvist, K. *The Report of the Amman Lots of the Qumran Silver Coin Hoards. New Chronological Aspects of the Silver Coin Hoard Evidence from Khirbet Qumran at the Dead Sea*, Amman, 2007.

76. Seyrig's notes propose a dating between 9 and 1 BC, but his knowledge of Tyrian coinage was less complete than Meshorer's.

358. Near East. *CH* 2.129. 1974

Burial: late 1st cent. BC
Contents: 6+ AR

Phraates IV: tetr.
Phraataces: tetr.
Disposition: Dispersed

Bibliography:
Anonymous. "A hoard of test-cut Athenian tetradrachms", *Journal of Numismatic Fine Arts* 4 1975, 32.

359. Nablus. *IGCH* 1629. 1935–1936 [rejected hoard]

Burial: 1st cent. BC or AD ?
Contents: 89 AR

Ptolemy II: 1 tetr. Sidon (Sv. 729, 258 BC?); 1 Joppa (Sv. 303, year 32 = 254 BC), both very worn.
Tyre: 23 tetr. (from 126/5 BC to 65/6 AD)
Jewish Revolt: 64 shekels (year 3 = 68/9 AD)

The description of this hoard comes from Hill 1938. p. 79, who supposes that a single deposit is not improbable. This would mean a very long period of accumulation from the mid-third century BC to AD 68/9. The editors of *IGCH*, on the contrary, think there are two: under no. 1629, they gather the non-Jewish coins and date them from the second to the first century BC. Houghton, Lorber, Hoover 2008 do likewise. This is at odds with the chronology of Tyrian coins provided by Hill 1938, which Kadman 1967 accurately reprises in his conspectus on p. 323.

IGCH does not clearly explain why its description differs from that of earlier authors, nor what would justify connecting this lot with *IGCH* 1630 (290).

Disposition: Unknown

Bibliography:
Hill, G. F. "The shekels of the first revolt of the Jews," *Quarterly of the Department of Antiquities in Palestine* 6 (1938), pp. 78–83.
Kadman, L. "The monetary development of Palestine in the light of coin hoards," in A. Kindler (ed.) *International Numismatic Convention, Jerusalem, 27–31 December 1963. The Patterns of Monetary Development in Phoenicia and Palestine in Antiquity*, Tel Aviv, 1967, no. 12.
Houghton, Lorber, Hoover 2008, p. 117.

2.7. UNCERTAIN HOARD

360. Northern Syria? *CH* 8.290, pl. 36, 7–32 = *CH* 9.491. 1983 [rejected hoard]

Contents: AR

Aradus: 3 st. of the 4th cent. BC; 4 dr. with bee (years 88 (?), 89, 91, 14[–])
Ephesus: 16 dr. with bee

Only on the plates:
Demetrius I: 1 tetr.
Antiochus III: 1 dr. with elephant; 1 silver fraction of which the photograph, very dark, does not allow identification

Kinns 1999, p. 55, was able to examine the photos of the coins of the Ma'aret en-Numan hoard (**193**) that Mattingly did not publish. 4 drachms from that hoard were mistakenly included with this lot, which accordingly ought to be removed, as *CH* 9.491 notes: "This entry to be deleted: it is contaminated with coins attributable to the Ma'aret En-Nu'man hoard (*CH* 6.37; 7.98; 8.433; 9.511)."

Bibliography:
Elayi, J. and A.-G. Elayi. "Nouveaux trésors de monnaies phéniciennes (*CH* VIII)," *Transeuphratène* 11 (1996), pp. 95–114, p. 97.
Kinns, P., "The Attic weight drachms of Ephesus: a preliminary study in the light of recent hoards," *Numismatic Chronicle* 159 (1999), pp. 47–97, 55.

3. Unpublished Hoards

175. Jablah, Msaitbe Quarter, Syria. 2005

Burial: after 190/189
Contents: 53 AE

All axes are 12 o'clock, unless stated otherwise.

Aradus

Obv. Head of Tyche turreted r.; border of dots.
Rev. Prow l., Athena as figurehead, monogram in field above, date in exergue.

Duyrat 2005a, nos. 1357–1454.
1. Exergue illegible, 6.25 g, 17 mm.
2. Year 24+? (236/5 BC?), 7.83 g, 21.5 mm.

Obv. Head of Tyche turreted r.; border of dots.
Rev. Prow l., Athena as figurehead, Σ? and monogram in field above; date in exergue: year 38? (222/1 BC?).

Duyrat 2005a, nos. 1446–1451.
3. 3.66 g, 15.5 mm.

Obv. Head of Tyche turreted r.; border of dots.
Rev. Prow of galley curving upwards l., Phoenician letters to either side of monogram in field above ; date in exergue.

Date illegible: Duyrat 2005a, nos. 1643–1732.
4. Year 40+ (45? = 215/4 BC?), *M'* in field above, 4.51 g, 16 mm.
5. Year 40+, *Ḥ'* in field above, 3.41 g, 16 mm.
6. ? ? in field above, 3.39 g, 15.5 mm.
7. ? ' in field above, 2.86 g, 15 mm.

8. ? ? in field above, 2.79 g, 14 mm.
9. Year 40+,? ? in field above, 3.41 g, 14.5 mm.
10. ? ? in field above, 2.89 g, 14.5 mm.
11. ? ? in field above, 3.01 g, 16 mm.
12. ʾ? T in field above, 3.92 g, 13 mm.
13. *Q* ? in field above, 2.72 g, 12.5 mm.
14. Year 43+,? ? in field above, 2.31 g, 16 mm.
15. ? ʾ in field above, 2.36 g, 13 mm.
16. ? ? in field above, 6.85 g, 20 mm. Fused with 23.
17. ? ? in field above, 2.45 g, 11 h, 15 mm.
18. Year 66? (194/3 BC),? *D*? in field above, 3.24 g, 11 h, 15 mm.

Year 54? (= 206/5 BC), Duyrat 2005a, no. 1690.[77]
19. *N* ? in field above, date off flan, 2.57 g, 14 mm.

Year 65? (= 195/4 BC?), Duyrat 2005a, nos. 1704–1705.
20. ? ? in field above, 3.43 g, 15 mm.

Year 66? (= 194/3 BC), Duyrat 2005a, no. 1706.
21. Same obv. die as Duyrat 2005a, 1706, ʿ *D* in field above, 2.97 g, 16 mm.

Obv. Head of Tyche turreted r., palm behind head, border of dots.
Rev. Tyche standing r., resting l. on sceptre and holding wreath in r., date in Phoenician vertically in r. field.

Year 52 (= 208/7 BC), Duyrat 2005a, no. 1733 var.
22. 7.88 g, 21.5 mm.

Year 53 (207/6 BC), Duyrat 2005a, no. 1733 var.
23. 8.75 g, 24 mm, fused with 16.

Date illegible: Duyrat 2005a, nos. 1733–1768.
24. 11.48 g, 26 mm.
25. 8.26 g, 22 mm.
26. 7.91 g, 21 mm.

Aradus or Carne?

Obv. Head of Tyche turreted r.; border of dots.
Rev. Prow of galley curving upwards l.

Duyrat 2005a, nos. 1643–1732 Aradus, or Duyrat 2002 Carne 73–74.
27. Rev. Monogram in field  or  ? Exergue, year 70? (190–189 BC?), 7.32 g, 20 mm.
28. Obv. Head of Tyche turreted r. or head of goddess veiled r. Rev. Prow of galley curving upwards l.? 3.10 g, 15 mm.
29. Rev. Prow of galley curving upwards l.? 3.41 g, 14 mm.
30. Rev. Prow of galley curving upwards l.? 3.04 g, 14 mm.
31. Rev. Prow of galley curving upwards l., year 42+, 2.77 g, 11 h, 15 mm.
32. 3.91 g, 14 mm.

77. This year is the only one recorded in Duyrat 2005a with *N* to the left of the monogram.

33. 3.40 g, 14 mm.
34. 3.16 g, 16 mm.
35. 3.46 g, 15.5 mm.
36. 4.62 g, 13.5 mm.
37. 2.94 g, 14 mm.
38. 3.18 g, 16 mm.
39. 3.62 g, 15 mm.
40. Year 60+, 3.34 g, 14 mm.
41. 6.12 g, 19 mm.
42. 3.24 g, 14 mm.
43. 3.69 g, 14.5 mm.

Aradus, Carne, Gabala or Simyra?

Obv. Head of Tyche turreted r.; border of dots.
Rev. Prow l., Athena as figurehead, field and exergue illegible unless noted.

Duyrat 2005a, nos. 1357–1454 Aradus or Duyrat 2002 Carne 15–34, Gabala 2–6 or Simyra 6.
44. 6.33 g, 22 mm.
45. 6.21 g, 1 h, 20 mm.
46. 5.81 g, 21.5 mm.
47. 7.20 g, 20 mm.
48. 5.93 g, 17.5 mm.
49. 6.22 g, 18 mm.
50. 7.52 g, 20 mm.
51. 6.97 g, 19 mm.
52. Date: 20+, 3.83 g, 11 h, 15 mm.
53. Year 40+?, 6.98 g, 20 mm.

This hoard was discovered in 2005 in the Msaitbe quarter, during excavations conducted by Massoud Badawi for the Directorate of Antiquities of Jablah in a zone of the Hellenistic city that had to be cleared for the construction of a hotel. Some fragments of burnt ceramic accompanied these 53 bronzes. Coins 16 and 23 were stuck together. Numbers 22 and 23 bear dates not reported in my monograph on Aradus.[78]

Hesitancy over attributions to one or another mint of northern Phoenicia arises because the represented series belong to currencies common in the Aradian Peraea: Gabala, Carne, and Simyra, during the 220s and again during the 180s, struck some bronze series with the same types as Aradus, but identified with each city's mint mark.[79] Nonetheless, it is probable that the majority of these coins come from the Aradus mint. Indeed, excavations in the region have turned up Aradian coins in large quantities, from the fourth century onward, supporting the idea that the island mint provided the bulk of the currency used in its Peraea.[80]

Legible dates stretch between 236/5 and probably 190/189 BC, assuming that the widest possible scope for these series, in the four mints that could be represented, covers the years 242/1–167/6 BC. Moreover, bronze can circulate for several years after being struck. It seems prudent to avoid fixing the burial date too precisely: "after 190/189" must suffice.

Disposition: Directorate of Antiquities, Jablah, Syria.

78. Duyrat 2005a, p. 55.
79. Duyrat 2002a, pp. 54–56; Duyrat 2005a, pp. 242–43.
80. That is the case at Al-Mina from the fourth century, at Ibn Hani, Ras el-Bassit, Tell Sukas, and Tell Arka.

284. Amrith (ancient Marathus). 1955

Burial: after 112/1
Contents: 50 AE

This hoard is described in the Seyrig Archives.[81] The file containing this list carries the notation "uninteresting," but the marking on the coins is painstakingly described and enables us to reconstitute the find.

Aradus

27 bronzes. The types are not specified, but the control marks (generally three Phoenician letters spread over the fields left and right and in the exergue) as well as the noted years correspond to series 7 of this mint,[82] a series common elsewhere in excavations in the region.

Obv. Head of Tyche r., border of dots.
Rev. Prow r., Athena fighting as figurehead, Poseidon seated on the prow, sceptre in l., crowning Athena with r.; Phoenician letters under the r. arm of the god; in r. field, and in exergue, date in Phoenician.

Years 126–129 (= 134/3–131/0 BC), Duyrat 2005a, nos. 2296–2356:

1. Year 126+, under the arm of the god, *N*?; in r. field, ‘.

Years 127–129 (= 133/2–131/0 BC), Duyrat 2005a, nos. 2302–2356:

2. Year 127+, under the arm of the god, *N*; in r. field, ‘.
3. Year 127+, under the arm of the god, *N*; in r. field, ‘.
4. Year 127+.

Year 128 (= 132/1 BC), Duyrat 2005a, nos. 2308–2351:

5. Year 128; in r. field, ‘; in exergue, *G*.
6. Year 128; under the arm of the god, *G*; in r. field, ‘.

Year 130 (=130/129 BC), Duyrat 2005a, nos. 2357–2424

7. Year 130, under the arm of the god, *N*; in r. field, ‘; in exergue, *D*.

Year 130 (= 130/129 BC), Duyrat 2005a, nos. 2425–2435:

8. Year 130+; in r. field, *B* ; in exergue, *D*?
9. Year 120+, under the arm of the god, *Q*?; in r. field, *B*.
10. Year?, under the arm of the god, *Q*?
11. Year 130+; in r. field, *B*.
12. Year 120+ ; under the arm of the god, *Q*.

Year 130?

81. Bibliothèque nationale de France, dossier 227, "Amrit 1955."
82. Duyrat 2005a, nos. 2237–2492, pp. 66–70.

13. Year 130+.
14. Year 130+.
15. Year 130.

Year 143, 144, 145, 147 or 148, Duyrat 2005a, nos. 2439–2446, 2456–2467:

16. Year 142+ ; under the arm of the god, -; in r. field, *B*; in exergue, *MY*??

Year 148 (= 112/1 BC), Duyrat 2005a, nos. 2459–2467:

17. Year 148, under the arm of the god, - ; in exergue, *MYTT*.
18. Year 148, under the arm of the god, -; in r. field, *B*; in exergue, *MYTT*.

Date and Phoenician letters illegible:

19.
20.
21.
22.
23.
24. In r. field, *B*.
25. Under the arm of the god, *N*; in r. field, ʿ.
26. Under the arm of the god, *N*; in r. field, ʿ.
27. In r. field ʿ; in exergue, *G*.

1 bronze noted "Athena on prow/D Zeus" and dated year 136 by Seyrig. Duyrat 2005a does not record this year for this series.[83]

Obv. Head of Zeus laureate r., border of dots.
Rev. Prow with ram l., Athena as figurehead, Phoenician letters in field above; date in Phoenician and Phoenician letters in exergue.
Year 136 (= 124/3 BC), Duyrat 2005a, nos. 4383–4386 var.

28. In field above, ??*NṢ*; in exergue, *B*.

Marathus

22 bronzes of which the types are not described, but the years and control marks can only correspond to series 13.[84] Seyrig undertook a die study that shows that the 22 coins were struck from only seven obverse dies (he seems not to have studied the reverses). By comparison, Duyrat 2002a found 22 obverses in 45 examples studied.

Obv. Head of Zeus laureate r.; border of dots.
Rev. Double cornucopia; three Phoenician letters in the outer l. field above; a Phoenician letter in the inner r. field below; a Phoenician letter in the inner l. field below; date in Phoenician vertically to r.

Year 131 (= 129/8 BC), Duyrat 2002a, nos. 322–325:

83. Duyrat 2005a, series 10, p. 107.
84. Duyrat 2002a, p. 35–36.

29. D1, year 131, in field above to l., *'??*; in inner r. field, *D*; in inner l. field, *N*.
30. D1, year 131, in field above to l., *'MG*; in inner r. field, *D*; in inner l. field, *N*.
31. D1, year 130+, in field above to l., *'MG*; in inner r. field, *D*; in inner l. field, *N*.

Year 131, Duyrat 2002a, nos. 322–324:

32. D1, year 120+, in field above to l., *'LG*; in inner r. field, *D*; in inner l. field, *N*.
33. D1, year 131, in field above to l., *'LG*; in inner r. field, *D*; in inner l. field, *N*.
Year 131, Duyrat 2002a, nos. 322–325:

34. D2, year 131, in field above to l., *'LG*; in inner r. field, *D*; in inner l. field, *N*.
35. D2, year 131, in field above to l., *'?G*; in inner r. field, *D*; in inner l. field, *N*.
36. D2, year?, in field above to l., *'LG*; in inner r. field, *D*; in inner l. field, *N*.
37. D2, year?, in field above to l., *'LG*; in inner r. field, *?*; in inner l. field, *N*.

Year 142 (118/7 BC), Duyrat 2002a, no. 336:

38. D3, year 142, in field above to l., *TTG*; in inner r. field, *'*; in inner l. field, *T*.
39. D4, year 142, in field above to l., *TTG*; in inner r. field, *'*; in inner l. field, *T*.

Year 142 (118/7 BC), Duyrat 2002a, no. 337:

40. D5, year 142, in field above to l., *TTG*; in inner r. field, ?; in inner l. field, *T*.
41. D5, year 140+, in field above to l., *???*; in inner r. field, ?; in inner l. field, *T*.
42. D5, year 120+, in field above to l., *TTG*; in inner r. field, '; in inner l. field, *T*.

Year 142 (118/7 BC), Duyrat 2002a, nos. 328–335:

43. D3, year 142, in field above to l., *BNG*; in inner r. field, ?; in inner l. field, *T*.
44. D5, year ?, in field above to l., *BNG*; in inner r. field, *'*; in inner l. field, *T*.

Year 142 (118/7 BC), Duyrat 2002a, nos. 328–336:

45. D5, year 141+, in field above to l., *BNG*; in inner r. field, *'*; in inner l. field, *T*.

Year 142 (118/7 BC), Duyrat 2002a, nos. 328–337:

46. D5, year 142, in field above to l., *BNG* ; in inner r. field, ?; in inner l. field, *T*.
47. D5, year 142, in field above to l., *???*; in inner r. field, *'*; in inner l. field, *T*.
48. D5, year 142, in field above to l., *???*; in inner r. field, *'*; in inner l. field, *T*.
49. D6, year 140+, in field above to l., *??G*; in inner r. field, *'*, in inner l. field, *?*.
50. D7, year 142, in field above to l., *BNG* ; in inner r. field, ?; in inner l. field, *T*.

To these 50 bronzes of Aradus and Marathus, 3 bronzes of Gabala were added, with the types Tyche/Three ears of corn,[85] noted at the bottom of the last page and crossed out, with the comment "different patina." A bronze of Alexander I Balas is also mentioned, with the comment "probably different patina." I have excluded them.

85. Duyrat 2002a, series 7, pp. 41–42.

The latest Aradian bronze is from 112/1 BC, that from Marathus 118/7 BC. Burial therefore probably occurred a little after 112/1 BC. It would have been tempting to associate the Gabala bronzes with this find, but one of them, dated year 207 (53/2 BC), presents too low a dating in addition to the different patina. Given the nature of Seyrig's notes, one may suppose that he saw these coins in trade. He clearly identified them as a hoard. The die connections among the bronzes of Marathus support this supposition, and the fact that the group is said to have been found at Amrith corresponds very well with its content.[86] The latest coin is Aradian and dates from 112/1 BC, suggesting burial after this date.

Disposition: probably dispersed.
Bibliography:
H. Seyrig Archives, Bibliothèque nationale de France, dossier 227 "Amrit 1955."

338. Unknown Findspot (Aradian Peraea?). Before 1991

Burial: after 51/0
Contents: 115 AR + 82 AR

At the beginning of the 1990s, two groups of Aradian tetradrachms were dispersed in succession on the Parisian and New York markets. I reported the existence of the lot sold in Paris in 1991 in *Arados hellénistique*.[87] M. Amandry and D. Gerin, curators at the Cabinet des Médailles in the Bibliothèque nationale de France, were able to examine and photograph it and to acquire 12 specimens for the Cabinet's collection. I am grateful to them for providing me with the Polaroids and the data they could gather at the time and for permitting me to present this documentation in its entirety.[88] It happens that, at the time of writing *Arados hellénistique*, I had only one box of files (out of two) in my possession. The lot sold off in Paris contained, in fact, 115 tetradrachms, not 73. The 42 additional specimens are included in the current catalogue with identification of the obverse dies used to strike them, following the catalogue published in Duyrat 2005a. These new coins revealed no new obverse die.

Year 124 (136/5 BC), *H*, ΔΣ
1. Duyrat 2005a, no. 3025, D5–R14, Paris, BnF, 1991.101. 15.29 g, 30.9 mm.

Year 165 (95/4 BC), *D*, ΒΣ
2. Duyrat 2005a, no. 3274, D52–R202. 15.13 g.

Year 166 (94/3 BC), *G*, ΓΣ
3. Duyrat 2005a, no. 3313, D54–R232. 14.82 g.

Year 167 (93/2 BC), ', IN
4. Duyrat 2005a, no. 3331, D57–R246. 15.15 g.

Year 168 (92/1 BC), *G*, ΔΣ
5. Duyrat 2005a, no. 3341, D59–R254. 14.98 g.
6. Duyrat 2005a, no. 3362, D59–R267. 15.19 g.
7. Duyrat 2005a, no. 3364, D59–R268. 15.18 g.
8. Duyrat 2005a, no. 3369, D59–R269. 15.06 g.

86. Cf. also *IGCH* 1545 (**187**) and esp. *IGCH* 1566 (**283**), whose composition and burial date are completely similar.
87. Duyrat 2005a, p. 170.
88. I am indebted to Dominique Gerin who digitized the content of these Polaroids for me before they faded too much.

Year 168 (92/1 BC), *Q*, ΔΣ
9. Duyrat 2005a, no. 3379, D60–R278. 14.88 g.

Year 169 (91/0 BC), *H*, ΘΣ
10. Duyrat 2005a, no. 3398, D61–R289. 15.13 g.

Year 172 (88/7 BC), *D*, ΜΣ
11. Duyrat 2005a, no. 3436, D63–R309, Paris, BnF, 1991.102 (15.08 g). 15.09 g, 28.3 mm.

Year 173 (87/6 BC), ʿ, ΜΣ
12. Duyrat 2005a, no. 3456, D64–R319, Paris, BnF, 1991.103. 15.22 g, 29.9 mm.
13. Duyrat 2005a, no. 3457, D64–R320. 14.50 g.

Year 173 (87/6 BC), *B*, ΜΣ
14. Duyrat 2005a, no. 3464, D65–R326. 15.06 g.
15. Duyrat 2005a, no. 3479, D66–R334. 14.89 g.
16. Duyrat 2005a, no. 3481, D66–R335. 14.76 g.
17. Duyrat 2005a, no. 3483, D66–R336. Holleman Munten, Enschede, 87, September 1991, no. 24. 15.03 g.
18. Duyrat 2005a, no. 3484, D66–R337. Poinsignon, Strasbourg, List 34, 1992, no. 400; Poinsignon, Strasbourg, 38, Nov. 1994, no. 659; Poinsignon, Strasbourg, 41, June 1996, no. 682. 14.99 g.
19. Duyrat 2005a, no. 3485, D66–R338. 15.13 g.

Year 174 (86/5 BC), *H*, ΘΕ
20. Duyrat 2005a, no. 3501, D67–R348, Paris, BnF, 1991.104. 15.00 g, 26.4 mm.

Year 174 (86/5 BC), *Q*, ΘΕ
21. Duyrat 2005a, no. 3509, D67–R353. 14.84 g.
22. Duyrat 2005a, no. 3513, D67–R354. 15.18 g.

Year 176 (84/3 BC), ʿ, ΘΣ
23. Duyrat 2005a, no. 3530, D68–R366. 15.16 g.

Year 176 (84/3 BC), *D*, ΘΣ
24. Duyrat 2005a, no. 3532, D68–R368. 15.15 g.

Year 177 (83/2 BC), *B*, ΘΕ
25. Duyrat 2005a, no. 3536, D69–R370. 14.99 g.
26. Duyrat 2005a, no. 3538, D69–R371. 15.12 g.

Year 177 (83/2 BC), *H*, ΘΕ
27. Duyrat 2005a, no. 3550, D69–R379. 15.23 g.

Year 178 (82/1 BC), *D*, ΜΣ
28. Duyrat 2005a, no. 3566, D71–R392. 14.75 g.
29. Duyrat 2005a, no. 3570, D72–R395. 15.04 g.
30. Duyrat 2005a, no. 3571, D72–R396. 15.15 g.
31. Duyrat 2005a, no. 3572, D72–R397. G. Barré, Saint Malo, winter 1991–1992, no. 30 (15.13 g). 15.12 g.
32. Duyrat 2005a, no. 3574, D72–R398. 15.15 g.
33. Duyrat 2005a, no. 3575, D72–R? 15.15 g.

Year 179 (81/0 BC), *G*, ΜΣ
34. Duyrat 2005a, no. 3600, D73–R413. 15.27 g.

Year 181 (79/8 BC), *H*, ΜΣ
35. Duyrat 2005a, no. 3630, D76–R437. 14.94 g.
36. Duyrat 2005a, no. 3631, D76–R437. 15.32 g.

Year 182 (78/7 BC), *Q*, ΜΣ
37. Duyrat 2005a, no. 3658, D76–R455. 14.96 g.

Year 183 (77/6 BC), *Q*, ΜΣ
38. Duyrat 2005a, no. 3668, D77–R463. 15.24 g.

Year 184 (76/5 BC), *D*, ΜΣ
39. Duyrat 2005a, no. 3680, D79–R471. 14.90 g.
40. Duyrat 2005a, no. 3681, D79–R472. 15.11 g.
41. Duyrat 2005a, no. 3682, D79–R473. 14.99 g.
42. Duyrat 2005a, no. 3689, D79–R474. 14.99 g.

Year 185 (75/4 BC), *B*, ΜΣ
43. Duyrat 2005a, no. 3706, D79–R487, Paris, BnF, 1991.105. 15.00 g, 25.9 mm.

Year 185 (75/4 BC), *G*, ΜΣ
44. Duyrat 2005a, no. 3713, D79–R492, double-struck. 14.70 g.
45. Duyrat 2005a, no. 3715, D79–R493. 15.16 g.
46. Duyrat 2005a, no. 3718, D79–R495. 15.00 g.
47. Duyrat 2005a, no. 3719, D79–R496. 15.01 g.
48. Duyrat 2005a, no. 3720, D79–R496. 15.01 g.
49. Duyrat 2005a, no. 3724, D79–R497. 15.27 g.

Year 187 (73/2 BC), *B*, ΑΣ
50. Duyrat 2005a, no. 3739, D79–R508. 15.12 g.
51. Duyrat 2005a, no. 3745, D79–R512. 15.10 g.

Year 188 (72/1 BC), ʾ, ΜΣ
52. Duyrat 2005a, no. 3752, D79–R515. 15.03 g.

Year 188 (72/1 BC), *Q*, ΜΣ
53. Duyrat 2005a, no. 3761, D79–R521. 15.25 g.
54. Duyrat 2005a, no. 3764. D79–R522. 15.13 g.
55. Duyrat 2005a, no. 3777, D81–R531. 15.08 g.

Year 192 (68/7 BC), *D*, ΜΣ
56. Duyrat 2005a, no. 3800, D83–R550, Paris, BnF, 1991.106. 15.16 g, 26.5 mm.
57. Duyrat 2005a, no. 3802, D83–R551. 13.75 g.
58. Duyrat 2005a, no. 3803, D83–R552. 15.06 g.

Year 193 (67/6 BC), *G*, ΑΣ
59. Duyrat 2005a, no. 3839, D84–R578. Poinsignon, Strasbourg, 36, Nov. 1993, no. 406; Poinsignon, Strasbourg, 41, June 1996, no. 683. 15.17 g.

Year 193 (67/6 BC), *G*, ΜΣ
60. Duyrat 2005a, no. 3843, D83–R580. 15.06 g.

Year 193 (67/6 BC), *H*, ΑΣ
61. Duyrat 2005a, no. 3859, D85–R591. 14.91 g.
62. Duyrat 2005a, no. 3860, D85–R591. 15.26 g.
63. Duyrat 2005a, no. 3861, D85–R592. 15.16 g.
64. Duyrat 2005a, no. 3863, D85–R593. 15.16 g.
65. Duyrat 2005a, no. 3864, D85–R594. 15.10 g.

Year 194 (66/5 BC), ⁏ ΑΣ
66. Duyrat 2005a, no. 3876, D86–R604. 14.89 g.
67. Duyrat 2005a, no. 3878, D86–R605. 14.85 g.
68. Duyrat 2005a, no. 3881, D86–R606, Paris, BnF, 1991.107. 15.02 g, 27.0 mm.

Year 195 (65/4 BC), *G*, ΑΣ
69. D 88. 15.12 g.
70. D 88. 15.25 g.
71. D 88. 15.07 g.
72. D 88. 15.16 g.
73. D 88. 14.91 g.

Year 196 (64/3 BC), *H*, ΑΝ
74. D 89. 15.18 g.
75. D 89. 15.13 g.

Year 196 (64/3 BC), *H*, ΑΣ
76. Duyrat 2005a, no. 3946, D90–R641, Paris, BnF, 1991.108. 14.93 g, 28.3 mm.
77. D 90. 14.91 g.
78. D 91. 15.24 g.
79. D 91. 15.25 g.
80. D 91. 14.67 g.
81. D 91. 14.90 g.
82. D 91. 14.57 g.
83. D 91. 14.90 g.
84. D 91. 15.45 g.

Year 196 (64/3 BC), *Q*, ΑΝ
85. Duyrat 2005a, no. 3989, D89–R663, Paris, BnF, 1991.109. 15.15 g, 28.9 mm.

Year 196 (64/3 BC), *Q*, ΑΣ
86. D 88. 14.93 g.
87. D 88. 15.16 g.
88. D 88. 15.07 g.
89. D 88. 15.27 g.
90. D 88. 15.09 g.
91. D 88. 15.03 g.
92. D 88. 15.10 g.
93. D 91. 14.97 g.

94. D 91. 14.92 g.
95. D 91. 15.16 g.

Year 197 (63/2 BC), ', AN
96. D 89. 15.23 g.
97. D 89. 15.27 g.

Year 197 (63/2 BC), ', AΣ
98. D 95. 15.16 g.
99. D 95. 15.14 g.

Year 197 (63/2 BC), *D* (re-engraved from ') AN
100. Duyrat 2005a, no. 4085, D89–R711, Paris, BnF, 1991.110. 15.02 g, 27.5 mm.

Year 198 (62/1 BC), *B*, EΣ
101. D 98. 14.86 g.

Year 198 (62/1 BC), *G*, AN
102. D 89. 15.07 g.
103. D 89. 15.11 g.

Year 198 (62/1 BC), *G*, AΣ
104. D 95. 15.26 g.

Year 198 (62/1 BC), *G*, EΣ
105. D 99. 15.17 g.
106. D 99. 15.16 g.
107. D 99. 15.10 g.
108. D 99. 15.00 g.
109. D 99. 15.19 g.

Year 199 (61/0 BC), ', AN
110. Duyrat 2005a, no. 4163, D89–R747, Paris, BnF, 1991.111. 15.35 g, 27.9 mm.
111. D 89. 15.13 g.

Year 199 (61/0 BC), ', EΣ
112. D 99. 15.01 g.
113. D 99. 15.17 g.

Year 199 (61/0 BC), *Q*, AN
114. D 89. 15.12 g.

Year 200 (60/59 BC), *D*, EΣ
115. Duyrat 2005a, no. 4208, D99–R764, Paris, BnF, 1991.112. 15.14 g, 26.3 mm.

This lot must be seen in light of the one sold in New York in 1994:[89]

89. Classical Numismatic Group, New York, 32, December 7, 1994, lots 1411 to 1416.

Table 1.1. Comparative table of Paris and New York lots of unknown findspot (Aradian Peraea?), before 191 (**338**)

	Paris	**New York**
Earliest year	Year 124 = 136/5 BC	Year 130 = 130/129 BC
Latest year	Year 200 = 60/59 BC	Year 201 = 59/8 BC
Best represented year	Year 196 = 64/3 BC	Year 181 = 79/8 BC
Issues not represented	Years 127–164	Years 131–157
	Years 170–171	Years 169–172
	Years 189–191	Years 189–191

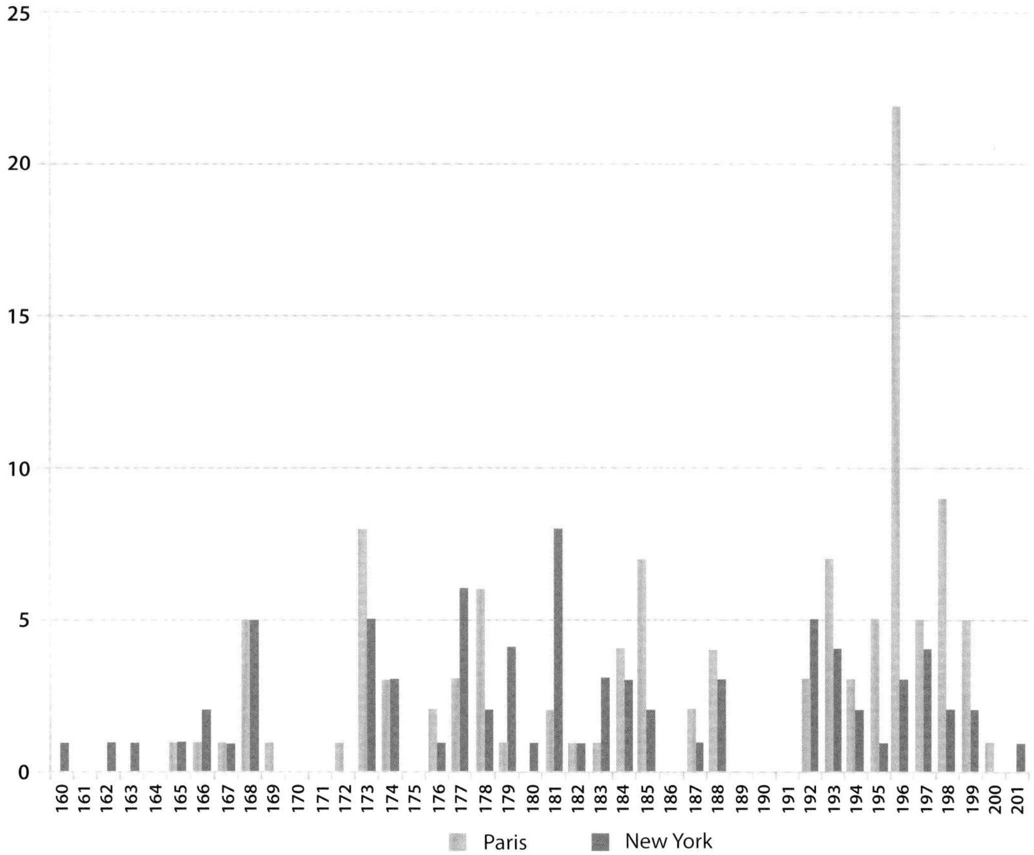

Figure 1.2. Comparative graph of Paris and New York lots of unknown findspot (Aradian Peraea?), before 191 (**338**)

Aradus: 80 tetradrachms, years 130, 160, 162, 163, 165, 166 (2), 167, 168 (5), 173 (5), 174 (3), 176, 177 (6), 178 (2), 179 (4), 180, 181 (8), 182, 183 (3), 184 (3), 185 (2), 187, 188 (3), 192 (5), 193 (4), 194 (2), 195, 196 (3), 197 (4), 198 (2), 199 (2), 201 (1).
Laodiceia ad Mare: 2 tetradrachms, year 30 (52/1 BC) and year 31 (51/0 BC).

Some similarities connect these two groups (Table 1.1).

Figure 1.2 illustrates the annual volumes represented in each lot. The two lots' similarity—one year of early production,[90] then noticeable gaps, an identical final year, the homogeneity of the content—leads one to think that this is indeed a single hoard.

Contrary to what I wrote in 2005, the addition of the new Parisian tetradrachms shows that the hoard reflects the rhythm of production of the Aradian mint. The peak in year 196 (64/3 BC) illustrates the increasing production noticeable between 64/3 and 62/1 BC (7 obverse dies in service in 64/3 BC, then 5 in 63/2 BC and 62/1 BC).[91] These three years are represented by 45 tetradrachms, roughly one quarter of the hoard (23%), if it is complete. Yet it is noteworthy that accumulation occurs over a production period of forty years, with a stray representation of two issues separated by more than 70 years from the final date. The autonomous tetradrachms of Aradus were issued at a rather slow pace, with one or two obverse dies in service each year, the same die often being reutilized several years in a row. It would not be surprising that these coins remained in circulation a long time. This hoard might perfectly illustrate not that is was accumulated over a long time but simply that its coins were still in use several decades after their manufacture.

The two tetradrachms of Laodiceia are characteristic of hoards from the Aradian Peraea at the end of the Hellenistic period. The Tartus (**348**) and Syria (**340**) hoards connect Aradus and this city and were themselves buried towards the middle of the first century, after 44/3 and c. 50 BC respectively. Mørkholm showed long ago that the Aradian standard formed a relatively closed system in the first century, and the circulation map I published in 2005 confirms this amply.[92] This leads me to conclude that the hoard probably comes from the Aradian Peraea. The dating of the coins from Laodiceia justifies putting its burial after 51/0 BC.

90. For clarity of presentation, the early years have been excluded from the graph (Paris year 124, New York year 130).

91. Duyrat 2005a, p. 282.

92. Mørkholm 1982; Duyrat 2005a, pp. 260–64.

Chapter 2

Coinage from Levantine Excavations

1. Introduction

1.1. Included Sites

In contrast to the approach taken for hoards, the catalogue below does not seek to be exhaustive. Only Israeli archaeologists could achieve this; their work has produced a multitude of references in Hebrew or English appearing in journals such as *'Atiqot* and *Hadashot Archeologiot*. A full accounting for the Hellenistic period does not look feasible for many years to come. H. Gitler has already published two instructive studies showing what is to be gained from assembling this sort of data. The first compares the coinage finds from eight excavations undertaken in Jerusalem as well as coins discovered at Masada between the third century BC and the Arab Conquest in 640.[1] The article, however, consists only of graphics and tables and draws no historical conclusions, since Gitler wanted merely to make the body of material available to scholars. Yet the collection of these data is hard to exploit without catalogues of the actual physical material and knowledge of the context in which it was found. A second article, written in collaboration with D. Weisburd and devoted to the Byzantine period, gathered together a considerable amount of material (15,236 coins) from 62 villages and six cities in Palestine between AD 383 and 696/7.[2] This evidence mostly derives from rural contexts and therefore provides us with a valuable source for a world generally less well known than the urban one. Statistical analysis shows that the number of coins found declines sharply after the fourth century AD but then remains stable from the fifth to the seventh century. This long-term stability might indicate that the volume of coins in circulation reverted to a normal level and that the fourth century, with its copious issues, represents an exception.

For a numismatist, working in France, it would be unrealistic to hope to give a complete list of excavations that have yielded Hellenistic coins in Syria. The following catalogue is therefore a selection. It would not be possible within the limits of this study to present the hundred or so

1. Gitler 1996b.
2. Gitler, Weisburd 2005.

sites I have surveyed. I have not included excavations that are too sketchily published, which mention only a portion of the specimens found without clarifying the nature and number of those excluded. Likewise, indications of single finds at sites appearing in the Seyrig Archives were too scattered and incomplete to be included. I have not aggregated the different excavations made in a same city (Beirut, Caesarea Maritima, Jerusalem, Tel Michal), since it would have given the false impression of a homogeneous and complete survey of coin finds. On the contrary, as they were conducted by different teams at different periods on different levels, they provide scattered data concerning the history of these cities.

Foreign sites such as Athens, exploited for comparative purposes, although they are entered into the database, are kept out of the catalogue. In fact, contrary to what I expected, it is extremely difficult, in the present state of excavation publication, to propose a comparative study with other regions of the Mediterranean. This sort of approach will surely be possible in the future, when the documentation is better controlled, but seeing how hard it is to get past the difficulties peculiar to regional comparisons, a more limited undertaking seemed preferable. For the same reason, the large excavations on Cyprus (Citium, Salamis, Paphos, Kourion) have been investigated but excluded from the catalogue. I have, however, included sites that only offered up very few Hellenistic coins, especially in Seleucid Syria, because the sources are scarce for this region and because even the poorest among them seemed to me informative.

The site of Tell el-Herr, in the eastern part of the Egyptian delta, has been included as a boundary. It provided only Ptolemaic material, clearly delineating the difference between the Seleucid domains, which all have complex coin profiles mingling different currencies, and the kingdom of Egypt, where the only Hellenistic coins are the royal currency.

1.2. Material Difficult to Compare

Generally speaking, the condition of coins from excavations is poor: they have spent time in the ground, without the protection of a container, in direct contact with the earth and humidity. The vast majority, moreover, are bronze; some are lead, an alloy and a metal that oxidize rapidly, sometimes beyond repair. The editors of the Masada excavation note that 158 out of 4,699 coins found were destroyed in cleaning.[3] The condition of the physical material does, however, vary greatly from one site to another. Not all publications necessarily give information on illegible coins or coins destroyed in cleaning, but Table 2.1 brings together a sampling of sites with more than a hundred coins to give an idea of the extreme variation of cases. This variation surely results from the nature of the soils, the abundance of rainfall, and the techniques used for cleaning[4] as well as the competence of the restorers.

En-Gedi and the City of David, in Jerusalem, show the worst results since a third to a half of the material was unusable. Moreover, the numbers go from negligible (under 5%) to a fifth of

3. Y. Meshorer in Yadin, Naveh, Meshorer 1989, p. 80.

4. On advances in this area, rarely mentioned in numismatic publications, cf. an example in Rotroff 1997, pp. 9–10.

Table 2.1. Proportion of illegible coins from excavations

Site	Illegible	Total Coins	% of Illegible AE Coins
Caesarea Maritima	2	259 AE	0.77
Si' 8, Hauran	2	261 AE	0.77
Si', Hauran	3	293 AE	1.02
Jerash–Gerasa	16	1,468 AE	1.09
Hama	15	545 AE	2.75
Gamala	428	6,200 AE	6.90
Jebel Khalid	23	317 AE	7.20
Caesarea Maritima	300	3,119 AE, 3 AR	9.62
Jerusalem	25	231 AE	10.64
Jerusalem, Jewish Quarter 2006	102	934 AE	10.92
Tell Abu Danne	32	115 AE	14.88
Tel Anafa	59	7 AR, 312 AE	18.91
Khirbet Qumran	135	689 AE	19.59
Jerusalem, Jewish Quarter 2003	120	577 AE	20.80
Jerusalem, City of David	125	355 AE	35.21
En-Gedi	640	1,247 AE	51.32

the total. These percentages create an uncertainty so that excavated coins, although having an historical context, must be treated statistically with this range in mind.

In addition to the coins' partial destruction, the fact is that this material has generally been little published. Numismatists are not that numerous, and the coins are often only partially or poorly reported, if at all, despite their importance for chronology. One of the most telling examples is surely Qumran, which revealed along with the famous Dead Sea Scrolls, discovered starting in 1947, some 1,250 coins that Father Roland de Vaux used with pottery to date the site's periods of activity. These coins have never been systematically published and are no more accessible today. K. and M. Lönnqvist were the first to offer a complete list of them, in 2006, based upon de Vaux's notes and (of course) without illustrations.[5]

5. Lönnqvist, Lönnqvist 2006.

As for the hoards (Chap. 1), the bibliography is in some cases obsolete, and it is generally impossible to update the classification of coins from excavations. Few are published with a picture that would allow a re-examination of the attribution and dating. The problem is particularly acute with the Ptolemaic bronze coins. Their descriptions rarely provide an indication of the issuing king and what little information is provided in the publications makes any attempt at reattribution nearly hopeless. Moreover, the reattribution of several bronze series of Tyre from Ptolemy II to Ptolemy III by C. C. Lorber changes the general distribution of Ptolemaic coins currently shown in my catalogue. Instead of a significant bronze production in the name of Ptolemy II in Syria and Phoenicia, the coins of his reign are mostly imported from Alexandria, and it is Ptolemy III who seems to have increased the local production.[6]

Confronted with this evidence so difficult to control, the temptation to publish only "useful" coins has sometimes won out. Thus, from the excavations of Balatah-Shechem the only Seleucid and Ptolemaic coins known are those that advance the argument of O. R. Sellers. Not a word is said of the other finds, which have never, apparently, been published, and the very existence of which must be surmised.[7] For the site of Gamala, D. Syon gives only a percentage of the total coinage for the Ptolemaic bronzes, and an overall number, combining all periods, for civic bronzes.[8]

This abundant evidence, repetitive and tricky to identify, occasions many errors. Thus, at Hama, a clear disagreement is noticeable between the general presentation of the Greco-Roman city[9] and the publication dealing with coins.[10] Hoards 1[11] and 3[12] are described, and especially dated, incorrectly.[13] Ploug also provides a rather confused description of the site's oldest coins: "The earliest Hellenistic coins from the mound dated from the 2nd century BC The oldest is perhaps the copper coin 128 (7N 1) struck by Antiochus Epiphanes, perhaps Antiochus IV (175–164 BC)."[14] On page 21, the same coin is mentioned this way: "Immediately west of the last wall, beneath a statue of a couched lion ascribed to period C.3 was a Hellenistic coin 128 (7N 1), showing the name of the presumed founder of Hellenistic Hama, Antiochus Epiphanes." In fact, the definitive identification attributes this coin to Antiochus VIII (121–96 BC), whose bronzes, along with those of Antiochus IX, are the most numerous on the site. These errors occur in the pages devoted to the dating of the reoccupation of the site in the second century. "The finds that could be ascribed to the first half of the 2nd cent. were not numerous, and no actual repre-

6. Lorber 2007–2008. I am grateful to D. T. Ariel for drawing my attention to this problem, and to C. C. Lorber for information and interpretation of this difficult question.

7. Sellers 1962.

8. Syon 1992–1993.

9. Ploug 1985, esp. p. 45.

10. Thomsen 1986.

11. Antiochus IV instead of Antiochus VIII.

12. Tetradrachms from Aradus dated 144–125 BC instead of 92/1–73/2 BC.

13. Ploug 1985, p. 21, the hoard of bronzes from Antioch (*IGCH* 1580, **337**) is described as containing 49 bronzes instead of 51.

14. Ploug 1985, p. 45.

sentative collection appeared before that of the second half of this century."[15] Indeed, the coins provide the only precise chronological marker, and a certain number are dated to the year. So the refoundation would belong to Antiochus VIII, or the end of the second century.

This type of mistake is evident for other sites. At Al Mina, C. L. Woolley describes the hoard of coins *IGCH* 1488, **37** as being accompanied by, amongst other things, a gold and electrum necklace[16] and "small bars of silver"[17] that become, p. 140, "the fine necklace of gold and silver beads … and two lead ingots." The same author commits another descriptive error for the hoard *IGCH* 1487, **36** despite its publication by E. S. G. Robinson in 1937.[18]

Summary lists in excavation catalogues are another occasion for mistakes. They are often very complicated, especially when the editor's chosen classification system is not chronological. Thus, the totals presented, often at the end of a volume, must be chronologically sorted, and this can cause errors. If *bis* numbers appear and possibly revisions that confuse the numbering, there is little chance that the results, give or take a few specimens, will be precise in a publication dealing with several hundred coins. For example, the excavation of the castle of ʿAtlit mentions 41 pre-Hellenistic coins in the general presentation of the Persian period, p. 110, but 46 in the catalogue under the same heading, including a bronze of Alexander and a Phoenician bronze struck with a Tyche on the obverse and which can only be Hellenistic.[19]

Archaeological sites also present highly varied occupation profiles. In the welter of preliminary and final reports, it is necessary to eliminate those not dealing with the Hellenistic period. But even within this period, the phases of occupation of the sectors excavated and the quantities of coins found differ enormously. One may well dream of a typology of sites, but, out of the dozens included here, it has been impossible to find a sufficient number of common traits. Even the chronological exploitation of the evidence is not easy. Bronze coins often remained in use for a long time, possibly more than a century.[20] Accordingly, they are a reliable chronological marker only when put in context and compared with the rest of the available remains, especially the pottery.[21] These variations in longevity, density, and circulation lead Butcher, with his experience of the enormous amount of material from the excavations of the souks of Beirut, to conclude that "it is certain that the patterns of coin deposition across the Near East were very diverse, with huge variations in the sorts of coins being deposited from site to site."[22] Establishing any numismatic typology for the sites based upon their activity (temples, military venues, etc.), as has been done for the Roman world, would risk erasing each site's individual characteristics.

15. Ploug 1985, p. 45.
16. According to the legend accompanying the photograph, fig. 9, p. 25.
17. Woolley 1938a, p. 13.
18. Woolley 1938b, pp. 141–42.
19. Metcalf, Kool, Berman 1999. The *BMC Phoenicia*, moreover, to which the authors refer for this last coin, shows a dating to the end of the second century BC.
20. This is a well known phenomenon in the Roman period (cf., e.g., Walker 1997, p. 24; Augé 1987). It is far less studied for the Hellenistic Age.
21. Cf., e.g., Rotroff 1997, pp. 13–15; Butcher 2001–2002, pp. 27–31.
22. Butcher 2001–2002, p. 114.

1.3. Surface Finds, the Geography of Finds, and Statistics

A not insignificant portion of the coins in this catalogue result from surface finds.[23] Although these finds are automatic in a well-managed dig, they are rarely mentioned since publications do not normally include a complete numismatic study. The example of Ras Ibn Hani, nevertheless, gives an idea of the importance of this evidence when it is appropriately handled.[24] The guardian of the site, a Syrian who actually lived there, systematically gathered the coins. He noted the place and date of discovery for all the finds. The mapping of his collection shows that a majority of the Hellenistic coins were found in the area of the cape. Most prominent are Ptolemaic bronzes (doubtless related to the occupation of 246–219 BC) and coins from Aradus, the latter mint flooding the region with its output in the Hellenistic era. By contrast, the north of the site offered up instead late Roman and Byzantine coins (fourth to fifth century AD). This division probably reflects the places and periods of occupation on the site, at present only partially excavated. It provides valuable information, useful when deciding on the location of sondages to establish new zones for excavation.

Excavation coins make an important contribution to these issues of spatial dispersion, density, and chronology. F. de Callataÿ considers it

> . . . a pity that, as a rule archaeological publications of coins fail to mention excavated surfaces. It would be of prime interest to get some quantitative ideas about the number of coins recovered per unit of surface, and some cases favor such a treatment: the Hellenistic block of houses in Delos known as 'L'ilôt de la maison des Comédiens' (about 50 x 100 m) fully excavated by the French School; and the Hellenistic 'House of Dionysos' in Paphos (roughly 48 x 40 m), fully excavated as well.... To take these numbers at face value, and with everything else equal, it appears that Delos was more monetized than Paphos, hardly a surprising conclusion.

He concludes, with a sensible call for caution, "it is much to be hoped that, in the future, such kinds of calculations may be extended."[25] However, a cautious approach to these kinds of statistics is necessary. For coins found on the surface as for those catalogued at the time of excavations, a very wide variation is observable across the zones and occupation periods of one and the same site. The nature of the soils is not irrelevant, as R. Reece notes in one of his attempts at statistical comparison for the Roman sites of Great Britain: "The Roman palace at Fishbourne with its mosaic floors, built about AD 75, followed a supply base constructed in wood with few mortar floors. The coins recovered reflected this fact in that the first 30 years of the site produced 122 coin losses and the 125 years of occupation of the palace produced 31

23. Ras Ibn Hani, Castle of 'Atlit, Umm el-Mara, and Tell Abu Danne, Ain el-Beida, Megiddo, 'Arab el-Mulk, Tell Daruk, Tell Keisan, Tel 'Ira.

24. Augé 2000, p. 61, note 7.

25. Callataÿ 2006b, p. 192.

coin losses.... Thus a muddy builder's yard is better for archaeology than a mosaic pavement swept every day."[26] A blunt comparison of the number of coins found in this building's two stages of remodeling would easily lead to false conclusions about its economic activity and the extent of coin use therein.

Butcher has elaborated on the problem of spatial dispersion of coins for the site of the Beirut souks: "If different sorts of site or different sorts of building commonly produce radically different sorts of coins (for example if the small change in the houses of the poor turn out to be from totally different mints to those from rich houses), then the meaning of coin finds is very much dependent on the function of the site or buildings, and comparison between sites becomes extremely difficult without that knowledge."[27] This observation, a call for the greatest caution in efforts at modeling complicated sites like Beirut, also applies to quantification initiatives that, when applied to sites highly varied in nature and period, could lead to unjustified conclusions about their monetization. Cahill, in his general study of coinage distribution on the site of Olynthus, has also insisted firmly on the differing nature of the numismatic evidence, depending on whether the location is the region of large houses in the city's southeast or among the lots of the north instead.[28] Thus, the stoa of the north zone turned up the greatest concentration of coins on the site. The houses revealed 20 coins each on average, but the houses on the streets around the agora show a heavy concentration; they produced on average four times as many as the other quarters. Ten of the 15 houses with the most coins are located around the agora; two are in a more distant street, while the large houses of the southeast reveal few coins but have huge storage spaces for agricultural commodities. In the same city, the daily use of coinage has not left the same traces and was probably not the same in the zone nearer the agora, where numerous workshops are clustered, and in the southeastern zone where, clearly, the large houses were principally engaged in agriculture.

Any statistical analyses that do not take account of the fact that the same site offers sharp monetary contrasts at any given period would be doomed to give a false impression of the place's monetization. Statistical models employed for the Roman period cannot be transferred, therefore, without serious adjustments, because they are adapted to a time when coinage was considerably more frequent in everyday exchanges. It seems to me that, in the example Callataÿ provides,[29] it is more prudent to conclude that the block of the House of the Comedians on Delos is more monetized than the House of Dionysus on Paphos. Trying to extrapolate the level of monetization of a whole site based upon the statistics derived from one house is a risky venture. The example of Olynthus shows the clear disparity among the finds throughout the city. No doubt the Delian economy in the Hellenistic Age was comparatively more monetized than that of any number of other cities; but from this strong probability for a well-known site, it is easy to slip into estimates that rapidly become false for other excavations, especially in regions where coin use was not widespread.

26. Reece 1996, p. 345.
27. Butcher 2001–2002, p. 27.
28. Cahill 2002, pp. 265–73.
29. 2006b, p. 192.

1.4. Some Principles for the Publication of Excavation Coinage[30]

When, happily, excavation coinage does get published, there is still no prevailing editorial standard, leading to results that are difficult to compare, and even sometimes just difficult to use. As an example, we might take the excavation of Hama, where the coins are not even numbered.[31] The absence of a common standard greatly complicates any comparative effort. Between full publications, detailing all the specimens, and those that offer only a rapid synopsis of the whole, it is difficult to establish a basis for comparison. Butcher's publication of the coinage from the Beirut souk excavations is exemplary and should serve as a guide.[32] The catalogue gives the necessary details for a comparative exploitation of the material. It is, moreover, preceded by some thoughts on the nature of coins from excavations, the manner in which they have survived, and the historical information that one might or might not hope to draw from them.

The following suggestions derive from consideration of the catalogue's web of data, and they try to adhere neither to a purely archaeological nor a numismatic logic. Instead, they offer a structure easy to apply, allowing for appropriate use and facilitating comparisons across sites.

In the general presentation of material, it is desirable that the total number of coins found stand out clearly, as well as the number of specimens destroyed in cleaning and those that remained illegible despite restoration. These data are important in estimating how much information has been lost, which inevitably impacts final conclusions.

A major problem arises because civic coinages are often considered the product of autonomous entities and are therefore presented geographically. Thus specimens of the same mint are gathered under the same heading, all periods together, and are artificially separated from contemporary royal or imperial coins. This requires deconstructing the catalogue completely in order to exploit it by period, necessitating careful trawling and thorough organization of the raw data to make any use of them. This choice of classification certainly facilitates the editor's work, but it seems surprising from the viewpoint of an archaeologist, who has every interest in laying out material clearly classified by periods. When results are not specified, as in the case of Gamala mentioned above, the material becomes unusable from a diachronic perspective.

In their introduction the editors of the coinage from the Meiron excavations entertain two possible classifications:[33] chronological, as for Antioch[34] or Dura,[35] or by mint, as for Seleucid coinages[36] or the coins from the Susa excavations.[37] They opt for the first, while offering a con-

30. I only intend to make suggestions for publishing. On the practical aspects of handling coins in excavations, cf., e.g., Johnston, Buttrey 1991.

31. Thomsen 1986.

32. Butcher 2001–2002. The quality of the publication results from the utterly complete nature of the catalogue and from its commentary, which clearly delineates differences in numismatic character depending on the nature of the buildings excavated and the nature of the soils (mosaics and pavement versus clay, p. 27).

33. Raynor, Meshorer, Hanson 1988.

34. Waage 1952.

35. Bellinger 1949.

36. Newell 1938a and 1941.

37. Le Rider 1965.

cordance table for the mints: "This system was chosen for the Meiron catalogue to facilitate the identification of the historical periods represented there and to compare the Meiron coin profile with those of other sites" (p. 1). Chronological classification with an index by mint is by far the best because it permits historical use of the catalogue. This does not mean presenting the coins in a year-by-year manner (something partially possible for the Hellenistic era in Syria, with a number of mints dating their production), but grouping the material by eras—Persian, Hellenistic, Roman, Byzantine—and by mint within these larger divisions. This system makes it possible to distinguish eras, while taking account of problems in classification and dating peculiar to excavation coins.

Classification by mint, on the other hand, requires separating Roman provincial coins from the Classical and Hellenistic output of the same mints and multiplies the chances for error. Obviously, such a choice is not justified on an historical basis, because Syria is noted for the marked permanence of coin types from the Hellenistic era to the first century AD. Only beginning with the second century AD does it fully adopt a Romanized typology.[38] Yet a catalogue ought first of all to be employable over the long-term without the need for major recasting by the user, whether an archaeologist looking easily to retrieve means of dating or an historian looking for points of comparison. The critical commentary and other complementary aids—maps, graphics, indices—should make the extraction of historical information by mint possible. Callataÿ has stressed the rarity in publications about the Greek world of a practice common amongst Roman numismatists: chronological tables that allow quick assessment of the quantity of the material.[39]

In the same vein, one has to ask whether the presentation of mints in Strabo's geographic order, the classic numismatic procedure, is appropriate today for the publication of excavation coins.[40] This system describes the regions of the Roman Empire clockwise from Spain to Africa and classifies mints alphabetically under each rubric. Yet in an archaeological publication the material is mostly of local provenance and associated with rather disparate mints. Geographical classification often emphasizes this dispersion and requires pointless mental contortions from a user little familiar with the habits of numismatists. Ernest Babelon vigorously stressed the need for a purely intra-regional geographical classification, justifying it thus in his *Traité des monnaies grecques et romaines*: "The geographic approach offers such advantages from the scientific, historical, and even artistic point of view, that it ought to be preferred in a book aspiring to be more than a dictionary and to rise to the level of accepted truth. With a geographical arrangement, one does not bounce around the four corners of a province, empirically speaking..."[41] Babelon

38. Burnett 2002.

39. Callataÿ 2006b, pp. 187–90. Table 7, p. 188, points out the rarity of maps and chronological tables in these publications, whereas summary charts of the material are clearly more common.

40. Pellerin 1763 used this method of classification, followed by Eckhel 1792. It has become standard for general catalogues, but not for coins on individual sites. Despite criticisms, it remains the norm for classifying Greek coins, absent a better solution.

41. "la marche géographique offre de tels avantages au point de vue scientifique, historique, artistique même, qu'elle doit être préférée dans un livre qui a la prétention d'être autre chose qu'un Dictionnaire et de s'élever jusqu'à la Doctrine. Avec l'ordre géographique, on n'est pas transporté aux quatre coins d'une province, empiriquement...." Babelon 1901–1907, part 2, vol. III, p. vi.

stresses the interest of those geographical connections that manifest reciprocal influences, the shared types, the activity of engravers from one mint to another, etc. Such observations are perfectly legitimate in a synthesizing work like the *Traité des monnaies*. So, too, are Louis Robert's when he proposes breaking up the traditional numismatic classification by Strabonian region in favor of a purely micro-regional system: "First would come the mass of coins from the local mint, next the neighboring mints, and then would appear the cities farther and farther away."[42] Since each site has its own character, there probably does not exist a single solution universally applicable. To ensure ease of handling for the ensemble, an index by mint is indispensable, as well as an introduction explaining the guiding principle of the chosen classification. As for the mint itself, a chronological classification is necessary: the autonomous coins of Tyre found at Meiron are classified by types, with an inevitable mixing of periods that makes investigation difficult and requires reconstituting the catalogue if one hopes to compare it with others.[43]

Once the classification system is settled, one might have thought that its actual format was automatic. Far from it. Mention has already been made of the publication of the excavations at Hama, which do not provide any numbering for the coins. The published excavations at Antioch and Seleuceia on the Tigris are even worse: they assign a numeration to the types and then give the number of specimens for the two sites. The summary tables by reign and mint, at the end of the volume, do not differentiate the Antioch material from that of Seleuceia: these are cumulative tables! So it is still necessary to assimilate all the data before being able to use them. It is a veritable headache for the user and inevitably leads to mistakes. Callataÿ, thinking he was presenting only results from Antioch, thus used cumulative results from Antioch and Seleuceia in the summary tables of his article "Greek Coins from Archaeological Excavations: A Conspectus and a Call for Chronological Tables."[44] His table for the Seleucids is incorrect because the table of D. B. Waage on which it is based does not count the bronze coinage (1 at Seleuceia, 26 at Antioch).[45] One could multiply the examples. I will offer one last, cases of insertions of coins into a catalogue with *bis* numbers that are overlooked in summary tables and falsify their totals. This happened with the publication of the Masada excavations.[46] These problems of numbering are quite frequent and discourage the most well-intentioned: the only way to limit them is to recount the coins oneself.

A crucial remaining problem is the reference bibliography that becomes progressively out-of-date and makes the material less and less usable. All authors who have depended on publication of excavated coins have raised this point.[47] To limit this problem and permit later possible

42. "En tête viendrait la masse des monnaies de l'atelier local, puis feraient encore quelque figure les ateliers des environs, tandis qu'au-delà on verrait se disperser de plus en plus les villes." Robert 1951a, p. 89.

43. Raynor, Meshorer, Hanson 1988.

44. Callataÿ 2006b.

45. Waage 1952, p. 173.

46. Yadin, Naveh, Meshorer 1989.

47. E.g., Rotroff 1996, p. 12, or the scathing comments of Robert 1966, pp. 95–104, on Bellinger's publication of the coins excavated at Troy.

corrections, the quality of descriptions and illustrations is key. The latter are often wanting, with the poorly preserved nature of the specimens used as an excuse. But today digital photography greatly facilitates coverage of the material. It would be ideal, however, to publish casts, which are often more legible. Illustration must absolutely be on a 1:1 scale, and enlargements ought to be only twice the size of the actual photographs.

A word needs to be said on hoards: the small number found in excavations can itself tell us about the conditions in which these riches were buried. Hoards alone can provide us with some of the means to understand the historical context. So it is essential they be scrupulously described. The identification of the coins is central, but it is remarkable that, most of the time, archaeologists do not attribute much importance to the container, describing it poorly in general, if indeed at all.

1.5. Data Usage

Material from excavations is therefore no more easy to use than that from hoards, although for different reasons. The graphs and tables of this book do not recognize uncertain attributions. Indeed, it frequently occurs, for example, that the coins' condition makes attribution to one king difficult. Certain coins are therefore labeled "Antiochus I–Antiochus III" or "Ptolemy I–Ptolemy II." Differences regularly obtain between the totals of the tables and the summary results of each dig. This is particularly evident for Ptolemaic coinages, since the classification is old, and the repetition of the same types from one reign to another provokes numerous doubts about attributions that are, accordingly, removed from the statistics. I will not enter here into the debate on the use of numismatic data in archaeology.[48] It is already the object of an abundant literature, and this essay aims mostly at opening up a few paths to utilizing these data once they have been assembled.

2. Catalogue[49]

The vast majority of coins found in excavations are bronzes. All figures, therefore, refer to bronze coinage, unless otherwise indicated. Each excavation has an entry; thus, the same site can appear several times in the catalogue. The sites are presented in alphabetical order.

1. Al Mina, 1936
Syria
Finds: 307 + 30–40 fragments AE

Persian Period: 61 (16 AR [of which 5 plated] + 45 AE)
Athens: 2 tetr., 4 plated tetr., 1 plated dr.

48. Briefly, one may cite Casey, Reece 1974; Reece 1987 and 1996; Sheedy, Papageorgiadou-Bani 1997; von Kaenel, Kemmers 2009.

49. Following the practice of the original excavation publications, the catalogue identifies the Ptolemaic bronze coins by reigns according to Svoronos 1904–1908, but the recent publication of the coins from the French excavations in Alexandria suggest now a classification by series. See Picard et al. 2012.

Aradus: 1 tetrob. (Bearded head/Galley), 4 obols (idem)
Sidon: 4 sixteenths (Galley/King fighting a lion)
Cities 45 AE: Cyzicus 1; Ephesus 2; Phygela 2; Cos 1; Rhodes 2; Citium 1; Salamis in Cyprus, Evagoras II: 3 + 4; Aradus 12 + 7 + 1; Sidon 2 + 1; uncert. Aradus or Sidon 6

Hellenistic Period: 6 AR, 197 AE, 30–40 illegible fragments
Philip II: 5 AE
Alexander III: 1 tetr. (Myriandros), 2 dr. (Amphipolis, Pella), 1 obol, 179 AE (Byblos, Aradus, Salamis, Tarsus, Uncert.)
Philip III: 2 dr.
Diadochoi (?): 1
Seleucid 4: Antiochus III 1; Antiochus IV 1 + 1; Antiochus IX 1
Ptolemaic 8: Ptolemy I 7; Ptolemy III 1
30–40 illegible frags. of bronzes of Aradus or Alexander

Commentary:
According to Woolley 1953, p. 188, the building of Seleuceia caused the final downfall of Al Mina (which he identifies as Posideion). The site was abandoned around 300 BC, according to the excavators: it reveals almost no coinage after this date, until the seventh century AD (Robinson 1937, p. 182). The finds come from level I, but this level intermingles with level II (375–300 BC) as a result of various reworkings connected to the site's medieval occupation. Coins testify to a Byzantine and mediaeval reoccupation. Robinson 1937, p. 183, emphasizes that large transactions were made in Athenian tetradrachms, while small exchanges were done in fractions from Aradus and Sidon. Moreover, most of the bronzes that the site reveals date from the period of the Macedonian Conquest.

In sum, counting coins from excavations and hoards of the fourth century before Alexander, the totals are as follows:

Aradus 69 AR and 20 AE;
Sidon 16 AR and 3 AE.
Elayi 1987, p. 261, n. 63, collects the allusive references to coins in Wooley 1938a and b.

Hoards:
Three hoards of the fourth century BC contain Athenian coins and fractions of Aradus and Sidon. Woolley 1938a, p. 13, describes their place of discovery: "Thus Room 2 of House E (Level E, sq. E.7) seems to have been the workshop of a jeweller, for in it were found small bars of silver and various bits of jewellery, including the fine necklace of gold and silver illustrated in Fig. 9. Small hoards of silver coins and numerous weights testify rather to retail trade than to the business of the importers."
IGCH 1486, **33**: 51 Aradus, 3 Sidon
IGCH 1487, **36**: 18 Athens, 7 Aradus
IGCH 1488, **37**: 26 Athens, 6 Aradus, 9 Sidon.

Bibliography:
Robinson, E. S. G. "Coins from the excavations at Al-Mina (1936)," *Numismatic Chronicle* (1937), pp. 182–196.
Woolley, C. L. (1938a). "Excavations at al Mina, Sueidia I. The Archaeological Report," *Journal of Hellenic Studies* 58 (1938), pp. 1–30.
________. (1938b). "The Excavations at al Mina, Sueidia II," *Journal of Hellenic Studies* 58 (1938), pp. 133–170.
________. A Forgotten Kingdom, London, 1953.
Elayi, J. "Al Mina sur l'Oronte à l'époque perse," E. Lipinski (ed.) *Phoenicia and the East Mediterranean in the First Millennium B.C.*, Studia Phoenicia V, Leuven, 1987, pp. 249–266, especially pp. 262–263.
Elayi, Elayi (1993a) provide a status update on the hoards.

2. Antioch on the Orontes, 1932–1939
Turkey
Finds: The total found is not given; the summary tables combine the results of the excavations at Antioch and Seleuceia.

Persian Period: not mentioned in the publication

Hellenistic Period: 1086 (3 AR, 1083 AE)
Alexander III 6: Aradus 1 tetr.; Uncert. 1 dr.; 4 AE (1 Cyprus, 3 Uncert.)
Demetrius Poliorcetes: 1 AE
Seleucid 869: Seleucus I 27; Antiochus I 74; Seleucus I or Antiochus I 1; Antiochus II 9; Interregnum (246–244 BC) 3; Seleucus II 37; ΔΕΛ mint 26; Seleucus III 75; Antiochus III 268; Seleucus III or Antiochus III 14; Seleucus IV 6; Antiochus IV 40; Seleucus IV or Antiochus IV 10; Demetrius I 71; Alexander I 31; Demetrius II (1) 11; Antiochus VI 12; Tryphon 3; Antiochus VII 34; Demetrius II (2) 1; Alexander II 27; Cleopatra and Antiochus VIII 11; Antiochus VIII 42; Antiochus IX 30; Antiochus VII, VIII or after 1; Seleucus VI 3; Antiochus X 1; Antiochus XI 1
Ptolemaic 11: Ptolemy I 1; Ptolemy II 2; Ptolemy III 2; Ptolemy V 1; Ptolemy VI 4; Uncert. 1
Cities 197: Antioch before Augustus 147; Seleuceia Pieria before Augustus 23; Thessalonica 1 (before 168 BC); Histiaea 1 (4th cent. BC); Athens 1 (220–83 BC); Pergamum 5 (133–27 BC); Phocaea 1 (4th cent. BC); Side 2 AE, 1 tetr.; Mopsus 1 (2nd cent. BC); Tarsus 3 (2nd–1st cent. BC); Apamea 1 (1st cent. BC); Laodiceia ad Mare 1; Aradus 6; Byblos 1 (82/1 BC); Marathus 1 (*BMC* 19–23); Sidon 2? (1st cent. BC–2nd cent. AD); Tripolis 1 (1st cent. BC); Tyre 5?; Uncert. of Phoenicia 3; Ascalon 1 (1st cent. BC)
Hasmonean: 1
Aretas III of Nabataea (97–82 BC): 1

Commentary:
The catalogue, originally classified by Newell, contains all the coins found in the excavations of Antioch and its vicinity (Daphne), including Seleuceia Pieria, during 1932–1939.

1932: excavation of a tower, of a part of the Byzantine stadium, three baths, a house, and a villa (both Roman), a part of the circus, and a temple.

1933–1936: church, chapels, plateau, and theatre of Daphne, villa.

1937–1939: excavations interrupted by the War.

Hoards:
IGCH 1526, **138**
IGCH 1565, **272**

Bibliography:
Waage, D. B. Antioch-on-the-Orontes, IV, 2, *Greek, Roman, Byzantine and Crusaders' Coins*, Princeton, 1952.

3. 'Arab el-Mulk—Paltos
Syria
Finds: 5 AE

Persian Period: 0

Hellenistic Period:
Aradus: 1 Zeus/Prow (168/7 BC?)

Commentary:
Oldenburg, Rohweder 1981, p. 5, make clear that we are dealing here, in fact, with broad sondages carried out on the perimeter of the excavation of Sukas in 1958–1959. The village is located on the coast, 4.5 km from Tell Sukas and 33 km south of Latakia, at the mouth of the Nahr es-Sinn, which runs through it. The northern shore is called ʿArab el-Mulk, the southern one Balda el-Mulk. The latter was identified by Renan 1964, p. 111 as Paltos. This city had a mint during the Roman Imperial period, but is hardly known before Cassius used it as a military base during the Roman civil war, although we have a mention of it in Strabo 16.2.12. Ancient and mediaeval remains are still visible (columns, column capitals, walls, port constructions). The coins come from surface finds.

Bibliography:
Oldenburg E., Rohweder J. *The Excavations at Tall Daruk (Usnu?) and ʿArab el-Mulk (Paltos)*, Copenhagen, 1981.

4. Auja Hafir—Nessana, Negev
Israel
Finds: 146

Persian Period: 0

Hellenistic Period: 1 AR, 3 AE
Ptolemaic 2: Ptolemy IV 1 Alexandria; Ptolemy VIII 1 tetr. Cyprus
Hasmoneans 2: John Hyrcanus or Alexander Jannaeus 2

Commentary:
Auja Hafir–Nessana is located 160 km southwest of Jerusalem, near the Egyptian border. Occupation was essentially Byzantine but remains of a fortified Hellenistic building razed to the ground have been discovered. Ceramics date it to the second century BC and it seems to be the earliest phase of the site.

Bibliography:
Bellinger, A. R. "Coins," in H. D. Colt (ed.) *Excavations at Nessana (Auja Hafir, Palestine)* I, London, 1962, pp. 70–75.

5. Balatah (ancient Shechem), Drew-McCormick Excavation
Israel
Finds: ?

Persian Period:
1 AR Thraco-Macedonian: Satyr carrying off a Maenad/Incuse square[50]

Hellenistic Period: 2 AR, 51 AE
Alexander III: 1 dr.
Ptolemaic 27: Ptolemy I 8; Ptolemy II 17; Ptolemy III or IV 1 (Tyre, 72.2 g); Ptolemy V 1.
Seleucid 19: Antiochus III 7; Antiochus IV 3; Demetrius I 1; Antiochus VII 1; Demetrius II (2) 1 dr. and 1 AE; Alexander II 5.
Cities 6: Ake-Ptolemais 6 (Dioscuri/Cornucopia, of which 1 dated 126/5 BC).

50. The publication indicates in error that this is an electrum coin.

Commentary:
A Thasian or Thraco-Macedonian silver coin ("a rare silver and white gold coin" [*sic*], Wright 1957, p. 32) dated from the sixth or the very beginning of the fifth century was discovered at the time of the American excavations of 1956 that brought to light chiefly Bronze Age remains. Wright does not specify the circumstances of the discovery, which would appear to come from the same zone as the hoard *IGCH* 1584 (**125**), near the east gate and a Hellenistic tower. The reproduction of this coin is poor in quality (Fig. 10, p. 29).

The 1960 excavations (Campbell 1960, pp. 104–105) sought to uncover the Hellenistic and Iron Age strata. The first efforts, undertaken by the Germans from 1913 to 1934, had neglected the center of the tell, on which they were encamped. The American excavations of 1960 focused on this area, and Hellenistic remains surfaced immediately. No Seleucid bronze, but numerous Ptolemaic specimens characterized level II. Nearby, a small jar was found containing 35 Ptolemaic tetradrachms (*IGCH* 1588, **169**), and a second hoard was buried near the east gate (*IGCH* 1584, **125**). The site was occupied from the end of the fourth until the end of the second century BC. The city was probably not abandoned until the campaign of John Hyrcanus, upon his accession in 107 BC. Throughout this period, Samaritans populated it. They had fled their own city at the time of Alexander the Great's reprisals when he returned from Egypt: the Samaritans had assassinated the governor he left them, Andromachus. He had turned Samaria into a pagan city and authorized the construction of a temple on Mt. Garizim. During the Achaemenid period, some traces of activity (pottery, a silver coin) are attested. The excavations of July–August, 1960, discovered 90 Ptolemaic and Seleucid coins. Sellers 1960, p. 88, clearly states that "At Shechem, however, all the coins so far found in stratified deposits are Ptolemaic or Seleucid." From that he deduced the absence of occupation during the Achaemenid period until reoccupation by the Samaritans, forced from their city by Alexander. A Hellenistic house excavated in 1957 revealed an Alexander drachm and 12 bronzes that are not described in detail but that range from Ptolemy I to a coin of Ake-Ptolemais dated to 201 (Seleucid Era = 112/1 BC).[51] Sellers 1962, p. 96, stipulates that no Jewish coinage was found on the site, but that the campaigns of 1957 and 1960 unearthed, respectively, 2 and 13 coins dating later than the destruction of the temple on Mt. Garizim by Alexander Jannaeus in 128 (that is, for the campaign of 1960, the specimens of Demetrius II, Alexander II, and Ake-Ptolemais). In total, Sellers 1962 describes only 52 coins from the excavation of 1960 (I have added the Alexander drachm and the electrum stater from the 1957 excavations). To arrive at the total of 90, the missing specimens must be illegible coins, although the author does not specify.

Hoards:
IGCH 1584, **125**
IGCH 1588, **169**
The context and the contents of these deposits should be compared with those of the hoards from Wadi Daliyeh (*IGCH* 1503, **87**), Tell Abu Hawam (*IGCH* 1502, **55**), and Tell el-Fukhar (*IGCH* 1501, **84**).

Bibliography:
Campbell, E. F. "Excavations at Shechem, 1960," *The Biblical Archaeologist* 23/4 (1960), pp. 102–110.
Sellers, O. R. "Coins of the 1960 Excavations at Shechem," *The Biblical Archaeologist* 25/3 (1962), pp. 87–96.
Wright, G. E. et al. "Shechem, the 'navel of the land,'" *The Biblical Archaeologist* 20/1 (1957), pp. 2–32.

6. Beirut Bey 006 and 045
Lebanon
Finds: 3,196

Persian Period: 1 plated AR, 8 AE
Sidon: 3 (407/2–357/4 BC); 1 AR plated (Galley/Archer)
Side: 5 (350–250 BC)

51. Sellers 1962, p. 88–89.

Hellenistic Period: 301 of which 2 dr. (Demetrius I; Ephesus?)
Alexander III: Macedonia? 2
Ptolemaic 59: Ptolemy I 2 (Alexandria); Ptolemy II 42 (Alexandria 19, Tyre 18, Sidon 2, Uncert. 3); Ptolemy II or III 9 (Tyre? 7, Uncert. 2); Ptolemy III 4 (Alexandria 2, Ake-Ptolemais 2); Ptolemy VI 1 (Alexandria); Uncert. ruler 1 (Cyprus, end of the 2nd–beginning 1st cent. BC)
Seleucid 167: Seleucus I? 1; Antiochus II 1 (Antioch or Sardis); Antiochus III 99 (Antioch and others? 91, Uncert. 8); Seleucus IV 2 (Antioch 1, Tyre 1); Antiochus IV 39 (Antioch or Seleuceia 1, Berytus 15, Tyre 1, Ake-Ptolemais 15, Ake-Ptolemaïs? 1, Uncert. 2, Uncert. 4 (Tyre, Antioch)); Demetrius I 2 (Antioch 1 dr., Tyre 1); Alexander I 3 (Antioch 1, Berytus 2); Demetrius II (1) 5 (Antioch 3, Sidon 1, Tyre 1); Antiochus VII 3 (Antioch); Demetrius II (2) 6 (Antioch 2, Berytus 3, Sidon 1); Alexander II 1 (Antioch); Uncert. ruler: 5
Hasmonean: 1 illegible
Cities 47: Berytus: 18 undated 2nd–1st cent. BC, 5 dated 1st cent. BC, 1 Uncert.; Aradus 8; Marathus 2; Byblos 1; Sidon 4; Ake-Ptolemais 1; Dora 1; Antioch 1; Chalcis 3 (Lysanias 2, Zenodoros 1); Ascalon 2;
Asia Minor 10: Pergamum 1 (200–133 BC); Ephesus 1 dr.; Miletus 1 (313–290 BC); Cnidus 1 (250–210 BC); Cos 1 (190–167 BC); Rhodes 3 (404–84 BC); Perge 1 (220–189 C); Etenna 1 (1st cent. BC)
Italy: Rhegion 1
Uncert.: 9
Illegible: 5

Hoards:
11 hoards of the late Imperial and Byzantine period

Commentary:
Butcher 2001–2002 (whose figures are reproduced here) published the excavations of the souks and baths of Beirut (sites BEY 006 and BEY 045). Of the roughly 7,000 coins or coin fragments unearthed, more than half were illegible or too corroded to be restored. They provide evidence of human occupation from the fourth century BC to the seventh century AD. Later finds are to be published in another volume.

Bibliography:
Butcher, K. "Bey 006. The Coins – Preliminary Report," *BAAL. Bulletin d'archéologie et d'architecture libanaises* 1 (1996), pp. 207–211.
________. *Small Change in Ancient Beirut: the Coin Finds from Bey 006 and Bey 045. Persian, Hellenistic, Roman and Byzantine Periods. Archaeology of the Beirut Souks: AUB and ACRE Excavations in Beirut, 1994–1996. Berytus* 45–46, 2001–2002.

7. Beirut Bey 020
Lebanon
Finds: 85 + 24

Persian Period: 4 AR?
Sidon: Straton I (370–358 BC) 3
Uncert.: Berytus? 1 (Suggested par Z. Sawaya, but this mint has never been attested for this period)

Hellenistic Period: 10 AE
Ptolemaic 4: Ptolemy III 2 (1 Tyre); Ptolemy V 1 (Tyre); Uncert. ruler 1
Seleucid 2: Antiochus III 1; Antiochus IV 1 (Berytus)
Cities 4: Aradus 1; Berytus 1; Side 1; Uncert. 1

Commentary:
The rest of the volume of *Berytus* 45–46 is devoted to this excavation that concentrates on the oldest occupation of the site: Bronze Age, defensive slope and oldest fortifications; Iron Age, with a Persian occupation in the quarter of the souks (p. 90).

Bibliography:
Sawaya, Z. "BEY 020: The Coins," in U. Finkbeiner, H. Sader, 'Bey 020. Preliminary Report of the Excavations 1995', *BAAL. Bulletin d'archéologie et d'architecture libanaises* 2 (1997), pp. 150–156.

8. Caesarea Maritima 1986
Israel
Finds: 259 of which 2 are illegible

Persian Period: 0

Hellenistic Period: 4 AE
Seleucid 3: Antiochus III 1; Demetrius II 2
Cities: Ascalon 1 (2nd cent. BC)

Commentary:
These excavations focused on the city at the time of the Crusades. The remains are principally Byzantine or mediaeval. See Caesarea Maritima 1995 for further data on ancient levels.

Bibliography:
Ariel, D. T. "The Coins," Levine, L. I. and L. I. Netzer (eds.) *Excavations at Caesarea Maritima, 1975, 1976, 1979. Final Report*, Qedem 21, Jerusalem, 1986, pp. 137–148.

9. Caesarea Maritima 1995
Israel
Finds: 3,119 AE, 3 AR, of which around 300 are illegible

Persian Period:
Cyme 1 (c. 350–250 BC)

Hellenistic Period: 55 AE
Ptolemaic: 4
Seleucid: 47
Hasmonean: 4

Commentary:
The original settlement on the site of Caesarea, Tower of Strato, was founded by Straton of Sidon in the fourth century BC. A Ptolemaic possession until 275 BC, it was disputed by the Seleucids. The city of Caesarea was founded by Herod the Great. After the revolt of the Maccabees, the city came under Hasmonean control, except for a time under Zoilus. Some defensive walls dated to the second century (?) could be related to the reign of this tyrant who was opposed to Alexander Jannaeus.

DeRose Evans 1995 provides a table of the coins found in the excavations from the years 1971–1984, 1984, 1985, 1986, 1992.

Bibliography:
DeRose Evans, J. "Ancient Coins from the Drew Institute of Archaeological Research Excavations of Caesarea Maritima, 1971–1984," *The Biblical Archaeologist* 58/3 (1995), pp. 156–166.

10. Castle of 'Atlit
Israel
Finds: c. 570 originally; 509 published

Persian Period: 23 AR + 5 AE + 16 AR unspecified (sixteenth-shekels)
Aegeae: 1 eighth-stater (Goat/Incuse square), in a tomb
Athens: 1 tetr.
Sidon 19+: 17 sixteenth-shekels (4 Galley/Royal archer; 13 Galley/King fighting a lion); 1 AE (Galley/King in a chariot), 1 AE (Galley/Royal archer), + AR?
Tyre: 3 didr. (Hippocamp and dolphin/Owl)
Phoenicia: 3 AE uncert. (nos. 386–388)
Philistia: 1 AR

Hellenistic Period: 22 AE
Alexander III: 1 AE
Ptolemaic 11 AE: Ptolemy II 1; Ptolemy III 1; Ptolemy VI 2; Uncert. 7
Seleucid 4 AE: Antiochus III 1; Antiochus IV 3
Cities 6: Uncert. 1 (no. 389, Tyche/Galley); Hellenistic or Roman 5

Commentary:
Located 21 km south of Haifa on a promontory facing the sea, the castle of 'Atlit was built by the Knights Templar and the Teutonic Knights in AD 1217–18. It was abandoned when the Knights Templar left the Holy Land in 1291. Metcalf et al. 1999 present coins that are the fruit of the excavation campaigns of C. N. Jones in 1930–1934, which had not been systematically published before. They are in the keeping of the Israeli Antiquities Authority. They were discovered in the castle proper and its enceinte on the mainland, called the "faubourg." In the southeast corner of the latter, there was a Phoenician cemetery, dating from the sixth to the fourth century BC, containing more than one hundred tombs. It revealed 16 silver sixteenth-shekels from Tyre and Sidon that are impossible to locate today (nos. 390–405 of the catalogue). Some other coins cannot be fitted into Jones' reference system. The published catalogue therefore collects 509 coins of the 570 initially brought to light. An area of the excavation situated 100 meters east of the castle's moat, on a tell, revealed continuous occupation from 1500 BC to the beginning of the Byzantine period. Coins dating from the Persian period to the reign of Heraclius (AD 610–41) have been unearthed. Late Roman coins have also been found at the base of the castle.

Bibliography:
Metcalf, D. M., R. Kool, and A. Berman. "Coins from the Excavations at 'Atlit, Pilgrims' Castle and its Faubourg," *'Atiqot* 37 (1999), pp. 89–164.

11. Dura Europos
Syria
Finds: 14,074[52]

Persian Period:

52. This is the total figure given in the publication of the coins. However, the total number of coins described is different.

Persia: 1 AR siglos

Hellenistic Period: 1,210: 3 AR, 1,207 AE
Alexander III 4: 1 plated tetr. (uncert. mint); 3 AE (Tarsus; Phoenicia?; uncert.)
Lysimachus: 1 dr.
Attalus I of Pergamum: 1 dr.
Seleucid 1,024: Seleucus I 13; Antiochus I 89; Antiochus II 19; Seleucus II 19; Seleucus III 80; Antiochus III 463; Seleucus IV 16; Antiochus IV 26; Seleucus IV or Antiochus IV 47; Demetrius I 22; Alexander I 6; Demetrius II (1) 1; Antiochus VI 3; Tryphon 5; Antiochus VII 62; Demetrius II (2) 6; Alexander II 2; Cleopatra and Antiochus VIII 19; Antiochus VIII 100; Antiochus IX 12; Antiochus X 3; Antiochus XI 1; Philip Philadelphus 4; Demetrius III 1; Antiochus XII 2; Tigranes I 3
Parthia: 61
Characene: 2
Cappadocia: Ariobarzanes I 1 (95–62 BC)
Commagene: Mithridates I 1 (96–70 BC)
Hasmoneans 36: John Hyrcanus I 3; Alexander Jannaeus 10; imitation of Alexander Jannaeus 1; John Hyrcanus or Alexander Jannaeus 22
Ptolemaic: Ptolemy II 1 (Cyprus)
Cities 78: Seleuceia on the Tigris 17; Antioch 6; Seleuceia Pieria 1; Laodiceia ad Mare 4; Apamea 1; Aradus 13; Tyre 26; Ascalon 1; Soli in Cilicia 1; Tarsus 1; Mopsus 1; Aegeae 1; Hierapolis-Castabala 1; Abydos 1; Cyme 1; Rhodes 1; Side 1.

Commentary:
Coinage confirms the foundation of Dura c. 300, like Antioch, and by the same authority: Seleucus I.[53] Earlier coins are non-existent: a Persian siglos and a few bronzes of Alexander could have arrived with the first settlers. The weak presence of civic Hellenistic coinages must be connected to the Parthian domination over Dura at a time when cities began to issue their autonomous coinages.

The introductory note on p. ix mentions a total of 14,074 coins, but the breakdown by categories in the catalogue approaches 14,500, excluding the numerous hoards. Of 1,024 Seleucid coins, Bellinger 1949, p. 196, stresses that 953 come from the Antioch mint: "Dura normally drew her money from Antioch, though not, of course, exclusively.… Whether this was in part an administrative arrangement we do not know, but considering the continual contact with Antioch during the Parthian domination, it is obvious that convenience was the basic reason." Seleucid bronzes indeed continue to circulate after the Parthian conquest. On p. 200, Bellinger specifies that they form the core of the small change until Parthian coins supplant them during the first century.

According to Bellinger 1949, p. 199, the first Jewish coins attested date from John Hyrcanus, whom Antiochus VII compelled to accompany his campaign against the Parthians. This seems to have opened relations between Dura and the Hasmonean kingdom, since excavations have discovered coins of Alexander Jannaeus.

Hoards:
21 hoards, the majority dating to the last years of the occupation of the city.
Hoards 8–9: probably a single deposit, found under the floor of the same room of a building close to the south-west gate of the city (complete catalogue in ANS NNM 85 (1939)). It contained 2,281 coins, of which 1 AE of Seleucus III (Antioch) and an imitation of a tetradrachm of Philip Philadelphus (Antioch). The remainder is Roman, from Domitian to Trajan Decius.
Hoard 13 (*IGCH* 1770, **212**): Antiochus III 206 (1 Seleuceia on the Tigris; 203 Antioch; 1 Tyre); Mithridates I 1 (Bactria).

53. Bellinger 1949, p. 196.

Bibliography:
Bellinger, A. R. *The Excavations at Dura-Europos Conducted by Yale University and the French Academy of Inscriptions and Letters, Final Report, VI, The Coins*, New Haven, 1949.

12. En-Gedi
Israel
Finds: 1,247 of which 640 are illegible

Persian Period: 0

Hellenistic Period: 52 AE
Ptolemaic 3: Ptolemy II 3 (Tyre).
Seleucid 5: Antiochus III 1 (Antioch); Antiochus IV 2 (Ake-Ptolemais); Demetrius I 1 (Ake-Ptolemais); Uncert. ruler 1.
Hasmoneans 44: John Hyrcanus I 2 (Jerusalem); Alexander Jannaeus 33 (Jerusalem); Uncert. 9 (Jerusalem).

Commentary:
The oasis of En-Gedi, on the western shore of the Dead Sea, is mentioned in the Old Testament. The excavations focused on the most prominent site called Tel Goren. The village excavated expanded from the top of the hill during the Iron Age. There was an interruption during the Babylonian period and then a period of development during the 5th century before complete destruction around 400 BC. The coins bear witness to some activity at the time of the Diadochoi and especially during the Hasmonean period: numerous coins of Alexander Jannaeus and his successor were found throughout the oasis. The fortress built on the tell seems to have been destroyed during the Parthian invasions and the war of the Hasmoneans against Herod. Before that destruction, En-Gedi seems to have been a "flourishing agricultural settlement" (Bijovsky 2007, p. 157).

The coins published by Ariel 2007 number only 30. They cover the excavation years 1961–1965, but take no account of earlier finds. The catalogue of Bijovsky 2007 summarizes all the available data. But her table (p. 158) does not give a complete account of her catalogue, which follows the different areas excavated: the village (areas A, B, C), the Roman bathhouse (area E), Metzad ʿArugot (area B), the Essene site (area H), the terraces and pools (area G), and the surface coin finds. My list is based on this catalogue.

Bibliography:
Ariel, D. T. "Coins of En-Gedi," E. Stern (ed.) *En-Gedi Excavations, 1. Conducted by B. Mazar and I. Dunayevsky. Final Report (1961–1965)*, Jerusalem, 2007, pp. 423–427.
Bijovsky, G. "The coins," Y. Hirschfeld (ed.) *En-Gedi Excavations, 2. Final Report (1996–2002)*, Jerusalem, 2007, pp. 157–233.
Stern, E. "The history of En-Gedi in the light of the excavations: summary and conclusions," Y. Hirschfeld (ed.) *En-Gedi Excavations, 2. Final Report (1996–2002)*, Jerusalem, 2007, pp. 361–365.

13. Gamala
Israel
Finds: 6,200 of which 428 are illegible

Persian Period: 0

Hellenistic Period: 5,408 AE
Ptolemaic: they are listed in the "others" section,[54] without complete descriptions. Among them one notes a coin of Ptolemy I c. 300; several examples from the end of the 3rd cent. BC; Ptolemy IX 5 Cyprus (110–100 BC)

54. 1% of the total, also including the Nabataean kings, Roman Provincial issues and bronzes later than AD 67.

Seleucid, 584: Antiochus I 2 (Carrhae); Antiochus III 3 (Tyre); Seleucus IV 4 (Antioch 2, Tyre 2); Antiochus IV 27 (Tyre 24, Sidon 1, Ake-Ptolemais 1, Ascalon 1); Antiochus V 1 (Tyre); Demetrius I 13 (Tyre 12, Sidon 1); Alexander I Balas 13 (Tyre 12, Antioch 1); Demetrius II (1) 69 (Tyre); Antiochus VI 1 (Antioch); Antiochus VII: 36 (Tyre 27, Jerusalem 4, Antioch 5); Demetrius II (2) 45 (Tyre 43, Sidon 1, Gaza (?) 1); Alexander II 3 (Antioch 2, Damascus 1); Cleopatra Thea and Antiochus VIII 8 (Antioch 2, Ake-Ptolemais 6); Antiochus VIII 4 (Antioch); Antiochus IX 12 (Antioch 10, Damascus 2); Seleucus VI 1 (Antioch); Demetrius III 7 (Damascus 6, Seleuceia Pieria 1); Antiochus XII 8 (Damascus); Uncert. ruler 304 (Tyre. Bust of king/Palm tree, abundantly struck before the autonomy of Tyre in 126 BC)
Hasmoneans: 3,883
Cities 941: Uncert. 31 (2nd–1st cent. BC); Balanea 1 (1st cent. BC); Aradus 1 (2nd cent. BC); Marathus 1 (110 BC); Berytus 1 (1st cent. BC); Sidon 128 (112 BC–AD 58); Tyre 721 (126 BC–AD 64); Ake-Ptolemais 28 (2nd cent. BC–AD 66); Gadara 4 (63 BC–AD 43); Hippos 1 (37 BC); Apamea 1 (75 BC); Antioch 5 (c. 80 BC); Seleuceia 2 (2nd–1st cent. BC)

Commentary:
Gamala, located on the western Golan Heights, is first mentioned only in Josephus' account of the conquest of the Golan by Alexander Jannaeus (*Jewish Wars* 4.2). Syon 1992–1993 notes that at the time of his publication the site had been the object of 14 excavation campaigns. A total of 6,200 coins have come to light, broken down as follows: Seleucids 584 (9.5%), Hasmoneans 3,883 (62.9%), Herodians and procurators 270 (4.4%), autonomous 941 (15.3%), others 63 (1%), unidentified 428 (6.9%). The article presents only a sample of the best specimens; the numbers cannot, therefore, be used for detailed statistical analysis. The city, surely a Hasmonean possession from 129 BC (first issues of John Hyrcanus I) to 76 BC (death of Alexander Jannaeus), was besieged and seized by the Romans in AD 67 and subsequently abandoned. The absence of coins of Antigonus Mattathias and the generally poor representation of issues from the first century BC argue in favor of the departure of the Hasmoneans after the death of Alexander Jannaeus. The latter's coins, exceptionally numerous on the site, circulated until the first century AD, in the strata of which they have sometimes been discovered.

The finds of coins of the 3rd cent. BC "remain an enigma" (p. 42), leading Syon to suppose the existence of a military camp on the site. The coins of Ptolemy IX are connected by the excavators with his campaign in the region after the raising of the siege of Ake-Ptolemais by Alexander Jannaeus in 102 BC.

Bibliography:
Stern, E. (ed.) *The New Encyclopedia of Excavations in the Holy Land, Jerusalem*, 1992, 2 vol., s.v. Gamala, pp. 459–463 (S. Gutman).
Syon, D. "The Coins from Gamala - Interim Report," *Israel Numismatic Journal* 12 (1992–1993), pp. 34–55.

14. Hama
Syria
Finds: 545 of which 15 are illegible

Persian Period: Not listed

Hellenistic Period: 99 AE
Seleucid 24: Antiochus II 1; Seleucus III 1; Tryphon:1; Antiochus VII 2; Cleopatra Thea and Antiochus VIII 1; Antiochus VIII 6; Antiochus IX 6; Uncert. ruler 6
Cities 67: Antioch 6 (1st cent. BC); Apamea 25; Laodiceia ad Mare 3; Seleuceia Pieria 3; Aradus 24 (2nd–1st cent. BC); Marathus 4; Uncert. 2
Uncert. 8

Commentary:
The coins are not numbered.

Excavations of the summit of the tell of Hama have revealed Iron Age remains that were violently curtailed until Hellenistic reoccupation (Sargon II destroyed the site in 720 BC). According to Ploug 1985, pp. 45–46, life actually resumed in the second half of the second century BC, since there is little evidence dating from its previous decades. "Archaeological documentation from the mound indicates that the town was founded very late in the reign of Antiochus IV, or just after." The name of the Greco-Roman agglomeration remains uncertain: in Aramaic, it is called *HMT*; St. Jerome, *Gen.* 10.15–18, writes that it was called Epiphaneia under the Seleucids, but this is a common name among Seleucid cities. The Elder Pliny, in his *Natural History* 5.82, mentions an Epiphaneia on the Orontes. According to Josephus (*Jewish Antiquities* 1.6.2), Hama may have taken this name from a Hellenistic prince, an epithet distinguishing Antiochus IV and Antiochus VIII. But the lack of inscriptions and autonomous coins at Hama has made archaeologists cautious.

Hoard 1 (Thomsen 1986, p. 63) is, in fact, a bronze of Antiochus VIII discovered beneath a statue of a lion couchant on a rectangular base that is said to date from period C3 of the site (Ploug 1985, p. 189), in other words, from 35 BC to AD 100 (Ploug 1985, p. 56). Perhaps it is a foundation or votive deposit that would connect this bronze of the second century BC and the sculpture. (Note that Ploug 1985, p. 45, dated this bronze to the reign of Antiochus IV, but Thomsen 1986, p. 63, corrects the attribution: it is a coin of Antiochus VIII.)

1 modern forgery of an Athenian tetradr., p. 63.

Hoards:
11 "hoards," of which:
1. 1 AE of Antiochus VIII under a limestone lion.
2. 1 AE, 1 AR: Antiochus IX and a Roman quinarius.
3. 5 tetr. of Aradus (years 92/1, 87/6, 73/2 BC), *IGCH* 1576, **325**.
4. 49 AE of Antioch (1st cent. BC) and 2 frags. AE not identified, *IGCH* 1580, **337**.
8. 7 AE or frags. of AE: Antiochus VIII; 1 uncert. Hellenistic; 5 Roman, 4th–5th cent. AD.

Bibliography:
Ploug, G. *Hama, Fouilles et recherches de la fondation Carlsberg, 1931–1938*, III.1, *The Graeco-Roman Town*, Copenhagen, 1985.
Thomsen, R. "The Graeco-Roman Coins," in A. Papanicolaou-Christensen, R. Thomsen, G. Ploug, *Hama, fouilles et recherches de la fondation Carlsberg, 1931–1938*, III.3, *The Graeco-Roman Objects of Clay, the Coins and the Necropolis*, Copenhagen, 1986, pp. 59–69.

15. Hippos-Sussita
Israel
Finds: 885

Persian Period: 0

Hellenistic Period: 68 AE
Ptolemaic 10: Ptolemy I 1 (Alexandria); Ptolemy II 4 (Alexandria 1, Tyre 3); Ptolemy III 1 (Tyre); Ptolemy V 1 (Alexandria); Ptolemy VI 1 (Alexandria); Uncert. ruler of the end of the second century BC 2
Seleucid 33: Seleucus III 1 (Antioch); Antiochus III 4 (Antioch 2, Apamea 1, uncert. 1); Seleucus IV 1 (Antioch); Antiochus IV 11 (Tyre 8, Ake-Ptolemais 3); Demetrius I 3 (Tyre); Alexander I Balas 2 (Antioch 1, Tyre 1); Antiochus VI 2 (Antioch); Anonymous Seleucid before 132 BC 1 (Ake-Ptolemais); Alexander II Zebinas 2 (Antioch); Antiochus VIII 1 (Antioch); Demetrius III 2 (Damascus); Antiochus XII 3 (Damascus)
Hasmonean 2: John Hyrcanus I 1; Alexander Jannaeus 1

Ituraeans 2: Ptolemy son of Mennaios 1; uncert. ruler 1
Cities 21: Aradus 1 (162/1 BC); Sidon 2 (2nd cent. BC); Tyre 13 (2nd–1st cent. BC); Demetrias/Damascus 1 (1st cent. BC); Gadara 2 (1st cent. BC); Hippos 2 (41/0 BC)

Commentary:
Hippos-Sussita is situated on the Eastern shore of the Lake Tiberias, on the top of a hill. The remains date from the Hellenistic period to 749 AD, when the city was entirely destroyed by an earthquake. It is an Hellenistic foundation with a regular plan, and it could have been founded by Antiochus III or Antiochus IV since it is known as Antiocheia-Hippos during the Hellenistic period. However, the first archaeological remains—coins and pottery—date back to the third century BC. A Hellenistic sanctuary is the oldest building excavated. It is dated to the second half of the second century, but very little remains from that period.

The catalogue is based on the conspectus of the coins from the 2000–2011 excavations published by Berman 2013. The team used a metal detector rather frequently, and the finds made with that tool were catalogued in separate files.

Bibliography:
Berman, A. "Hippos-Sussita 4th season (July 2003). The Coins find Catalogue," A. Segal et al. (ed.) *Hippos-Sussita. Fourth Season of Excavations (June–July 2003)*, Haifa, 2003, pp. 89–101.

________. "The Coins find Catalogue - Hippos-Sussita 5th season (2004)" followed by "General Conspectus of Coins Chronology and Mints found at Hippos-Sussita," A. Segal et al. (ed.) *Hippos-Sussita. Fifth Season of Excavations (September–October 2004) and Summary of all Five Seasons (2000–2004)*, Haifa, 2004, pp. 123–126 and 127–134.

________. "The Coins Catalogue - Hippos-Sussita 6th season (2005)," A. Segal et al. (ed.) *Hippos-Sussita. Sixth Season of Excavations (July 2005)*, Haifa, 2005, pp. 108–112.

________, "The coins catalogue - Hippos-Sussita 7th season (2006)," A. Segal et al. (ed.) *Hippos-Sussita. Seventh Season of Excavations (July 2006)*, Haifa, 2006, pp. 144–153.

________. "The Coins Catalogue - 8th season (2007)," A. Segal et al. (ed.) *Hippos-Sussita. Eighth Season of Excavations (July 2007)*, Haifa, 2007, pp. 155–171.

________. "Hippos-Sussita - 9th season (2008) - Coins Catalogue," A. Segal et al. (ed.) Hippos-Sussita. *Ninth Season of Excavations (June–July 2008), Haifa*, 2008, pp. 143–162.

________. "Hippos-Sussita - 10th season (2009) - Coins Catalogue," A. Segal et al. (ed.) *Hippos-Sussita. Tenth Season of Excavations (July and September 2009)*, Haifa, 2009, pp. 157–172.

________. "Hippos-Sussita - 11th season (2010) - Coins Catalogue," A. Segal et al. (ed.) *Hippos-Sussita. Eleventh Season of Excavations (July 2010)*, Haifa, 2010, pp. 153–169.

________. "The Coin Finds of Hippos-Sussita," A. Segal et al. (ed.) *Hippos-Sussita of the Decapolis. The First Twelve Seasons of Excavations. 2000–2011*, Vol. I, Haifa, 2013, pp. 279–301.

16. ʿIraq al-Amir, Monumental Gateway
Jordan
Finds: 13 of which 3 are illegible

Persian Period: 0

Hellenistic Period: 8 AE
Seleucid: Antiochus III 6 "halves" (Antioch); Uncert. ruler 1 (2nd cent. BC)
Maccabees: 1

Commentary:
These few coins were found in the excavations of the monumental gateway of the city, 150 m from the Qasr.

Bibliography:
Dentzer, J.-M., F. Villeneuve, and F. Larché. "Iraq el-Amir: Excavations at the Monumental Gateway," in *Studies in the History and Archaeology of Jordan I*, Amman, 1982, pp. 201–207 (coin study by C. Augé).

17. Jablah, Necropolis of al-Jbeibat
Syria
Finds: 13

Persian Period: 3 AR
Aradus: 3 tetrob. (Bearded head/Prow)

Hellenistic Period: 1 AV, 5 AR
Alexander III: 5 dr. (Salamis in Cyprus, Colophon 2, Lampsacus, Magnesia? perhaps plated)
Ptolemaic 1: 1 Attic weight gold stater of Ptolemy I (Head of Alexander in elephant scalp/Prow).[55]

Commentary:
Badawi's thesis only details the coins found in the necropolis of al-Jbeibat, to the north of ancient Gabala. Most were found in the same tomb (K-2002): a gold stater, two tetrobols of Aradus, and five Alexander drachms. The majority of these coins are in precious metal, contrary to what is usually found in an excavation, since they were selected to accompany the deceased. The yield is small despite the number of excavated tombs. This is the result of the repeated plundering the necropolis has endured: no tomb is intact.

Badawi notes several dozen coins discovered during the excavation of the baths and in the archaeological investigation of the city.

Bibliography:
Badawi, M. *Jablé (Syrie) et son territoire à l'époque hellénistique et romaine: développement urbain et culture matérielle*, 2 vol., unpublished thesis, University of Paris I, 28 March 2009.

18. Jaffa
Israel
Finds: 677

Persian Period:
Sidon: 2 AR, 22 AE

Hellenistic Period: 138 AE
Alexander III: 12 (Macedon 11, Babylon 1)
Ptolemaic 39: Ptolemy I 5 (3 Alexandria, 2 incert.); Ptolemy II 10 (1 Sidon, 2 Tyre, 1 Ake-Ptolemais, 3 Alexandria, 3 incert.); Ptolemy III 2 (1 Alexandria, 1 incert.); Ptolemy VIII and Cleopatra 1 Ake-Ptolemais; Uncert. ruler (2nd cent. BC) 21
Seleucid 51: Antiochus III 11; Antiochus IV 18; Antiochus V 1; Demetrius I 2; Alexander I 1; Demetrius II 3; Alexander II 2; Antiochus VIII and Cleopatra 2; Uncert. ruler (2nd cent. BC) 11
Hasmonean: 30
Cities: 6 (unspecified)

Hoard:
IGCH 1611, **313**

55. On this issue see Lorber forthcoming, no. 38.

Commentary:
These coins are the fruit of excavations from 1955–1978, zones A, C, D, G, J, T, Y (note 5). The author reminds us that Jaffa (Joppa) was under Sidon's power during the Persian period, which explains the exclusive presence of Sidon's currency. This is also an important Ptolemaic mint, but its bronze currency is curiously absent from excavations. John Hyrcanus took the city from the Seleucids at the start of his reign.

Bibliography:
Meir, C. "The Historical Evidence of the Ancient City of Jaffa," in B. Kluge and B. Weisser (eds.) *XII. internationaler numismatischer Kongress*, Berlin 1997. Akten I, Berlin, 2000, pp. 123–130.

19. Jebel Khalid
Syria
Finds: 317 of which 23 are illegible

Persian Period: 0

Hellenistic Period: 264 AE, 1 AR + 2 tetr. plated
Alexander III: 1 dr. Lampsacus (?); 1 tetr. uncert.
Seleucid 239 (146 identified): Seleucus I 2 (Antioch); Antiochus I 6 (Antioch 4, Seleuceia Pieria 1, Uncert. 1); Antiochus II 2 (Antioch 1, Seleuceia in Pieria 1); Antiochus I or II 1 (Antioch); Seleucus II 5 (Antioch 4, Sardis 1); Seleucus III 8 (Antioch 7, Ecbatana 1); Antiochus III 37 (Antioch); Seleucus III or Antiochus III 1 (Antioch?); Seleucus IV 3 (Antioch); Antiochus I–Seleucus IV 1 (Uncert.); Antiochus IV 9 (Antioch 8, Hierapolis-Bambyce 1); Demetrius I 3 (Antioch); Alexander I Balas 1 dr., 1 AE (Antioch); Demetrius II (1): 6 (Antioch 3, Uncertain mint in Northern Syria 3); Antiochus VI 3 (Antioch); Antiochus III–Demetrius II (1) 1 (Tyre); Serrate bronzes before Antiochus VI 7; Antiochus VII 9 (Antioch); Cleopatra Thea and Antiochus VIII 3 (Antioch); Antiochus VIII (1): 7 (Antioch); Antiochus VIII (2): 2 (Antioch); Antiochus VIII (3): 1 (Antioch); Antiochus IX (1): 10 (Antioch); Antiochus IX (2): 2 (Antioch); Antiochus IX (3) 6 (Antioch 1, Uncert. 5); Demetrius III 1 (Damascus); Antiochus XII 1 (Damascus); Antiochus III–XII 1 (Uncert.); Antiochus I–XII 2 (Uncert.); Uncert. rulers 93
Cities 24: Tarsus 1 (c. 130–80 BC); Antioch 21 (92–72 BC); Sidon 1 (c. 100–80? BC); Aradus 1 (c. 175–140 BC) + 2 plated tetr. with types Tyche/Nike, (Duyrat 2005a, D89 and D91).[56]

Commentary:
Nixon 2002 describes the site of Jebel Khalid, located on the west bank of the Euphrates at a crossing point, about 60 km south of Jerablous, 200 km east of Antioch. It is a site with impressive fortifications, including those around the acropolis. Excavations started in 1987 and brought to light a palace and a residential quarter. No inscription has been found, and the ancient name of the city remains conjectural. It is situated on the route from Hierapolis to the Euphrates and on the road that runs along the Euphrates between Zeugma and Dura Europos, in the direction of Seleuceia on the Tigris.

The archaeological material is typically Hellenistic. More precisely, 85% of the coins can be dated by the Seleucid Era (Nixon 2002, p. 293). The oldest finds are two posthumous coins of Alexander the Great. Nearly all reigns are then represented, peaking under Antiochus III. The civic coins of Antioch date basically from 90–70 BC. Later occupation of the site is then very sporadic, if one relies on the coins. "To judge from the numismatic evidence alone, the excavated site would seem to be almost purely Seleukid" (p. 293). The site seems abandoned following the years 70–60 BC, with the bronzes of Antioch from the time of Caesar, common at Antioch, Seleuceia Pieria or, even closer, Tell Abu Danne, totally absent at Jebel Khalid. At Tell el-Hajj, there is a noticeable interruption in the provision of coins from Antioch after Seleucus II, but

56. The photographs of these two coins, of which only the bronze core remains, were sent to me by Oliver Hoover in October 2009. For other plated examples of the same period: Duyrat 2005a, nos. 3973 and 3974.

it resumes under Augustus (p. 297). Additionally, roofing material and anything transportable seem to have been removed from the site during the first century BC.

Antioch's preeminence as a coinage source contrasts with the total absence of Mesopotamian mints. Yet, "Jebel Khalid commands a crossing of the Euphrates, near major routes east," and docks have been discovered. Nixon 2002, p. 299, accordingly concludes that there was a transfer of currency, meant to pay the garrison, from the regional capital. The Antioch coinage would then have vanished at the same time as the garrison.

Bibliography:
Nixon, C. E. V. "The Coins," in G. W. Clarke, et al., *Jebel Khalid on the Euphrates: Report on Excavations 1986–1996*, Volume 1, Mediterranean Archaology Suppl. 5, Sydney, 2002, pp. 291–335.
Clarke, G. W. and H. Jackson. "Jebel Khalid on the Euphrates: An Overview," *Annales archéologiques arabes syriennes 45–46 (2002–2003)*, pp. 189–206.

20. Jerash – Gerasa
Jordan
Finds: 1,468 of which 16 are illegible

Persian Period: 0

Hellenistic Period: 5 AE
Ptolemaic: 2 AE
Hasmonean: 3 AE

Commentary:
The excavations in Gerasa unearthed remains from the Neolithic and the second millennium BC. But the foundation of the city seems to date back to the second century BC, after the conquest of Syria and Phoenicia by the Seleucids. Gerasa received the name of Antiocheia ad Chrysorrhoam. The region was then under Hasmonean power until the reduction of Syria to a Roman province. However, the remains of the Hellenistic period are rather scarce. The coins come from the Spanish excavations of the Roman market building (2nd century AD) that also revealed a Hellenistic wall and some ceramic of the same period as the few coins catalogued here. The stratigraphy of these layers was disturbed by later building works.

Bibliography:
Marot, T. *Las monedas del Macellum de Gerasa (Ŷaraš, Jordania). Aproximación a la circulación monetaria en la provincia de Arabia*, Madrid, 1998.

21. Jericho
Israel
Finds: 877

Persian Period: 0

Hellenistic Period: 599 AE
Seleucid 6 AE: Antiochus IV 2; Alexander I Balas 2; Alexander II Zebinas 2
Hasmoneans 593: John Hyrcanus I 15; Alexander Jannaeus 549; Alexander Jannaeus or John Hyrcanus II 8; Antigonus Mattathias 21

Commentary:
Excavations of the palaces of Jericho have turned up Hasmonean and Herodian coins, as was to be expected, but the oldest coins are attributed to Antiochus IV. The coins of Alexander Jannaeus and Antigonus Mattath-

ias are the most abundant of the Hasmonean issues; the majority of those of Mattathias are actually gathered in a hoard found in a pool (*CH* 2.128, **349**). Hasmonean bronzes constitute about half of all the numismatic finds.

Hoard:
CH 2.128, **349**

Bibliography:
Meshorer, Y. "The Coins," E. Netzer and R. Laureys-Chachy (eds.) *Hasmonean and Herodian Palaces at Jericho: Final Reports of the 1973–1987 Excavations. II. Stratigraphy and Architecture*, Jerusalem, 2004, pp. 289–312, pl. IX.

22. Jerusalem, Muristan, 1970–1974
Israel
Finds: 231 of which 25 are illegible

Persian Period: 0

Hellenistic Period: 18 AE
Ptolemaic 2: Ptolemy I–III 1; Uncert. ruler 1
Seleucid 5: Antiochus I 1 (Sardis); Antiochus IV 2; Demetrius II (1) 2
Hasmoneans 9: Alexander Jannaeus 7; Antigonus Mattathias 2
Cities 2: Antioch 1 (82/1 BC); Uncert. 1

Commentary:
This is the site of a mediaeval church.

Bibliography:
Carradice, I. A. "The Coins," K. J. H. Vriezen (ed.) *Die Ausgrabungen unter der Erlöserkirche im Muristan, Jerusalem (1970–1974)*, Wiesbaden, 1994, pp. 311–330.

23. Jerusalem, 1961–1967, Armenian Garden, west hill
Israel
Finds: 392

Persian Period:
4th cent. BC: 1 Uncert.

Hellenistic Period: 169 AE
Ptolemaic 1: Ptolemy III or IV 1 (Tyre)
Seleucid 14: Antiochus III 1 (Tyre); Antiochus IV 7 (Ake-Ptolemais); Demetrius II (1) 3 (Ake-Ptolemais); Antiochus VII 3 (Jerusalem)
Hasmonean: 153
Cities 1: Sidon (2nd cent. BC) 1

Commentary:
This site was occupied in the Bronze Age, then under the Hasmoneans at the time of the first Jewish revolt, and then again in the Byzantine period.

Bibliography:
Miles, G. C. (ed.) "The Coins from the Armenian Garden," in A. D. Tushingham, *Excavations in Jerusalem, 1961–1967*, vol. 1, Royal Ontario Museum, Toronto, 1985, pp. 156–177.

24. Jerusalem, City of David
Israel
Finds: 355 of which 125 are illegible

Persian Period:
Lycia: 1 AR (5th cent. BC)

Hellenistic Period: 132, 1 plated shekel, two AE flans
Ptolemaic, 9 AE: Ptolemy II 2; Uncert. rulers 7
Seleucid, 12 AE: Antiochus III 5; Antiochus III or IV 1; Antiochus IV 5 (Ake-Ptolemais); Antiochus VII 1 (Jerusalem)
Uncert. 1
Hasmoneans, 109 AE: Alexander Jannaeus 79; Judah Aristobulus 1; John Hyrcanus 4; Uncert. 24; Antigonus Mattathias 1
2 Hasmonean or Herodian flans, of which one double flan (not separated)
Cities 2: Antioch 1 AE; 1 plated imitation of a shekel of Tyre (126/5 BC)

Commentary:
These finds come from different places in the City of David. According to Mørkholm 1967, the coins of Antiochus IV were struck in Ake and used to pay his troops in the war against the Maccabees. The bronze of Antiochus VII belongs to a series D. T. Ariel attributed to Jerusalem, on the basis of finds in the excavation. The plated Tyrian shekel is the first found in an excavation. It has been cut. 81% of the coins are of local manufacture.

The excavations have also uncovered blank disks in unseparated strips, as well as moulds for blanks.

Bibliography:
Mørkholm, O. "The Monetary System of the Seleucid Kings until 129 BC," *International Numismatic Convention, Jerusalem, 27–31 December 1963. The Patterns of Monetary Development in Phoenicia and Palestine in Antiquity*, A. Kindler (ed.) Tel Aviv/Jerusalem, 1967, pp. 75–86.
Shiloh, Y., and D. T. Ariel (eds.) "Coins, Flans, and Moulds," *Excavations at the City of David 1978–1985. 2. Imported Stamped Amphora, Handles, Coins, Worked Bone and Ivory, and Glass,* Jerusalem, 1990, pp. 99–118.

25. Jerusalem, Jewish Quarter 2003
Israel
Finds: 577 of which 120 are illegible

Persian Period: 0

Hellenistic Period: 240 + 2 AE
Ptolemaic 6: Ptolemy I 2; Ptolemy II 4
Seleucid 16: Antiochus III 4; Antiochus IV 7; Antiochus VII 4 (Lily/ Anchor); Demetrius III 1
Hasmoneans 218: John Hyrcanus I 14; Alexander Jannaeus 191; Uncert. 10; Antigonus Mattathias 3
Prutot (1st cent. BC): 2

Commentary:
Excavations in the Jewish Quarter of the Old City of Jerusalem occurred after the annexation of the West Bank following the Six Day War in 1967. The excavations were possible since the quarter had suffered destruction in 1948 and was the place of an intensive building program after 1967. The excavations took place in scattered areas of the Jewish Quarter, and the publication is a synthesis of the results. The first settlement dates back to the 8th century BC. There are few archaeological remains from the 6th to the 3rd cent. BC., but the settlement is denser from the second half of the 2nd cent. The Hellenistic architectural remains were mostly destroyed by the Herodian buildings (Geva 2000).

Bibliography:
Geva, H. "General Introduction to the Excavations in the Jewish Quarter," H. Geva (ed.) *Jewish Quarter Excavations in the Old City of Jerusalem Conducted by Nahman Avigad, 1969–1982*. Vol. I. Architecture and Stratigraphy: Areas A, W and X2. Final Report, Jerusalem, 2000, pp. 1–30.
Gitler, H. "The Coins," H. Geva (ed.) *Jewish Quarter Excavations in the Old City of Jerusalem Conducted by Nahman Avigad, 1969–1982. Vol. II. The Finds from Areas A, W and X-2, Final Report*, Jerusalem, 2003, pp. 453–492.

26. Jerusalem, Jewish Quarter 2006
Israel
Finds: 934 of which 102 are illegible

Persian Period: 0

Hellenistic Period: 759 AE
Ptolemaic: 3 Uncert.
Seleucid 17: Antiochus III 5 (Antioch); Antiochus IV 2 (Ake-Ptolemais); Demetrius I 1 (Ake-Ptolemais); Uncert. ruler 2 (Ake-Ptolemais); Antiochus VII 2 (Lily/ Anchor); Uncert. rulers 5
Hasmoneans 737: John Hyrcanus I 10; Alexander Jannaeus 696; Uncert. 6; Antigonus Mattathias 3; Uncert. 22
Cities 2: Berytus 1st cent. BC 1; Tyre or Sidon 1

Commentary:
This site was occupied during the Iron Age, then in the Hellenistic and Roman periods. All the coins discovered were in bronze, with one exception in lead.

Ariel 2006, pp. 192–93, identifies a significant number of coins as probably or possibly of Alexander Jannaeus. In a postscript, Lönnqvist, Lönnqvist 2006, p. 146, connect them to the group L of Meshorer 2001, pp. 40 and 210, consisting of light *prutot* with an Aramaic inscription instead of the expected Hebrew. They could be post-78 imitations that reused the types, but not the legends, of the original models.

The site also revealed blank moulds.

Bibliography:
Ariel, D. T. "The Coins," H. Geva (ed.) *Jewish Quarter Excavations in the Old City of Jerusalem Conducted by Nahman Avigad, 1969–1982. Vol. III. Area E and Other Studies, Final Report*, Jerusalem, 2006, pp. 192–217.
Lönnqvist, Lönnqvist, "The Numismatic Chronology of Qumran: Fact and Fiction," *Numismatic Chronicle* 166 (2006), pp. 121–166.
Meshorer, Y. *A Treasury of Jewish Coins. From the Persian Period to Bar Kokhba*, Jerusalem, 2001.

27. Jerusalem, Valley of Tyropoion, Mt. Ophel
Israel

Finds: The total number of finds is unknown.

Persian Period: 0

Hellenistic Period: 56 AE
Ptolemaic: Ptolemy VI? 2
Seleucid 10: Antiochus IV 3; Demetrius II (1) 2; Demetrius II 1; Antiochus VII 2; Uncert. 2
Maccabees 13: Simon Maccabeus 1; Maccabees 12
Hasmoneans 31: John Hyrcanus I 1 (now reclassified as John Hyrcanus II); Alexander Jannaeus 28; Uncert. 2

Commentary:
Along with the Cedron and Gehenna valleys, the valley of Tyropoion defines the plateau on which Jerusalem is built, but this wadi has a gentle current that has not carved out a very deep bed. The excavated site is located 120 m south of the "City of David" wall. It reveals occupation levels from the Bronze Age to the Emperor Titus, followed by a gap and a resumption of occupation from around 300 to 600 AD (p. 10). The later levels appear much poorer (p. 11).

Three, perhaps four hoards have been discovered in the excavations, but the publication offers no details (pp. 19, 25). Only one is listed in *IGCH*. Noted under Number 1, p. 106, are "90 coins together, fragmentary and corroded. Among the types distinguishable are a lion, a palm tree, and human heads; others are conjectural. ... The majority probably belong to the 4th century BC"; one coin might conjure up a late Roman bronze. Mentioned under number 2, p. 106, are 43 coins "apparently of the same class as 1." Under number 3, p. 106, we read simply "coins, apparently of the same class as 1." *IGCH* 1623 (**342**) has the benefit of an itemized inventory.

Hoard:
IGCH 1623, **342**.

Bibliography:
Crowfoot, J. W. and G. M. Fitzgerald. *Excavations in the Tyropoeon Valley, Jerusalem, 1927, Palestine Exploration Fund Annual*, Jerusalem, 1927, pp. 103–120.

28. Khirbet Qumran
Israel
Finds: 689 (+ 561 AR hoard = 1,250) of which 135 are illegible

Persian Period: 0

Hellenistic Period: 175 AE, 5 AR
Seleucid 9: Antiochus III 1 AE; Antiochus IV 1 AE; Demetrius II 1 AR; Antiochus VII 4 AR, 2 AE
Hasmoneans 171: John Hyrcanus I 14 AE; Alexander Jannaeus 145 AE; Antigonus Mattathias 6 AE; illegible 6 AE

Commentary:
The discovery of the Dead Sea Scrolls in the caves of Qumran also brought to light numerous objects, including several hundred coins. The latter have never been systematically catalogued and, since the 1960s, their place of deposit is unknown (Lönnqvist, Lönnqvist 2006, p. 121). Roland de Vaux's chronology of the site, based on the coinage and pottery, supposes a first settlement during the second century BC (before the reign of John Hyrcanus I, 135–104 BC), until an interruption between the earthquake of 31 BC and the reign of Archelaus (4 BC–AD 6). The site's most intense period of activity is the first century AD, until its destruction during the Jewish revolt of AD 66–73.

The catalogue of coins found at Qumran presented here is that published by Lönnqvist, Lönnqvist 2006, which synthesized previous editions drawn from de Vaux's excavation notebooks. Supplementing the list of 681 coins found in the excavations are seven identified silver coins and one illegible coin which Lönnqvist, Lönnqvist 2006, p. 126, catalogue as "stray finds." The large hoard of 561 silver coins (**357**) brings the total of numismatic discoveries to 1,250.

The 145 coins of Alexander Jannaeus constitute the largest share, or 25%, of the total bronzes. The Herodian kings plus Roman procurators and the Jewish revolt form the other important groups. All periods are represented, without break. The number of coins of John Hyrcanus I and the Seleucid kings leads Lönnqvist, Lönnqvist 2006, p. 133, to conclude that the site was occupied from the years 150–130 BC, thus confirming de Vaux's dating.

Hoard:
Qumran Hoard, not in *IGCH*, **357**.

Bibliography:
de Vaux, R. "Fouilles de Khirbet Qumrân. Rapport préliminaire," *Revue biblique* 60 (1953), pp. 93–94.
_______. "Fouilles de Khirbet Qumrân. Rapport préliminaire sur la deuxième campagne," *Revue biblique* 61 (1954), pp. 229–231.
_______. "Fouilles de Khirbet Qumrân. Rapport préliminaire sur les 3e, 4e et 5e campagnes," *Revue biblique* 63 (1956), pp. 565–569.
_______. *L'archéologie des manuscrits de la Mer Morte*, Oxford, 1959.
_______. *Archaeology and the Dead Sea Scrolls*, London, 1973, index s.v. "Coins". Revised English version of the 1959 edition.
_______. *Fouilles de Khirbet Qumran et de Ain Feshkha, Album de photographies. Répertoire du fonds photographique. synthèse des notes de chantier du Père Roland de Vaux*, I, Humbert J.-B., Chambon A. (ed.) Göttingen, 1994, pp. 291–368.
de Vaux, R., F. Rohrhirsch, and B. Hofmeir. *Die Ausgrabungen von Qumran und En Feschcha. Die Grabungtagebücher*, Göttingen, 1996.
Humbert, J.-B., A. Chambon, and S. Pfann. *The Excavations of Khirbet Qumran and Ein Feshkha. Synthesis of Roland de Vaux Field Notes*, Fribourg, 2003.
Hirschfeld, Y. *Qumran in Context. Reassessing the Archaological Evidence*, Peabody, Mass., 2004, p. 143. (old-fashioned interpetation of coinage as a sign of economic activity)
Lönnqvist, K. and M. Lönnqvist. *Archaeology of the Hidden Qumran. The New Paradigm*, Helsinki, 2002.
_______. "The Numismatic Chronology of Qumran: Fact and Fiction," *Numismatic Chronicle* 166 (2006), pp. 121–166.

29. Marisa (Ancient Maresha)
Israel
Finds: 950

Persian Period: 2

Hellenistic Period: 948 AE
Ptolemaic: 135
Seleucid: 716
Hasmonean: John Hyrcanus I 2; other unidentified Hasmoneans 12
Nabataea: 29 (before 108/7 BC)
Cities 54: Side 7 (end of the 3rd cent. BC–middle of the 2nd cent. BC); Ascalon 45 (175–108 BC); Gaza 1 (c. 130–120 BC); Ake-Ptolemais 1 (before 126/5 BC)

Commentary:
Marisa is located 38 km to the southwest of Jerusalem. In 259 BC, the Zenon papyri show it to be a Ptolemaic administrative seat, while an epitaph from the huge Hellenistic necropolis shows the existence of a Sidonian colony as well. Everything indicates that the city was important under the Seleucids, both militarily and economically. John Hyrcanus I destroyed it in 108/7 BC.

Barkay's article gives an account of the numismatic finds from the excavations of Kloner between 1989 and 2000 (to appear in the *Israel Antiquities Authorities Reports*). She pays particular attention to the coinages of Side, Ascalon, Gaza, Ake-Ptolemais, and Nabataea. The last are autonomous types (helmeted head of Athena/standing Nike) difficult to date, but their presence at Marisa shows that they were issued before the city was abandoned in 108/7 BC. Their rather worn state suggests they were struck at the very beginning of the reign of Aretas II (c. 110–96 BC).

Hoard:
CH 9.544, **285**.

Bibliography:
Barkay, R. "Undated Coins from Hellenistic Marisa," *Israel Numismatic Journal* 15 (2003–2006), pp. 48–55.

30. Masada
Israel
Finds: 4,699 of which 785 illegible and 158 destroyed in cleaning

Persian Period: 0

Hellenistic Period: 117 AE
Ptolemaic 12: Ptolemy I 1 Alexandria; Ptolemy II 9 (5 Alexandria, 2 Tyre, 1 Sidon, 1 Ake-Ptolemais); Ptolemy IV 2 (1 Alexandria, 1 frag.)
Seleucid 5: Seleucus II 1; Seleucus IV 3; Demetrius II 1 (128 BC)
Hasmoneans 91: Alexander Jannaeus 84; John Hyrcanus I or John Hyrcanus II 4; Antigonus Mattathias 3
Cities 9: Side 1 (190–36 BC); Antioch 1 (35 BC); Tyre 2 (1st cent. BC); Sidon 1 (1st cent. BC); Ascalon 4 (1st cent. BC)

Commentary:
Meshorer, p. 71, attributes the weak presence of Seleucid coins to the construction of a citadel on the site by Alexander Jannaeus (103–76 BC), as reported in Josephus, *Jewish Wars* 7.285. Since the oldest coins date to Ptolemy II (283–246 BC)—except one isolated bronze of Ptolemy I—Masada's foundation would go back to this sovereign's reign. Seleucid bronzes and those attributed to John Hyrcanus I would presumably have arrived at the same time as those of Alexander Jannaeus. The abundance of the latter's coins is a function of the very large volumes struck, especially those with the anchor and star types. As was to be expected, coins from the war against Rome are omnipresent in the excavations. Generally speaking, the bronzes are rather well preserved.

The third hoard of coins from the Roman War included a shekel (no. 3668) and a half-shekel (no. 3670) whose types had been deliberately effaced. The Mishna (Kellim 12.7) also mentions a sela (tetradrachm) used as a weight, its types destroyed.
N. B. There are bis numbers in the catalogue with the result that the totals do not square with the numbering.

Hoards:
Three hoards of shekels from the period of the Jewish Revolt. The first was made up of 37 coins fused together "with clear traces of the cloth bag in which they were put" (p. 73). The second (12 coins) was protected by "a medicinal cup, used as a pyxis" (p. 74), published by M. Hershkowitz, "A Roman Cupping Vessel from

Masada," *Eretz Israël* 20 (1989), in Hebrew. The heavy corrosion of the vessel affected the coins. The third hoard was dispersed beneath the debris of a wall in which it had undoubtedly been hidden.

Bibliography:
Meshorer, Y. "The coins of Masada," in Y. Yadin, J. Naveh, and Y. Meshorer. *Masada I. 1989: The Yigael Yadin Excavations 1963–1965, Final Reports: The Aramaic and Hebrew Ostraca and Jar Inscriptions. The Coins of Masada*, Jerusalem, 1989 (coins pp. 69–132, pl. 61–81).

31. Megiddo
Israel
Finds: 102

Persian Period: 2 AE + 2 AR
Sidon: 2 AE Straton I (Galley/Chariot)
Tyre: 2 Attic didr. (God on hippocamp, dolphin/Owl)

Hellenistic Period: 10 AE
Ptolemaic 4: Ptolemy II 3 (Alexandria 2, Tyre 1); Uncert. ruler 1
Seleucid 3: Seleucus III 1 (Antioch); Antiochus III 1 (Antioch); Antiochus IV 1 (Babylon)
Hasmonean: Alexander Jannaeus 1
Cities 2: Tyre 2

Commentary:
The present Tell el-Mutesellim is the ancient Megiddo, the Armageddon of the Bible. It is strategically located overlooking the plain of Esdralon. The site was inhabited from c. 1050–1000 to c. 350 BC. A Roman camp has left some archaeological traces nearby. The last phase (650–350 BC) has turned up signs of active occupation, with animal stables, ovens and pipes. The pottery points to a pre-Hellenic type of settlement. The authors do not give any reason for the site's abandonment. Some Roman period tombs are the last vestiges of activity here (4th century AD).
Of 102 coins found, mostly on the surface, 7 were silver, the rest bronze.

Bibliography:
Newell, E. T. "The coins," in R. S. Lamon and G. M. Shipton, *Megiddo I. Seasons of 1925–1934, Strata I–V*, Chicago, 1939, pp. 196–212.

32. Meiron
Israel
Finds: 1,017

Persian Period: 2 AR
Tyre: 1 AR (Dolphin/Owl) 1.02 g
Sidon: 1 AR (Galley/King fighting a lion) 0.99 g

Hellenistic Period: 160 AE
Ptolemaic 2: Ptolemy I 1 (Alexandria); Ptolemy II 1 (Cyprus)
Seleucid 39: Antiochus III 6 (Antioch 2, Tyre 4); Antiochus IV 6 (Tyre); Demetrius I 1 (Tyre); Demetrius II (2) 26
Hasmoneans 108 AE: Alexander Jannaeus 89; John Hyrcanus II 18; Judah Aristobulus 1
Cities 11: Sidon 1; Tyre 10 (8 Tyche/Galley; 2 Tyche/Palm tree, down to 36/5 BC)

Commentary:
Meyers et al. 1981, p. xix, show that the first level of occupation is Hellenistic and dated basically by the coins and the remains of a single structure between 200 and 50 BC. "The number of Hasmonean coins is too great to be understood merely as chance finds. Rather, they suggest a small nucleus of a Jewish community here in the late Second Temple period or pre-Herodian era." The site then develops until attaining its zenith (c. AD 250–365), during which one of the largest synagogues in Palestine was built. The modern village of Meiron was founded in 1949 (p. 1).

Raynor et al. 1988, p. 1, note that the excavation did not turn up any hoards. Almost all the coins were discovered in stratigraphic levels. They are currently kept in the Israeli Department of Antiquities or at Duke University in Durham, North Carolina. Of the 1,017 specimens, 3 are gold, and 5 silver.

Bibliography:
Meyers, E. M., J. F. Strange, C. L. Meyers, et al., *Excavations in Ancient Meiron, Upper Galilee, Israel 1971–72, 1974–75, 1977*, Cambridge (Mass.), 1981.
Raynor, J., Y. Meshorer, and R. S. Hanson. *The Coins of Ancient Meiron*, Winona Lake (Ind.), 1988.

33. Pella Tabaqat Fahl, Areas III, IV, V, XXIII, XXIX, XXXII, XXXIV
Jordan
Finds: 1,076

Persian Period: 0

Hellenistic Period: 81 AE
Ptolemaic 5: Ptolemy II 3; Ptolemy IV 1; Ptolemy VI 1
Seleucid 20: Antiochus III 1; Antiochus IV 2 + 1?; Antiochus IV–VI: 1; Demetrius I 1; Antiochus VII 1; Alexander II 2; Antiochus VIII 1; Demetrius III 3; Antiochus XIII 4; Antiochus XII or Demetrius II: 1; Uncert.: 2
Hasmoneans 25: Alexander Jannaeus 17; Uncert. Hasmonean 8
Uncert. Jewish: 3
Cities 17: Antioch 1 (1st cent. BC); Ake-Ptolemais 12 + 1?; Tyre 1 (2nd cent. BC); Tyre? 2
Uncert. Hellenistic: 11

Commentary:
Excavations by the University of Sydney and Wooster College (Ohio) focused on the site of Pella in the Decapolis, in the hills, 28 km south of Lake Tiberias, and 5 km east of the Jordan. It is a crossroads between the north-south route connecting Damascus to Arabia and the east-west road to the Mediterranean. This study's results show continuous settlement from the Hellenistic period to the Islamic.

Bibliography:
Sheedy, K., R. Carson, A. Walmsley, *Pella in Jordan 1979–1990. The Coins*, Sydney, 2001.

34. Ras el-Bassit—Posideion
Syria
Finds: 94

Persian Period: 4 AR
Athens: 1 tetr.
Aradus: 3 obols

Hellenistic Period: 90 (6 AR, 84 AE)

Alexander III 40: Posideion 13 AE; Tarsus 1 tetr. and 2 AE; Mylasa 1 dr.; Lampsacus? 1 dr.; Uncert. 2 dr. and 20 AE
Antigonus Monophthalmus?: 1 AE
Seleucid 23 AE: Seleucus I 3 AE; Seleucus III 3 AE; Antiochus III 4 AE; Antiochus IV 1 AE; Demetrius I 1 AE; Demetrius II (1) 2 AE; Antiochus VII 3 AE; Demetrius II (2) 3 AE; Alexander II 1 AE; Antiochus VIII 2 AE
Ptolemaic: Ptolemy II 1 AE; Ptolemy III 7 AE
Cities 12: Posideion 1 AE; Seleuceia Pieria 2 AE; Aradus 6 AE; Berytus: 1 AE; Seleuceia on the Calycadnus 1 AE; Byzantium 1 AE
Hasmonean: Alexander Jannaeus 2 AE
Uncert: 1 AR, 3 AE

Commentary:
A French team excavated Ras el-Bassit, 25 km south of Latakia, beginning in 1971. Its foundation goes back to c. 1600 BC. From the fourth century BC, the excavations revealed Attic pottery. The city seems to have been prosperous at the time of Alexander's conquest, which led to fresh construction, new equipping of the port, occupation of the acropolis, and fortification of the city, as well as issues of bronze coins using Alexander types and bearing the city's distinctive mark (Courbin 1986, pp. 205–206). Ras el-Bassit is generally identified with the Posideion mentioned in Classical sources.

Le Rider's article only deals with pre-Roman coins.

Hoard:
CH 8.476, **279**

Bibliography:
Courbin P. "Recherches archéologiques dans la région de Marathus. Note préliminaire," *Annales archéologiques arabes syriennes* 3 (1953), pp. 165–170.
_______. "Bassit," *Syria* 63 (1986), pp. 175–220.
_______. "Bassit," *Contribution française à l'archéologie syrienne 1969–1989*, Damascus, 1989, pp. 102–106.
Le Rider, G. "L'atelier de Posideion et les monnaies de la fouille de Bassit," BC*H* 110 (1986), pp. 393–408.

35. Ras Shamra environs
Syria
Finds: 145

Persian Period: AR
39 AR Thraco-Macedonian and Cypriot, ingots (hoard 1)
Athens: 2 AR
Sidon: 1 shekel
Aradus: 2 obols

Hellenistic Period: 3 AR, 22 AE
Alexander III 8: Byblos 1 tetr.; Tarsus 2 AE; Aradus 1 AE; Uncert. 1 dr. and 3 AE
Antigonus Monophthalmus: Salamis in Cyprus 1 AE
Demetrius Poliorcetes: Pella 1 tetr.
Lysimachus: 1 AE
Ptolemy I: 2 AE
Seleucid 10 AE: Seleucus I 5; Antiochus III 1; Seleucus IV 1; Antiochus IV 1; Demetrius II 1; Uncert. 1
Cities 2: Aradus 1; Side 1

Commentary:
These are coins discovered as surface finds around the excavation of Ras Shamra during other operations, except for the hoard found in the dig of 1936. Stucky 1983 previously published a portion (74) of them.
Hoard:
IGCH 1478, **1**

Bibliography:
Callot, O. "Les monnaies des environs de Ras Shamra," in C. Augé and F. Duyrat (eds.) *Les monnayages syriens. Quel apport pour l'histoire du Proche-Orient hellénistique et romain? Actes de la table ronde de Damas, 10–11 novembre 1999*, Beirut, 2002, pp. 93–103.
Stucky, R. "Fundmünzen," in *Ras Shamra. Leukos Limen, die nach-ugaritische Besiedlung von Ras Shamra*, BAH 110, Paris, 1983, pp. 29–54.

36. Samaria, Palestine Exploration Fund, 1931–1933, 1935
Israel
Finds: 692

Persian Period: 3 AR + 3 AE?
Philistia: imitations of Athenian tetr.: 3
Sidon: 3

Hellenistic Period: 308 AE
Alexander III: 2
Ptolemaic 92: Ptolemy I 2 AR, 5 AE; Ptolemy I or II 9; Ptolemy II 48; Ptolemy II–IV 11; Ptolemy III 2; Ptolemy IV 4; Uncert. 11
Seleucid 111: Seleucus I 1; Seleucus III 1; Antiochus III 18; Antiochus IV 34; Demetrius I 4; Alexander I 1; Demetrius II (1) 7; Antiochus VI 1; Antiochus VII 5; Demetrius II (2) 1; Alexander II 22; Cleopatra Thea and Antiochus VIII 1; Antiochus VIII 2; Antiochus IX 1; Uncert. 12
Hasmonean: 52
Cities 51: Antioch 11; Ascalon 1; Gaza 2; Ake-Ptolemais 25 (2nd cent. BC); Rhodes 1; Side 4; Sidon 1 (1st cent. BC); Tyre 2 (1st cent. BC); Uncert. 4

Commentary:
The variety of coinages reflects the different political regimes the city experienced: in the third century, the Ptolemies; in the second, the Seleucids; in the first, the Jews. John Hyrcanus I seized and destroyed the city in 108/7 BC, and it declined from the first century BC. Samaria is rich in agricultural land (grains, olives, vineyards) and had to export to the coast, perhaps via Joppa and, after the latter's destruction in 146 BC, via Ptolemais.

Bibliography:
Kirkman, J. S. "The Evidence of the Coins," in J. W. Crowfoot, G. M. Crowfoot, and K. M. Kenyon, *Samaria Sebaste III: The Objects from Samaria*, London, 1957, pp. 43–70.
Meshorer, Y. *Ancient Jewish Coinage*. Vol. 1, *Persian Period through Hasmoneans*, New York, 1982, pp. 43–44.

37. Sea of Galilee
Israel
Finds: 57 of which 14 are illegible, 1 lead flan

Persian Period: 0

Hellenistic Period: 19 AE
Ptolemaic 8: 3rd cent. BC 1; Ptolemy IX 4; Ptolemy IX or XIII 3
Seleucid 6: Alexander I Balas 2 (Sidon 1, Tyre 1); Antiochus VIII 1; Antiochus VIII (1) 3 (Antioch 1, Uncert. 2)
Hasmonean: 1 (103–40 BC)
Cities 4: Ake-Ptolemais 2; Tyre 2 (end 2nd cent. BC; 1st cent. BC–1st cent. AD)

Commentary:
A shipwreck about 8 m long was discovered when the Sea of Galilee retreated markedly at the end of January, 1986. The vessel's pottery cargo dated from the first century BC. Bronze coins were found on the surface during the excavations and cannot be used directly for dating the boat. A number of these bronzes, however, were struck in the name of Ptolemy IX on Cyprus. They are rare in the region and must be seen in the context of this monarch's campaign against Alexander Jannaeus at Ake-Ptolemais, in Galilee, and in the north of Peraea until 102 BC. The finds also included one lead coin blank.

Bibliography:
Gitler, H. "The Coins," in S. Wachsmann (ed.) *The Excavations of an Ancient Boat in the Sea of Galilee (Lake Kinneret)*, *'Atiqot* 19 (1990), pp. 101–106.

38. Seleuceia Pieria
Syria
Finds: The total is not given and the summary tables combine the finds from Antioch and Seleuceia.

Persian Period: not mentioned in the publication.

Hellenistic Period: 273 (3 AR, 270 AE)
Alexander III 3: Uncert. 1 plated dr.; Cyprus 1 AE; Uncert. 1 AE
Antigonus Monophthalmus: 1 tetr.
Demetrius Poliorcetes: 1 tetr., 16 AE
Seleucid 167: Seleucus I 20; Antiochus I 20; Seleucus I or Antiochus I 2; Antiochus II 3; Seleucus II 3; ΔΕΛ mint 1; Seleucus III 7; Antiochus III 29; Seleucus III or Antiochus III 2; Seleucus IV 1; Antiochus IV 9; Seleucus IV or Antiochus IV 2; Demetrius I 11; Alexander I 5; Demetrius II (1) 6; Antiochus VII 6; Demetrius II (2) 7; Alexander II 1; Cleopatra and Antiochus VIII 4; Antiochus VIII 17; Antiochus IX 6; Antiochus X 1; Philip Philadelphus 4
Ptolemaic 22: Ptolemy I 2; Ptolemy II 8; Ptolemy I or II 2; Ptolemy III 9; Uncert. 1
Hasmonean: 2
Cities 61: Antioch before Augustus 3; Seleuceia Pieria before Augustus 42; Pergamum 2 (133–27 BC); Magnesia on the Maeander 1 (3rd cent. BC); Cos 1; Rhodes 2 (4th cent. BC); Side 2; Tarsus 2 (2nd–1st cent. BC); Salamis in Cyprus 3 (4th cent. BC); Aradus 1; Berytus 1 (2nd cent. BC); Uncert. Phoenicia 1

Commentary:
The publication of the coins from the Antioch excavations also includes those from Seleuceia Pieria.

Hoards:
IGCH 1526, **138**: 10 Ptolemaic tetr., 1 of Antigonus Monophthalmus, 1 of Demetrius Poliorcetes discovered together, but without container (p. vii).
IGCH 1573, **316**.

Bibliography:
Waage, D. B. Antioch-on-the-Orontes, IV, 2, *Greek, Roman, Byzantine and Crusaders' Coins*, Princeton, 1952.

39. Sepphoris
Israel
Finds: 84

Persian Period: 0

Hellenistic Period: 4 AE
Seleucid or autonomous civic?: 1
Hasmonean: Alexander Jannaeus 2
Tyre: 1 (2nd–1st cent. BC)

Commentary:
The city of Sepphoris, well attested in the Roman-period sources, is not mentioned in the Old Testament. It is situated on a small hill in Lower Galilee. The excavations unearthed a fortified building (citadel or tower) and a villa dating to the Imperial period.

Bibliography:
Strange, T. F., T. R. W. Longstaff, and D. Groh. *Excavations at Sepphoris*. Vol. I., Leiden, 2006 (coins p. 119).

40. Si' 8, Hauran
Syria
Finds: 261 of which 2 are illegible

Persian Period: 0

Hellenistic Period: 3 AE
Ptolemaic: Ptolemy II or III 2
Seleucid: Antiochus IV 1 (Antioch)

Bibliography:
Augé, C. "Les monnaies de Si' 8," in J. Dentzer-Feydy, J.-M. Dentzer, and P.-M. Blanc (eds.) *Hauran II. Les installations de Si' 8: du sanctuaire à l'établissement viticole*, I, Beirut, 2003, pp. 230–266.

41. Si', Hauran
Syria
Finds: 293 of which 3 are illegible

Persian Period: 0

Hellenistic Period: 4 AE
Ptolemaic: Ptolemy II or III 2
Seleucid: Antiochus IV 1; Antiochus VIII 1

Bibliography:
Augé, C. "Les monnaies de la fouille de Si' et la circulation monétaire antique dans le Hauran," in J.-M. Dentzer (ed.) *Hauran I. Recherches archéologiques sur la Syrie du Sud à l'époque hellénistique et romaine*, I, BAH 124, Beirut, 1985, pp. 205–218.

42. Tel 'Ira
Israel

Finds: 56 of which 5 are illegible

Persian Period: 1 AR
Sidon: 1 AR (denomination not noted, no photo) 'Abdashtart (370–358 BC)

Hellenistic Period: 40 AE
Alexander III: 1 AE (Macedonian shield/?);
Ptolemaic 8: Ptolemy I 1; Ptolemy II 7
Seleucid 22: Antiochus III 8; Antiochus IV 14
Hasmonean: John Hyrcanus I 5
Nabataeans 3: Aretas II or III 3 (110–96 or 87–62 BC)
Uncert.: 1 fragment

Commentary:
Tel 'Ira is located in the valley running from Arad to Beersheba, an area widely studied and surveyed by teams from the Archaeological Survey of Israel. All its important sites have been excavated. This valley seems to have been inhabited since Paleolithic times and to have reached its zenith in the seventh century BC, which witnessed the fortification of several places, including Tel 'Ira. Archaeologists have explained these fortifications as defense against neighboring Arab tribes or the Edomites, whose troubled relations with Judah the Bible mentions on several occasions (p. 2). The population decreases during the Persian period but picks up again in the Hellenistic age. (p. 6). The site belonged to the *limes* under Diocletian. A new phase of expansion opens with the Byzantine period, before a new decline at the onset of Islam (p. 6).

All the coins, with two exceptions, are bronze and come basically from surface finds. 73% are Hellenistic. The absence of Seleucid coins after Antiochus IV is not reflected in the archaeological material, which seems to show no interruption in activity. Coins of John Hyrcanus might have arrived at Tel 'Ira following his conquest of Edom in 112/11 BC. The Nabataean coins are no surprise. No Herodian or Roman coin prior to the fourth century AD is known. In contrast, a rare coin of the Axumite king Ezana (AD 330–358) confirms other discoveries of the same type at Caesarea, Jerusalem, and Beth-Shan. Later coins remain quite rare.

The breakdown proposed here is based on the list published by Kindler 1999, p. 439 (with a repeated typographical error: coins of Antiochus III are said to belong to Antiochus II), not on the table of Hellenistic coins found on p. 440, which gives slightly different results.

Bibliography:
Kindler, A. "The Numismatic Finds," in I. Beit-Arieh (ed.) *Tel 'Ira. A Strongold in the Biblical Neguev*, Jerusalem, 1999, pp. 438–441.

43. Tel Anafa
Israel
Finds: 7 AR, 312 AE

Persian Period: 0

Hellenistic Period: 242 AE + 1 plated tetr.
Alexander III: 2
Ptolemaic 16: Ptolemy I 2 Alexandria; Ptolemy II 13 Alexandria; Ptolemy I or II 1
Seleucid 102: Antiochus III 5; Antiochus IV 7; Antiochus V 1; Demetrius I 2; Alexander I 2; Demetrius II (1) 2; Demetrius II (1 or 2) 7; Uncert. 25 + 1 plated tetr.; Antiochus VII 10; Demetrius II (2) 3; Alexander II 19; Antiochus VIII 10; Antiochus IX 1; Demetrius III 6; Antiochus XII 1
Hasmonean: 3
Cities 120: Chalcis, Lysanias 1; Aradus 2; Ake-Ptolemais 2; Sidon 76; Tyre 24; Uncert. Sidon or Tyre 20

Commentary:
Tel Anafa is a small site (a small city at best) that flourished from 150 BC. Abandoned after 71 BC, it was reoccupied at the beginning of the first century AD. 70% of the coins date from the second half of the second century BC to the first century AD.

Meshorer 1994, p. 241, emphasizes that "The bronze of Ptolemy II occurs very frequently and very widely spread about the eastern Mediterranean, so that there is no surprise in finding it here. What is notable is that not a single Ptolemaic piece dates any later. There is a total break between these and the subsequent Seleucid coinages." Most of the finds come from Sidon and Tyre (the royal coinages likewise).

The site produced very large quantities of glass, in amounts unparalleled elsewhere.

Bibliography:
Meshorer, Y. "Coins 1968–1986," in S. C. Herbert, *Tel Anafa I, i. Final Report on Ten Years of Excavations at a Hellenistic and Roman Settlement in Northern Israel. Journal of Roman Archaeology* Supplementary Series 10, Ann Arbor, 1994, pp. 241–260.

44. Tel Dor
Israel
Finds: 116

Persian Period: 3 plated AR, 7 AE
Sidon: 2 plated AR (0.58 g; 0.35 g); 6 AE
Tyre: 1 plated AR (7.59 g)
Philistia: 1 AE

Hellenistic Period: 5 AR, 67 AE
Alexander III: 5 AE
Ptolemaic 38: Ptolemy I 6 AE (Cyprus, Alexandria, Uncert.); Ptolemy I or II 6 AE (Alexandria, Uncert.); Ptolemy II 4 tetr. (Sidon 1 (285/4 BC), Tyre 2 (279, c. 260 BC), Alexandria 1 (c. 285–270 BC)), 10 AE (Alexandria, Sidon, Tyre, Uncert.); Uncert. ruler 8 AE (3rd cent. BC); Ptolemy IX Lathyrus 4 AE
Seleucid 15: Antiochus III 6 AE (Antioch, Apamea, Uncert.); Antiochus IV 2 AE (Ake-Ptolemais, Uncert.); Demetrius II (1) 1 AE (Tyre); Tryphon 1 tetr. (Ake-Ptolemais); Antiochus VII 2 AE (Antioch); Demetrius II (2) 1 AE (Damascus, 129/8 BC); Uncert. 2 AE (Tyre)
Hasmonean: Alexander Jannaeus 2 AE
Cities 12: Ake-Ptolemais 8 AE (of which one of 112/1 BC, the others of the second half of the 2nd cent. BC); Uncert. city 1 AE (65/4 BC?); Gaza? 1 AE (1st cent. BC); Dora 2 AE (64/3 BC)

Commentary:
Stern 1995, pp. 1–3, states that the site of Dora, well-attested in Biblical and Hellenistic sources, is located on a tell, between Mt. Carmel and the Tower of Strato. Written sources confirm a city from the 13th century BC, but archaeological remains go back to the end of the third millennium (Bronze Age). Like the Palestinian coast in general, it prospered under the Achaemenids. In the fourth century, it is part of the Sidonian realm. In the Hellenistic period, it was fortified sufficiently to thwart seizure by Antiochus III in his campaign of 219 BC. The strong enclosure and towers found in excavations are attributed to the reign of Ptolemy II (283–246 BC). Ptolemaic coins represent 30% of the coins found (38 of 116, Meshorer 1995, p. 461). Antiochus VII besieged the city, to no avail, when Tryphon sought refuge there in 139/8 BC (1 Mac. 15.10–38; Josephus, *Jewish Wars* 1.2.2, *Antiquities of the Jews* 13.7.2). At the end of the second century, the tyrant Zoilus governed it and the Tower of Strato, and it suffered terrible destruction before falling into the hands of Ptolemy IX Lathyrus and, then, Alexander Jannaeus. Yet, apart from a few coins of the latter, Hasmonean bronzes are missing from the site. Pompey closed the period by annexing Dora to the Roman province of Syria in 63 BC. Until that time,

the city presents a marked Semitic-Phoenician character (Stern 1995, p. 278). Under Roman rule, Hellenization grows as the lower city develops.
Plated coins date from the 4th century.

Bibliography:
Meshorer, Y. "Coins from Areas A and C," in E. Stern (ed.) *Excavations at Dor, Final Reports, Areas A and C: the Finds. Qedem Reports* 2, Jerusalem, 1995, pp. 461–472.
Stern E. (ed.) *Excavations at Dor, Final Report. IA. Areas A and C: Introduction and Stratigraphy*, Jerusalem, 1995.

45. Tel Michal
Israel
Finds: 182

Persian Period: 11 AR, 7 AE
Evagoras II, Cyprus: 1 sixteenth
Sidon: end of the 5th cent. BC: 1 thirty-second; ʿAbdashtart I 1 thirty-second, 1 sixteenth, 1 half-shekel, 7AE
Tyre: 1 AR (4th cent. BC, 0.20 g)
Philistia: 1 dr., 1 fraction of an obol, 2 obols(?) (0.50 g, 0.95 g), 1 hemidr.

Hellenistic Period: 128 (66 AR, 62 AE)
Alexander III 16 AR: Babylonian lion type 1 fraction of an obol; Aradus 2 tetr., 1 hemidr.; Ake-Ptolemais/Tyre 1 tetr.; Babylon 2 tetr.; Pella 1 tetr.; Uncert. 8 dr.
Ptolemaic 50 AR, 25 AE: Ptolemy I 10 tetr., 4 AE; Ptolemy II 30 tetr. (Sidon, Tyre, Joppa, Gaza and 'Uncertain Era' (2)), 16 AE (5 Tyre, 1 Sidon, 1 Joppa, 1 Gaza); Ptolemy III 9 tetr. (Sidon, Tyre, Ake-Ptolemais, Joppa, Gaza and uncertain (2)); Uncert. rulers 5 AE (3rd cent. BC); Ptolemy IV or V 1 didr.
Seleucid 23 AE: Antiochus III 6 AE (Antioch); Antiochus IV 1 AE (Seleuceia on the Tigris), 12 AE (Ake-Ptolemais); Demetrius I 1 AE (Antioch); Demetrius II (2) 3 AE (Antioch)
Philip V of Macedon: 5 AE
Hasmonean 7: Alexander Jannaeus 7 AE
Cities 2: Side 2 AE

Commentary:
Tel Michal is situated in the plain of Sharon, 12.5 km north of Jaffa and 6.5 km south of the river Yarkon. The University of Tel Aviv excavated it between 1977 and 1980. The ancient settlement is located on a group of five hills along the sea. The soil is sandy and saline, marshy in the eastern part during the several winter months. This environment does not encourage permanent settlements in the area. The authors therefore think that the site's strategic and commercial aspects guided its occupation (p. 8).

The first settlement dates from the middle of the Bronze Age (17th century), and the site experienced three interruptions in settlement before the Persian period; habitation then continues until the first half of the first century AD, when the site was completely abandoned. It was reoccupied in the eighth and ninth centuries and then left for good. It flourished particularly in the Persian period, with strong population growth. Viticultural equipment and pottery workshops are attested. Numerous metal objects have been found. Forts protect the settlement on the north of the highest hill, facing the sea (pp. 8–9). The presence of Sidonian coins proves Tel Michal's inclusion in the lands between Dora and Joppa under Sidon's rule in the mid-fourth century BC (p. 320).

In the Hellenistic period, construction of a fortress on the main hill strengthened the settlement's military character. An extensive vine growing operation was established on the north hill. The settlement declines under the Hasmoneans and then the Romans (p. 9). The site apparently turned up several small Hellenistic hoards, their specimens counted with those of isolated finds. They seem to have been ignored by the authors of *IGCH* who did not consider these lots as hoards.

Hoards:
CH 9.498, **158**
CH 10.256, **91**
146
155
178

Bibliography:
Kindler, A. "Numismatic Report," in Z. Herzog et al. (eds.) *Excavations at Tel Michal, Israël*, Tel Aviv, 1989, pp. 320–329 et 443.

46. Tel Michal 1996
Israel
Finds: 38 of which 5 are illegible

Persian Period: 11 AR, 1 AE
Tyre 3: 1 AR (0.76 g), 1 AR (0.46 g), 1 AE (0.63 g)
Sidon 8 AR: Straton I 5 sixteenth, 1 (4.98 g); 1 (2.46 g), 1 (3.95 g)
Philistia: 1 AR (0.56 g)

Hellenistic Period: 7 AE
Alexander III: 4 AE
Seleucid 2: Antiochus III 2 AE (Antioch)
Cities 1: Side 1 AE (3rd cent. BC)

Hoard:
CH 10.226, **26**

Bibliography:
Ariel, D. T. "Coins from Tel Mikhal (Tel Michal)," *'Atiqot* 52 (2006), pp. 71–88.

47. Tell Abu Danne
Syria
Finds: 115 of which 32 are illegible

Hellenistic Period: 68 AE
Seleucid 48: Seleucus I 2; Seleucus II 4; Antiochus III 25; Antiochus IV 1; Alexander I 1; Demetrius II (1) 2; Antiochus VII 3; Alexander II 2; Cleopatra and Antiochus VIII 1; Antiochus VIII 3; Uncert. 4
Cities 20: Antioch 16; Tyre 1 (1st cent. BC); Uncert. 3

Commentary:
Tell Abu Danne lies in the region of the salt lake of Djabboul, in northern Syria, east of Aleppo. As at Umm el-Mara, the coins are the result of very numerous surface finds and date from the Seleucid period to the reign of Augustus. With the Roman period, settlements on tells were forsaken in favor of dwelling on the plain. The number of ancient sites around the lake attests to the region's fertility in antiquity.

Bibliography:
Doyen, J.-M. *Les monnaies du Tell Abou Danné et d'Oumm el-Marra (campagnes 1976–1985). Aspects de la circulation monétaire en Syrie du Nord sous les Séleucides*, Brussels, 1987.
Le Rider, G. Compte rendu de J.-M. Doyen, *Les monnaies du Tell Abou Danné et d'Oumm el-Marra (campagnes 1976–1985). Aspects de la circulation monétaire en Syrie du Nord sous les Séleucides,* Brussels, 1987, *Revue numismatique* (1989), p. 362–363.

48. Tell Ain el-Beida
Syria
Finds: 17

Persian Period: 0

Hellenistic Period: 1 AR, 10 AE
Alexander III: 1 dr.
Seleucid 10: Antiochus II 1; Seleucus III 2; Antiochus III 2; Demetrius I 2; Alexander I 1; Antiochus VI 1; Uncert. 1

Commentary:
Villagers collected these coins and showed them to the authors.

Bibliography:
Raymaekers, P. and J.-M. Doyen. "Un lot de monnaies hellénistiques, romaines et byzantines en provenance de Tell Ain El-Beida, et de ses environs immédiats (Syrie du Nord)," *Bulletin du cercle d'études numismatiques* 39/1 (January–April 2002), pp. 181–183.

49. Tell Arka, 1974–1980
Lebanon
Finds: 39

Persian Period: 0

Hellenistic Period: 39 AE
Ptolemaic: Ptolemy II: 3
Seleucid 7: Seleucus III 1; Demetrius I 3; Antiochus VII 1; Tryphon 4; Philip Philadelphus 1; Uncert. 1
Cities 25: Marathus 3 (175–169 BC, 170/169 BC, Uncert.); Carne 1; Aradus: 16 (170/169, 159/8?, 150/149, 148–145, 2 145/4, 149–141, 137–127 BC, Uncert.); Tyre 4; Uncert. 1

Commentary:
Thalmann 1978 does not mention any coinage despite excavating late Hellenistic strata. My figures derive from C. Augé for the excavations during 1974–1980 (an unpublished list entitled "List of 39 identifiable coins," which Augé kindly sent me).

Bibliography:
Starcky, J. "Arca du Liban," *Cahiers de l'Oronte* 10 (1972), pp. 103–117.
Thalmann, J.-P. "Tell Arqa (Liban nord), campagnes I–III (1972–1974). Chantier I. Rapport préliminaire. Introduction d'Ernest Will," *Syria* 55 (1978), pp. 1–151.
_______. "Tell Arqa de la conquête assyrienne à l'époque perse," *Transeuphratène* 2 (1990), pp. 51–58.

50. Tell Beydar (survey)
Syria
Finds: 2

Persian Period: 0

Hellenistic Period: 1 AR, 1 AE
Seleucid 2: Antiochus I 1 tetr.; Antiochus VI 1 AE (Antioch)

Commentary:
The Tell Beydar program is based on a survey and "focuses on the reconstruction of the ancient environment of the Beydar region aiming at a better understanding of the mechanisms that helped create settlements and early urbanisation in the region" (Van Lerberghe, G. Voegt, p. I). These are the only coins discovered on the site during the campaign of 1994. The tetradrachm of Antiochus I came to light in a tomb. Corrosion makes identification of the mint impossible.

Bibliography:
Scheers, S. "Seleucid Coins from Tell Beydar 1994," in K. Van Lerberghe, G. Voegt (eds.) *Tell Beydar, Environmental and Technical Studies, Subartu VI*, Turnhout, 2000, pp. 135–137.

51. Tell Daruk—Usnu
Syria
Finds: 20 AE

Hellenistic Period: 9 AE
Alexander III: Aradus (?) 3, Uncert. 1
Demetrius Poliorcetes: Tarsus 1
Cities 4: Ake-Ptolemais 1 (125–120 BC); Aradus? 1; Uncert. 2

Commentary:
The excavations seeked to give a confirmation of the identification of the tell with Usnatu, mentioned in Ugaritic texts, and Usnu/Usana known from Assyrian texts of the 9th and 8th cent. BC. Oldenburg, Rohweder 1981, p. 5, make clear that their information derives from soundings carried out on the perimeter of the excavation of Sukas in 1958–1959. The tell lies halfway between Gabala and Baniyas, near Tell Daruk and the navigable Nahr es-Sinn river. The remains go back to the Bronze Age, but those from the Iron Age are especially abundant. Hellenistic and Roman occupation has left a few traces (pp. 12–13), meager when compared to those from the Middle Ages. The coins are discussed on pp. 64–66, with a plate on p. 115; they come from surface finds, with just one exception: the bronze of Demetrius Poliorcetes struck at Tarsus.

Bibliography:
Oldenburg, E. and J. Rohweder. *The Excavations at Tall Daruk (Usnu?) and 'Arab el-Mulk (Paltos)*, Copenhagen, 1981.

52. Tell el-Hajj
Syria
Finds: 45 of which 16 are illegible

Persian Period: 0

Hellenistic Period: 1 AR, 4 AE

Seleucid 3: Seleucus III 1 (Antioch); Antiochus III 1 (Antioch); Antiochus IV 1 (Antioch)
Cities 1: Aradus 1 (Tyche/Stern)
Uncert.: 1 dr.

Commentary:
The site is an oval tell, 21 m high, overlooking the Euphrates, a few kilometers to the north of Meskene. Figures are those of Stucky 1972.

Bibliography:
Stucky, R. A. "Die Münzen," in C. Krause et al. (eds.) *Tel el Hajj in Syrien. Ersten vorlaüfiger Bericht. Grabungskampagne 1971*, Bern, 1972, pp. 35–39.
Stucky, R. A. and S. Zellweger, "Die Münzen," in C. Krause et al. (eds.) *Tel el Hajj in Syrien. Zweiter vorlaüfiger Bericht. Grabungskampagne 1972*, Bern, 1974, pp. 59–65.

53. Tell el-Herr
Egypt
Finds: 18

Persian Period: Not studied

Hellenistic Period: 11 AE
Ptolemaic 11: Ptolemy I 6; Ptolemy II 3; Ptolemy III 1; Ptolemy VI–VIII 1

Commentary:
The publication only takes account of the Hellenistic remains and those from the High Roman Empire, which construction of a late imperial Roman camp and recent military occupation of the site have largely destroyed. Wind and water erosion have also contributed to destruction of the higher parts of buildings. Only those with very deep foundations have left any vestiges; little associated material remains. A Hellenistic fortress was rebuilt several times; residential quarters have come to light. The High Roman strata are even fewer and more damaged than those of the Hellenistic period.

The number of specimens found is very low, compared to the roughly 150 Late Imperial coins that the site has revealed. Finds are practically non-existent between the Ptolemaic coinage reform of 262/1 and the beginning of the first century AD. Carrez-Maratray 2007 obtains "the impression of a quasi-demonetization of the citadel" ("l'impression d'une quasi démonétarisation de la citadelle"), which might be explained in different ways: weak economic activity, remelting of metal currency, payment in kind for soldiers (land allotments), or, more probably, landowners residing at Pelusium, their *kleroi* rented out to farmers dwelling at Tell el-Herr.

Bibliography:
Carrez-Maratray J.-Y. "Les monnaies," in D. Valbelle (ed.) *Tell el-Herr, les niveaux hellénistique et du Haut-Empire*, Paris, 2007, pp. 226–235.

54. Tell er-Ras, Giv'at Yasaf
Israel
Finds: 10

Persian period: 0

Hellenistic Period:
Ptolemaic: 1 AE?

Seleucid 2 AE: Antiochus III 1; Uncert. 1
Commentary:
The excavations unearthed remains from the Bronze Age to the Mamluk period. Area C revealed a building from the Persian period apparently still in use during Hellenistic times. Another building and a cistern were found in area D with tombs of Persian and Hellenistic periods. Preceding excavations had unearthed Hellenistic presses (Rochman-Halperin). The 10 coins are from all periods.

Bibliography:
Berman, A. and D. T. Ariel, "Coins from Excavations at Giv'at Yasaf, Tell er-Ras," *'Atiqot* 37 (1999), pp. 23–24.
Rochman-Halperin, A. "Excavations at Giv'at Yasaf (Tell er-Ras), 1984–1985," *'Atiqot* 37 (1999), pp. 83–123 (Hebrew) and pp. 172–173 (English summary).

55. Tell Keisan, Galilee
Israel
Finds: 56

Persian Period: 4 AR, 2 AE
Tyre: 4 AR
Sidon: 1 AE
Tyre or Sidon?: 1 AE

Hellenistic Period: 1 AR, 25 AE
Ptolemaic 7: Ptolemy I 1 tetr.; Ptolemy III 1 AE; Uncert. 4 AE; illegible 1
Seleucid 12: Seleucus IV 1 AE; Antiochus IV 3 AE; Demetrius II (2) 1 AE; uncert. 7 AE
Ake-Ptolemais: 7 AE

Commentary:
The site is a few kilometers southeast of Akko (Ake-Ptolemais). Settlement starts at the beginning of the Iron Age (11th cent.) and is interrupted around 150 BC, the strata from c. 450 to c. 150 BC being largely destroyed. Occupation resumes only in the sixth cent. AD. Abundant red-figure Attic pottery imported from Greece and Asia Minor characterizes the strata belonging to the end of the Persian period and the Hellenistic era. The site has revealed pottery dumps (table, p. 27). Most of the coinage derives from surface finds.

Pl. 132, murex shells have turned up in the Iron Age strata.

Bibliography:
Briend, J. and J.-B. Humbert (eds.) *Tell Keisan (1971–1976), un cité phénicienne en Galilée*, Fribourg, 1980.

56. Tell Sukas
Syria
Finds: 35 of which 4 are illegible

Persian Period: 2 AR
Aradus: 1 tetrobol (Ichthyomorphic god/Galley and winged hippocamp, Lund 1986, p. 113 n. 15 and fig. 108 p. 146 = *SNG Copenhagen* 37, nos. 3–5); 1 AR (Lund 1986, p. 152 n. 2 = *SNG Copenhagen* 37, nos. 10–13)

Hellenistic Period: 29 (of which 4 are AR?)
Alexander III 14: Aradus 1 tetr. (Lund 1986, p. 171 n. 190 = *SNG Copenhagen* 10, no. 803); 1 dr. (Lund 1986, p. 137 n. 180 = AE Aradus *SNG Copenhagen* 9, no. 1051); 1 dr. (Lund 1986, p. 149 n. 1 = *SNG Copenhagen* 10, nos. 1091–1107); 1 AR (Lund 1986, p. 165 n. 124 = *SNG Copenhagen* 10, nos. 1052–1063 AE); Aradus 1 AE (Riis

1979, pp. 35–36 = Uncert. *SNG Copenhagen* 9, no. 1063), 1 AE (Lund 1986, p. 157 n. 34 = *SNG Copenhagen* 10, nos. 1052–1063), 1 AE (Lund 1986, p. 157 n. 40 = *SNG Copenhagen* 10, nos. 1052–1063), 1 AE (Lund 1986, p. 157 n. 41 = *SNG Copenhagen* 10 nos. 1052–1063), 1 AE (Lund 1986, p. 158 n. 44 = *SNG Copenhagen* 10 nos. 1052–1063), 1 AE (Lund 1986, p. 158 n. 48 = *SNG Copenhagen* 10, nos. 1052–1063), 1 AE (Lund 1986, p. 160 n. 60 = *SNG Copenhagen* 10, nos. 1052–1063), 1 AE (Lund 1986, p. 160 n. 67 = *SNG Copenhagen* 10, nos. 1052–1063), 1 AE (Lund 1986, p. 160 n. 69 = *SNG Copenhagen* 10, no. 1051), 1 AE (Lund 1986, p. 171 n. 176 = *SNG Copenhagen* 10, nos. 1052–1063)
Lysimachus: 1 tetr. (Lund 1986, p. 138 n. 184 = *SNG Copenhagen* 2 nos. 1095–1102)
Seleucid: Antiochus VII 1 AE (Lund 1986, p. 158 n. 47 = *SNG Copenhagen* 35 nos. 323–325)
Cities 13: Aradus 3 (1 AE (Lund 1986, p. 145 n. 223 = *SNG Copenhagen* 37, nos. 26–29), 1 AE (Lund 1986, p. 152 n. 4 = *SNG Copenhagen* 37, no. 42), 1 AE (Lund 1986, p. 172 n. 205 = *SNG Copenhagen* 37, nos. 36–44)); Marathus 2 (1 AE (Lund 1986, p. 168 n. 144 = *SNG Copenhagen* 10, no. 167), 1 AE (Lund 1986, p. 169 n. 152 = *SNG Copenhagen* 10, nos. 165–166); Uncert. 8 (1 AE (Lund 1986, p. 156 n. 22), 2 AE (Lund 1986, p. 157 n. 28), 1 AE (Lund 1986, p. 160 n. 70), 1 AE (Lund 1986, p. 161 n. 81), 1 AE (Lund 1986, p. 166 n. 128), 1 AE (Lund 1986, p. 169 n. 169), 1 AE (Lund 1986, p. 171 n. 188))
AR illegible: 1 (Lund 1986, p. 127 n. 122)
AE illegible: 1 (Lund 1986, p. 112 n. 9), 1 (Lund 1986, p. 113 n. 22), 1 (Lund 1986, p. 127 n. 120)

Commentary:
Lund 1986, p. 171, mentions a hoard of 10 silver tetradrachms.[57] The site was destroyed during the earthquake of 68 BC (p. 200). The publication does not include any list of the numismatic finds, which have to be sought out page by page (with no description guaranteed). Riis 1979 also fails to provide an inventory of numismatic finds, and they merit no commentary, even when he mentions Aradus: “Paltos may originally have been founded by colonists or fugitives from Arados… Sukas belonging to Paltos, whose mother city was Arados, a town under Tyrian sway, might well have had cults of the same kind as the Tyrian ones” (p. 67). He concludes that Tell Sukas was part of the Aradian Peraea, basing himself on Strabo 16.2.12, which is only valid for the end of the Hellenistic period. He gives no further information beyond the hoard already mentioned in Riis 1958/59.

Lund 1990, p. 90, makes clear that Aradian coins predominate on the site.

Making use of Riis 1979 and Lund 1986 is trying: references to *SNG Copenhagen* are habitually incorrect (*SNG Copenhagen* 7 instead of 37, for example; a silver coin of Alexander mentioned in the publication with a reference to a bronze coin in *SNG Copenhagen*). According to the references given, all the Alexander bronzes come from Aradus.

Hoard:
IGCH 1528, **145**

Bibliography:
Lund, J. *Sukas VIII. The Habitation Quarters*, Copenhagen, 1986.
_______. “The Northern Coastline of Syria in the Persian Period. A Survey of the Archaeological Evidence,” *Transeuphratène* 2 (1990), pp. 13–36.
_______. “The Archaeological Evidence for the Transition from the Persian Period to the Hellenistic Age in Northwestern Syria,” *Transeuphratène* 6 (1993), pp. 27–45.
Riis, P. J. “L'activité de la mission archéologique danoise sur la côte phénicienne en 1958,” *Annales archéologiques arabes syriennes* 8–9 (1958/1959), pp. 107–132.
_______. *Sukas VI. The Graeco-Phoenician Cemetery and Sanctuary at the Southern Harbour*, Copenhagen, 1979.

57. Riis 1958/1959, p. 125–126; Lund 1986, p. 171; Seyrig *IGCH* 1528.

57. Umm el-'Amed
Syria
Finds: 131 of which 32 are illegible

Persian Period: 0

Hellenistic Period: 80 AE
Ptolemaic 18: Ptolemy I 1 (Alexandria); Ptolemy II 17 (Tyre 9, Sidon? 1, Uncert. 1, Alexandria 5, Cyprus? 1)
Seleucid 49: Antiochus III 30 (Tyre 29, Uncert. 1); Antiochus V 1 (Tyre); Demetrius I 1 (Sidon); Demetrius II (1): 5 (Tyre, 4 Uncert. 1); Antiochus VII: 8 (Tyre 7, Uncert. 1); Demetrius II (2) 4 (Tyre)
Cities 13: Tyre 12; Aradus 1 (*BMC* p. 13, no. 88)

Commentary:
Umm el-'Amed is situated 19 km south of Tyre on a hill facing the sea. The settlement began during the 5th cent. BC but the main occupation dates to the Hellenistic period. The excavations unearthed a temple dedicated to Milk'ashtart, another temple and several houses. The 3rd and 2nd cent. are the period of highest activity of what seems to have been an agricultural and religious center. The remains are more scarce during the 1st cent. BC and the site declined until the 4th cent. AD.
Some remains date from the Byzantine era.

Bibliography:
Seyrig, H. "Monnaies," in M. Dunand, R. Duru, *Oumm el-'Amed*, Paris, 1962, pp. 227–231.

58. Umm el-Mara
Syria
Finds: 10

Persian Period: 0

Hellenistic Period: 5
Seleucid 5: Seleucus I 2 (Antioch, Seleuceia on the Tigris); Antiochus III 1; Demetrius II (2) 1; Uncert. 1

Commentary:
Umm el-Mara is located in the area south of the salt lake of Djabboul in northern Syria, east of Aleppo. These coins are the result of numerous surface finds. Most of the coins fall between "the start of the Seleucid period and the end of the reign of Augustus" (p. 11). This is prosperous farming country with scattered habitation, in which the tell sites were abandoned at the beginning of the Roman Empire in favor of life on the plain made possible by the pax Romana.

The region's arid character is quite recent: "all the evidence from travelers in the last [19th] century confirms the memories of the oldest inhabitants of Djubb es-Saffa, the village closest to the site [Tell Abu Danne, neighbor of Umm el-Mara], deserted today and transformed into a necropolis: even at the beginning of the [20th] century, water flowed abundantly in the area, and the small streams forming the watershed of the lake of Djabboul made it look quite different from the vast stretch of salt it presents nowadays" (p. 18).[58] The plethora of ancient sites around the lake attests to the region's fertility in antiquity.

58. "tous les témoignages des voyageurs du siècle dernier confirment les souvenirs des plus vieux habitants de Djubb es-Saffa, le village le plus proche du site [Tell Abou Danné, voisin d'Oumm el-Marra] aujourd'hui déserté et transformé en nécropole: au début du siècle encore, l'eau coulait en abondance dans la région et les petites rivières formant le bassin hydrographique du lac de Djabboul lui conféraient un aspect fort différent de la vaste étendue de sel qu'il présente de nos jours."

Bibliography:
Doyen, J.-M. *Les monnaies du Tell Abou Danné et d'Oumm el-Marra (campagnes 1976–1985). Aspects de la circulation monétaire en Syrie du Nord sous les Séleucides*, Bruxelles, 1987.
Le Rider, G. Compte rendu de J.-M. Doyen, *Les monnaies du Tell Abou Danné et d'Oumm el-Marra (campagnes 1976–1985). Aspects de la circulation monétaire en Syrie du Nord sous les Séleucides,* Brussels, 1987, *Revue numismatique* (1989), pp. 362–363.

Chapter 3

A Source to be Reconstituted

Historical knowledge is tailored on the body of mutilated documents.
—Paul Veyne[1]

Introduction

It is more than likely that the majority of coins in precious metal sold on the market come from hoards, whether discovered recently or long ago. They have therefore lost their archaeological context. Despite that, this material remains a useful source of information, in the first place for its abundance. Thus certain series in the corpus of *Arados hellénistique* are chiefly known through the evidence of sale catalogues, evidence that is therefore probably hoard-derived.[2] Some specimens of crucial importance come from the same source. Lorber and Houghton were able to show that tetradrachms with the types of Antiochus VII were in fact posthumous productions from Cappadocia, an insight prompted by a rare tetradrachm seen in the trade. The portrait of Antiochus VII appeared on its obverse; the reverse carried the name of Ariarathes VII, while the obverse was die-linked to other reverses with the name of Antiochus VII.[3] Even when information on the original hoard is lost, such coins remain extremely useful, whether the specimens are unpublished or they simply add to the sample of examples known. Knowledge of the material's archaeological origin separates the museum numismatist from the archaeologist-numismatist who alone works with evidence in context. In the present volume, most of the data derive from hoards out of context.

1. Veyne 1996, p. 26.
2. Duyrat 2005a, p. 5, series VI, VII, and VIII.
3. Lorber, Houghton 2006.

1. Reassembling Hoards

The task of bringing the material together and comparing all the publications of hoards has been particularly long and rather thankless, but it was indispensable in the effort to minimize mistakes that range from mere misprints, like a wrong *IGCH* entry number in Lorber 2007, to commingling within a hoard (*CH* 8.467, **227**) or problems that are insoluble in the absence of sufficiently detailed information (Akken, *CH* 2.95, **213**). The complexity of the data they entail makes hoards particularly susceptible to compound errors. For example, even in a reference work like *Coin Hoards*, discrepancies occur between the brief description of a hoard's contents in the general conspectus and the article devoted to the hoard later in the volume. So it is with the Ascalon hoard, *CH* 9.548 (**294**), where a coin of Antiochus II struck at Antioch according to the conspectus actually turns out to be a coin of Antiochus Hierax at Sardis. Such mistakes are easy to make; doubtless the catalogue presented here will not escape criticism. Published photographs, even for the poorest specimens, prove enormously valuable because they facilitate correction of errors and reattribution of coins when establishing new classifications.

This problem of reliable information arises because a substantial portion of the documentation is reconstituted on the basis of groups that appeared on the antiquities market and that had to be pieced back together, rather like a jigsaw puzzle. Indeed, excavations only very rarely reveal Hellenistic coins in precious metal.

Table 3.1 gives the numbers for gold and silver coins found in excavations and their percentages in relation to all Hellenistic coins. Note, first, that of 58 sites studied, 38 produced only bronzes, and that of the remaining 20, 10 provided under 4% of coins in precious metal.[4] Among the final 10 sites, seven revealed 30 coins or less, skewing ratios once one precious coin was found. Jablah is a special case. It is an excavated necropolis, and the coins were not lost but deliberately placed in the tombs to accompany the dead, and they are of higher value since the only gold coin inventoried in the 58 excavations was found here.[5]

In sum, therefore, the gold and silver coins coming on to the antiquities market probably derive almost entirely from hoards, old or new. This origin explains why a number of them are well, indeed very well, preserved. Either the container in which they were buried or just the piling up of the other coins have protected them from oxidation. When loose silver coins have spent several centuries in the ground, they generally suffer damage, as the nice example of the Byblos hoard shows (*IGCH* 1496, **69**): seven coins dropped out of the vases containing the hoard and were no longer protected. They are much less well preserved than those that stayed in the vases. The market rarely presents these groups as hoards. In the overwhelming majority of cases, the coins are sold individually, often because they come from already established collections or because they arrive on the market after a long time, sometimes as a way to disperse a hoard more discreetly.

4. These percentages are comparable to those reported in Callataÿ 2006b, p. 180, for the Greek world.
5. It is a rather rare gold stater of Ptolemy I: Svoronos 1904–1908, pl. I, 22–23, c. 311. Lorber forthcoming, 38.

Table 3.1. Coins in precious metal by archaeological site[6]

No.	Site	Total Hellenistic	AR	%	AV
11	Dura Europos	1,210	3	0.25	
2	Antioch on the Orontes, 1932–1939	1,086	3	0.28	
19	Jebel Khalid	265	1	0.38	
44	Tel 'Ira	243	1	0.41	
6	Beirut (Bey 006 and 045)	301	2	0.66	
40	Seleuceia Pieria, 1932–1939	273	3	1.10	
28	Khirbet Qumran	180	5	2.78	
1	Al Mina, 1936	203	6	2.96	
5	Balatah (anc. Shechem), Drew-McCormick Excavation	53	2	3.77	
57	Tell Keisan, Galilee	26	1	3.85	
36	Ras el Bassit–Poseideion	90	6	6.67	
46	Tel Dor	72	5	6.94	
50	Tell Ain el-Beida	11	1	9.09	
37	Ras Shamra, environs	25	3	12.00	
58	Tell Sukas	30	4	13.33	
54	Tell el-Hajj	5	1	20.00	
4	Auja Hafir–Nessana, Negev	4	1	25.00	
52	Tell Beydar	2	1	50.00	
17	Jablah, necropolis of al-Jbeibat	6	5	83.33	1
	Total: 19 sites	**4,085**	**54**		**1**

1.1. Physical Appearance of a Hoard

"A prime test of a hoard's homogeneity is uniformity of incrustation or coloration," Hill wrote in 1936.[7] The most palpable way to get an idea of what a hoard is like when it gets into the hands of a researcher is undoubtedly to read the first scholar who offered a scientific description of such an ensemble. Pellerin, in his *Mélange de diverses médailles*, in 1765, mentions the antiquities that arrived from the Near East in Europe and whetted appetites for collecting at the time: "the majority of the coins reported in the first part of this volume came to the author from the Levant after the peace."[8] Among them was a collection of coins (he uses the older French word

6. The site of Tel Michal (chap. 2, **47**) has been eliminated because the hoard's description is combined with that of the isolated coins and makes distinguishing between the two categories difficult.

7. Hill 1936, p. 236.

8. "la plupart des médailles qui sont rapportées dans la première partie de ce volume sont venues du Levant à l'auteur depuis la paix." Pellerin 1765, p. 1. The peace referred to is the end of the Seven Years' War (1756–63).

Figure 3.1. Broken tetradrachm of Alabanda, Latakia hoard (*IGCH* 1544, **184**; BnF, Paris, fonds général 2).

"*médaillons*," medallions) from the Latakia hoard (*IGCH* 1544, **184**), which were uncleaned. "They were as black as old lead, and most were so covered with a sticky dirt adhering to the metal that no one would have taken them for silver unless he had broken a few on the spot before buying them. The dirt was tenacious as though a natural component, so that only enormous pains and patience succeeded in removing it. One supposes there was a fire in the place where they lay, since several coins have blisters that seem to have been caused by a violent fire. Otherwise, they are quite handsome and intact for the most part"[9] (Fig. 3.1).

The individual who gets his hands on a hoard compromised by encrusted dirt and oxidation usually tries to improve the condition of his find or acquisition.[10] Seyrig's archives thus preserve a highly instructive message from one of his correspondents in Aleppo, H. Bachellier, a collector who had just bought a hoard of 92 tetradrachms (*IGCH* 1524, **123**) on the local market.[11] In his letter he explains how he removed the obstinate oxidation from the coins: "I toiled, for the oxidation was resistant, to vinegar, lead, lemon, gasoline, alcohol, even fire, which didn't burn it; rather, the oxidation melted, leaving a sticky residue on the coin when it became red hot, leading one to suppose that it contains a metallic salt; finally, after having boiled the coins in oil with no success, and in soda with only minimal success, I tried ammonia. That worked."[12]

9. "ils étaient noirs comme du vieux plomb, et la plupart si couverts d'une terre tenace et adhérente à la matière qu'on n'auroit jamais pu les prendre pour de l'argent si l'on n'en avoit pas rompu quelques uns sur le lieu avant que de les acheter. La terre y étoit attachée, et comme incorporée, de façon que ce n'a été qu'avec une peine et une patience extrême qu'on est parvenu à les en dépouiller. On estime qu'il y a eu un incendie dans le lieu où ils estoient déposés, plusieurs ayant des soufflures qui semblent provenir de ce qu'ils ont souffert un feu violent. Du reste ils sont très beaux et entiers pour la plus grande parti." Pellerin 1765, p. 106.

10. An allusion to the excesses of such cleaning efforts for the hoard from the Aradian Peraea (*CH* 9.368, **66**).

11. Seyrig Archives, Bibliothèque nationale de France, dossier 214, letter from Aleppo, dated May 10, 1933.

12. "j'ai travaillé, car elle résistait, au vinaigre et au plomb, au citron, à l'essence, à l'alcool, au feu même ou (*sic*) elle ne calcinait pas, elle fondait, elle laissait un résidu adhérent à la pièce quand elle était chauffée au rouge, ce qui laisserait supposer qu'elle contient un sel métallique, enfin, après les avoir fait bouillir dans l'huile, sans résultat, et dans de la soude, avec un petit résultat, j'ai essayé l'amoniaque (*sic*). C'était gagné."

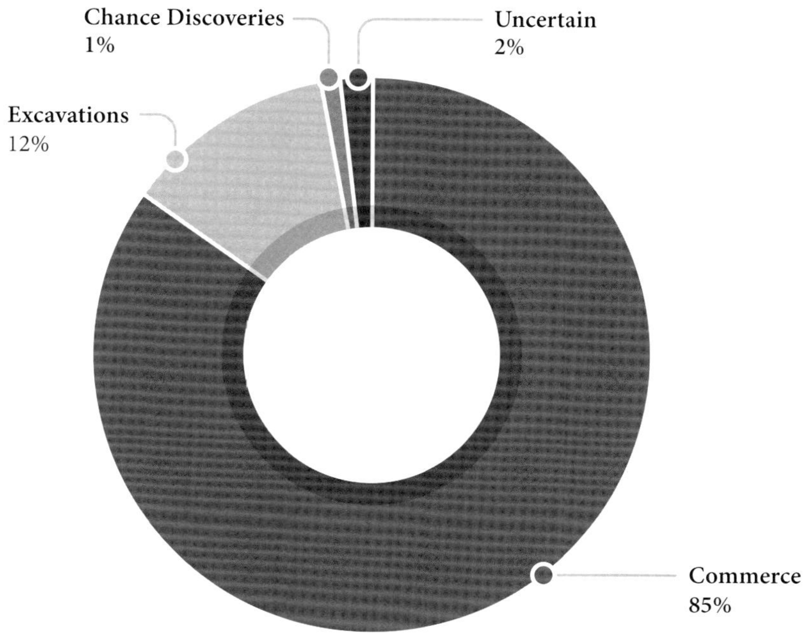

Figure 3.2. Allocation of hoards by conditions of discovery.

1.2. Conditions of Discovery

The vast majority of hoards studied come from the trade, as Figure 3.2 shows.[13] Accordingly, all the information about their contexts has been lost. The very integrity of some groups is occasionally doubtful. In all cases, hoards on the market must be examined carefully to guarantee their content, to determine their geographic origin, and to establish their probable date of burial.

In some cases, we do know the conditions of discovery for hoards revealed fortuitously. These finds often occur as the result of public works projects (**66**, **93**, **135**, **147**, **172**, **255**) or agricultural endeavors (**170**), in one case, by someone strolling on the beach between Beirut and Tyre (**40**), in another by a hoard hunter skilled in scuba diving (**281**). More rare, a hoard of bronzes from the second century was discovered during the dragging of a river (**185**). A dig worker found the Tell Abu Hawam hoard (*IGCH* 1502, **55**). He failed to share the news and managed to pocket 47 coins, which he immediately sold to an antiquities dealer from Haifa before disappearing. Bulldozing in a field belonging to the commune of Hüseyinli köyü, nine kilometers west of Antakya, revealed the Hüseyinli hoard (*CH* 9.489, **135**). The next day, the local authorities managed to reassemble the whole find, which the three discoverers had divided up amongst themselves and some of which still lay buried in the ground. The precipitate haste of discoverers sometimes makes recovering part of the find possible, but in most cases without any proper excavation.[14]

13. Many hoard discoveries are fortuitous, but the only ones included in the Chance Discoveries category here are those that did not end up on the antiquities market or pass directly into a private collection.
14. Davesne, Yenisoğanci 1992, pp. 24–25.

Dispersion need not happen immediately. The two years it took to release the Kessab (**288**) and Tell Kotchek (**198**) hoards are a relatively short delay for such lots. Concerning the Aleppo (?) hoard (*IGCH* 1562, **235**), thought to have been found c. 1930, Seyrig warns: "If I can believe my informants, the date of 1930 would only be when the hoard appeared on the market: discovery was many years prior, the hoard having remained a long time in the possession of an antiquities dealer in Aleppo."[15] The reliability of the most immediate informants is itself occasionally subject to suspicion. The tetradrachms from the El-Aweinyie hoard (*IGCH* 1550, **211**), in the Aradian Peraea, which their discoverers released onto the market over a period of years, were taken to Beirut by a man claiming to have discovered them with a collection of jewels. Seyrig absolutely rejects this association, basing himself on the two groups' chronological criteria. In some cases, it is nearly impossible to make a definitive determination. Thus, the Abu Shusheh hoard (*IGCH* 1507, **80**), in Judaea, has an apparently quite curious composition. If one accepts the additions proposed by J. and A.-G. Elayi,[16] one ends up with a composite group: coins from before Alexander as well as Alexanders, imitations, tetradrachms and fractions, bronze and silver, all mingled together.

1.3. Reconstitution of Hoards

This dispersal method sometimes leads to complicated reconstitutions of hoards. Some instances are especially noteworthy. The most celebrated, which set the original standard for Greek numismatists, remains without any doubt Newell's reconstitution of the Demanhur hoard. This collection of several thousand tetradrachms of Alexander the Great went on sale by lots beginning in 1905 in the city of Demanhur, in the Egyptian Delta. Newell initially devoted several publications to it in 1911 and 1912, following them with a magisterial synthesis in 1923. In those intervening years, he engaged in an endurance test to reassemble the lots dispersed among various collectors. The result is the publication of a hoard fundamental for our knowledge of Alexander's coinage. It is one of the coin hoards not derived from excavation that are the best known and studied, both by Newell and by others subsequently inspired, directly or indirectly, by his work.[17] In Syria, other hoards, less spectacular, are also the product of complicated reconstitutions. Thus, Seyrig's archives inform us how he reconstituted the Kessab hoard (*IGCH* 1568, **288**), which he had to separate from a lot of Alexanders found at Tell Kotchek (*IGCH* 1773, **198**). These coins were sold at Homs, Idlib, and Beirut between June, 1952, and May, 1954, in no fewer than 19 lots. Tigran Sarrafian was the original source of information, one of the informants who appear most often in Seyrig's notes and who himself provided Seyrig with numerous specimens from his own collection, according to data available in the French

15. "A en croire mes informateurs, la date de 1930 ne serait que celle où le trésor est apparu sur le marché : il aurait été découvert bien des années auparavant, et serait resté longtemps dans la possession d'un antiquaire d'Alep." Seyrig archives, Bibliothèque nationale de France, dossier 260.
16. Elayi, Elayi 1993a, pp. 209–16.
17. For a fuller narrative of tracking down the Demanhur hoard, along with its bibliography, cf. Duyrat 2005b.

national coin cabinet. This same dealer also sold coins to the American University of Beirut. Six intermediaries permitted Seyrig to study these lots and, exceptionally, he cites them by name.[18] More recently, Mattingly has reassembled 536 coins from the Maʿaret en-Numan hoard (*CH* 9.511, **193**) that were scattered about in private collections (A. Houghton in the U.S., P. Girardi in Trieste, A. Spaer in Jerusalem) or in public collections (in the displays and storage cabinets of the British Museum in London, the Nationalmuseet in Copenhagen, and the Bibliothèque nationale de France), or, finally, with dealers (Bank Leu in Zurich, Münzen und Medaillen in Basel, Numismatic Fine Arts in Beverly Hills).[19] The contrast between Seyrig's quest and Mattingly's is striking. Seyrig appealed to local informants and worked quite close to the source, having the good fortune of residing there, while Mattingly had to set up an international network, a mélange of public institutions, collectors, and professional numismatists. Meadows exemplifies yet another method. Thanks to painstaking "digging," this time in the archives of the American Numismatic Society, he is preparing to publish a reconstitution of the Syria hoard (*CH* 7.90, **168**) found before 1981.[20] Work on the ground is not necessarily any easier. J. and A.-G. Elayi amply demonstrate this when they try to distinguish hoards in a group of 496 coins dispersed in Lebanon in 20 lots to several continents between 1983 and 1988 (**28**, **29**, **72**). "Among the multiple rumors that inevitably float around, we have only considered information from individuals reputed to be trustworthy: some already published authors, others reporting to us orally, with permission to make their findings public."[21] Without rehearsing J. and A.-G. Elayis' entire investigation, one may note that the local press made it possible to discern one initial hoard by echoing news of one of the finds, as relayed in the *Counterfeit Report* and the *Bulletin of Counterfeits*. "The very year of its discovery, this hoard gave rise to the fabrication of counterfeits relatively easy to uncover and rather quickly denounced."[22] A second hoard is known through more academic channels: archaeologists obtained the material, which a collector and a numismatist subsequently recognized.[23]

The hoard's physical appearance is an important factor that, when it comes from the trade (the most common occurrence), is a serious indicator of the lot's unity. This is the criterion ad-

18. Cf. the catalogue, hoard **288.**

19. Mattingly 1993.

20. Meadows 2016a.

21. "Parmi les multiples rumeurs qui n'ont pas manqué de circuler, nous n'avons considéré que les informations données par des personnes réputées dignes de foi : les unes ayant déjà été publiées et les autres nous ayant été communiquées oralement avec l'autorisation de les diffuser." Elayi, Elayi 1993a, p. 107. Other examples of complications the same authors encountered with hoards: **59** (*CH* 9.429), **61** (*CH* 9.431), and **62** (*CH* 8.149).

22. "L'année même de sa découverte, ce trésor a donné lieu à la fabrication de faux relativement faciles à déceler et assez vite dénoncés." Elayi, Elayi 1993a, p. 107. This is not an isolated phenomenon. Other finds have encouraged the production of counterfeits placed on the market coincidentally or a little afterwards: cf. the Tartus hoard (*CH* 8.471, **277**). I myself had the occasion to observe this phenomenon in Damascus in 1997. A visitor presented me with a small hoard of Byzantine solidi, among which was an obviously counterfeit mould, scarred all over with small blisters, the result of clumsy casting. This collection, said to have been discovered in the region of Christian villages north of Damascus (Maaloula, Sednaya), had also prompted the discoverer to enlist a local silversmith in the attempt to improve the revenue he hoped to obtain from the sale of the lot by adding some supplementary coins, as my visitor finally admitted to me.

23. Byblos, *CH* 9.374 (**29**).

vanced in 23 cases,[24] often for old hoards because the severe cleaning that dealers today inflict eliminates the coins' surface oxidation.[25] This oxidation is sometimes so great that is causes the coins to cling together, forming a block that has to be pulled apart by mechanical or chemical means.[26] The patina, in one instance, is not homogeneous, which could be the result, in Hill's opinion, of a difference in metallic composition (**359**). In rare cases, hoards have arrived on the market with earth still on them (**112**, **132**) and even occasionally with their container (**50**, **66**, **130**, **131**, **161**). Noticeably similar wear can also be a criterion of unity (**242**, **259**). Most of the time, nevertheless, it is internal factors and comparison with well-attested hoards that help to guarantee that a coin lot arriving as an entity on the market actually constitutes a hoard.

Not all finds, however, take the form of agglomerations. Coins can wash away in the soil and appear scattered to the discoverer. This is undoubtedly the case especially for hoards enclosed in perishable containers, cloth or leather, which degrade before oxidation clumps the coins together. Geographical context can play an aggravating role: the Qasr Naba hoard (*IGCH* 1493, **53**) was found in the alluvial deposits left by a raging torrent. The elements of Khan el-Abde (*IGCH* 1597, **255**) might have been washed away by water, which would explain their dispersion on the site. A shepherd found the Kırıkhan hoard (*CH* 10.310, **231**) while he was watering his flock, the coins capturing his attention as they dropped one by one into the water from the bank where they had been buried.[27] Elsewhere, ensembles have even been reconstituted during surface gatherings (Tel Gamma **81**, Tell el-Fukhar *IGCH* 1501, **84**).

The Seyrig Archives inform us of the purchase price of these coins only once: Newell acquired the tetradrachms from the Ain Tab hoard (*IGCH* 1542, **242**) at the start of the 1920s for $3 to $5 a coin.

It does happen that these attempts at reconstitution fail, even when an expert in the field oversees them. Seyrig became resigned over a hoard of Alexander staters discovered at Sidon in 1961.[28] The file with the name and date of the hoard also states "will be published by N. Waggoner." As the correspondence preserved in the file shows, the latter envisioned publishing this lot in her study of Babylon, today still unpublished. Seyrig presents this collection as follows: "In 1961, an important hoard of staters of Alexander the Great appeared on the Beirut market; discovery near Sidon was reasonably claimed."[29] He inventoried the specimens he found at various dealers, but he caught himself registering the same coin twice at different shops. "The confusion became overwhelming, I had to give up the task." He estimates the total as at least 100 coins, some of which were quickly put on sale with European dealers. They are easily recognizable because only four varieties were represented, "still in mint condition." In a message to Waggoner dated October 26, 1972, Seyrig clearly states that he bought a specimen of each variety:

24. **52, 66, 80, 82, 99, 123, 127, 133, 162, 184, 190, 202, 208, 214, 226, 235, 281, 296, 305, 314, 320, 326, 359.**

25. Seyrig, in both his archives and his publications, pays particular attention to this criterion.

26. A hoard separated under the observation of Meshorer: **133.**

27. I thank A. Meadows for informing me of Levante's description of this discovery, now preserved in the archives of the American Numismatic Society (see Appendix 2).

28. H. Seyrig Archives, Bibliothèque nationale de France, dossier 233.

29. "en 1961 apparut sur le marché de Beyrouth un important trésor de statères d'Alexandre le Grand, qui passait avec vraisemblance pour avoir été trouvé près de Sidon."

- Sidon: Newell 1916, no. 49. Serpent with single volute on the helmet.
- Sidon: Newell 1916, no. 49, but serpent with double volute on the helmet. Seyrig did not record any specimens with a griffon on the helmet.
- Sidon: Newell 1916, no. 51.
- Babylon: Müller 1855, no. 731s, to the left MI beside a monogram surrounded by a crown.[30]

Waggoner suggests dating the Babylonian staters to 313/2–311/0 BC. Newell 1916 gives the years Σ = 316/5 BC and T = 315/4 BC for the Sidon specimens.[31] A final note mentions some sale catalogues containing specimens from the hoard:

- Leu, April 12–13, 1962,[32] no. 180 (Babylon)
- Leu, April 4, 1963, no. 49 (Babylon).
- Münzen und Medaillen, Basel, 25, Nov. 17, 1962, no. 441 (Babylon).
- Münzen und Medaillen, Basel, 25, Nov. 17, 1962 no. 442 (Sidon Σ).

Despite all the efforts of the two numismatists, this hoard has therefore remained unpublished, and I have not included it in the catalogue here. It should surely merit, however, a notice in *Coin Hoards*.

1.4. "Uninteresting" Hoards

More surprising is the mention of "uninteresting" hoards in the Seyrig Archives. In the following two cases, Seyrig saw some lots, probably on the Beirut market, the source of most of his information. He studied them relatively quickly and dismissed them. The first, to the contrary, is highly interesting because it is a hoard of bronze coins, something still relatively rare in the Hellenistic period outside the Hasmonean kingdom. This is the Amrith hoard (**284**), which has been included here in the catalogue because Seyrig's notes were very detailed, providing dates and control marks for the 50 specimens studied. Seyrig does not inform us about the criteria that led him to dismiss this lot in an apparently unjustified way. Its characteristics, it seems to me, leave no doubt about its authenticity and unity. The coins belong to mints and dates suitable for the findspot, as another Amrith hoard (**283**) shows. Was the hoard's unprepossessing character enough to cast it aside? Yet that was not Seyrig's way, who was always so attentive to sources.

A second lot is mentioned much more cursorily.[33] This is a "hoard brought from Homs, Nov. 18, 1951. 12 tetradr. of Alexander." The folder containing the group's description has the following information: "eliminated as without interest," the reason being "All these coins in bad

30. Price 1991a, no. 3749.
31. Letter from Seyrig to Waggoner, October 26, 1972.
32. In fact, sale at Hess-Leu, as for the next coin, too.
33. H. Seyrig Archives, Bibliothèque nationale de France, dossier 230.

condition" at the end of the list. They are nonetheless quickly described, with, in parentheses, mention of the countermarks they received and the words "dotted border", probably when the latter was visible on the obverse. I append the reference to Price's catalogue of Alexanders.[34]

Perge
  Year 17, dotted border (Helios): Price 1991, no. 2929.
  Year 18, dotted border: Price 1991, no. 2930.
  Year 20, sphinx left (anchor): Price 1991, no. 2933.
  Illegible, dotted border (anchor).

Temnos
  Oinochoe, vine; effaced monogram: Price 1991, nos. 1671–1690.

Aspendus
  Year 8 or [.]8 (anchor, dotted border): Price 1991, nos. 2888 or 2897.
  Year 10 (anchor): Price 1991, no. 2890.
  Year 17 (anchor): Price 1991, no. 2896.
  Year 23 (anchor): Price 1991, no. 2902.
  Year 23: Price 1991, no. 2902.
  Year 25 (anchor): Price 1991, nos. 2904–2905.
  Year 26: Price 1991, nos. 2906–2907.

Apart from the tetradrachm of Temnos and one of those from Perge, the coins appear to have been sufficiently legible for study. The latest Alexander is the one from Aspendus of year 26, that is, 188/7 BC, according to Meadows' recently proposed chronology.[35] But the anchor countermark is usually considered dating c. 175–170 BC.

1.5. Circulation of Antiquities

The discovery of a hoard outside the context of authorized excavations generally remains a mystery. The account given by individuals of a find's circumstances sometimes reaches us when the hoard is exceptional. Thus, W. M. Thompson, a missionary in Syria and Palestine when the second lot of the enormous hoard of gold coins from Saida (1852) was discovered, describes the frenzy for hoard-hunting that took hold of the local populations:

> I have heard of diggers actually fainting when they have come upon a single coin. They become positively frantic, dig all night with desperate earnestness, and continue to

34. Price 1991a.
35. Meadows 2009, p. 69; the system of Boehringer 1972 dates the Aspendus Alexander to 185/4 BC.

> work until utterly exhausted. There are, at this hour, hundreds of persons thus engaged all over the country. Not a few spend their last farthing in these ruinous efforts. I heard a respectable man in Sidon declare that if he had been one of these fortunate diggers in this garden he would have killed all the rest, and fled with the treasure out of the country. These operations are carried on with the utmost secrecy, accompanied with charms and incantations against the *jan* and other spirits which are said to keep guard over hidden treasures. The belief in the existence of these guards, and of their dangerous character, is just as prevalent now as in the time of the Thousand Nights. Intelligent and respectable people have assured me that they have come upon some slabs of stones, closing up doors to secret chambers, which no power on earth could remove, because the proper password or charm is lost. Others soberly assert that they have been driven away by terrible *jan,* who threatened them with instant death if they attempted to force the doors.[36]

It is common knowledge that a hoard, once discovered, always winds up on the antiquities market. This may happen quite rapidly, in the form of lots quickly noticeable, or in small groups, even a coin at a time, when the discoverer or his intermediaries want to be discrete or to avoid lowering the value of their goods by flooding the market with too much material, or if he or they want to hold something of value in reserve. These networks began operating a long time ago. Sarmant lists the French and European correspondents with whom Pellerin (1684–1782) dealt.[37] The correspondence of the Count of Caylus, studied by Callataÿ, provides numerous examples, including some outside Europe. Thus, in mentioning the engraving of the plates in Pellerin's *Recueil*, in which he seems to have participated, Caylus writes: "So far, Pellerin has only presented the three volumes of which you speak to me. My plan is to send the Infante of Spain the fourth volume, on which I am currently working. But the author is waiting for some coins from Aleppo in order to finish, and which I am having sent to him. They are en route from Marseilles to Paris, and this book will be just like the others" (Letter LXXII, from Caylus to Paciaudi, Oct. 24, 1763, cited by Callataÿ).[38] There is an established and efficient system, although the middlemen are not always reliable, as Pellerin's mishaps in Italy attest. Marseilles is the port of entry for finds coming from the Levant: "Those curious to witness the surge in new discoveries became much more committed to overseas voyages. That is why, moreover, Parisians envied the people of Marseilles for their proximity to the Levant. The state financed foreign expeditions, not digs on native soil."[39] Deals can be made long-distance, upon guaran-

36. Cited by Sharp 1870.

37. Sarmant 2003, pp. 213–14.

38. "Jusqu'ici M. Pellerin n'a donné que les trois volumes dont vous me parlez. Mon dessein est bien d'envoyer à l'Infant le IVème volume auquel je travaille. Mais l'auteur attend, pour finir, quelques médailles d'Alep, et que je lui fais venir. Elles sont en chemin de Marseille à Paris, et ce livre sera de la même condition que les autres." Callataÿ 2010, p. 1347.

39. "C'est beaucoup plus aux voyages outre-mer que se fiaient les curieux pour voir surgir des nouveautés. C'est d'ailleurs pourquoi les Parisiens enviaient aux Marseillais leur proximité avec le Levant. L'Etat finançait des missions à l'étranger, non des fouilles sur le territoire métropolitain." Sarmant 2003, p. 271.

tee of finding dependable intermediaries. Sarmant mentions the cool response of the abbé de Rothelin who, apprised of a sale of coins in Aleppo, ultimately declines: "on the one hand, the catalogue is not ready and perhaps there is no one in Aleppo who can be found capable of doing it; what's more, the catalogue aside, one would have to be certain of the antiquity and to know the degree of preservation of each coin in order to determine its price. We do not dare to flatter ourselves that such a deal can be concluded in the face of these, rather major, obstacles."[40] The French were not the only ones in Aleppo, where the English were prominent. A letter of Jean-François de Lacroix, dated April, 1672, recounts how "for coins, I can tell you that there are several Englishmen here looking with extraordinary eagerness and they have amassed a large number; the English representative in Constantinople has a sizeable quantity of them."[41] Concerning Constantinople, the principal commercial center for antiquities destined for Europe: "the number of interested parties or, better, their agents is so large at Constantinople that gold coins are exceedingly scarce."[42]

In the twentieth century, and despite advances in communications, the local network remains primary, and circulation of material on the regional scale appears very important. This can be seen in the case of the Kessab hoard (*IGCH* 1568, **288**) above, which passed through the hands of at least six intermediaries in three cities, Idlib, Homs, and Beirut. In addition, such intermediaries introduce themselves to each other, from one place to the next. Seyrig's archives provide rather numerous examples, including one J. and A.-G. Elayi cite. A dealer from Saida showed Seyrig a group of Sidonian coins at a dealer's in Beirut in November, 1959.[43] In another case (*IGCH* 1613, **300**), a peasant from southern Syria brought 40 bronzes to Damascus. The lot's composition "seems to indicate a findspot within Palestine, probably Golan, ancient Gaulanitis, near Lake Tiberias, a region that is a rich source of coins and antiquities for the Damascus bazaar."[44] It is interesting to observe that, c. 1940, the antiquities circuit in the Golan region funnelled them in quantity towards Damascus, a situation the Israeli occupation has obviously altered since 1967. In the '60s, Spaer confirms this flow of antiquities to the north, noting that the most natural export route for a coin hoard found in Israel is "Beirut, the most likely outlet for a large hoard," with direct exports to Europe and the U.S. in mind.[45] Instances of lots sold in Beirut are quite numerous: **4**, **17**, **18**, **60**, **67**, **148**, **157**, **173**, **190**, **208**, **209**, **211**, **213**, **228**, **261**,

40. "d'une part le catalogue n'est pas fait et peut-être ne trouveroit-on personne à Alep capable de le faire, de l'autre, indépendamment du catalogue, il faudroit être assuré de l'antiquité et connoître le degré de conservation de chaque médaille pour décider de son prix. Ce sont là des embarras trop grands pour oser se flatter de conclure un pareil marché."

41. "pour les médailles, je vous diray qu'il y a icy plusieurs Anglois qui en cherchent avec un empressement extraordinaire et qui en ont ramassé un grand nombre, et le résident d'Angleterre à Constantinople en a une très grande quantité." Letter to P. de Carcavy, keeper of the Royal Coin Collection, cited by Sarmant 2003, p. 293, n. 110.

42. "le nombre des curieux ou pour mieux dire des commissionnaires des curieux est si grand à Constantinople que les médailles d'or y sont fort rares." Letter, November 7, 1738, to the Marquis de Caumont, cited by Sarmant 2003, p. 272, n. 18.

43. Elayi, Elayi 1993a, p. 126.

44. "semble indiquer un lieu de trouvaille des confins de la Palestine, probablement du Jaulan, de l'ancienne Gaulanitide, près du lac de Tibériade, région qui approvisionne beaucoup le bazar de Damas en monnaies et en Antiquités." H. Seyrig Archives, Bibliothèque nationale de France, dossier 224.

45. Spaer 1965–1966, p. 1.

262, **266**, **276**, **288**, **292**, **301**, **305**. Today, hoards from the Palestinian territories leave directly through antiquities dealers in the Old City of Jerusalem.

Current borders are not impregnable, often severe laws against trafficking in antiquities notwithstanding. Thus I had the occasion in October 1997, to examine a hoard of 36 tetradrachms in Tripoli that had moved from Syria to Lebanon in the mid-'90s. The collector who showed it to me had a reputation for buying anything offered him, and he had an abundance of objects such as coins found in northern Syria. The peasant who brought the hoard said he had found it in a pot in his garden. The collector, anxious to preserve anonymity, only reluctantly revealed to me that the find came from Tell Hmiayra on the plain of Akkar. I was unable to study the hoard in depth, having to content myself with rapidly jotting down its composition. The lack of detail in these identifications precluded my presenting this ensemble in the catalogue, but one may observe that tetradrachms with the types of Philetairos are rare in Syria (**166**, **181**), like those of Philip V (**174**).[46]

27 tetradrachms with types of Alexander
- 9 Chios
- 10 Miletus
- 1 Cos
- 1 Argos
- 2 Rhodes
- 1 Aradus (Price 1991, no. 3365)
- 3 unidentified

3 Lysimachus
2 Philetairos
1 Philip V
1 Antigonus Gonatas
1 Prusias I
1 tetradrachm of Alabanda in Caria

Rouvier in 1902[47] describes the removal of hoards from their findspots to western markets: the 179 coins of the Beithir hoard (*IGCH* 1489, **18**) not melted down "were acquired by a tourist interpreter"[48] who sold Rouvier 11 of them, keeping 80–90 for himself; "the rest he put on the market, whether locally or abroad, in London, Europe, and America. I am personally aware that a young Russian diplomat, sometime envoy to a German royal court, acquired around 30 items."[49] He further states that the Russian consul-general in Beirut, a Monsieur de Lischine,

46. Hoard **323** also contains a tetradrachm of Philip V, but it is dated 72 BC.
47. Rouvier 1902, pp. 256–57.
48. Rouvier's French reads: "un drogman de voyageurs."
49. "le reste a été écoulé par lui, soit sur place, soit à l'étranger, à Londres, en Europe et en Amérique. A ma connaissance, un lot d'une trentaine de pièces aurait été acquis par un jeune diplomate russe, quelques temps accrédité auprès d'une cour allemande."

bought two specimens. Without mentioning the hoards from which these coins probably come, Rouvier writes that "the double staters of Sidon attributed to Bagoas and Mazaeus, which appear in numismatic collections, were found within the borders of the ancient Sidonian territory or nearby. The majority of those in the de Luynes collection, today in the Cabinet de France, like all the other coins of the ancient kings of Sidon, were conveyed to the illustrious Member of the French Academy by the chancellor of the French consulate in Beirut, Monsieur Pérétié. The coins of the same sort that Monsieur de Démétrio acquired in Alexandria and which he bequeathed to the Athens Museum would appear to be an exception because of their apparent origin. Yet one knows these coins were of Syrian provenance and that there has never been a similar find in Egypt."[50] Sidonian coins from the Persian period only circulated in very limited fashion in Egypt. J. and A.-G. Elayi mention only five hoards, which mostly contain just one to three Sidonian coins.[51] It is quite possible that the Démétrio coins reached him via channels of the antiquities network, coming from Syria. These few remarks of Rouvier well illustrate how easily coins circulate in the region until they find a buyer.

2. HOARD PROVENANCE AND WARS IN THE MIDDLE EAST

Such networks raise the problem of locating findspots. Hoards are usually routed to commercial venues where their owners know they can dispose of them quickly. Beirut and Jerusalem principally played this role at the end of the nineteenth and in the twentieth centuries. Such market concentration can muddy provenance identification. The so-called "Lebanon" hoard (*IGCH* 1483, **17**),[52] upon further study, thus became the Syrian hoard or, more strictly speaking, the Massyaf hoard. A mere note indicates that "before it had become apparent that the hoard was actually found in Syria, I had referred to it as 'the Lebanon hoard' since it was exported to Western Europe through Lebanon."[53] These changes in origin, involving name changes, are important because the bibliography is hard to keep up with, so that later writers sometimes use out of date nomenclature. Thus, Starr still calls this hoard "Lebanon" two years after Kraay, Moorey 1968.[54]

Editors of hoard catalogues continually repeat the uncertainty that weighs on hoard provenances, given that most hoards are chance discoveries. This phenomenon grows between the first publications and later volumes of *Coin Hoards*: "An increasing number of hoards has no

50. "doubles statères de Sidon attribués à Bagoas et à Mazaios, qui figurent dans les collections numismatiques, ont été trouvés dans les limites de l'ancien territoire sidonien ou à proximité. La plupart de ceux de la collection de Luynes, aujourd'hui au Cabinet de France, avaient été transmis à l'illustre académicien, comme toutes les autres pièces des anciens rois de Sidon, par M. Pérétié, chancelier du consulat de France à Beyrouth. Sembleraient faire exception, comme origine apparente, les monnaies de la même catégorie acquises à Alexandrie par M. de Démétrio et léguées par lui au Musée d'Athènes. Mais on sait que ces pièces étaient de provenance syrienne, et que jamais trouvaille analogue n'a été faite en Egypte." Rouvier 1902, pp. 254–55.

51. Elayi, Elayi 1993a, hoards 30, 71, 72, 74, and 75, fig. 24.

52. Kraay 1964a, p. 20; 1964b, p. 78.

53. So Kraay writes in Kraay, Moorey 1968, p. 210.

54. Starr 1970, p. 88.

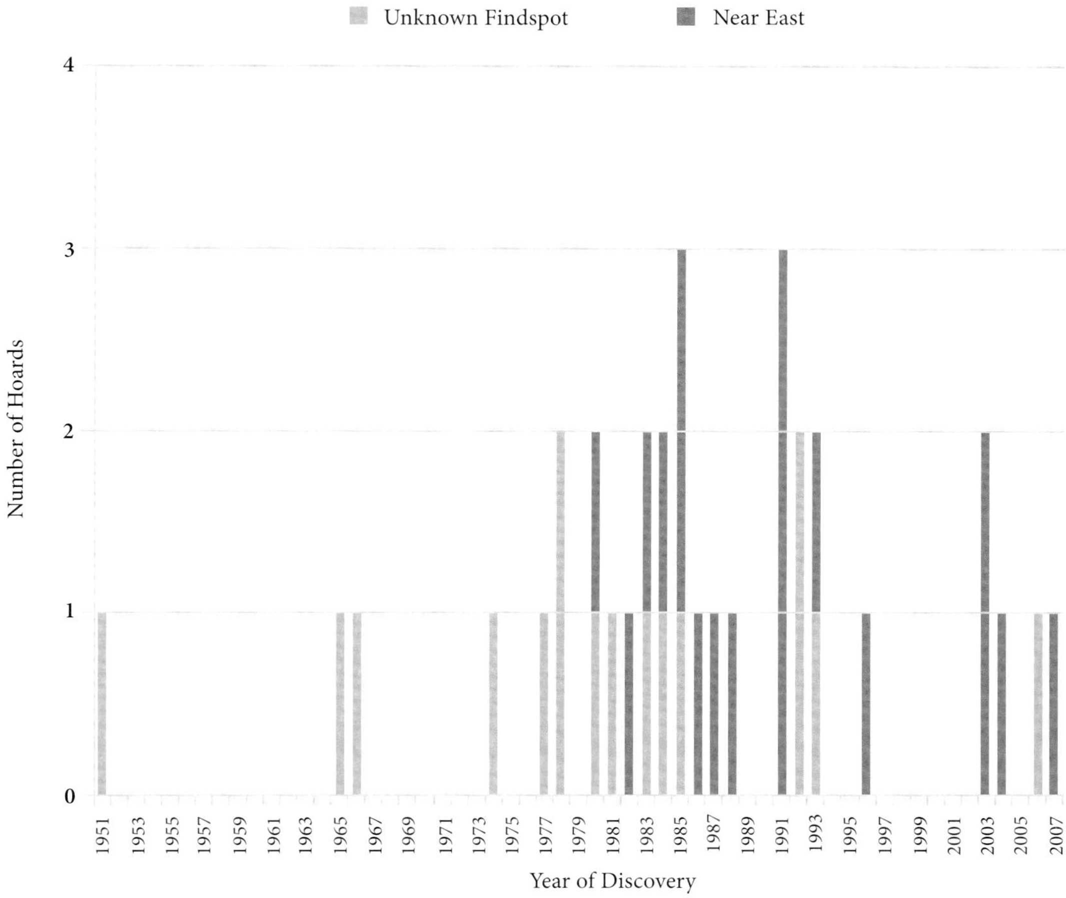

Figure 3.3. Hoards without a verified provenance by find-date.[55]

known findspot, and it should be noted that only hoards from controlled excavations have an accurate and definite provenance, whereas the majority of locations are based on contributors' speculations."[56] In his preface to the book of Paunov and Prokopov on Roman Republican coin hoards in Bulgaria, Crawford identifies one of the reasons for this increase: "the devastation of the record by use of metal detectors: one has only to peruse any recording journal to see the ruin of knowledge caused by *soi-disant* scholars who support the trade in coins."[57] Near Eastern sites are not immune. The main archaeological sites in Syria since the beginning of the civil war are an obvious example. Aï Khanoum in Afghanistan is striking too. This is quite certainly the primary reason hoards are discovered nowadays, which, accordingly, can no longer be judged really fortuitous finds. Nercessian gives another reason for this phenomenon: "The laws in Near Eastern countries do not encourage reporting hoard discoveries. Governments confiscate coin finds from the hand of the public, thus encouraging secrecy and smuggling. As a result the exact

55. Hoards are considered discovered prior to the given date.
56. *CH* 8, p. vi.
57. Paunov, Prokopov 2002, p. 7.

provenance of coin hoards unearthed in this area remains unknown."[58] This is particularly true in the case he describes. Of the 25 coin hoards of Tigranes he inventoried, nearly half have an unknown origin.

These are general observations with no special bearing on Hellenistic Syria. For this region, hoards of unknown origin are listed as "Unknown Findspot" or "Near East." Figure 3.3 provides an overview by year of discovery.

No hoard before 1951 comes from a totally unknown provenance. Editors always name the assumed country of origin. Beginning with the 1970s especially, the general appellation "Near East" appears, so broad that it is tantamount to admitting in fact that the hoard's provenance is unknown. This habit became the norm in most cases with the 1980s. The graph in Figure 3.4 also shows a spike in hoards of uncertain origin between the 1970s and the beginning of the 1990s, a period corresponding to the war in Lebanon (1975–1990) that led to looting of the country's antiquities and increased regional trafficking in them. It is impossible to make an exact accounting of this looting and its perpetrators in the absence of available official documents. At best, one can refer to press reports whose accuracy is unverifiable. Thus, Hakimian notes excavations by the Israeli army in the region of Tyre, which was the most pillaged. The army penetrated into the area the first time as far as the Litani River in 1978, and overran the whole in 1982. In the summer of 1982, it occupied the region south of Tyre for the long term. Figure 3.4, which collects all finds by date of discovery, shows a first peak in 1978, followed by a second, more spectacular, in 1983, which would coincide with the Lebanese occupation. In 1987, Hakimian, relying on the Lebanese press that regularly reported the most outrageous lootings, mentions "the proliferation of clandestine digs and illegal trafficking in antiquities" in a country where the official archaeological service no longer functioned and where the currency had been severely devalued, depriving the Lebanese of a portion of their wealth. Selling antiquities enhanced the income of some of the population. They rapidly joined the network of intermediaries "who plow the country from north to south and east to west, overcoming all obstacles, barriers and front lines."[59] Hakimian describes a progressive rummaging that began with the dumps of the Antiquities Service and moved on to sites excavated long before, notably Byblos, before opening up zones untouched by any exploration. The archaeological holdings of the Constituency of Northern Lebanon, of the Castle of Tripoli, the Roman-Byzantine Museum of al-Mina, the Mediaeval Museum of the Castle of Tripoli, were all plundered and destroyed. The newspaper Al-Nahar for April 27, 1978, and October 8, 1985, mentions looting by the Israeli army which Hakimian sums up as follows: "At the time of the Israeli army's invasion of southern Lebanon in 1978, an Israeli archaeological mission visited the tomb of Hiram situated in the region of Hanawayh… After having investigated the tomb site and an ancient well nearby, the Israelis dug up the sarcophagi; after having pierced a hole into the bottom of the tomb of Hiram, they removed, local inhabitants say, ancient objects, which were transported by helicop-

58. Nercessian 2006.

59. "la prolifération des fouilles clandestines et [le] trafic illégal des antiquités"; "qui sillonnent le pays du nord au sud et d'est en ouest, surmontant tous les obstacles, barrages et lignes de fronts." Hakimian 1987, pp. 199–200.

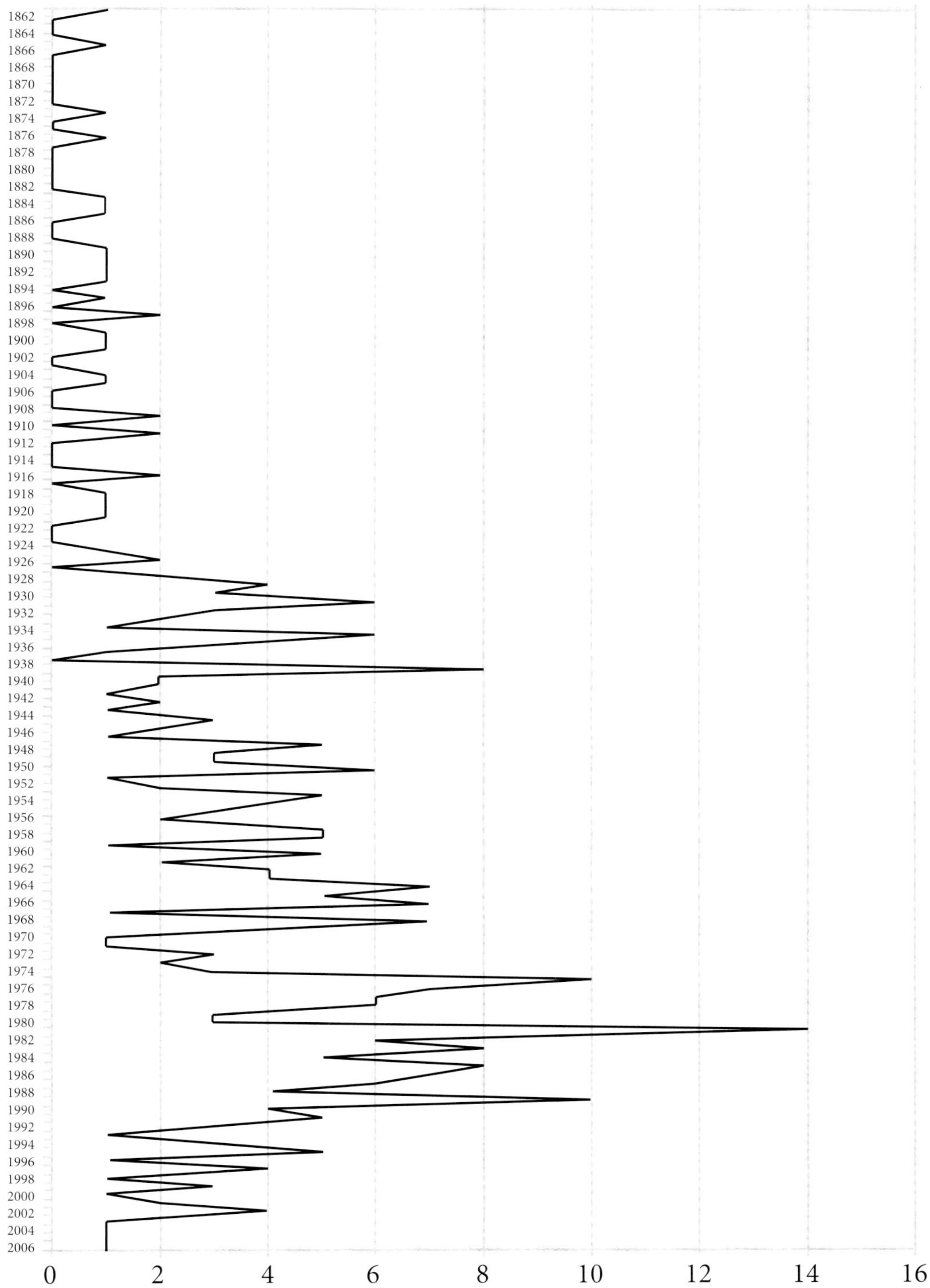

Figure 3.4. Hoards by date of find.[60]

60. This graph takes account of 332 hoards. The find dates of those not included here are unknown. The hoards of Latakia (*IGCH* 1544, **184**) and Saida (*IGCH* 1508, **93**) have been excluded. Since they were discovered in 1759 and beginning in 1829, respectively, their presence in the graph would have overwhelmed the data for the 20th century.

ter to Israel. During the 1982 invasion, another mission visited the site and its environs, as the Antiquities Service of Southern Lebanon has confirmed."[61] Other reports recount Israeli "prospecting." Sometimes they are hardly credible, decked out with more than improbable details: diamond jewellery and highly fanciful estimations of stolen asset values. In addition to Israeli invasions, the National Museum, situated on the Green Line in Beirut, suffered severely during the Lebanese War. Part of the collection was destroyed, another part plundered, and another, happily removed to safety, survived the events unharmed. As an example, there is the publication by Bordreuil and Gubel of Phoenician weights that were put on sale in Cologne,[62] though they had been stolen from the Beirut Museum.[63]

The war's destabilization of the region did not only entail an increase in illicit antiquities trafficking in Lebanon but surely also contributed to turning the country into a favored transit center for antiquities found throughout the area. A quick sampling of the 34 hoards with no mention of provenance shows, indeed, that, if their find dates cluster mostly in the 1970s to 1990, their contents are just as likely to belong to the hinterland of Aradus (**338**) as they are to the zone where the Ptolemaic (**125**, **130**, **133**) or the Attic weight standard prevailed (**124**, **128**, **134**, **137**, **186**, **197**, **202**, **203**, **228**, **243**, **318**, **319**, **325**, **330**). But the territory of Lebanon is entirely within the Ptolemaic standard zone. The Lebanese War represents a sharp growth spurt in the number of hoards sold on the antiquities market, all countries included, as the graph above (Fig. 3.4) demonstrates.

The French and British Mandates in the Levant began in 1920. It is tempting to attribute the spike in the number of hoards arriving on the market at the end of the '20s to this European presence that opened the doors of the antiquities market. From 1929, two to six new hoards are known each year, with a noticeable spike in 1940 followed by a falloff during World War II. In his introduction to *Trésors du Levant*, Seyrig suggests an explanation for the finds during the 1950s: "If one goes through the list of 48 hoards we published, one will observe that 31 of them were found between 1948 and 1957. This skewing cannot be by chance. I would say, rather, that the frequency of finds, in the course of this special decade, was owing to the use of new agricultural machinery, which enabled the laborer to open up deep, still unexplored layers. After a while, the archaeological content of these strata was exhausted, and the discoveries diminished."[64] After 1929, the only year lacking a hoard is 1939. From 1974 to 1994, the number grows appreciably, from two to 14 hoards annually, never less. Throughout the Lebanese War

61. "Lors de l'invasion du Liban-Sud par l'armée israélienne en 1978, une mission archéologique israélienne a visité le tombeau de Hiram situé dans les parages de Hanawayh.... Après avoir prospecté le site du tombeau et un puits antique avoisinant, les Israéliens ont fouillé les sarcophages et après avoir creusé un trou dans le sol du tombeau de Hiram, ils en ont extrait, aux dires des habitants, des objets antiques qui ont été transportés par hélicoptère en Israël. Lors de l'invasion de 1982, une autre mission a visité le lieu et ses environs, ce qu'a confirmé le Service des Antiquités au Liban-Sud." Hakimian 1987, p. 207.

62. Münz Zentrum Auktion 49, November 23, 1983, vol. IV.

63. Bordreuil, Gubel 1990, IV.6 and IV.7, pp. 510–12.

64. "Si l'on parcourt la liste des 48 trésors que nous publions, on remarquera que 31 d'entre eux ont été trouvés entre 1948 et 1957. Cette prépondérance ne doit pas être due au hasard. Je croirais plutôt que la fréquence des trouvailles, au cours de cette décennie privilégiée, a été due à l'emploi de nouvelles machines agricoles, à l'aide desquelles le laboureur a pu entamer des couches profondes, encore inexplorées. Après quelques temps, le contenu archéologique de ces couches s'est épuisé, et les découvertes ont diminué." Seyrig 1973, p. 7.

Table 3.2. Origin of coins in *CH* 9 and *CH* 10 (Asia Minor, Levant, East)

	Trade	**Excavations**
CH 9 (2002)	18,844	3,702
CH 10 (2010)	21,378	4,002

and the following five years during which institutions recovered little by little (1973–1995), 125 finds cluster, 37.7% of the 332 whose find date is known. This concentration occurs in 23 years out of 150.[65] It is not easy to assess the role of metal detectors: their use developed during the 1980s, when the curve slopes downward.[66]

The first decade of the 2000s falls back to clearly weaker levels, from one to four hoards a year. But those years have also produced some hoards of unknown provenance but striking size. The "Demetrius I hoard" (*CH* 10.301, **202**), placed on the market in 2003, comprised 532 silver coins and three gold; the "Near East hoard" (*CH* 10.244, **68**), in 2006, contained 475 silver coins.

These overall results do not allow us to appreciate other, more regional variations. Thus, the Six Days War profoundly altered the supplying of the antiquities market. The Israelis invaded the West Bank and East Jerusalem in June, 1967. Spaer describes the new situation: "There was a dramatic change in possibilities in Jerusalem after the Six Days War of 1967, when we gained access to the Old City and the eastern part of Jerusalem and the West Bank. In these areas, there was a huge amount of coins for which no customers had been found earlier. In particular, it was easy to obtain bronze issues, which explains their preponderance in my collection. Usually, they could be bought at flat rate, about 30–50 U.S. cents each."[67] This alteration, essentially affecting bronze currency, is not discernible in the global statistics, but all the same one observes a spike in 1967 and successive years.

The large variability in these results is closely connected to the political situation in the region. Ten-year averages, such as those Callataÿ published for all the hoards listed in *Coin Hoards* between 1980 and 1990, would give contrasting results for Syria.[68] It would be interesting to extend his study to the decades 1970–1979 and 1990–1999 to see if these regional variations are noticeable or if they disappear on a Mediterranean scale. A review of *Coin Hoards* 10 recently published by Iossif shows that, between the publication of *CH* 9 (2002) and *CH* 10 (2010), the vast region Asia Minor-Levant-East displays a certain stability in volumes (Table 3.2).

These numbers, however, conceal one development. During the same time, the ratio of precious metal to bronze, stable in hoards coming from excavations, greatly changed in the trade, where the share of bronze goes from more than a third in 2002 to 6.5% in 2010. No overall explanation can be given.[69]

65. 15.3% of the period under consideration (1862–2011).
66. On the use of these devices in archaeological excavations, cf. Connor, Scott 1998.
67. In Houghton, Spaer, Lorber 1998, p. 3.
68. Callataÿ 1996, pp. 61–63.
69. Iossif 2011b, pp. 442–43.

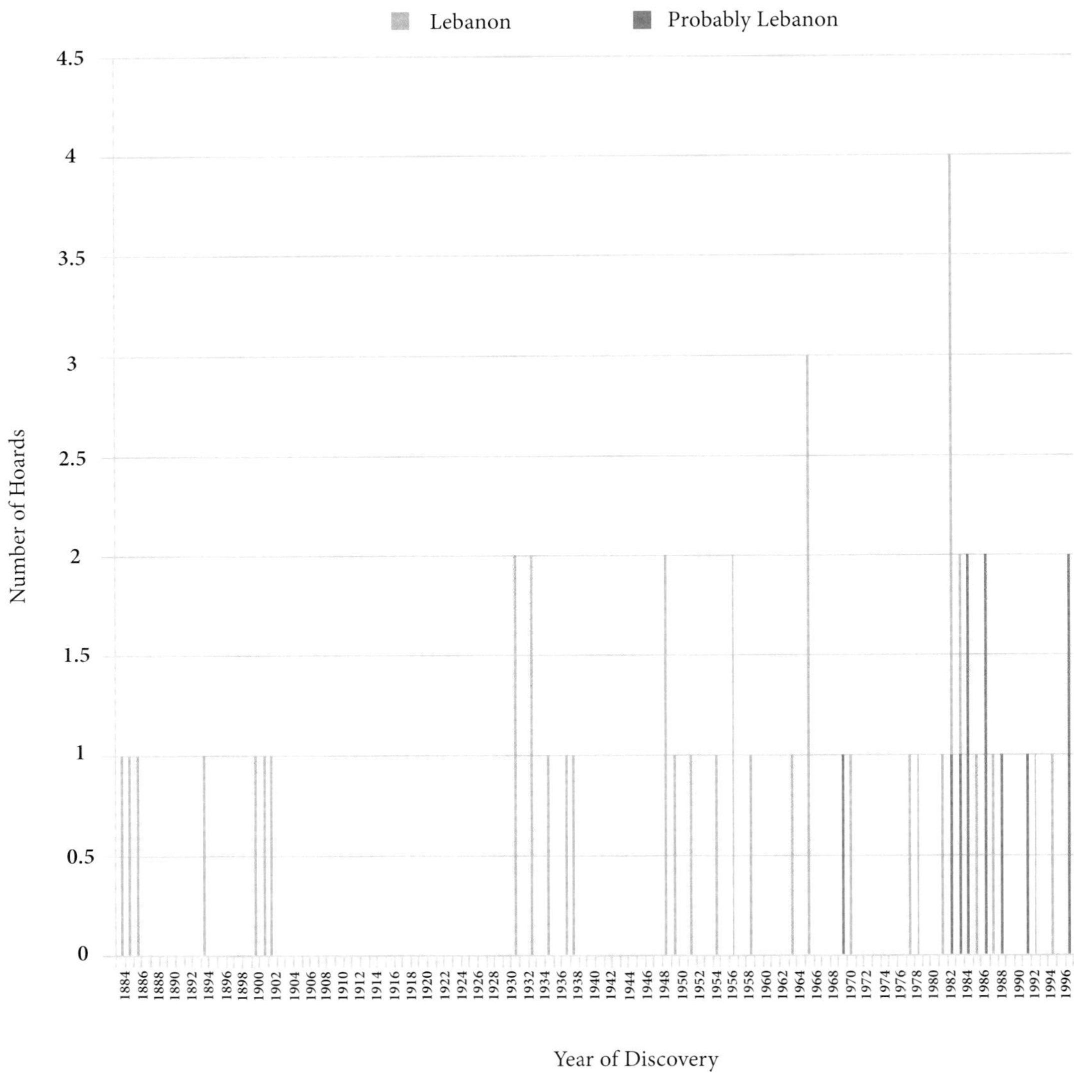

Figure 3.5. Hoards with Lebanese provenance.[70]

The current lack of transparency in these networks, through which coins deriving from hoards pass, is closely linked to the illegal character of the objects' discovery and sale. Laws, indeed, do protect the objects; and after countries gained their independence, they toughened the laws in order to combat what the states concerned considered looting. In 1936, Hill collected the then available data on the legislation of European countries over time. The *Comptes rendus* of the International Numismatic Commission since 1955 have offered articles by country under a heading called "The Law and Practice Regarding Coin Finds." Up to now they have

70. The hoards called "Probably Lebanon" have reached us with mention of only the country as origin. The rest have a precise location. Hoards prior to 1884 (**93**, **239**, **332**) have been excluded to avoid an excessive stretching of the data.

concerned only Europe and the U.S., with the exception of Israel, and more recently Turkey.[71] This would be worth doing for Italy and the countries of the eastern Mediterranean that are the chief sources of hoards. It would certainly give a very useful insight into the judicial arsenal of each country, its definition of antiquities, and the effectiveness of such laws, in comparison with the material I have collected here. To my knowledge, in the Levant such an overview exists only for Israel, the publication of this article being clearly intended to make known to numismatists their rights and duties: "It has been selected for numismatists interested in understanding their rights and obligations regarding the discovery and ownership of ancient coins or other antiquities in Israel, and the possibility of export of those coins/antiquities."[72] The Israeli texts define an antiquity as follows: "any object, whether detached or fixed, which was made by man before the year 1700 of the general era, and includes anything subsequently added thereto which forms an integral part thereof." It is understood that the state is the owner of every object discovered on Israeli soil answering this description, that it has sole power to authorize excavations, sale, and export, and that any sale of a copy or imitation of an antiquity must clearly indicate that it is not an original. "A person who contravenes is liable to imprisonment for a term of two years or a fine of 100,000 pounds." Illegal exports and imports are liable to a special penalty: six months imprisonment and a fine of 30,000 pounds. Despite the severity of the stipulated penalties, the withholding of information is rampant, as much here as in the rest of the Near East.

A certain number of hoards are mentioned only by country of origin. As already noted, this information may in fact merely indicate the country where the coins were sold, not necessarily where they were found. Although incomplete, this source is nonetheless instructive, as Figure 3.7 shows for Lebanon.

Seven out of 11 hoards known only as "Lebanon" date from the time of the Lebanese War, confirming the concentration seen with the hoards of unknown origin. The tendency is not at all noticeable for the hoards said to come from Jordan and the four from Israel (**269**, **275**, **291**, **326**).[73] Syria *in genere* is mentioned as the provenance for 32 hoards, 12 of them dating from the period of the Lebanese War (37.5%).

3. ARCHAEOLOGICAL POLICIES AND PUBLICATION OF EXCAVATED COINS

The importance of material coming from excavations, whether legal or not, no longer needs to be demonstrated. New discoveries constantly emerge from the soil, as Hoover's recent article on Nabataean lead coins shows. "The coinages of the Nabataeans have long been studied, and numerous collections have examples in silver and bronze. However until recently Nabataean lead coins have been extremely rare [two known coins]. Numerous new examples that have

71. Israel (Ariel 2002), Turkey (Pfeiffer-Taş 2012), Scotland (Sheridan 1995 and Saville 2008), England and Wales (Bland 1995 and Burnett 2000), whose laws were extensively amended at the beginning of the twenty-first century, Belgium (Van Heesch 1996), France (Petit, Meissonnier 1996; Aubin 2012), Denmark (Moesgaard 1998), Austria (Dembski 2001), Spain (Roma Valdés 2001), Russia (Malkov 2005), the U.S. (Kleeberg 2006, 2007, 2010).

72. Ariel 2002, pp. 63–64.

73. The latter are all later than the Six Days War, and one has to wonder if they do not, in fact, come from the Palestinian Territories.

appeared on the Israeli antiquities market are now greatly expanding our knowledge of this formerly rare series."[74] The market is no longer interested only in coins in precious metal or in specimens of exceptional quality, but also in coins of historical interest, even in a material as base as lead.

The historian's natural tendency is to consider material from excavations as unfiltered, without the mediating view of an ancient author and likely to provide us particularly reliable information, if it is interpreted correctly. Yet these coins, too, call for critical assessment, if only because excavated coins, albeit less so than those from hoards, are affected by the market. Meshorer, one of the leading lights of Israeli archaeology, with his keen appreciation of Israeli archaeology, recognizes as much in his study of the coins excavated from Qumran: "The absence of late coins of the Jewish War does not mean that the site was abandoned after the third year of the war. At Masada, 2,170 coins of 'year two' and 'year three' were found and only 105 of 'year four.' (Coins of 'year four' have a tendency to disappear from some excavations – stolen by workers who sell them in the antiquities market for high profit)."[75] According to this observation, workers know the value of what they are stealing and choose their targets carefully. This is a variable almost impossible to quantify, but other oral testimony from archaeologists of different nationalities, working in Israel and Syria, confirms that a portion of excavated coins winds up in workers' pockets, not in the excavations' safekeeping.

Political factors are also fundamentally important and produce conflicting data, whence the need to sketch in broad strokes the context in which national archaeological efforts developed in the countries of the Near East.

3.1. The Wars of the Twentieth Century

In the twentieth century, the Near East was the theater of several wars.[76] They have had consequences difficult to evaluate archaeologically, since no one has tried to develop an exact assessment. I have mentioned above the effects of the Lebanese War and Israeli invasions for the Lebanese archaeological record. Some further observations made in passing allow us to surmise the extent of these episodes for our sources. So Donceel, in studying the coins of Canatha in the Decapolis, is especially intrigued by the information he can extract from the excavations of Khirbet Qumran. Yet he warns the reader: "5/7ths of the coins excavated on the site have disappeared, most probably during the hostilities of 1967."[77] I have already mentioned the coins flooding the Israeli market that Spaer observed in the aftermath of the Six Days War.[78] One sees here the consequences from the Jordanian side.

74. Hoover 2006, p. 105.

75. Meshorer 2003–2006, p. 21.

76. Creation of the State of Israel (1948), Suez War (1956), Six Days War (1967), Yom Kippur War (1973), Lebanese War (1975–1990), spillover effects of the wars in Iraq (1980–1989, 1990, 2003–2006) and, more recently, wars in Syria and Iraq (from 2012 to today).

77. "Les 5/7e des monnaies de fouilles du site ont disparu, assez probablement lors des épisodes guerriers de 1967." Donceel 2007, n. 352.

78. In Houghton, Lorber, Spaer 1998, p. 3.

The heavy devastation Beirut suffered during the Lebanese civil war also led to necessary reconstruction beginning in the second half of the 1990s. A large archaeological program of exploration preceded it in the city, wherever buildings had to be razed and particularly in the ancient center. The Square of the Martyrs and neighboring quarters, the ancient quarter of the souks, thus revealed remnants of the Phoenician and then Greco-Roman city, thanks to the joint efforts of international teams.[79] Thousands of coins surfaced; Butcher has published, magisterially, those from the souks quarter.[80]

3.2. Archaeological Policies and National Identities

Intensifying this context of endemic war since the 1960s is a close association between archaeology and the definition of national identities. Finding useful information on the different governments' archaeological policy is no easy matter, especially because of the large imbalance that exists between the countries concerned. In the occupied territories, the latent state of war makes archaeological activity difficult. The *Ecole biblique et archéologique française* in Jerusalem nonetheless succeeded in opening a dig at Gaza.[81] Yasser Arafat's introduction to a catalogue of the exhibition that resulted is eloquent. The late president of the Palestinian Authority wrote of his joy in seeing the fruit of these Franco-Palestinian excavations presented in Paris. "This joy emanates from the fact that the Gaza Strip as well as the city itself will receive the esteem that is their due. Indeed, Gaza is profoundly rooted in the memory of Palestine and in our present consciousness, it plays a crucial role in the ongoing struggle of the Palestinian people and their National Authority to recover their rights and to proclaim the State of Palestine, of which Jerusalem is our only acceptable capital." In his brief exegesis on the archaeological and historical aspects of the city, he states that "Gaza is known as the first Palestinian city to strike coins, from the 5th century B.C."[82]

A strongly worded two-page note written by young Lebanese archaeologists emphasizes how the governments of the Near East use history for propaganda: "The majority of these regimes impose a research policy as focused on the interpretation of historical sources as on the results of archaeological excavations, which superimposes present geopolitical reality onto the past in order to justify their existence." The article does not provide concrete examples and sticks to generalities. It does mention the poor funding for archaeology: "Archaeological activity is reduced to a few scattered campaigns, directed by foreign entities and expeditions. Local

79. Cf. Perring 1997–1998 for a partial presentation of these works.
80. Butcher 2001–2002.
81. Humbert 2000.
82. "Cette joie émane du fait que la Bande de Gaza ainsi que la ville elle-même bénéficieront de l'estime qui leur est due. En effet, Gaza est profondément enracinée dans la mémoire de la Palestine tout comme de nos jours, elle joue un rôle crucial dans la lutte assidue du peuple palestinien et de son Autorité Nationale pour récupérer les droits et déclarer l'Etat de Palestine, pour lequel nous n'accepterons que Jérusalem pour Capitale." "Gaza est connue comme la première ville palestinienne qui ait frappé des monnaies dès le Ve s. av. J.-C." Yasser Arafat in Humbert 2000, p. 7. The text is opposite a recent photo of the Shatti refugee camp in Gaza City.

entities and universities are practically absent in this regard."[83] Here, too, the article lacks statistics, but it is obvious that Lebanon and Syria have archaeological services and archaeological budgets far more restricted than those of Israel. Foreign expeditions in partnership with the local governments' antiquities departments and Lebanese and Syrian universities (University of Lebanon, the American University in Beirut, University of Damascus) underwrite a large portion of archaeological exploration. This makes the latter a seasonal activity dependent on the expeditions' presence. It was not always thus. Valter indeed has shown the importance of archaeology and the budget she enjoyed in Syria in the 1950s. This interest in the country's rich past won Palmyra, Damascus, Aleppo, and Bostra designation as world heritage sites in the 1970s. Currently the country has 5,000 sites so classified. If the budget no longer adequately accommodates the number of remains, history and its role in creating the national identity and legitimating the current regime are, by contrast, quite sensitive and entrenched subjects.[84]

Outlets for publication are relatively few: *BAAL. Bulletin d'archéologie et d'architecture libanaises* (Directorate General of Antiquities in Lebanon) and *Berytus* (American University of Beirut) are the principal Lebanese journals. In Syria the *Annales archéologiques arabes syriennes* and in Jordan the *Annual of the Department of Antiquities in Jordan* are the only local publications in a foreign language specializing in archaeology. None of these is specifically concerned with numismatics. Local numismatists are rare, but a young generation, mostly educated in Paris, is once again taking interest in this source.[85] Most work therefore is done through foreign journals and by foreign numismatists, who naturally do not devote all their time to this area of research.

Table 3.3. Number of articles on antiquity/total published

Journal	2006	2007	2008	2009
American Journal of Numismatics	5/10	4/8	24/28	5/7
Israel Numismatic Research	13/16	16/19	13/15	12/16
Numismatic Chronicle	16/25	15/20	11/17	13/19
Revue Numismatique	9/12[86]	8/11	6/10[87]	6/10

The other problem evident in Syrian and Lebanese archaeological excavations is the excavators' failure always to provide thorough accounts of coin finds in their reports, including the ex-

83. "La majorité de ces régimes impose une politique de recherche bien orientée dans l'interprétation des sources historiques ainsi que dans les résultats des fouilles archéologiques, en superposant la réalité géopolitique actuelle au passé afin de justifier leur existence." "L'activité archéologique est réduite à quelques missions éparses, dirigées par des organismes et des missions étrangères. Les organismes et les universités locales sont pratiquement absents à cet égard." Abou Diwan, Khalil, Khreich 2006.

84. Valter 2002, pp. 234–40. The situation described here is of course prior to the Arab Spring.

85. Z. Sawaya and G. Abou Diwan in Lebanon, Kh. Kiwan, Q. El-Adra and A. Al-Mohanna in Syria.

86. Omits the special section in ancient numismatics honoring H. Nicolet.

87. Omits the special section in mediaeval numismatics honoring F. Dumas.

cavation's comprehensive, final report.[88] Thus, in his preliminary account of the late Hellenistic strata of Tell Arka, Thalmann expatiates at length on the pottery but says not a word about the coins.[89] In the final report on Tell Sukas, the Danish expedition publishes a highly detailed description of the excavation of this small town in the northern hinterland of Aradus, but no coin inventory. Coins are mentioned from time to time, usually without description, with a simple "cf." with a reference to a standard catalogue. The unsystematic nature of their presentation makes exploiting these discoveries very difficult.[90] Moreover, when an expedition's program focuses on a period prior to the Hellenistic, Hellenistic and later strata are archived and usually not published.

By contrast, Israeli archaeology is particularly active.[91] A highly developed archaeological service supports it, financed with budgets reflecting the large number of open excavations, rich in trained personnel with mastery of English, especially a numerous and effective team of field-numismatists. Israel also enjoys specialized publication resources. The *Israel Numismatic Journal* has been published since 1963, but its irregular appearances in later years prompted the creation of a new periodical in 2006 devoted entirely to numismatics, *Israel Numismatic Research*. It is introduced thus in the first issue: "The ability to publish a true annual reflects the advances in the field of numismatics in Israel over the past decades. The title of the journal signals the Society's wish to encourage comprehensive and innovative research in the field. The focus of *Israel Numismatic Research* will be on coinage circulating in the Southern Levant, from antiquity to the modern era."[92] In fact, Israeli ancient numismatics is by far the most prolific in the region. The journal's self-proclaimed chronological scope notwithstanding, the first issue (2006) contains 13 items concerning antiquity, against three dealing with later periods; the second volume (2007) has a ratio of 16:3. One might add that this dominance of ancient numismatics is also evident in the majority of other national journals (Table 3.3).

It is worth stressing the international reach of this young journal that has already welcomed the efforts of numerous foreign authors. Other Israeli journals regularly apportion space to numismatic articles: *Scripta Classica Israelica, 'Atiqot, Hadashot Arkheologiyot – Excavations and Surveys in Israel, Israel Antiquities Authority Reports, Qadmoniot, Israel Exploration Journal and Salvage Excavation Reports* of the University of Tel Aviv, archaeological journals that publish excavation results, including coinage. Such resources of scholarly dissemination are remarkable for a country the size of the state of New Jersey or two or three *départements* in France.[93]

88. Israel, although less affected by this problem, is not immune, as Barkay 2003–2006, p. 51, laments.

89. Thalmann 1978.

90. Cf. their chaotic description of the coinage material, mentioned in the catalogue of excavations here, Chap. 2, Tell Sukas.

91. In conversation, D. T. Ariel (Jerusalem, June, 2012) estimated that 700,000 coins have emerged from Israeli excavations. Only a tiny fraction is currently published.

92. *INR* 1 (2006), p. 3.

93. Israel (leaving out the occupied territories of Gaza and the West Bank) is 8000 sq. miles (20,770 sq. km). New Jersey, the 47th US state ranked by size, covers 8,722 sq mi. The département of the Gironde is 10,000 sq. km. For an itemized list of Israeli publications, I will merely refer to my periodic bibliographies in *Syria* that gather all these works since 1995.

The internet offers possibilities for extending still further the capacity to disseminate these efforts, notably through the website "Hadashot Arkheologiyot, Excavations and Surveys in Israel," http://www.hadashot-esi.org.il/search_eng.asp, which gives full access to the results of recent Israeli excavations.

Israel also has the distinction of having hosted a numismatic congress in Jerusalem in 1963, sanctioned by the International Numismatic Commission, but devoted exclusively to questions of ancient local numismatics, unlike the usual congresses the commission organizes every six years. Indeed, discussion was limited to *The Patterns of Monetary Development in Phoenicia and Palestine in Antiquity*.[94]

In numismatics, these publications are the work of a generation of scholars very well integrated into the international research network, where their energy is much esteemed. The substantial increase in publications on this region, modestly called "Southern Levant," is noticeable in the *Surveys of Numismatic Research* published every six years to coincide with the international congress of numismatics (compare Figs. 3.4 and 3.5). The authors of most of the works included are Israeli, but not only. It is not easy to present a true statistical study of this increase because the breakdown by region varies from one *Survey* to another.

Table 3.4. The southern Levant in *Surveys of Numismatic Research*, 1972–1984

Survey	Region	Entries
1972–1977[95]	Syria and Palestine	26
1978–1984[96]	Judaea, Samaria, Galilee only	18

The following entries cover the southern Levant: Persian Phoenicia and Palestine, Jewish and Nabataean coinages. The Seleucids are treated separately, illustrating the development of work in general on Hellenistic numismatics.

The noticeable increase in numismatics from the southern Levant does, in fact, accompany a marked development in numismatic publications in recent decades. The editors of the *Survey* published in 2007 take note of this: "Summing up, this *Survey of Numismatic Research* 2002–2007 lists more than 12,000 articles written by some 4,000 authors."[97] The decline in the number of works focused on the Levant in the last volume is closely connected with the fact that Bijovsky had to make a selection to keep within the limits imposed on the authors. So she was unable accurately to reflect the entirety of undertakings in this region, especially the growth in the number of excavation reports mentioning coinage (Table 3.6).

94. This congress took place, out of normal sequence, between the international numismatic congresses in Rome (1961) and Copenhagen (1967).
95. Mørkholm 1979.
96. Meshorer 1986.
97. Amandry, Bateson 2009, p. xii.

Table 3.5. The southern Levant in *Surveys of Numismatic Research*, 1985–2007

Survey	Region	Entries
1985–1990[98]	Phoenicia (Persian period)	65
	Palestine (Persian period)	33
	Jewish Coins (Hellenistic and Roman periods)	16
	Nabataeans	28
		Total: 142
1990–1995[99]	The Levant[100]	110
1996–2001[101]	The Levant	256
2002–2007[102]	The Levant	179

Table 3.6. Coins from excavations in *Surveys of Numismatic Research*

1990–1995[103]	27
1996–2001[104]	85
2002–2007[105]	52

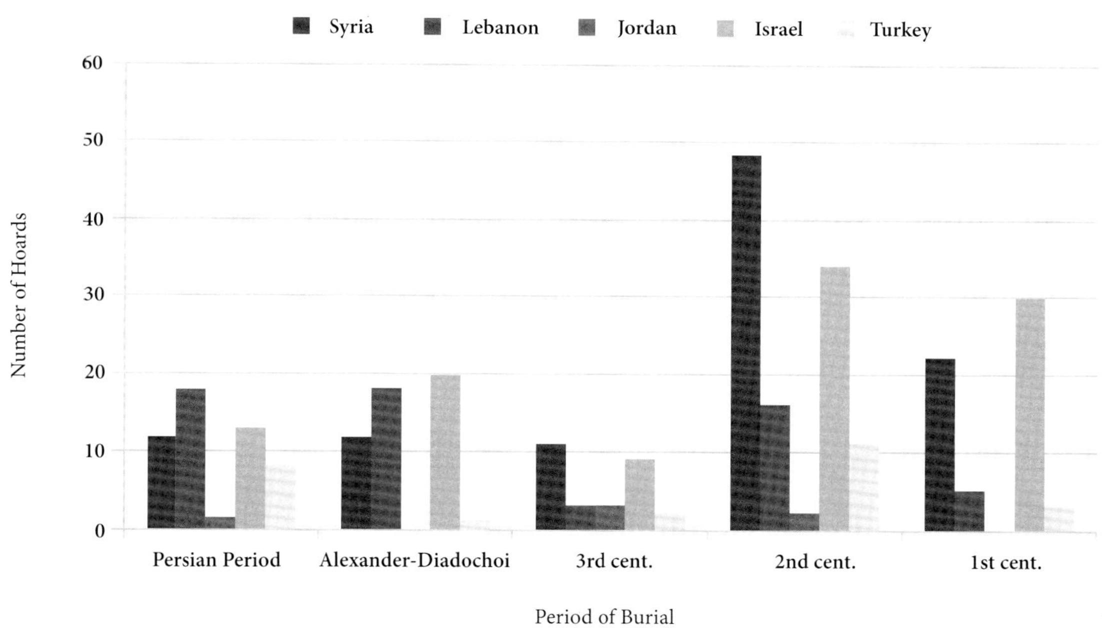

Figure 3.6. Provenance of hoards by country.

98. Lemaire 1991, Mildenberg, 1991, Barag 1991, Wenning 1991.
99. Gitler 1997.
100. This region covers in fact the same coinages as those listed in the Survey 1985–1990.
101. Gitler 2003b.
102. Bijovsky 2009.
103. Gitler 1997.
104. Gitler 2003b.
105. Bijovsky 2009.

Figure 3.7. Israeli two shekel coin (2008).

Figure 3.8. Bronze of John Hyrcanus II (76–67 BC), ANS 1944.100.62765.[106]

The archaeological material therefore comes, overwhelmingly, from Israel: of the 58 archaeological sites in my catalogue of excavated coins, 31 are from this country. Paradoxically, hoards with the same provenance are also quite numerous, although many of them are illegal in origin.

The graph in Figure 3.6 shows that Israel provided as many hoards as Syria (106), despite the small size of its national territory. There are surely two explanations for this. One is closely connected with legal and illegal archaeological activity: 25 of the 43 hoards we know of from legal excavations come from this country.[107] The other also surely reflects the favored zone of coin circulation along the coastal strip, whereas coinage is much less common east of the line Aleppo-Antilebanon-River Jordan-Dead Sea.[108] This same phenomenon explains the larger representation of Lebanon from the Persian period to the time of the Successors: coin use is then concentrated in this narrow region.

As in neighboring countries, ancient history is an important element in Israeli national identity. Coin types currently used by the State of Israel are the best evidence of this, since they reprise types from ancient coins (Figs. 3.7 and 3.8), and the shekel is the basic currency unit.

The weight of contemporary history is also apparent in some introductions to Israeli books. The origin of the collector Reuben Hecht's taste for numismatics is a good example. While visiting the British Museum in the 1920s, he explained to G. F. Hill that "as a Zionist he was moved by the sight of the word 'Jerusalem' inscribed in ancient Hebrew letters on an early Jewish coin." Mazar elaborates: "This coin, small though it was, sufficed to create an intimate tie linking the young Zionist with his ancestors who had lived in the Land of Israel in the periods in which the ancient Jewish commonwealth had reigned."[109] This bond between past and present is very much alive in the mind of Zionists of the 1930s, and it extends to coin types. In the conclusion of an unpublished article written for a German journal, Hecht transmitted "a fervent Zion-

106. Reverse: two corncupiae joined at the base, a pomegranate between them, dotted border.

107. Some of the production from illegal finds in the Occupied Territories is sold in Jerusalem, as a visit to antiquities dealers in the Old City will show.

108. Duyrat 2004.

109. Mazar in Meshorer 1998, pp. 7–8.

ist message, together with the hope to speedily see Jewish coins with Hebrew inscriptions in the renewed Jewish state." Meshorer picks up on this message in his introduction to the same catalogue: "Coins struck by Jewish authorities such as high priests and kings, not only teach us about them; they may be regarded as a direct greeting from our forefathers or from the distant past, a greeting which lessens the distance separating them from us."[110] The preface of the *Treasury of Jewish Coins*, by the same author, states: "The present volume is an English edition of the above-mentioned Hebrew work. Some changes have been made, which were obligatory not only on account of the need to modify certain aspects of importance to the Hebrew reader but not relevant to the English reader."[111]

The energetic Israeli research activity skews our data especially in favor of Israel. More than 50% of our most reliable information persistently comes from this country. This holds for hoards issuing from controlled excavations and isolated coins found on these sites. Such material possesses a well-established archaeological context and has elicited scholarly discussion. When, however, one considers the Israeli share of hoards throughout the catalogue, which is largely based on material seen in the trade, the ratio falls to less than 30% (Table 3.7).

Table 3.7. Israeli share of evidence

	Israel	**Total**
Hoards from Controlled Digs	25 (55.8%)	43
Archaeological Sites	31 (53.4%)	58
All Hoards	106 (29.9%)	355

The bias in our records is quite noticeable, and it must be borne in mind when drawing general conclusions from both hoards and excavations. Israeli territory is qualitatively the best-documented, in the number of official archaeological digs and in the quality and regularity of publications that are the work of internationally recognized scholars. The illegal record partially compensates in the representation of other countries, but at the price of a marked loss in data and uncertainties about hoards' authenticity.

110. Meshorer 1998, p. 11.
111. Meshorer 2001, p. vii.

4. A RELIABLE SOURCE?

Hoards are difficult to evaluate because usually the circumstances of neither formation nor burial can be determined with any certainty. A single hoard may be wholly untypical and its contents may thus provide misleading evidence. If, however, a number of hoards show common features or combine to produce a coherent picture, their evidence obviously deserves much more attention.

—Colin M. Kraay[112]

The several preceding pages underline the chance character of discoveries and the uncertainties that weigh on reconstituting some hoards: origin, date of discovery, and exact content are sometimes subject to notes of caution. Numismatists have always been alert to these difficulties, which are enumerated and illustrated here, to the extent possible. But must one still toss out every hoard from our database, as soon as legal and scientifically established conditions of discovery have not duly guaranteed a hoard's integrity? Such strictness would allow us to keep only hoards resulting from official excavations. A few years ago, in a study dealing with a hoard of dispersed Athenian tetradrachms, Flament voiced very vigorous doubts on the validity of scientific information obtained from such a source. Having observed that dealers typically "enrich" a hoard of coins otherwise difficult to sell, or remove the handsomest specimens, he adds that the more intermediaries there are, the less reliable a find is, and that discoverers are severely tempted to obfuscate a hoard's actual origin in order to elude the authorities. He concludes that "out of a desire to be exhaustive, the editors of *IGCH* and *Coin Hoards* have undertaken to point out the varying groups of coins that could constitute hoards, but very many of them certainly are not..."[113] In fact, careful examination of the present catalogue reveals that actually doubtful lots are few. Only two are probably not hoards (**245**, **360**). They are not included in our statistics. The case of the hoard said to come from the region of Antioch (**245**) is a good example of editorial prudence: after careful analysis of the groups and confirmation that several hoards were surely combined, the numismatists who have had the opportunity to work on these specimens have extracted as much new data as possible from them, but they have not published this assemblage as a hoard.[114] Similarities between groups seen on the market can sometimes prompt thoughts that they are one and the same ensemble. When indications are particularly encouraging, groups have been gathered under the same inventory number. Alternatively, notices of the individual hoards point out this relationship.[115] On the other hand, a collection like

112. Kraay 1956, p. 48.

113. "dans un souci d'exhaustivité, les responsables de l'*IGCH* et des *Coin Hoards* ont entrepris de signaler les différents ensembles monétaires qui pourraient constituer des trésors, mais beaucoup n'en sont certainement pas...." Flament 2005, p. 32.

114. Hoover, MacDonald 1999–2000.

115. For a quick overview of the lots concerned: **33–34**, **22–132**, **28–47**, **59–61–62**, **69–107**, **160–162**, **209–210**.

Khan el-Abde (*IGCH* 1597, **255**) seems composed of several distinct lots, and Seyrig notes it as such.[116]

Furthermore, the content of finds can sometimes help us to overcome our ignorance of their precise origin. The hoard that appeared in the trade in Paris in 1991 and in New York in 1994 (**338**) is one example: it consists entirely of autonomous Aradian tetradrachms that circulated almost exclusively in the mainland zone controlled by the island city of Aradus.[117] In this case, this peculiarity of regional coin circulation in the first century BC can correct for the absence of any indication of provenance.

Necessary revisions to hoard publications are a good deal less numerous than expected, and editors had already caught most of them. Thus, true uncertainty weighs only on those hoards whose documentation is a note in *IGCH* or *CH* without further actual specifics. For these, indeed, Flament's calls for the greatest caution are clearly justified. Figure 3.8 gives percentages of hoards by degree of reliability.

Since we are able to certify that only 12% of hoards are complete, it is impossible to draw any very precise conclusions from the numbers they provide. Still, they do establish a floor for values hoarded that enables us to gain an impression of the wealth of Syrians during the Persian and Hellenistic periods, and potentially to uncover trends. By comparison, out of the 132 hoards containing Roman Republican *denarii* found in Bulgaria before 1990, Paunov and Prokopov reckon only 32 (24%) have been published, often incorrectly.[118] Including the 25 hoards seen in the trade since 1989/1990, but unstudied, reduces the ratio to 15.9% (see Table 3.9).

Table 3.8. Reliability of hoards

Found in Excavations	43	12.1%
Known only through a notice in *IGCH* or *CH*	52	14.6%
Content not Itemized[118]	14	3.9%

Table 3.9. Hoards of Roman Republican *denarii* in Bulgaria

Published Hoards	32
Partially Inventoried Hoards	6–7
Dispersed, Unstudied Hoards 1982–1990	25
Officially Inventoried, Unpublished Hoards	70
Total Inventoried	**132**

(Hoards dispersed without study since 1990: 25+)

116. Seyrig 1950, pp. 1–7.
117. Duyrat 2005a, map 11, p. 359.
118. Paunov, Prokopov 2002, pp. 9–10.
119. The number of specimens is unknown, even approximately.

Table 3.10. Comparison of excavation hoards and illegal hoards[120]

Category	Silver		Bronze	
	Excavations	*Trade*	*Excavations*	*Trade*
Unknown	0	14	0	2
1–10	8	56	6	5
11–50	**13 (44.8%)**	**115 (41.8%)**	**6 (37.5%)**	**6 (24%)**
51–100	3	37	2	4
101–500	3	41	2	5
501–1000	1	7	0	2
1001–2000	1	5	0	0
4000	0	0	0	1
Total	**29**	**275**	**16**	**25**

In his previously cited article, Flament states "deposits discovered during controlled excavations are normally above suspicion, since they are customarily placed in a museum and rather quickly published."[121] While not wishing to be overly skeptical, we need to qualify this assertion: all archaeologists know that workmen are expert in pocketing coins during digs. So even these official finds may not be absolutely complete. They nonetheless remain our most complete source. Were we to content ourselves with working on the 43 reliable hoards, those found in excavations, where we think we have entire contents, we might gain in confidence, but it would be wrong to think that the resulting perspective would be more accurate. For example, no hoard found in an excavation contained a gold coin, whereas seven hoards with gold coins, including two quite voluminous ones, are attested among chance finds and clandestine digs. The result of official excavations therefore gives us a clear, but incomplete picture because of the small quantity of material they represent. The question then arises, whether the mass of hoards of illegal origin gives us a false sense of hoarding. A comparative table (Table 3.10) leads to some observations.

Hoards found without scientific control give averages that are not too far from those of hoards found in excavations. The best-represented category is 11–50 coins, for both silver and bronze hoards, whether found in legal circumstances or not. Generally speaking, hoards found outside the scientific pale are larger than those found in authorized excavations. 90 illegal hoards (32.7%) of silver coins consisted of more than 51 specimens versus 8 legal hoards (27.6%). This

120. The bold figures signal the most numerous class, which is also where the median lies. Calculation is based on the total coins actually studied by editors, not on estimates of the lot's original total. Hoards containing both silver and bronze are counted twice.

121. "les dépôts découverts lors de fouilles régulières sont normalement au dessus de tout soupçon, puisqu'ils sont habituellement déposés dans un musée et assez rapidement publiés." Flament 2005, p. 29.

observation is all the more interesting in that hoards in the trade are often thought to be just portions of hoards whose original totals are judged to be substantially higher. This is the case, for example, with the ʻIraq al-Amir hoard (Jordan, *CH* 10.268, **147**), of which 315 specimens are currently in the Amman Museum, but which probably contained more than 1,200 tetradrachms at the time of its discovery. One has to conclude, therefore, that the hoards known to us through the antiquities market, for all their difficulties of reconstitution, are a source that can be used, with caution. Excavated hoards do not provide evidence at all, or only a little, for large and very large deposits or those with gold coins. In contrast, hoards seen in the trade, despite the margin of error they introduce into our evaluations, do not seem to present a notably skewed aspect of what hoarding in Syria might have been from the fifth to the first centuries BC.

5. PROBLEMS OF CHRONOLOGY

Even when a hoard or isolated coin derive from controlled excavations, they are not necessarily easy to use, especially because the question of how to date them remains. This is a central issue, since coins are chronological markers both for archaeology and history. The temptation is all the more strong when dealing with coin series dated by well-established eras. The feeling of precision this type of material gives can, however, be illusory.

There are different sorts of chronological problems. They concern, first of all, the way in which scholars determine the periods when undated coins were struck. There is no intention here of inventorying the bibliography on this topic, only to draw some examples by way of illustration. The problem is most pressing for Persian era coins, when the practice of dating by local eras was not yet developed. For Phoenician coinages, abundant in the fourth century, the work of the J. and A.-G. Elayi is the chief reference point at present, and most authors accept their proposed chronologies in the absence of alternatives. But J. and A.-G. Elayi push back all the dates of reigns, so that in effect Phoenician coins allegedly ceased being struck in the first years of the Macedonian conquest. Thus, the Tyrian shekels Newell dated to the late fourth century[122] have been reattributed by J. and A.-G. Elayi to the years 340–330,[123] against the advice of most of the editors of the papyri of Wadi Daliyeh. J. and A.-G. Elayi date the last year of production for ʻOzmilk of Tyre by the last dated papyrus from the Wadi, 335 BC. Overall, they tend to think that the last year of the Phoenician kings' coin production coincided with the conquest. They also date numerous hoards immediately before Alexander's conquest: 11 buried in 335 and 334[124] versus only six clearly linked to the year 333.[125] I have deliberately not omitted datings different from theirs; indeed they are favored in the statistics: the importance of the Macedonian invasion is such that increased hoard burials upon the armies' arrival is highly plausible.

122. Newell 1923b, pp. 15–23.
123. Elayi, Elayi 1993a, p. 146 and p. 218.
124. **58**, **59**, **60**, **61**, **62**, **65**, **66**, **67**, **71** ("end of the Persian period"), **75** (after 335 BC), **84** (before 333 BC).
125. **69**, **70**, **72**, **73**, **74**, **76**. That Phoenician dynasties may have continued under Alexander is recognized, but in practice dating of reigns is done retrospectively from 333 BC. Elayi 2006; 2008.

The same authors provide another example of problematic chronology. Athenian "owls" are traditionally classified according to stylistic criteria that focus on the shape of the eye: a frontal eye marks an issue as fifth century.[126] J. and A.-G. Elayi tend to date as fifth century all heads where the eye is frontal, in imitation of the Athenian model: this is the case with the bearded god of Arwad and the Janus-like head on the coins of Philistia.[127] For Arwad they spell out their thinking:

> As the motive of Athena on Athenian coins inspired Aradian engravers, the evolution of the shape of the eye on Aradian coins was probably parallel to that of Athena: the full eye of Athena begins to change at the end of the fifth century and becomes profile-shaped from the beginning of the fourth. Aradian engravers certainly had instant knowledge of this evolution because the Athenian coins were exported in large quantities like ordinary goods to the whole Near East. The persistence of archaizing Aradian style at the beginning of the fourth century cannot be ruled out, but it is less likely than the progressive evolution of the representation of the eye following the Athenian pattern. The series with full eye should therefore, in this case, be dated prior to the beginning of the fourth century.[128]

This hypothesis does not take account of the interruption in Athenian issues between 404 and 393 and its definite repercussions in the area that prized this currency. It is one of the reasons for the development of the imitative coinage of the fourth century. If the latter was developed to confront the shortage of those Athenian tetradrachms, it must have taken as a model those that were available, and it is perfectly possible that the fifth century type became the standard type.

Other coinages pose chronological problems and are often the subject of numerous debates. One has to mention, among others for the Hellenistic Age, the tetradrachms with types of Alexander struck in Pamphylia[129] and the Ptolemaic coins said to be of "uncertain era."[130] At least a debate among specialists allows a better idea to emerge of the arguments favoring one solution or another, but that is not the case for the Persian period.

Once chronology is established for the different issues present, the whole hoard itself can be dated. In some happy instances, the group's very content provides clear indications. In Egypt, the Demanhur hoard is a textbook case: the Alexanders from Phoenicia are dated and all years are represented down to 318 BC; then nothing.[131] In Syria, a recent find of unknown provenance offers another interesting example. This group of 535 coins arrived on the market without having been cleaned, and its editor called it the "Demetrius hoard" (*CH* 10.301, **202**). The burial

126. Cf. most recently Flament 2007, p. 34.
127. Elayi, Elayi 1993a, pp. 215, 216, 248.
128. Elayi, Elayi 1986, pp. 6–7.
129. Most recently, Meadows 2009; 2013, p. 172, n. 54.
130. Most recently, Lorber 2007; Olivier, forthcoming.
131. Newell 1923a, pp. 152–54.

date of the hoard is very precise thanks to coins of Demetrius I dated 152/1 BC and New Style Athenian tetradrachms dated 151/0 BC by the low chronology.[132] It remains, however, to determine whether the absence of certain Asia Minor mints that struck wreathed tetradrachms means that they had not yet commenced this production in 150 BC.[133] This is a type of reasoning frequently adopted in trying to date difficult series by way of other, clearly dated, coins accompanying them in a hoard. When combining several hoards, the practice must be exercised with great care. The "Demetrius hoard" thus contains Aradian "bee" drachms, the latest of which is from 156/5 BC, while this well attested series extends to 152/1 BC. In each of these cases, one must not make too much of the absence in an individual hoard of various series assumed to be contemporary. The Gaziantep hoard (*CH* 10.308, **228**) provides a very favorable instance: the presence of Athenian New Style wreathed tetradrachms and royal Seleucid coins leads one to propose an exceptionally exact burial date, perhaps autumn, 143 BC.

Countermarks placed on some series have also been used to date the coins bearing them. Yet the chronology of the best-known countermarks remains imprecise. In Syria, the most studied are the famous "anchor" countermark and that with the head of Helios.[134] Metcalf provides a fine example of relative dating for hoards of 170–150 BC through these countermarks (**184**, **189**, **190**, **193**, **198**, **242**, **253**).[135]

But this argument is generally considered insufficient. So it is necessary to employ a range of means to establish a burial date successfully. The date of the latest series generally serves as a *terminus post quem*. The real difficulty comes in determining the date of the burial itself, which may be much later than the date of the latest issue. Coin wear has become the subject of a relatively abundant bibliography.[136] Without entering the particulars of the debate, two points seem to me important to remember. The first concerns length of circulation. We are very poorly informed on the recall of coinage. Countermarks give an idea of how a coin's exchange value could be modified without recourse to a recall, melting-down, and new striking, all costly and time-consuming undertakings.[137] But the actual recall that renders a coin useless as a medium of exchange has left us no trace except the disappearance of the coinage concerned from hoards and excavations. Now, certain coinages circulated for a very long time, as their degree of wear attests. The most telling case is surely the 'Ain Tab Hoard (*IGCH* 1542, **242**). It comprised roughly 200 tetradrachms of Alexander-type. Metcalf has shown that a burial as late as 130–120 BC cannot be excluded, even though the hoard's contents placed it instead before 160 BC.[138] Alexanders circulated far longer than all other coinages,[139] with the sole exception, perhaps, of Classical Athenian tetradrachms. Such longevity in itself is not that surprising, but

132. Mattingly 1990, p. 67.
133. Lorber 2010, p. 156.
134. Cf., selectively, Seyrig 1958b; Le Rider 1999a, p. 229; Mattingly 1993; Metcalf 1994, 1998.
135. Metcalf 1994, pp. 48–53.
136. Most recently, Velde 2013.
137. Le Rider 1975.
138. Metcalf 1998.
139. Le Rider 1986b.

it is difficult to assess and so obscures burial dating. This becomes all the more complicated to assess since, in one and the same hoard, some coins may be worn and others less so. Wear is not a constant value. This is the second point on which I would like to linger. In a hoard, the coins were gathered one last time; but they circulated separately most of the time, and some may have been hoarded for several years before being restored to circulation that other coins never left.[140]

Generally, burial dates remain approximate. It appears prudent, in most cases, to stick closest to the latest dated coin. Hellenistic Syrian mints usually dated their production, and it seems good methodology to date burials according to this information, without envisioning a year's lapse, as many publications do that add a "time of burial" based upon an inevitably arbitrary calculation. Seyrig's proposed dating of the Kessab hoard (**288**) is a model of good sense. The tetradrachms of Seleuceia Pieria dated year 5 (105/4 BC) are the most recent, and the village of Kessab is within the city's territory. "Since they show signs of circulation, moderate but unmistakable, one will allow at least a few months between their striking and their burial," but not more, since issues from later years are absent.[141] Only particularly noticeable wear seems to me to justify serious consideration. In other uncertain cases, "after such-and-such a date" is definitely the most appropriate formula.

Once dated, hoards and coins from excavations can serve to establish the chronology of a site's occupation or the absolute dating of series that are otherwise hard to pinpoint. Hoards are often used to enable dating of new issues. One could easily multiply the examples for Hellenistic Syria alone. Thus Le Rider was able to propose a chronology for the spread of Alexanders in the Seleucid Empire based on 11 hoards he studied and securely dated.[142] Kinns proceeded similarly with Ephesian bee drachms that circulated deep within the same realm.[143] Some of the most complex dating, still widely debated, was initially based on the chronology of hoards containing disputed series. Tetradrachms with types of Alexander struck by cities in Pamphylia during the second century are one instance. Boehringer first proposed fixing the starts of the periods used to date these coins with the aid of a helpful table matching up the hoards.[144] The controversy between Lewis and Thompson on the chronology of New Style Athenian tetradrachms is largely based on hoards, especially Syrian hoards, each author rebutting the other's interpretations using the same evidence.[145]

It is always tempting to relate wars and hoarding. Numerous, well-documented examples have been published. This is one of the arguments Meadows uses to revise the beginning of periods for Pamphylian tetradrachms that circulated widely in Syria during the second century.

140. This is one of the issues in the debate between Thompson and Lewis over the dating of the Kessab hoard (*IGCH* 1568, **288**), part of the larger controversy over the dating of New Style Athenian tetradrachms: Thompson 1961, pp. 475–77; Thompson 1962, pp. 311–12; Lewis 1962, p. 279.

141. "Comme ils portent des traces de circulation, modérées mais certaines, on comptera au moins quelques mois entre leur frappe et leur enfouissement." Seyrig 1973, p. 102.

142. Le Rider 1986b.

143. Kinns 1999.

144. Boehringer 1972, table I; cf. most recently Meadows 2009 with revision in Meadows 2013, p. 172, n. 54.

145. Lewis 1962; Thompson 1961, 1962.

Mentioning a collection of hoards whose burial date is decisive in the debate, he writes: "But it seems highly unlikely that any of these hoards belong after the campaign of Antiochus III into Asia Minor in 203 BC. In fact it is tempting to suggest that a number of these hoards represent deposits made in anticipation of, or even in reaction to the beginning of this campaign, and thus reflect circulation down to as late as 204 or 203 BC in areas that had fallen out of direct Seleucid control."[146] This argument seems to me the weakest of those Meadows employs. Indeed, I have recently been able to show that wars do not entail noticeable increases in hoards, except when they are particularly long. None of the Syrian wars, especially not the fifth, which occurred entirely on Syrian territory, led to any surge in our evidence. Only the Macedonian conquest and the Wars of the Successors, as well as the conflicts of the 140s and the Hasmonean wars, had an effect on the volume of our surviving hoards.[147] It would be prudent to wait for a thorough study of the effects of the wars of Antiochus III on hoarding before justifying war as an argument for hoard dating.

6. TYPOLOGY OF HOARDS

Many hoard studies commonly speculate on the motives for hoarding, based on the given hoard's content and burial date. The *Dictionnaire de numismatique* even defines four types of hoards in this light: "chance losses;[148] emergency burials (wherein the coins reflect circulation at their time of hiding); savings hoards or treasures (which sometimes display the savings of several generations and tend to skew in favor of higher weight specimens); and finally, ritual hoards (which take the form of foundation deposits, deposits at a river crossing, offerings by pilgrims, and funerary deposits).[149] The *Oxford English Dictionary* gives the following definition of the verb "to hoard": "to amass and put away (anything valuable) for preservation, security, or future use, to treasure up: esp. money or wealth," including in the word's very definition the owner's intentions for his treasure.[150] The examples could be multiplied endlessly. The *Diccionario de Numismática* thus presents more a typology than a definition of the word "find."[151] J. and A.-G. Elayi devote an entire section of their volume on the circulation of Phoenician coins to the same effort.[152] At first glance, these attempts might seem useless speculation, given that the archaeological context is missing most of the time and our knowledge of Hellenistic Syrian society is especially lacunose. Yet great is the temptation to try to pierce through the hoard owners' privacy, to understand what conditions drove them to store currency and, eventually,

146. Meadows 2009, pp. 60–61.

147. Duyrat 2011a.

148. This first definition is not compatible with the legal definition of "hoard," which posits that a hoard is hidden deliberately.

149. "les pertes fortuites, les enfouissements d'urgence (dont les monnaies reflètent la circulation au moment où elles sont cachées), les trésors d'épargne ou de thésaurisation (qui représentent parfois les économies de plusieurs générations et ont tendance à sélectionner les exemplaires de bon poids), enfin les trésors liés à un rite (dépôts de fondation, dépôts de gué, offrandes de pélerins, dépôts funéraires)". Amandry 2001, s.v., "trésor."

150. *OED*, Oxford, 1989, s.v. "hoard."

151. Alfaro Asins et al., 2009, s.v. "*hallazgo*."

152. Elayi, Elayi 1993a, pp. 322–37.

other sorts of wealth in this particular manner. According to the type of hoard, the historian thus hopes to get a little closer to a social, historical, and, it must be said, psychological reality difficult of access.[153]

6.1. Abandoned Riches

The nagging question, invariably, for anyone studying hoards is "Why?" Why were these riches not recovered? In other periods, written sources enable us to obtain an idea of why the hoard was abandoned. For modern times, Bercé gives some well-developed examples in which war plays a prominent role.[154] In relating the discovery of the second parcel of the Saida hoard, W. H. Thomson explains the reasons for the burial of valuables in Lebanon during the first half of the nineteenth century. The government, the nobility, the clergy stole from a population already enduring Arab raids, even as insecurity increased from internecine warfare "such as laid Lebanon in ruins in 1841,[155] and again in 1845. At such times multitudes bury their gold and jewels, and in many cases the owners are killed, and no one knows where the treasure was concealed. Then, again, this country has ever been subject to earthquakes, which bury everything beneath her ruined cities. On the first days of 1837, Safed was thus dashed to the ground in a moment, house upon house down the steep mountainside, and many entire families were cut off. Some were known to have had money, and it was a shocking spectacle to see hardened wretches prowling about under the ruins, amid putrefying carcasses, in search of these treasures."[156] In the twentieth century, Kadman cites two rather spectacular examples of hoards that were not reclaimed by their owners. The first goes back to 1918: the German army was supposed to retreat before the advance of troops under Lord Allenby. The German command wanted to protect its booty and buried it in precisely delineated locations around Beth-Shan. The value of the hoard was estimated at 20,000 pounds of gold, whether in coin or ingot. Despite numerous searches undertaken after the war with German officers who had participated in the operation, the hoard was never relocated. The second example is more personal: in 1922, Kadman's kibbutz at Heftzibah underwent an Arab attack, and the population retreated to the neighboring village. Before leaving, the inhabitants buried silver chargers and candelabra in their possession: "they were put into boxes and buried in the sand-dunes. The exact spot was marked on a sketch." Returning a week later, the inhabitants found the village intact. Despite weeks of digging, they never succeeded in finding their sterling.[157]

One might have thought that, at a time when most wealth is notional and coinage has no intrinsic worth, the practice of hoarding would have mostly disappeared. As the following example, cited by Noe, shows, this is not so: "According to recent newspaper reports certain paper notes of the Bank of England, whose value as legal tender ceased after a date fixed by law, be-

153. Grierson 1976, pp. 164–78, gives an example of well-documented typology with hoards that are textbook cases.

154. Bercé 2004, pp. 16–22.

155. In 1841, the English expelled Egypt from the province of Syria, to which Mt. Lebanon belonged. This area then reverted to the Ottoman Empire and experienced a period of instability.

156. Cited by Sharp 1870.

157. Kadman 1967, pp. 312–13.

gan to appear in surprising numbers. This, it was explained, was due to their withdrawal from hoards. That some of these hoards have been buried was indicated through the deterioration which the notes had suffered from dampness or other soil conditions."[158] The practice is risky since these notes, which do not have any intrinsic value, always end up being recalled from circulation or losing their worth owing to inflation, not to mention the risks of physical degradation inherent in the burial of paper items. But it does demonstrate the continuing attachment to a physical form of wealth materially represented in these bills.

Current practice distinguishes primarily savings hoards, accumulated over a long time with an eye to the finest specimens, and emergency hoards assembled in haste from a shop's till or ready cash.[159] The distinction is not, however, always that simple. "Fear is generally conceded as the commonest cause for the secreting of a hoard," according to Noe.[160] But he adds that most of the time the best specimens were chosen.[161] Similarly, one often supposes, as Bercé writes, "the constitution of a hoard must have occurred in trying circumstances that are hard to rediscover. The image immediately arises of anxiety and urgency. When enemies are at the gate, when escape seems cut off and survival uncertain, a rich man at his wits' end digs a deep hole in the earth to bury his coins and most precious goods." Bercé then provides a counterpoint to this somewhat romantic scenario by recalling that burial may occur "in calm, serenity, and silence, out of mature deliberation."[162] Droulers, in his study of royal French coins, offers a quite detailed list of the alleged reasons for burial: foreign war, troop movements or the apprehension thereof; civil or religious war, revolution, or the apprehension thereof; tax investigation; avarice, prudence, whether of an ecclesiastic, merchant, estate owner, traveler, or pilgrim, etc.; no major historical cause; illicit currency speculation, currency debasement; accidental (?) fire; shipwreck.[163] In his statistics, 80% of the reasons for burial are connected to war. The precision of modern sources partly justifies these nuanced profiles, but it is illusory to think that personal motivations, when there is no historical event or private source of information, can be clearly identified.

J. and A.-G. Elayi have tried to analyze the nature of the 75 hoards of Phoenician coins they published in 1993.[164] Their presentation of the Jablah hoard (*CH* 9.405, **42**) well illustrates the difficulty of this endeavor: "it is easier to say what this hoard is not rather than define what it

158. Noe 1949, p. 239.

159. Giard 1979, pp. 8–9; Elayi 1999, p. 138.

160. Noe 1949, p. 239.

161. The same difficulty in Elayi 1999, p. 138.

162. "la constitution du trésor a dû survenir dans des circonstances émotionnelles qu'il est bien difficile de retrouver. L'image qui s'impose d'abord est celle de l'angoisse et de l'urgence. Alors que des ennemis s'approchent, que la fuite semble coupée, que la survie est incertaine, un homme riche, aux abois, creuse dans la terre un trou profond pour enfouir ses pièces de monnaies et ses biens les plus précieux." "dans le calme, la sérénité et le silence, de propos mûrement délibéré." Bercé 2004, p. 15.

163. Droulers 1980, p. 236, Table E. The case of Samuel Pepys hiding a considerable sum in June, 1667, when he feared a Dutch invasion of England, and his description of how he recovered these coins a few months later is a rare case documented in detail by a private source. *Diary of Samuel Pepys*, 10 June, 1667.

164. Elayi, Elayi 1993a, pp. 322–37.

is: it is obviously not a hoard amassed by a rich owner choosing the handsomest pieces issued; nor is it a savings deposit by an owner of modest means since he would have hoarded different currency denominations. In view of the wear of the coins, one could imagine the coins were set aside for recasting, but why only thirds of a shekel? … The hypothesis of a loss or voluntary abandonment, a votive deposit, for example, can neither be supported nor refuted."[165] The final hypothesis, assumed reluctantly, is that it was an emergency burial of a sum received or readied as a payment, which would explain why it is composed uniquely of thirds of a shekel. This example shows, I think, the limits of such an exercise: defining criteria too narrowly on the basis of hoard contents ultimately restricts one to limited categories that certainly do not reflect the multiplicity of possible individual and general circumstances leading to a hoard's constitution. In this particular instance, the causes explaining the absence of denominations other than thirds of a shekel might be various and dependent on specific circumstances (owner's resources, nature of a payment, abundance of this denomination in circulation, etc.). It is difficult to base a solid conclusion on this. Still, one has to say a few words on the hoard categories most commonly cited in publications, since in any case they do appear in the relevant scholarship.

6.2. Emergency Hoards and Currency Deposits

Content felt to reflect the currency in circulation at the time of hoarding is what characterizes the "currency deposit," a concept frequently used in numismatic writing.[166] Kadman clearly delineated the nature of the "currency deposit" in 1967: "It will mainly be in time of political, social and economical unrest that a man will feel forced to hide his property … The date of the last coins contained in the hoard will, therefore, give a strong hint of the time when the hoard was hidden, and with this of the historical events which brought about his concealment."[167] It is this contextual aspect that the term "emergency hoard" captures in English, or "*trésor d'urgence*" in French. Assembled in haste, such a collection is grabbed from circulation, as its composition reflects. Logically, the oldest coins ought to be more worn than the newer issues. The argument carries weight especially in some very favorable cases. Thus, the ʿIraq al-Amir hoard (**147**) consists mainly of Ptolemaic tetradrachms struck in Phoenician cities. The latter date their issues by years, and this hoard contains almost all the issues from 295–293 to 243/2 BC. The wear on the oldest tetradrachms is quite pronounced, whereas the more recent have a fresher look. One might then conclude that we are probably dealing here with a sample drawn from the currency circulating in the late 240s.

165. "il est plus facile de dire ce que ce trésor n'est pas que de définir ce qu'il est : ce n'est évidemment pas un trésor amassé par un riche propriétaire avec sélection des plus belles pièces émises ; ce n'est pas non plus le trésor d'épargne d'un propriétaire modeste parce qu'il aurait thésaurisé différentes catégories de divisionnaires. Etant donné l'usure des pièces, on pourrait envisager qu'elles aient été mises de côté pour la refonte, mais pourquoi seulement des tiers de sicles ? […] L'hypothèse d'une perte ou celle d'un abandon volontaire, tel qu'un dépôt votif par exemple, ne peuvent pas, à notre avis, être argumentées ni réfutées." *Ibid.*, p. 60.

166. Even as a misnomer, for example the Susiana hoard (*IGCH* 1812) that, precisely, does not reflect the currency circulation of its time of burial. Metcalf 1994, p. 52.

167. Kadman 1967, p. 313.

6.3. Savings Hoards

In his analysis of the typology of hoards, Aubin clearly contrasts this type of deposit, "reflections of saving and consisting of selected coins, sometimes amassed over a long time," with emergency hoards.[168] In general, these so-called savings hoards require the greatest prudence when drawing conclusions from them, conclusions that often seem gratuitous and insufficiently supported to win assent. Price provides an example in his publication of the Jericho hoard (*CH* 8.215, **109**).[169] The tetradrachms with types of Alexander in this hoard, buried around 305, are not noticeably worn. "It would seem that the hoard represents the savings of an individual who had received payment in this form of coin over a number of years." This assertion is questionable. In 305, Alexanders were the prevailing coinage in circulation in the Near East. The velocity of coin circulation is not constant, and tetradrachms from different periods will show wear differently, depending on whether they spent more or less time as a currency reserve or were used instead in numerous transactions. To this must be added the fact that certain payments may require coins in good condition, hence not worn, necessarily leading to a choice of specimens irrespective of their date of production but focused rather on their current state at the time of payment. Price's hypothesis is plausible, but unsubstantiated.

In general, the largest hoards are often taken to be savings hoards. The Byblos hoard (*IGCH* 1496, **69**, and 1515, **107**) lends itself well to such an interpretation because it was contained in two bronze vases and the question remains whether this is a single find or two distinct hoards. The two pots were close to one another, but their contents were rather different: one consisted of 217 shekels of Byblos, the second of 137 tetradrachms with types of Alexander, except for two double shekels of Sidon and one tetradrachm of the satrap Ptolemy. The time of hoarding is thus almost coextensive with the fourth century. J. and A.-G. Elayi suggest seeing here "a reserve successively augmented by several individuals, like a family endeavor, for example."[170] But this again is mere conjecture.

6.4. Votive Deposit

This category of hoard is in theory linked to a cult site. The catalogue contains no find of this sort explicitly. Only the hoard from the region of Arwad (*CH* 9.386, **31**) has a content that might come close to a votive deposit: 27 silver coins[171] were accompanied by fragments of the same metal, three lion figurines, a pair of silver earrings, a bronze arrowhead, and seven terracotta statuettes. According to J. and A.-G. Elayi, some of the terracotta statuettes were of the "Persian rider" type, while others were plaques of Astarte, prompting the authors' votive deposit conclusion. Since the find was clandestine, it is impossible to determine what sanctuary was its provenance. The marked presence of Aradian thirds of a shekel, which circulated little beyond

168. "reflets de l'épargne et composés d'espèces sélectionnées, amassées parfois depuis longtemps." Aubin 2007, p. 55.

169. Price 1990, p. 24.

170. "une réserve alimentée successivement par plusieurs individus, de type familial par exemple." Elayi, Elayi 1993, p. 87.

171. Including 23 thirds of a shekel of Aradus.

the city's territory, inclines one to look for it in the continental hinterland of this island city-state.[172]

The excavation of Hama has also turned up a coin that was hidden beneath the base of a limestone lion dating from 30 BC to AD 100. The coin is a bronze of Antiochus VIII, and it is not at all certain that it was put there deliberately.

6.5. Travelers' Hoards

Some hoards present atypical contents, unusual compared to the overall profile of contemporary finds in the same area. They have usually been taken as evidence of their owner's travels, which would explain their disparate nature. This rubric is generally applied to finds of overly varied content, such as the Sarnakunk hoard from Armenia (*IGCH* 1746), assumed to be a soldier's nest egg.[173] The hoard found on the beach south of Beirut (*IGCH* 1500, **40**), dated between 368 and 333 BC, has elicited a good deal of comment. Its editor, Sheridan, hypothesized that it was the hoard of a traveler who sailed from the Propontis to Byblos, the gathered coins witness to his ports of call. This itinerary, according to J. Elayi, does not explain the presence of coins of Sicyon, Sidon, and Tyre, especially Tyrian bronzes that did not circulate far afield. But J. and A.-G. Elayi do not exclude the hypothesis of a "capricious itinerary" in their later study of Phoenician hoards.[174] Destrooper-Georgiades particularly emphasizes the large chronological gap among the find's different coins: she finds it hard to believe that they all circulated in the lifetime of the traveler who is assumed to have collected them.[175]

Much later, around 100 BC, the Ascalon hoard (*CH* 9.548, **294**) has the advantage of having been found in an excavation. Composed of bronzes, it groups Seleucid and Ptolemaic issues from various mints of western Asia Minor dating from the fourth to the second centuries BC. Gitler and Kahanov propose seeing here too a traveler's purse that ended up under the floor of a Hellenistic house in Ascalon. They reconstitute the route he allegedly took by comparing the hoard's coins with what we know of maritime routes at the end of the Hellenistic Age, chiefly those of St. Paul. The broad chronological spread of this hoard answers—only partially—the doubts expressed by Destrooper-Georgiades apropos of the previous hoard. In the same vein, a hoard found, perhaps, in northern Syria contains some coins marking the route taken by the Macedonians at the time of the Conquest (**68**). The hoard found in a shipwreck off Megadim (**298**), on the coast of Mt. Carmel, while quite small—seven bronzes in an amphora—also presents a diversity that marks it as a traveler's hoard.

One of the hoards found at Saida (*IGCH* 1521, **118**) presents a completely unusual appearance. Buried around 300 BC, it consisted of at least 17 hemidrachms from the Thracian Chersonese and six drachms and hemidrachms of Amisos. Both the standard and the denomina-

172. Elayi, Elayi 1990, p. 14.
173. Cf. the summary concerning this hoard's interpretation in Duyrat 2005a, p. 170.
174. Elayi, Elayi 1993a, p. 206.
175. Destrooper-Georgiades 1987, p. 351 and n. 48.

tions, under a drachm, as well as the mints of origin are completely atypical and can only be explained by the presence of travelers who saved some currency from a distant stay.

6.6. An Appeal for Prudence

These classifications sketch in the somewhat fluid contours of the motives for hoarding, without the ability to go too much further, however. That would risk being locked into a preconceived interpretation of the burial context. For all his carefulness, Barag illustrates this.[176] He tries to date a hoard of Idumaea to 111/10 BC, although the lot's composition only justifies saying that it is later than 128 BC (**259**). The reason he gives is that the coins are very worn. A withdrawal from circulation in 111/10 BC would allow connecting this hoard to the conquest of Idumaea by John Hyrcanus I and so make it an emergency hoard. This interpretation is debatable: 17 years separate the last date attested in the hoard from Hyrcanus' conquest. The hoard may not be complete, because it was seen in the trade and dispersed. Barag's proposal seems imprudent; nothing in the material justifies drawing such a conclusion that, clearly, strains the sources. The typology of hoards is not a bad thing in itself, in certain, well documented cases; but it ought not to be applied systematically. In addition to our unfamiliarity with the actual context, there is the fact that certain segments of the population must never have seen some denominations: a double shekel of more than 25 g of silver or even a tetradrachm of Attic weight were probably not normal coins for an entire part of the population that instead would have had access to silver fractions and bronzes. This reality surely had consequences for the contents of money-boxes. Some worn tetradrachms, perhaps rubbish to a rich merchant whose transactions were supervised by the civic authorities, may have been treasure to an individual who did not necessarily use coinage on a daily basis. So we must recognize that in most cases we cannot discern the motives for hoard burials and that in the rest we must speculate with the greatest caution. The excavations around Vesuvius provide a good example of this, when the eruption of AD 79 stopped in their flight hundreds of inhabitants. Among them, at Oplontis, a woman carried in a linen sack a motley collection that Andreau describes thus: "Some of these coins correspond to the coin circulation in AD 79; others show that there has been a process of 'hoarding' (for instance, there were 110 Republican *denarii*)."[177] If, instead of taking these coins with her, this woman had left them in the ground, she would have created a typological head-scratcher.

176. Barag 2007–2008.
177. Andreau 2008, p. 216.

Table 3.11. Number of surviving hoards by period

Period	Total Hoards	In Excavations
Persian period	68	7 (10.1%)
Alexander's successors (333–280)	61	8 (13.3%)
3rd cent. (280–200)	33	6 (17.6%)
2nd cent. (199–100)	126	8 (6.3%)
1st cent. (100–1 BC)	67	14 (20.3%)
Total	**355**	**43**

CONCLUSION

The following chapters propose a matrix for interpreting this uneven database. They elicit from it the most general historical insights, leaving more particular studies for the future. Table 3.11 is provided as a point of reference amidst the mass of hoards. The Hellenistic Age by itself, from Alexander to 8 BC, yields 289 hoards. Scientifically controlled conditions of discovery guarantee only 6% to 20% of them, with the first century offering the best evidence.

Chapter 4

Before Alexander

To understand coin circulation in Hellenistic Syria, it is essential to know about practices in the region before Alexander the Great's armies arrived and profound upheavals ensued. The area that Persian sources called the *Transeuphratene* was familiar with coinage from the end of the Archaic period (Ras Shamra hoard, *IGCH* 1478, **1**), and Phoenician mints were active from the second half of the fifth century.[1] During this period of almost two centuries (c. 525–333 BC),[2] monetary practices change. The fifth and fourth centuries present quite different circulation profiles, just considering the number of hoards: 19 for the fifth century[3] versus 48 for the fourth before 333,[4] a total of 68 hoards from the Persian period including the Ras Shamra deposit (**1**). But this number would rise to 89 were one to extend the fourth century cutoff to the 320s, which mark the real change.[5]

1. Weighed Silver, Greek Silver

1.1. First Finds

The Ras Shamra hoard is the oldest found in Syria, dating from the years 525–520 BC (*IGCH* 1478, **1**). It essentially contains coins from Macedonia and Thrace, with the exception of six coins from Cypriot Salamis, which leads one to suppose a transit via this island, according with navigation routes to the East. The coins were found in a pot in the middle of a hearth, and some were partially melted. The case is interesting: Syria at the end of the sixth century used weighed metal, and the value of these coins depended on this metal, of great purity, instead

1. Elayi 1992.
2. The Ras Shamra hoard was buried about 425–420 BC.
3. Hoards **2–20**, including hoards **18** and **19** dated between the end of the fifth and the beginning of the fourth century.
4. Hoards **21–68**, leaving aside the Dinar hoard (**51**), omitted from the catalogue. Hoard **114**, which does not contain Alexanders and must predate the Macedonian conquest, has been added to this list.
5. Hoards **1–89** and **114**, leaving aside **51**.

of their shape. Other excavations have produced unusually old coins: a Thasian piece struck c. 510–480 BC, with chiseling on the obverse, was found in the excavation of Balatah (Shechem). It was discovered even though the American expedition was exploring primarily Bronze Age strata. The editors of the excavation report, while stating "It is the oldest coin known to have been found in Palestine thus far,"[6] did not clarify the find's context. In fact, other coins of the same period have since been discovered. Gitler and Tal's survey of Archaic and Classical period coins found in authorized excavations in Palestine or by surface survey mentions 13 others that are possibly earlier than 500 BC.[7] They remark that "some of the Archaic coins retrieved from controlled archaeological excavations come from Persian-period contexts...; therefore, it is evident that they arrived at these sites shortly after they were issued."[8]

1.2. *Hacksilber* and Denominated Money

All these early coin discoveries on Levantine soil mark the beginning of the slow disappearance of *Hacksilber*. "*Hacksilber* (irregularly cut silver) are broken pieces of silver ingots, jewelry and varia used as currency or money. Material in this form was weighed on scales against standardized weights for the purposes of exchange or payment before and after the development of coinages," according to Gitler's excellent definition.[9] Schlumberger offers a similar observation: "Often associated in finds with this coinage of the Greek world is silver in various other forms: pieces of wrought silver and jewelry, ingots, foundry residues, "cut" silver ("*Hacksilber*": all sorts of silver scrap, including coin fragments). Exchanges of silver are, in fact, usually controlled by weight. Silver, whether bullion, crafted, or coined, is all the same on the scale; no matter its shape, the metal is suitable for circulation."[10] Hoard editors have some difficulty in naming these objects, often remnants or fragments without definite form. They are a kind of money that has to be weighed to establish its value, unlike coinage of the Greek sort, whose weight and worth are guaranteed by the issuing authority through the expedient of types placed on the coin's obverse and reverse. This information frees the user from systematically verifying the value and weight. The use of denominated money depends on trust. Accordingly, there is a distinction between weighed money (here, *Hacksilber*) and denominated, marked money (Greek coinage).

6. Wright 1957, p. 32, who, mistakenly, says it was struck in electrum. Correction and supplementary bibliography in Gitler, Tal 2006, p. 15.

7. Gitler, Tal 2006, pp. 15–20. This table highlights the limits of my own catalogue of excavations, which cannot rival the quality of information at the disposal of Israeli archaeologists.

8. Ibid., p. 13. There is no up to date overview on the beginnings of coin circulation in the region. Several articles deal with specific cases: Kraay, Moorey 1968, and, more recently, van Alfen 2004–2005a and b.

9. Gitler 2006b, p. 5, n. 2.

10. "A cette monnaie du monde grec est souvent associé, dans les trouvailles, de l'argent sous diverses autres formes: pièces d'orfèvrerie et bijoux, lingots, résidus de fonte, argent 'cisaillé' ('*Hacksilber*': débris d'argent de toutes sortes, y compris des fragments de monnaies). C'est que les échanges d'argent sont habituellement contrôlés par la pesée. Argent brut, travaillé ou monnayé, c'est tout un pour la balance; sous quelque forme que ce soit, le métal est propre à la circulation." Schlumberger 1953, p. 17.

Figure 4.1. Part of the Massyaf hoard (*IGCH* 1483, **17**; BnF, Paris).

In the Near East, weighed silver is well attested as a medium of exchange before the invention of coinage.[11] The evidence is abundant, whether textual[12] or archaeological.[13] Joannès has shown that there was a difference in Mesopotamia between silver intended for exchanges and that used by silversmiths. Cuneiform tablets reveal rather numerous names for silver, depending on the metal's degree of refinement and its purpose. One may adopt a broad classification in three categories that bear witness to a certain refinement in criteria: very pure silver (90–95%) reserved for silversmiths, pure silver (80–90%) for exchanges. Under 80%, the metal is unfit for exchanges. These distinctions blur—above 80%—from the mid-fifth century: the appearance of Greek coinage, with its heightened standard, changes practices. Highly refined silver is now no longer limited to silver working but also shows up in exchanges.[14] Kraay and Moorey consider that the monetary metal in hoards contain-

11. *Contra* Flament 2007, p. 43, who proposes a primitivist view of *Hacksilber*: "Silver did not circulate, or only a little, in these territories, since it was principally meant for hoarding. (L'argent ne circulait pas ou très peu dans ces territoires, puisqu'il était principalement destiné à la thésaurisation)" For an accessible presentation of weighed silver coinage in Mesopotamia, cf. Le Rider 2001a, pp. 1–39.

12. Numerous examples in the chapter on silver and coinage in Jursa 2010, pp. 469–753. Monerie 2013 points out two examples of *Hacksilber* hoards in Mesopotamia in the Achaemenid period, both partially or totally sent off to the foundry after discovery, which could explain the rarity of this sort of find.

13. The site of Ekron in Israel has thus revealed six *Hacksilber* hoards from the seventh century BC. They consist of cut jewelry, folded silver leaf, metal clippings, etc. Gitin, Golani 2001. Other examples of *Hacksilber* found in the Levant during the Iron Age in Balmuth, Thompson 2000, Thompson 2003, and Kletter, De Groot 2007.

14. Joannès 1994, p. 144. For the distinction in degrees of fineness in silver in Egypt during the Persian period, cf. van Alfen 2004–2005a.

ing *Hacksilber* is of excellent quality. Reade's analysis of pieces of *Hacksilber* and coins from the Babylon hoard (*IGCH* 1747) confirms this: their fineness falls between 96–98% pure.[15]

The presence of *Hacksilber* remains one of the characteristics of coin circulation in the Near East and Egypt in the fifth century. Van Alfen has noted this in a study where he concludes "unmarked silver appears to be wholly absent from Cilician and Cypriot hoards, a significant observation if true, since it restricts the monetary use of bullion during the Persian period to the Levant and Egypt."[16] The transition from weighed silver (*Hacksilber*) to denominated silver is a slow process, as the physical evidence and several studies show.

In 1968, Kraay and Moorey offered a study of eastern coin circulation in the fifth century that compared the hoards of Bostra (*IGCH* 1482, **13**) and Massyaf (*IGCH* 1483, **17**) for Syria (Fig. 4.1), Benha (*IGCH* 1640) and Zagazig (*IGCH* 1645) for Egypt, and Malayer (*IGCH* 1790) for Iran. They all contained from 50 to about 100 coins and some uncoined metal, ingots, and/or jewelry, except the Malayer hoard, which amounted to at least 400 items, apparently only currency, although its contents are poorly identified.[17] Despite these differences, the composition of the last is quite similar to that of the Syrian hoards: it presents the currency in circulation in Syria in the last quarter of the fifth century. The authors emphasize, however, that the presence of fractions, absent from the other finds, distinguishes the Syrian hoards. "This may, therefore, be a characteristic of this particular area of circulation."[18]

The Benha hoard, the oldest, consists principally of Thraco-Macedonian and Athenian silver. In the Bostra and Zagazig hoards, from the mid-fifth century, Athenian coins are now more numerous than the Thraco-Macedonians, and they are also later, most from after 480. By the end of the fifth century, the hoards of Malayer and Massyaf show the advance of Athenian coinage, very well represented, and the appearance of Phoenician issues from Sidon and Tyre (Fig. 4.2). Kraay and Moorey relate the beginning of the Phoenician production to the influx of Athenian coins and the start of issues from Aspendus, Celenderis, and Side that would have provided the metal necessary for the striking. The increasing local productions, they argue, would have displaced Athenian silver in hoards, the latter being melted for restriking, unlike in Egypt, which continued to use "owls" in the absence of an important mint of its own.[19] This is a debatable hypothesis: Levantine imitations of Athenian tetradrachms are attested, demonstrating continued interest in this currency, which remains abundant in the region during the fourth century. One has to wonder, instead, if the Phoenician coinages were not started and then encouraged by the growing tendency to pay in coin and by the interrupted supply of Athenian coins between 404 and 393 BC.

15. Reade 1986.
16. Van Alfen 2004–2005a, p. 16.
17. I thank A. Meadows for sending me his work in progress on this hoard. The catalogue he has assembled with E. Askari includes over 330 coins.
18. Kraay, Moorey 1968, p. 223.
19. Ibid., p. 227.

Figure 4.2. Shekel of Tyre (ANS 1944.100.72689).

The jewelry associated with these hoards is well crafted but reflects the fashions current in the region during the Achaemenid period. "The workmanship of these earrings . . . may be taken to illustrate a selection from the standard repertoire of an urban jeweler, regularly reproduced to a set of established patterns."[20] The silver used is very pure. The lots of intact jewelry, in good condition and not accompanied by fragments, must not be automatically likened to *Hacksilber*; they may simply have been safeguarded as pieces of silver work.[21]

The finds from Ras Shamra (**1**) and the Antilebanon (**8**) contain melted silver. These are the only instances listed in the entire catalogue. They are evidence for the practice of recasting coins: the Antilebanon hoard revealed foundry products in which the coins' original form is still recognizable. This practice is not surprising at a time when weighed silver dominates, but it surely persisted for overly worn or damaged coins in later periods. The number of listed hoards (Table 4.1) containing *Hacksilber* is geographically (Map 3) and temporally quite diverse. It is often a matter of small quantities of objects, of a few fragments. Hoards **7** and **8** are exceptions since they contain some 20 kg of *Hacksilber*, which means that the weight of the metal represents much more than the value of the various coins accompanying it. Hoards **13** and **17** are more evenly spread between the two types of objects. In total, only seven hoards out of 48 contain *Hacksilber* in the fourth century, versus seven out of 19 in the fifth. Hoards containing coins and jewelry or other objects after the Macedonian Conquest are omitted from this table. They are rare, and their non-monetary content always seems either haphazard (a bracelet, **111**; a lead weight, **291**) or uncertainly identified (a silver statuette?, **267**; a marble head ?, **314**).

Callataÿ has used the presence of *Hacksilber* to revise the location of two hoards: *CH* 1.15 (65 drachms of Sinope out of 108 coins) and a considerable collection of nearly 900 objects, including 594 coins of Sinope and some *Hacksilber*.[22] Based on the abundance of Sinopean issues, the original editors situated them on the Black Sea, even though *Hacksilber* is never present in such proportions in local circulation of that region. Callataÿ saw them instead as coming from the Near East or Egypt. I have not included them in my catalogue precisely because they contain too many Sinopean coins by comparison with the usual contents of Syrian hoards (see

20. Ibid., p. 228.
21. Ibid., pp. 230–31.
22. Pfisterer 2000 and Callataÿ 2003.

Table 4.1. Hoards containing *Hacksilber*

No.	Location	*IGCH* or *CH*	Burial Date	Contents
1	Ras Shamra	*IGCH* 1478 = Noe 851	525–520	39 AR, 2 frags. AR, some fused, in a pot in the middle of a hearth
7	Syria	*CH* 6.4–5 = *CH* 7.12	480	8+ AR, 20+ kg of ingots and of cut coins, perhaps a decadr. of Athens
8	Antilebanon	*CH* 6.4 = *CH* 8.45	475	70 AR (including 2 cut pieces); c. 20 kg *Hacksilber*
11	Byblos	*CH* 8.587 = *CH* 9.356	450	18 AR, in a bronze box, authorized excavation, found with some silver flans cut up, and one, in gold, intact; also with some casting residues, jewelry and silver toiletry accessories, some fragmentary.
13	Region of Bostra, Hauran	*IGCH* 1482 = *CH* 9.355	445	113 AR, jewelry and frags. of coins, 10 small frags. of silver (51.01 g), 32 pieces of jewelry (beads, elements of bracelets and necklaces, earrings) and frags. of silver
16	Region of Jbeil?		425	54 AR and 3 ingots AR Athens: 3 tetr.
17	Massyaf	*IGCH* 1483 = *CH* 8.587 = *CH* 9.362	425–420/400	104 AR, jewelry: unidentified and frags.: 17; frags. of uncoined silver: 4; 2 silver spirals for hair(?), silver fragments
31	Region of Arwad	*CH* 8.123 and 8.587 = *CH* 9.386	390–350	27 AR and frags., 3 figurines and a pair of silver earrings, a bronze arrowhead, 7 terracotta statuettes
37	Al Mina	*IGCH* 1488 = *CH* 8.587 = *CH* 9.397	375	43 AR, plated coins, jewelry
46	Near East	*CH* 8.126	350	21 AR, 2 ingots
50	Samaria	*CH* 8.587 = *CH* 9.413	355 or 345	334 coins and frags. in a pot, with beads and frags. of jewelry. 328 AR, 6 AE
54	Near East	*CH* 10.253	340–330	76 and 2 coin-shaped dumps AR
77	Nablus	*IGCH* 1504 = *CH* 9.440	333/2	965+ AR, plated coins, jewelry
114	Samaria	*CH* 10.237	End 4th cent.	32 pieces of *Hacksilber*, including Athens: 5 frags. of tetr., of which 1 plated.

Table 4.2. Coins of Sinope in Syrian hoards

No.	Location	*IGCH* or *CH*	Burial Date	Coins of Sinope/Total Studied
8	Antilebanon	*CH* 6.4 = *CH* 8.45	475	1 dr./70
68	Near East	*CH* 10.244	334–330	3 dr./475
76	Syria, 100 km east of Aleppo	*CH* 8.158	333	4 dr./164
77	Nablus	*IGCH* 1504 = *CH* 9.440	333/2	2 dr./965

Table 4.2). This does not mean that these hoards may not be exceptional—this is Callataÿ's argument[23]—but the criterion seemed to me too slender to justify such a localization.[24]

The find published by Pfisterer is enormous with its 899 entries, 108 of which are *Hacksilber*.[25] Among hoards larger than 150 silver coins catalogued in Syria, only two contained *Hacksilber* (**50**, **77**). The Nablus hoard (*IGCH* 1504, **77**) would be the "closest" to Pfisterer's. But it contained hundreds of fractions, reflecting a profoundly different economic profile. *Hacksilber* is still attested in the region at the end of the fourth century (**54**, **114**), but in modest proportions. Only hoards from the start of the fifth century would be comparable (cf. Fig. 4.1), but it seems that the burial date of Pfisterer's hoard lies in the second half of that century.[26]

1.3. Currencies of the Fifth Century

Schlumberger, in 1953, proved that Greek cities provided most of the currency available in the Persian Empire. "Coin circulation in the Persian Empire depends on two major sources. One is outside the empire: it is the small region of Attica and the Saronic Gulf in Greece proper, where the great city producing coins for export is, first, Aegina (the mines of Siphnos), then Athens (the mines of Laurium). The other is part of the empire, namely, the zone of cities of ancient Greek civilization lining the coast of Asia Minor, from the Hellespont to Cilicia, including Cyprus. As for the Thraco-Macedonian mining district, whose importance is so clear, it plays its role only through the intermediary of the cities already mentioned."[27] The Syrian hoards

23. "In this case, we are asked simply to believe in the occasional over-representation in a series of finds (two, so far) of the currency of Sinope. And nothing more. I do not see other obstacles to this interpretation. (Dans ce cas, on nous demande simplement de croire à la sur-représentation ponctuelle dans une série de trouvailles (deux jusqu'ici) du numéraire de Sinope. Et rien de plus. Je ne vois pas d'autres obstacles à cette interpretation)" Callataÿ 2003, p. 271.

24. Thus, contra Gitler 2006b and Van Alfen 2004–2005a.

25. Pfisterer 2000, nos. 791–899, pp. 68–76.

26. Callataÿ 2003, pp. 269–70.

27. "La circulation monétaire dans l'empire perse se ramène à deux grandes sources. L'une est extérieure à l'empire : c'est la petite région attico-saronique de la Grèce propre, où la grande cité productrice de monnaies pour l'exportation est d'abord Egine (mines de Siphnos), puis Athènes (mines du Laurium). L'autre fait partie de l'empire, et c'est toute la zone de cités de vieille civilisation grecque dont est bordée l'Asie Mineure, de l'Hellespont à la Cilicie, Chypre inclus. Quant au district minier thraco-macédonien, dont l'importance est si manifeste, il ne joue son rôle que par l'intermédiaire des dites cités." Schlumberger 1953, pp. 18–19.

Table 4.3. Hoards containing Persian *sigloi*[28]

No.	Location	*IGCH* or *CH*	Burial Date	Contents
8	Antilebanon	*CH* 6.4 = *CH* 8.45	475	70 AR and c. 20 kg *Hacksilber* Sardis: 1/6 *siglos*, 3 *sigloi*
11	Byblos	*CH* 8.587 = *CH* 9.356	450	18 AR, in a bronze box, *Hacksilber* Sardis: 1 *siglos* (type 3)
12	Northern Syria	*IGCH* 1481 = *CH* 8.587 = *CH* 9.357	450	4+ AR Sardis: 1 *siglos*
13	Region of Bostra	*IGCH* 1482 = *CH* 9.355	445	113 AR, jewelry and frags. Sardis: 1 *siglos*
15	Northern Syria	*CH* 1.14 = *CH* 8.587 = *CH* 9.363	425	16+ AR Sardis: 1 *siglos* (type 2)
17	Massyaf	*IGCH* 1483 = *CH* 8.587 = *CH* 9.362	425–420/400	100 AR, jewelry and frags. of jewelry Sardis: 1 *siglos*
24	Near East	*CH* 7.28	4th cent.	Sardis: 12 *sigloi*
46	Near East	*CH* 8.126	350	21 AR, 2 ingots Sardis: 1 *siglos* (?)

Schlumberger collected did not contain a single *siglos*.[29] His sample for Syria-Palestine consisted of only 11 hoards. That of Carradice, in his study of "royal" coinage of the Persian Empire, encompasses 36 hoards of Persian *sigloi* but only four with a Syrian provenance.[30] Of the 68 hoards from the Persian period in the catalogue presented here, eight hoards contain *sigloi* (Table 4.3). Despite the substantial increase in material, it is evident that Persian *sigloi* circulated only marginally in Syria. It is also necessary to stress that they are particularly rare in the fourth century,[31] although they appear just at this time in Mesopotamia and Iran.[32]

In total, the number of *sigloi* is derisory and seems purely accidental, except for hoard 24: it is the only one containing so many *sigloi* and no other coinage, such that one has to wonder

28. The origin of these *sigloi* is not Persia, but more probably Sardis or mints in Asia Minor, Le Rider 2001a, pp. 133–39. "Persia" designates the issuing authority, not the geographical provenance. This is a good example of the problems in nomenclature with identifications.

29. Ibid., pp. 7–8.

30. Carradice 1987, p. 79. One of these hoards (Lebanon 1983) is catalogued neither in *IGCH* and *CH*, nor in the present catalogue, in the absence of bibliographical references. Consisting of 150 *sigloi*, it would represent an exception in the table below.

31. Especially if hoard **24** comes, in fact, from Asia Minor.

32. According to the table in Carradice 1987, p. 79: the Persia (*IGCH* 1795), Babylonia (*IGCH* 1747), Tchaman-i Hazouri, Afghanistan (*IGCH* 1830), Susa (*IGCH* 1792), and Bhir Mound, Pakistan (*IGCH* 1831) hoards are dated between 400 and 300 BC. No hoard of *sigloi* from the fifth century is located east of Syria.

whether it does not come from Asia Minor. The seven other hoards provided only nine *sigloi* and one fraction, out of a total of at least 352 coins. The record from archaeological excavations is no better: only Dura Europos has yielded a *siglos*.

The great coinage of the late fifth century is unquestionably that of Athens. Starr sums up its position: ". . . Athenian coinage of the period 480–449 does not, as far as present knowledge extends, turn up in the western Mediterranean at all and appears only sporadically on the eastern shores of the Mediterranean; the issues of the Athenian mint did not become in any sense the standard medium of exchange generally until the point when Athens had come almost to monopolize the silver of the Aegean."[33] The absence of "owls" in the Athenian Empire has been long observed. "Indeed, only two of the 42 hoards buried between 480 and 400 in these areas contained any, and what is more, in totally insignificant proportions. Paradoxically, it is in the East, in the territories governed by the Great King, that owls were hoarded in large quantity."[34] These tetradrachms are indeed well documented in fifth-century Syrian hoards.

Before studying the catalogue's hoards with Athenian coins, it is necessary to mention several exceptional finds that have not yet been fully published. First among them is the so-called Carchemish hoard or North of Aleppo hoard (**A**), or even "second decadrachm hoard" as opposed to the "first decadrachm hoard" found at Elmalı in Lycia (*CH* 8.48, 10.212).[35] A study in progress of a lot from Carchemish/North of Aleppo, which went on sale in Zurich, has allowed Meadows and Wartenberg to put together 456 specimens, of which six decadrachms and 344 tetradrachms are Athenian.[36] The other mints are located chiefly in northern (Thrace-Macedonia) and central Greece. Two coins from Asia Minor, two from Sidon, three from Tyre, and two from Barce represent the paltry showing from the eastern Mediterranean and Africa. The exact provenance of this hoard remains obscure; the authors suggest a burial between 440 and 430, if the lot is representative of the original collection. Just as difficult to evaluate is a lot of 10,000 Athenian tetradrachms, accompanied by a tetradrachm of Cyrene and also perhaps an Athenian decadrachm and a Syracusan tetradrachm, identified as coming from the "North of Aleppo" hoard in 2006 (**B**). Burial was c. 400.[37] These two hoards have in common their huge number of Athenian tetradrachms. The Elmalı hoard is better known than the others, and it consists mostly of coins of Lycia, the area where it was discovered.[38] Since hoards **A** and **B**

33. Starr 1970, p. 85.

34. "En effet, seuls deux des quarante-deux trésors enfouis entre 480 et 400 dans ces régions en contenaient, et de surcroît, dans des proportions tout-à-fait insignifiantes. Paradoxalement, c'est en Orient, dans les territoires gouvernés par le Grand Roi, que les chouettes furent massivement thésaurisées." Flament 2007, p. 45.

35. This hoard of more than 1,900 coins appeared on the market in 1984 and contained coins from mints of northern Greece, from Athens, Ionia, Caria, and Lycia. In addition to its unusual size, it was characterized by the presence of numerous coins of large dimension (more than 70 octadrachms of the Bisaltae, Getae, and Derrones, 13 Athenian decadrachms). It was presumably buried c. 460 BC. Fried 1987, Kagan 1987, Fischer-Bossert 2008, p. 17.

36. I would like to thank here the authors who have generously conveyed to me the data at their disposal.

37. Buxton 2009, p. 4. The article is based on personal examination of 2,626 specimens, including the coin from Cyrene.

38. 970, according to Fried 1987, p. 9.

are only partially known, they may have also contained local coins. In the present state of our knowledge, their provenance depends solely on hearsay, which puts them north of Aleppo. This approximate location has the advantage for sellers of avoiding mention of any Turkish origin. The dispersal of the Elmalı hoard in the 1980s provoked legal proceedings for the first time by the Turkish government against dealers and the repatriation of some of the coins to Turkey. The stiffening of control on the traffic in antiquities with provenance in a country like Turkey, Egypt or Italy in recent years has driven dealers to conceal the provenance of the objects they sell. As a result, it is very difficult to know exactly where these sizeable hoards containing Athenian coins and decadrachms in large quantity come from. They do not fit Syrian coin circulation as it appears from the material collected in our catalogue, but repeated big finds may be connected to exploration with metal detectors in areas previously spared these methods, like Syria.[39] More unusually, the presence of Athenian decadrachms is otherwise only attested in a purely anecdotal manner and uniquely in the form of fragments (**13** and perhaps **7**, with some *Hacksilber* in both cases[40]). If they really do come from Syria, these hoards would be evidence for hoarding habits peculiar to a long west-east strip running from Lycia to the foothills of the Syrian Taurus, with the three decadrachm hoards and the large hoard of tetradrachms (Elmalı and **A** and **B**), and perhaps into Iran. Meadows, who is preparing a new publication of the Malayer hoard (Iran, *IGCH* 1790), has indeed drawn my attention to the characteristics that it shares with the aforementioned large hoards. Out of some 330 coins, 22 Greek and Thracian mints and others from Italy to Lycia have each provided some individual items, but Athens (142 tetradrachms), Sidon (19 specimens), and Tyre (71 specimens) are especially well represented. These features could make this a hoard constituted in the Levant and buried in Iran during the third quarter of the fifth century. This continuity between the south of Anatolia, the southern Taurus foothills, and Iran is not out of the question: the route along the foothills is well attested by the textual sources from before the first millennium, and it runs all the way to Iran. It was sufficiently frequented to have revealed a highly discernible concentration of hoards in the Hellenistic Age in Mesopotamia.[41] If, then, hoards **A** and **B** should be properly located in Syria, it seems that both were found in the north and that the practice of these large burials extended from the 460s to the end of the century. The sole hoard located north of Aleppo in our catalogue may provide confirmation. It was discovered at Marash in 1898 (*IGCH* 1484, **2**) and is quite poorly documented. It apparently consisted of 100 Athenian tetradrachms and was buried during the fifth century; nothing more is known. It contains the largest number of Athenian tetradrachms in the catalogue for the fifth century (Table 4.4).

Foreign coins (cf. Fig. 4.3), especially Athenian tetradrachms, figure prominently in fifth-century hoards. Out of the total volume of coins (819 specimens, all denominations included), Athens and its imitations constitute 35%, Phoenician mints 38%, other mints, scattered around the Aegean basin, in southern Anatolia and on Cyprus, 25%, while Samaria and Philistia, confined to local circulation, account for only 2% of the whole. The number of hoards where they

39. This surmise may also apply to the hoard of coins of Sinope mentioned earlier.
40. But they served as a model for the coins of Ascalon: Gitler, Tal 2006, pp. 96–101.
41. Duyrat 2004.

Table 4.4. Fifth-century hoards containing coins with Athenian types (Map 4)[42]

No.	Location	*IGCH* or *CH*	Burial Date	Contents
2	Marash	*IGCH* 1484	5th cent.	100 AR Athens: tetr.
3	Vicinity of Gaza	*CH* 8.29	500–400	16 AR, in a pot Athens: 2 tetr.
4	Jablah	*IGCH* 1479	500–490	16+ AR Athens: 12 tetr.
6	Latakia	*CH* 6.5	480	25+ AR Athens: 2 tetr.
7	Syria	*CH* 6.4–5 = *CH* 7.12	480	8+ AR, ingots and cut coins Athens: 1 tetr. Among the cut coins, perhaps a decadr. of Athens
8	Anti-lebanon	*CH* 6.4 = *CH* 8.45	475	70 AR and 20 kg *Hacksilber* Athens: 17 tetr.
13	Region of Bostra	*IGCH* 1482 = *CH* 9.355	445	113 AR, jewelry and frags. Athens: 11 coins and 20 frags., including 1 Wappenmünzen ob. with wheel, 1 frag. of a decadr., 1 dr.
14	Ramallah	*CH* 8.59	430	76+ AR Athens: tetr.
16	Region of Jbeil?		425	54 AR and 3 ingots AR Athens: 3 tetr.
17	Massyaf	*IGCH* 1483	425–420 Kraay, Moorey; 425–400 Elayi, Elayi	100 AR, jewelry and frags. of jewelry Athens: 14 tetr., 19 frags., 2 dr. of which 1 plated? (1.52 g)
18	Beithir	*IGCH* 1489	407–368 (370 *IGCH*)	510+ AR Sidon: 170+ or 177+ double shekels, Athens: 2+ or 9+ tetr. with frontal eye
20	Aleppo	*IGCH* 1490	End of the 5th cent.?	AR, in a pot Athens, imitations: fractions Tyre, Sidon

appear supports the significant share of Athenian types: 12 out of 19 in all, or 63% of the fifth-century hoards. In many hoards in the catalogue, Athenian tetradrachms form a minority, with the exception of those from Phoenicia (**21**), Marash in Commagene (**2**), and Ramallah (**14**) that approach those of the fourth century. The coins are sometimes cut, mixed with *Hacksilber*. Fragments of Archaic coins, such as Athenian *Wappenmünzen*, still circulate in the mid-fifth centu-

42. Contents have been simplified. Only details on small hoards have been retained.

ry because of their metallic value. The practice of chiseling tetradrachms continues throughout this time, to the end of the fourth century. It is no longer a question of cutting up coins to make *Hacksilber* out of them, but of marking them with a chisel blow. It is generally believed that this practice aimed at disclosing plated coins. Van Alfen emphasizes the frequency of chisel marks observed on two-thirds of the tetradrachms from the three hoards he published in 2004 and 2005.[43] He concludes from this that the practice is related to the phenomenon of countermarking rather than a verification of the coin's underlying nature.[44] So interpretation vacillates between two hypotheses: does chiseling aim to guarantee the value of worn denominated money, or is it the sign of continuing use of weighed silver that does not accord confidence to the metal until it has been duly verified? It seems probable, especially on the coast from the second half of the fifth century, when Phoenician mints begin to strike coinage, that use of denominated silver spread. It is noteworthy that, after 450, nearly all hoards of known origin containing *Hacksilber* are from inland (Map 3). Gitler and Tal point out a large number of Athenian tetradrachms in excavations or in isolated finds in Palestine on sites from the second half of the fifth century. My catalogue also reveals some Athenian tetradrachms, uniquely on the coast, at Al Mina, 'Atlit, Ras el-Bassit, and Ras Shamra. This abundance leads Gitler and Tal to conclude that "since hundreds of Athenian and Athenian-styled issues from this period are found in Palestine in both archaeological excavations and as stray finds, it seems obvious that during the second half of the fifth century a partial monetary economy was practiced in the region."[45] Callataÿ has qualified the idea of an already partially monetized economy in the second half of the fifth century: "as stated, these coins, Athenians or not ..., were not accepted as coins but as silver bullion. The distinction between 'a partial monetary economy' and 'a real monetary economy' is a nuanced debate that has engaged specialists of periods as late as the eighteenth century, and disagreement continues."[46] The hoards do not justify maintaining the idea that coins circulating in Syria during the second half of the fifth century were only exchanged for their metallic value. The start of Phoenician coin production, the coexistence of an increasingly abundant currency and the persistence of *Hacksilber*, and cut coins suppose the existence within the very same region of combined practices: silver is weighed or denominated depending on place and circumstance.

The fifth century, therefore, marks the beginning of the use of coinage, but also of local issue. Athenian tetradrachms play an early role in this process, from the time of the second Persian war; and one may pose the question of this historical episode's part in introducing coinage into the region. The Phoenicians participated, Herodotus witnessing in several passages to their major contribution to Xerxes' fleet (at Salamis, for example: Herodotus 8.85). Athenian "owls" and their standard, from this time forward, are accepted throughout the entire region, on the coast as well as in the mainland interior (Map 4). This phenomenon grows in the fourth century.

43. Van Alfen 2004–2005b, p. 49.
44. Van Alfen 2002, pp. 6–7.
45. Gitler, Tal 2006, p. 25.
46. Callataÿ 2006c, pp. 168–69.

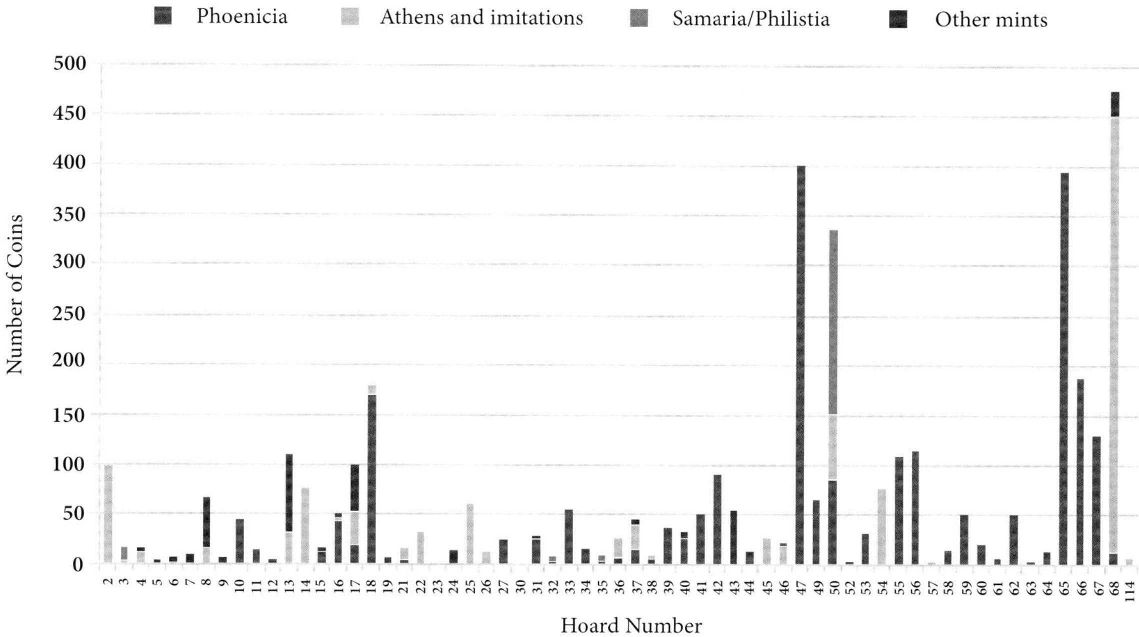

Figure 4.3: Provenance of coins in hoards of the fifth and fourth centuries, before 333 BC[47]

2. THE FOURTH CENTURY

In the fourth century, currency circulation clearly changes, with three new characteristics. Denominated money dominates from now on in our data: of 48 hoards, only four contain *Hacksilber*: cut up fragments of silver objects (**50**, **54**, **114**) or ingots (**46**). Coins are also more rarely chiseled.[48] The second characteristic of this period comes from the Phoenician mints whose production now appears in numerous deposits. Finally, the place of "owls" and their imitations, still important, is transformed. Mildenberg has shown that a wide variety of monetary supply characterized the Persian Empire: royal issues, satrapal coinages, provincial coinages (Samaria and Judaea), foreign imports, eastern imitations of Athenian owls, coins of local dynasts and cities in the empire.[49] This general description is only partially valid for Syria, where official imperial productions are largely absent.

2.1. Phoenician Silver (Map 6)

Sixty-nine Syrian hoards contain Phoenician coins: 10 from the fifth century and 37 from the fourth prior to 333 BC, to which are added 22 hoards buried at the time of Alexander the Great, almost all before 325 BC.[50]

47. The numbers on the X-axis are hoard numbers. Hoards **29** and **48** have been excluded, in the absence of firm numbers, as well as hoard **28**, composed of 1,600 shekels of Byblos, an amount that would overwhelm the other data. It only reinforces the impression of Phoenician coinages' dominance.
48. Van Alfen 2004–2005a, pp. 35–39.
49. Mildenberg 1993.
50. Only hoards **97**, **99**, and **107** are later than this date.

Figure 4.4. Double shekel of Sidon (ANS 1944.100.71290).

Figure 4.5. Silver stater of Aradus (ANS 1944.100.71164).

Figure 4.6. Double shekel of Tyre (ANS 1967.152.578).

The fourth century has a completely different profile from the fifth. Phoenician coins have an increasing place. They even constitute the sole currency present in 25 hoards.[51] Figures 4.3 and 4.7, based on the number of coins studied by hoard, reveal the growing role of these issues in time and in number of specimens. Sidon vastly dominates, with 48% of hoard content and an area of circulation that goes beyond the limits of its own regional zone of influence (Fig. 4.4). Aradus (Fig. 4.5) and Tyre (Fig. 4.6) have produced between 11% and 9% of hoard specimens and demonstrate a strong regional circulation, Tyre having a wider reach outside of Syria. The diffusion of the coinage of Byblos is strictly confined to the city's immediate vicinity.[52] The decline in non-Athenian foreign coins is particularly noticeable: from 25% in the fifth century to merely 2% of specimens buried in the fourth century.

I have had occasion to remark on the abundance of fractions in these fourth-century hoards, at a time when local mints produced a great deal of them.[53] The coins of Philistia, Judaea, and Samaria struck in the fourth century are drachms at the largest (with the exception of some tetradrachms produced at Gaza), but in the majority of cases are fractions thereof, highlighting the marked preference in the region for either larger-sized coins—tetradrachms with Athenian types, Phoenician shekels and double shekels—or small denominations, with little in between.[54]

51. **23, 27, 28, 29, 30, 33, 34, 39, 41, 42, 44, 47, 48, 49, 55, 56, 58, 59, 60, 61, 62, 63, 64, 65, 67**.
52. Cf. the comments of Elayi, Elayi 1993a, pp. 354–58, and the diffusion maps for mints, figs. 20–26.
53. Duyrat 2011b and here below, pp. 429–433.
54. Gitler, Tal 2006; Meshorer, Qedar 1991, 1999; Meshorer 1982.

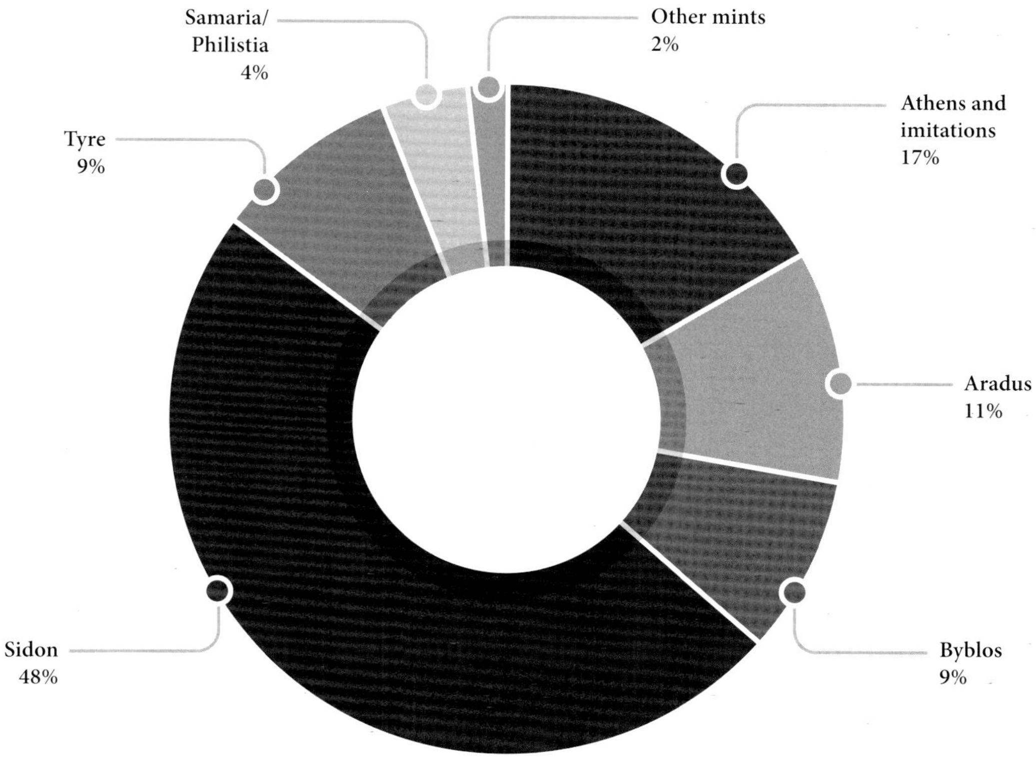

Figure 4.7. Proportion of Athenian and Phoenician coins in hoards of the fourth century.

Speaking of the development of Phoenician coinages, Kraay and Moorey have suggested that "it would be reasonable to suppose that the activity of the new Phoenician mints may have constituted a bar which did not previously exist to the eastward dispersion of Cypriot coins; such examples which continued to arrive may well often have been intercepted in the coastal areas and melted down to provide bullion for the mints of Tyre and Sidon."[55] This hypothesis is rather tentative. Cypriot mints were not particularly prominent in the fifth century (**8**, **9**, **13**, **16**, **17**), no more so than other Greek mints. Elayi and Elayi have also questioned this hypothesis by arguing that the melting down of coins has not been attested.[56] This may not be the most forceful argument since we do possess two hoards that contain partially melted coins (**1**, **9**).

Compared to the fifth century, Phoenician coinages therefore experience a real flowering in the fourth century that translates into strong representation in hoards, where they amount to 77% of the content. The important place coins with Athenian types held in the fifth century evolves differently in the fourth.

55. Kraay, Moorey 1968, pp. 220–21.
56. Elayi, Elayi 1993a, p. 245.

Table 4.5. Development in the representation of coins with Athenian types in hoards, fifth and fourth centuries

	Fifth Century	Fourth Century
Athenian Coins in Hoards	35% (310/819 coins)	17% (796/4,740 coins)
Hoards Containing Coins with Athenian Types	63% (12/19 hoards)	35% (17/48 hoards)

2.2. Athenian Owls and Their Imitations

The relative share of coins with Athenian types apparently drops in the fourth century, both within hoards (17% vs. 35% in the fifth century) and in the number of hoards themselves displaying this currency (35% vs. 63% in the fifth century, Table 4.5). Yet the numbers show a progression in absolute amount (from 310–796 specimens) that coincides with the rise in the currency supply in circulation. The latter surely also explains the increase in the size of finds (Fig. 4.3). Nonetheless, taking account of the two very large hoards of Athenian tetradrachms described above (**A** and **B**), the latter thought to have contained several thousand of these coins, one has either to acknowledge that the share of "owls" in circulation declined, especially in northern Syria, or to conclude that finds of this size from the fourth century have yet to occur. Be that as it may, the nomenclature "Athenians and imitations" in fact covers several categories of coins. Precision on this point is necessary because some of these owls are actually local productions.

The quality of their metal and the abundance of issues from Athens made owls into an accepted international currency from the fifth century. Imitations are attested from the beginning of the fifth century.[57] Numerous works have focused on the nature of Athenian tetradrachm imitations. The present endeavor seeks only to define the different types of imitations found in Syria, with the aim of clarifying their role in the region's circulating currency.[58] They divide into two main groups: imitations able to be exchanged at parity with Athenian prototypes and imitations merely inspired by Athenian types. Within the first group, there are two further subdivisions. The first seeks to copy the original exactly. This is the situation for a good number of tetradrachms with Athenian types struck in Egypt if one follows Buttrey's, probably exaggerated, hypothesis that millions of these coins were produced.[59] Thus, the way to distinguish

57. Reflections on the causes of imitating Athenian coins and their geographic and chronological spread in van Alfen 2005 and 2011.

58. van Alfen 2005 has distinguished six sorts of imitations. 1. Artistic: copies of major features of Athenian types, obverse and/or reverse, sometimes embellished by local legends; 2. Anonymous: exact copies, sometimes difficult to distinguish from the originals; 3. Marked: identical copies with non-Athenian marking; 4. Superficial: also called barbarian imitations, having remote connections to the prototypes; 5. Plated or of inferior metal standard; 6. Counterfeits. Flament 2007, p. 56, distinguishes simply between exact copies and all the rest, "from mere addition of a secondary symbol to a more or less noticeable alteration, to the point, sometimes, of making it hard to recognize the original model. (de la simple adjonction d'un symbole secondaire à une altération plus ou moins sensible, jusqu'au point, parfois, de ne laisser reconnaître qu'avec peine le modèle de départ)."

59. Buttrey 1982, p. 138.

Figure 4.8. Athenian tetradrachm (ANS 1968.34.40).

Figure 4.9: Imitation in the name of Sabaces (ANS 1944.100.75461).

Figure 4.10. Obol of Samaria (ANS 2010.77.257).

an imitation from an authentic coin is occasionally nonexistent or debatable, as Flament has shown: an obverse judged authentic is sometimes paired with a reverse previously thought an imitation.[60] Recent analyses of Athenian coins found at Tel Michal (**26**) tend in this direction: first thought to be imitations, they appear to have been struck in a metal with the characteristics of silver from Laurium.[61] A second subcategory in the group reproduces the types of Athenian tetradrachms well but adds a mark foreign to Athens, a letter, symbol, satrapal name (Fig. 4.9) or even the name of Artaxerxes III.[62] This feature makes the imitation clear but did not prevent the coins from circulating together with the prototypes.

The second main group of imitations makes no pretence at being exchangeable for authentic tetradrachms. It has two subcategories. The first always employs good types, but on a coin size different from the tetradrachm that represents the overwhelming majority of exported Athenian coins (Figs. 4.8 and 4.10). The second includes coins inspired by Athenian models, but only inspired: one surface uses another type, or else highly altered versions of the originals. I would be reluctant to call these last two categories imitations: the change in coin size and/or iconography makes the difference with the model patently clear. It is no longer a matter of circulating coins that could be exchanged for the same value as Athenian tetradrachms, but only of winning the user's confidence by employing a familiar and recognized typology.

60. Flament 2003; 2005; 2007, p. 58.
61. Gitler, Ponting, Tal 2009.
62. Some examples in Flament 2007, p. 56.

2.2.1. Circulation of Authentic and Imitation Tetradrachms

The Near East produced a large variety of owl imitations in each of the categories mentioned above. The earliest date from the 420s, according to Mildenberg.[63] Interest in these coinages has grown markedly during the last decades, and the bibliography grows apace, on the hoards as well as on the typology. No general study, however, exists on the topic.

Tetradrachms constitute the overwhelming majority of coins with Athenian types in hoards from the Persian period. Originals and copies circulate easily together, the quality of the latter theoretically adequate in terms of metal and weight. The circulation zone of the owls covers the entire region that employs the coinage in no particular concentration, in contrast to the pattern for Phoenician coins (Map 5). An especially telling example is the hoard found east of Aleppo (*CH* 8.158, **76**), buried c. 333/2 BC: alongside more than roughly a hundred authentic and imitation Athenian tetradrachms, it contained Egyptian tetradrachms with the name of Artaxerxes and his satraps in Egypt, Sabaces, who died at the battle of Issus, and Mazaces, who was in charge at Memphis at the time of the Macedonian conquest in 332 BC.[64]

This raises the problem of identifying originals when they do not bear any distinctive mark, an issue far from being resolved. Van Alfen, publishing the tetradrachms with Athenian types from a hoard in Syria (**76**), distinguishes 41 imitations from authentic tetradrachms on the following criteria: "The non-Athenian quality of the following owls leaves little doubt that they were made outside of Athens, in the Levant or Egypt."[65] However, Athenian production in the fourth century is often poor in quality. One might add the three pages of tables in Gitler and Tal reclassifying as imitations 10 Athenian tetradrachms or didrachms found in officially sanctioned digs in Palestine out of 27 sites mentioned, essentially on stylistic criteria established by Kroll.[66] These changes in attribution, between Athenian prototypes and imitations, based only on style, partly depend on *ex cathedra* statements. It is worth recalling here with Flament how fragile these criteria can sometimes be. This prevailing opinion, that a large number of imitations were struck in the Near East, could be born, he adds, "of a poor interpretation of the numismatic data." The frequency of fifth-century Athenian types characterizes Eastern hoards, yet their context clearly indicates fourth-century circulation; hence the conclusion that these were coins imitating fifth-century originals. Flament, however, defends the idea that these are authentically Athenian coins from the fifth century, which simply circulated for a longer time in the East.[67] He apparently dismisses completely the idea of fourth-century oriental issues imitating fifth-century Athenian tetradrachms that continued to circulate in the region. Without being able to settle the question, I draw attention to the fact that owls appear in 17 hoards in the fourth century (26, if one includes finds later than 333 BC), compared with 12 in the fifth century, a palpable increase (from 310 to 796 well documented tetradrachms). It would require

63. Mildenberg 1993, p. 64.
64. van Alfen 2002, pp. 3 and 24–32.
65. Ibid., p. 12.
66. Gitler, Tal 2006, pp. 27–29, following Kroll 1993.
67. Flament 2007, p. 58.

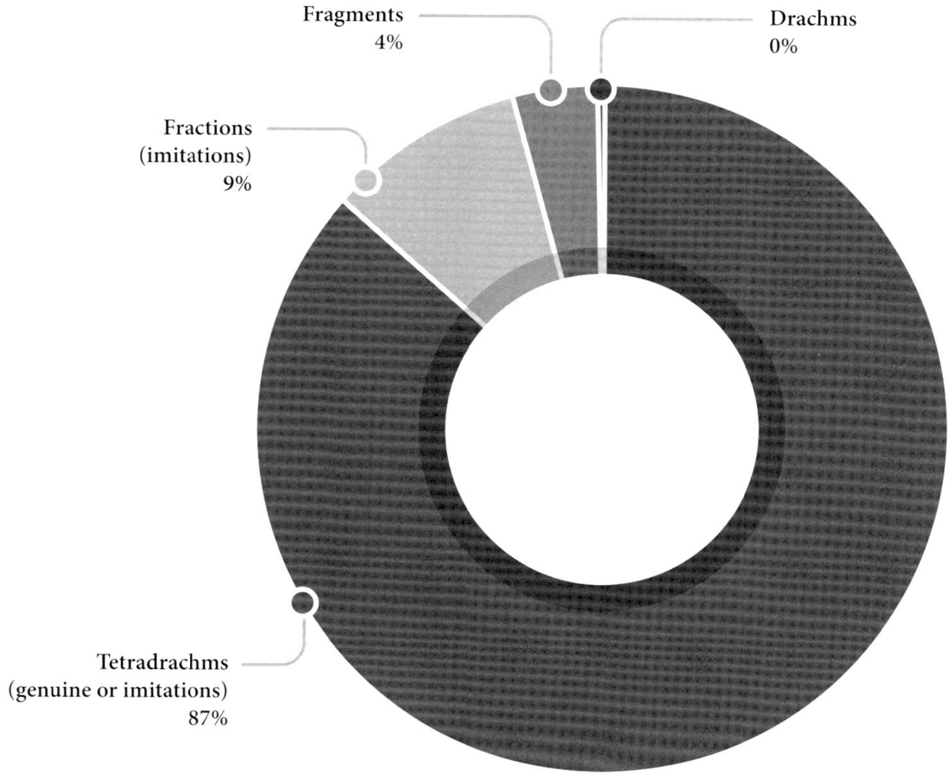

Figure 4.11. Coins with Athenian types in hoards: tetradrachms, fractions, and fragments.

a stylistic study of the tetradrachms from these finds to determine how many belong to the fifth-century categories, but they are indeed numerous, as Flament himself recognizes. Their numerical increase within hoards thus poses a problem: if one is to think that the large majority of them are authentically Athenian, where would they come from, since they were less numerous in hoards of the fifth century, at the very time of mass production in Attica? The technical criteria ordinarily used to date, at least roughly, authentic Athenian tetradrachms (the shape of Athena's eye, the incuse square on the reverse, etc.) pose another difficulty. Imitations did not have to follow changes in style and may have only copied these features to a varying degree. Thus the incuse remained current on the coinage of Bactria with Athenian types down to the end of the fourth century, while it disappeared on tetradrachms from Athens by the end of the fifth century.[68] Paradoxically, if authentic tetradrachms found in Levantine excavations are primarily in the Pi style, that is to say, fourth century, the imitations prefer to copy fifth-century tetradrachms, especially the mass strikings from the years 454–415/13 BC.[69] Flament's view cannot, therefore, be held without qualification.

68. Nicolet-Pierre, Amandry 1994, p. 45.
69. Gitler, Tal 2006, p. 25.

Identification of the mints striking imitation Athenian tetradrachms remains highly conjectural.[70] In some rare, very fortunate cases, the signature of the responsible issuer is clearly indicated (Artaxerxes and his satraps in Egypt, Mazaces in Babylonia).[71] But a large number of imitations do not have any explicit signature allowing us to identify the issuing authority: some letters or supplementary symbols are added to the original types and make the imitation clear but nothing else. The only two specimens published from hoard **57** (*CH* 8.152) are known just from photographs of casts of the obverses that seem quite beautiful and like authentic tetradrachms, from which they are distinguished only by the Semitic letters, *aleph* and *kaph*, engraved directly on the die in the middle of the type. Hypotheses about the mints supposed to have struck Athenian imitations suggest Cilicia,[72] Phoenicia?,[73] Gaza (*ʿ* and *M* for the name of the city and its principal god, Marnas), Philistia,[74] Babylonia,[75] attested by local finds that did not circulate far, Bactria,[76] and Egypt, whose production ended up largely in Transeuphratene. The striking of imitation Athenian tetradrachms is therefore widespread, far beyond Syria. The popularity of the Athenian coinage prompted, at the same time, production of fractions with Athenian types and also types derived from those of Athens. Since these coins cannot be confused or exchanged at par with the originals, I classify them separately.

2.3.2. Fractions with Athenian Types and Coins with Derivative Types

One of the characteristics of coin circulation in fourth-century Syria is the use of silver fractions, some of them very tiny. The recent publications of the numismatic *corpora* of Sidon and Tyre for the Persian period amply show this.[77] For fractions of less than 0.1g, a reference to the hoard found in the 1936 excavations of Al-Mina (**33**) will suffice: a silver purse, measuring 6.7 × 2.5 cm in diameter, contained 55 coins of Aradus (from 0.04 g to 0.11 g; 4 mm diameter), and four of Sidon (0.5 g). The entire find weighed less than 6 g of silver. The burial occurred in c. 375 BC. This is an extreme case, but it well illustrates the development of small denominations in the Levant. Coins of larger diameter are also prevalent—double shekels, shekels, tetradrachms—and that is also the average size of the only Athenian coins appearing in Syria (Fig. 4.11).[78] The

70. The absence of homogeneity in engraving style, control marks, and legend that permit identification of the issuer leads van Alfen 2005, p. 77, to suppose the existence of private issuers in the Levant. Nothing in the current state of our knowledge supports this.

71. Cf. the hoards of Syria and Iraq published by van Alfen 2000 and 2002a.

72. Flament 2000.

73. Gitler, Tal 2006, p. 26.

74. Ibid., p. 25.

75. Seven Mesopotamian hoards from the fourth and early third centuries have revealed owls: *IGCH* 1747, 1752, 1753, 1757, 1761, 1762, *CH* 8.188. Cf. Nicolet-Pierre 1973 (*CH* 2.45); Nicolet-Pierre, Amandry 1994 (*CH* 9.452); Reade 1986 (*IGCH* 1747); Price 1991a and 1991b; van Alfen 2000 (*CH* 8.188).

76. Six hoards from Iran and Afghanistan containing owls dating from the 440s BC (Malayer, communication from Meadows) to 180/170 BC: *IGCH* 1790 (Malayer), 1820, 1830, 1822, *CH* 2.45, *CH* 9.452. Cf. Schlumberger 1953; Curiel, Schlumberger 1953; Troxell, Spengler 1969; Nicolet-Pierre, Amandry 1994.

77. Sidon: Elayi, Elayi 2004b; Tyre: Elayi, Elayi 2009b. Cf. the comparative study offered here, pp. 429-433.

78. Hoards have revealed only four Athenian drachms, one of which is plated (**17**) while another two are imitations struck in Egypt (**46**), out of a total of 1,084 coins and fragments with Athenian types.

latter's abundance and quality made them popular, and so their types were adapted to fractions, especially in southern Levantine mints. These silver coinages have become much better known over the last decade. Highly active Israeli archaeology has unearthed a lot of material, leading to numerous publications, three of which revolutionize our knowledge of these coins.[79]

Issues from Samaria, Judaea, and Philistia are distinctive because of some shared features. They all date from the fourth century, before the Ptolemies' conquest in 301 BC. The Ptolemies subsequently closed all the mints, with the notable exception of Jerusalem, where the types are then derived from Ptolemaic royal coins.[80] Only small silver denominations were issued, the drachm being the largest in size, with few exceptions. Thus circulation is basically local. Numerous types exactly copy or take their inspiration from Athenian tetradrachms, which were abundant, as we have seen. Since the fractional denominations were in high demand throughout the region, issues from the southern Levant were a response to the demand, which then evolved towards variations on the reverse and, finally, to alteration of the Athenian types.[81] The area of circulation, relatively modest and well attested by excavations, assures their identification, as does the placement of an ethnic or an entire or abbreviated city's name on some of the specimens. Thus, *YHWH* or *YHD* distinguishes Judaean coins.

Samarian coinage has emerged from limbo in the last 20 years. It consists of small silver coins struck between c. 372 and 332 BC, dates that Meshorer and Qedar established in their study of 1991. These coins are overwhelmingly obols (8–9 mm in diameter) and hemiobols, along with some quarter-obols and the occasional drachm. Their inscriptions, most often in Aramaic or Hebrew, are quite varied: name of city and province of Samaria (*ŠMRYN* and variants), names of individuals, some proper names in Greek as well, and, of course, the legend AΘE.[82] The types are those of classic tetradrachms, only they appear on uniquely miniscule coin sizes (Fig. 4.10). The same mint produced obols with types of Athenian decadrachms, some specimens or fragments of which are observable in fifth-century hoards (hoards **A** and **B**, pp. 309–310; **7**, **13**).[83] The replication of types from Athenian tetradrachms can be only partial, on just the obverse or the reverse.[84] These variations in Athenian types are not unusual in the East, but Samaria surprises with an obol with a composite obverse—a triple-bearded male head wearing a rounded hat—and, especially, a reverse that shows what appears to be a heap of five Athenian coins seen from the reverse (owls), unless these are shields.[85]

79. Meshorer, Qedar 1991; Meshorer, Qedar 1999; Gitler Tal 2006. Judaean coins have yet to be the subject of a fresh overview; a useful presentation in Meshorer 2001; Gitler, Lorber 2006.

80. Cf. Barag 1994–1999; Deutsch 1994–1999; Gitler, Lorber 2000–2002.

81. Mildenberg 1997, p. 11.

82. One example among many: an obol of 0.79 g with Athenian types and legend mentions additionally, in retrograde Aramaic, *HNNYH*, *Hananyah*, which happens to be the name of the governor of Samaria, mentioned in papyri 7 and 9 from Wadi Daliyeh, and is also a fairly common name in contemporary Samaria. Meshorer, Qedar 1999, pl. 6, 38.

83. Meshorer, Qedar 1999, pl. 13, 87. On the reverse, an Aramaic legend: *ŠN* = contracted abbreviation of the name Samaria.

84. Thus an obol displays on the obverse a helmeted head of Athena, left, but on the reverse a lion attacking a deer. Legend in Aramaic: *ŠMRYN*. Meshorer, Qedar 1999, pl. 12, 77.

85. Meshorer, Qedar 1999, nos. 141–42. A hemiobol exists with the same reverse but only a Janus head on the obverse.

Table 4.6. Pre-Hellenistic coins from excavations[86]

Site	Pre-Hellenistic Mint
Al Mina, 1936	61: 16 AR (including 5 plated) + 45 AE Athens: 2 tetr., 4 plated tetr., 1 plated dr. Aradus: 1 tetrob. (Bearded head/Galley), 4 obols (*idem*) Sidon: 4 sixteenths (Galley/King fighting lion) Cities 45 AE: Cyzicus 1; Ephesus 2; Phygela 2; Cos 1; Rhodes 2; Citium 1; Salamis in Cyprus, Evagoras II: 3 + 4; Aradus 12 + 7 + 1; Sidon 2 + 1; uncert. Aradus or Sidon 6
Balatah (anc. Shechem),	1 AR Thraco-Macedonian: Satyr carrying off a Maenad/Incuse square
Beirut, (Bey 006 and 045)	8 AE, 1 AR Sidon: 3 (407/2–357/4 BC); 1 (Galley/Archer) plated Side: 5 (350–250 BC)
Beirut, Bey 020	4 AR ? 3 Sidon (Straton I, 370–58); 1 uncert.
Caesarea Maritima	1 AR Cyme (Aeolis), c. 350–250 BC
Castle of ʿAtlit	23 AR + 5 AE + 16 AR unspecified (sixteenth-shekels) Aegae: 1 eighth-stater (Goat/Incuse square), in a tomb Athens: 1 tetr. Sidon 19+: 17 sixteenth-shekels (4 Galley/Royal archer; 13 Galley/King fighting a lion); 1 AE (Galley/King in a chariot), 1 AE (Galley/Royal archer), + AR? Tyre: 3 didr. (Hippocamp and dolphin/Owl) Phoenicia: 3 AE uncert. (nos. 386–388) Philistia: 1 AR
Dura Europos	Persia: 1 AR
Jablah, Necropolis of al-Jbeibat	3 AR Aradus: 3 tetrob. (Bearded head/Prow)
Jaffa	Sidon: 2 AR, 22 AE
Jerusalem, 1961–1967, Armenian Garden, west hill	4th cent. BC: 1 Uncert.
Jerusalem, City of David	Lycia: 1 AR (5th cent. BC)
Marisa (anc. Maresha)	2 AR
Megiddo	2 AE + 2 AR (Hellenistic period?) Sidon: 2 AE Straton I (Galley/Chariot) Tyre: 2 Attic didr. (God on hippocamp, dolphin/Owl)
Meiron	2 AR Tyre: 1 AR (Dolphin/Owl) 1.02 g Sidon: 1 AR (Galley/King fighting a lion) 0.99 g

86. Bronze is highlighted in gray.

Site	Pre-Hellenistic Mint
Ras el Bassit – Posideion	4 AR Athens: 1 tetr. Aradus: 3 obols
Ras Shamra, environs	5 AR Athens: 2 AR Sidon: 1 shekel Aradus: 2 obols
Samaria, Palestine Exploration Fund, 1931–1933, 1935	3 AR + 3 AE? Philisto-Arabian imitations of Athenian tetr.: 3 Sidon: 3
Tel ʿIra	Sidon: 1 AR, ʿAbdashtart (370–358 BC)
Tel Dor	3 plated AR, 7 AE Sidon: 2 plated AR (0.58 g; 0.35 g); 6 AE Tyre: 1 plated AR (7.59 g) Philistia: 1 AE
Tel Michal	11 AR, 7 AE Evagoras II, Cyprus: 1 sixteenth Sidon: end of the 5th cent. BC. 1 thirty-second; ʿAbdashtart I 1 thirty-second, 1 sixteenth, 1 half-shekel, 7AE Tyre: 1 AR (4th cent. BC, 0.20 g) Philistia: 1 dr., 1 fraction of an obol, 2 obols(?) (0.50 g, 0.95 g), 1 hemidr.
Tel Michal 1996	11 AR, 1 AE Tyre 3: 1 AR (0.76 g), 1 AR (0.46 g), 1 AE (0.63 g) Sidon 8 AR: Straton I 5 sixteenth, 1 (4.98 g); 1 (2.46 g), 1 (3.95 g) Philistia: 1 AR (0.56 g)
Tell Keisan, Galilee	4 AR, 2 AE Tyre: 4 AR Sidon: 1 AE Tyre or Sidon?: 1 AE
Tell Sukas	2 AR Aradus : 2 AR

The most southerly Syrian mints to have struck fractions imitating Athenian types are Ashdod, Ascalon, and Gaza, which Gitler and Tal have now gathered under the Biblical name "mints of Philistia," in preference to the former nomenclature "philisto-arabian" that Mildenberg chiefly defended against other tags (Greco-Persian of Palestine, Egypto-Arabian, etc.).[87] Viewing the coinage with Athenian types as the premier coinage of the region, these authors uniformly present these types at the head of their catalogues. These mints produced the whole gamut of denominations: tetradrachms, didrachms, drachms, hemidrachms, and especially obols, hemiobols, and smaller fractions. There are no decadrachms, however. But there, as in Samaria and Judaea, drachms and fractions are the core issues. Identification poses no problem since most

87. Gitler, Tal 2006, pp. 31–36.

of the coins carry the city's complete or abbreviated name.[88] The presence of owls depends on the mint: Ashdod shows only five varieties versus 23 at Ascalon and 25 at Gaza. Variations on the theme of Athenian tetradrachms are very numerous. Investigation of circulation through isolated hoards and, especially, excavation coins shows that Philistine issues travel farther than those of Samaria and Judaea, both of which are limited to their region of origin: the coins of Philistia were also accepted in those northern territories.[89]

Gitler, Tal, and van Alfen have highlighted some curious coins with Athenian types in the form of a dome, struck with worn dies that were re-engraved and polished. These drachms, accompanied by some obols, show a generally smooth obverse, with the head of Athena still discernible on some specimens. The owl on the reverse remains more easily visible in outline. Dating from the fourth century, they are attributed to the region of Edom, south of Hebron and in the regions of Beersheba and Arad. A highly unusual instance of currency, they recall the silver dumps found in several *Hacksilber* hoards, which leads the three authors to suggest seeing here a transition from weighed silver to denominated money: "it may have helped to ease the acceptance of this new form of money to those who were reluctant to use it."[90]

In all, southern Levantine mints produced a large number of types inspired by Athenian tetradrachms. This widespread practice of iconographic borrowing means that these coins no longer belong, strictly speaking, to the "imitations" from which they diverge so much. Such proliferation is characteristic of these mints and their highly original typology that blends Persian, Cilician, Greek, and Egyptian influences with great creativity.[91] The popularity of Athenian tetradrachms and the flowering of derivatives they prompted in the southern Levant probably influenced the Arabian Peninsula. Gaza is the endpoint of the spice and incense route that begins in Arabia. The numerous owl imitations found there are usually seen in relation to this commercial route and the connections maintained between the peninsula and the Mediterranean coast. Owl issues start there rather late, at the end of the fourth century or the beginning of the third, at the time, that is, when the southern Levant under Ptolemaic domination ceases its own production. The connection, however, is not so simple, since no hoard from the Arabian Peninsula has turned up coins from the southern Levant, which are admittedly quite rare in local hoards, too.[92] The different kingdoms that dot the spice route along the west coast of Arabia produced coins with types inspired by Athenian owls, with some common features among them. A range of different sizes exists, from tetradrachms to hemidrachms. The metal is not necessarily pure silver: gold,[93] silver of varying grade, and bronze were also used. The

88. Ibid., p. 69.

89. Ibid., pp. 49–51; Gitler 2006a.

90. Gitler, Tal, van Alfen 2007, p. 52.

91. Cf., among others, Mildenberg 1997; Gitler 2000; Gitler, Tal 2006 for the catalogue. The coinage is not a special case, as Phoenician art shows: the *naos* with *uraei* of Amrit demonstrates Egyptian influence, the *ma'abed* of the same sanctuary borrows from the ancient East, the column capitals of the sanctuary of Eshmun at Sidon are perfectly Achaemenid, the anthropomorphic sarcophagi of Amrith or Sidon are in the Greek style.

92. Gitler, Lorber 2006, pp. 25–28.

93. Qataban: Huth 1999, p. 40, points out a very rare gold coin known only through two public sales (MMAG 25, 1962, 478; Crédit Suisse, 1, 1983, 157). It has a value mark on the cheek of Athena (*T*); assuming the gold/silver ratio is 13⅓, it is worth a tetradrachm.

techniques employed are sometimes startling: thus there is an incuse drachm of 4 g,[94] acquired by J. de Morgan at Muscat in Oman.[95] Other coins are struck on flans formed out of old coins hammered and then restruck.[96]

Owls are imitated in Arabia until the second century BC, whereupon the typology increasingly departs from the original types, preserving only one side and finally abandoning references to Athenian coinage altogether. The degradation is occasionally such that scholars wonder if they are not looking at imitations of imitations. The crude character of these coins should not deceive us as to their intent: neither cut nor chiseled coins are known. They were used as denominated money, not as ingots. Their face-value is sometimes exaggerated because some are in low-grade silver, or even bronze.

In the Sinai, in Jordan, and along the Red Sea, coins are typologically impoverished: overwhelmingly pseudo-Athenians, but impossible to mistake for the originals.[97] Athena is transformed into an Arab goddess and the reverse carries Aramaic inscriptions.[98] In the south, the kingdoms of Saba, Qataban, Ma'in, and Hadramaut essentially occupy present day Yemen. Their issues are principally imitations of Athenian tetradrachms.[99] The kingdom of Qataban first strikes light Attic tetradrachms (c. 16.80 g), but also didrachms (rare), drachms, and hemidrachms whose axis is generally at nine o'clock, as on the originals. All styles are represented, from imitation conforming to the prototype, to coins of completely local inspiration. Tetradrachms of the Pi style close to the originals are accordingly dated to the years 350–300 BC. Coins with degraded Athenian types continue to be struck until the second century. In eastern Arabia, the peoples occupying the present United Arab Emirates and Bahrain also struck owls, notably on flans made from old coins previously defaced and reshaped with a hammer.[100]

To sum up, the Near East lies at the geographic heart of a vast zone of diffusion for Athenian types, in the absence of authentic owls themselves. It also stands out for its early adoption of coinage compared to neighboring regions, and for its own currency production from the second half of the fifth century in Phoenicia and the fourth century in Samaria, Judaea, and Philistia. Mesopotamia, Iran, and Arabia, by contrast, did not really adopt coinage until the Hellenistic Age and only then, essentially, along trade routes.[101]

94. In the Levant, Phoenician coins from the end of the fifth century sometimes use this technique.

95. *BMC Arabia*, pl. L, 4; Huth, Qedar 1999, p. 297, pl. 27, 7.

96. Huth, Qedar 1999, p. 298, pl. 27, 11. For a similar practice in Athens in the latter half of the fourth century: coins struck on silver foil, folded in two, Flament 2007, pp. 32–33.

97. Cf. *BMC Arabia*; Munro-Hay 1996; Huth 1999.

98. Huth, Qedar 1999, pp. 295–96.

99. Huth 1999; Munro-Hay 2003.

100. Huth 1998.

101. Duyrat 2004; Duyrat 2014; Monerie 2013; Huth, van Alfen 2010.

Figure 4.12. Bronze of Sidon (ANS 1944.100.71326).

3. DAILY USE AND LOST COINS

Coinage from the Persian period appears in excavations in far smaller proportions than from the Hellenistic Age. Pre-Hellenistic coins from excavations in the catalogue amount to only 223 coins, silver and bronze combined, or roughly the number of Hellenistic coins discovered on the site of Tel Anafa alone (243 items), for example (Table 4.6).

Callataÿ, comparing results from 38 sites across the Greek world, entitles a paragraph "The Absolute Preponderance of Bronze since the Fourth Century BC."[102] This observation is not true for Syria prior to Alexander. Of the 223 Persian era coins found in excavations, 65 were bronze, or less than one-third.

The preponderance of silver is directly tied to the production of the region's mints, essentially in this metal, even if bronze makes an appearance at a date that is difficult to specify. The recent *corpora* of the Persian period for Tyre and Sidon entitle us to say that these two mints started striking bronze probably not much before the mid-fourth century, with a developed system of four denominations at Sidon (Fig. 4.12),[103] but only one at Tyre.[104] The fact that silver fractions are so numerous also reflects local production. Shekels, double shekels, and other tetradrachms are rare, as everywhere, large coinage being rarely lost. The Sidon mint is by far the best represented for bronze in Samaria and Galilee, where Sidonian influence was directly felt, as well as on the coast, where the city's fleet had anchorages as far as Al-Mina. The latter site also turns up some Aradian material in quantity, since Aradus contributed to currency circulation in northern Phoenicia from the fifth century.[105]

CONCLUSION

The circulation of Athenian tetradrachms and their high quality imitations is wide and varied, with a clearly international role. In contrast, fractions copying Athenian types enjoyed only local use and have a typology that, over time, departs from their originals. Their use is limited to the issuing mint's zone of influence. For both Arabian coins and those from Samaria-Judaea-Philistia, the prevailing sense is of an imitation at first careful, followed by adaptation that progressively combines Athenian obverses and local reverses, until only local types remain. Mildenberg sees in this the deep impression Athenian types made on the imagination. At least one of the types survives for a rather long time: the head of Athena in Asia Minor and the

102. Callataÿ 2006b, p. 178.
103. Elayi, Elayi 2004b, pp. 349–86.
104. Elayi, Elayi 2009b, pp. 192–200.
105. Elayi, Elayi 1993a, fig. 21.

Levant, the owl in Arabia.[106] He also considers this popularity a common system of reference, a constant for coinages that had no default, in contrast to what Schlumberger suggested in *L'argent grec dans l'empire achéménide*.[107] These imitations also display the mints' great adaptability. Consistency of types usually marks a successful coinage.[108] These imitations are not an indication of the issuing authorities' inability to create their own types.[109] On the contrary, they are the prolongation of the established original types. Allusion to Athenian coins guarantees exchange by endowing the coinage with features that reinforce the users' confidence. It permits inclusion in general currency circulation, where this coinage served as the standard.

Enquiry creates the impression that at the time of the Macedonians' arrival a large variety of coinages was available, a variety that innovations regularly enriched. To the general circulation of "owls", we may add that of Phoenician coinage, each mint with its own diffusion: wide for Sidon and Tyre, narrower for Aradus, and for Byblos limited to the city's own territory.[110] The coins from Samaria and Judaea, as well as from Philistine mints, circulate strictly regionally. Practices remain varied: denominated money seems to dominate, but it sometimes verges on bullion, at least in shape.[111] At the same time, weighed money, in the form of *Hacksilber*, continues in use, as a hoard dated to the late fourth century and found in the environs of Samaria attests.[112]

106. Mildenberg 1998 p. 65.
107. Schlumberger 1953, p. 25.
108. Kroll 2011, pp. 27–38.
109. Their inventiveness sometimes leads to weird results like the "Alexander owl" published in Wartenberg 1998.
110. Elayi, Elayi 1993a, pp. 322–37.
111. Like the drachms in the shape of a dome, Gitler, Tal, van Alfen 2007.
112. Gitler 2006b.

Chapter 5

Alexander and the Successors (333–280 BC)

Alexander's arrival in 333 BC at the head of powerful armies provoked political and rapid monetary upheavals. It is interesting to observe that, according to the chronology in the most recent studies of the hoards and Alexander's mints, the break, where currency is concerned, did not happen until the 320s. Until then, the traditional circulation described in the previous chapter carried on as usual, characterized by the dominance of Phoenician issues and Athenian tetradrachms and their imitations, along with the coinages of Judaea, Samaria, and Philistia in the southern Levant. It is only in the late 320s that these currencies disappear from hoards, displaced by tetradrachms with the types of Alexander. The Conqueror probably did not begin striking his own tetradrachms with personalized types until the autumn of 333 BC, in Tarsus. Up to that time, he continued his father's standard issues, on the Attic system for gold and the Macedonian for silver.[1] Thereafter, the output of initial silver issues seems to have been relatively modest until 323/2 BC at the earliest.[2] So it is only following Alexander's death that the volume of coins produced with his personal types grows to sizeable proportions in all mints. Monetary circulation in the third century is dependent upon these changes that occurred during this brief period.

1. A World in Transition: Alexander and his Successors in Syria

Alexander was victorious at the battle of Issus in November 333 BC, and advanced into Syria immediately after. We know that he spent the winter of 333/2 BC at Marathus, opposite the island of Aradus.[3] Achaemenid domination in Syria crumbled within a few months. Macedonian power, however, took some time to establish itself. Entrusted by Alexander to the weak Laomedon of Mytilene (Diodorus 18.3.1), the region endured the upheavals of the Successors' strug-

1. Le Rider 1977, pp. 393–95 (silver), 441–42 (gold); Le Rider 2003, pp. 47–63 (= Le Rider 2007, pp. 31–43).
2. Le Rider 2003, pp. 189–93 and pp. 299–319 for the eastern mints (= Le Rider 2007, pp. 139–43, 225–40); Duyrat 2005a, pp. 214–22 for Aradus.
3. Arrian, *Anabasis* 2.14.

gles. It was the transit point for fresh troops coming from the Mediterranean to join up with the army and for veterans returning home. After Alexander's death in 323, Perdiccas and his armies crossed through en route to Egypt (321 BC). Coveted by Ptolemy in 319 BC (Diodorus 18.33.1), Syria witnessed the flight of Eumenes before Antigonus Monophthalmus (Diodorus 18.73.2–4), domination by the latter and his son, Demetrius (Diodorus 19.85.4–5; 20.47.5), then, in 301 BC, conquest by Seleucus, even as Ptolemy grabbed for himself Syria and Phoenicia to the south (Diodorus 21.1.5; Justin 15.4.21–22). During this troubled period, currency circulation underwent comparatively slow changes, which nonetheless proved profound in the end.

1.1. Former Coinages in a New World (333–c. 325 BC)

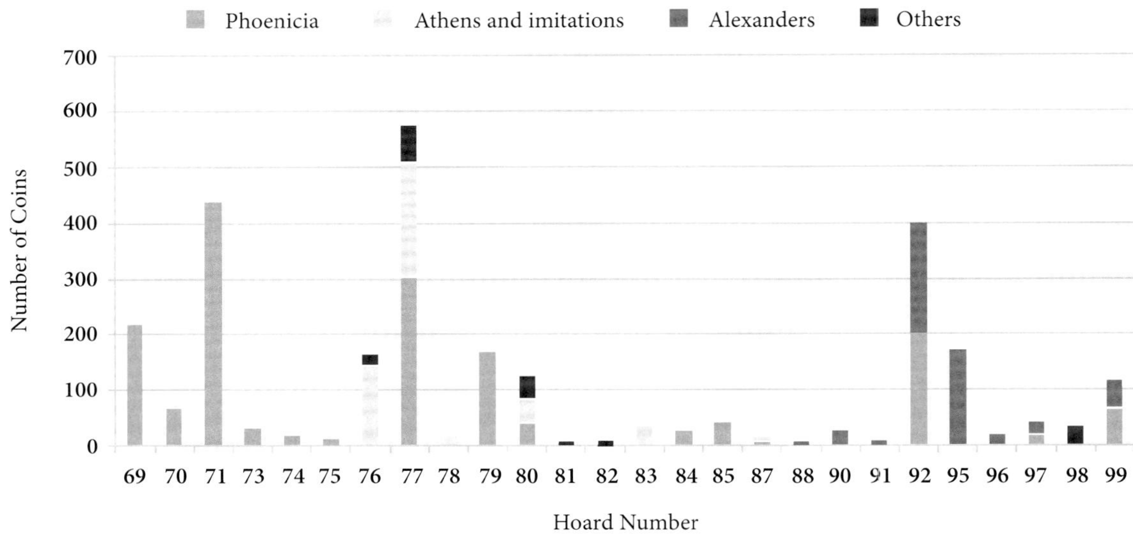

Figure 5.1. Evolution in the content of Syrian hoards, 333–319 BC.[4]

Figure 5.1 clearly reveals circulation little changed from what is observable before 333 BC (Fig. 4.6). Phoenician mints, Athenian owls and their imitations dominate in the first 17 hoards dated between 333 and 330 BC (**88**). Phoenician mints represent 70% of the coins found, Athens and its imitations 23%, and other mints just 7%.[5] These proportions are comparable to those existing before the Macedonian Conquest: 77%, 17%, and 4% respectively, with Philistine coins an additional 2%. Alexanders appear in hoards starting in 330 BC, a little after their production began.

Issues of tetradrachms with Alexander's own types began at Tarsus a little before or after the Battle of Issus, according to the generally accepted chronology.[6] He struck his first gold staters,

4. Hoards **93** and **94** have been eliminated from this chart because their considerable size (1,400 drachms and 7,200 gold staters) skewed the data from other hoards. The chart takes account of all hoards, no matter their content.
5. Including three hoards of coins from Philistia (**77**) and Judaea (**81**, **82**).
6. Le Rider 2003, pp. 15–26 and 155–70 (= Le Rider 2007, pp. 6–14, 113–125) summarizes the debate over this chronology.

Figure 5.2. Tetradrachm of Alexander struck at Sidon (ANS 1944.100.35184).

Figure 5.3. Tetradrachm of Alexander struck at Tyre (ANS 1944.100.35337).

Figure 5.4. Tetradrachm of Alexander struck at Aradus (ANS 1944.100.34594).

with head of Athena and a Nike, following the siege of Tyre (January–July, 332 BC), probably at Tarsus in 332/1 BC.[7] The output of mints in this region was not very important during his reign. It grew considerably after his death, however, probably from 323/2 BC, and was sustained during the following years. Le Rider compiled a comparative inventory of die studies from the mints of the region: Tarsus, Sidon (Fig. 5.2), Tyre (Fig. 5.3), Aradus (Fig. 5.4), Myriandros/Alexandria ad Issum, and Soli.[8] The volume increase in their emissions after 323 BC is not very meaningful (one–five dies a year[9]); only Aradus shows substantial numbers.[10] The chronology of Syrian hoards reflects that of the Alexander issues. Of the 19 hoards buried between 333 and 325 BC (**69–90**), only three contain Alexanders (**85**, **88**, **90**). The low level of output explains this relative rarity. The traditional currencies of the Persian Empire continue to be produced and exchanged. Hoards do not segregate the new currency from the old, proving the latter's validity. This is not always the case when a new coinage appears. In contrast, Ptolemy Soter's reform in Egypt at the end of the fourth century completely eradicated the former coinages in a

7. Ibid., pp. 182–88 (= Le Rider 2007, pp. 134–139).
8. Ibid., pp. 194–205 (= Le Rider 2007, pp. 143–152); summary table in Duyrat 2005b, p. 26.
9. Le Rider 2003, p. 200 (= Le Rider 2007, p. 149).
10. Duyrat 2005a, p. 215.

very short time.[11] In Syria, the old habits endure. The marked preference of southern Levantine populations for fractions during the Persian period has been noted. Around 320 BC, two hoards present us with, respectively, obols and hemiobols of Sidon with Alexander types, accompanied by a Philistine coin (**113**) and some bronzes of Alexander amidst bronzes of Tyre (**97**).

The combined circulation of Alexanders and coins from the Persian period is relatively poorly documented (**80**, **85**, **88**, **92**, **97**, **99**, **107**). Two finds at Byblos (*IGCH* 1496, **69**; *IGCH* 1515, **107**) illustrate this brief transition: the two vases, one ceramic, the other bronze, were buried beside one another, and the editors have seen this as a sign of common origin, despite the long burial time between these two caches, composed of Phoenician coins and Alexanders. Naster believed that "one may surely conclude from this that local coins still circulated for several years under Alexander and that then the new currency, on the Attic standard, because it was rather abundant, was able to replace the former currency on the Phoenician standard; the latter was then withdrawn, held in reserve in a pot by its owner. Then, a few years later, but prior to the Seleucid era, he safeguarded an amount of tetradrachms of Alexander and Philip Arrhidaeus in another vase, the two pots being buried or hidden together, perhaps in an emergency during the campaigns of the Successors."[12] While the details of this reconstruction for the history of these two deposits may be debatable, it nonetheless remains true that the hoards are evidence indeed of profound changes in currency circulation. Naster's commentary points up an anomaly in the transition: Attic owls and their imitations share the same standard as Alexander's new tetradrachms. Yet they are never hoarded together. In contrast, Phoenician coins are. Two other hoards combine Alexanders and earlier coinages: Khirbet el-Kerak hoard (**99**) was buried between 323 and 319 BC, according to its authors; the hoard from the region of Akko (**97**) was buried c. 320 BC.[13] These are the only two to have revealed an actual mix of currencies. Thus the transition seems to have been brief and relatively abrupt.

1.2. The Dominance of Alexanders (after c. 325 BC)

Beginning in 325 BC, there is an unmistakable swing: owls disappear completely from circulation. Phoenician mints represent no more than 35% of the coinage discovered, versus 61% for Alexanders and 4% for other currencies.[14] The end of the 320s also marks a turning point in the

11. Duyrat 2005b; Picard 2005. In the excavations by the Centre d'études alexandrines, Marcellesi 2012b, p. 172, identifies only seven foreign coins (nos. 1310, 1311, 1328–1330, 1335, 1338) later than Ptolemy Soter's reform compared with 1022 Ptolemaic issues.

12. "on peut dès lors sans doute en conclure que les monnaies locales ont encore circulé pendant plusieurs années sous Alexandre et qu'alors, le nouveau numéraire, de poids attique, étant assez abondant, a pu se substituer à l'ancien de poids phénicien; ce dernier a été alors retenu, mis en réserve dans un pot par son propriétaire, puis après quelques années, mais avant l'ère des Séleucides, ce dernier a mis en sécurité dans un autre vase une somme de tétradrachmes d'Alexandre et de Philippe Arrhidée, les deux pots étant déposés ou cachés conjointement peut-être à la suite d'un danger lors des campagnes des diadoques." Naster 1987, p. 46.

13. One silver fraction compared with 40 bronzes of Tyre and Alexander.

14. The dominance of Alexanders is even more overwhelming if one adds hoards **93** and **94** to the total: Alexanders then constitute 97% of the hoards' content. The three lots of gold coins from Saida (**93**) form, however, an exceptional find that does not reflect the ordinary circulation of the region.

production of coins with the types of Alexander the Great. Having begun at Tarsus in 333/2 BC for silver and after July 332 BC for gold, it remained modest until Alexander's death.[15] Numerous mints become active only after 325, probably even after June 323 BC.[16] Production grows substantially only after 323 BC, in Cilicia, Phoenicia, Cyprus,[17] and Babylon[18] simultaneously. This clearly noticeable increase certainly explains why Alexanders rapidly become omnipresent in Syrian hoards.

After 324 BC, while the number of preserved hoards rises substantially, local coinages current in the Persian period now appear in only eight hoards (**97**, **98**, **99**, **107**, **112**, **113**, **132**, **133**[19]), often haphazardly. A fraction and 22 bronzes of Tyre in a hoard overwhelmingly consisting of bronzes (**97**), 34 obols from a southern Levantine mint weighing in total 11.41 g of silver (**98**), eight other obols (**112**), two double shekels buried amidst 139 Alexanders (**107**), and one fraction from the southern Levant (**113**) represent tiny amounts. Only the Khirbet el-Kerak hoard (**99**), c. 320/319 BC, revealed a majority of higher denominations from Sidon and Tyre. This break in the nature of circulation does not therefore mean that Alexander, and especially his successors, sought to impose an imperial currency on their new possessions. If such were the case, Alexander would not have waited so long to create a coinage with his types, and he would surely have sought to expand it, which was not the case. The jump in output is after his death and is the work of his successors. But the volume produced, especially at Amphipolis, Babylon, and Aradus, was enough to penetrate the market, leading to a substantial increase in available coinage. Map 7 illustrates this dense circulation from the last quarter of the fourth century, notably in southern Syria, between Byblos and Gaza. Their quality and quantity certainly contributed a great deal to the popularity of these coins. Must we infer a systematic restriking of existing coinages, as Kraay and Moorey have suggested for Cypriot coins of the Persian period?[20] Metal analyses might perhaps provide at least a partial answer to this question.

The influx of tetradrachms with types of Alexander in the region is clear during the last quarter of the fourth century. I studied the provenance of these coins in 2005 through 10 hoards.[21] The present corpus doubles the number of hoards containing tetradrachms of Alexander and of Philip III with the Conqueror's types (21 in total).[22] Their provenances break down as shown in Table 5.1:

This increase in evidence does not significantly alter the dispersion by number of hoards. There are twice as many hoards in all regions except Alexandria, still attested by just four hoards.

15. Le Rider 2003, pp. 26–28 (= Le Rider 2007, pp. 14–16).
16. Le Rider 2003, pp. 124–28 and 131 (= Le Rider 2007, pp. 88–92 and 94).
17. Le Rider 2003, pp. 195–98 (= Le Rider 2007, pp. 144–147).
18. Le Rider 2003, pp. 316–19 (= Le Rider 2007, pp. 238–40).
19. The last two hoards are later than 261 and consist of coins of Judaea, the Jerusalem mint being the only one to continue issuing.
20. Kraay, Moorey 1968, pp. 220–21.
21. Duyrat 2005b, p. 34.
22. Hoards **85**, **90**, **91**, **95**, **96**, **99**, **100**, **101**, **103**, **104**, **105**, **106**, **107**, **108**, **109**, **110**, **111**, **115**, **117**, **119**, **122**. Other hoards contained Alexanders, but their exact content is not known: **92**, **102**.

Table 5.1. Provenance of tetradrachms of Alexander in Syrian hoards of the fourth century

Origin	1st Place[23]	Hoards[24]	n[25]
Macedonia	0	14	262
Asia Minor	0	13	146
Cyprus	1	10	78
Syria-Phoenicia	11	20	535
Babylon	9	19	490
Alexandria	0	4	18
Total	**21**	**21**	**1,630**

The progression in number of specimens also remains similar, as the following table (Table 5.2) shows.

The only real change occurs with the switch in first place, held by Babylon in my earlier observations, but nosed out now by Syria-Phoenicia. The latter holds first place by number of specimens in the current state of the corpus. Moreover, Syria-Phoenicia dethrones Babylon overall in the number of hoard first places. In 2005, these mints were first in only two hoards out of 10, versus seven out of 10 for Babylon. The catalogue's new entrants raise the local mints to 11 out of 21 hoards, versus nine out of 21 for Babylon. The question then arises of squaring these results with what we know about the output of local mints from Babylon to Amphipolis. Waggoner never published the catalogue by dies that she was preparing for Babylon, and the data are therefore missing.[26] In contrast, Troxell provided an imposing study of the dies of Amphipolis that revealed no fewer than 740 obverse tetradrachm dies.[27] In the current state of our knowledge, Macedonian output leads in Alexander's empire. Levantine productions are more difficult to get a grasp on. The following chart (Fig. 5.5) gives the percentages of silver coins from Babylon, Amphipolis (to which are sometimes added tetradrachms attributed to Pella or "Macedonia"), and Levantine mints (Myriandros, Aradus, Byblos, Sidon, and Tyre). Some other mints, such as those of Cyprus or Asia Minor, are not mentioned because they are still quite insignificant.

These hoards contain only tetradrachms, hence only silver. The Levantine mints are often well represented compared to Babylon, and especially Amphipolis. If we add in gold production, their output indeed seems far from negligible. Aradus (Fig. 5.6), whose production totals permit us to think that it was the one of the foremost mints on the coast,[28] is nevertheless not

23. Number of times a region occupies first place in a hoard total.
24. Number of hoards containing coins coming from this region.
25. Total number of coins coming from this region.
26. An outline of this study in Waggoner 1979.
27. Troxell 1997, p. 26.
28. Duyrat 2005a, p. 214; Duyrat, forthcoming.

Table 5.2. Provenance of tetradrachms of Alexander in Syrian hoards of the fourth century: Duyrat 2005b and current study compared

Origin	% in Duyrat 2005b	% in Present Corpus
Macedonia	16%	17%
Asia Minor	10%	10%
Cyprus	5%	5%
Syria-Phoenicia	32%	35%
Babylon	36%	32%
Alexandria	1%	1%

well represented in these hoards, compared to neighboring mints. Appearing in 13 hoards, issues from Aradus constitute 27% of the total of Levantine tetradrachms therein, but they are not the most numerous in hoards **91** and **95**. A die study based on an up-to-date corpus of the mints of Tyre and Sidon might give different results from those currently apparent.

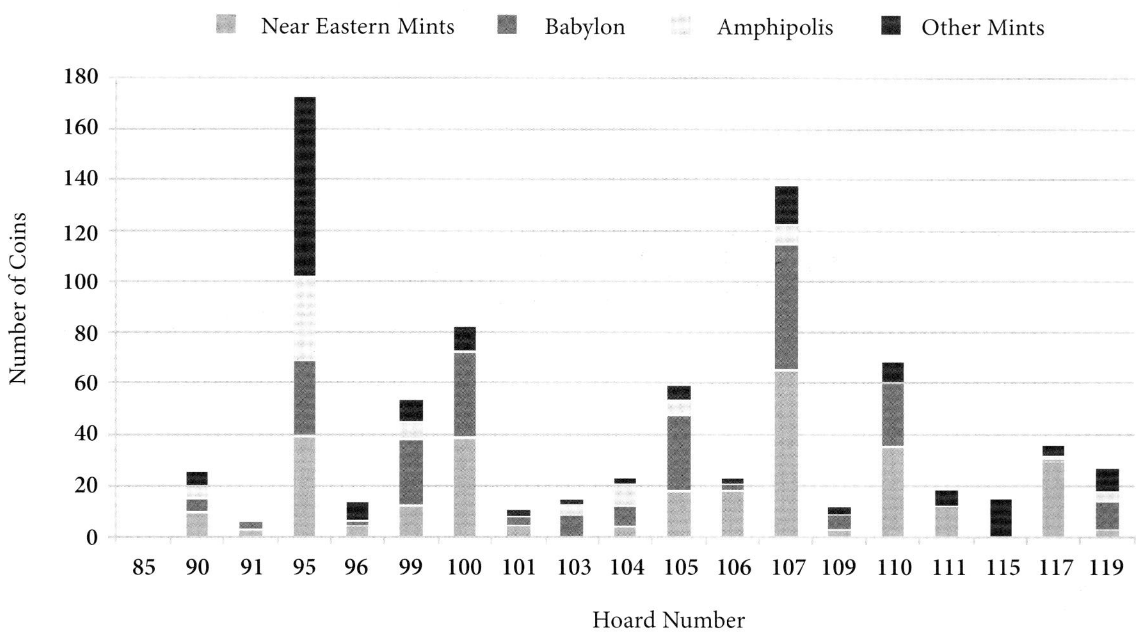

Figure 5.5. Provenance of silver Alexanders in fourth-century hoards.[29]

29. Hoard **108** has been left out of this chart because its unusual volume skewed the findings. It consists of 221 tetradrachms from Levantine mints, 248 from Babylon, 156 from Amphipolis, and 213 from diverse other mints, only confirming the results from other hoards.

Figure 5.6. Gold stater of Alexander struck at Aradus (ANS 1944.100.34548).

As well studied as Alexander's silver currency is, the bronze has remained just as much on the research periphery. Price lists five Syrian mints that struck this metal for the Conqueror: Myriandros, Ake/Tyre, Aradus, Byblos, and Sidon.[30] All these issues come after Alexander's death. According to Le Rider, one must probably add the mint of Posideion, which marks its output with the letters AP: "Since so many specimens of this issue were discovered at Bassit (13, it seems, out of 17 legible Alexander bronzes), and since some others were found at Al-Mina (7 out of 70 legible Alexander bronzes), I would definitely suggest looking for a local attribution. Now there happens to be the village of Posideion, generally located at Bassit, despite an attempt to situate it at Al-Mina. The inhabitants of Posideion, in the last part of the fourth century, struck a silver issue and a bronze issue in their name and types: they therefore had the means to operate a mint, and so the attribution of the issue of bronzes with the letters AP to Posideion does not seem impossible."[31] None of these series has benefited from a die study. But archaeological evidence can provide some enlightenment (Table 5.3).

The distribution of bronzes is also interesting because it is very uneven (Map 8). The 21 sites where they have turned up show that they are an imperial coinage, just like gold and silver, insofar as their circulation is not limited to the few mints that produced them. Quantities are, however, negligible: these coins seem to have been only a very modest addition to the production with types of Alexander in precious metal. Al Mina has revealed a completely exceptional number: 179 specimens from neighboring mints, Aradus, Byblos, Tarsus, Cypriot Salamis, and, according to Le Rider's identification, some specimens from Posideion. Since Al Mina, despite the presence of some later bronzes, was abandoned c. 300 BC, this concentration is not insignificant and suggests a strong Macedonian presence there for a sufficiently long enough time for these coins to have been used and lost. The presence of five coins of Philip II, not found on other sites studied, reinforces this feeling. The 30–40 illegible fragments attributed to Aradus or Alexander are most assuredly also Macedonian bronzes, since the Aradus mint did not begin to issue its own autonomous bronzes until the late 240s.[32] They could be Aradian bronzes from the

30. Price 1991a: no. 3232 for Myriandros, 3268 and 3269 for Ake/Tyre, 3311, 3334, and 3335 for Aradus, 3425, 3427, and 3428 for Byblos, 3469, 3492, and 3493 for Sidon.

31. "Puisque tant d'exemplaires de cette émission ont été découverts à Bassit (13, semble-t-il, sur les 17 bronzes alexandrins lisibles), et que quelques autres ont été trouvés à Al-Mina (7 sur 70 bronzes alexandrins lisibles), je suggèrerais de rechercher une attribution résolument locale. Or il existe la ville de Posideion, qu'on place généralement à Bassit, malgré une tentative de la situer à Al Mina. Les habitants de Posideion, dans la dernière partie du IVe siècle, ont frappé à leur nom et à leurs types une émission d'argent et une émission de bronze: ils avaient donc les moyens de faire fonctionner un atelier monétaire, et, de ce fait, l'attribution à Posideion de l'émission de bronzes aux lettres AP ne paraît pas impossible." Le Rider 1986a, p. 399.

32. Duyrat 2005a, p. 44.

Persian period, although these are not attested in other excavations and appear only in the Samaria hoard (**50**). This hypothesis, however, need not necessarily be excluded, given the strong representation of Aradian silver in the Al Mina excavations. The other coins revealed on the site are two drachms of Philip III with types of Alexander, a bronze struck perhaps by a Successor, and 12 others of the Seleucids and Ptolemies. The early years of the Macedonian presence are therefore over-represented.

Al Mina aside, Alexander issues are not so frequent in excavations. Twelve sites out of 21 have revealed silver: Al Mina, Antioch on the Orontes, Balatah, Dura Europos, Jablah (necropolis of al-Jbeibat), Jebel Khalid, Ras el Bassit-Posideion, Ras Shamra, Seleuceia Pieria, Tel Michal, Tell Ain el-Beida, and Tell Sukas. The majority of single finds from the Persian period are in this metal. The end of the fourth century resembles what was observed before the conquest. Only Ras el Bassit-Posideion (**40**), Ras Shamra (**8**), and Tell Sukas (**10** or **12**[33]) have more than five bronze specimens. Alexanders are, moreover, everywhere incidental. The location of these sites is not fortuitous: they are all in a perimeter close by Al Mina, to the north of the continental hinterland of Aradus (Map 8), leading one to suppose that the phenomenon observed on that site has affected the entire region, which for a few years was able to use bronzes with the types of Alexander. The fact that Macedonian troops, because of the coast's strategic importance,[34] were stationed in the Aradian Peraea during the winter of 333/2 BC justifies an assumption of longer term garrisoning that would explain the more intensive use of these coins. This concentration of coins tied to the presence of a foreign army is not a unique case.[35] At the time of the Chremonidean War (267–261 BC), the admiral of the Egyptian fleet, Patroclus, established military camps on the east coast of Attica, where a significant number of Ptolemaic coins have turned up.[36] Similarly, bronzes of Antiochus II reveal the presence of a Seleucid garrison at Kabyle in Bulgaria.[37]

North of Aradus, the excavation of the necropolis of Al-Jbeibat, at Jablah (the ancient Gabala), conducted by Badawi, uncovered a particularly interesting tomb in September, 2009.[38] Eight coins of quite different nature accompanied the deceased. The oldest were two fractions of Aradus struck in the fourth century.[39] There were, additionally, five Alexander drachms struck at the mints of Salamis on Cyprus,[40] Colophon,[41] Lampsacus and one uncertain mint.[42] The last

33. The references in Lund 1986 to *SNG Copenhagen* are mistaken twice: he mentions two silver coins, but the citation in the Copenhagen collection is for bronze coins.

34. Arrian, *Anabasis*, 2.17.

35. See the case of Ras Ibn Hani, p. 357.

36. Chryssanthaki 2005, pp. 165–66.

37. Draganov 1993, pp. 57–60; Draganov 1994, pp. 280–82.

38. Badawi 2009, tomb K-20002, pp. 327–28.

39. Bearded head right/ ship right on three wavy lines; Phoenician legend *M'* in the field above. *BMC Phoenicia* 27–34.

40. Price 1991a, no. 2578 or 2580.

41. Price 1991a, nos. 1750 and 1761.

42. Price 1991a, no. 1385 or 1389 or 1394.

Table 5.3. Alexander-type coins on Syrian sites

Site	Hellenistic Mints
Al Mina, 1936	6 AR, 197 AE, 30–40 illegible fragments Philip II: 5 AE Alexander III: 1 tetr. (Myriandros), 2 dr. (Amphipolis, Pella), 1 obol, 179 AE (Byblos, Aradus, Salamis, Tarsus, uncert.) Philip III: 2 dr.
Antioch on the Orontes, 1932–1939	1086: 3 AR, 1083 AE Alexander III 6: 1 tetr. Aradus, 1 dr. uncert., 4 AE (1 Cyprus, 3 uncert.)
Balatah	2 AR, 51 AE Alexander III: 1 dr.
Beirut (Bey 006 et 045)	299 AE and 2 dr. AR Alexander III: 2 AE Macedonia?
Castle of ʻAtlit	22 AE Alexander III: 1 AE
Dura Europos	1,207 AE, 2 dr., 1 tetr. plated Alexander III 4: 1 tetra. plated, mint uncert.; 1 AE Tarsus; 1 Phoenicia?; 1 uncert.
Jablah, necropolis of al-Jbeibat	1 AV, 5 AR Alexander III: 5 dr. (Salamis on Cyprus, 2 Colophon, Lampsacus, Magnesia? perhaps plated)
Jaffa	138 AE Alexander III: 12 (11 Macedonia, 1 Babylon)
Jebel Khalid	264 AE, 1 AR Alexander III: 1 dr. Lampsacus (?); 1 tetr. uncert.
Ras el Bassit - Posideion	90: 6 AR, 84 AE Alexander III 40: 13 AE Posideion; 1 tetr. and 2 AE Tarsus; 1 dr. Mylasa; 1 dr. Lampsacus?; 2 dr. and 20 AE uncert.
Ras Shamra, environs	3 AR, 22 AE Alexander III 8: 1 tetr. Byblos; 2 AE Tarsus; 1 AE Aradus, 1 dr. and 3 AE uncert.
Samaria	308 AE Alexander III: 2 AE
Seleuceia Pieria , 1932–1939	273: 3 AR, 270 AE Alexander III 3: 1 dr. plated uncert., 1 AE Cyprus, 1 AE uncert.
Tel ʻIra	40 AE Alexander III: 1 AE (Macedonian shield/?)
Tel Anafa	242 AE + 1 tetr. plated Alexander III: 2
Tel Dor	5 AR, 67 AE Alexander III: 5 AE
Tel Michal	128: 66 AR, 62 AE Alexander III 16 AR: 1 obol fraction with Babylonian lion; 2 tetr., 1 hemidr. Aradus; 1 tetr. Ake/Tyre; 2 tetr. Babylon; 1 tetr. Pella; 8 dr. uncert.
Tel Michal 1996	7 AE Alexander III: 4 AE

Site	Hellenistic Mints
Tell Ain el-Beida	1 AR, 10 AE Alexander III: 1 dr.
Tell Daruk - Usnu	9 AE Alexander III: 3 Aradus (?), 1 uncert.
Tell Sukas	29 (incl. 4 AR?) Alexander III 14: 1 tetr., 2 dr., 1 AR or AE, 1 AE Aradus?; 9 AE uncert.

coin was a rare gold stater of Ptolemy Soter on the Attic standard, representing, on the obverse, the head of Alexander right, draped in an elephant skin, and on the reverse a ship's prow right, without legend. Svoronos dates it to 311 BC.[43] An officer stationed at Saida acquired another specimen of the same type prior to 1860.[44] Besides the rarity of this coin of Ptolemy Soter, a *hapax* in Syria, the content of this tomb brings together coins of the Persian period, Alexander, and one of the Successors. This is a rather rare piece of evidence, in view of what the hoards tell us, from this relatively brief transitional period when all these currencies were in circulation.

2. ALEXANDER'S GOLD

The striking of gold was exceptional in Syria and chiefly seen in coinage with the types of Alexander. Later, the Seleucids and Ptolemies also produced coins in this metal, but these did not circulate widely in the region. The production of gold with types of Alexander therefore represents a singular moment in Syria's monetary history. Even without its own production, the region could have revealed hoards with foreign coins in this metal if there had been a demand for gold. Western Asia Minor struck electrum in Ionia and in Lydia in the sixth century, then gold in the form of Croeseids and *darics*. Investigation of Syrian hoards of the fifth and fourth centuries has shown that *sigloi* are found only exceptionally in this region. There are no *daric*s either, and certainly no electrum issues or Croeseids.

Philip II of Macedon, thanks to the mines around Pangaeum, produced significant quantities of gold coins, and the success of these issues meant that his son continued them after his death and that the Celtic peoples of northern Europe copied them. Alexander the Great, up until 332 BC, employed coinage with his father's types. The total output of Philips rises to 250 obverse dies. It is difficult to differentiate these strikings of Alexander from his father's. The Philips of Alexander could represent 160 obverse dies placed in service between 336 and 332 BC in the Amphipolis mint(?).[45]

Some staters of Philip II were found in the hoards of Saida (*IGCH* 1508, **93**) and Beirut (*IGCH* 1518, **116**), probably in large amounts. These two deposits were impressive: around 7,200 gold coins for the former and probably a thousand (intermingled with bronze?) for the latter. In the case of Saida, the Philips apparently total 302 at least. Their volumes notwithstand-

43. Svoronos 1904–1908, pl. I, 22–23; Lorber, forthcoming, 38.
44. Mentioned in Westermark 1979–1980, apropos of the discovery of the Saida hoard (*IGCH* 1508, **93**).
45. Le Rider 2003, pp. 55–60 (= Le Rider 2007, pp. 37–41), based on Le Rider 1977.

ing, these two hoards are still quite isolated when compared to the heavy density of finds of staters of Philip in the northern Aegean and Thrace.

Alexander began his gold issues with personal types in the year following his invasion of Syrian territory. In July, 332 BC, his victory over Tyre, after a siege on land and sea, was his sole naval triumph. This perhaps explains the choice of type on the reverse of his gold coins. It represents a Nike holding a *stylis*, the ship's ensign on which the name of a vessel's protecting deity was inscribed, and which the winner of a naval battle seized and appropriated as a trophy. This is a very apposite choice, since the recruiting of the kings of Aradus and Byblos with their fleets in 333 BC, soon followed by the kings of Cyprus, and the final victory over Tyre in July, 332 BC, gave Alexander uncontested maritime supremacy.[46]

Tarsus was surely the first mint to strike gold with types of Alexander, as it was for tetradrachms.[47] Phoenician mints probably followed quite rapidly. Although other mints have revealed a large gamut of denominations, from the distater to eighths by way of the stater, half-stater, and quarter-stater, the mints of Aradus, Byblos, Tyre, and Sidon kept mainly the stater, with the exception of some distater issues at Aradus, Byblos and Sidon.[48] Because Syria had no gold mines, the metal had to be procured elsewhere. Callataÿ has attempted to evaluate the amounts of precious metal Alexander confiscated in Persian treasuries. He estimates 180,000 talents were seized at Damascus, Gaugamela, Susa, Persepolis, and Pasargadae between November, 333, and the winter of 331/30 BC, and stored temporarily at Ecbatana.[49] Although financial accounts do not generally distinguish between the two metals, following the Greek practice of viewing silver as the standard of reference, the quantities of gold available were clearly considerable.

Metallic analyses now provide ways to characterize the gold and to attempt to follow the coined metal's evolution. Using the results of Gondonneau's thesis, which were based on analyses through proton activation and LA-ICP-MS,[50] Guerra and Gondonneau tried to determine if Alexander reused Persian gold to strike his own gold staters. They analyzed gold Croeseids (7), *darics* (18), Philips (from his lifetime or posthumous: 42), and Alexander staters (from his lifetime or posthumous: 44). These analyses show that "the coinages struck in the former Persian Empire ... have a similar chemical composition, characterized by higher levels of platinum and palladium."[51] In contrast, Macedonian issues of Philips and Alexanders divide into two groups: until Alexander, the gold contains tiny amounts of platinum; beginning with Philip III, platinum is clearly present. This chronology coincides perfectly with Le Rider's, which shows an interruption in striking between 328 and 323 BC. Between these two dates, supplies surely changed. These analyses therefore allow us to distinguish two golds, one probably Macedonian

46. Le Rider 2003, pp. 27–28 (= Le Rider 2007, pp. 15–16).
47. Le Rider 2003, pp. 186–87 (= Le Rider 2007, pp. 134–39).
48. Duyrat 2005a, no. 538; Price 1991a, nos. 3331A, 3459, 3462.
49. Callataÿ 1989, pp. 260–62.
50. Gondonneau 2001.
51. "les monnayages frappés dans l'ancien empire perse [...] ont une composition chimique proche, caractérisées par de plus fortes teneurs en platine et en palladium." Guerra, Gondonneau 2000, p. 99.

Table 5.4. Mints striking gold with Alexander types

Period	Amphipolis	Aegae	Pella	Lysimacheia	Sestos	Lampsacus	Abydos	Alex. Troas	Colophon	Chios	Ephesus	Magnesia	Miletus	Teos	Sardis	Side	Tarsus	Citium	Salamis	Amathous
332–317	x	x	x			x	x					x	x	x	x	x	x	x	x	x
317–300				x	x	x	x		x			x		x	x				x	
300–280	x					x	x				x		x							
280–270	x					x														
270–225						x		x		x										
225–200																				

Period	Myriandros	Ake/Tyre	Aradus	Beirut	Byblos	Sidon	Babylon	Carrhae	Ecbatana	Seleuc. ad Tigrim	Susa	Alexandria	Cyrene	Mesambria	Odessus	Callatis	Istros	Tyras	Sinope
332–317	x	x	x	x	x	x	x				x	x							
317–300		x	x			x	x	x	x	x	x	x	x						
300–280		x					x		x	x									
280–270															x				
270–225														x	x	x	x	x	
225–200															x				x

Table 5.5. Number of mints striking gold Alexanders

Period	Active Mints
332–317	23
317–300	19
300–280	9
280–270	3
270–225	8
225–220	2

(Pangaeum?), with little platinum and palladium content, the other, however, characterized by manifestly higher amounts. In this group are the *darics* and Alexanders of the eastern mints, which might then be the result from melting the Great King's gold reserves, coined or not.

Alexander, therefore, probably had the wherewithal to monetize quite large quantities of gold at the Babylonian and Syrian mints. The six coastal mints, moreover, struck this metal in his lifetime, as the table in Table 5.4, based on Price's catalogue, demonstrates.[52]

Table 5.4 situates Syrian mints within the context of all gold production with the types of Alexander. They rank among the leaders, out of 23 mints active between c. 332 and c. 317 BC, representing more than a quarter of estimated production. But they maintain these gold issues only for the reigns of Alexander and the Successors. Thus they share a general tendency as revealed by the number of mints involved with these issues established in Table 5.5.

Even though their production did not last long, it is all the same noteworthy that Alexander felt the need to have six official sites striking gold on the Levantine coast. It is not insignificant that, generally speaking, the mints striking Alexanders preferred silver to gold, always; Price counted 110 issuing silver versus only 39 that put out gold. These mints were located just where Alexander and his successors needed them: as close as possible to where payments in these currencies were to be made. In contrast, east of Babylonia, there is no known Alexander mint. Le Rider, relying on a passage in Arrian (*Anab.* 4.18.7), concludes that the Macedonian conqueror did not open mints in the East because he employed the *daric* there, which he had in abundance after capturing the royal treasuries at Gaugamela, Babylon, Susa, Persepolis, and Pasargadae. In the Eastern regions, the use of silver bullion and payments in kind complemented this highly valued currency, not to mention Greek silver coins, especially Athenian tetradrachms and their imitations, which the Macedonian coffers must have held in quantity.[53]

To assess the relative ranking of eastern mints, it would be useful to know their production volume. Die studies, reflecting its importance, are much more numerous for gold than for the other metals or alloys,[54] but they still remain rather few. Even so, it is possible to compare the

52. Price 1991a, pp. 72–76.
53. Le Rider 2003, pp. 323–27 (= Le Rider 2007, pp. 243–46).
54. Callataÿ 1997b, pp. 322–23.

Table 5.6. Gold coin production of some Alexander mints[55]

Mint[56]	d	n	d x 20	d of Drachms
Amphipolis ("lifetime")[57]	108	347	2,160	3,516[58]
Lampsacus (329/8–302/1)	73	160	1,460	384
Abydos (325/4–302/1)	73	230	1,460	254
Sardis (330–298/7)	56	181	1,120	242
Miletus (325–300/294)	44	160	880	150
Aradus (333?–316)	25	80	500	1,056[59]

sole Phoenician mint for which a complete die study exists, Aradus, with the neighboring mints of Asia Minor and with Amphipolis (Table 5.6).

Thompson studied the gross gold production of Asia Minor mints.[60] Callataÿ has shown that it was more important, in absolute value, than that of the silver issued by these mints essentially in the form of drachms. Although the number of drachm dies put in service is quite important—between 150 and 384—one gold stater is worth 20 drachms, and so the output from gold dies surpasses that from silver in value.[61] The Asia Minor mints are thus preeminently producers of gold staters, by absolute value. Amphipolis presents a more balanced ratio. On the other hand, the production of Aradus, by absolute value, is chiefly tetradrachms (Table 5.7).

Table 5.7. Place of gold in Aradian output, by absolute value[62]

Period	% of Production
333–323 BC	42%
323–320 BC	21%
320–316 BC	49%

The drop in the years following Alexander's death is owing to the considerable increase in strikes of tetradrachms, which represent 182 obverse dies, or 77% of production. These few

55. The first three columns of this table refer to production of gold coins: d = number of stater obverse dies observed; n = number of known specimens; d x 20 = number of obverse dies multiplied by 20 to obtain an artificial equivalence in drachms (1 gold stater = 20 silver drachms). The last column indicates the number of known silver drachm obverse dies for the mint, to be compared with the previous column.

56. For Lampsacus, Abydos, Sardis and Miletus see Callataÿ 1997b, nos. 200, 204, 213 and 223.

57. Troxell 1997, p. 100.

58. The Amphipolis mint in fact employed 879 tetradrachm dies between c. 332 and c. 310 BC (Troxell 1997, p. 26),which are multiplied by 4 to arrive at a result comparable with the Asia Minor mints. The gold/silver ratio cannot be calculated like for like, since Troxell's study does not deal with exactly the same production periods for gold and silver. So these figures are provided as merely indicative, for want of anything better.

59. The Aradus mint employed 264 tetradrachm obverse dies during this period. They are multiplied by 4 here.

60. Thompson 1983 and 1991.

61. Callataÿ 1994.

62. Following Duyrat 2005a, p. 215.

Table 5.8. General circulation of Alexander's gold staters (*IGCH* and *CH*)

Region	c. 330–230 BC	c. 230–130 BC	c. 130–30 BC	Total
Greece	*IGCH* 47 (= *CH* 9.102), 77, 92, 121, 123, 134 (= *CH* 2.62), 143, 148, *CH* 7.64 (= *CH* 9.129), 8.169, 175, 177, 181, 203, 259, 261 (= *CH* 10.66), 276, 10.40			18 (22.5%)
Macedonia-Black Sea	*IGCH* 395, 396, 399 (= *CH* 9.105), 400 (= *CH* 9.119), 401, 408 (= *CH* 9.88), 409 (= *CH* 9.94), 410, 414, 774, 775, 777, 796, 797, 798, 799, 800, 801, 840, 853, 865, *CH* 2.50, 3.29 (?), 4.28, 6.15, 8.191, 9.106, 107, 10.33, 34, 46, 60, 81	*IGCH* 866 (= *CH* 10.93), 958 (= *CH* 1.93 = 3.44)	*CH* 8.122	36 (45%)
Russia	*IGCH* 1108, 1109, 1110, 1111			4
Asia Minor	*IGCH* 1369 (= *CH* 8.324), 1396, 1441, 1442, *CH* 7.48	*IGCH* 1404, 1449 (imitations)		7
Cyprus	*IGCH* 1472			1
Near East	*IGCH* 1508 (= *CH* 9.190), 1518, *CH* 2.70 (8.312), 5.35			4 (5.8%)
Egypt	*IGCH* 1672, 1673			2
Italy	*IGCH* 1932, 1937 (= *CH* 10.401?), 1955, *CH* 8.183			4
Sicily	*IGCH* 2143, 2196, 2204, *CH* 7.59			4
Total	**75 (93.75%)**	**4**	**1**	**80**

numbers show that, while the amount of gold dies in service in the mints is not necessarily very high, their share in output, by value, has to be reconsidered.

The table by periods (Table 5.5) shows that the end of the wars of the Successors at the beginning of the third century brought about a reduction in issues and the end of striking gold in numerous mints: of roughly 20 between 333 and 300 BC, no more than nine mints remain in 300–280 BC, and only three in 280–270 BC. It is likely that gold was only struck in the East for military purposes. Local mints had never issued gold coins previously, and finds in Syria are rare, although they do occur in numerous foreign hoards.

The geographic dispersion of hoards with Alexander staters (Table 5.8) does not align with the mints' geography. Between 330 and 230 BC, the area from Greece to the Black Sea has revealed 54 hoards, 67.5% of the total, versus four for the Near East. Everywhere Alexanders circulate jointly with Philips, and these two currencies are the only ones hoarded in two-thirds of these finds. The final third also contain Lysimachi, staters of Demetrius Poliorcetes, Seleucus I,

Table 5.9. Hoards of gold staters with types of Alexander in Syria

No.	Find Spot	No. IGCH or CH	Date	Content
93	Saida	*IGCH* 1508 = *CH* 8.190 = Noe 881, 882, 884	323–320	7,200+ AV in three lots Philip II: Westermark: 6+ st. (2 Pella, 4 Amphipolis). *IGCH*: 302+ Alexander III: Westermark: 17+ st. (2 Amphipolis, 2 Salamis, 1 Citium, 1 Lampsacus, 2 Miletus, 3 Sardis, 5 Sidon, 1 uncert.). *IGCH*: 6,000+ st. and some double st., many of Sidon down to local year 10 and Ake-Ptolemais to year 24 Ptolemy I: 1+ st. (intrusion?) Chios: Westermark: 10+ st.; 8 in Le Rider 1963 Panticapeion: 1+ Pergamum: 2+ st. Rhodes: 3+ Salamis on Cyprus, Pnytagoras: 2
116	Beirut	*IGCH* 1518 = Noe 133	300	1,000 AV, AE, in a pot Philip II Alexander III
137	Near East	*CH* 5.35	250	Some AV Alexander III: staters Seleucids: staters

and some municipal issues. This exclusivity is even more marked north of the Aegean: out of 36 hoards found from Macedonia to the Black Sea, only six contain anything else but Philips and Alexanders. This region absorbs gold currency, to the extent of compensating for the decrease in production in the Mediterranean world after 270 BC, by opening up its own mints that are the last to issue coins with these types at a time when all the other mints shut down.[63]

Nearly two-thirds of these hoards were buried before 300 BC, that is, during the time when the largest number of mints are open and production reaches its highest level. Circulation ceases completely after the third century, with the closure of nearly all the mints after 230 BC. One has to conclude that the hoarding of these high-value and quite rare coins was almost immediate, as Touratsoglou, using a totally different approach, shows for Macedonia.[64]

In this circulation with its northern orientation, hoards found in Syria appear marginal, but still instructive (Table 5.9).

Hoard **137** is only known from a brief mention in *Coin Hoards* and seems to have contained just some staters, with no further clarification. The Beirut hoard (**116**) is no better documented and may have consisted principally of bronzes accompanied by a few staters. The Saida hoard

63. The numerous hoards of gold metalwork found in the Thracian and Scythian worlds are further evidence of the particular predilection of the peoples of this region for this metal. Callataÿ 2006a, pp. 57–60, offers some detailed estimates and a comparison using jewelry weight.

64. Touratsoglou 1998.

(*IGCH* 1508, **93**) is what really captures the attention. First, there is the manner of its discovery, in three tranches beginning in 1829—although nothing is known of this lot, which was probably melted down—and then successively in 1852 and 1863. The find was so large that numerous specialist journals reported it, as did a book by an American missionary who was clearly versed in numismatics. The six lead vases found fortuitously in the gardens of Saida contained at least 7,200 gold coins, including several hundred Philips and several thousand Alexanders. They held gold distaters and staters. Even granting that the hoard consisted only of staters, 7,200 units in this denomination represent the equivalent of 144,000 Attic drachms or 24 talents of silver. This considerable sum looks very much like an official treasury and is highly unlikely to represent private assets. According to data that could be rescued, especially thanks to the research of Westermark, the vases contained many coins of Sidon, dating down to the local year 10, as well as of Ake/Tyre down to the local year 24. Thus burial would have occurred c. 323/320 BC, right in the midst of the wars of the Successors over Alexander's empire. The situation in Syria then was particularly confused, if we may trust the account in Book 18 of the *Universal History* of Diodorus Siculus. The weak Laomedon, once satrap of the region, let the armies of Perdiccas pass through, only to be removed by Ptolemy I, before Eumenes and then Antigonus Monophthalmus took control of Syria by turns in 318–316 BC. The considerable holding that the Saida hoard represents was not buried just anywhere. Despite the continuing debate on its precise role, Sidon seems to have had close relations with Persian power.[65] Between the strategic importance of Sidon's port and its powerful navy, it is highly likely that Alexander himself paid the city close attention. In the troubled context of his conquest, the idea naturally occurs that this hoard may be an official fund. Alexander's gold staters almost never circulated in Syrian territory. In any case, none are buried there. By contrast, they are found in abundance in the northern Aegean and in the Black Sea region. The generally accepted opinion is that this currency was used to pay Thracian mercenaries accompanying the Macedonian armies. The currency's limited time in circulation and the fact that it was quickly hoarded after being struck rule out a slow accumulation through the roundabout means of commerce and exchange. Thus it is very tempting to connect this enormous hoard with a military fund being transported to meet a payroll, only to be buried in an emergency to avoid an imminent danger. That was how Le Rider and Davesne explained the burial of the Meydancıkkale hoard, in admittedly a far clearer archaeological context.[66] This theory has the virtue of explaining the abundance of gold as well as the huge presence of Philips in the Saida hoard, two anomalies for the region.

On the other hand, the exceptional character of this hoard, in metal, nature, and number of hoarded coins, highlights the absence of gold in our Syrian documentation. Coins of greater value (gold or electrum, larger denominations of silver) are exceptions in excavations. It is interesting to consider here the example of the Athenian Agora excavations, because they deal with a large commercial city where exchanges must have been highly monetized in comparison with Syria at the same time. Moreover, the Agora is surely the place in the city where coinage

65. Briant 1996, pp. 505–506, 624–26.
66. Davesne, Le Rider 1989, pp. 346–48.

circulated the most.[67] The American excavations have been systematic and very well published. Kroll catalogued 14,604 coins, dating from the sixth to the first century BC.[68] This impressive total yielded only two gold coins: one Alexander and one Persian *daric*, as well as a single electrum coin, from Cyzicus. The complete absence of gold coins in Syrian excavations, apart from the funerary deposit of Jablah, is not, therefore, surprising. On the other hand, the exceptional character of gold coin hoards is certainly a better indicator about circulation in this metal, emphasizing its rarity in the region. While silver on the Attic standard was already circulating internationally in the Persian period, the gold of Alexander is the only currency to be accepted at such a distance and in such large quantities. Its near complete absence in Syrian finds seems to be a solid argument for concluding that it was not meant for the local market.

CONCLUSION

The period encompassing the Macedonian Conquest and the stabilization of the kingdoms of the Successors also marks a monetary turning point. The traditional circulation of the Persian Empire continued until the 320s. If coinage were to be used to establish the frontier between the Achaemenid period and the Hellenistic Age, the latter would date from c. 325 BC on the basis of hoard contents: with or without Alexanders, with or without fractions. Next, the monetizing of the reserves of the Great King sweeps out the old currencies and imposes Alexanders, their Attic standard, and the near disappearance of fractions. Gold issues, massive and related to specific need, were probably meant for sizeable payments in other regions. The role of shifting military populations from east to west probably explains a great deal of this phenomenon: all throughout the period, fresh troops were sent to the East, even as demobilized veterans returned home with their pay. Some of these soldiers received tetradrachms,[69] while others may have received gold coins.[70] They probably contributed significantly, therefore, to the spread of Alexander's currency, no matter what other reasons can be found amid these flows.

67. Cahill 2002, pp. 266–73.
68. Kroll 1993, conspectus, p. xvii–xxvi.
69. Callataÿ 1997a, pp. 389–416 surveys these practices.
70. The hoards are the chief witness of this practice.

Chapter 6

The Two Syrias

The salient feature of third-century Syria is its partition between Ptolemy Soter and Seleucus I. In theory, sovereignty should have reverted to the latter in the wake of the coalition's victory over Antigonus Monophthalmus in 301 BC, but Ptolemy was quicker off the mark. He seized Syria, the defensive buffer that previously protected the Egypt of the pharaohs. He must have deemed it indispensable for the safety of his own kingdom after the failed assault by Perdiccas in 321 BC. This frontier divided two zones with very different monetary practices. The north, Seleucid, employed the Attic standard and accepted all currencies of this weight. The south, Ptolemaic, became a part of the closed Egyptian system, with a tightly controlled currency exchange at the borders. Scholars such as Mørkholm, Jenkins, and, more recently, Le Rider have carefully studied the specific aspects of currency circulation in the two regions, especially through the examination of hoards.[1]

The third century is the century of the Syrian wars; the region's partition was the cause of these confrontations, five in all before 198 BC. They did not affect hoarding, doubtless because some of the conflicts occurred outside Syria, despite their name. Their brevity was certainly a factor as well. These wars were each settled in a few years and probably did not involve lasting displacement of the populace.[2]

This period, marked by the struggle between the region's two great dynasties, is also one of the least well known. Written sources are scarce. Archaeology is not much help either, even though this is the time when what Strabo calls the Seleucid Tetrapolis fully develops.[3] Surveys in the region of Antioch (Amuq Valley), which have gathered evidence of occupation from the third millennium BC to the Arab period, underline the paucity of data for the Seleucid era beginning with the founding of Antioch.[4]

1. Cf. esp. Mørkholm 1967, Jenkins 1967, and Le Rider 1986b and 1995.
2. Duyrat 2011a.
3. Strabo 16.2.4.
4. Casana 2007.

The hoards of the third century form the smallest contingent of the present catalogue, with only 33 lots. The period is admittedly abbreviated, since only hoards thought to have been buried between 280 and 200 are taken into account. Of these, six come from authorized excavations (**138**, **142**, **145**, **146**, **155**, **158**).

1. SELEUCID SYRIA

1.1. Seleucid Sites

Le Rider devoted a major article to currency circulation in the Seleucid Empire during the third century.[5] His focus was the role that Alexanders played in this empire, and in the process he highlighted the contrast between the monetary policies of the Seleucids and the Ptolemies. After a detailed study of the type of currency found in the hoards of Asia Minor and the Seleucid East, he analyzed 11 well-documented hoards. He drew the following conclusions: coins with the types of Alexander dominate; the drachms of Alexander are quite abundant in the hoards consisting of this denomination; Ptolemaic and Rhodian coins are absent; circulation is open to every coin of Attic weight. This article has served ever since as the foundation for all studies of Seleucid monetary organization. It so happens that of the six hoards Le Rider used for the study of the "Seleucid East," five are located outside of Syria, in Babylonia (*IGCH* 1761), Qazvin (Media, *IGCH* 1976), Mashtal (Bagdad, *CH* 4.33), Tell Halaf (Mesopotamia, *IGCH* 1763), and Mesopotamia (*IGCH* 1764). Only the Bab hoard is located in Syria, east of Aleppo (*IGCH* 1534, **140**). The catalogue presented here, therefore, should help to fill out the picture Le Rider created for the central part of the empire, the least well represented in his documentation.

The first observation is the impermeability of the monetary zones: in the third century, Ptolemaic coins do not circulate at all in Seleucid Syria. As Table 6.1 shows, the archaeological sites of northern Syria in particular confirm this. It leaves out sites occupied by the Ptolemies between 246 and 219 BC, which are dealt with later on.[6] The first three columns give the totals for the entire Hellenistic period. With the exception of Hama, Seleucid issues represent from 60% to 100% of the finds. If only issues of third-century Seleucid kings are taken into account, the dominance of the royal currency is even more imposing.[7]

Seleucid coins dominate on these sites, sometimes to the exclusion of every other currency. For modest, essentially rural settlements like Umm el-Mara, Tell Abu Danne, and Tell Beydar, the fact that the official mints furnished the basic currency is not surprising. There was no local mint, and commercial activity was probably also not as dependent on coinage as in a large town.

5. Le Rider 1986b. In Duyrat 2004, I myself provided a view of currency circulation in the Seleucid Empire overall based on the hoard information. The concentrated focus on Syria in the present work is not meant to slight the larger orbits in which Seleucid coinage participated.

6. Also not included are sites too small that did not reveal Seleucid and/or Ptolemaic coins of the third century: 'Arab el-Mulk Paltos, Tell Daruk Usnu, and Tell Sukas.

7. This is not quantified here because it would require an especially fine sifting of excavation publications where the coins are not always dated precisely or clearly.

Table 6.1. Sites of northern Syria not occupied by the Ptolemies

Site	Total Hellenistic Bronzes	Total Seleucid Bronzes	Percentage of Seleucid Bronzes	SI	AI	AII	SII	SIII	Total
Dura Europos	1,210	1,024	84.6%	13	89	19	19	80	**220**
Hama	99	24	24.2%			1		1	**2**
Jebel Khalid	265	239	90.2%	2	6	2	5	8	**23**
Tell Abu Danne	68	48	70.6%	2			4		**6**
Tell Ain el-Beida	11	10	90.9%			1		2	**3**
Tell Beydar	2	2	100%		1				**1**
Tell el-Hajj	5	3	60%					1	**1**
Umm el-Mara	5	5	100%	2					**2**

At Jebel Khalid, life on the site seems to have been connected to the presence of a garrison. The majority of coins come from Antioch, not Mesopotamian mints, even though they are nearby.[8] The same observation is valid for Dura: 93% of the Seleucid bronzes come from Antioch, which Bellinger considered to be the result of an administrative arrangement, not currency circulation.[9] Hama has produced relatively few Seleucid coins owing to the tell's marked slowdown in activity during the third century: occupation really does not recommence until the second century.[10]

In sum, these northern sites are highly similar in their supply of bronze coins, no matter their size and political or economic importance, from the great city on the Euphrates to the garrison outpost, with rural settlements in between.

1.2. Silver Currency Circulation

Le Rider, in his article on the circulation of silver Alexanders in the Seleucid Empire, especially stressed the nature of the 12 hoards he had included. Two were very large (2,000–3,000 coins), three came from authorized digs, and the content of all of them seemed well documented.[11] I noted above that only the Bab hoard came from Syria. I should add that it is composed of drachms, whereas tetradrachms are ordinarily hoarded in Syria. Only 32 of the 247 listed hoards of silver coins buried after 333 BC contained drachms. Examination of the 11 hoards

8. Nixon 2002, p. 293.
9. Bellinger 1949, p. 196.
10. Ploug 1985, pp. 45–46.
11. Le Rider 1986b, p. 25.

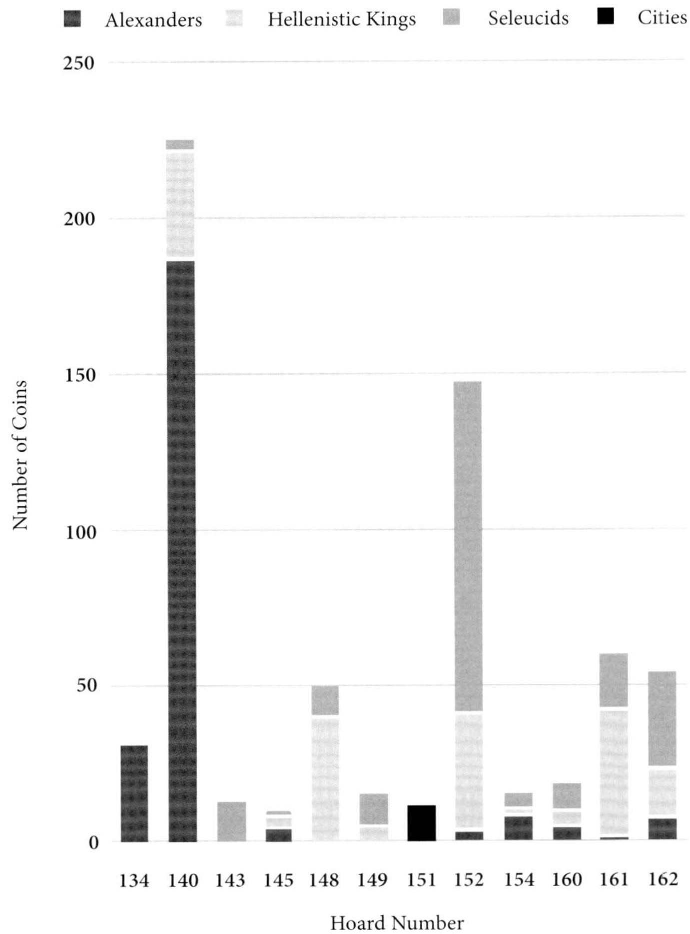

Figure 6.1. Hoards on the Attic standard.

solely on the Attic standard buried in the third century and presented together in the catalogue should permit further clarification of the picture of coin circulation in this period (Fig. 6.1).

Le Rider's first conclusion dealt with the dominance of Alexanders: "In the eleven hoards, the coins with types of Alexander form the majority. This majority is sometimes overwhelming: the Denizli hoard contained only Alexander drachms; these likewise constitute nearly the entirety of the Bab Hoard (95.9%)."[12] The presence of Alexanders in Syrian hoards is not negligible; Map 9 shows their spread in third-century Seleucid Syria. But that presence is not as overwhelming as Le Rider suggests, firstly because five of the listed hoards do not contain any at all. One of these comes form Homs (**148**). A second from Homs (**161**) produced only an insignificant number of Alexanders, as did another said to come from Syria (**160**). One must

12. "Dans les onze trésors, les monnaies aux types d'Alexandre forment la majorité. Cette majorité est parfois écrasante: le trésor de Denizli ne contenait que des drachmes alexandrines; celles-ci constituent également la quasi-totalité du trésor de Bab (95,9 %)." Ibid.

Figure 6.2. Tetradrachm of Antiochus I, Ecbatana (ANS 1944.100.73522)

certainly not draw too many conclusions from possibly incomplete hoards lacking a precise origin, but I would be inclined to temper Le Rider's remarks on the Alexanders' overwhelming presence, as least for the geographic zone under consideration here.

Maps well attest to the homogeneity by reign of the circulation of Seleucid royal coinage: from Seleucus I (312–281 BC) to Seleucus III (226–223 BC), hoards containing their issues are all concentrated in Seleucis and stretch from the sea to the northeast, following the route towards the Mesopotamian provinces (Fig. 6.2).[13] The change in type with each reign has no effect on the circulation of the royal coinage of the third-century. On the other hand, the orientation of the supplies does alter. Golenko had already shown that 80% of the coins of Seleucus I found in published hoards came from eastern mints, versus 2.4% from the Antioch mint.[14] This observation should be extended: from Seleucus I to Seleucus II (246–226 BC), royal coins from Syrian hoards basically came from eastern mints, no matter when they were buried. Beginning with Seleucus III, western and Syrian mints are better represented, reflecting the geography of royal minting activity during this period.[15]

Currency circulation in Seleucid Syria, therefore, essentially consists of royal tetradrachms, among which Alexanders and Seleucid issues hold pride of place.[16] So the few hoards that are exceptions deserve to be mentioned. One contained only Athenian tetradrachms of the third century, with no further clarification (**151**). It was allegedly found in northeastern Syria. Insofar as these coins are on the Attic standard, nothing prevented them from circulating, although they are civic issues. Their absence from Syrian hoards may merely be connected with the paucity of Athenian issues in the third century.[17] Amidst its otherwise ordinary content, another hoard contained two civic tetradrachms: one from Perge, a city in southern Asia Minor, and the other from Sinope. These issues are relatively rare in third-century Syria (**152**). Seyrig, who reconstituted this collection in commerce, was uncertain whether to locate it in Syria or Asia Minor. Its content would be unremarkable in Seleucis, and the presence of two unusual civic coins is not a strong enough reason to exclude it from the catalogue. Civic coinages are small in number because cities struck few tetradrachms in the third century: Aradus issued civic tetradrachms with types of Alexander beginning c. 246–244 BC (Fig. 6.3);[18] cities in Asia Minor employing their own types are few.

13. Cf. the general maps of circulation in the Seleucid Empire found in Duyrat 2004.
14. Golenko 1993, p. 154.
15. Houghton, Lorber 2002, 2, pp. 133–49.
16. Cf. Map 12 for the hoards containing Lysimachi and tetradrachms of Demetrius Poliorcetes.
17. For a description of these issues, cf. Flament 2007, pp. 133–41.
18. Duyrat 2005a, p. 38.

Figure 6.3. Civic tetradrachm of Aradus with Alexander types, 202/1 BC (ANS 1944.100.70381).

The absolute dominance of royal coinages, Seleucid or others, on the Attic standard, is an interesting phenomenon because it eliminated automatically the problem, so common in the cities of Greece, of calculating the weight equivalence between common coinage and local coinage.[19] The silver coinage circulating at this time in Syria was universal from the outset: the Attic standard tetradrachm definitively replaced, from the 320s, coins of varying standard that were the norm in the Persian period and that had led to differing currency zones requiring money-changers. Bronze coinage does not even play such an epichoric role: in this alloy, excavations at Seleucid Syrian sites have overwhelmingly produced royal Seleucid coins, which one has to suppose were related to silver, in a way that has been debated.[20]

In this homogeneous environment, the autonomy of Aradus stands out: beginning in the mid-third century, the city develops a production of tetradrachms, silver fractions, and bronze coins that circulate in its mainland territory, but not to the exclusion of other coinages.[21] Marathus, Carne, Gabala, and Simyra, four mints under Aradian control, introduce issues partially with types shared with Aradus.[22] Civic coinages from other cities in Syria start only during the last quarter of the second century.

Gold is totally missing from this picture. Le Rider published a die-study of the gold struck at Antioch in the third century. Production volumes are quite small: no issue under Antiochus I, one to two dies per reign for the other kings down to Seleucus II. The latter put 15 dies into service, but they are known from only a few specimens; and some also struck silver coins, leading one to suppose their output was not great.[23] Seleucus III and Antiochus III increased production, notably striking octadrachms,[24] but even here in negligible amounts compared to contemporary Ptolemaic output.[25] From the third century, no Seleucid gold coins have been found in Syria, and they are rare throughout the empire's extent. Hoards from this period that have revealed any, always in small quantities, are located in the far north, in Anatolia, Greece, Thrace, and Russia.[26]

19. Picard 1996; Marcellesi 2000.
20. Most recently, Hoover in Houghton, Lorber, Hoover 2008, pp. 43–52.
21. Duyrat 2005a, chap. VI.
22. Duyrat 2002a.
23. Le Rider 1999, p. 59.
24. Ibid., and the compilation tables in Duyrat 2002b, p. 410.
25. Duyrat, Olivier 2010, pp. 78–81.
26. Ibid., map, p. 81.

A tiny area of Seleucid Syria, however, stands apart from the highly homogeneous circulation just described: a few sites on the coast have produced coinage that preserves traces of the history of the third century. For north of the border between the Seleucid and Ptolemaic territories, it is only in Seleuceia Pieria that Ptolemaic bronzes of the third century have been found.

1.3. A Ptolemaic Enclave (Map 10)

Hoards and excavation coins attest to the presence of Ptolemaic coinage on Syrian territory. The Hüseyinli hoard (**135**), from between Seleuceia and Antioch, consisted of 58 gold coins of Ptolemy I and II and may also have contained a bronze of Antiochus I. Its editors date it between 264/3 and 258/7 BC and connect it to the Second Syrian War (260–253 BC), the events of which are obscure.[27] This collection is the result of a voluntary burial, and absolutely not a loss. Its content is atypical in Syria, both for being on the Ptolemaic standard, which restricts the circulation of such coins to Ptolemaic possessions, and for the metal, which, as we have seen, is not usual in Syrian hoards. Since Ptolemy II struck coinage briefly at Tarsus in 261/0 BC, Davesne and Yenisoğancı suggested a Ptolemaic incursion into Seleucis during this Second Syrian War. The hoard would be its unique evidence.

Excavation coins attest to another episode in the Ptolemaic presence in Seleucid Syria (Table. 6.2).

The coastal concentration of these bronzes has already been noted several times without anyone to my knowledge drawing up a complete inventory.[28] To be added to this table are the important results from the excavation of Ras Ibn Hani, which Augé has published only incompletely. The following numbers (Table 6.3) come from his notes for the campaigns prior to 1992, which he has generously shared with me. They include only civic coins. I have included the numbers given in his article on Ibn Hani and the Syrian wars.[29] In all, more than 500 Hellenistic coins have turned up on the site.

The Ptolemies held the region between 246 and 219 BC, that is, from the Third to the Fourth Syrian War.[30] Polybius, emphasizing Seleuceia's strategic importance, attests to their presence on the eve of the Fourth Syrian War: "[Seleuceia] was of first-class practical importance. 'While held by the enemy,' he [Apollophanes, an adviser to Antiochus III] said, 'it is the greatest possible hindrance to all our enterprises; for in whatever direction we decide to advance, the precautions we have to take to protect our own country from the menace of this place give us just as

27. Davesne, Yenisoğanci 1992.

28. I have already mentioned the available material in Duyrat 2005a, pp. 230–31. One should add the rare gold stater of Ptolemy Soter discovered in a tomb of the Jablah necropolis. Some silver coins of Attic weight accompanied it, and its presence cannot be taken as evidence for the region's currency circulation. This is a funerary deposit and may have been chosen for its intrinsic value and been brought by a traveller through Ptolemaic lands.

29. Augé 2000.

30. *OGIS* 54; Justin, *Epitome* 27.1; Holleaux 1952, on the Third Syrian War and the capture of Seleuceia Pieria and Antioch.

Table 6.2. Sites with Ptolemaic coins of the third century (Map 10)

Site					Seleucid Coins							Ptolemaic Coins			
	Total Hellenistic	SI	AI	AII	Inter-regnum	SII	ΔΕΛ Mint	SIII	Total	PI	PII	PIII	PIV	PV	Total
Al Mina, 1936	203 + 30–40 frags.								**0**	7		1			**8**
Antioch	1,086	27	74	9	3	37	26	75	**251**	1	2	2		1	**6**
Ras el Bassit – Posideion	90	3						3	**6**		1	7			**8**
Ras Shamra	25	5							**5**	2					**2**
Seleuceia Pieria	273	20	20	3		3	1	7	**54**	2	8	9			**19**

much trouble as our preparations for attacking the enemy."[31] The excavations of Seleuceia Pieria have brought to light an interesting hoard of mixed composition (*IGCH* 1526, **138**):

Antigonus Monophthalmus: 1 tetr. of Alexander type, Antigoneia on the Orontes
Demetrius Poliorcetes: 1 tetr.
Ptolemy I: 1 tetr. Alexandria
Ptolemy II: 3 tetr. Alexandria, 1 tetr. Tyre, 1 tetr. Sidon, 1 tetr. Joppa, 1 tetr. Gaza
Ptolemy I or II: 2 tetr.

The editors of the *Inventory of Greek Coin Hoards* put its burial around 250. If this dating accords with the content of the hoard, it still makes no historical sense. The presence of 10 Ptolemaic tetradrachms in a Seleucid capital in 250 BC is hard to explain, short of conjuring up a merchant who, foreseeing commerce with the southern ports, may have saved a coinage that he must have found useful. I wonder whether we ought not to connect this hoard with one of the two wars surrounding its burial date: perhaps the Second Syrian War (but nothing indicates that Seleuceia was occupied by Egyptian forces), or the Third and, thus, related to the Ptolemies' long occupation of Seleuceia.

Although the literary sources do not say so, it is clear that the Ptolemies occupied not only Seleuceia but also surrounding territory of unknown extent. Thanks to excavation coins, the

31. Polybius 5.58.5–7 (tr. Patton, Loeb Classical Library).
32. Augé 2000, p. 65.
33. Augé 2000, p. 67.
34. Augé 2000, p. 62.

Table 6.3. Overview of coins from the excavation of Ras Ibn Hani

Seleucids	Around 260[32] of which 6 Seleucus III more than 140 Antiochus III Antioch.[33]
Ptolemies	Around 170,[34] principally of Ptolemy II Ptolemy III Berenice II
Cities	8 Antioch 1 Antioch or Seleuceia 5 Seleuceia 19 Laodiceia around 50 + 3 (1987 campaign) Aradus 2 Gabala 3 Carne 5 Marathus 2 Orthosia 2 Tripolis 2 Sidon 1 Tyre 17 Uncert.
Hasmoneans and Herodians	2

boundaries of this zone held by Ptolemaic garrisons between 246 and 219 BC can be clarified. At Ras Ibn Hani, nine Ptolemaic bronzes published in 1978 already prompted the excavators to affirm "the control of Ptolemy III Euergetes over the region at the beginning of the Third Syrian War."[35] Later campaigns of excavation largely corroborated this opinion: nearly 170 Ptolemaic coins were unearthed. This puts Ibn Hani in the first rank of Ptolemaic settlements in the region. Rey-Coquais also published a stele bearing the names and ethnics of 28 mercenaries on the Ptolemies' payroll: these men were probably stationed there during the first phase of the Third Syrian War.[36] Unsurprisingly, Antioch and especially Seleuceia have provided identical monetary evidence, as the written texts had already led us to believe. Seleuceia gave better results than Antioch, though they were still modest, considering the length of the Ptolemaic garrison's occupation. This small amount may be a function of the areas excavated in the city.[37] Al Mina revealed not one Seleucid coin for this period, and for good reason: the site was abandoned after the foundation of the Seleucid capitals, c. 300 BC, which probably entailed movement of population.[38] It is all the more remarkable that eight bronzes of the first two Ptolemies were found there. Likewise, the site of Ras Shamra–Leukos Limen declines and disappears between

35. Bounni, Lagarce, Lagarce, Saliby 1978, p. 299.

36. Rey-Coquais 1978.

37. The harvest is, in any case, relatively poor at Seleuceia, with a total of 275 Hellenistic coins, four of which are silver.

38. Wooley 1953, p. 180. On population shifts to Antioch or Seleuceia: Diodorus 20.47.6; Strabo 16.2.4; Le Rider 1999a, pp. 117–18, 137–38.

Table 6.4. Percentage of coins of Ptolemy II in hoards of the Third Century (Map 11)[39]

No.	Place of Discovery	% of Ptolemaic Coins
168	Aradus?	46%
150	Jordan	56%
146	Tel Michal, Palestine	60%
158	Tel Michal, Palestine	64%
153	Syria	67%
135	Hüseyinli, near Antakya	76%
139	Hebron Region	80%
147	ʻIraq al-Amir, Jordan	81%
141	Amman	83%
144	Saida	84%
142	Beth-Shan (anc. Nysa-Scythopolis)	90%
131	Sikka, southwest of Hebron	100%
136	Nuba, Hebron	100%

280 and 250 BC.[40] It is represented here only by surface finds that yielded two Ptolemaic coins out of a meager total of 25.

Some of the numbers reported here may seem rather weak support for the presence of the Ptolemies. Yet one must bear in mind that Ptolemaic coinage does not travel abroad and that the remarkably closed nature of the border between Seleucid Syria and Ptolemaic Syria and Phoenicia characterizes the third century.[41] This is even more axiomatic for bronze, which was worthless outside the issuing mint's zone of influence. The complete absence of Ptolemaic coins on other Syrian sites is the best evidence for this. Systematic archaeological survey in the region would no doubt be very useful because it would probably make feasible a relatively precise mapping of the Ptolemies' presence. It is necessary to conclude, therefore, that, for all its sparseness, apart from Ras Ibn Hani and Seleuceia, the presence of these coins shows the region under Ptolemaic influence between 246 and 219 BC, yet with one imponderable. It is possible that the Seleucids retook certain outposts earlier, without leaving us any traces.

39. Most of the identifications are based on the work of Svoronos, which is currently being revised by C. C. Lorber. There may be some changes in the ratios once her catalogue is published, but at this point it seems they will be marginal.

40. Stucky 1983, p. 54.

41. Duyrat 2013, pp. 7–11.

2. PTOLEMAIC SYRIA AND PHOENICIA

2.1. The Closed Border

In the south, starting with the reform of Ptolemy Soter at the end of the fourth century, all foreign coinages disappear. Hoards and excavations testify to the highly effective establishment of the closed monetary system.[42] The latest hoards of coins on a foreign weight standard in this region are dated c. 300 BC: in Galilee (**117**), at Sidon (**118**), and at Beirut (**119**). The earliest hoard of Ptolemaic coins consists of 15 bronzes of Ptolemy Soter found in the excavation of Balatah, the ancient Shechem, and dated c. 285 (**125**). The transition from the system of Attic weight inherited from Alexander and the new organization desired by the first two Ptolemaic kings thus occurred between c. 300 and c. 285 BC. After this date, only two third-century hoards are on the Attic standard. One is said to be from Phoenicia (**126**), but its contents correspond perfectly with finds from Seleucid Syria. It is impossible to decide definitively, inasmuch as its burial conceivably falls between 285 and 280: the hoard could be a relic of the former monetary system. The second hoard consists of five bronzes of Philip V of Macedon found during the excavation of Tel Michal (**155**). *Coin Hoards* has not included this lot as a hoard. A traveller or soldier may have brought these bronzes, hoarded c. 215/4 BC, and they do not suffice to call into question the region's remarkable monetary impregnability. This chronology for the establishment of Ptolemy Soter's reform accords well with what we know about Egypt itself through hoards. In the third century, few hoards have been inventoried containing coins of Attic weight, always in the company of Ptolemaic coins.[43] They are dated, respectively, c. 285, mid-third century (?), and 200–180 BC.

The archaeological sites of the southern Levant confirm the new system's remarkable effectiveness: until the region's conquest by Antiochus III, they yield Ptolemaic coins exclusively.[44]

2.2. Origin of the Currency Used in Ptolemaic Syria and Phoenicia

The matter of "initial silver money supply" has been debated notably by Davesne and criticized by Callataÿ on the basis of the Meydancıkkale hoard. Davesne, using his study of the dies of the 2,158 Ptolemaic coins in this find, attributed to Ptolemy I a silver output that constituted a considerable starting supply. "Maintenance strikes" would have subsequently replenished this stock under the reign of Ptolemy II.[45] In 2005, Callataÿ revised this die study and divided Davesne's results by 10. But he confirmed that the silver issues of Ptolemy Soter, and especially

42. Le Rider 1995, pp. 398–402; Duyrat 2013, pp. 7–11.

43. Phacous (*IGCH* 1678); Delta (*IGCH* 1684); Delta (*IGCH* 1701) by my reckoning in 2002, Duyrat 2005b, pp. 36–37. C. C. Lorber informs me that according to Newell's manuscript held at the American Numismatic Society, *IGCH* 1684 most probably dates to soon after c. 294 and doesn't contain the Arsinoe coins that led to a lower dating. *IGCH* 1701 could come from Macedonia or Greece.

44. The sole exception is a bronze of Antiochus I found in the excavation of the Muristan quarter in Jerusalem (site **22**).

45. Carcassonne, Davesne 1987.

Figure 6.4. Tetradrachm of Ptolemy II, Alexandria (ANS 1944.100.75455).

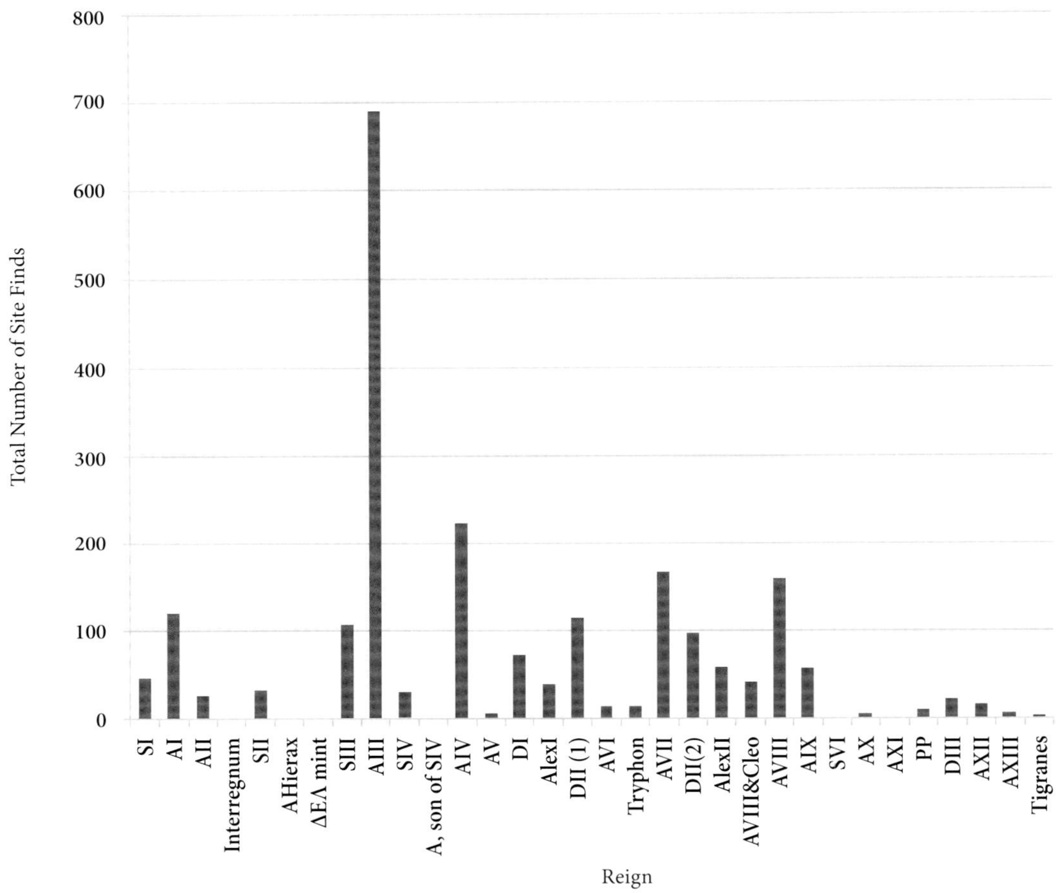

Figure 6.5. Seleucid coin totals on all sites.

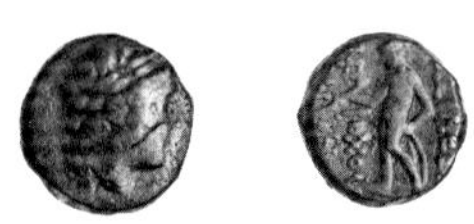

Figure 6.6. Bronze of Antiochus III struck at Antioch (ANS 1944.100.75145).

those of Ptolemy II had been sustained by putting into service some 200 obverse dies in a few years.[46] This heavy output finds an echo in Syrian and Phoenician hoards buried in the third century: the tetradrachms of Ptolemy II are always in the large majority, as Table 6.4 shows.[47] These numbers provide a minimum because they do not take into account tetradrachms whose attributions editors have been unable to determine, and which appear in catalogues under the heading "Ptolemy I–II" or "Ptolemy II–III."

Of 13 hoards, 12 consist mostly of coins of Ptolemy II, and the ratio rises to more than 75% for eight of them. Meadows draws attention to the highly worn condition of the tetradrachms of Ptolemy I and II in the numerous hoards of the region, suggesting even "the comparative monetary neglect of the region on the part of the Ptolemaic kings, outside of periods of warfare."[48] The detailed study Keen is preparing on the Iraq al-Amir hoard refines these observations.[49] The allotment by reign of this hoard's coins gives pride of place to the coins of Ptolemy II Philadelphus (Fig. 6.4). More important, Keen shows that, if the issues of the Alexandria mint prior to 261 BC are numerous, those following are almost non-existent. This disappearance is contemporary with the start of production from the Syrian-Phoenician mints and the drop in Alexandrian issues between c. 260 and c. 240 BC.[50] "This may, if one is willing to allow that this hoard is representative of coin circulation in the region, indicate that the coins of the regional mints were sufficient to meet the needs of the regional economy and that additional influxes of coins from the primary mint in Alexandria were, for some reason, no longer coming to mingle with the coins of the regional mints."[51]

In this picture, hoards **132** and **134** are the sole exceptions: they consist of Judaean coins, the only production of the Persian period to have continued in circulation under the Ptolemies.[52]

3. THE GREAT SYRIA OF ANTIOCHUS III

The majority of the other bronzes found on southern Levantine sites come from Seleucid mints after the conquest of the region, with a considerable spike, everywhere evident, for the coinage of Antiochus III (Fig. 6.5). At Antioch, Beirut, and Dura Europos these small coins represent respectively almost 31%, 59%, and 45% of the Seleucid bronzes found.

All sites confirm the spike for the bronzes of Antiochus III.[53] Nixon qualifies this observation. In the excavation of Jebel Khalid, the overrepresentation of Antiochus III's currency declines

46. Callataÿ 2005, p. 124.
47. Hoards without coins of Ptolemy II in the third century in Syria and Phoenicia: **132** and **133** (*YHD* coins), **157** (Ptolemy IV), **159** (Ptolemy I).
48. Meadows, 2016a.
49. Keen, 2016. I want especially to thank this author for sharing with me the conclusions of his article before its publication.
50. Lorber Forthcoming. Oral communication to Keen.
51. Keen, 2016.
52. Cf. Gitler, Lorber 2000–2002 and 2006; Gitler 2006a.
53. Cf., e.g., the comparative graph in Nixon 2002, p. 300.

if regnal lengths are taken into account: Seleucus III is proportionally better represented than Antiochus III.[54] The excavation of the Beirut Souks has yielded ninety bronzes of Antiochus III (Fig. 6.6).[55] Butcher remarks that, "their high rate of deposition may be a combined consequence of large numbers originally produced and demonetization or obsolescence through inflation. Unfortunately, we cannot know how rapidly these coins fell out of circulation."[56] Examination of coins from the site BEY 045 allows him to suggest, without complete confidence, a withdrawal from circulation in the mid-second century (c. 164 BC?[57]).

The volume of the production during the reign of Antiochus III meets the needs of regions previously deprived of Ptolemaic bronze coinage. There has been no in-depth study of the motives guiding the king's choice. Butcher suggests that "the influx of new coin may be viewed as part of a more general program whose aim was to create a Seleucid identity for recently annexed territory. The use of the Seleucid era stamped on amphorae (probably from Sidon: Paul Reynolds, personal communication) in the years immediately following the conquest would appear to be part of the same fairly aggressive process."[58] A few pages later, the same author writes, "the adoption of Seleucid coinage is probably best seen as part of a wider programme of 'Seleucidization' of the region, including the adoption of the Seleucid era and the renaming of some urban centres using Seleucid dynastic names."[59] I am inclined to think that coin production is always guided, first of all, by practical considerations. As soon as Antiochus III decided against changing the currency system of his new possessions, only stocks already in circulation could support the region. Importing coins on the Ptolemaic standard was necessary so long as the Seleucids did not opt themselves to produce the necessary coinage. On the other hand, since bronze did not suffer from the problem of weight standard, it was probably much easier to produce on site, especially when demand seems to have been great. That the typology additionally contributed to the diffusion of the royal countenance goes without saying, but the continuation of Ptolemaic silver shows that this was not the coinage's principal purpose, at least in this particular instance.

The abundance of Antiochus III's bronze and silver coins, however, ought not to be taken too hastily as the sign of an increase in output. Le Rider has published a corpus of Seleucid gold and silver issues from Antioch based on a very respectable sample.[60] He clearly shows that, while the surviving tetradrachms are more numerous than those of Antiochus' predecessors and successors down to Antiochus IV, the mint's annual production nonetheless remained stable.[61] No die study of the bronze issues exists, but the longevity of Antiochus III's reign ought to qualify the impression of size the raw data create.

54. Ibid., p. 301.
55. Butcher 2001-2002, pp. 130–32.
56. Ibid., p. 49.
57. Ibid., p. 114.
58. Ibid., p. 47.
59. Ibid., p. 54. Thus, Berytus (Beirut) becomes Laodiceia in Canaan and strikes coinage with this name.
60. Le Rider 1999.
61. Summary tables in Duyrat 2002b, pp. 413–14, esp. the table of annual dispersion of issues, which indicates an average of two obverse tetradrachm dies per year under Seleucus III, 1.88 under Antiochus III, and two under Seleucus IV.

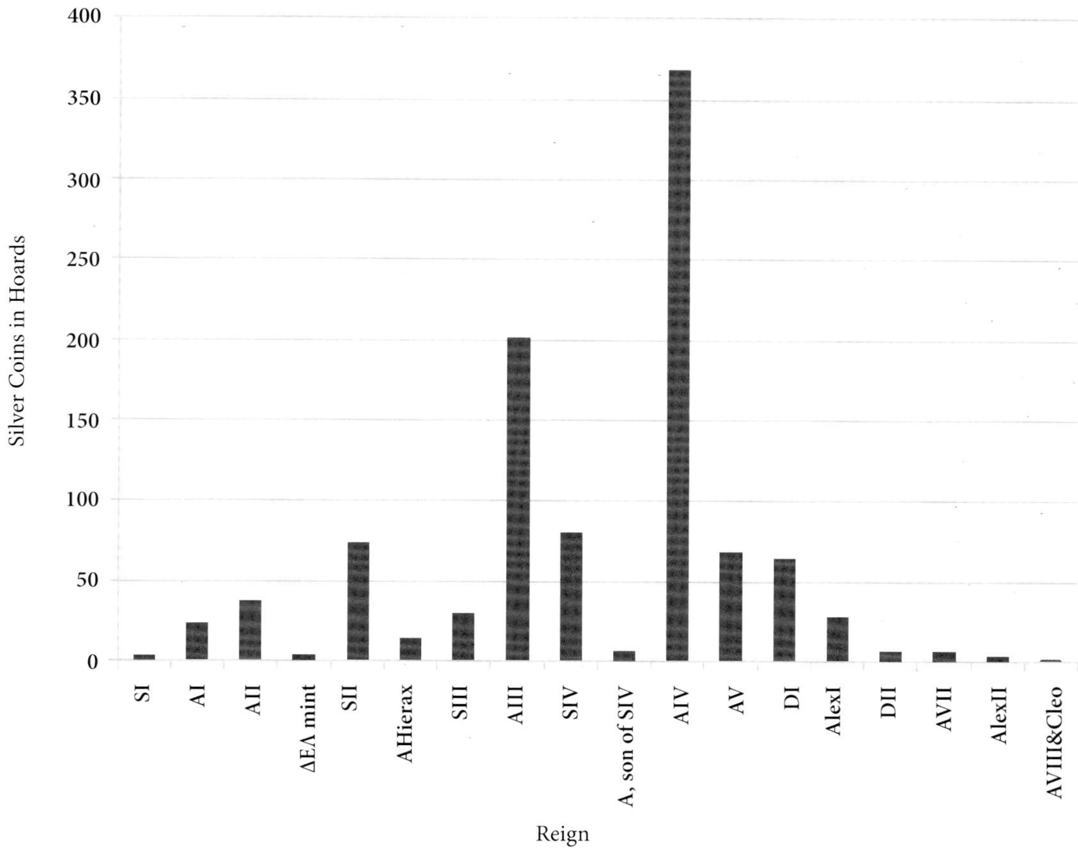

Figure 6.7. Silver coins of the Seleucids in hoards (c. 220–121 BC).[62]

As we can see from Fig. 6.7, the silver coinage of Antiochus III does not predominate in the hoards: that of Antiochus IV is more numerous. This outcome is even more striking when taking into account the length of reign of the two kings, in which case Antiochus III shows about five coins per year and Antiochus IV more than 30. The reign of Antiochus III does not stand out from those of his predecessors and immediate successors.

Unlike what can be observed under Ptolemy II, the output of silver and bronze does not seem to have been correlated under Antiochus III if one relies on the evidence of the hoards and the Antioch mint. Unlike silver, this king's bronze issues played an important role in circulation. Most sites have revealed them, in some cases in large numbers. More important, this currency literally drives out that of the Ptolemies from their former province of Syria and Phoenicia.[63] Leaving aside the smallest sites, where very little material has turned up, the bronze coinage of Antiochus III is omnipresent, while that of the Ptolemies practically disappears.[64] Starting with his reign, Seleucid coins in this alloy become the region's ordinary currency.

62. This chart assembles the share of each Seleucid king in Syrian hoards containing coins of Antiochus III, from c. 220 to 121 BC.

63. This phenomenon had already been noted, esp. by Houghton, Lorber 2000–2002.

64. For another representation of this change, cf. the table published in Duyrat 2013, pp. 16–17.

The rapidity with which the bronze of Antiochus III establishes itself is surely explained in part by the military campaign itself: it lasted several years and necessitated *ad hoc* production, some in mints that accompanied armies. Houghton and Lorber thought the phenomenon too rapid and too complete not to have been preceded by a political decision to withdraw the Ptolemaic bronze coinage.[65] It is difficult to determine how long this latter coinage was used, and there is no indication that it did not continue to circulate for a time with other Ptolemaic coins. The supply had clearly been cut, since after Ptolemy V they are rare, but that does not necessarily mean that they were no longer legal tender. One hoard (**275**), published by Hoover, leads to the same cautious stance: buried c. 121 BC in northern Israel, it still contains Ptolemaic coins. Hoover concluded that "the evidence of the present hoard and others makes it seem more likely that the Ptolemaic bronzes in the region were not pulled out of circulation at once but rather disappeared over time just like the Ptolemaic silver which was ultimately replaced by new Phoenician-weight coinages of Alexander I in 150 BC"[66] The minuscule hoard **291** also contained one bronze of Ptolemy I; in addition, the Kessab hoard (**305**), buried c. 95 BC, contained three Ptolemaic bronzes, evidence of a certain indifference among users to the official character of the coinage in this metal. A few rare specimens from Ptolemy VI to Ptolemy VIII have also been found during excavations,[67] but they only serve to highlight by contrast the wide spread of Seleucid coins. The absence of a supply of Ptolemaic bronze may explain the disappearance of this currency for which Antiochus III produced a replacement coinage. On the other hand, the Ptolemaic silver already available was the sole source of currency in this metal and continued to circulate until the Seleucids decided to strike coinage on this standard.[68]

Le Rider devoted a long article to the preservation of the Ptolemaic standard in Syria and Phoenicia after the Seleucid conquest. He stressed that suppression of the lighter silver standard would surely have disrupted the region's economy to some degree and would have deprived Antiochus III of the advantages of a closed system that permitted the ruling government to collect a lucrative exchange tax in a commercial region.[69] Of these two reasons, the first is doubtless the more compelling. Written evidence does not give us a clear insight into the role coinage played in economic life. A die study of the royal issues from the regional mints would give a more precise idea of the volumes produced in the third century. The work remains to be done. Up to 261 BC, however, everything argues for the importance of the influx of coins struck in Alexandria. Moreover, it is certain that the Ptolemaic system pervaded all levels of society as the legal tender, since all previous coinages disappeared, and the Ptolemaic king dealt only in his own coinage. One has to conclude that the region made do with the currency of the third century during the first half of the second century. The worn character of the surviving hoard specimens shows this. This preservation of a previous system is not original with the Seleucid Empire. Heirs of

65. Houghton, Lorber 2000–2002, pp. 57–58.
66. Hoover 2010, p. 229.
67. Beirut (Bey 006 and 045), Pella, Jaffa, Auja Hafir, Castle of 'Atlit, Jerusalem (site **27**), Hippos-Sussita.
68. I do not think that the population had any choice, contrary to Barag 2007–2008, pp. 28–29, who thinks that it preferred the small Seleucid bronze fractions, easier for transactions, while rejecting Seleucid silver.
69. Le Rider 1995.

Table 6.5. Seleucid bronzes in the excavations of Beirut[70]

King	Mint	n
Antiochus III	Antioch	91
	Uncertain	8
Seleucus IV	Antioch	1
	Tyre	1
Antiochus IV	Antioch or Seleuceia	1
	Berytus	15
	Tyre	1
	Ptolemaïs	15 + 1 ?
	Uncertain	6
Demetrius I	Antioch	1
	Tyre	1
Alexander I	Antioch	1
	Berytus	2
Demetrius II (1)	Antioch	3
	Sidon	1
	Tyre	1
Antiochus VII	Antioch	3
Demetrius II (2)	Antioch	2
	Berytus	3
	Sidon	1
Alexander II	Antioch	1

the Achaemenids in this regard, the kings of Syria, from the start of the dynasty, exercised their authority over peoples who maintained their ancestral practices. The unpublished thesis of Julien Monerie on Hellenistic Babylonia makes abundantly clear the continuation of traditional means of payment, which the habits of new masters did not eradicate as they superimposed themselves.[71] Syria and Phoenicia may have benefited from this tendency. Such Seleucid pragmatism probably sought to avoid disturbing a region where a closed monetary system requiring exchange at the borders had strongly prevailed for a century.

Bronze coinage, on the other hand, did not warrant such precautions, and it is hard to imagine a Seleucid king striking this alloy with the types of his adversary without taking any financial or political advantage from it. Separating the two sorts of currency is easy to bring about technically: the bronze coinage possesses the face value that the issuing authority gives it, since this alloy does not have great value. So under Antiochus III one observes the establishment of a dual system where silver preserves the types and metal content it had under the Ptolemies, while bronze is struck in the name of the Seleucid king. Nonetheless, bronze is a division of silver. Results from the Beirut excavations (Table 6.5) well demonstrate that the coins of An-

70. Based on the catalogue in Butcher 2001–2002, pp. 130–37.
71. Monerie 2013.

tiochus III are chiefly of small diameter (around 10 mm), with the head of Apollo and Apollo standing for types Fig. 6.6), and that they are essentially imported from the north.[72] Those of his successors, by contrast, come indifferently from both northern and southern mints.

104 coins were struck at Antioch, versus 53 in the other mints. The metrological analysis presented by Hoover in *Seleucid Coins* 2 shows that the royal Seleucid coins belong to systems based on five, occasionally six, denominations,[73] but their flan sizes do not exactly correspond from one mint to another.[74] Hoover prudently concludes: "While the evidence seems to point to an empire-wide system of bronze denominations, with Phoenicia as a special case during the Antiochus IV–Demetrius I period, it is hard to be sure how it really operated on the ground."[75] He presents two tables of silver/bronze equivalencies that show that the A denomination (22–29 mm, 11–24.25 g) was a tetrachalkon (or hemiobol) in the Attic system, but an obol in the Ptolemaic system prior to the reform of Alexander I Balas, who standardized everything.

CONCLUSION

The documentation assembled here shows that in the third century the monetary border between Seleucid Syria and Ptolemaic Syria and Phoenicia was completely closed. On either side, circulation responded to similar criteria on the whole, albeit on different standards: above all, the silver coinage was royal. While in the south this came solely from Ptolemaic mints, in the north in most cases it took the form of tetradrachms with the types of Alexander or of the Seleucid kings. Other royal currencies of Attic weight were also accepted, but they do not constitute the largest portion of the hoards. Excavations confirm this disposition, yielding predominantly Seleucid bronze coinage. The only "mixed" zone is the region held by the Ptolemies from 246–219 BC, around Seleuceia Pieria. Here the two dynasties succeeded one another during this century, and the coinage we possess shows as much.

The Fifth Syrian War altered this landscape partially. The bronze coinage then provided a monetary unity not found in the silver, since for this alloy the Ptolemaic system endured in Syria and Phoenicia. The second century confirms this situation.

72. Butcher 2001–2002, p. 47, for Beirut, but the observation can be extended to other sites.

73. This number is often reduced to three, or even fewer, over time.

74. On the special case of the royal issues of the Phoenician mints, Houghton 2003–2006; Houghton, Lorber, Hoover 2008, 2, pp. 9–29.

75. Houghton, Lorber, Hoover 2008, p. 51.

Chapter 7

From Kings to Cities

After the victory of Antiochus III and the conquest of Ptolemaic Syria and Phoenicia, the currency zones remained unaltered. Seleucid Syria and the eastern possessions continued to use the Attic standard; the southern Levant preserved a closed monetary system organized around the Ptolemaic standard despite the Ptolemies' defeat. The second century also witnessed the gradual weakening of the Seleucid dynasty, first, in confrontation with Roman might, and then through dynastic rivalries encouraged by powerful neighbors, chiefly the Ptolemies and Attalids. This political context fostered the development of civic autonomy and local powers. It also influenced the production and circulation of coinage. Thus the first Hasmonean coins found in a hoard date from 110/109 BC. The cities of Phoenicia established eras of autonomy between the end of the second century and the beginning of the first: in 126/5 at Tyre, in 111 at Sidon, in 102/101 BC at Byblos. Civic coinages appeared in the wake of the grants of freedom. The second century is the time when Syrian mints were most active, across all standards. The number of hoards buried is very high compared to the third and first centuries: 126 are dated between 200 and 103 BC, or 35% of all hoards and nearly 44% of Hellenistic hoards.

1. Common Coinage in Northern Syria

The previous chapter briefly broached the question of common coinages: in the third century, the almost total absence of local coins meant that the royal coinage of Attic standard in the north and the Ptolemaic in the south constituted currency circulation zones devoid of local features. This situation changed in the second century, and it seems worthwhile to explain the term "common (or Hellenic) coinage." This expression, used by Plato, designates a coinage to which several states grant legal status, making it in effect a common medium of exchange among them (*Laws* 5.742a–b):

> As regards the common Hellenic coinage (*koinon Hellenikon nomisma*), needed for military expeditions and foreign visits, as well as for embassies or any other essential

> state business when someone has to be sent abroad, for purposes such as these the state must have readily available Hellenic money. In the case of a private individual needing to travel abroad, he may do so, after first obtaining permission from the authorities; and should he come home from his trip with leftover foreign currency (*nomisma xenikon*), he is to deposit it with the state for an equivalent amount of the local coinage (*to epikhorion*).[1]

Plato here distinguishes two types of coinage: local and common or Hellenic. The term "foreign," which could delineate the common coinage as well as the local coinage of another city, remains ambiguous. Thus Plato distinguishes local coinage from the coinages of other cities and the common coinage. This description, applicable to Plato's ideal city, is not, for all that, a fiction. Cities, like private individuals, use alternatively one or the other coinage, depending on the payment they have to make. These mechanisms are now better known thanks to the combined study of coins and epigraphic and literary texts.[2]

From the last quarter of the fourth century, as we have seen, Alexanders performed this role of common coinage: they were accepted everywhere within the possessions of the Macedonian conqueror and his successors, with the notable exception of the Ptolemaic kingdom, which assumed its own standard at the very end of the fourth century. Subsequently, all coinage on the Attic standard was accepted and circulated in these regions following the Alexanders. The content of second century hoards changes perceptibly compared to the preceding period. Alexanders are less numerous and lose their preeminence. By contrast, Seleucid silver and new coins arrive and feed into the circulating currency.

1.1. Alexanders

The enormous stock of Alexanders struck during the last third of the fourth century continued to circulate throughout the second century but dwindled naturally. New, posthumous, issues were put into circulation in large quantities. Le Rider, using Price's catalogue, listed the 23 mints of Asia Minor that, in his opinion, chose to carry on these types from 188 or slightly later, by mint, down to 170–160 BC.[3]

Le Rider emphasizes that the bulk of this production is found in hoards of the Seleucid Empire, save for some rare exceptions.[4] The Alexander output from the cities of Pamphylia (Table 7.1)

1. Κοινὸν δὲ Ἑλληνικὸν νόμισμα ἕνεκά τε στρατειῶν καὶ ἀποδημιῶν εἰς τοὺς ἄλλους ἀνθρώπους, οἷον πρεσβειῶν ἢ καί [742b] τινος ἀναγκαίας ἄλλης τῇ πόλει κηρυκείας, ἐκπέμπειν τινὰ ἂν δέῃ, τούτων χάριν ἀνάγκη ἑκάστοτε κεκτῆσθαι τῇ πόλει νόμισμα Ἑλληνικόν. ἰδιώτῃ δὲ ἂν ἄρα ποτὲ ἀνάγκη τις γίγνηται ἀποδημεῖν, παρέμενος μὲν τοὺς ἄρχοντας ἀποδημείτω, νόμισμα δὲ ἄν ποθεν ἔχων ξενικὸν οἴκαδε ἀφίκηται περιγενόμενον, τῇ πόλει αὐτὸ καταβαλλέτω πρὸς λόγον ἀπολαμβάνων τὸ ἐπιχώριον· Tr. Meadows 2014 p. 185, with adaptation.

2. Tréheux 1992, pp. 22–23; Picard 1996; Marcellesi 2000, pp. 333–57; Chankowski, forthcoming.

3. Le Rider 1999b, p. 40: Alexandria Troas, Assos, Cyme, Myrina, Temnos, Methymna, Mytilene, Clazomenae, Colophon, Erythrae, Magnesia on the Maeander, Miletus, Teos, Chios, Samos, Alabanda, Antioch on the Maeander, Euromos?, Mylasa, Cos, Sardis?, Phaselis, Aspendus. A study by Lorber, 2010, pp. 155–56, based on a close analysis of the hoards in which they appear, suggests a later dating for the Alexanders of Temnos: from the late 160s to before 143/2 BC.

4. Le Rider 1999b, p. 44.

is particularly interesting because the issues are dated by eras that have been the subject of numerous studies. The most recent of these proposes an overall revision of the dates of the hoards where these coinages appear and consequently of the start of the Pamphylian eras.[5] Meadows has based himself specifically on Le Rider's publication of the Syria 1971 hoard (**174**) to support his new chronology.[6] Upon examination of the list of hoards that do not contain these tetradrachms, he writes that "the general conclusion that we may draw from this table is that Pamphylian Alexanders tend to be absent from hoards in Asia Minor and the Seleucid kingdom that were deposited in the period c. 229–210 BC."[7] A subtle and convincing demonstration follows, tying the Alexander production of Pamphylian mints and Aradus closely to the campaigns of Seleucus III and Antiochus III in Asia Minor. In 223 BC, Seleucus III undertook an expedition against Attalus I that led him to Phrygia, where he died from poisoning the next year. In 225/4 BC, Gabala, Carne, and Marathus issued civic Alexanders[8] while Simyra struck Seleucid tetradrachms.[9] All these series are unique. Their coincidence signals a particular event that could be the participation of the Aradian fleet in military operations in Asia Minor, perhaps transporting troops from Syria to Pamphylia.[10] The same phenomenon can be observed in the mid-190s, the expedition of Antiochus III in Asia Minor provoking some alterations in currency production in the Aradian hinterland and in Pamphylia.[11]

Meadows' article, focused on a reexamination of the production of Pamphylian mints (Figs. 7.1–7.3), does not elaborate on Syria. It is interesting to note that, while these coinages are closely linked to the two kings' campaigns in Asia Minor, most of their output is nonetheless found in Syria.

This influx even led Seyrig, discussing Pamphylian mints, to speak of "a veritable export industry in their coinage."[12] Le Rider explained this comment: "The cities in question would have striven to produce, in view of trade with the Seleucid kingdom, as many Alexanders as they could, to profit monetarily from the favorable currency rate. This motivation, in my opinion, would not only have spurred the issuing activity of these mints, but would also have probably focused a larger number of merchants on the Seleucid kingdom."[13] Meadows has clearly shown that production meant for Syrian export is not the question here; rather, it was meeting royal

5. Meadows 2009, recalling previous suggestions. The same author corrects his own dating for the beginning of the era of Phaselis, which would now start at the latest in 216/5 BC: Meadows 2013, p. 172, n. 54.

6. Le Rider 1998b.

7. Meadows 2009, p. 58.

8. And perhaps also Balanea, if that is the mint to which two very rare Alexanders appearing on the market in 2013 are to be attributed. For an example see Gemini 11 (2014) 62; another one in MNL Collection, San Rafael, CA. My thanks to Andrew Meadows for having brought this discovery to my attention.

9. Duyrat 2002a and forthcoming.

10. Meadows 2009, p. 71. I retain here only those parts of Meadows' presentation that shed light on the role of Syria in these developments.

11. Ibid., p. 76. At Aradus, the period of Antiochus III's campaigns in Asia Minor coincides with the resumption of civic Alexanders: Duyrat 2003, p. 38, chart 1; Duyrat 2005a, p. 153, chart 1.

12. "une vraie industrie de leur monnaie pour l'exportation," Seyrig 1973, p. 35.

13. "les villes en question se seraient efforcées de produire, en vue du commerce avec le royaume séleucide autant d'alexandres qu'elles pouvaient, pour obtenir le profit monétaire qu'apportait la cotation favorable de ce numéraire. Cette motivation, à mon avis, non seulement aurait développé l'activité émettrice de ces ateliers, mais aussi, probablement, aurait orienté un plus grand nombre de commerçants vers le royaume séleucide," Le Rider 1999b, p. 53.

Table 7.1. Hoards containing Alexanders of Perge, Aspendus, and Phaselis (Map 13)[14]

No.	Findspot	Date of Burial	Content
162	Syria	210	Aspendus 1 (year 1); Perge 1 (year 13)
166	Oylum Höyüğü	200–195 (Özgen, Davesne); 203/2 (Houghton, Lorber)	Perge 1 tetr. (201/0 BC according to Boehringer); Aspendus: 2 tetr
171	Kosseir	c. 190	Phaselis 4 (to year 24); Perge 3 (to year 20); Aspendus 3
172	Latakia	c. 190	Phaselis 1 (year 10)
173	Dniye	c. 190	Phaselis 1 (year 26)[14]
174	Syria (hinterland of Aradus?)	c. 190/189	Phaselis 5; Aspendus 3; Perge 6
176	Beqaa Valley	187/6?	Phaselis (1) + 31
177	Baiyada	c. 180–175	Phaselis 2; Aspendus 2
179	Unknown findspot	175–170	Perge 4
183	Syria	170–160	7 Phaselis (to year 26); 4 Perge (to year 32); 12 Aspendus (to year 26)
184	Latakia	169	Pergé 1; Aspendus 1
189	Aleppo?	165	Phaselis 2; Perge 5; Aspendus 10
190	Khan Cheikhoun	165	Phaselis 18; Perge 28; Aspendus 25
193	Maʿaret en-Numan	162	Phaselis 57; Aspendus 71; Perge 63
198	Tell Kotchek	160/150–142	Phaselis 15; Perge 7; Aspendus 20
202	"Demetrius I hoard"	151/0	Phaselis 6; Phaselis (?) 1; Aspendus 10; Perge 3
225	Teffaha	After 145/4	Aspendus 1
242	Ain Tab	140–120	Phaselis 18 (to year 26); Aspendus 48 (to year 28); Perge 33 (to year 33)
253	Eastern Anatolia?	130–120	Phaselis 68; Aspendus 118; Perge 44; uncert. 11

14. 188/7 BC, according to the table in Meadows 2009, p. 69, corrected to 191/0 BC in Meadows 2013, p. 171, n. 54.

Figure 7.1. Tetradrachm of Perge, from the Aleppo 1931 hoard (*IGCH* 1546, **189**; ANS 1944.100.33186).

Figure 7.2. Tetradrachm of Aspendus from the Aleppo 1931 hoard (*IGCH* 1546, **189**; ANS 1944.100.32323).

Figure 7.3. Tetradrachm of Phaselis, from the Ain Tab 1921 hoard (*IGCH* 1542; **242** ANS 1944.100.32276).

military demands. Surely one must see in the massive presence of these issues in Syria a phenomenon bound up with the return of soldiers paid in this currency once the military campaigns were over. Meadows' article is additionally interesting, from the Syrian perspective, insofar as it shows that the currency production of Aradus during these years responded to the same criteria as those of the Pamphylian mints. There thus emerges a large region, extending from northern Syria, including the hinterland of Aradus, to Pamphylia, where royal needs influenced output directly.

Alexanders, counting all mints, are present in 32 hoards, often in quite significant proportions, usually above 40% (Fig. 7.4).

Down to the 150s, the only hoards lacking Alexanders were buried in Coele Syria and Phoenicia and are on the Ptolemaic standard (**164**, **165**, **168**, **169**, **182**, **191**, **194**, **203**) or consist of

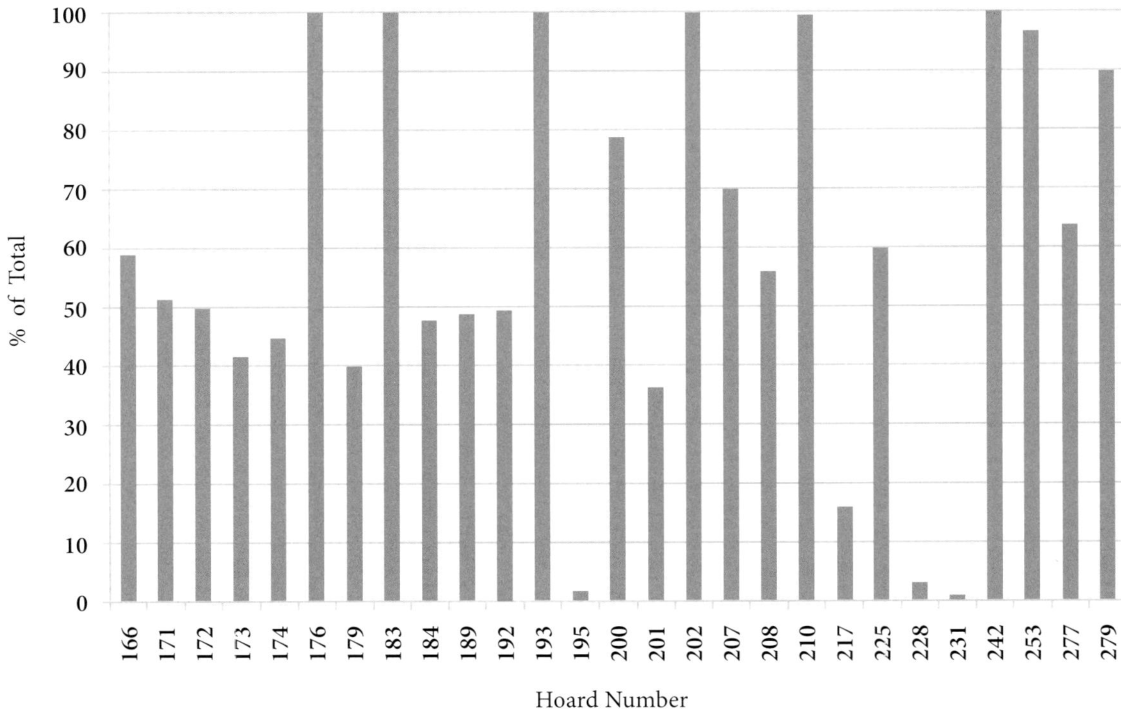

Figure 7.4: Percentage of Alexanders in second-century hoards.[15]

bronze coins (**175**, **178**, **185**, **187**). They show the continuance of practices prior to 200 BC: northern Syria was familiar with Alexander coinage and preferred it to the extent that Le Rider, following Seyrig, saw in this the sign of a premium accorded by the State. The persistence of the cities of Asia Minor, and subsequently Aradus, in striking Alexanders could be explained by the financial benefit from their use in Syrian territory.[16] In my view, perhaps one ought to see here only evidence of the users' confidence and the specific demand of certain populations—among which the mercenaries—that will have encouraged both the continued production in numerous mints and the special hoarding of a currency whose value did not weaken. Meadows' article on the striking of Pamphylian Alexanders and the wars of Seleucus III and Antiochus III in Asia Minor especially highlights the relationship between the production of these tetradrachms and military operations. That Aradus and its Peraea aligned their production periods in this currency with these events, to the point of opportunistically creating new varieties of posthumous Alexanders in mints that had never struck any before,[17] or of starting and stopping issue between 203 and 190 BC, as Aradus did,[18] speaks volumes about the close connection between campaigns, and therefore military expenditures, and the choice of Alexanders.

15. Five hoards do not appear in this chart because of insufficient data on their content: **167**, **170**, **176**, **186**, **197**.
16. Le Rider 1999b, p. 55.
17. Duyrat 2002a, pp. 54–55.
18. Duyrat 2005a, p. 153, chart 1; Duyrat 2003, p. 38, chart 1.

The Asia Minor Alexanders share another specificity: they have been widely countermarked, especially those from Perge, Aspendus, and Phaselis, as the civic tetradrachms of Side that circulated in Syria during the same period. That practice has been commented on by different authors, as the date of the countermarking episodes since they are of crucial importance to establish the date of burial of the hoards. The anchor countermark (Fig. 7.14), the most common, is usually considered dating c. 175–170 BC and being a royal mark which purpose is not entirely clear. The Latakia hoard (**184**) is the first well dated with anchor countermarks, which means they appeared before 169 BC.[19] Mørkholm links these countermarks with the new light standard of Antiochus IV's coinage at Antioch and the issue of large bronze and some silver fractions to conclude to a specific monetary policy of that king.[20] The link between the reduction of the Attic standard and the countermark is not certain, but the beginning of the countermarking episode can safely be dated c. 175–170 BC, at the eve of Antiochus IV's reign.[21] Boehringer suggests a date just before 170 BC.[22] It was probably of short duration since the hoards show countermarked and non-countermarked coins circulating together. With the anchor countermark were sometimes found coins bearing a countermark with the head of Helios facing or, a little later, a "cistophoric" countermark with a bow-case and letters.[23] In our catalogue, the hoards of the Beqaa Valley (**177**), Unknown Findsport (**179**), Syria (**183**), Latakia (**184**), Aleppo (**189**), Khan Cheikhoun (**190**), Ma'aret en-Numan (**193**), Tell Kotchek (**198**), Ain Tab (**242**), and Eastern Anatolia (**253**) contained countermarked Alexanders from Asia Minor (Map 14).

Little by little, however, other coinages contested this omnipresence of Alexanders: Seleucid issues, occasionally supplemented by some others, constitute the core of hoards **180**, **181**, **190**, **196**, **204**, **205**, **206**, all without Alexanders. Some more short-lived coinages on Syrian territory, like the bee drachms of Ephesus and Aradus, are sometimes the only, or almost the only coins in a hoard (**188**, **200**, **201**).[24] Yet when it comes to silver in the Attic standard zone, Alexanders are present in 21 hoards[25] out of 30 prior to c. 150, 70% of cases.

From the 150s, however, Alexanders become far more rare in hoards. They appear in only 10 from the second half of the century out of the 32 discovered in the northern zone (31%).[26] This development is linked with the cessation of production in these types in the Asia Minor mints and at Aradus from 170–160 BC.[27] Thus, they slowly disappear in our sources. Metcalf has shown that the tetradrachms of the 'Ain Tab hoard (**242**) were very worn and had circulated a

19. Seyrig 1958b, p. 194–195.
20. Mørkholm 1982b. Le Rider 2001b discusses the purpose of the anchor countermark and the hypothesis of a monetary reform of Antiochus IV.
21. See Seyrig 1973, p. 55.
22. Boehringer 1972, p. 21–22.
23. Metcalf 1994, p. 44–47 gives a useful summary of the discussions about these second-century countermarks.
24. Le Rider 1991; Duyrat 2005a, pp. 163–66.
25. **166**, **167**, **170–174**, **176**, **177**, **179**, **183**, **184**, **186**, **189**, **190**, **194**, **196**, **198**, **199**, **202**, **203**.
26. **208**, **209**, **217**, **225**, **228**, **231**, **242**, **253**, **277**, **279**.
27. In the 140s for Temnos, according to Lorber 2010, pp. 155–56.

Figure 7.5. Wreathed Tetradrachm of Myrina (ANS 1944.100.44224).

Figure 7.6. Wreathed Tetradrachm of Cyme (ANS 1954.203.178).

long time, justifying a late dating for the burial, perhaps between 140 and 120 BC.[28] The last lot containing Alexanders is dated precisely: it was discovered in the excavation of Ras el-Bassit, rolled up in lead foil (**279**). Nine Alexanders of Alabanda and Temnos were accompanied by a tetradrachm of Antiochus VIII struck at Damascus in 119/8 BC. After this date, Alexanders disappear completely from hoards.

1.2. Wreathed Tetradrachms

Tetradrachms with civic types and, on the reverse, an encircling wreath represent an important component of second-century hoards (Table 7.2). Unlike posthumous Alexanders, these coins have benefited from detailed studies that often come with classification by die.[29] Until recently, most publications placed their issue during the years 160–140 BC among the different coastal cities of Asia Minor. Their chronology has undergone detailed revision in the last volume of *Coin Hoards*. Lorber stresses the fact that the earliest hoard to produce these coinages is now the "Demetrius I hoard" (**202**), which was buried c. 151/0 BC. At this date, the production of Myrina is well underway (Fig. 7.5), Cyme's is starting, but other mints do not seem to have begun wreathed issues (Fig. 7.6).[30] Her lowering of the chronology of the Alexanders of Temnos places them at the point of transition to the first wreathed tetradrachms of Myrina and Cyme.[31]

28. Metcalf 1998, p. 66. Lorber 2010 suggests a burial after 151 BC, but is not opposed to a later date.
29. Le Rider 1999b, p. 46, provides an overview up to that date.
30. Lorber 2010, p. 156.
31. Ibid., p. 157.

The wreathed issues of these two mints might have taken over from the Alexanders when the latter ceased being struck, so between 160 and 151 BC.[32] The reexamination of several hoards enables Meadows and Houghton to propose a closer dating for the chronology of wreathed tetradrachms, in three waves: first, Cyzicus and Tenedos, from c. 165 to c. 155 BC, which circulated little in Syria; then Myrina and Cyme, followed by Aegae, Magnesia, and Smyrna during the 140s. These issues penetrated deeply throughout Syria. A last wave brought together Heraclea, Lebedos, and the tetradrachms in the name of the Theoi Kabeiroi, their production commencing only in the mid-140s.[33]

The wreathed tetradrachms of the cities of western Asia Minor circulated systematically together. Only hoards **222** and **277** contained specimens from just one mint.

Wreathed tetradrachms appear in 11 silver hoards out of 19 recorded in northern Syria between 151/0 and 139/8 BC (Fig. 7.7).[34] In these 11 lots, they represent from nearly a quarter (**202**) to the entirety of the find (**211**). This currency's circulation seems to have been concentrated and brief throughout Syrian territory. Le Rider explains this density: "One may suppose that the Syrian authorities considered these coins with varied types as a single currency, placed under the aegis of the crown, and it is not impossible that this currency also won a certain popularity and an advantageous rate in transactions."[35] These observations, and bearing in mind that the coins are almost never found outside the Seleucid realm, lead to the logical conclusion that "like Alexanders, wreathed tetradrachms from 160–140 BC were manufactured primarily for Syria, which their Attic weight and findspots also indicate."[36] The articles of Lorber, Meadows and Houghton in the most recent volume of *Coin Hoards* clearly show that, contrary to what has long been thought, the issues of wreathed tetradrachms follow successively upon those of the civic Alexanders. This typological change had no effect on the flow of coins of Attic weight from the mints of Asia Minor to Syria. The long-term trust accorded to the types of Alexander is transferred without apparent difficulty to the civic coins struck with a wreath. The common denominator of these issues—Attic weight and Asia Minor provenance—seems to have sufficed. The Seleucids maintained their custom of accepting all coinage of Attic weight within their territory, including those coming from their lost possessions in Asia Minor.

In this group, the *stephanephoroi* of Athens (Fig. 7.8)[37] are less numerous, as Seyrig[38] and Thompson had already shown. The latter, having gathered the finds of these coins, noted that

32. Meadows, Houghton 2010, pp. 180–81.

33. Ibid., pp. 185–86. Callataÿ 2013, p. 235, mentions the indemnity of 100 silver talents that Prusias had to pay in 153 to the cities of Methymna, Aegae, Cyme, and Heraclea for having pillaged their territory (Polybius 33.13.8), noting that this weight of metal could have been coined by just eight obverse tetradrachm dies. The list of those cities that, a little later, begin to issue wreathed tetradrachms is probably not accidental.

34. Hoards containing coins from just one mint have not been integrated in this figure.

35. "on peut supposer que ces monnaies à types variés furent considérées par les autorités syriennes comme un seul numéraire, placé sous le signe de la couronne, et il n'est pas exclu que ce numéraire ait obtenu lui aussi une certaine faveur et une cote avantageuse dans les transactions," Le Rider 1999b, p. 56.

36. Ibid., p. 53.

37. On the name of these coins, cf. Robert 1951b and 1977. They are also often called "New Style tetradrachms."

38. Seyrig 1973, pp. 85–86, 125.

Table 7.2. Dispersion by mint of wreathed tetradrachms in hoards (Map 15)[39]

Area	**Mint**	**d**	**202**	**209**	**210**	**211**	**214**	**217**	**222**	**225**	**228**	**231**	**232**	**235**	**277**
Mysia	Cyzicus										x				
Troad	Tenedos		x												
Aeolis	Myrina	97	x	x	x	x	x	x	x	x	x	x	x	x	
	Aegae	36		x		x					x	x	x		
	Cyme	79	x	x	x	x	x	x		x	x	x	x	x	
Ionia	Smyrna	13		x	x		x				x	x	x		x
	Lebedos	8										x		x	
	Magnesia on Meander	36		x	x	x		x			x	x	x	x	
	Heraclea of Latmos	25		x								x		x	
	Theoi Kabeiroi	13		x								x			

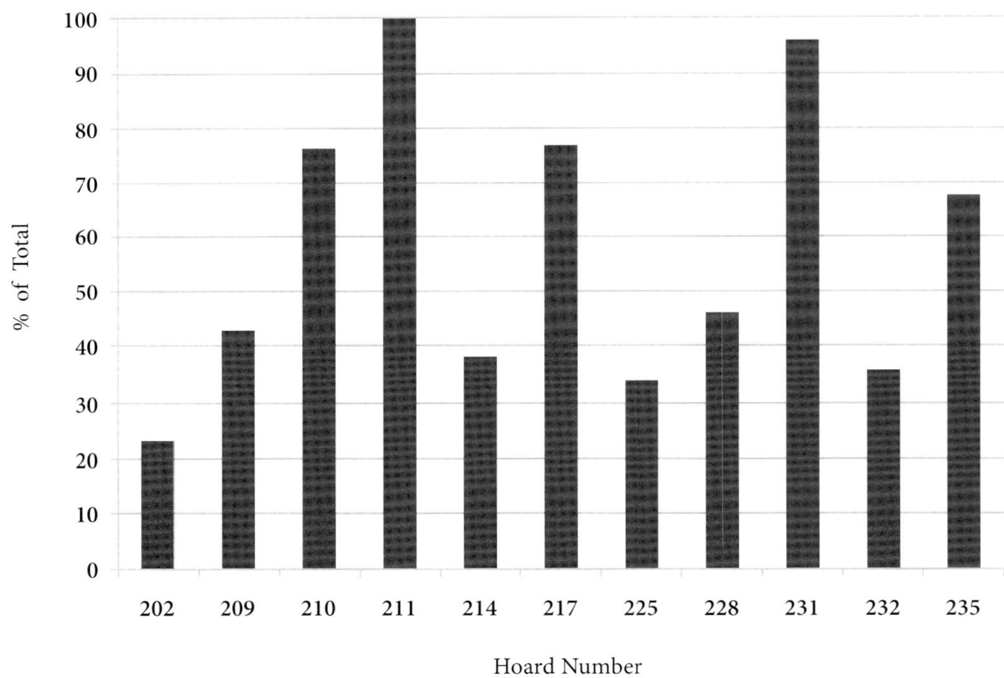

Figure 7.7. Percentage of wreathed tetradrachms in hoards.[40]

39. Callataÿ 2013, p. 233, provides the estimates of obverse dies. Shading designates hoards with wreathed tetradrachms from only one mint.

40. Including Athenian *stephanephoroi*.

Figure 7.8. New Style Athenian Tetradrachm, 136/5 BC (ANS 1944.100.24615).

"the material from Crete and the other islands, from Anatolia, Syria and Italy is scanty."[41] The current state of the hoard evidence is presented in Table 7.3.

With the exceptions of the Demetrius hoard (**202**) and of the Syria (?) hoard (**249**), they constitute only a limited portion of Syrian finds. This weak representation of what was an abundant coinage[42] raises the question of the channels that brought the coinage from its production site to its burial place. Clearly, despite the masses of tetradrachms Athens issued from c. 165 BC, they did not reach Syria.[43] The contrast with Thrace, for example, is sharp, where these tetradrachms flooded in during the 120s.[44] Le Rider suggested, without elaborating, that Athenian commerce favored Delos over the East.[45] It is noteworthy that Athenian *stephanephoroi* are basically present only during the time when Alexanders and wreathed tetradrachms from western Asia Minor mints appear. One has to wonder whether they did not arrive through the same channels as those much more popular coinages, caught up in a surge that first involved the output of mints in Asia Minor to which their Attic weight related them.

The dating by month of new style Athenian tetradrachms allows Meadows and Houghton to assess how quickly these coins circulated between their issuing mint and their burial in Syria in the Gaziantep hoard. They suggest that the last of these coins were struck during the period from July to September 143 BC and that the hoard was buried between August and October of the same year, the closing month of the year 169 on the Seleucid calendar, the date on the latest coin of Antiochus VI present in the hoard.[46] Their small number notwithstanding, the Athenian *stephanephoroi* were imitated: four tetradrachms of Myrina were overstruck with rather clumsily made dies reprising Athenian types. Hoover and MacDonald concluded that "the overstriking of Myrina tetradrachms with imitations of Athenian types reflects the ascendancy of the new foreign currency and probably represents an attempt to avoid depreciation of the obsolete coins in the market place. The poor style of the imitation types and their apparent rarity

41. Thompson 1961, p. 538, thus contrasting with Hoover, MacDonald 1999–2000, p. 116, who suggest that "By 140–130, Athenian New Style coinage was entering the Seleucid realm in great quantity and replacing Myrina tetradrachms as the dominant foreign currency in circulation."

42. Flament 2007, pp. 148–50.

43. Thompson 1961, vol. I, pp. 649–57; for a convenient overview of the production, cf. Callataÿ 1997b, nos. 157–59.

44. Most recently Picard 2008, p. 472. The importing of these coins is connected to the wars the Romans waged against the Thracian peoples.

45. Le Rider 1999b, p. 57.

46. Meadows, Houghton 2010, p. 179.

Table 7.3. New Style Athenian tetradrachms in hoards (Map 16)

202	"Demetrius I hoard"	151/0	532 AR, 3 AV Athens, New Style: 105 tetr.
222	Lebanon	145	Athens New Style: any?
228	Gaziantep	144/3	1916 AR Athens New Style: 197
231	Kırıkhan	143/2	1104 AR Athens New Style: 3
232	Ras Baalbek	After 143/2	45 AR Athens New Style: 2 tetr.
249	Syria?	after 133	15 AR Athens: tetr. New Style
260	Syria	Late 120s?	23 AR Athens New Style: 17 tetr.
277	Tartus	120	200 tetr. AR Athens New Style: 6
288	Kessab	After 105/4	392 tetr. AR Athens New Style: 41

indicates the overstrikes were the product of a small scale forger's workshop."[47] These imitations confirm that wreathed coins were particularly sought after in Syria.

The strong concentration in time and space of the distribution of the wreathed tetradrachms demands further comment. Le Rider supposed that they circulated in a privileged manner towards Syria because they were more highly valued. This production might have ceased, in his opinion, in the wake of civic unrest, or because of the deregulation of commercial relations with Syria between Demetrius II's return there in 147 BC and the accession of Antiochus VII in 139/8 BC.[48] Generally speaking, the scholars who have considered the matter assume a commercial and/or military cause amidst these upheavals. So, recently, Psoma has cited the festivals that were perhaps the occasion for the cities of Asia Minor to continue striking silver on the Attic standard, with types of Alexander and then the wreathed type, even as the Attalids henceforth used a lighter standard. The large numbers attending these festivals meant the cities had to have available common coinages accepted by all. Very probably the production of coins of Attic weight, at a time when the Attalids were striking *cistophoroi* for closed circulation, is the fruit of a reciprocal accord between the king and the cities where each party benefitted.[49] Callataÿ has stressed the coastal origin of wreathed tetradrachms of Attic weight, while the mints issuing *cistophoroi* of reduced weight are, on the contrary, located in the interior of the Attalid realm.

47. Hoover, MacDonald 1999, p. 116.
48. Le Rider 1999b, pp. 57–58.
49. Psoma 2013, pp. 288–89.

He also observes that it was often mints with previously insignificant production that struck the wreathed issues.[50] These factors do not support an exclusively commercial explanation for the production of these coins.

The arrival of tetradrachms of Asia Minor in Syria might be tied to the well-attested aid the Attalids provided Alexander I Balas in his overthrow of the royal power. The subsidies used to pay his troops were necessarily on the Attic standard. Hoover and MacDonald have neatly summed up the connection between the two: "The Myrina issues first began to be struck about the time Alexander was raising an army in Anatolia for his invasion of Syria and ceased around the year of his death. These coins are frequently found in hoards in Seleucid territory in conjunction with the coins of Alexander and his two rivals, Demetrius I and Demetrius II.... They are only rarely encountered elsewhere. Myrina tetradrachms and related issues were struck to fulfill a specific purpose in Syria: Attalid support of Alexander I Balas. When Alexander was killed by his own associates in 145 BC, the purpose of Myrina's tetradrachms died with him."[51] Commercial activities, probably intense between the Levant and western Asia Minor, certainly contributed to this flow, but the chronological and geographical coincidence of these coins and the period's political events favor seeing here military payments.[52] One hoard upsets this edifice a little: the "Demetrius Hoard" (**202**) is dated 151/0 BC at the earliest. The preciseness of this dating leads Lorber to revisit the chronology of the Alexanders of Temnos and wreathed coins and to suggest that the unrepresented mints in this hoard did not issue these tetradrachms in 151/0 BC. In her view, this would partially call into question the association of these tetradrachms with Alexander Balas' seizure of power, unless we are to think that "the 'Demetrius I' hoard simply failed to capture many wreathed tetradrachms because it was formed by a supporter of the legitimate king at the time when the wreathed tetradrachms were used to pay Alexander's partisans."[53] The hoard also contained some gold coins of unknown issues of Demetrius I that served to finance defensive preparations against the armies of Alexander I Balas. The wreathed tetradrachms were perhaps not created for supporting the latter, but the heyday of these coinages nonetheless falls between 151 and 143 BC,[54] and I do not think that we ought to discard too quickly the circumstantial ties they had with this reign.

2. SELEUCID ROYAL SILVER

2.1. Growth in Royal Production

One of the most striking features of the second century is undoubtedly the increase in the number of Seleucid coins in hoards (Table 7.4). Taking into account all standards, they appear

50. Callataÿ 2013, p. 234.
51. Hoover, MacDonald 1999, p. 116.
52. Psoma 2013, pp. 292–93, for similar conclusions.
53. Lorber 2010, p. 156.
54. Meadows, Houghton 2010, pp. 185–86.

in 101 of 122 deposits, or almost 83%.[55] The large quantity makes an individual breakdown difficult, but the number of hoards in which the royal coinages are present is very suggestive and is visible on the maps.

Table 7.4. Hoards containing Seleucid coins (by reign)

King	Number of Hoards	Map
Antiochus IV (175–164)	22	Map 17
Antiochus V (164–162)	10	-
Demetrius I (162–150)	25	Map 18
Alexander I Balas (150–145)	31	Map 19
Demetrius II (146–138; 129–126/5)	52	Map 20
Antiochus VII (138–129)	44	Map 21
Alexander II (128–122)	11	-
Antiochus VIII (121/0–96)	20	Map 22

All numismatists have observed the paucity of Seleucid issues in the third century.[56] Le Rider notably stressed it in the context of his study of hoards where Alexanders predominate: "By permitting Alexanders to circulate freely in their realm, [the Seleucids] accepted limitations on their own coinage,"[57] and, further on: "The limited number of coins the Seleucids struck in the third century leads one to wonder about the pace of their currency production. One may surmise that the rulers at this time issued coins only occasionally, whether for reasons of prestige (at the time of accessions, for example) or because of exceptional circumstances (wars, unexpected events), when a fund of available resources was shown to be crucial."[58] More recently, examination of gold and silver output at Antioch has allowed us to quantify precisely how production developed in one of the empire's largest mints. The following chart (Fig. 7.9) is based on the results of Le Rider's die studies.[59]

With an average of 7.33 obverse tetradrachm dies annually under Antiochus V, the production level was not at all sizeable, compared to the initial output of Ptolemy Soter and Ptolemy Philadelphus,[60] or to that of Aradian tetradrachms with the types of Alexander issued at the

55. Excluding the five hoards of bronze coins: **175**, **187**, **283**, **284**, **289**.
56. Houghton 2002, pp. 14–15, tables 4A and 4B.
57. "en laissant les alexandres circuler librement dans leur royaume, ils acceptaient que leur monnayage personnel fut très restreint," Le Rider 1986b, p. 34.
58. "Le nombre limité de monnaies que frappèrent les Séleucides au IIIe siècle amène à s'interroger sur le rythme de leur production monétaire. On peut supposer que les souverains, à cette époque, n'émirent des monnaies qu'occasionnellement, soit pour des raisons de prestige (lors des avènements par exemple), soit dans des circonstances exceptionnelles (guerres, événements inattendus), quand un complément de ressources disponibles se révélait indispensable," Ibid., p. 36.
59. Le Rider 1999, with summary tables in Duyrat 2002b.
60. Callataÿ 2005, p. 124.

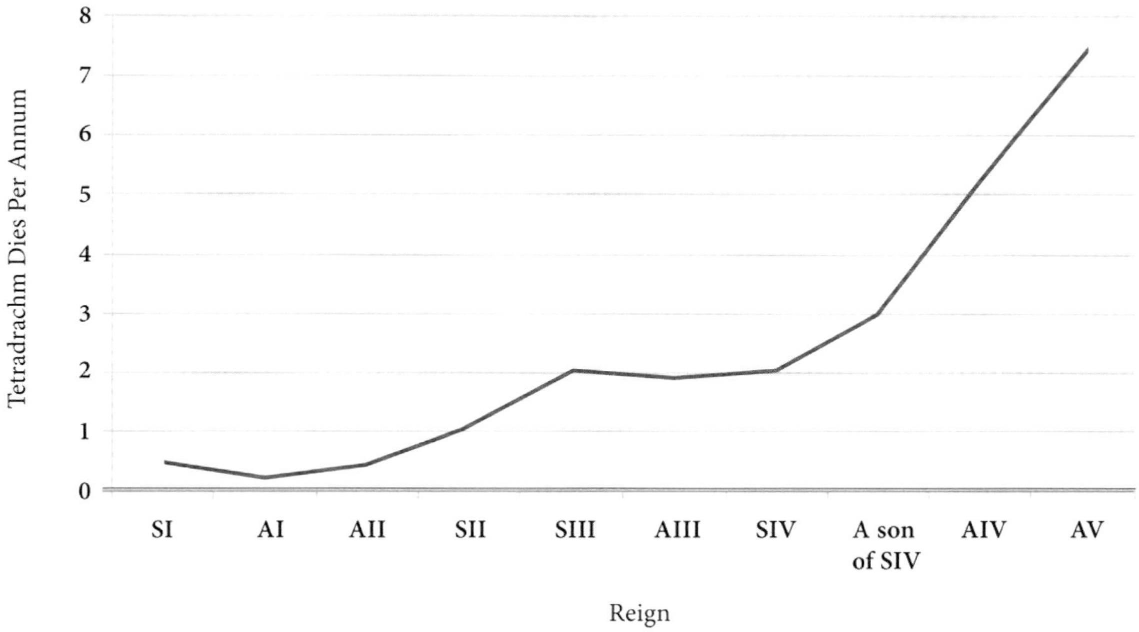

Figure 7.9. Number of obverse tetradrachm dies in use each year at Antioch.

end of the 320s.[61] But increase is noticeable in a single mint, although at least 37 were active under Antiochus IV.[62] At Antioch, Houghton asserts more than 10 obverse dies annually under Demetrius I and his successors. Production was clearly growing.[63]

Succeeding reigns confirm this increase. The number of hoards producing coins of Demetrius I, Alexander I Balas, Demetrius II, and Antiochus VII is particularly high. Various causes explain the rise. The first is certainly the endemic state of war in the region from the Sixth Syrian War (170–168 BC) and the Maccabees' Revolt that followed (166–161 BC). The succession after Antiochus IV also provoked dynastic wars between the two branches that claimed him, those of Demetrius I and Alexander I Balas. Revolving door reigns are certainly their most salient feature, Demetrius II being in power, for example, from 146–138 and again from 129–125 BC. This chronic instability led to a clear increase in the number of surviving hoards (Map 17 to Map 20).[64] Their number does not have any necessary connection with the volume of coins produced. But other factors point to a significant rise.

The amount of material makes a presentation of the hoard content for each sovereign difficult, but it is possible to give one example. I have chosen the turbulent reign of Antiochus VII (Fig. 7.10) because it is well documented and unified, unlike that of Demetrius II, who reigned twice, for instance. From the first hoard containing tetradrachms of Antiochus, during the 130s

61. Duyrat 2005a, pp. 214–18.
62. Taking account only of well-attested mints and uncertain mints itemized in *SC* 2, 1, pp. 51–52.
63. Houghton 1991, p. 80, for Antioch after Antiochus III; Houghton 2002, pp. 14–15, tables 4A and 4B for "the Seleucid Core."
64. Duyrat 2011a.

Figure 7.10. Tetradrachm of Antiochus VII, Antioch (ANS 1944.100.76630).

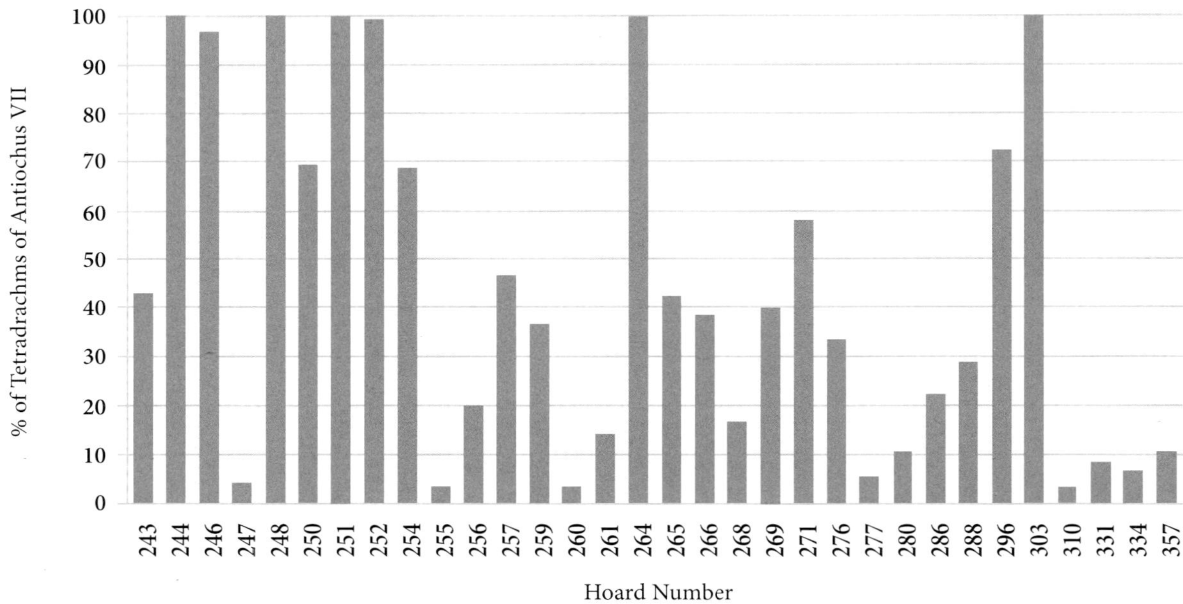

Figure 7.11: Percentage of tetradrachms of Antiochus VII in hoards.

(**243**), and the end of the century (**289**), the catalogue shows 47 hoards of which 30, or nearly two-thirds, have issues of this king. Thirteen others date from the first century. The percentage of coins of Antiochus VII can be assessed in 33 of these hoards (Fig. 7.11).

In more than two-thirds of cases (69%), Antiochus VII's tetradrachms represent more than 20% of the total hoarded; in more than a third (38%), they are over 50%. One hoard in six consists of coins of Antiochus VII exclusively. One should add that coinage in the name of Antiochus VII often circulates together with that of Demetrius II, whose two reigns (145–140, 129–126/5 BC) frame that of Antiochus. The following table (Table 7.5) lists all the hoards in which only tetradrachms of Antiochus VII and Demetrius II appear, sometimes with civic issues.

The last six hoards produced coins of Antiochus VII and Demetrius II accompanied by coins of a single city in each instance, Ascalon (**269**) and Tyre (**271**, **276**, **290**, **334**, **357**), illustrating the progressive development of local civic issues at the end of the second century. Hoards **250**, **260**, and **261** should be added, in which the coins of these two kings are mixed with those of other Seleucids or of the Ptolemies (**259**).

Table 7.5: Joint circulation of coins of Antiochus VII and Demetrius II

No.	Findspot	No. *IGCH* or *CH*	Date of Burial	Cities
252	Syria	*CH* 10.314	130	
254	Tyre	*CH* 9.533	129/8	
256	Latakia	*IGCH* 1563 = *CH* 1.75	c. 128/7	
257	Samaria	*CH* 9.534	128/7	
258	Golan	*IGCH* 1600 = *CH* 1.75	128/7–126/5 (autonomy of Tyre)	
262	Phoenicia	*IGCH* 1599	127/6	
263	South of Jerusalem	*CH* 8.469	126/5	
264	Bethlehem, region of Hebron	*IGCH* 1603	126/5	
265	Beth Ummar	*CH* 10.315	126/5	
266	Capernaum	*IGCH* 1602 = *CH* 1.75	After 126/5	
268	Hebron	*CH* 7.111	125	
269	Israel	*CH* 4.65, fig. 8	125	1 Ascalon
271	Unknown findspot	*CH* 8.468	125	9 Tyre
276	Thalalaia, near Zahle	*IGCH* 1604 = *CH* 1.75	After 121/0	10 Tyre
290	Palestine	*IGCH* 1630 = Noe 788	2nd–1st cent.	Tyre
334	Palestine	*IGCH* 1617	After 61	10 Tyre
357	Khirbet Qumran		8 BC	448 Tyre

Lorber and Houghton have recently reassessed the currency of Antiochus VII. They have shown that an important portion of the issues previously attributed to Antiochus were probably, in fact, excellent imitations made in Cappadocia.[65] This phenomenon is arguably the best illustration of the success of Antiochus' coinage.

2.2. Alexander I Balas, Ptolemy VI, and Coinage

Although short (152/0–145 BC), the reign of Alexander I Balas brings a certain number of monetary changes that warrant further attention. The first change, as we have seen, was the flow of wreathed tetradrachms from the cities of Asia Minor into Syrian territory. Attalus II of Pergamum may have used these coins to support his candidate for the Seleucid throne against Demetrius I.[66] Alexander I opposed Demetrius I for two years before finally overcoming him

65. Lorber, Houghton 2006. One of these hoards appears in the catalogue (**303**). Of late date, its specific findspot is uncertain, as is that of the other hoards Lorber and Houghton inventoried. The latter are situated in eastern Syria, in eastern Anatolia, or in Mesopotamia, without further clarification.
66. Diodorus 31.32a.

Figure 7.12. Tetradrachm of Alexander I Balas, Tyre 148/7 BC, Ptolemaic standard (ANS 1944.100.77689)

in 150 BC. He ascended the throne with the backing of Ptolemy VI, whose daughter, Cleopatra Thea, he married at Ptolemais.[67] Ptolemaic involvement puts Coele Syria and Phoenicia at the center of Alexander's reign. This geopolitical positioning has noticeable consequences for currency, and they must be seen in light of remarks already made on the wreathed coinages to achieve a global perspective.

It was Alexander I Balas who developed a genuinely Seleucid currency on the Ptolemaic standard. Until this time, the Seleucids were content to let Ptolemaic coinage circulate. Antiochus V was the author of a short-lived first issue of Ptolemaic weight struck at Ptolemais, with an eagle on the reverse but his own portrait on the obverse.[68] Under Alexander I Balas, three other mints in addition to Ptolemais were active: Laodiceia in Phoenicia (Beirut), Sidon, and Tyre (Fig. 7.12) began regular issues in 151/0 BC. All struck Seleucid tetradrachms of Ptolemaic weight, with an eagle on the reverse. This clear change of orientation in royal monetary policy probably stems from varied motives. One is likely to have been quite basic: Ptolemaic coins of the second century are rare in second-century Syrian hoards.

Table 7.6 shows that following the burial of the Balatah hoard (**169**), in c. 199 BC, the coins of the first five Ptolemies become rare in hoards. The next three hoards (**182**, **191**, **194**), buried probably in the 160s, reveal a few coins of Ptolemy VI (Fig. 7.13). In all, nine hoards contain tetradrachms of Ptolemy VI. Their geographical and chronological spread is not without interest.

Table 7.7 highlights three periods for the burial of coins of Ptolemy VI: the 160s, the 140s, and the 120s. I have had occasion to show elsewhere that these waves of hoarding correspond to military episodes, the duration and consequences of which were sufficiently long and profound for the local populations as to be conducive to a palpable increase in this phenomenon.[69] The 140s are particularly interesting: they witness the confrontation of Alexander I Balas, backed by Ptolemy VI, and Demetrius II. In his unpublished dissertation, Olivier presents the results of metallurgical analyses of both Alexander's coins on the Ptolemaic standard and contemporary Ptolemaic output.[70] It is very illuminating that the copper content of the coins of Coele Syria and Phoenicia groups them with Cypriot Ptolemaic issues. Olivier also observes that several

67. Josephus, *Antiquities of the Jews* 13.81–82; I *Maccabees* 10.51–58; wedding tetradrachm: Houghton, Lorber, Hoover 2008, no. 1841.

68. Houghton, Lorber, Hoover 2008, no. 1583.

69. Duyrat 2011a, pp. 427–28.

70. Olivier forthcoming, pp. 760–63.

Table 7.6: Dispersion of Ptolemaic coins in the hoards of Coele Syria and Phoenicia in the second century[71]

	PI	PII	PIII	PIV	PV	PVI–PVIII
164	10	25	1			
168	301	431	24	31	147	
169		19	1	3	12	
182		1	1			2
192					1	7
195						4
216	1	1	1	1	2	1
218						1
226						34
236						6
259						2
267		1				
268						1
Total	**312**	**478**	**28**	**35**	**162**	**58**

Figure 7.13. Tetradrachm of Ptolemy VI (ANS 1944.100.78720).

hoards buried in the 140s contain coins struck in Cypriot mints (**218**, **226**, **236**). This convergence is indicative of the financial support Ptolemy VI provided Alexander I Balas, although written sources are not explicit on this point.

The peak in hoarding in 146/5 BC is all the greater if one takes into consideration the "coins of uncertain era." These tetradrachms and didrachms with Ptolemaic types, struck according

71. Hoard **255** has been omitted from this table. Buried after 129/8 BC, it contains coins on the Attic and Ptolemaic standards. The latter have attributions dating from Ptolemy II to Ptolemy IV. Doubt remains about this collection that could, in fact, be a compilation of several hoards.

Table 7.7. Coins of Ptolemy VI in hoards of Coele Syria and Phoenicia

No.	Findspot	No *IGCH* or *CH*	Date of Burial	Content
182	Jericho(?)	*CH* 8.412	c. 170/169	Ptolemy II: 1 tetr. Ake-Ptolemais Ptolemy III: 1 tetr. Ake-Ptolemais Ptolemy VI: 2 tetr. Alexandria "Uncertain Era": 12 tetr.
192	Near Bethlehem	*CH* 8.432	c. 165	10 AR Ptolemy V: 1 Salamis Ptolemy VI: 3 Alexandria, 4 Paphos Ptolemy uncert.: 1 tetr., 1 didr.
195	Southern Palestine	*CH* 4.58	Late 160s	15+ AR Ptolemy VI: 1 tetr. Salamis; 3 tetr. Alexandria
216	Madaba, Jordan	*IGCH* 1592	After 146/5	Ptolemy I: 1 tetr. Ptolemy II: 1 tetr. Ptolemy III: 1 tetr. Ptolemy IV: 1 tetr. Ptolemy V: 2 tetr. Ptolemy VI: 1 tetr.
218	Yatta, Region of Hebron	*CH* 9.531	146	10 AR "Uncertain Era": 4 didr. Ptolemy VI: 1 tetr. Paphos Alexander I Balas: 1 tetr. Laodicaeia in Phoenicia/Berytus, 4 tetr. Sidon
226	Region of Hebron		After 145/4	50 tetr. AR Ptolemy VI 34; 15 Paphos, 7 Citium, 12 Salamis Alexander I Balas 14: Berytus, Sidon, Tyre, Ake-Ptolemaïs Demetrius II (1): 1 Berytus, 1 Tyre
236	Hebron	*CH* 7.109	140	44+ AR Lot 1 Alexander I Balas: 1 tetr. Berytus; 2 tetr. Sidon; 4 tetr. Tyre Demetrius II (1): 8 tetr. Sidon Antiochus VI: 1 tetr. Ptolemaïs Tryphon: 1 tetr. Ptolemaïs Lot 2 Ptolemy VI: 5 tetr. Salamis Ptolemy VIII: 1 tetr. Citium (year 26) "Uncertain Era": 21 didr.
259	Region of Hebron		After 128/7, c. 111/0?	11 AR Ptolemy VI and VIII: 1 tetr. Salamis Ptolemy VI: 1 didr. Alexandria Antiochus VII: 1 tetr. Tyre ; 3 didr. Tyre Demetrius II: 1 tetr., 4 didr.

No.	Findspot	No *IGCH* or *CH*	Date of Burial	Content
268	Hebron	*CH* 7.111	125	6 tetr. AR Antiochus VII: 1 Tyre Demetrius II (2): 5 Tyre Ptolemy VI: 1 Salamis (year 28) was seen with this lot

to an era the start of which is now better established, although its mints are still debated,[72] also undergo more marked hoarding between 146 and 140 BC.[73] The date of 146/5 BC is not insignificant. In 147 BC, Demetrius, the son of Demetrius I, recruited an army and proceeded into Cilicia with the intention of reconquering his father's kingdom.[74] As Alexander went to meet him, Ptolemy VI moved into Coele Syria and Phoenicia and their chief cities. After Alexander tried to have him assassinated, Ptolemy allied himself with Demetrius II and advanced as far as Antioch.[75] During all these operations, the written sources speak just of captured coastal cities. Jerusalem is the only city in the interior mentioned, owing to Jonathan Maccabeus' participation in Ptolemy's VI's campaign. It so happens that four of the seven hoards buried in the years 146–140 BC are densely concentrated in the region of Hebron (Map 23). Such a chronological and geographic conjunction must be meaningful: in the mid-140s, a sufficiently violent and defining event occurred in this region that a group of four hoards was buried there, never to be recovered by the owners. It is tempting to connect this fact with Ptolemy VI's campaign, but without being to able to go any further.

It is conceivable that the worn condition of Ptolemaic coins circulating regionally in a closed zone prompted Alexander's decision to develop a substantial Seleucid issue on the Ptolemaic standard. This made it possible to resupply Coele Syria and Phoenicia with a means of payment that was its own and that was critical to the smooth functioning of the region and the royal treasury. In Egypt, in 258 BC, the letter of Demetrius to the chief financial officer Apollonius, known from the Zenon archive, explicitly calls attention to the difficulties in restriking foreign coins into Ptolemaic, and the problems attendant upon use of a worn coinage, which was all that was available in the absence of newly minted issues.[76] Similarly, it is possible that the fiscal administration set up in the ports of Coele Syria and Phoenicia alerted the central Seleucid administration to this type of predicament. Nevertheless, the sources do not justify going beyond the mere hypothesis, and political and military motivations remain the most obvious.

Be that as it may, the change in the origin of the coin supply is quite evident in monetary circulation: the maps show a large number of Seleucid tetradrachms on southern sites where

72. Most recently, Lorber 2007.

73. **218, 220, 221, 232, 236, 237.**

74. I *Maccabees* 10.67; Josephus, *Antiquities of the Jews* 13. 86; Justin 35.2.2.

75. I *Maccabees* 11.1–12; Josephus, *Antiquities of the Jews* 13.103–110; Justin 32.9c.

76. *PCZ* 59.021. http://papyri.info/ddbdp/p.cair.zen:1:59021; Orrieux 1983, pp. 28–29; Le Rider, Callataÿ 2006, pp. 142–43.

they had been excluded before the reign of Alexander Balas (Maps 19 to 22). The increasing rarity of Ptolemaic silver coins accompanies this switch: out of 28 hoards buried in Coele Syria and Phoenicia after 140 BC, only three consist of this coinage, in rather modest proportions in each instance[77] (**259**, **267**,[78] **268?**[79]). This change is confirmed under Alexander I's successors.

To sum up, this king played an important role in his kingdom's monetary evolution. He initiated an abundant issue of coins of Ptolemaic weight with his portrait and name. This coinage effectively drove out the Ptolemaic currency that had continued to circulate in Coele Syria and Phoenicia after the conquest by Antiochus III. It was also during his reign, it seems, that wreathed tetradrachms and, more generally, non-Syrian tetradrachms of Attic weight disappear from circulation. This pivotal reign, therefore, would mark major changes in the monetary landscape: from this point on, the royal Seleucid coinage played a preeminent role it never had before. At the same time, the kingdom refocussed itself around Syria following the loss of Mesopotamia, where Parthian coins replaced Seleucid royal coinage progressively after 140 BC.[80]

3. COMPARTMENTALIZATION OF THE MONETARY SYSTEM

The disappearance of Alexanders and wreathed tetradrachms of the mints of Asia Minor is a major development. Other factors, however, point to a gradual compartmentalization of currency circulation starting in the 140s.

3.1. End of the Supply of Tetradrachms from Asia Minor

The fact that the Attic standard was the sole norm imposed on coinage in the Seleucid Empire allowed the circulation of foreign civic coins with autonomous types. Though far less numerous than Alexanders and the wreathed tetradrachms of Asia Minor, they are no less significant. Tetradrachms of Side in Pamphylia (Fig. 7.14), sometimes in noticeable amounts, have turned up in 13 hoards buried between c. 200 and 130–120 BC (Fig. 7.15).[81] These silver coins are concentrated in northern Syria, in the Attic standard zone.

More unexpectedly, bronzes of Side have been found in excavations in relatively sizeable proportions.[82] These coins date from the third century BC, but they are often worn; Barkay suggests that they were still circulating down to the mid-second century because, on the site of Marisa, they are associated with coins of Antiochus III and IV.[83] The reasons for the circulation

77. Bronze coin hoards are not included.
78. Just one tetradrachm.
79. The presence of a coin of Ptolemy VI in this lot is not certain.
80. Le Rider 1965, p. 356; Duyrat 2004, pp. 397–98.
81. A third of the Aleppo hoard (**189**), which, however, is only fragmentary.
82. Cf. Map 36. Barkay 2003–2006, pp. 51–52, offers a more complete accounting than my catalogue for Israeli excavations. Ariel 2000, p. 46, has also published a list of 73 coins of Side found on 37 Near-Eastern sites, mostly Israeli.
83. Barkay 2003–2006, pp. 50 and 52.

Figure 7.14. Tetradrachm of Side from the Aleppo 1931 Hoard (*IGCH* 1546, **189**; ANS 1944.100.50917).

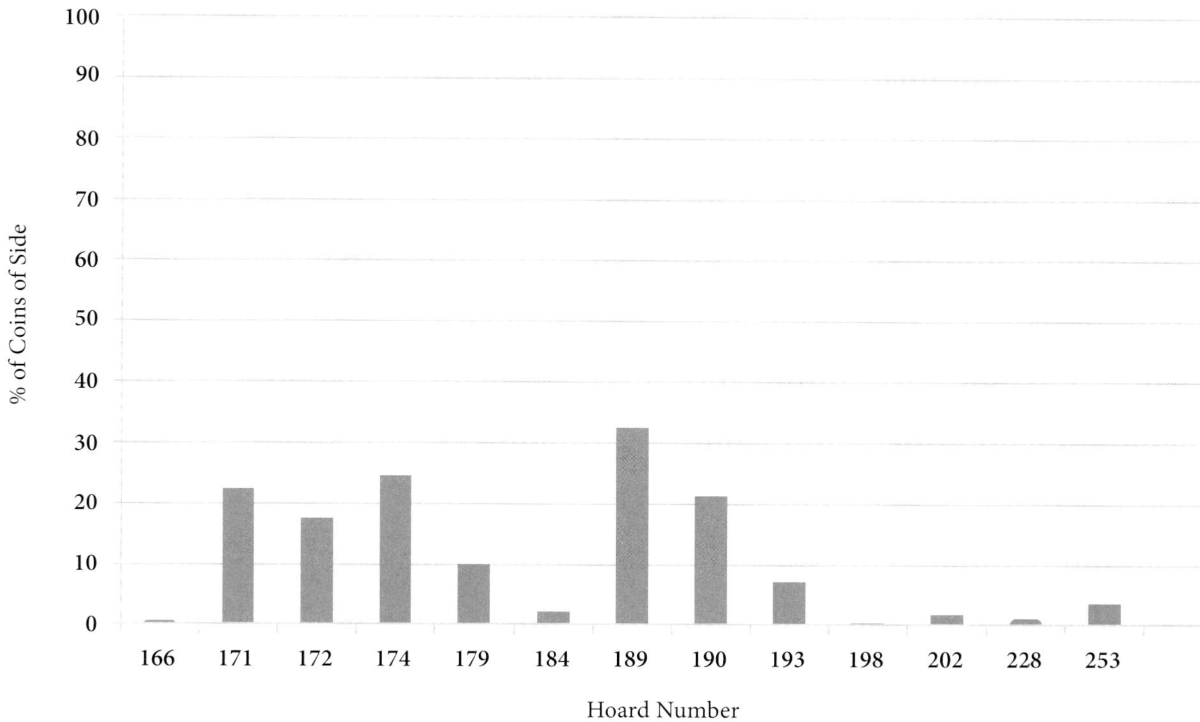

Figure 7.15. Percentage of Coins of Side in Hoards.

of bronze coins are always difficult to discern. Barkay recalls that Pamphylia is a region that traditionally supplied mercenaries. The end of the third century is also the time when Seleucus III and, later, Antiochus III were active in Asia Minor. Meadows' observations on these military undertakings and how they influenced the production of tetradrachms with types of Alexander are probably just as valid for explaining the presence of these Sidetan bronzes in Syria.[84]

Other coinages, by contrast, only appear in smaller proportions. Cos is represented by one tetradrachm in three hoards (**193**, **202**, **275**), Alabanda by scarcely more, probably because they were struck in smaller quantities (Table 7.8, Fig 3.1).

84. Meadows 2009.

Table 7.8. Tetradrachms of Alabanda of autonomous type

No.	Findspot	No. *IGCH* or *CH*	Date of Burial	n
172	Latakia	*IGCH* 1536	c. 190	1
174	Syria, perhaps Aradian Peraea	*CH* 2.81 = *CH* 10.289	c. 190	1
184	Latakia	*IGCH* 1544 = Noe 603	169	5
202	"Demetrius I hoard"	*CH* 10.301	151/0	1
228	Gaziantep	*CH* 9.527	144/3	4
235	Aleppo?	*IGCH* 1562 = *CH* 1.75	After 142/1–139/8	2

It is noteworthy that these tetradrachms with civic types disappear from hoards in the decade of the 130s, even though the coinage continued to be struck.[85] Thus it seems that the removal of wreathed tetradrachms during the 140s is not unique to that coinage but affected all the issues of Asia Minor. Psoma suggests that the loss of Attalid interest in Syria upon the death of Attalus II in 139 BC may be a cause for the interruption in the flow of these coins to Syria.[86] Such a hypothesis would have the attraction of explaining the substantial increase in royal Seleucid production as compensation, at a time when the multiplication of dynastic struggles and usurpations imposed on the different claimants the need to pay their troops in silver coinage. These changes entail a *de facto* monetary compartmentalization of Syria: for the first time since Alexander the Great, Syria no longer obtained abundant supplies of coins on the Attic standard from foreign sources.

3.2. Aradus and Changes in Common Coinages

The variety of coinages circulating in Syria in the first half of the second century shows the wide acceptance of "common coinages." Certain cities went so far as to make new common coinage as needed. This is the case for the Aradians who, probably in 172/1 BC, began to strike drachms imitating those of Ephesus (Figs. 7.16–17).[87] These were rather popular in Syria, where they are found in eight hoards. In Syrian territory, Ephesian drachms are most often accompanied by their Aradian imitations, in proportions favoring the latter (Fig. 7.18).

Thus Aradus maintained a common coinage in a novel way, by choosing an acceptable coinage but not one as widely recognized as Alexanders. Perhaps the relative disaffection with Alexanders, which progressively disappeared during the 160s, explains this choice. But the Aradians would then have anticipated by a few years a widespread movement. They discontinued their issues of Alexanders in 168/7 BC and selected the types of Ephesian drachms to meet their silver

85. Cf. Meadows 2006b for the chronology of the autonomous tetradrachms of Side and their imitations in the first century.

86. Psoma 2013, pp. 275, 292–93.

87. Le Rider 1991 and Kinns 1999 have studied this coinage; catalogue in Duyrat 2005a, pp. 73–81, commentary, especially pp. 162–66, 249–52, 261–62.

Figure 7.16. Drachm of Ephesus (ANS 1968.57.94).

Figure 7.17. Drachm of Aradus (ANS 1944.100.70416).

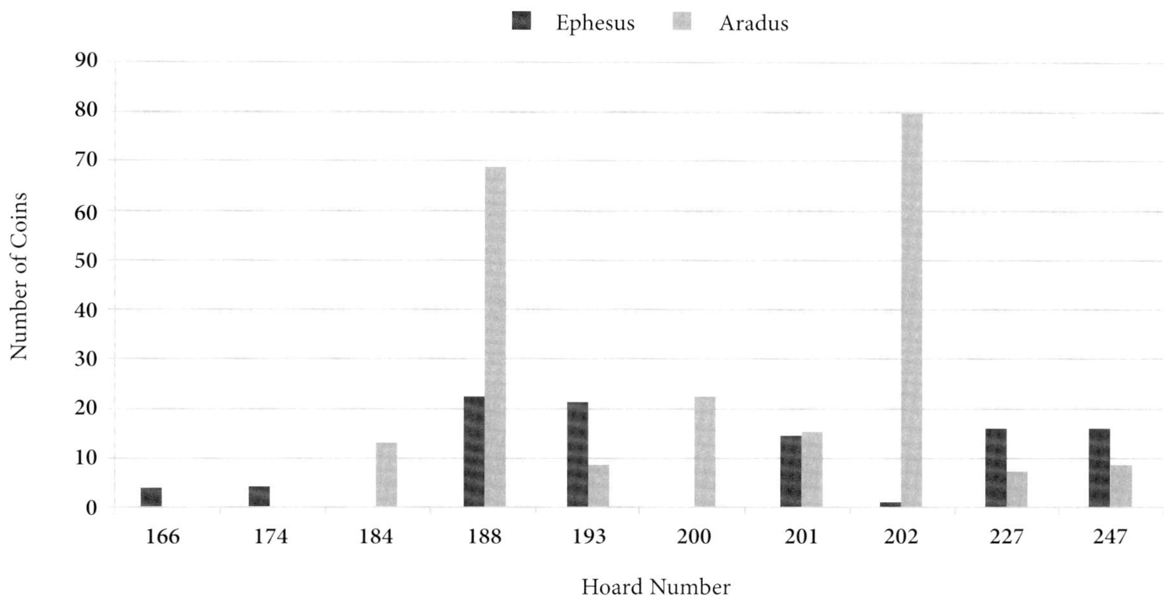

Figure 7.18. Aradian bee drachms and drachms of Ephesus in hoards.

coinage needs.[88] Le Rider thought that the fiscal attraction of a widely accepted coinage guided their choice. I wonder if demand was not the compelling factor. Aradus is a port that must have seen a lot of foreign coinages pass through, which were acceptable to different users in different ways. The letter of Demetrius to the *dioicetes* Apollonius, as analyzed by Le Rider and Callataÿ, highlights the Ptolemaic authorities' ability to adapt to the requirements of their foreign exchange operations by producing sufficient money supply whenever a really dire need arose.[89] It is very likely that this attention to overall monetary conditions also influenced the choice of types when it came to placing in circulation a currency meant for universal use.

88. Duyrat 2005a, pp. 249–50.
89. *PCZ* 59.021 (above n. 72). Le Rider, Callataÿ 2006, pp. 222–23.

Figure 7.19. Autonomous Tetradrachm of Aradus (ANS 1944.100.70509).

This choice is relatively opportunistic: while the Aradian bee drachms were issued rather abundantly in the early years, at the time of the Sixth Syrian War their production rapidly became sporadic. When the city resumed a regular silver coinage, beginning in 138/7 BC, it selected civic types, with a wreath on the reverse (Fig. 7.19). But this wreath was no longer the recognizable sign of a common coinage, like the wreath on the tetradrachms of western Asia Minor. The choice of a reduced weight standard officially made this coinage one of limited circulation. This change of standard occurred at a time impossible to pinpoint, between 152/1 and 138/7 BC. It is tempting to place it in the 140s, when the numerous monetary changes described above took place. Yet this new weight did not limit these coins to a strictly epichoric circulation, because these tetradrachms have a regional distribution, beyond the continental hinterland of Aradus (Map 24), and their standard is common with those of Tripolis and Laodiceia ad Mare.[90]

It is interesting to note that, probably in response to the disappearance of the wreathed tetradrachms of Asia Minor in the 140s, the Aradians chose to strike wreathed coins themselves, all the while restricting the coins' ability to circulate, through the selection of a reduced standard. The wreath probably served as a guarantee for users. As with the imitations of Ephesian drachms or the choice of Alexander types, the wreath surely guided the authorities as they picked a coin type. The wreath, in this instance, turns these tetradrachms into a regional common coinage, but not an international one. Their starting date, 138/7 BC, is also very interesting, because it leads one to suppose that the Aradians sought to remedy a general lack of currency that must have made itself rapidly felt. The last hoard containing Attic-weight wreathed tetradrachms is the so-called Aleppo hoard, whose burial apparently dates after 142/1–139/8 BC.

3.3. Adaptations

At the time the Aradians decided to strike their reduced standard tetradrachms, Seleucid currency becomes dominant in hoards throughout Syria. In the south, the Seleucids were the sole suppliers for the Ptolemaic standard zone in which Ptolemaic issues penetrated only slightly. In the north, most hoards consist of Seleucid coins. The coincidence between the disappearance of foreign currencies in the north during the 140s and the development of Seleucid issues on

90. I list here the articles of Mørkholm 1982 and Callataÿ 2002, as well as an elaboration on my thesis, Duyrat 2005a, pp. 258–64, map 11, p. 359. A study by Olivier and Parisot 2013 tries to connect the tetradrachms of Antony and Cleopatra struck at Antioch to the Aradian standard or to a reduced Attic standard.

the Ptolemaic standard in the south during the reign of Alexander I Balas is remarkable. There, as well, Ptolemaic coins gradually disappear from hoards, in favor of royal Seleucid currency.

The Aradians' conduct shows an obvious pragmatism as well as an ability to adapt rapidly to changes in Syrian monetary circulation. So they opted to strike tetradrachms on a reduced standard at the start of the 130s. In a short space of time, it appears that the Seleucid mints must have assumed sole responsibility for the manufacture of most silver coinage used in Syrian territory. Reasons for the disappearance of Alexanders and wreathed tetradrachms have already been suggested. This would explain why a powerful city like Aradus selected a reduced standard, which would limit circulation of these coins to the territory of the issuing state and, in this particular case, to that of neighboring cities with the same system. Beyond the fiscal attraction,[91] which the Ptolemaic example suggests as an explanation, I wonder if this choice was not foremost a precautionary measure to guarantee sufficient liquidity for local transactions at a time when coined silver was no longer so plentiful. Without going so far as to speak of regulating the money supply, which seems highly unlikely in this era,[92] the simple demands of commercial centers must have sufficed to alert the authorities. It seems that in the Ptolemaic system, where currency exchange was mandated at the borders, a lack of royal currency could occur, requiring merchants to wait around in Alexandria and complain urgently to the royal bureaucracy in order to obtain Egyptian legal tender. "The royal bureaucracy, one presumes, awaited complaints of this sort before ordering issue of a new series of coins. This risked disturbing commercial operations momentarily and foregoing income; on the other hand, it calculated currency needs better and avoided placing too great a quantity of coins in circulation."[93] "The Seleucids probably proceeded in the same, or comparable fashion. ... Presumably, in normal times, they issued coins only when the need was palpable, when they did not have on hand sufficient reserves to meet an unexpected outlay (for example, during a military campaign)."[94] Given the importance of the major eastern commercial centers, especially the ports, and the power of the royal bureaucracies with their numerous local representatives,[95] one may suppose that most of the time officials must have been able to anticipate well enough to avoid extreme situations of insufficient funds. This system of information directly based on demand was certainly rapidly informed when Alexanders and especially wreathed tetradrachms became scarce. Seleucid production increased progressively, from the reign of Antiochus IV, although

91. Le Rider's preferred approach, cf. Callataÿ 1999.

92. Callataÿ 2005, p. 129; Le Rider, Callataÿ 2006, pp. 221–22.

93. "L'administration royale, on peut le présumer, attendait des protestations de ce genre avant d'ordonner la frappe d'une nouvelle série de monnaies. Le risque était de gêner momentanément les opérations commerciales et de subir un manque à gagner ; en revanche, les besoins en numéraire étaient mieux mesurés et on évitait de lancer dans la circulation une trop grande quantité d'espèces," Le Rider, Callataÿ 2006, pp. 142–43, commentary on the letter of Demetrius to the financial officer Apollonius in 258 BC.

94. "Les Séleucides procédaient probablement de la même façon, ou d'une façon comparable. [...] on peut présumer que, en temps ordinaire, ils émettaient des pièces seulement quand le besoin s'en faisait sentir, quand ils n'avaient pas à leur disposition des réserves suffisantes pour régler une dépense inattendue (par exemple au cours d'une campagne militaire)," ibid., pp. 222–23.

95. On the importance of the Seleucid administrative network, cf. Capdetrey 2007, pp. 277–329.

it is impossible to say whether this was a response to the growing lack of foreign coins, or was what caused it. The ability of a city like Aradus to adjust quickly to changes in circulation leaves the impression that this information was also available to civic communities that obtained it through their own devices—Aradus was a large port—or through their close connections with the Seleucid administration; both hypotheses are probably correct.

4. NEW REGIONAL POWERS

From the second half of the second century, the dissolution of the Seleucid kingdom in a troubled context favored the emergence of new regional powers. Amid rampant brigandage and piracy, Arab dynasts and "tyrants" seize cities or regions.[96] The Hasmonean kingdom expanded and quickly confronted the Arabs, notably the Nabataeans, who became a constant political opponent at the end of the second and beginning of the first centuries BC.[97] Against such a backdrop, the most powerful cities asserted their own autonomy and rapidly announced it with their individual coinages. At the same time, bronze coinage enjoyed an increase which archaeological excavations reflect.

4.1. Civic Coinages

The breakdown of the Attic standard is probably the most defining phenomenon of the end of the second century. Mørkholm, studying its development, concluded that three zones emerged in Syria with different standards: the Seleucid zone, using a reduced Attic standard of c. 16.8 g after 172/1 BC; the Ptolemaic zone, which maintained its existing standard (c. 14.3 g); and the Aradian zone with its tetradrachm of c. 15.3 g.[98] The fragmentation of royal bronze production coincides with this phenomenon. Butcher has emphasized the broad sweep of provenances on the different sites of the southern Levant: Beirut received royal coins from Antioch, Sidon (Fig. 7.20), Tyre, and Ptolemais, in addition to its own mint; Samaria was supplied by Tyre, Ptolemais, Antioch, and, with one specimen, Gaza.[99]

In addition to these changes in royal production, local civic coinages appear. The cities of Phoenicia, in particular, initiated autonomous eras at the end of the second century and generally began to strike coinage with their own types shortly after on the Ptolemaic standard. They ceased, *de facto*, their royal issues. The unpublished thesis of Abou Diwan on Sidon contains a catalogue of autonomous tetradrachms with head of Tyche and eagle on a prow that amounts only to 104 specimens, which seems relatively few.[100] A catalogue by dies for Tyre is still lacking.[101] Comparing the circulation of these two mints and Aradus in the second and first cen-

96. Sartre 2001, pp. 381–84.
97. Ibid., p. 414.
98. Mørkholm 1982, p. 144.
99. Butcher 2001–2002, p. 55.
100. Abou Diwan 2010. His study of output greatly overestimates the number of obverse dies employed, so I prefer not to repeat his figures.
101. Callataÿ 2002, p. 81, says he has assembled a catalogue of 411 tetradrachms struck between 108/7 and 60/59 BC with 205 obverse dies (p. 83).

Figure 7.20. Tetradrachm of Sidon (ANS 1944.100.71466).

turies is, however, instructive (Map 24). Sidon's autonomous tetradrachms are quite rare in hoards (**311**). By contrast, those of Tyre appear in 16 hoards[102] and those of Aradus in 25,[103] all issues combined (civic Alexanders, autonomous drachms and tetradrachms). In Coele Syria and Phoenicia, Tyrian coins circulate everywhere, perpetuating the Ptolemaic standard zone and, for Callataÿ, counterbalancing that of Aradus in the north.[104] Sidon and Ascalon fall within this orbit.

The Seleucid standard degrades to such a degree in the first century that it approaches the lighter standards. Mørkholm, working from a catalogue of coins of Ake, Antioch, and Babylon, came up with a tetradrachm basically weighing under 16 g.[105] The calculations of Hoover and Iossif for the mints of Antioch and Sidon are more detailed: they track the variations in the weight of Seleucid tetradrachms between 16.2 g and 13.7 g from 113/11 to c. 47 BC.[106] The distinction between Ptolemaic and reduced Attic standards gradually disappears in effect, giving way to a regionally closed circulation.

4.2. Hasmoneans, Autonomous Cities, and Bronze Coinage

Despite their variations in weight, making determination of the standard difficult, the silver coins of the Seleucid kings continued to circulate as widely as those of their predecessors;[107] but they competed increasingly with civic coinages and bronze: 20 out of 67 hoards dating from the first century are composed of bronze, versus 15 out of 126 in the previous century. They are overwhelmingly concentrated in the southern Levant where the expansion of an independent Jewish power following the Maccabean Revolt (166–161 BC) strongly encouraged the development of circulation in this metal. The Hasmonean kings struck only bronze, and Alexander Jannaeus (103–76 BC) did so in remarkable amounts (Fig. 7.21), to judge by the abundance especially of his output in hoards: several hundred coins are not uncommon (**312**, **327**, **342**), the largest find reaching about 4,000 (**326**). Excavations amply confirm these observations (Map 26). This abundance resulted in the driving out Seleucid coins, probably during the reign of

102. **267**, **271**, **276**, **280**, **282**, **290**, **293**, **295**, **296**, **311**, **313**, **334**, **336**, **347**, **355**, **357**.

103. Civic Alexanders: **171**, **172**, **173**, **174**, **176**, **184**, **193**, **203**, **242**; bee drachms: **188**, **193**, **200**, **201**, **202**, **227**, **247**; autonomous tetradrachms: **301**, **308**, **310**, **313**, **325**, **332**, **333**, **338**, **340**, **347**.

104. Callataÿ 2002, pp. 84–85.

105. Mørkholm 1982, p. 144.

106. Houghton, Lorber, Hoover 2008, 2, pp. 2–3.

107. Antiochus VII, Map 21; Antiochus VIII, Map 22; Antiochus IX, Map 25.

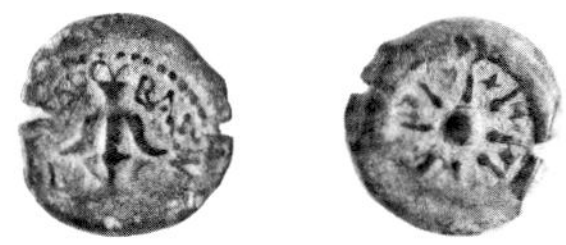

Figure 7.21. Bronze of Alexander Jannaeus (ANS 1952.142.377).

Alexander Jannaeus.[108] The unusual number of limestone flan moulds and of flans still attached by their sprues, indeed of unused flans in hoards (**352**) discovered in Israeli excavations bears witness to the enormous production of Jannaeus' reign.[109] Shachar notes that this king's bronzes represent 87% of the Hasmonean coins in the 44 excavations conducted in Jerusalem and 52% of those in Gamala.[110] They continued to be struck after the king's death and were imitated in bronze and lead.[111] They are so numerous that Shachar uses variations in their presence on sites to determine phases of occupation. Silver did not disappear from circulation: autonomous tetradrachms of Tyre circulated widely in Hasmonean possessions, where they were joined by those of Ascalon from the first century BC (Maps 28 and 33).[112] There is a clear symbiotic relationship between Hasmonean bronze and Tyrian silver in the Hasmonean territory, as Biblical sources testify.[113]

In addition to the Hasmoneans, numerous civic mints struck bronze at the turn of the second and first centuries. The 12 best represented in excavations are gathered in the following table (Table 7.9; cf. Map 27 to Map 37). All other mints produced fewer than 13 coins across the 58 sites examined.

The dispersion of each mint's coins is linked to complex factors. The production volume of the mints is relevant: excavations at cities without a mint or with little output have yielded more coins of other mints than cities with imposing production. Butcher has studied this phenomenon in the Orontes valley at the end of the Hellenistic Age and during the High Roman Empire. He even notes a selection of foreign types that circulate on these sites in a privileged way.[114]

It is very difficult to distinguish the bronzes in excavations by period in the current state of the catalogue. To enter each coin in the database with its date of production represents a considerable task impossible to accomplish within a reasonable timeframe. Furthermore, the fact that bronzes sometimes circulated for lengthy periods obfuscates the chronology. This is especially true for cities where the autonomous coinages are longstanding, like Aradus and Side. The two well-documented examples of Antioch and Berytus will help to depict this problem (Table 7.10).

On the two sites, the role of foreign mints, which had increased in the second century BC, diminishes in the first, perhaps as a result of the appearance of local issues. The late-won auton-

108. Meshorer 1982, p. 47.
109. Shiloh, Ariel 1990, among others.
110. Shachar 2004, p. 10.
111. Fontanille 2007, e.g.
112. Meshorer 1982, pp. 57–59.
113. Hendin 2010, pp. 476–77.
114. Butcher 2002, p. 150.

Table 7.9. Autonomous cities best represented in excavations

Mint	Total	Map
Antioch	214	27
Tyre	95	28
Aradus	88	29
Sidon	87	30
Ake Ptolemais	66	31
Seleuceia Pieria	60	32
Ascalon	55	33
Apamea	28	34
Beirut	28	35
Seleuceia on the Tigris	17	-
Side	14	36
Marathus	13	37

omy of the cities of ancient Syria and Ptolemaic Phoenicia probably explains in part this progressive alteration. The local mint is not necessarily very well represented. The excavations of Beirut show this: they have revealed only 24 coins of Berytus over three centuries. In contrast, the imposing character of Antioch's output revealed on site is unmistakable.

In the north, Aradus achieved autonomy early, celebrated by an era beginning in the autumn of 259/8 BC. The city then quickly began to produce autonomous coins. Their production increased amply during the second century (Fig. 7.22). Counting all denominations, 75 obverse dies have been identified for issues of the third century, versus 506 for the second and 89 for the first.[115] These numbers are even more suggestive if we take into account the fact that they probably understate the reality. The specimen-to-die ratios are low in general (Table 7.11), and the assembled sample is probably only poorly representative, even though the collected number of specimens is occasionally rather large.

This would make the mean specimen to die ratio for Aradian bronzes 1.98.[116] Given that, for silver, an index under 3 renders the estimation of the original number of dies hypothetical, the sample probably understates actual production. But bronze is a hard alloy, it must be remem

115. Duyrat 2005a, p. 293.
116. This is an average number compared to the studies of bronze dies summarized in Annexe 1 of Callataÿ 1997b, pp. 309–18.

Table 7.10. Dates of civic bronzes in the excavations of Antioch and Beirut

	3rd Century		2nd Century		1st Century	
Mint	**Antioch**	**Beirut**	**Antioch**	**Beirut**	**Antioch**	**Beirut**
Antioch					147	1
Apamea					1	
Aradus	1	4	5	4		
Ascalon					1	2
Berytus						5[116]
Byblos					1	1
Dora						1
Marathus			1	2		
Ptolemais				1		
Seleuceia Pieria			13		10	
Sidon				2		2
Tripolis					1	
Tyre					5	
Foreign Coins	1	4	6	4	5?	1
Total	**2**	**8**	**25**	**13**	**166**	**13**

Figure 7.22. Bronze of Aradus, 130/29 BC (ANS 1944.100.70652).

bered, and must have caused dies to break much sooner than silver did, requiring a much larger number, therefore, to achieve an equivalent level of unit production. This is an area where one depends on experimentation.[119] Other evidence for the abundance of Aradian bronze coinage comes from the six surviving hoards (Table 7.12).[120]

The hoarding of this metal only became common in the first century, an impression heavily influenced by the weight of Hasmonean hoards in our evidence. Their number results from two

117. Based on the catalogues of Waage 1952 and Butcher 2001–2002.
118. 18 coins are dated from the 2nd or 1st cent. BC, one is uncertain.
119. Faucher, Téreygeol, Brousseau, Arles 2009.
120. To compare, we know of five Tyrian bronze hoards: **287** (1 specimen), **294** (1 specimen), **300**, **302**, **322**.

Table 7.11. Specimen-to-die ratios for the series of Aradian bronzes[121]

Series	n	d	n/d
1	96	40	2.4
2	13	9	1.44
3	86	51	1.68
4	35	28	1.25
5	397	266	1.49
6	16	13	1.23
7	247	97	2.54
8	75	41	1.82
9	139	59	2.35
10	22	9	2.44
12	176	44	4
13	15	9	1.66
Total	**1,317**	**666**	**1.98**

related causes: the actual abundance of this dynasty's issues and the activity of Israeli archaeologists. The latter means that our evidence comes mostly from authorized excavations.[122] Seen in this light, the six hoards of Aradian coins,[123] five of which are from the second century, are evidence that bronze was in common use and that its value was enough to warrant significant hoarding.

5. EPILOGUE: THE FIRST CENTURY

Beginning in the 80s BC, it becomes difficult to draw any clear information from numismatic data. Hoard studies show some breakdown in circulation zones. Aradus' sphere of influence remains truly homogeneous thanks to its reduced standard: 11 out of the 46 hoards with silver coins from the first century have turned up there. They date from 89/8 (**301**) to 44/3 BC. (**348**).[124] All come from the continental hinterland of Aradus or its environs, the neighboring cities of Tripolis and Laodiceia ad Mare having adopted the same standard, as mentioned above. Outside this favored space, the geography of hoards is more difficult to read.

121. Series 11 and 14–18 have been excluded: they were struck with only one or two obverse dies. Based on the catalogue in Duyrat 2005a, pp. 155–74.

122. Ten of the 20 bronze hoards from the first century come from authorized digs.

123. I include the bronzes of Marathus, which belongs to the Aradian Peraea and whose coins are generally associated with those of Aradus.

124. **301**, **308**, **310**, **313**, **325**, **332**, **333**, **338**, **340**, **347**, **348**.

Table 7.12. Hoards of Aradian bronzes

No.	Findspot	No. *IGCH* or *CH*	Date of Burial	Total Studied	Content
175	Jablah quarter of Msaitbe		After 190/189	53	53 AE, legal excavations Aradus 26 AE Aradus or Carne: 17 AE Aradus, Carne, Gabala or Simyra? 10 AE
187	Amrith (anc. Marathus)	*IGCH* 1545 = Noe 650	168 or later		AE of Aradus and Marathus
275	Northern Israel	*CH* 10.319	121	327	329 AE Ptolemies: 9 Seleucids: 309 Cos: 1 Side: 3 (end 3rd cent.) Aradus: 3 (of which 1 from 126/5 BC) Ake-Ptolemais: 4
283	Amrith	*IGCH* 1566	112/1	27	27 AE Aradus: 12 Marathus: 15
284	Amrith		After 112/1	50	50 AE Aradus: 28 Marathus: 22
305	Kessab	*IGCH* 1571	95	22	22 AE Seleucids: 16 Ptolemies: 3 Aradus: 1 Byblos: 2

It seems that Seleucid issues continued to circulate everywhere. They are present in 20 out of the 46 silver hoards, or more than a third of the burials (43.5%).[125] The latest hoard dates from c. 8 BC (**357**). In nearly half the cases, royal tetradrachms are comingled with civic coins of Aradus, Tripolis, Sidon, Tyre, or Ascalon.[126] We have seen how Aradus, protected by its local standard, enjoyed a special circulation zone. The mint of Tyre became the most important of the southern Levant and is represented in 10 hoards, or 21.7% of the silver deposits.[127] This equals what has been observed for Aradus autonomous tetradrachms (10 out of 46) and continues the situation noted since the end of the second century.[128] The circulation of these civic coins is concentrated in the former Syria and Phoenicia, with the exception of a stray tetradrachm in a

125. **292, 296, 301, 303, 304, 309, 311, 314, 315, 317, 322, 328, 330, 331, 334, 335, 339, 345, 355, 357**. Hoard **310** has not been counted here: the Seleucid tetradrachms are apparently intrusive.

126. **292, 296, 301, 311, 322, 331, 334, 355, 357**.

127. **293, 295, 296, 311, 313, 334, 336, 347, 355, 357**.

128. On this, cf. the remarks of Callataÿ 2002.

Table 7.13. Hoards of Ptolemaic coins of the first century BC

No.	Findspot	No. *IGCH* or *CH*	Date of Burial	Content
299	Megadim		100/99	Ptolemy VIII: 1 Salamis, 2 Citium Ptolemy IX: 1 Alexandria Ptolemy X: 2 Alexandria 2nd cent. BC?: 13 uncert.
306	Phoenicia		95/4	Ptolemy IX: 4 Alexandria Ptolemy X: 5 Alexandria
307	Gaza Strip	*CH* 4.69	94	19+ AR Ptolemy IX: 4 tetr. Ptolemy X and Cleopatra III: 8 tetr. Ptolemy X: 7 tetr.
324	Coast of Mt. Carmel		72/1	Ptolemy IX or X: 14 tetr. Alexandria Cleopatra III and Ptolemy X: 89 tetr. Alexandria. Cleopatra III and Ptolemy X or Ptolemy X alone: 3 tetr. Alexandria. Ptolemy X: 402 tetr. Alexandria Ptolemy IX: 19 tetr. Alexandria Ptolemy XII: 848 tetr. Alexandria Cleopatra III and Ptolemy X–Ptolemy XII: 380 tetr. Alexandria
351	Palestine	*IGCH* 1626	40	43+ AR Cleopatra VII: tetr. Alexandria (years 10–12, Sv. 1824–26)

hoard of coins of Aradus at Tartus (**313**, Map 24). This preeminence of Tyrian tetradrachms in the southern Levant is destined to continue under Roman domination down to 65/6 AD. Their popularity in Palestine[129] even led Meshorer to suggest that certain series may have been struck at Jerusalem, an hypothesis numismatically as well as papyrologically inadmissible.[130] As for the tetradrachms of Ascalon, they are narrowly concentrated on the coast between Irbid and Gaza (**292**, **331**, **343**), with the exception of a few specimens in the Safed hoard in Galilee (**344**).

Some hoards of Ptolemaic coins, vestiges of the Ptolemaic standard zone, are still attested in the first century (Table 7.13). Hoard **351**, composed of coins of Cleopatra, is evidence for Antony's brief control of Coele Syria and Phoenicia and his alliance with Cleopatra.[131] The three other deposits, by contrast, are much more homogeneous. All contain coins from Ptolemy VIII to Ptolemy XII, and all come from the coastal zone, namely, Phoenicia, the Gaza Strip, or shipwrecks found along the Palestinian coast. This tight restriction to the littoral, when the coins of Tyre abound in the interior, raises a question. Was there a coastal zone that accepted

129. The Qumran hoard (357), revealed beneath a building on the Essene site, is particularly good evidence for this.

130. Bibliography on the debate in Duyrat 2008, p. 19.

131. Sartre 2001, pp. 464–68.

this currency, the last to do so? Or, rather, was this coinage meant for exchanges with Egypt in a commercial relationship with these ports?

Some Parthian coins also crop up in two hoards of Seleucid coins (**314**, **328**). They are an indication of the profound political and military troubles that characterize first-century Syria. The region experiences numerous foreign incursions between 84/3 and 69 BC, starting with that of Tigranes from Armenia. Curiously, this episode is almost absent from the numismatic record: a single hoard of tetradrachms is the only evidence (**329**), and the bronze coins of Tigranes are rare in Syria.[132] In contrast, alone among the royal issues of the first century, the coinage of Philip I Philadelphus (95/4–76/5? BC) is strikingly abundant. His immediate predecessors issued only paltry series. A strong showing of Philip I's tetradrachms, inventoried in half the hoards of Seleucid coins from the period, reveals this leap in royal output.[133] Hoards **335** (55 BC) and **345** (47/6 BC) contain tetradrachms of Philip I Philadelphus mixed in with imitations of these coins issued by the Roman authorities and discretely revealing Roman presence.[134] After 69 BC and the intervention of Lucullus against Tigranes, Syria fell more and more into the orbit of Rome. In 67 BC, Rome intervened in Syria as part of the struggle against piracy. Actions taken at Pompey's command multiplied, reducing Syria to a Roman province in 64 BC. These changes seem to echo only faintly in currency circulation: Roman coins are absent down to the last hoard in the catalogue. At Khirbet Qumran (**357**), in 8 BC, the first six *denarii* appear amidst 561 coins, otherwise overwhelmingly Seleucid and Tyrian.[135] Several mints in the region experienced an increase in tetradrachm production between 64/3 and 62/1 BC principally, coinciding with Pompey's stay in Syria, the area's pacification, and its subsequent subjection to provincial status.[136] The increase in volume, however, seems moderate compared to the extensive political and military upheavals of these years, which witnessed the end of the Seleucids and, shortly after, the Hasmoneans.[137]

We have seen that two Syrian hoards contain Parthian coins mingled with Seleucid specimens (**314**, **328**). Others consist entirely of coins of the Parthian dynasty (**356**, **358**). Mesopotamia was definitively under the control of the Arsacids probably following the capture of Dura around 113 BC.[138] Present in Commagene at the start of the first century, they made several Syrian incursions during the century. Hoard **314**, found on the plain of Akkar, contains only one Parthian coin, which could be an intrusion because it dates from 33/2 BC, while the remaining coins place the burial in the 70s. The other lots come from northern Mesopotamia c. 70–57 BC (**328**) or from unknown findspots in the last quarter of the first century.

132. Duyrat 2012.

133. **309**, **315**, **316**, **317**, **318**, **319**, **330**, **335**, **345**, buried between 88/7 (?) and after 47/6 BC.

134. On the circumstances of the Romans' striking of these imitations, cf. Houghton, Lorber, Hoover 2008, pp. 596–97. For an interesting parallel with late tetradrachms of Side, which could be Roman-issued imitations, cf. Meadows 2006b.

135. The Roman presence is also evident in certain issues bearing "era of Pompey," "era of Caesar," etc., like the bronzes of Antioch from hoard **337**. I presented a summary table of these eras in Duyrat 2005a, pp. 309–10.

136. Callataÿ 1997a, p. 384; Callataÿ 2002, p. 83; Duyrat 2005a, p. 282.

137. Sartre 2001, pp. 442, 447–49.

138. Sartre 2001, p. 428.

CONCLUSION

Thus the fragmentation of monetary circulation characterizes the first century. Coins on the Aradian standard, those from Tyre, and Ptolemaic coins do not mix, or do so only slightly. The contrast with the second century and its two sharply differentiated zones, Attic standard in the north, Ptolemaic in the south, is clear. In terms of monetary practice, the reign of Alexander I Balas is a turning point, distinguished by an end to the flow of tetradrachms from Asia Minor and a compensatory increase in royal issues. At the same time, royal coins produced on the Ptolemaic standard pour into Coele Syria and Phoenicia. The incessant rivalries between the dynasty's different branches, Hasmonean expansion, and the assertion of civic autonomy all lead to a political partitioning of Syria that is reflected in increasing closure of currency zones. Strangely, the Armenian and subsequent Roman invasions and Syria's reduction to provincial status have not left numismatic traces matching their historical significance. The real changes in this regard will only occur at the end of the first century AD.[139]

139. Burnett 2002.

Chapter 8

Wealth and Coinage

The ability to accumulate coinage for hoarding signifies, in principle, one form of wealth. Since we do not know what percentage of fortunes consisted of coined money, it is impossible to evaluate them precisely. Yet, for those questions on which written sources provide little assistance in Syria, hoards can be suggestive. Containers are usually quite unprepossessing, and the choice of a hoard's protective packaging shows no trace of luxury, whatever the hoard's value. In contrast, contents vary greatly, from extremely modest sums to princely riches.

1. Containers

> *Elle y prit une grosse bourse en velours rouge à glands d'or, et bordée de canetille usée, provenant de la succession de sa grand-mère. Puis elle pesa fort orgueilleusement cette bourse et se plut à vérifier le compte oublié de son petit pécule.*
>
> —Honoré de Balzac[1]

Eugénie Grandet's purse, like the Miser's casket in Molière's play, is strongly suggestive to the historian who tries to imagine what container might preserve money in eras when fortunes were tangible. The following presentation cannot be exhaustive because publications do not always specify if there were any container remnants and because my own inventory is certainly not without lacunae (Appendix 1).[2] However, it does permit some useful observations. We have

1. H. de Balzac, *Eugénie Grandet* (1833), *La comédie humaine*, III, Pléiade ed. (Paris, 1977), p. 1127. [She picked up a plump purse, red velvet with golden tassels and trimmed in worn gold thread, its provenance her grandmother's estate. Then she weighed said purse very proudly and was delighted to confirm the forgotten worth of her little nest egg. —WEH]
2. Paunov, Prokopov 2002, p. 184, is just an index of containers.

an idea of the containers for only 30 out of 355 hoards, or just 8.5%.[3] In 70% of the cases (21 hoards out of 30), they are terracotta pots, vases, or jugs, editors' nomenclature being highly imprecise.[4] Only the archeologists at Marisa (**285**) bother to clarify that the container here is a type of jug widespread in the city; they also give its dimensions. J. Elayi and Lemaire, thanks to a photograph from the publication of Dunand's excavation of Byblos, identify the container of that hoard (**69**) as a small jug of local manufacture, a type attested at Tell Kazel and in Palestine during the Persian period.[5] Some of these terracotta containers have kept their stopper mechanisms. At Khirbet Qumran (**357**), two of the three vases still had covers made of palm. The Tell Tsippor hoard (**105**) was deposited within an already closed jug that had a hole pierced into its side large enough to insert the coins, transforming the jug into a cashbox. Only in one case is the terracotta container a more highly wrought object: the Samaria hoard (**50**) was enclosed in a pyxis made locally that, while not being a valuable object, was not just any old vase either.

Metal containers are a good deal less frequent (six out of 31, or 19.3%) and much more varied. The oldest is a bronze box in the shape of an uninscribed Egyptian cartouche with a pivoting opening mechanism, discovered during Dunand's excavations at Byblos (**11**). The staters it contained date the burial to c. 450 BC. A small silver purse 6.7 cm high is probably the most valuable container among this small sample (Al Mina, **33**). Tubular in shape (2.5 cm in diameter), it has a well-fitted cover and dangling rings, suggesting attachment to a belt, for example. J. and A.-G. Elayi aptly observe that its diameter precludes saving large-denomination coins.[6] At the time of discovery, it contained only fractions, 55 in number. They date this object's loss to c. 375 BC. Exactly at the other end of the value scale, 10 tetradrachms with types of Alexander were rolled in a humble lead sheet found in the excavation of Ras el-Bassit (**279**).[7] This malleable metal was also used to make six vases protecting the spectacular Saida hoard discovered in three tranches during the nineteenth century (**93**). This material, usually considered base, was employed to bury the greatest hoard—both in value and number—ever found in Syria. It contained more than 7,200 gold coins. One of the two associated deposits found at Byblos (**69** and **107**) was buried in bronze vases. As with the Saida hoard, this is a numerically important ensemble, amounting to 358 silver coins (shekels and tetradrachms). Apart from the humble lead foil of Ras el-Bassit, metal containers are either in valuable material (bronze cartouche, silver purse) or have dimensions capable of protecting a hoard of rather respectable worth. This is sometimes also the case for terracotta containers that are amenable to hoards of every size.

The catalogue of hoards and excavations has no mention of perishable containers, which completely or almost completely elude us. It indicates only four hoards as coming from this type of material, but this may be mere conjecture.[8] The excavators of Samaria say they discovered

3. Twenty were found in excavations, i.e., 64.5% of the hoards whose containers are known.

4. **1, 36, 50, 55, 66, 105, 130, 131, 142, 145, 158, 161, 166, 169, 184, 272, 285, 296, 298, 357.**

5. Elayi, Lemaire 2009, p. 90.

6. Elayi, Elayi 1993a, p. 64.

7. The practice of preserving coins in wrapper rolls exists elsewhere in the Roman period. Aubin 2007, p. 66, n. 46, provides a brief survey.

8. *Hacksilber* hoards wrapped in linen have been carefully examined by Thompson 2003, pp. 78–80.

Figure 8.1. Terracotta of an actor sitting on an altar with a purse in his hand. (Acquisition 1889 CA 265). © RMN-Grand Palais (musée du Louvre) / Hervé Lewandowski.

hoard **322** wrapped in some cloth, without further specification. At Ascalon (**22**), the excavation apparently revealed traces of linen, justifying the assertion that a fourth-century hoard of obols was enclosed in a sack of this material. But on the same site (**294**) it is only the coin pile that prompts the supposition that a canvas sack or "a small container"[9] enclosed the coins. The same observation, connected with identical corrosion of the coins, leads the editors of hoard **323** to conclude that this had originally been wrapped in an organic material. These few statements invite the thought that purses could be buried as is in the ground. Greek purses do not seem markedly different from those known from later periods. They are mentioned in literature, without description, however. Lafaye has reconstituted their various features based on literary references,[10] and his description squares with the iconographic evidence. A terracotta in the Louvre provides a good example: it shows an actor emptying a purse in his hand. The purse is a simple canvas or leather sack tied with strings (Fig. 8.1).[11] Excavations, farther afield, of the cities in the region of Vesuvius provide some information on those types of containers that were utilized by people fleeing the eruption of 79 AD. Near a woman's body found at Oplontis, some 400 coins were preserved in a linen sack. Another woman carried her fortune in a box.[12] Such everyday packaging was used as much for burying as it was for carrying.

It is impossible to obtain a clear idea of the ancients' preferences for containers when they were deciding to bury their possessions. If it seems obvious that metal containers are exceptional, probably just because of the material's value (lead excepted), it may be that containers made of organic matter were much more common than this modest sample leads one to suspect. All the same, this small list highlights the large variety of possibilities. Most editors' lack of precision is certainly regrettable, especially when it comes to the fragments of ordinary pottery that do not catch the attention of archeologists; container-loss obviously lurks also in hoards dispersed in trade. One thing does stand out, however: there was no normal form of container, and it appears that most of the time the chosen vessel was simply picked from among the household furnishings, probably with an eye to the most suitable volume, occasionally with adaptations, as in the case of the pierced jug at Tel Tsippor (**105**). To my knowledge, there is no systematic study of hoard containers, and the only lists available are epigraphic, from Greek sanctuaries, where sums of cash are often contained in strongboxes and different vessels, the names of which regularly recur in the temple accounts. Comparing the information provided by archeology and written sources would therefore help somewhat, but it remains to be done. One can still make some observations from the data gathered here. The standardized nomenclature for materials used in Greek sanctuaries is not evident in the practices of individuals in the Near East. No regular procedure is therefore identifiable. One could accordingly argue that individuals did not have any reasons for concealing their goods in a common way. Yet examples do exist. From

9. Gitler, Kahanov 2002.
10. In Daremberg, Saglio 1877-1919, s.v. "*marsupium.*"
11. Cf. http://www.photo.rmn.fr/archive/02-016051-2C6NU0G29OUP.html.
12. Andreau 2008, pp. 216, 222.

the end of the first century BC, "lamp hoards" begin to appear in the southern Levant. These are hoards enclosed in oil lamps and hidden in houses.[13] In his publication of a hoard in En-Gedi, Meshorer, going back to one of his earlier publications without a catalogue,[14] explains that the lamp is a symbol of eternity. The hoard, meant to chase away the evil eye, had been placed in a rather large lamp (big enough to protect 139 *prutot*) and was carefully plastered into the wall. The lamp itself is of the contemporary Herodian type, but its diameter is 11 cm and larger than usual models.[15] It is an apotropaic deposit. This sort of practice is not discernible in Hellenistic deposits. If regularity in burial manner is not evident, the present catalogue does not reveal unusual objects altered to hold coinage such as we find elsewhere or in later periods.[16]

No evolution is discernible, either, although the period we consider stretches from the end of the sixth century to the end of the first century BC. All one can say is that the most highly wrought containers belong to the Persian period: terracotta pyxis (**50**), bronze box-cartouche (**11**), and silver purse (**33**). The obvious conclusion would be that when coinage was less common and only in silver it was more precious, and its container was chosen with more care. But the small sample calls for caution.

2. THE RICH AND THE POOR

The containers provide no information about the owners, their wealth, or the circumstances of hoarding. Conversely, an overview of the hoards gives a general idea of what the owners' fortunes might or might not have been.

2.1. Median Fortunes

Wealth is an important element of personal identity in all societies. For classical antiquity, it is a truism to say that we are quite familiar with the super rich—the Hellenistic kings—and the merely wealthy, especially if they are Athenians and lived in the fourth century. Literature has left us striking descriptions of the unheard of wealth of the Ptolemaic and Seleucid monarchs, on which Callataÿ has even based some quantitative studies.[17] The processions (*pompai*) of Alexandria or Daphne, the royal luxury (*tryphē*), which earned the usurper Diodotus his nickname (Tryphon), the public benefaction (*euergesia*) hailed by cities have all been thoroughly examined. Yet the financial means of private individuals, even the well-off, have been almost completely ignored, especially in Hellenistic Syria. In the absence of written sources, there is no hope of reconstituting in detail the socio-economic fabric, but the wealth of a household, an *oikos*, can be partially gauged by its ability to amass currency, especially at a time when coinage becomes more common. In this sense, hoards give us a small insight into what a nest egg or

13. Some examples of lamp hoards from different periods in Spijkerman 1961; Hendin 2000–2002; Syon 2000–2002.

14. Meshorer 1976.

15. Meshorer 2007, p. 412.

16. As, e.g., the bracelet-purse of Volubilis that contained 115 *denarii* and three bronzes dating from Nero to Hadrian in a hollowed out compartment; cf. Ruhlmann 1933.

17. Callataÿ 2004, 2006a; Callataÿ, Depeyrot, Villaronga 1993.

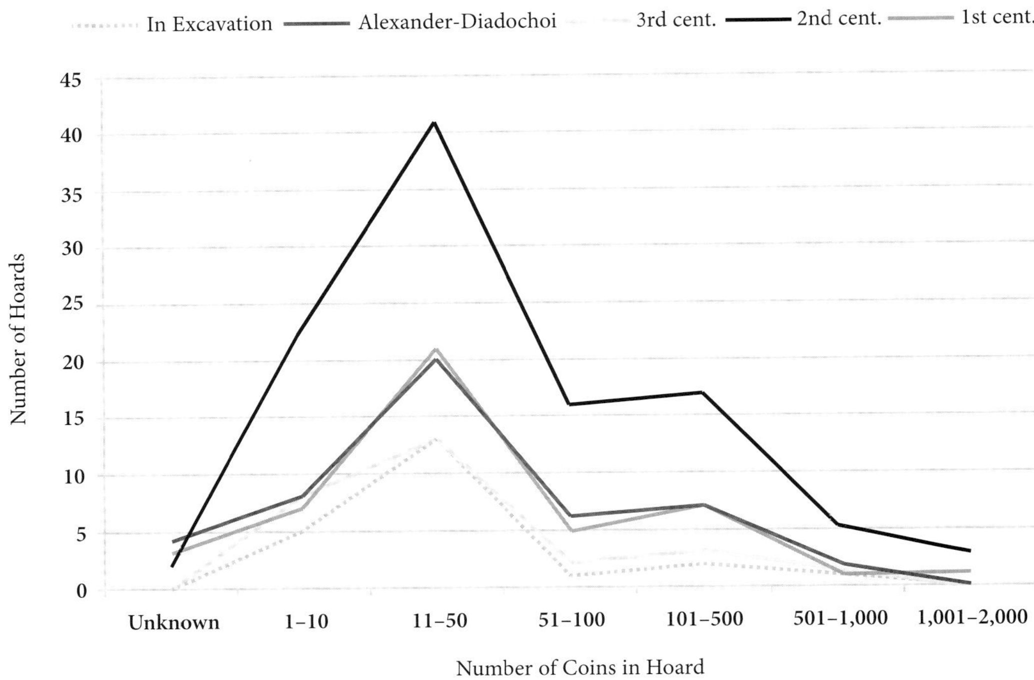

Figure 8.2. Classification by size of hoards containing tetradrachms.[18]

large fortune might amount to and how they were composed. The numerical data supporting this section come from the investigations of hoard editors. When an original sum was an estimate, it has not been used further, since this type of information is never verifiable. All numbers provided, therefore, should be understood as *minima*.

We know that between 67% and 85% of Hellenistic hoards contain tetradrachms (Fig. 8.2).[19] This chart only takes account of the number of tetradrachms, whereas 11% of Hellenistic hoards also contain drachms that would have to be added to the total value hoarded.[20] So this chart illustrates *minima*. The results are remarkably constant over time, whether one considers evidence from excavations of all periods or from what has appeared on the commercial market. The best-represented group is hoards consisting of 11–50 tetradrachms. It would be desirable to relate this information to written evidence illuminating fortunes. The latter does not exist for Syria, but we still have some documents from the Greek world that give us an idea of what these caches could pay for, and hence an idea of the relative hierarchy of wealth they represent. Comparisons with the Greek world have been preferred to Egypt or Babylonia since it is a world of cities, as is Syria, with an extensive use of coinage.

18. Certain hoards contain some other denominations: silver didrachms, drachms, or fractions. They have been counted in the class corresponding to the number of tetradrachms they produced. Alexander-Successors: 77, **79**, **85**; third century: **132**; second century: **166**, **227**; first century: **328**.

19. Alexander and the Successors: 77%; 3rd cent.: 75.8%; 2nd cent.: 84.9%; 1st cent.: 67%.

20. Drachms: 77, **94**, **105**, **118**, **124**, **129**, **134**, **140**, **145**, **149**, **152**, **166**, **167**, **173**, **174**, **184**, **188**, **193**, **200**, **201**, **202**, **210**, **214**, **227**, **229**, **234**, **246**, **247**, **260**, **328**. **341**, **353**; 14 of 20 hoards with fractions date before 300 BC (77–**113**): 77, **79**, **80**, **81**, **82**, **84**, **85**, **86**, **87**, **89**, **97**, **98**, **112**, **113**, **124**, **132**, **133**, **173**, **269**, **311**.

Table 8.1. Major and minor artisans at Eleusis, Epidaurus, Delphi, and Delos

	Eleusis	Epidaurus	Delphi	Delos
< 100 drachms (25 tetradrachms)	107	127	46	305
100–799 drachms (25–200 tetradrachms)	28	64	48	96
> 800 drachms (> 200 tetradrachms)	2	35	25	12
Total	**137**	**226**	**119**	**413**

The class of small hoards, 1–10 tetradrachms, is the next best-represented. "Small hoard" is a deceptive label: they are small in the number of specimens, but certainly not in value. The parallels to be drawn here can only be orders of magnitude because it is impossible to be certain that the prices and wages known in Greece, Asia Minor, Seleucid Syria, and Ptolemaic Syria (on the Ptolemaic standard) are comparable. But they enable us to obtain an idea of what a tetradrachm meant in a world broadly using the Attic standard, at least in the third and second centuries. Mention of the Attic tetradrachm first brings to mind soldiers' pay. Studies relating currency output and wars are numerous, as are those that try to estimate the payroll and other expenses of warfare.[21] Based on epigraphic data, Launey was able to estimate the daily wage of a third century hoplite at 8 Attic obols for the salary (*misthos*) and, for the food allowance (*sitēresion*), "3 or 3⅓ obols if rations were entirely converted into cash."[22] This comes to 1⅓ drachm just for the salary.[23] Thus one tetradrachm would represent three days' salary, five tetradrachms half a month's. Some mercenaries were clearly less expensive, like the Galatians Antigonus Gonatas enlisted in 277 BC, whose monthly pay was a Macedonian *chrysous*, or 4 obols a day.[24] In this instance, our five tetradrachms would be an entire month's salary. Hoplites are generally thought of as well paid but also as a special case, since they received their remuneration in principle over several months, the duration of the campaign or their enlistment. Known wages of other categories of workers rarely have this regularity. The sanctuary artisans studied by Feyel were often paid by the day or, even more commonly, by the job or at a flat rate, making it extremely difficult to estimate their living standard.[25] Nonetheless Feyel undertook "an attempt to understand the wage scale. ... We propose a simple solution: select for each individual listed in our catalogues the best paid work order or, if not that, the largest sum paid for a job or delivery of various materials." When several workers win a contract, the payment is divided among the associates.[26] The result is tabulated in the table reproduced here (Table 8.1), where the amounts have also been provided in tetradrachms.[27]

21. I cite among these especially Launey 1950, pp. 724–812, and Callataÿ 1997a, pp. 389–415.
22. Launey 1950, II, p. 758.
23. The Attic drachm equals six obols.
24. Launey 1950, II, p. 759.
25. Feyel 2006, tables 13 to 17, pp. 396–401, Classical and Hellenistic periods.
26. Ibid., p. 408.
27. Ibid., p. 410.

Table 8.2. Hellenistic hoards over 200 tetradrachms

No.	Findspot	Date of Burial	Total Studied
77	Naplouse	333/2	206
69	Byblos	333	217
357	Khirbet Qumran	8 BC	364
253	East of Anatolia?	130–120	379
288	Kessab	After 105/4	392
92	Jdita	325–300	400
343	Gaza region	50–30	400
71	Byblos	333	439
263	South of Jerusalem	126/5	450
68	Middle East	334–330	471
202	Unknown findspot, so-called "Demetrius I hoard"	151/0	535
193	Ma'aret en-Numan	162	536
198	Tell Kotchek	150–142	604
234	Southeastern Turkey	142	750
147	'Iraq al-Amir, Jordan	240–235	914
168	Syria	199	941
108	Aleppo	c. 305	973
231	Kırıkhan	143/2	1,104
163	Citadel of Afamya	2nd cent.	1,160
324	Coast of Mt. Carmel	72/1	1,755
228	Gaziantep	143	1,916

The smallest artisans often appear only once in the accounts,[28] unlike the major entrepreneurs with multiple contracts. With the exception of Delphi, a large construction venue where contracts are more expensive than those for restoration efforts at Eleusis or Delos, the lesser artisans are more numerous. "Many of these workers offer themselves for small undertakings and earn ridiculously tiny sums: at Eleusis, among the 107 small earners, 72 received under 50 drachms at most and 30 got less than 10."[29] These sums are not ridiculous in themselves: they represent several weeks' pay for a hoplite, but they have to be adjusted because they are not monthly salaries but one-off payments.

28. This is the case for 152 artisans out of 239 at Epidaurus: ibid., p. 336. Cf. also Feyel's charts 5–9, pp. 333–34.
29. "Beaucoup de ces travailleurs se livrent à de petites affaires et gagnent des sommes dérisoires : à Eleusis, parmi les 107 gagne-petit, 72 ont reçu au mieux moins de 50 drachmes et 30 moins de 10 drachmes", ibid., p. 411.

Table 8.3. Distribution of gold coin hoards by value in tetradrachms

Number of Coins	Hoard	Value Expressed in Tetradrachms[30]
Unknown	**116**, **137**	
1–10		
11–50		
51–100	**207**	62.5 + 28
101–500	**237**[31]	72 + 29.5
501–1,000	**135**	870
	202	30 + 532
1,001–2,000		
> 2,000	**93**	36,000

If they had hoarded all of their earnings under 100 drachms, or 25 tetradrachms, the lesser artisans would fall in the first two classes of hoard sizes, confirming the notion that the smallest hoards are not so negligible. Hoarding supposes an ability to accumulate wealth, that is, surplus resources, something certainly not within the reach of those of the most modest means.

2.2. The Rich and the Super-Rich

2.2.1. Over 200 Tetradrachms

On the other hand, the payments over 200 tetradrachms, typical for large contractors, also correspond to sums rarely hoarded in Syria during the Persian and Hellenistic periods. Only 24 out of 355 hoards fall into this category, 21 of them from the Hellenistic period (Table 8.2).

The few hoards with gold coins must be added to these with silver. Assessing their worth in tetradrachms (Table 8.3) permits comparison with the latter.

Apart from the Saida hoard (**93**), whose exceptional character has already been noted, the largest hoard inventoried is Hüseyinli (**135**), comprising 58 *trichrysa*. That number is not so small, because it is in the form of large coins weighing c. 17.80 g each and valued at 60 Ptolemaic silver drachms (15 tetradrachms). The lot therefore represents the equivalent of 870 tetradrachms, placing it in the top rank of biggest silver hoards. The two hoards containing gold coins of Demetrius I, the Seleucid king most prolific in this metal,[32] are limited to a few

30. That is, the value of gold coins in tetradrachms + the value of silver coins in tetradrachms. Hoards **135** and **237** are Ptolemaic standard.

31. Julien Olivier, for whose help I am grateful, proposed this assessment to me. The exchange commission (epallage) incurred complicates conversion of gold into silver in the second century. In addition, the coin called here pentekontadrachmon was in fact worth 80 drachms according to Olivier. Cf. Olivier 2006.

32. Houghton, Lorber, Hoover 2008, 1, p. 166.

Table 8.4. Cost of Athenian liturgies according to Lysias and Demosthenes

Liturgy	Price in Drachms	Value in Tetradrachms	Reference
Choregia of Dithyrambic Chorus, Panathenaea	300	75	Lysias 21.2
	1,500	375	Lysias 21.4
	2,000	500	Lysias 21.1
	5,000[37]	1250	Lysias 21.2
Pyrrhic Dancers, Panathenaea	800	200	Lysias 21.1,
	700	175	Lysias 21.4
Gymnasiarchy	1,200	300	Lysias 21.3
Boat Race, Panathenaea	1,500	375	Lysias 21.5
Choregia of a Comic Chorus	1,600	400	Lysias 21.4
Choregia of a Tragic Chorus	3,000	750	Lysias 21.1
Trierarchy	4,000	1,000	Demosthenes 21.80
	4,800	1,200	Lysias 32.24, 27
	5,142 (6 talents for 7 years)	1,285	Lysias 21.2

specimens, but their very high face value marks them as reserves of substantial worth. In hoard **202**, two gold staters (each equal to 20 silver drachms) and one gold octadrachm (80 silver drachms) add the equivalent of 30 tetradrachms to the 532 actual tetradrachms in this find. In hoard **207**, the three octadrachms and the hemistater equal 250 drachms or 62.5 tetradrachms; in other words, the four gold coins are worth more than the 28 silver tetradrachms, their companions. Hoard **237** belongs in the same category, with its two *mnaieia* (27.8 g each) and its *pentekontadrachmon* (12.9 g) accompanied by 19 silver tetradrachms and 21 silver didrachms, the whole amounting to 870 Ptolemaic tetradrachms. The five gold coin hoards whose content is known break out as follows: hoards **135**, **202**, and especially **93** are, in value, off the charts of silver hoards. Hoards **207** and **237** fall within the category of hoards ranging from 50–100 tetradrachms. These last two collections constitute an accumulation of above-average wealth, but they do not represent the very greatest fortunes.

2.2.2. Defining a Great Fortune

Understanding what level of accumulated wealth Syrian hoards reveal requires searching for parallels in literary texts. The orators inform us about the fortunes of some fourth-century Athenians. Without launching into a full analysis of these complex estates, it is useful to recall

33. Including a commemorative monument.

here that Demosthenes' father at his death enjoyed an estate worth 14 or 15 talents, equal to between 21,000 and 22,000 tetradrachms if it were all in cash.[34] Eighty minas of silver, equivalent to 2,000 tetradrachms or 1.33 talents, were on hand at home.[35] The more modest estate of Ciron, submitted for probate, amounted to 90 minas (2,250 tetradrachms), not counting money lent out at interest.[36] This personal property consists of real estate, slaves, and other chattels, without taking account of currency kept at home or invested with others. The indicated worth is never all in currency. To define wealthy Athenians (*hoi plousioi, hoi euporoi, hoi ta ktēmata ekhontes*), Davies chose to use the liturgies they performed in the fourth century, about whose cost Lysias informs us (Table 8.4).[37]

Each of these sums would merit being discussed and put in context, but they provide an order of magnitude for what a rich Athenian in the early fourth century would have to pay assuming such a duty. This is Davies' understanding when he observes that "even the cheapest liturgy of Lysias XXI cost nearly as much as a contemporary skilled workman was paid a year."[38]

Epigraphy also presents some currency sums that provide an idea of what a rich civic benefactor would place at the disposal of an impoverished city. Table 8.5 gathers examples drawn from Migeotte's study of public loans in Greek cities. It only takes account of sums expressed in currency or accounting units. There is no attempt, therefore, to gauge Hellenistic fortunes; this is merely an overview of the funds at the disposal of these illustrious individuals. The range of values shown here is quite broad, from 500 silver drachms (Migeotte 10 and 27) to 6,700 gold staters (Migeotte 44). Certain sums represent several thousand coins, silver or gold. But caution is called for. These data come to us through the filter of honorary decrees that enumerate the civic benefactions of an individual and their accumulated worth, of which the city has been the beneficiary. Such is the case, for example, with the largest benefactor on the list, Protogenes of Olbia (Migeotte 44). Gauthier points this out in recalling that "the largesse of Protogenes (loans, advances, gifts) ... stretched over several years."[39] The biggest amount mentioned in the document is an advance of 1,500 gold staters (lines 40, 129–30) that therefore represent what Protogenes was able to afford on one occasion to support the city.

The source data belong to different times and to places distant from one another. They still allow us to get an idea of the currency sums that the richest individuals could raise at will. It is striking that the largest Syrian hoards are generally much smaller than these amounts. The biggest Syrian hoard (**228**) does not even equal the liquid funds that Demosthenes' father maintained (2,000 tetradrachms).[40] Fifteen of the 19 largest hoards of tetradrachms contained

34. Demosthenes, *Against Aphobos* 1.1: 14 talents; 1.9: 15 talents.
35. Ibid., 1.10.
36. Isaeus, *On the Inheritance of Ciron* 35.
37. Davies 1971, p. xxi.
38. Davies 1971, p. xxii.
39. Gauthier 1985, p. 71.
40. Leaving aside the Saida hoard (**93**), to which I return later. The content of the "Seleucus I hoard" (*CH* 10.272) approximates in value the cash on hand of Demosthenes' father.

Table 8.5. Amounts of loans granted to Greek cities by large benefactors, according to Migeotte 1984.[41]

No.	Date	City	Amount	Benefactor	Nature of Transaction
10	c. 200–180	Chorsiai	500 drachms	Kapon	forgiveness on loan grant
12	228–210	Orchomenos	16,093 drachms + 5,773 drachms 1 obol 1/2	Eubolos of Elateia	reimbursement of loan
13	223	Orchomenos	18,883 drachms	Nikareta of Thespiae	reimbursement of loan
16	3rd cent.	Akraiphia	672 drachms 5 obols 1/2 on a loan of 1,672 drachms 5 obols 1/2 and 835 drachms on the interest	Kallon	forgiveness on loan and interest
16	3rd cent.	Akraiphia	3,163 drachms 1 obol on 5,261 drachms 2 obols 1/2	Euklidas of Thebes	forgiveness on loan
20	c. 100	Argos	10,000 drachms	Augis	loan
24	71/0	Gytheion	3,965 drachms + 4,200 drachms and forgiveness of 1,500 drachms on the latter	Cloatii, Romans (2 brothers)	loans
27	67–59	Pagai	500 drachms	Soteles	interest-free loan
40	3rd cent.	Istros	500 gold staters	Diogenes	interest-free loan
40	3rd cent.	Istros	1,500 gold staters	Grandson of the preceding Diogenes	interest-free loan
41	3rd cent.	Istros	300 gold staters + interest, forgiveness of 400 staters on the total and only reimbursement of the face value loaned	Hephaistion of Callatis	loan and forgiveness of interest

42	3rd cent.	Istros	1,000 gold staters	Dionysius	loan
43	3rd cent.	Olbia	3,000 gold staters	Apollonius of Chersonesus	loan
44	3rd cent. or early 2nd	Olbia	6,700 gold staters[42]	Protogenes	loan and gifts
49	325–275	Arcesine	3 talents of Attic silver	Praxikles of Naxos	loan
64	Mid-1st cent.	Tenos	11,000 + 19,500 Attic drachms	Aufidius Bassus	loan
66	After 321	Samos	1,000 gold staters	Sosistratus of Miletus	interest-free loan
67	243/2	Samos	6,000 drachms	Boulagoras	advance
70	2nd cent.	Chalcis	13,500 drachms	Cleon of Lacedaemonia	interest-free loan
71	340	Oreos	1 talent	Demosthenes of Athens	loan
78	First half 3rd cent.	Sigeum	200 gold Phocaean staters	?	loan
79	c. 306	Ilion	300 gold staters+ 1,450 gold staters	Malousios of Gargara	interest-free loan
85	After 270	Erythrai	6,000 drachms of Alexander	Polycritus	interest-free loan
94	End of the 2nd cent.	Priene	1,000 drachms of Alexander + 2,158 drachms of Alexander and 4 obols + 1,200(?) drachms of Alexander	Moschion	advance
94	End of the 2nd cent.	Priene	Pledge of silver items valued at 4,000 drachms of Alexander	Moschion	advance
102	275–250	Halicarnassus	10,000 drachms	Diodotus	interest-free loan
105	1st cent.	Olymos	7,000 drachms	Ouliades	loan

41. According to the calculations of Migeotte 1984, p. 140.
42. The entry number in the first column is that for each document in Migeotte 1984.

fewer than 1,000 of those coins (Fig. 8.4). Only three sums loaned by benefactors fall within this category (Migeotte 10, 16, and 27). Also, in two of these cases (10 and 16), we are dealing with simple forgiveness of loans that the cities could not repay.

Sums coming closest to the amounts in our hoards are those Demosthenes' father invested in businesses or with bankers: 2,400 drachms with Pasion (600 tetradrachms), 600 drachms with Pylades (150 tetradrachms), 1,600 placed with Demomeles (400 tetradrachms). The investments are only a fraction of this Athenian's fortune, a fortune not all that remarkable among the wealthy of fourth-century Athens. But they fall at the high end of silver hoards from Hellenistic Syria. This observation is also valid for Athenian liturgies. Apart from the trierarchy, they are on a scale with the most noteworthy hoards.

The fact that Syrian hoards only rarely attain the level of ordinary contributions made by the Hellenistic world's benefactors and wealthiest citizens shows not that fortunes like that of Demosthenes' father did not exist but that, just like this rich Athenian, the wealthy men of Syria did not put their ready reserves into the ground. Thus, the super rich elude us by and large, and their fortunes are not well represented in our surviving hoards. Neither modest nest eggs nor huge fortunes, these surviving hoards nonetheless cover a rather broad range. To determine the value of these lots accurately, an idea of commodity prices in Syria during the Hellenistic Age would be ideal. Such information is basically lacking, chiefly because of the poor epigraphical record in this region before the Roman period. The archives of Zenon of Caunus help to fill in this gap to a certain extent. They principally deal with the *dorea* received by Apollonius, the treasury official of Ptolemy II, at Philadelphia in the Fayum; but they also inform us about the mission of his representative, Zenon, sent to Syria and Phoenicia between 260 and September 258 BC. The documents assembled—easily 60 or so texts—provide an idea of the transactions that occurred in Ptolemaic Syria and Phoenicia in the mid-third century BC: caravans, grain trade, slaves, furnishings, etc. Several papyri give prices and a few salaries, obviously expressed in drachms on the Ptolemaic standard. So we know that an adult slave could cost between 150 and 300 drachms on the Ptolemaic standard, or the equivalent of from 37 tetradrachms and 2 drachms to 75 tetradrachms.[43] The slave woman mentioned, at 300 drachms, is the most expensive in Zenon's Syrian dossier. These prices correspond to the highest represented hoard bracket, which could thus just about purchase one good quality adult slave. Whether this was an ordinary purchase or something special in third-century Syria is still unknown.

2.2.3. The Saida Hoard

The Saida hoard (**93**) is exceptional in content. I have already observed that 7,200 staters—the hoard also contained distaters in unknown proportions—represent the equivalent of 36,000 tetradrachms or 24 Attic silver talents (see pp. 345–346). For comparison, among the most

43. Durand 2003, no. 27.

imposing hoards found in the eastern Mediterranean, all silver, the Demanhur hoard, roughly 8,000 tetradrachms of Alexander type, only comes to 5.33 talents.[44] The Meydancıkkale hoard, 5,215 coins, "represents a total weight of some 66 kg, equivalent to about two and one-half talents on the Attic standard or three on the Ptolemaic."[45] In recent years, the antiquities market has dispersed several very large hoards of Seleucid coins. The "Seleucus III hoard" (*CH* 10.272), found in 2002, contained c. 6,500 silver coins.[46] Its description in *Seleucid Coins* 2 lists 4,326 coins, of which 2,266 are tetradrachms and 2,060 drachms, or 1.85 talents, and we should bear in mind that a third of the hoard is not described. More recently, the "Seleucus I hoard"[47] (*CH* 10.265), probably buried in Asia Minor c. 281, revealed 1,960 tetradrachms and 641 drachms, or 1.41 talents.

Private fortunes might be held in gold staters, as the list shows of loans and gifts granted by benefactors to certain Hellenistic cities in poor financial shape (Table 8.5, Migeotte 40, 41, 42, 43, 44, 66, 78, and 79). It should be noted, however, that these are periods or regions in which gold circulates more widely. Five inscriptions, including the spectacular decree honoring Protogenes of Olbia, come from Istros and Olbia in the third century. All the sums are expressed in gold staters or bronze coinage,[48] which were the two types of currency then available.[49] At Samos (Migeotte 66) and at Ilion (Migeotte 79), the time period explains the presence of gold coins. Alexander the Great and his successors struck them in large quantities in the mints of the Levant and Asia Minor. This gold was hoarded and stopped circulating. It disappears from the hoards in the early third century; but it is still in circulation at the time of these two documents (after 321 and c. 306 BC).[50] As for the gold staters of Phocaea, these are in white gold, in other words, electrum. Such references are not common in the third century, since Phocaea was no longer striking this alloy. Daux, in an earlier edition of this document, recalled mentions of Phocaean staters in texts that, in his opinion, establish the staters as "an internationally accepted coinage."[51] The decree from Sigeum would be a relic of this status. In fact, Phocaea in the Classical period struck only sixths of staters.[52] Hence we must conclude that these valuations are made in money of account and that the physical units employed were electrum fractions.

In contrast, hoards of gold coins are rare in Syria. If the regional mints struck them, the coins were not used there and are mostly found outside the region. So the metal of the Saida hoard

44. Newell 1923a and Duyrat 2005b for the relevant bibliography.

45. "représente un poids total de quelques 66 kg, qui équivaut à deux talents et demi environ selon l'étalon attique ou trois talents selon l'étalon ptolémaïque", Davesne, Le Rider 1989, vol. 1, p. 16.

46. Houghton, Lorber, Hoover 2008, 2, pp. 142–50. Although one lot of drachms is said to have come from Hama, the editors of *Coin Hoards* locate it instead in the Near East or in Mesopotamia.

47. Houghton, Lorber, Hoover 2008, 2, pp. 140–42.

48. In the Protogenes decree, two reimbursements of loans in gold are partially made in bronze coinage.

49. Olbia, bronze: *IGCH* 1071–1108 and 1112–1119; gold: *IGCH* 1108–1111 (staters of Philip II, Alexander the Great, and Lysimachus). The general region of Thrace and the Black Sea around Istros: bronze - *IGCH* 841–842, 843–848, 857, 861–864, 867–868, 878–885; gold: *IGCH* 840, 853, 865, 866, 876 (Philip II, Alexander the Great, Successors).

50. Cf. Chapter 5.

51. Daux 1954, p. 56.

52. Bodenstedt 1981: electrum issues end with series 4, produced between 387 and 326 BC.

is uncommon in Syria. Compared to the large hoards of silver found outside Syria presented above, or to the sums familiar from the textual evidence, it seems clear that the Saida hoard (**93**) far exceeds the savings of the richest contemporary individual. Its composition also provides clues that prompt me to see here an official, probably military, fund. Indeed, Macedonian coins, Philips and Alexanders, make up a large part of it; they were particularly used for army pay. There are some additional specimens: staters of Chios, Pergamum, and Rhodes. Callataÿ's recent die study of the Pergamene staters with head of Heracles and image of a warrior Athena facing[53] showed how rare they are (five obverses for seven reverses); their production was probably concentrated over a few months. More generally, the gold issues of Chios, Pergamum, and Rhodes are atypical in both their metal and their Attic standard. They predate the issues with types of Alexander. Callataÿ suggests that these coins were struck from requisitions from the cities of Asia Minor. These cities would have been responsible for producing this currency at the Conqueror's behest. "The episode occurs within the overall context of Alexander's need for replenished money to pay his troops and his lack of compunction in exacting heavy contributions from the available wealth of the cities on his path, while not intervening in the choice of coinage types."[54] The presence of these rare issues, connected to the Macedonian conquest, and coming from the west seems strange at a time when, on the contrary, a flow of bullion was occurring from east to west in a very pronounced manner (cf. Chap. Nine). It strengthens the feeling that the Saida hoard is an army fund in a metal of sound market value, containing rare coins arriving from the west with the Macedonian troops at the beginning of the conquest, and that it was buried in Phoenicia in a major port at a critical time for the empire, since Alexander had just died. Its burial date, probably c. 320 BC, invites a connection with the Wars of the Successors. It represents an accumulation of wealth on a par with what could be called royal.

2.3. Modest Nest Eggs

I borrow this expression from J. and A.-G. Elayi, who use it in a way that, it seems to me, must be reconsidered. Indeed, they consider a hoard a little under 400 g of silver from the second half of the fourth century as "rather modest."[55] But in the same work (p. 327), they note that hoards of 100–500 g of silver are the most common. I have shown above that most hoards of silver coins are not modest. On the other hand, some hoards of bronze coins are (Fig. 8.3).

The small number of hoards containing bronze coins does not permit any far-reaching conclusions, all the more so since, in several cases, they are hoarded with silver or gold, which noticeably alters the content's value (Tables 8.6 and 8.7).

The bronze hoarded in these mixed deposits is generally worth less than the silver and gold. It would require a close examination of each hoard to arrive at an estimate of the sums repre-

53. Callataÿ 2012.

54. "L'épisode s'inscrit dans le canevas global d'Alexandre ayant besoin d'argent frais pour payer ses troupes, n'hésitant pas à mettre lourdement à contribution les richesses disponibles des cités situées sur son passage, mais n'intervenant pas dans le choix des types monétaires", ibid., p. 192.

55. Hoard **42**. Elayi, Elayi 1993a, p. 60.

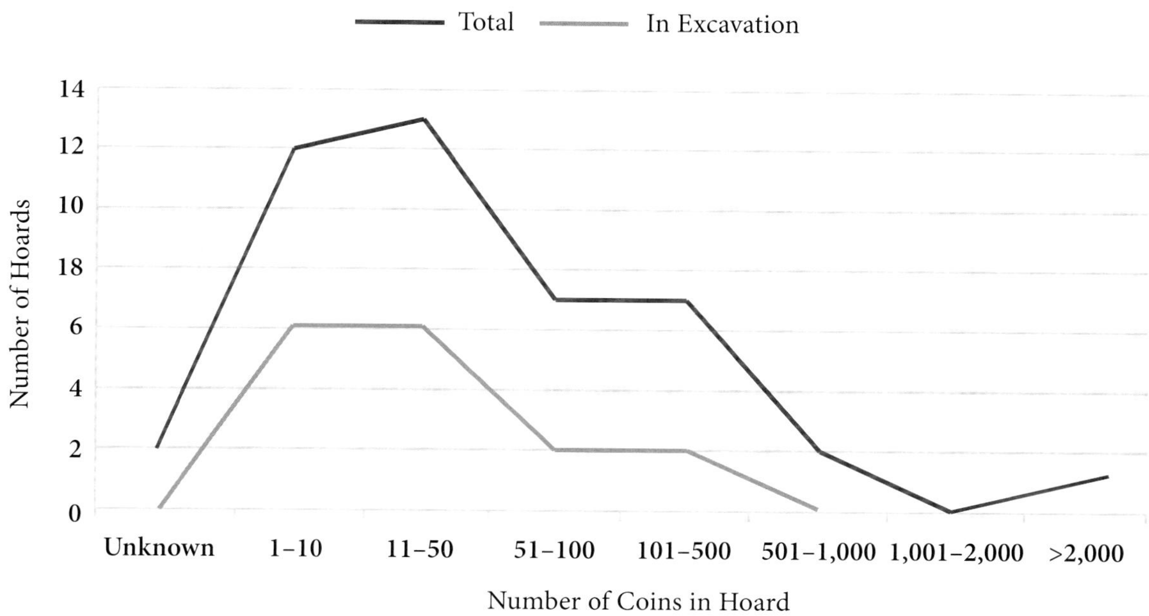

Figure 8.3. Breakdown of bronze hoards by size.[56]

sented. While awaiting the opportunity to do this, I will be content here to offer a quick assessment. We must bear in mind that the *chalkous* seems to have been the most hoarded denomination.[57] Following the Attic system adopted by the Seleucids,[58] one obol equals eight *chalkoi*; thus, 48 *chalkoi* make six obols or one drachm, and 192 *chalkoi* are required for a tetradrachm. In hoard **322**, the value of the hoarded tetradrachm is therefore clearly superior to that of the bronzes. This order of magnitude can be applied to all the Hellenistic hoards of Attic standard, even if they do not contain only Seleucid coins: the ratio is always highly favorable to silver. Thus a tiny hoard composed of two tetradrachms is equivalent to 384 *chalkoi*, and this places it in the upper bracket of the bronze hoard table. One has to assume that a person with this amount to save preferred to do so in silver coinage, a more durable metal with a higher intrinsic value. This would explain the very small number of hoards with more than 500 bronze coins. One also has to conclude that the hoards in this latter alloy, with rare exceptions, represent small amounts. Market prices known from Greek examples allow us to obtain a fair sense. At Delphi, in the third century, a mina of fish (c. 430 g) costs from 6–19 *chalkoi*.[59] At Akraiphia in Boeotia, at the end of the third century, a mina of fish varies, depending on the kind of fish, from 5 *chalkoi* to 2 obols plus 2 *chalkoi*.[60] The agoranomic inscription from the Piraeus, dated to the second half of the first century BC, amongst a whole list of butcher's prices, shows two

56. Some hoards contain both bronze and silver or gold. This chart only takes into account the number of bronze coins.

57. Hoover 2010, p. 227, n. 2.

58. Hoover in Houghton, Lorber, Hoover 2008, 2, p. 49.

59. Vatin 1966. The obol is worth 12 *chalkoi*.

60. Feyel 1936, pp. 27–36; Salviat, Vatin 1971, pp. 95–109.

Table 8.6. Hoards containing bronze and silver

No.	Silver	Bronze
40	27	6
50	326	6
80	114	10
97	1	60
294	1	47
322	1	22

Table 8.7. Hoards containing bronze and gold

No.	Gold	Bronze
116	?	?
135	58	1 ?

pig's trotters for 7 *chalkoi*.[61] These examples could be easily multiplied.[62] They throw into relief the modest nature of most bronze hoards, which could quickly have been spent in the agora purchasing the ingredients of an ordinary Greek meal.[63] This parallel is obviously only valid on the assumption of a similar organization of economic life in a Syrian city of the Hellenistic Age and in a Greek city.

Hasmonean coin hoards occupy a special place in this group: the three lots inventoried with more than 500 bronze coins contained only or mostly coins of this dynasty (**289**, 900 bronzes: **312**, 851 bronzes; **326**, at least 4,000 bronzes[64]). These kings, especially Alexander Jannaeus (103–76 BC), struck this metal in large quantities indeed. Elsewhere in Syria, the hoards follow the more ordinary pattern.

CONCLUSION

Thus we can see that the quality of the containers has no bearing on the contents, perhaps with the exception of the silver purse of Al Mina or the small case in cartouche form at Byblos from the Persian period. No precious vases for remarkable hoards, no modest purses for tiny sums in bronze. The containers show that coinage is a medium of exchange that has to remain transportable, no matter the amount gathered. The container's primary virtue lies in keeping the items together without loss. Its manufacture seems a matter of indifference.

61. Steinhauer 1994, p. 54, l. 2. Complementary analysis in Bresson 2002.
62. See Steinhauer 1994, p. 65, for other examples drawn from classical Greek literature.
63. Bresson 2002, p. 177.
64. If one converts the *prutah* to an Attic *chalkous*, this hoard would be worth a little over 20 tetradrachms.

To sum up, this brief survey of buried quantities demonstrates that our data poorly illustrate both the very greatest fortunes and the smallest nest eggs. It appears that hoards inform us most about a large, middle category extending from the piggy-bank to a handsome chest. Coined money, therefore, probably served an intermediate level of exchange, and all transactional levels did not require it. Hence the question of monetization arises, that is, the place of coinage in exchanges.

Chapter 9

Coin Use and Monetization

Syria is a region of north-south circulation, between the Mediterranean and the desert, down the coast through *cabotage* or on the mainland, but also via the Orontes, Beqaa, and Jordan valleys. There is an east-west vector as well, via the mouth and valley of the Orontes, the passes of the Bargylos, the saddle of the Homs Gap, the passes of Mt. Lebanon and the Antilebanon, and the coastal plains of the southern Levant. To reach Mesopotamia, caravans journeyed via Palmyra, braving the desert; but easier was the northern approach via Aleppo, the Taurus foothills, the upper reaches of the Tigris and, after Seleuceia Pieria, the lower Euphrates, a well-provisioned and highly travelled path. It comes as no surprise that along this age-old route Hellenistic coin hoards cluster, proof of coin penetration in these regions, especially along this highway, and in proportions quite inferior to what Syria has produced.[1] A crossroads between two continents and the Mediterranean, ancient Syria witnessed the interpenetration of traditional means of exchange and denominated money. The following pages seek to interpret this phenomenon.

The chapter title seems quite ambitious because it presumes a development in an economic history of expansion. The rate of monetization is an economic value with a precise definition: it is the ratio between goods that are the objects of monetary transactions and other goods. Grandjean has shown that, although we do not possess most of the necessary data for calculating the rate of monetization—GDP, evolution of prices, population numbers, velocity of the circulation of money—it is still possible to arrive at an estimate of the role of coinage using the circulation and geographic concentration of our finds (hoards, archaeological survey results, and excavations). She adds that "the development of monetary systems including numerous denominations with the creation of subdivisions of very little value seems to me to point in the same direction, namely the development of monetization."[2] The following presentation shares this perspective, which adheres closely to the physical evidence.

1. Duyrat 2004, pp. 400–405 and map 8, p. 424.
2. "le développement de systèmes monétaires comprenant de nombreuses dénominations avec la création de subdivisions de très faible valeur me paraît aller dans le même sens, celui d'un développement de la monétarisation", Grandjean 2006, pp. 199–200.

1. What Coinage?

Hoard contents do not allow of easy explanation. From the very first studies, numismatists have debated how to interpret these assemblages. Are they an accurate illustration of the currency available at the time of their burial or, on the contrary, are they the result of their owner's careful selection? Before attempting any deeper understanding, it is worth examining the general profile of the hoards by period.

1.1. Large Denominations and Small Change in Silver

1.1.1. Chronology

Possessions buried in the ground, both in the Achaemenid and Hellenistic periods, are essentially in silver: 310 hoards contain silver coins (87.3%), all eras combined. These hoards, in the Hellenistic Age, chiefly contain denominations larger than the drachm,[3] more rarely drachms (32 hoards) (Table 9.1). This dominance of silver accords with the practices of the Greek world at the time, and with those of the Mesopotamian world as well.[4]

Table 9.1. Distribution of silver denominations in hoards[5]

Period	Total Hoards	> Drachm	Drachms	< Drachm
Persian period	68	52	7	31
Alexander and Successors (333–280)	61	47	7	15
3rd cent. (280–201)	33	25	5	2
2nd cent. (200–101)	126	107	17	2
1st cent. (100–1 BC)	67	45	3	1
Total	**355**	**276**	**39**	**51**

Table 9.1 shows the numbers for hoards containing coins weighing more than a drachm, drachms, and fractions less than a drachm. The drachm has been retained as the base because that was its role in most of the Hellenistic Greek world. This choice is not relevant for the Persian period, when standards varied and drachms were rare and often foreign in origin; but this intermediate denomination does enable us to distinguish large coins (shekels, double shekels, etc.) from the sometimes tiny fractions that circulated then. A clear chronological evolution in hoard content is evident. A graph giving the percentage of hoards with large denominations, drachms, and fractions illustrates this better (Fig. 9.1).

3. 225 hoards out of the 287 from this period following the Macedonian Conquest, or 78.4%.
4. Cf. the contributions of Jursa 2010, pp. 469–753, on this issue, and Monerie 2013 for the Hellenistic period.
5. A single hoard may contain several denominations.

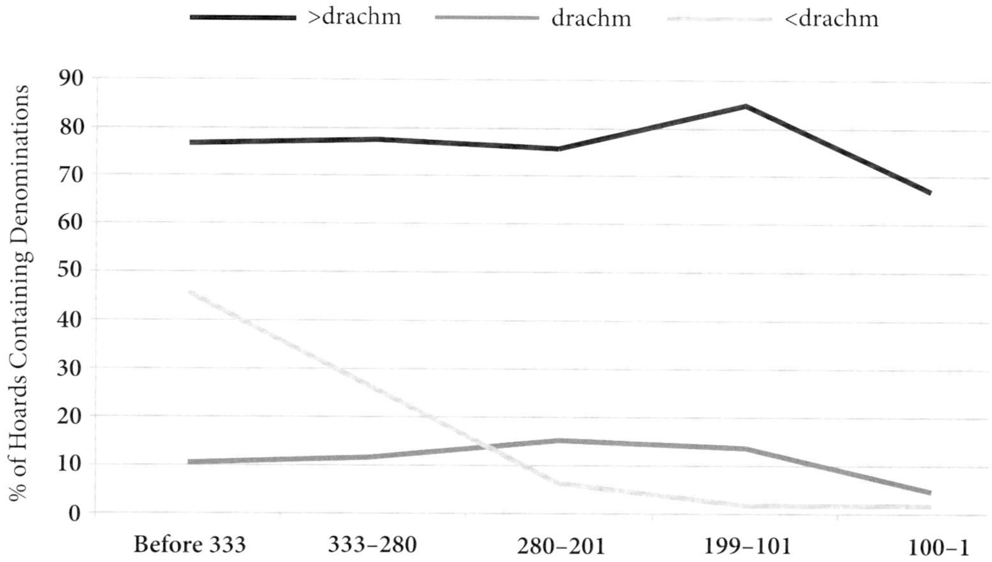

Figure 9.1. Percentages by period of hoards containing large denominations (> drachm), drachms, and fractions (< drachm).

Figure 9.1 demonstrates that in all periods large denominations overwhelmingly dominate: they are present in 75% to 85% of hoards, except for the first century. But even in that period, silver is still present in two-thirds of hoards as large denominations. Closer study brings out the importance of regional contrasts. A noticeable hoarding of bronze characterizes regions under Hasmonean control (Map 26), while in the rest of Syria the rates of representation for large silver denominations do not alter much from previous centuries. Hoards containing drachms show the same tendency as those with large denominations: these coins are present in 10% to 15% of hoards, except during the first century, where they appear in only 4% of finds.

The data do not support this relative stability for fractions, however; they undergo a clear and steady decline. They are present in nearly half of the hoards from the Persian period (45.6%), and are especially prominent in the southern Levant, where 11 of the 15 hoards have been found containing fractions dated between 333 and 280 BC.[6] Fractions still appear in a quarter of the finds from the period of Alexander and the Successors. Yet one must observe that two-thirds of them date from before 325 BC,[7] that is, the period of the Macedonian Conquest, when coin circulation still retained characteristics of the Achaemenid period.[8] As the production of Alexanders develops, fractions almost completely disappear from hoards. This evolution occurs only in the 320s, the time when production of Alexanders became sufficient and this currency became established in the region.[9] It is, however, also necessary to take into account regional practices that seem deeply embedded: during the years 333–320 BC, a hoard from Nablus or Gaza (*CH* 9.453, **113**) consists of a Philistine fraction and six obols and hemiobols. Four are

6. Hoards **77**, **80**, **81**, **82**, **84**, **87**, **89**, **97**, **98**, **112**, **113**. Duyrat 2011b, map 2.
7. Hoards **77**, **79**, **80**, **81**, **82**, **84**, **85**, **86**, **87**, **89**.
8. Cf. Duyrat 2011b.
9. Duyrat 2004, pp. 386–88; Duyrat 2011b.

Table 9.2. Production volumes of silver Hellenistic coins at Aradus (Duyrat 2005a, p. 293)

Series	Denomination	d
I	Autonomous tetradrachms with types of Alexander	50
II	Tetrobols	18
III	Hemidrachms	16
IV	Diobols Zeus/Prow	1
V	Tetradrachms Poseidon/Zeus	1
VI	Drachms	89
VII	Tetradrachms Tyche/Nike	105
VIII	Diobols Medusa/Aplustre	4

illegible, but two others are Alexanders from Sidon, for which we have little other evidence.[10] Schindel has provided a quick overview of the mints that struck hemidrachms of Alexander, highlighting the repeated presence in his surveys of Aradus, Marathus, and, to a lesser degree, Sidon. This concentrated production may reflect the greater use of fractions in this region, although Babylon and other mints are also represented.[11] After about 10 years of Macedonian rule, the local populations found themselves deprived of these fractions that figured in so many hoards of the Persian period. Bronze did not replace silver small change before the second half of the third century. The issuing authority did not seek to meet the needs of daily exchange but to answer only those of the state, leaving to users the problem of adapting to these transformations. The abrupt change in the last quarter of the fourth century makes clear the issuing authority's lack of concern for the customs of the population.

After 325 BC, the number of hoards containing small coins in silver is marginal: about 6% in the third century, it amounts to no more than 1.5% in the next two centuries, even as the use of bronze grows progressively for small transactions. From the 320s, the drachm is the smallest denomination hoarded, and it is much less frequent than the tetradrachm. This dominance of the tetradrachm does not reflect the diversity in production of the regional mints but rather the volumes they issued. The example of Aradus, for which we have actual numbers, reveals the variety in silver fractions, yet they were struck in amounts quite inferior to those of the larger denominations. During the Hellenistic Age, the city produced eight series of silver, only three of which were tetradrachms. The others range from the drachm to the diobol.[12]

The 26 hoards containing Aradian Hellenistic coins chiefly contain tetradrachms and drachms of this city, with the exception of one tetrobol (**173**) and six hoards of bronze coins. The production of silver fractions might have been greater than the Aradian *corpus* indicates

10. Another hoard, Qasr Naba (**85**), has produced a single obol of Alexander, also struck at Sidon.

11. Price's *corpus* confirms the rarity of silver fractions with types of Alexander, collected in two plates. Price 1991, pls. CXLI–CXLII.

12. Duyrat 2005a, pp. 300–301.

Table 9.3. Hoards of small weight, Persian period

No.	Findspot	Date of Burial	Total	Weight
113	Nablus Region? Gaza?	End of 4th cent., 333–320?	7	2.44 g
33	Al Mina	375	55	c. 6 g
98	Hebron Region or Gaza	320–270	34	11.41 g
43	Southern Asia Minor?	mid–4th cent.	54	12.25 g
40	Beach south of Beirut	368–333	27[13]	16.65 g

(Table 9.2), the ratio of observed specimens to dies being low for these coins. The quantity and nature of the available coinage conditions hoarding choices, but so does the relative importance users accord it. Thus, silver fractions were hoarded in the Persian period and bronze coins in the Hellenistic.

1.1.2. Silver Fractions of the Persian Period

Fractions are common in the Persian period, and they are sometimes quite small. The weight of certain hoards is perplexing (Table 9.3). The silver purse from Al Mina (**33**), although stuffed with 55 coins, actually contained scarcely more than six grams of silver, the lightest weighing 0.04 g, the heaviest 0.59 g. Other hoards or parts of hoards yield average weights of less than one gram per coin.

The denominational system of certain mints in the Persian period is particularly interesting because it allocates a very large place to fractions. The following tables (9.4–9.6) display this breakdown for the mints of Tyre, Sidon, and Philistia, which have been the subject of detailed studies.

For Tyre (Table 9.4), numerous fractions do not enter into this reckoning since they could not be classified. Elayi and Elayi did not succeed in placing them in the divisional system because, although struck with common types, their weights vary too noticeably. So their group III – absent from my table – includes 194 fractions that escape classification, as well as the five series of Tyrian bronzes (69 specimens) and the uncertain bronzes (12). The number of shekels preserved is obviously overwhelming in comparison with the subdivisions, but when considering the numbers one has to bear in mind that the fractions, especially the smallest, are less well preserved, endure greater wear, and are less easily noticed in excavations. This table shows especially that the sixteenth-shekels were a significant proportion of the city's production in the fourth century.

13. And six bronzes not counted in the weight total.

Table 9.4. Denominations struck by Tyre in the Persian period[14]

Group	Shekels 13.56 g, then 8.77 g	Quarters 3.16 g	Sixteenths 0.57 g	Thirty-seconds[15] 0.32 g	One hundred-sixtieths[16]
I. (c. 450–425)	160	47[17]	21	13	3
II.1.1. Phoenician standard, uninscribed (c. 425–333/2).	155	29	183	0	0
II.1.2.Phoenician standard, inscribed (c. 393–358)	102	0	81	0	0
II.2. Attic standard (c. 357–333)	744	0	0	0	0

The example of Sidon (Table 9.5) is even more telling than that of Tyre. The coin production rests on three denominations: double shekels, halves, and sixteenths down to the reign of Tennes (c. 351–347). After this king, only very large denominations endure, of more than 25 grams, and fractions of small size, always less than a centimeter in diameter. 136 half-shekels in bronze, 136 quarter-shekels, two eighths, and 13 sixteenths in the same alloy (group IV) are said to be unclassifiable.

The catalogue of Philistine coins published by Gitler and Tal tries to reconstitute the denominational system of the Ashdod, Ascalon, and Gaza mints (Table 9.6).[18] These struck some large denominations, but mostly significant quantities of fractions for which a die study would be invaluable, although probably very hard to realize

The close study of weights shows there is no question of an Attic standard, even though the standard nomenclature is Greek. "Although we could see them as corresponding to a lower Attic standard, we prefer to define their weight standard as local, Philistian, or even Palestinian, since the average weights of the Samarian drachms, obols and hemiobols are quite similar, albeit slightly higher."[19] All the difficulty derives from the abundance of fractions of often irregular weight for which we do not yet have a *corpus*. Nonetheless, this catalogue testifies to the dominance of fractions of the drachm. The situation is even more pronounced in Samaria and Judaea, neither of which issued any denomination higher than the drachm.[20] In Samaria, "the

14. Elayi, Elayi 2009b. Since Elayi and Elayi's die study is open to criticism, this table takes into account the number of catalogued specimens rather than die-counts. Their book offers a detailed study of the weights, from which the theoretical weights shown here are drawn.

15. Called half-sixteenths by J. and A.-G. Elayi.

16. Called tenths of sixteenths by J. and A.-G. Elayi.

17. Elayi, Elayi 2009b, p. 44, suppose the existence of eighths of shekels on the basis of a specimen of unclassifiable weight.

18. Gitler, Tal 2006.

19. Ibid., p. 315.

20. Summary table in Meshorer, Qedar 1999, p. 71.

Table 9.5. Denominations struck by Sidon in the Persian period[21]

Group	Double shekels c. 25.67 g	Shekels	Halves c. 6.94 g	Quarters	Sixteenths[22] 0.76–0.55 g	Thirty-seconds
I. (after 450)	0	1	1	15	0	0
II. (before 425)	26	0	75	1	64	8[23]
III. (425–c. 402)	81	0	87	0	88	10
IV.1. Baʿalšillem II (c. 401–366)	316	0	28	0	414	16
IV.2. ʿAbdʿashtart (c. 365–352)	139[24]	0	19	35	37 + 19	35
IV.3. Tennès (c. 351–347)	54	0	0	0	53	0
IV.4. "Evagoras" (c. 346–343)	106	0	0	0	55	0
IV.5. ʿAbdʿashtart II (c. 342–333)	123	0	4	1	8	0
IV.6. Mazday (c. 353–333)	98	0	0	0	128	0
IV.7. Uncertain (c. 401–333)	35	0	23	21	72	20

basic and most common denomination is the obol,"[25] supposed to have made the link possible between the local, light "drachm" and the Athenian drachm that was heavily represented in the region through tetradrachms and their imitations.

In sum, all these fractions were struck in probably important quantities, which it will be challenging, however, to estimate, since die studies on such small sizes are particularly difficult. Nonetheless, other indicators support this idea. Thus, concerning fractions of ʿAynel of Byblos, the city's last king before Alexander's conquest, Elayi and Elayi emphasize that "the study of the engraving technique, of the use of dies, of the technique of striking, and of style create the very

21. Elayi, Elayi 2004b. The first three groups are anonymous. The book offers a detailed study of the weights, providing the basis for the theoretical weights set forth in the table.

22. Elayi, Elayi 2004b, pp. 36-37, assume the existence of a 1/64th of a shekel on the basis of one specimen of unclassifiable weight.

23. Elayi, Elayi 2004b, pp. 53-54, assume the existence of a 1/128th of a shekel on the basis of one specimen of unclassifiable weight.

24. Elayi, Elayi 2004b, p. 221, assume the existence of a tetradrachm on the basis of one specimen of unclassifiable weight.

25. Ibid., p. 70.

Table 9.6. Denominations of Philistine mints

Tetradrachms	Didrachms	Drachms	"Obols" 0.92–0.40 g	"Hemiobols" 0.32–0.17 g	"Fractions" 0.15–0.04 g

Table 9.7. Hoards containing gold coins

No.	Findspot	Date of Burial	Total Studied
93	Saida	323–320	7,200 AV
116	Beirut	300	1,000 (AV, AE)
135	Hüseyinli, near Antakya	259/8	58 AV, 1 AE
137	Near East	250	?
202	"Demetrius Hoard"	151/0	3 AV, 532 AR
207	Antakya	150	4 AV, 28 AR
237	Syria	140	3 AV, 40 AR

clear impression, especially with the vast majority of 'Aynel's fractions, that one is dealing with issues rather carelessly produced at all stages of manufacture, the mint employing personnel more or less qualified and more or less pressed for time."[26] This observation squares with what Meshorer and Qedar, under the title "Quantity and Quality," write of Samarian coinage that "out of a certain weight of silver it was expected that a specific number of coins of a fixed denomination would be prepared. Examining the [Samaria] hoard [**50**]..., one can see that the value of a coin was determined by the die rather than by weight."[27] The weights of the fractions from the Samaria hoard indeed range from 0.46–0.90 g. "The smaller the denomination—hemiobols and quarter obols—the greater the deviation." The "hemiobols" weigh between 0.10 g and 0.45 g. The carelessness in striking is surely not owing to the coins' size: small fractions of very good manufacture were issued elsewhere in the Greek world. I would be inclined, as Meshorer and Qedar's title suggests, to think rather that the need to strike *en masse* is what prompted mints to neglect quality, since metrological precision could not be guaranteed in such conditions. These poorly standardized weights may also have another explanation that does not contradict the preceding. It is plausible that such small coins had a face value superior, indeed clearly superior, to their weight in silver. Their alignment to the weight standard would then be less important for two reasons. First, small coins can only lose small amounts of metal through wear. Secondly,

26. "l'étude de la technique de gravure, de l'utilisation des coins, de la technique de la frappe et du style donne la très nette impression que l'on a affaire, surtout pour la grande majorité des divisionnaire d''Aynel, à des émissions peu soignées à tous les stades de la fabrication, l'atelier utilisant un personnel plus ou moins qualifié et plus ou moins pressé par le temps." Elayi, Elayi 1993a, p. 113.

27. Meshorer, Qedar 1991, p. 67.

Table 9.8. Hoards containing bronze coins

Period	Total Hoards	Bronze Hoards	%
Persian period	68	2	2.9%
Alexander and Successors (333–280)	61	4	6.6%
3rd cent. (280–201)	33	4	12.1%
2nd cent. (200–101)	126	15	11.9%
1st cent. (100–1BC)	67	20	29.9%
Total	**355**	**45**	**12.6 %**

their face value being superior to their weight of silver, the necessarily limited irregularity of their weights had probably no consequence for the user.

It is noteworthy that this production of small silver coins was also abundant at a time when the Greek world had already switched mostly to bronze coinage for small transactions. Meadows has recently pointed out the disappearance of silver fractions from western Asia Minor hoards from c. 400, when numerous mints of the region were disposed to adopt the Chian standard under the pressure of the Spartan wars.[28] By comparison, Syria preserves and develops the use of occasionally tiny fractions at the same time as weighed silver prevails in Mesopotamia, in parallel with commodity currencies.[29] The monetary landscape of these three large regions of the Persian Empire evolved differently, in response to political history and local economics.

1.2. Rarity of Gold

Unlike silver, gold is very little represented, without any particular concentration either in time or place (Table 9.7). These hoards are for the most part poorly known and varied in content. They all date from the Hellenistic period. Syrian territory does not appear to have yielded a single daric. The absence of homogeneity in these hoards is also clear numerically, for they range from three gold coins to perhaps 7,200. The coinage is of every provenance and size: there are royal staters (Philip II, Alexander the Great, Demetrius I: **93**, **116**, **137**, **202**, **207**), *trichrysa* and other gold Ptolemaic denominations (**93**, **135**, **237**). The rare gold stater of Ptolemy Soter, found in tomb K–2002 at Jablah, must be added to this list. The hoarding of gold, therefore, seems exceptional and does not answer to any special rules beyond that of the standard that separates gold as well as silver between the zones of Attic and Ptolemaic weight.

28. Meadows 2011, pp. 275–77, figs. 1–3.
29. Monerie 2013.

1.3. Bronze

We are poorly informed about the circulation of bronze through hoarding because the coins in this alloy were not hoarded in proportion to their production volume. Once more, the example of Aradus is instructive. The city struck a large variety of bronzes during the Hellenistic Age. Between the middle of the third century and the end of the first, it put into service 670 obverse dies for bronze coins. They break out into 18 series.[30] Of this rich production, the hoards give only a pale reflection through six deposits (**175**, **187**, **275**, **283**, **284**, **305**). Unlike large silver coins, whose production volumes are rather well reflected in circulation, hoards illustrate bronzes very poorly.

The situation evolves over time (Table 9.8). In the Persian period, relatively little bronze was struck compared to silver. Sidon is an exception with its four denominations in this metal, known through several dozen specimens.[31] Only one has reached us through a hoard (**50**)! The bronzes of the four hoards from the time of Alexander and the Successors come from the mints of Alexander himself (**80**, **97**, **116**) and those of Ptolemy Soter (**125**). Third-century bronzes come from the Ptolemies (**130**, **131**) and from Philip V of Macedon (**155**). The increase in the second century is quite relative since it coincides with the overall increase in the number of surviving hoards. Seleucid coinages dominate (**178**, **185**, **212**, **230**, **270**, **272**, **275**, **287**, **289**, **291**), except in the Aradian Peraea, which produces only local coinage struck at Aradus and Marathus to the exclusion of everything else (**175**, **187**, **283**, **284**). There is a fresh development in the first century: bronze hoards now chiefly consist of Hasmonean coins that only circulate in the reg-

Table 9.9. Size of hoards of bronzes[32]

n	Persian Period	Alexander and Successors	3rd Cent.	2nd Cent.	1st Cent.
Unknown		1		1	
1–10	2	1	2	4	4
11–50		1		3	8
51–100		1		4	3
101–500			2	2	3
501–1,000				1	1
> 1,000					1
Total	**2**	**4**	**4**	**15**	**20**

30. Duyrat 2005a, p. 293.
31. Elayi, Elayi 2004b, pp. 349–86.
32. For hoards consisting of several metals, only the bronze coins are taken into account.

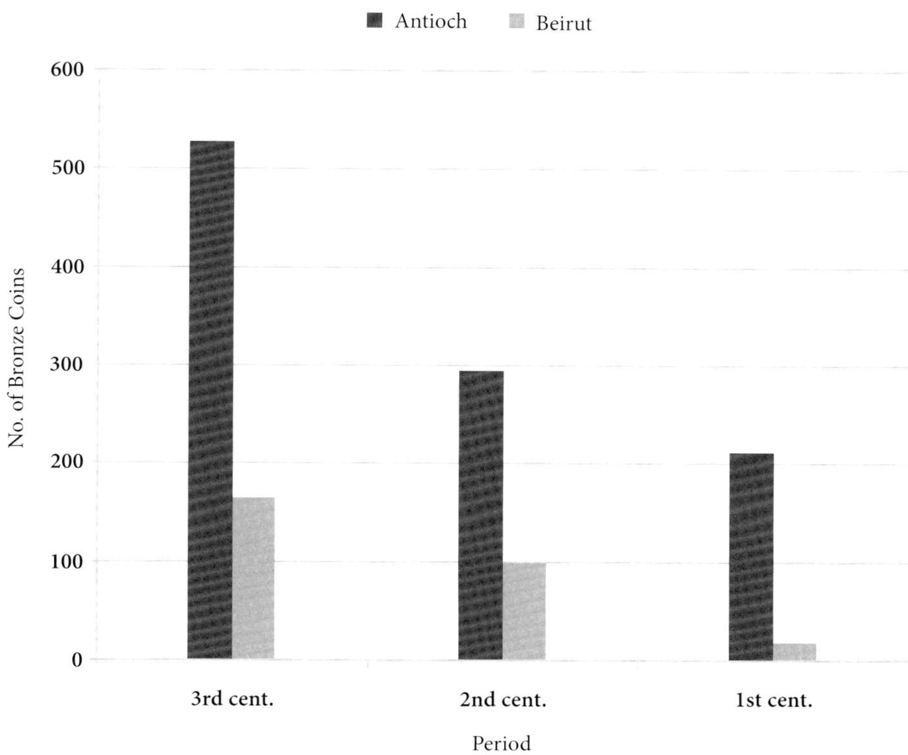

Figure 9.2. Hellenistic bronze coins in the excavations of Antioch and Beirut, 3rd–1st cent.

ions this dynasty controlled (Map 26). During this last century, bronze hoards also increase in size.

Table 9.9 shows that the size of hoards grows at the same time as their number. This phenomenon in the first century is closely connected with the fact that the Hasmoneans only produced bronze coins. The abundant issues of Alexander Jannaeus widely supplied circulation in the southern Levant. His coinage prompted a number of imitations that were cast and also struck in lead.[33] The hoards reflect the wide acceptance this currency gained, a currency of little intrinsic worth and so largely fiduciary, revealing a hoard value potentially rather more modest than that of previous centuries. The large size of certain finds partially compensates for this low value of bronze. The Jaffa Hoard (**314**) thus consisted of 851 coins of Alexander Jannaeus, plus some others in fragmentary condition. Even more spectacular are the roughly 4,000 *prutot* from a hoard found in Israel, without further information (**326**). The map of hoards of Jewish coins would therefore *de facto* be a map of bronze coin hoards, with the exception of the rare finds from the Persian period (*YHD* coins). It should be read together with the map of isolated coins found in excavations (Map 26) and with the map of Tyrian civic issues (Map 28): Hellenistic shekels struck with the head of Heracles/Melqart and an eagle constitute, indeed, the silver currency of the Hasmonean territories.

33. Meshorer 2001, pp. 47–48.

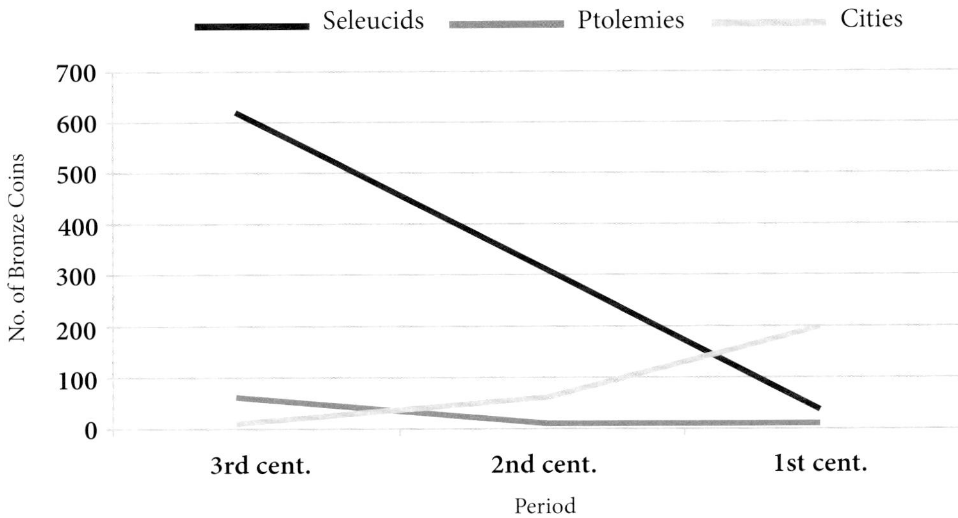

Figure 9.3. Seleucid, Ptolemaic, and civic bronzes in the excavations of Antioch and Beirut.

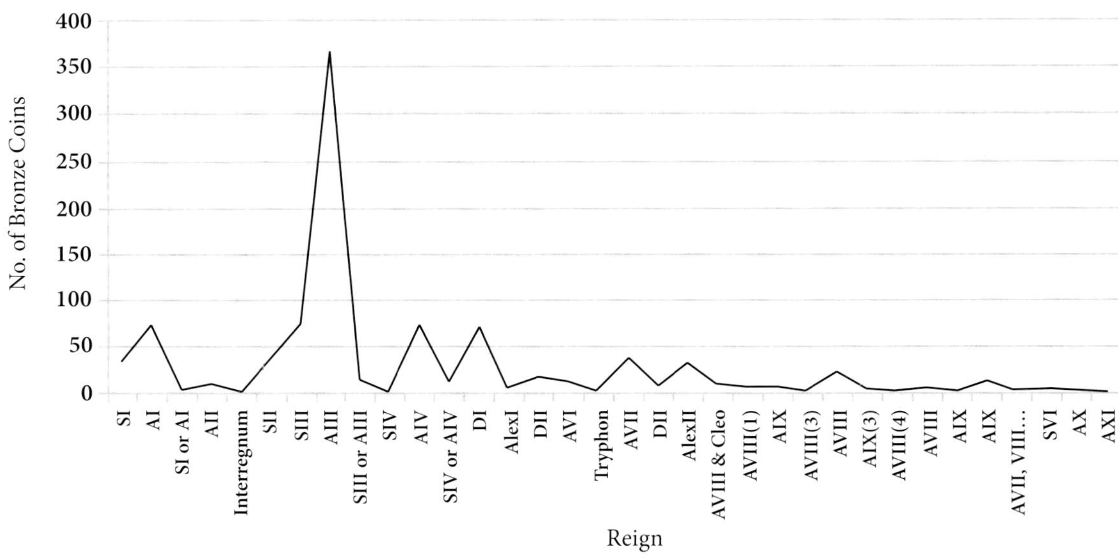

Figure 9.4. Seleucid bronze in the excavations of Antioch and Beirut.

The hoards give some indication of the increased production and use of bronze, but these data are variable. The low value of bronze prevented its becoming a privileged metal for hoarding, and the volumes discovered do not reflect production. Moreover, the fact that a large proportion of our archaeological information comes from numerous and well published Israeli digs, entirely concentrated on Israeli soil, accentuates all the more the considerable preponderance of Hasmonean output in our information. In contrast, a detailed examination of discoveries made in excavations ought to be a far more accurate indicator of the ordinary use of bronze coins. Such an examination is not possible in the present state of the *corpus*, which does not distinguish finds with sufficient precision. On the other hand, it is conceivable to dwell more specifically on the total volumes from two large, well-published sites, Antioch and Beirut (Fig. 9.2).

The quantity of Hellenistic bronzes found at Antioch and Beirut (Fig. 9.2) contradicts the impression given by the hoards: the number of coins in this metal clearly decreases between the third and first centuries. However, a few words of caution must precede any interpretation. The number of finds depends directly on the archaeological levels excavated in each of these cities. Moreover, bronze may circulate a long time; this table is based on the issue dates of the coins. Yet the decrease is parallel in both cases. A more in-depth analysis shows that the disappearance of Seleucid royal coins explains the phenomenon (Fig. 9.3). Very numerous in the third century, they were replaced only partially by civic bronzes in the first.

A cumulative graph of Seleucid bronzes found on the two sites confirms this observation (Fig. 9.4). It is uncertain whether Figure 9.4 exactly reflects the production of the different mints concerned, but it is surely a likeness. The graph highlights the greater presence of the coins of Antiochus I, Seleucus III, Antiochus IV, Demetrius I, and especially the considerable volumes issued during the long reign of Antiochus III. The falloff is clearly evident from the mid-second century.

To sum up, the hoards of the Hellenistic period are primarily composed of large silver denominations, and they roughly reflect the production of the mints in this metal. In contrast, bronze production was greater, in quantity and variety, than the hoards show, with the notable exception of the Hasmonean realms. The example of Antioch and Beirut creates the impression that, in the third century, bronze coinage is more abundant but less hoarded than in later eras. The impression that the hoarding of this metal increases is misleading due to the special case of the Hasmonean kingdoms.

2. THE REIGN OF SILVER

2.1. *Hacksilber* and Denominated Coinage: an Invisible Couple

Chapter Four showed that *Hacksilber* disappears from hoards towards the end of the fourth century BC. The natural tendency has therefore been to suppose that denominated money entirely replaced weighed money from that time forward. The scarcity of written sources in Syria makes it difficult to depict the transition between weighed and denominated silver, as well as the differentiation between these two currencies at a time when they were used simultaneously. Thus, more than half of the papyri of Wadi Daliyeh, discovered in 1962 by Bedouin in grottos 14 km north of Jericho, deal with slave sales. These documents date between 350 and 332 BC.[34] All the transactions are registered in shekels, penalties in minas. The price of a slave falls within a broad spectrum from 10–35 shekels. The sale of a house is attested in the same *corpus* at one mina and 10 (?) shekels. Gropp states that transactions are in actual coinage: "Clearly money has changed hands. In line 15 this money is explicitly mentioned as that 'which you gave m[e].'"[35] There can be no question here of denominated coinage but rather weighed silver must

34. Dušek 2007, pp. 441–45.
35. Gropp 2001, p. 110.

have been used, as Dušek explains: "The double contract WDSP 17, dated to the mid-fourth century BC, which appears to be a contract concerning a loan of money with collateral, explicitly contains the Hebrew verb לקת 'weigh' that, in this context, is quite probably related to the action of weighing the loaned money."[36] The shekel and mina employed may have been those of Babylon (1 mina = 60 shekels).[37] The coins discovered on the site belong to different standards. The Nablus Hoard (**77**) contained several hundred fractions, principally of Phoenician cities or with Athenian types. In addition, six stray coins have been recorded: an Athenian tetradrachm, one (or three) stater(s) of Mazaios, two Tyrian shekels (Baal on a winged hippocamp, dolphin/owl), a fraction with Athenian types, and a Sidonian fraction that is the only coin discovered in an archaeological context.[38] This small ensemble, essentially seen in the coin trade, suggests, despite Dušek, that there was no competition between the system of weighed money and denominated coinage.[39] These two currencies circulated together, the papyri employ the shekel and mina as accounting entities, payments were effected in silver, but what sort of silver (weighed or denominated) it is impossible to say most of the time. It is worthwhile, in order better to understand how weighed and denominated coinage interacted, to look at the written evidence available in other regions.

To reconstitute the actual monetary circulation—weighed or denominated—in the Persian period, one must first realize that a considerable amount of *Hacksilber* may have been lost. Monerie has pointed out the remarkable contrast between the numerous attestations of silver payments in Babylonian texts of the Hellenistic period and the extreme scarcity of any finds of *Hacksilber*.[40] So it is necessary to keep in mind that hoards probably inform us in only a very limited way about the actual circulation of silver money. Struck coinage never met the entirety of needs as a means of payment during the period under consideration, a point to which I will return below. The transition from traditional forms of money encompasses two centuries according to the hoard evidence and is only complete after the Macedonian Conquest. The available documentation in Babylonia and in Egypt can help in understanding the conditions of this coexistence.

Hellenistic Babylonian texts first mention payments in staters in 321 BC.[41] After this time, conversions between coins, always called staters, and the silver Babylonian shekel are fixed. This "Babylonian rate," explicitly mentioned in the texts, established an equivalence of two Babylonian shekels (16.6 g of silver) for one Greek stater. The latter may be Attic tetradrachms (Alexanders, Seleucid royal coins) or lion staters down to the 270s. After this date, the staters increasingly become the standard money for exchanges in Babylonia and the shekel a money

36. Dušek 2007, p. 496. WDSP 15.
37. Ibid., pp. 505–507.
38. Ibid., pp. 57–62.
39. Ibid., p. 496.
40. Monerie 2013 only catalogues two *Hacksilber* hoards: Babylonia (*IGCH* 1747) and Tigris (*IGCH* 1762). Cf. Jursa 2010, pp. 469–753, on the omnipresence of silver in the texts from the first millennium.
41. M. Jursa, "Florilegium babyloniacum: neue Texte aus hellenistischer und spätachämenidischer Zeit," in C. Wunsch (ed.), *Mining the Archives. Festschrift for Christopher Walker* (Dresden, 2002), pp. 107–30 (*non vidi*), cited by Monerie 2013.

of account. This system remains in effect until the first century BC. The texts only infrequently mention payments below two shekels, which one must suppose were paid in weighed money or in commodity currency (barley, dates, etc.) since silver fractional coins were extremely rare. Mentions of staters disappear from Babylonian texts in the second century BC, when struck coinage became more current. This is a sign that coins had become commonplace and were now completely integrated into the region's economic environment.[42] The Babylonian example is instructive because it shows how local accounting adapted to this new medium of struck coinage. The fixed rate between the Babylonian shekel and coins granted the latter official recognition as a standard currency. Commodity currency and *Hacksilber* are well attested in some temple archives, as is clear from Monerie's selection of examples from the late fourth and early third centuries with payments in barley, silver, dates, and wool.[43] Struck coinage does not replace traditional means of payment; it complements it.

Another example, well-documented by written texts, is the site of 'Ayn Manâwir, in the oasis of Khargeh in the Libyan desert, 200 km west of the Nile Valley.[44] A team headed by M. Wuttmann (Institut français d'archéologie orientale in Cairo) has excavated the temple and part of the inhabited area. These efforts have brought to light several hundred *ostraka* inscribed in demotic. Unlike Nile Valley *ostraka*, these are not rough notes but true archives—of matrimonial records, irrigation, credit, etc.—inscribed on a cheap and accessible medium: ceramic shards. We have here a rural society employing barley as a commodity currency. Yet this documentation contains the earliest written attestation of Greek staters in Egyptian sources, on an *ostrakon* dated between December 4, 412, and January 2, 411 BC. Agut-Labordère attributes this very early appearance of staters in the texts of an oasis far from the Nile Valley to the development of olive oil and wine production, the sale of which would have attracted silver money circulating in the valley. As in Babylonia, Greek staters are integrated within the traditional system of weighed silver: five staters for one *deben* of 91 g of silver. They are an addition, not a replacement, taking a well-defined place in the existing monetary system that now encompasses commodity currency and silver, weighed and coined. From 412 to 377 BC, *ostraka* of payments in *deben*s and staters are equally attested, mostly for payments of fines. The documents are clear about the actual presence of these coins and of the fact that they are not cut, so not transformed into *Hacksilber*, but easily exchanged for their face value. Contemporaneously, loan contracts are stated in barley. This commodity currency also serves to buy goods and to price other products. Each currency seems to have had different functions, silver being particularly used as collateral in transactions:

42. Monerie 2013.
43. Ibid., fig. 25 and 40.
44. Agut-Labordère 2014.

whether it was a matter of protecting the income from a wife's holdings or guaranteeing the purchase or renting of important quantities of irrigation shares, silver, so it seems here, served especially to reassure business partners. One who had some Greek coins or Egyptian ingots safe in his purse offered collateral that facilitated the transactions he was intending to conduct. In the relatively closed environment of the Egyptian village, silver seems to have had an utterly patrimonial value, embodying a wealth one could dispense only parsimoniously, chiefly for the purpose of increasing the means of production at the disposal of the domestic group.[45]

These two examples, dating from the end of the Persian period and the beginning of the Hellenistic, show how struck coinage came to be integrated into prior systems without destroying them. It occupies a growing place revealed by the Babylonian texts that, from the third century, reveal payments in staters identified by the names of Seleucid kings. This evolution is also probably true for Syria, where *Hacksilber* is attested before the fifth century and where one probably has to imagine payments in commodity currency, which have totally eluded us. In addition, these eastern examples more broadly provide food for thought on the manner in which struck coinage was progressively imposed in the Greek world and on what it replaced.

2.2. Silver Flow

Evaluating coin usage in Syria presupposes knowing the availability of precious metal and, especially, of currency in the region during the times under investigation. Major political upheavals repeatedly involve noticeable flows in coin circulation, to which hoarding is a witness. Three periods stand out rather sharply. Under the Achaemenids, money flowed in a west-to-east direction; the Macedonian Conquest marks a strong reversal, clearly identifiable, with a heavy draining of coins from east to west. From the third century BC and, above all, during the second century, monetary flows are shorter and more fractured, with Syria continuing to attract foreign coinages.

2.2.1. Greek Silver in the Achaemenid Empire

This section takes its title from the book by Daniel Schlumberger who so magisterially demonstrated that the coins available in the Achaemenid Empire were mostly Greek.[46] His use of coinage as an indicator of silver supplies is particularly pertinent: mints are identified and the

45. "qu'il s'agisse de protéger la rente d'une épouse ou de garantir l'achat ou la location de quantités importantes de parts d'irrigation, l'argent, tel qu'il apparaît là, servait avant tout à rassurer les partenaires en affaires. Celui qui possédait, serrés dans une bourse, quelques pièces grecques ou lingots égyptiens offrait des garanties qui facilitaient les transactions qu'il entendait mener. Dans le cadre relativement clos du village égyptien, l'argent se parait donc d'une valeur toute patrimoniale, cristallisant une richesse que l'on ne pouvait dépenser que parcimonieusement, essentiellement dans le but d'accroître les moyens de production dont disposait le groupe domestique." Ibid., p. 89.

46. Schlumberger 1953.

secondary origin of the metal is obvious, unlike *Hacksilber*, which is generally not datable and indeterminate in origin. The trajectory of coins, when the coins are sufficiently numerous, may thus give a general idea of the orientation of the flow of metal that is probably just as valid for uncoined metals.

The primary origin of the metal is, however, more complicated to discern. Metallurgic analyses provide indications about composition and manufacturing techniques, but they cannot trace the mining source, given the absence of mine samples in most cases. Written sources inform us about the existence of mining districts; the Thraco-Macedonian region, the island of Siphnos, and Laurium in Attica supplied the large mints of the Greek world.[47] We are poorly informed about silver resources in the East. Yet the tribute collected by the Great King consisted principally of precious metal.[48] The Achaemenid dynasty's hoarding of these resources was colossal, leading to a warehousing of precious metals that may partly explain the rise in the price of silver in their realm. In Babylonia, cuneiform sources reveal a progressive lowering of commodity prices from the beginning of the fifth century until 330 BC.[49] Jursa sets this alongside the increase in the price of silver during the same period.[50] The latter could be connected with the increase of taxation in this metal, in preference to commodity currency, in a context of heavy fiscal pressure. The sources are rather scanty for this period, and this reconstruction is not completely certain, but it has the merit of explaining the Achaemenid Empire's siphoning up of coins from Mediterranean mints in the fifth century. Athenian owls have been reported in quantity in Syria and farther east, as we have already seen. Some hoards had spectacular contents unparalleled in the Greek world.[51] The west-to-east silver flow created by he rise in the silver price in the heart of the empire beginning in the early fifth century could also explain this phenomenon. Xenophon does not contradict this in the *Poroi* 3.2, when he writes that merchants who do not wish to seek a return cargo leaving Athens can make a handsome profit by exporting silver.[52] From production areas where silver had a low price, owing to the mineral's availability, international commerce would therefore transfer the coinage to areas of greater demand where the metal's price was higher. Seyrig had concluded, concerning posthumous Alexanders from Pamphylia, that there was a veritable coinage industry.[53] Kroll extends this idea: "Subsequently, Georges Le Rider and Alain Bresson have applied it to the production of other Hellenistic coinages, Le Rider to posthumous, civic Lysimachi, and Bresson to the New Style Silver of Athens. Since these were all coinages that in their days enjoyed an enormous international demand, a fundamental incentive in minting them was the profit by supplying this

47. Howgego 1995, pp. 24–25; Doumergue 2008, p. 84.

48. Briant 1996, pp. 417–22; Monerie 2013.

49. R. Pirngruber, *The Impact of Empire on Market Prices in Babylon in the Late Achaemenid and Seleucid Periods ca. 400–140* BC, unpublished thesis, University of Amsterdam, 2012 (directed by R. J. van der Spek), cited in Monerie 2013.

50. Jursa 2010, pp. 751–52.

51. Especially the decadrachm hoards, see pp. 309–310.

52. Le Rider 1989b, pp. 159–61; Kroll 2011, p. 28. Van Alfen 2012, basing himself on this passage, tries to assess long distance trade between the Aegean and the East, in which he attributes a major role to silver.

53. Seyrig 1973, pp. 35–36.

demand. My contention is simply that this motivation was by no means restricted to the minting of popular coinages of the Hellenistic world, but was characteristic of several major mints in earlier times."[54] The gold of Cyzicus, Thraco-Macedonian silver, and Aeginetan turtles would thus belong to this category of production meant for export. Kroll suggests that the Aeginetans used their commercial network to sell their silver coins to the highest bidder, having obtained the raw metal on Siphnos since their own island did not possess an ore deposit. "The more silver was brought in, the more coins were struck, and the more profit that the coins made for the state and the merchants, who were able to trade for ever more silver." On Aegina as at Athens, "increasing supply and demand fed one another."[55] Cities and peoples would thus have produced very large quantities of coins because these were a means of profiting from their mineral resources—on their own soil or through their trade—more than to meet the needs of the state to pay its bills. This interpretation does away with traditional views that tend to favor the importance of military expenses in coin production. It posits a rational exploitation of silver resources based on market prices. The ancients were familiar with these mechanisms, as the attention that cities paid to grain provisioning shows as well as the speculation in grain prices that occurred on a pan-Mediterranean scale.[56] This hypothesis can be completely combined with other explanations, such as the need to cover military expenses, for example. Production at Athens with a view to demand or the city's expenses and the high price of silver in the Achaemenid Empire would at least partially explain the west-to-east drift evident through hoard-study.

2.2.2. The Liquidation of Royal Treasuries and the Reversal of the Flow of Silver

Alexander the Great's conquest of the Persian Empire provoked a remarkable change in that drift. He inaugurated a gold and silver coinage with his own types in 333–332 BC. Production was, however, modest until 323, in the view of most scholars.[57] Thus it was under the Successors that considerable quantities of drachms, tetradrachms, and gold staters were produced in the mints of the East and Macedonia. Callataÿ has tried to estimate how much precious metal was seized in the Persian treasuries and probably transformed, for a large part, into coin. According to his calculations, in the autumn of 330 BC, the Conqueror had at his disposal the equivalent of 180,000 talents of silver (some of it in gold), amounting to 4,680 tons of silver.[58] This came from the successive capture of the treasuries that the Great King maintained at Damascus (November, 333 BC), Gaugamela (October, 331 BC), Susa (autumn, 331 BC), Persepolis and Pasargadae (winter 331/0 BC). This enormous sum of precious metal remained at Ecbatana during the cam-

54. Kroll 2011, p. 33.
55. Ibid., p. 35.
56. Thus, Cleomenes of Naucratis, to whom Alexander the Great entrusted the administration of Egypt after 332, organized a grain trade, arbitraging the price quotes in different cities: Ps. Demosthenes, *Against Dionysodorus* 56.8; Le Rider 1997, p. 78. Bresson 2008 II, pp. 118–33, 178–210.
57. Troxell 1997, pp. 92–93; Le Rider 2003, pp. 122–32, 194–205 (= Le Rider 2007, pp. 88 ff., 143 ff.).
58. Callataÿ 1989, pp. 260–62.

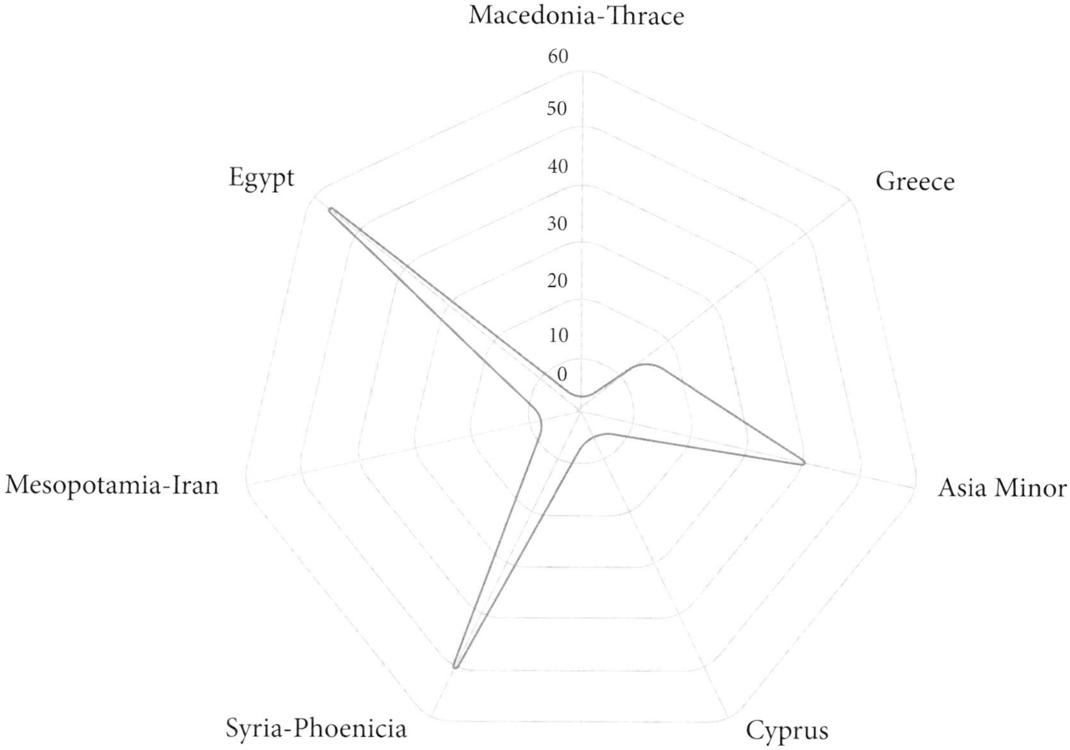

Figure 9.5. Number of silver coins of Aradus with types of Alexander in hoards according to Duyrat 2005a (c. 325–300 BC).[59]

paign in Asia.[60] These coins are easily traceable: all the mints of Alexander used the royal types and their own individual control marks that have enabled numismatists to identify them.[61] Thus it is possible to map the mints and hoards and so to follow the path traveled from place of issue to place of hoarding. This investigation clearly shows an east-to-west flow, reversing the previous direction. Gold coins with types of Alexander are generally hoarded in Greece and especially in Thrace. Callataÿ has calculated that 48.6% of the production of the mints of Asia Minor circulated towards the Balkans.[62] Silver coins follow a similar trajectory; the production of tetradrachms of Aradus provides a good illustration of this. In the fourth century, they are

59. The numbers provided for Phoenicia-Syria in Duyrat 2005a have not been revised in Figs. 9.5 and 9.6. The present study is in much greater depth and has doubled the numbers available for this region. That provokes an imbalance in the results and an artificial over-representation of Phoenicia-Syria. It seemed preferable to offer a picture based on a less complete but more homogeneous *corpus* that gives comparable orders of magnitude for each region.

60. Curtius 3.13.16 (Damascus); Diodorus 17,64.3, Curtius 5.1.10 (Gaugamela); Diodorus 17.66.1–2, Justin 11.14.9, Plutarch, *Alexander* 36.1, Strabo 15.3.9, Arrian, *Anabasis* 3.16.7, Curtius 5.2.11 (Susa); Diodorus 17.71.1, Curtius 5.6.9 (Persepolis); Curtius 5.6.10 (Pasargadae).

61. Newell 1923a, pp. 18–21; Price 1991a, pp. 34–36.

62. Callataÿ 1994, pp. 33–34. For an overall total of gold coin hoards by region, cf. Duyrat 2005b, p. 30; Touratsoglou 1998 on the Balkans.

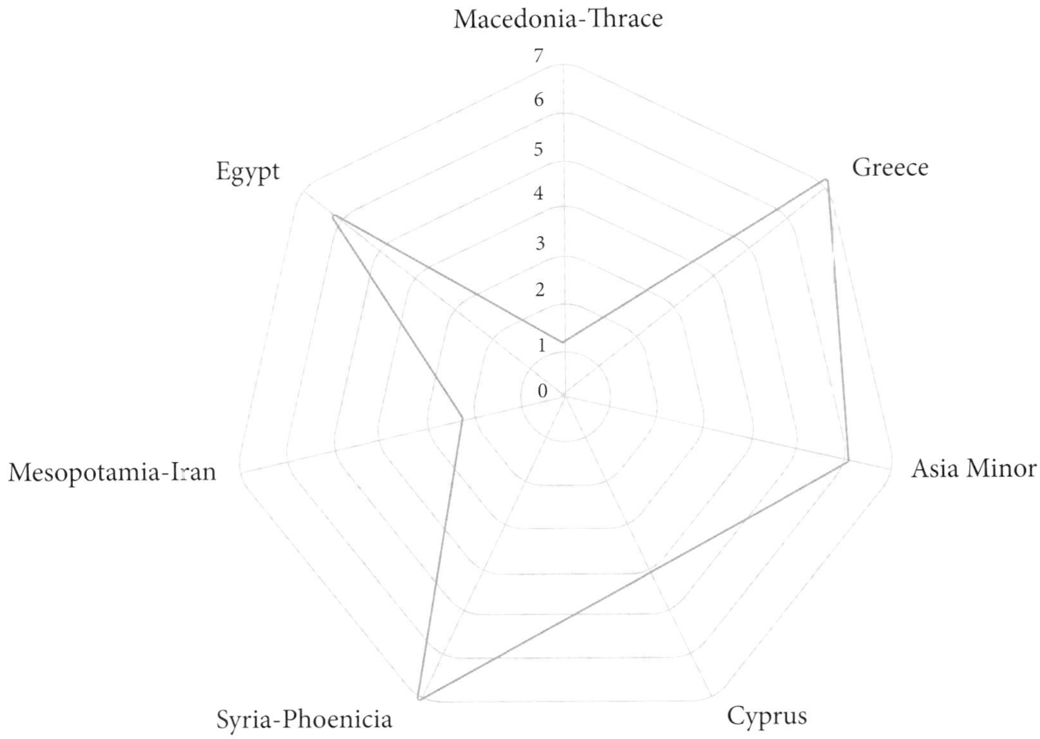

Figure 9.6. Number of hoards containing Aradian silver coins with types of Alexander according to Duyrat 2005a (c. 325–300 BC).[63]

found abundantly not only in Syria, but also in Egypt, Asia Minor, and in Greece proper, whether by numbers of Aradian tetradrachms (Fig. 9.5) or by number of hoards (Fig. 9.6).[64]

This example of a highly productive Phoenician mint could be an isolated case, or could be explained by the city's port status, which would have facilitated the transport of coins to the Mediterranean. The issues of Babylon, the principal mint east of the Mediterranean,[65] are a good indicator of overall silver movements and permit a better understanding of the metal's circulation. Table 5.2 and Figure 5.5 in Chapter Five highlight the role of this mint in Syrian monetary circulation in the last quarter of the fourth century, almost equal to the local mints that were nonetheless quite productive. A more general investigation based on hoards containing fourth-century Alexanders struck at Babylon illustrates the overall movement of silver between the time of their production and the third century.[66] *IGCH* lists 96 hoards containing silver Alexanders, mostly tetradrachms.[67] Figures 9.7 and 9.8 also take into account hoards containing

63. The Demanhur Hoard (*IGCH* 1664) has been excluded from these results. Its exceptional size skews the chart and gives to Egypt a pre-eminence other hoards do not confirm. For an evaluation of how misleading the Demanhur Hoard is, cf. Duyrat 2005b.

64. Duyrat 2005a, pp. 216–18; map 6, p. 353.

65. Waggoner 1979.

66. Only *IGCH* has been consulted. A more thorough study is in preparation. Some hoards are later than 190: Gorna Orjahovica, Bulgaria (*IGCH* 521); Basorah, Characene (*IGCH* 1786); Susa, Susiana (*IGCH* 1804).

67. A few hoards contained some other denominations: decadrachms (*IGCH* 1749, 1750), didrachm (*IGCH* 1760), drachm (*IGCH* 1831), and hemidrachm (*IGCH* 1758). Numbers are those of *IGCH* only, unrevised with the present

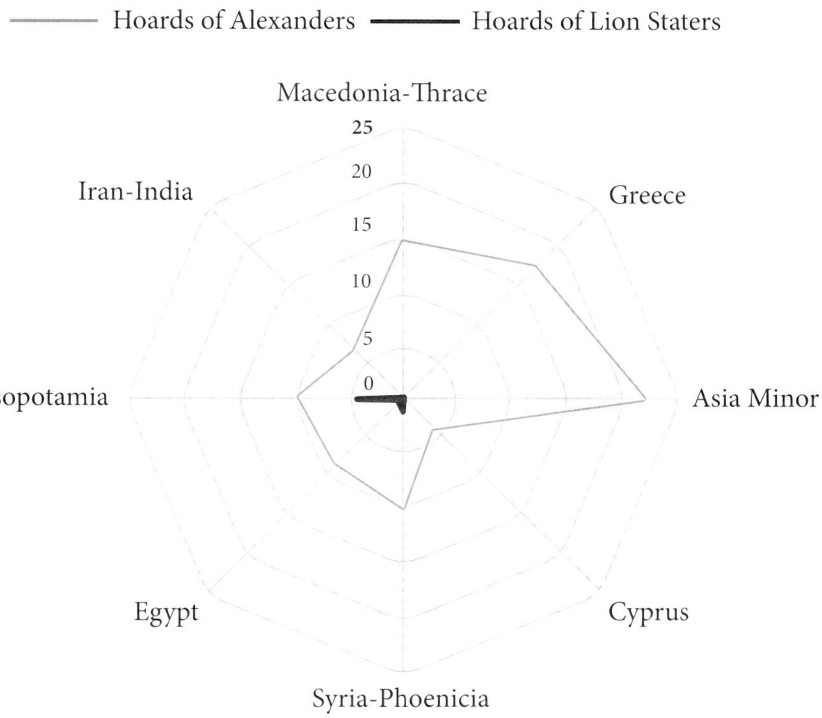

Figure 9.7. Hoards by region containing Babylonian lion staters and tetradrachms with types of Alexander struck at Babylon in the fourth century.

Babylonian lion staters, struck on a lighter standard than the Attic. The former counts hoards by region, the latter the total number of tetradrachms or lion staters.

The number of hoards by region clearly shows the westward drift of Babylonian Alexanders, which are present in more than twice as many Greek or Asia Minor hoards as they are in those of Mesopotamia or even Syria. Figure 9.8, based on the number of buried tetradrachms, offsets this impression. In this instance, Egypt and, to a lesser degree, Syria have furnished the most specimens. This amount is partly the result of some very large finds, such as the Aleppo Hoard (*IGCH* 1516, **108**) or the Demanhur Hoard (*IGCH* 1664), which rather outdistance the other hoards of these regions. But even excluding these two hoards, it nonetheless remains true that Mesopotamia has revealed only a reduced number of hoards and tetradrachms compared to areas situated farther west. This must illustrate the shift in flow occasioned by the liquidation of the Persian treasuries that led to a drop in the price of silver in the former Achaemenid Empire's heartland and a flow towards the west of the Babylon mint's production.

In contrast, the location of finds of Babylonian lion staters is telling.[68] These coins, issued from c. 331 BC, enjoyed a plentiful production between c. 308/7 and 302 BC, these years alone having witnessed the placing into service of some 100 obverse dies.[69] After 328 BC, the coins

catalogue for Syria. The intent is simply to provide comparable orders of magnitude for each region.

68. On this coinage, Nicolet-Pierre 1999; Iossif, Lorber 2007.

69. Iossif, Lorber 2007, p. 349.

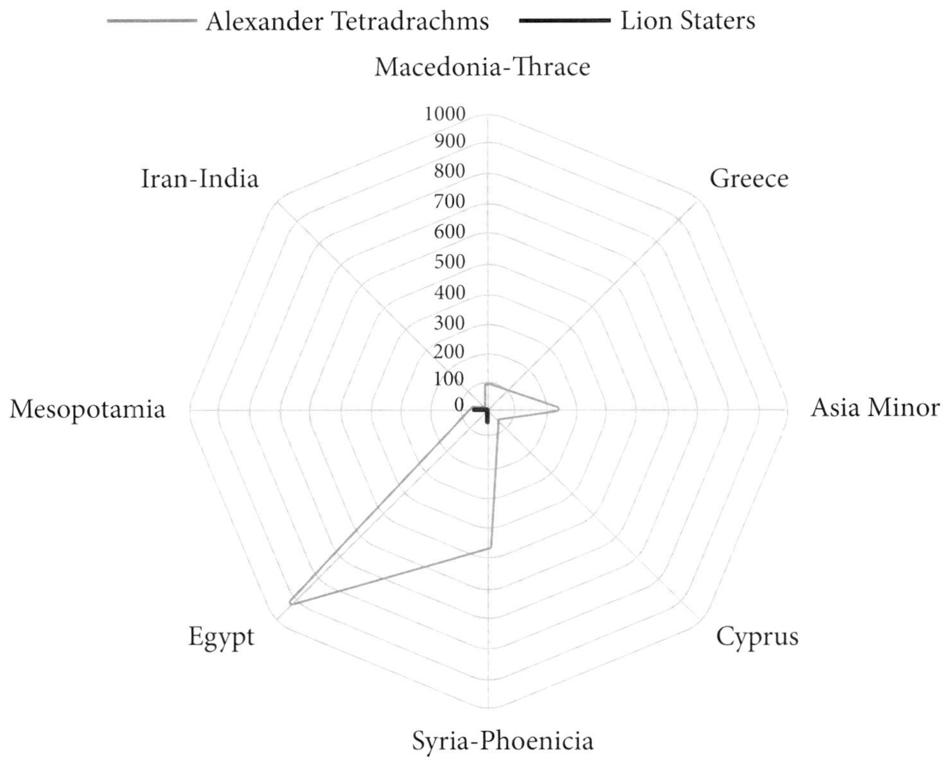

Figure 9.8. Number of lion staters of Babylon and tetradrachms with types of Alexander struck at Babylon in the fourth century by region.

are on a lower standard, 17 g, that steadily falls to about 15.52 g between 308/7 and 302 BC. This reduced weight explains the exclusively local circulation of these staters evident in Figures 9.7 and 9.8.[70] Nicolet-Pierre has also shown that their silver purity is slightly inferior to that of the Alexanders.[71] These staters continued to be struck until the 270s. Thus, between 311 BC and its termination, production of lion staters covered the period when the flow of Alexanders towards the west was strongest. Of the 96 hoards of Babylonian Alexanders collected in *IGCH*, 70 are earlier than 270 BC (73%), and those that are later are mostly divided up between Greek and Thracian locations. The hoards therefore reveal a heavy east-west circulation of Babylonian tetradrachms under Alexander and the Successors. Production of lion staters was probably an effective means of offsetting the coin flow that drew tetradrachms of Attic weight towards the Mediterranean, since production on a local standard was only usable in that region. The hoards illustrate the effectiveness of the parallel use of a local coinage and a common coinage.[72]

70. A hoard from Susa (*IGCH* 1522) contained lion hemidrachms and was not included in these charts. A hoard found in Syria (?), *IGCH* 1522, without a confirmed location, contained 40 staters.

71. Nicolet-Pierre 1999, p. 305.

72. Monerie 2013 correctly observes that Babylonia also had a system of local gold coinage: double darics struck under the Successors with a weight of 16.6 g. The 14 hoards of Babylonian gold staters with types of Alexander are located west of Syria (Cyprus 1, Asia Minor 3, Macedonia-Thrace 6, Greece 4), confirming the even more marked east-west flow for this metal.

Egypt completely disappears from the dispersion map of Hellenistic tetradrachms after the adoption of a reduced standard at the very end of the fourth century. Previously, this region received its fair share of Alexanders from pretty much all over. I have been able to show, by re-examining the Demanhur Hoard, that Egyptian hoards are composed in equal proportions of Alexanders from Macedonia, Asia Minor, Syria-Phoenicia, and Babylon. In contrast, the Levant produces an over-representation of Babylon and local mints.[73] Following Thompson, I sought a military explanation for the presence of Aradian Alexanders in Egypt before 300 BC, even though troop recruitment by Alexander and his successors in this region is not attested.[74] The broader study of silver movements would incline me now to raise the question of the silver price. A still more elevated price for this metal in Egypt possibly explains the influx of silver tetradrachms with types of Alexander and provenances from all the regions that struck them, even Macedonia, during a time when the massive un-hoarding occurring in the East created a drop in the metal's price. This phenomenon would allow for a better understanding of the arrival of Macedonian coins, the opposite of the east-to-west flow. The marked presence of Alexanders from Syria-Phoenicia and Babylon in Syrian hoards could also be the sign of a higher price for silver than in Babylonia, something that would have therefore frozen these coins in place, with only a portion drawn to Greece and the northern Aegean.

If the troop movements of Alexander and the successors may not have played a role in the influx of silver coins into Egypt, it is, however, difficult to deny completely their part in the general movement from east to west. The Macedonian Conquest provoked an unprecedented mixing of populations. Not just thousands of soldiers, but also an entire support corps, merchants, prostitutes, and families followed Alexander's army to India and then back west. Successive troop demobilizations returned these soldiers to the Mediterranean, along with their families and profits. This is the basis for Thompson's thesis that connects the increase in production of Alexanders with the demobilization decreed at Babylon in 325 BC. The location of the principal mints in port cities seemed to her to confirm this interpretation: "For troops returning by sea, and surely most must have taken that route, the mints chosen to compensate them were strategically located."[75] Le Rider has questioned this stand-alone explanation, arguing that many other plans and actions of Alexander might explain the production increase.[76] Moreover, this increase is now dated after Alexander's death and must be related to the long wars of the Successors. Still, the fact remains that massive troop movements automatically involved the coinage used to pay their wages and the army's expenses. Thus, for example, some tetradrachms of Amphipolis were hoarded in Syria in the last quarter of the fourth century, contrary to the east-west money flow (Chap. Five, Figure 5.5). The currency issued by Macedonian mints in very large quantities probably accompanied the fresh troops sent to join up with the Conqueror

73. Duyrat 2005b, p. 34.
74. Duyrat 2005a, pp. 214–15.
75. Thompson 1984, p. 246.
76. Le Rider 2003, pp. 301–303 (= Le Rider 2007, pp. 227–28).

Table 9.10. Origin of coins of Antiochus III in hoards

No.	Findspot	Date of Burial	Total Studied	Western Mints	Mints of Syria-Commagene	Eastern Mints
166	Oylum Höyüğü, Cyrrhestice	203/2	134	1	12	2
171	Kosseir	c. 190	40	1	2	1
172	Latakia	c. 190	34		6	
174	Syria, perhaps Aradian Peraea	c. 190	90	4	5	1
180	Syria	175	9		1	
181	Lebanon	175?	105	3	27	3
186	Unknown findspot	169	16			1
191	Qalʿat el-Moudiq	165	45	1	6	2
193	Maʿaret en-Numan	162	536	22		
196	Syria	160	65		2	
201	ʿArab el-Mulk, Paltos	After 152/1	28		1	
202	"Demetrius I Hoard"	151/0	535		1	
224	Northern Syria	145	54		1	
275	North of Israel	121	327		71	
	Total			**10**	**157**	**10**

and his successors in the East. Returns to the Mediterranean, in the opposite direction, initiated, accompanied, and amplified the east-to-west money flow at the end of the fourth century.

This phenomenon continued on a grand scale in the third century, with Alexanders of the fourth century continuing to dominate Syrian monetary circulation. The persistence of old coins in circulation prevents any definite assertions about the geography of monetary flows. The start of Seleucid royal issues, however, permits some conclusions. In Chapter Six, we saw that, until the reign of Seleucus III, the most active eastern mints were Syria's principal supplier. With Seleucus III, this abates.

2.2.3. The Attic Standard and the Price of Silver in the Second Century

A new change in direction is discernible through Syrian hoards at the start of the second century. The date it commences is difficult to pin down. Circulation is still mostly Alexanders and royal Seleucid coins. Table 7.1 in Chapter Seven shows the arrival of posthumous Alexanders from the southern cities of Asia Minor chiefly c. 190 BC with four hoards (**171**, **172**, **173**, **174**), all buried on Syria's northern coast between Kosseir and the Aradian Peraea (Map 13). It is tempting to connect this concentration with the end of the military operations of Antiochus III after the defeat at Magnesia and the Peace of Apamea. The troops engaged beyond the Taurus were repatriated, some probably via northern Syria and the ports, including Aradus, and this movement may have provoked a certain instability that could explain why the hoards were buried and not recovered. Pamphylia remained a bone of contention between the Attalids and Seleucids,[77] and Meadows has shown how relations between the Aradian mint and those of Pamphylia were close at this time.[78]

During the following decades, the Alexanders of Perge, Aspendus, and Phaselis continue to turn up in Syria. At the same time, if one examines the provenance of the silver coins of Antiochus III in Syrian hoards, all burial periods combined, one notices the major presence of coins issued by the central mints of the empire in his reign (Table 9.10). With the loss of Asia Minor and then the eastern provinces at the end of the second century, Syrian mints provided a significant amount of the currency in circulation. Syria *de facto* became the one large kingdom without a monetary border. The arrival of new tetradrachms from Asia Minor compensates for the steady disappearance of Alexanders from the middle of the second century. These civic coinages marked with a wreath flow in from the 160s to the 140s. It is only with the reign of Alexander Balas that the royal Seleucid coinage assumes a preeminent place in Syrian monetary circulation.

In the second century, Syria thus attracts at first quantities of silver coins struck in southern Asia Minor (Alexanders), and then coins from farther afield (civic "wreathed" tetradrachms). This led Seyrig to view the Asia Minor Alexanders as an export product[79] and Le Rider to explain the phenomenon by the premium attributed to Alexanders in Syria.[80] It is difficult to deduce an explicit orientation towards Syria in the activity of the mints of southern Asia Minor just from hoard study. Seyrig's conjecture recalls the passage from the *Poroi* cited earlier, where Xenophon mentions silver exports from Athens. It is conceivable that the higher price of silver in second-century Syria fostered this flow of Alexanders and subsequently wreathed tetradrachms to the Seleucid realm. But one should not exaggerate its extent. Between c. 210–205 and c. 180–170 BC, according to the hoard evidence, Pamphylian Alexanders also flow to the interior of Asia Minor, following the route leading to the mountain passes; some of those that travel as far as Syria return to Pamphylia, where they are hoarded, bearing Seleucid countermarks.[81] If the silver price was higher in Syria, this was not enough to drain all the Alexanders from the cities of southern Asia Minor or to prevent their return. Syria does, however, rapidly absorb most of the wreathed tetradrachms, their successors, evidence of a renewed flow towards Syria from 160–140 BC.[82] These developments with Attic-weight silver happen in a changing monetary context.

77. Livy 38.39.17.
78. Meadows 2009.
79. Seyrig 1973, p. 35.
80. Le Rider 1999b, p. 53.
81. Bresson, forthcoming. [AU : out yet ?] I am very grateful to Alain Bresson for having sent me a draft version of this article.
82. For an assessment of the production volumes of wreathed tetradrachms, cf. Callataÿ 2013, p. 233.

After the Peace of Apamea, probably between 175 and 166 BC, the Attalids adopted a new silver coinage of lighter weight, the cistophorus (c. 12.60 g). These tetradrachms and their fractions only circulate in the Attalid kingdom.[83] During the second half of the second century, Aradus, followed by the neighboring cities of Tripolis, Laodiceia ad Mare, and Seleuceia Pieria, adopted a reduced common standard.[84] A key region whose ties with southern Asia Minor Meadows has recalled, it had some large ports that were probably the first to benefit from the arrival of precious metals. The adoption of its own standard is therefore not unimportant.

The compartmentalization of circulation areas created by zones with a standard lighter than the Attic led to a splitting of the circulation of coined silver. Monetary flows towards Syria were henceforth limited to issues of Attic weight that represent only a part of the monetary production of Asia Minor.[85] Closed monetary systems were generally bound up with the income incentives that states obtained from them. This interpretation rests principally on the arguments Le Rider brought to bear on this topic.[86] But it seems to me that some other motivations may come into play, particularly in the second century. The increasing disappearance of Alexanders did, indeed, induce states to produce a replacement currency. Adopting a closed monetary system certainly offered possibilities for new fiscal returns, especially if one accepts the idea of an exchange of the reduced weight coinage at par with the international coinage on the Attic standard. But the steady disappearance of the stock of Alexanders that constituted the core of the international coinage must also have created pressure on the currency of Attic weight. This must have been keenly felt in a period when Rome's arrival in Asia and the fratricidal strife in Syria also kept demand high for the usual means to pay armies, tetradrachms of Attic weight. The numerous military operations converging on this territory in the throes of dynastic struggles certainly encouraged flows of silver money towards Syria.[87]

If the silver price in Syria was higher than in Asia Minor, the creation of a closed standard zone helped to prevent too heavy a flow of Attic standard coins from one region to another.[88] Creation of a special standard zone around Aradus in the latter half of the second century probably addressed the same concern to counter movements of Attic silver. From the time of Alexander Balas' reign, the royal Seleucid mints took up the slack of foreign output that disappeared even as the Attic standard was gradually debased. The pragmatism, always characteristic of this dynasty in monetary matters, inclines one to see here an adaptation rather than the desire to impose its own coinage. This could simply be one solution in the face of a decline in the influx of foreign coins. Bresson interprets the imposition of Seleucid countermarks on Pamphylian Alexanders as a first instance of a closed monetary system, beginning in the first half of the

83. Bresson, forthcoming [AU : out yet ?], and the discussions in Thonemann 2013.

84. Between 252/1 and 238/7 BC on Aradus and in its hinterland: Duyrat 2005a, pp. 258–60; after 100 BC at Tripolis, 81/0 BC at Laodiceia ad Mare, and 109/8 BC at Seleuceia Pieria: Mørkholm 1982a; weight study for Tripolis in Callataÿ 1993, p. 122. Cf. also Callataÿ 2002.

85. Clear listing in Meadows 2013 (by reign) and Callataÿ 2013 (by coinage). Overview on the mint of Pergamum: Marcellesi 2012a.

86. Summary in Callataÿ 1999, pp. 118–19 especially.

87. Thus the Attalids supported Alexander Balas financially when he seized power in 150 BC and thereafter; cf. above, Chapter 7.

88. This is the interpretation I have proposed above for Babylonian lion staters.

second century, which would be another argument supporting my interpretation.[89] Adoption of a closed monetary system could be seen as an adaptation to the decline in metal supplies, a means of assuring a stock of silver needed for the smooth functioning of exchanges and local tax collecting.

CONCLUSION

Examination of the hoard evidence reveals a contrasting diagnosis of metal flows in Syria. In the Persian period and then under Alexander the Great, the region is a way station for metal *en route* to the east until Alexander, and then in the opposite direction during the last quarter of the fourth century and perhaps still in the third. These major occurrences are closely connected with the differences in price of metals from one region to another in the ancient world. From the time of Alexander and the wars of the Successors, however, it appears that population movements tied to the wars and periodic troop demobilizations from the Mediterranean amplified them.

The second century is characterized by the progressive compartmentalization of the flow of silver money, along with the appearance of closed monetary systems. These closed systems, by locking in a part of the stock of metal within them, slowed the large flows previously evident. The Seleucid kingdom preserved the Attic standard, except in Coele Syria and Phoenicia. A higher silver price probably explains this decision, the price attracting metal to the region and not warranting any protectionist measures. Use of the Attic standard, geographic proximity, and political circumstances explain how the production of certain mints in Asia Minor circulated in a privileged way towards Syria from the 190s to the 140s.

Generally speaking, although Syria does not possess any silver mines, its location between the Mediterranean and Mesopotamia puts it at the center of these silver movements. From c. 150 BC, the royal Seleucid coinage rapidly assumes a preponderant place in Syrian monetary circulation. Supplying the mints with metal may have occurred in several ways. The first is recycling: the steady disappearance of Alexanders from circulation probably furnished an important amount of the metal for the new Seleucid tetradrachms. The second is direct supply from regions possessing the metal. The manner of these supplies remains to be determined. Must one imagine caravans or ships laden with coins arriving in Syria? Examples of bullion transport of American silver in modern times are numerous. The French mint of St. Lô, in the sixteenth and seventeenth centuries, for example, sent envoys to St. Malo to acquire American silver snatched by St. Malo pirates.[90] Be that as it may, and despite the likely absence of difficulties in securing metal supplies, Syria preserved an economy where the use of struck coinage remains partial.

89. Bresson, forthcoming.
90. Jambu 2013, pp. 117–20.

2.3. Doing without Coinage . . . or Not

2.3.1. Never Enough Coins

The title of this section is not meant to suggest that I am adopting a primitivist position. Different studies of production have made clear the inadequacy of coin issues vis-à-vis the needs of the issuing state.[91] Callataÿ in his work on the Mithridatic wars has shown that the coin production of Mithridates could not cover the totality of his military requirements.[92] So one must imagine other means of payment, notably in bronze or in kind. The fact that the production of tetradrachms and drachms of a mint like Aradus, for a large part of its history, was a function of wars, highlights in brief that it was not recurrent economic considerations that guided production, but, rather, urgent and specific needs.[93] This also reveals that coinage did not need to cover all levels of exchange.

Neither is coinage used all the time. In Aristophanes' *Acharnians* Dicaeopolis complains about having to use it during the Peloponnesian War.[94] The country bumpkin of Theophrastus views it with suspicion, for fear of being swindled.[95] Even if usage was widespread, especially in an urban milieu, numerous exchanges certainly continued to be made with more traditional means. If one readily imagines the countryside doing without coinage, one has to accept that the most active cities did so, too. Picard thus points out how on Thasos the period 340–280 BC witnessed especially ambitious public works programs: "whether we are dealing with private fortunes or public funds, it is nonetheless the case that colossal sums were expended then on these public works." Yet that is precisely when the production of the Thasian mint declines "before complete smothering."[96] Local tetradrachms, therefore, did not pay for these construction efforts, which may conceivably have been financed with something other than struck coinage. From peasant to wealthy city, people knew how to make do without silver coinage for payments. These remarks should not suggest that the economy of the Greek world was particularly archaic. Sargent and Velde have written a chapter providing examples of "coinage hunger" in mediaeval and modern Europe.[97] Modern France has often confronted inadequate cover in coinage for its needs owing to a lack of metal available for striking.[98] Credit among individuals, taking the

91. A good example in Jambu 2013, pp. 252–62, on the insufficiency of minted coinage in the modern era and the means of remedying it, beginning with deferred payments.

92. Callataÿ 1997a, pp. 281–388.

93. Tables showing these variations in Duyrat 2003.

94. Aristophanes, *Acharnians*, ll.33–36. τὸν δ' ἐμὸν δῆμον ποθῶν, ὅς οὐδεπώποτ' εἶπεν, ἄνθρακας πρίω, οὐκ ὄξος οὐκ ἔλαιον, οὐδ' ᾔδει 'πρίω,' ἀλλ' αὐτὸς ἔφερε πάντα χὠ πρίων ἀπῆν. "yearning for my own deme, that never cried 'buy coal,' 'buy vinegar,' 'buy oil'; it didn't know the word "buy"; no, it produced everything itself, and the Buy Man was out of sight." (tr. Henderson, Loeb Classical Library).

95. *Characters* 4.13.: καὶ τὸ ἀργύριον δὲ παρά του λαβὼν ἀποδοκιμάζειν, λίαν μὲν λυπρὸν εἶναι, καὶ ἕτερον ἀνταλλάττεσθαι. "He rejects a silver coin that he gets from someone because it looks too much like lead, and trades for another."(tr. Rusten, Loeb Classical Library).

96. "qu'il s'agisse de fortunes privées ou de fonds publics, il n'en reste pas moins que des sommes colossales ont alors été dépensées pour ces programmes édilitaires." … "avant un étouffement complet." Picard 1994, p. 34.

97. Sargent, Velde 2002, pp. 123–226.

98. Jambu 2013, pp. 252–53.

form of IOUs and promissory notes, made circumventing the lack of currency possible to a certain extent.[99] Recourse to debt is also well attested for fourth-century Athens,[100] as well as in Latin sources, the latter prompting Harris to conclude that "*pecunia* could include loans,"[101] and, further on, "*Nomina* were transferable, and by the second century BC, if not earlier, were routinely used as a means of payment for other assets."[102]

There is a tight connection between credit and coinage; both play an economic and social role that presumably existed in Syria as well. Hoards provide in outline the image of a society that used coinage to cover a portion of its needs as a means of payment but which also probably had an extensive and complex use of credit. Otherwise it is difficult to imagine how the major Phoenician and Palestinian ports could have financed their activity in a world where currency supplies were insufficient. At Athens in the fourth century, bottomry loans were extended by wealthy individuals as well as by professional lenders.[103] The developments in credit Harris discusses in the Roman world are, from this point of view, enlightening: all strata of society had recourse to them, going so far as to make payments in coins frequently useless, especially for those with good credit.[104] This evidence squares with a number of aspects in the picture Fontaine depicts of credit networks in modern Europe. Some examples give a clear idea of the way in which economic activity in a pre-industrial society could develop without coin circulation: "In the farms of the Netherlands, the owners and the peasants who worked for them constantly exchanged reciprocal services. Very little money circulated, but everything was recorded and once or twice a year the farmer and his day laborers settled accounts together, and the salaries owed were remitted against the goods and services provided."[105] These very flexible forms of credit, depending on trust and the social bond, are attested everywhere in modern Europe in the most diverse forms. Harris' assertion, "debt was in fact the life-blood of the Roman economy, at all levels,"[106] should probably be applied to any number of pre-industrial societies, including, no doubt, Hellenistic Syria.

In the Hellenistic period, bronze coinage probably compensated partially for this ability to do without silver currency in exchanges large and small. Picard has suggested that substantial payments could be made in bronze.[107] The enforced value of this coinage, with high fiduciary value and abundant production, leads to the conclusion that exchanges in a certain number

99. Ibid., pp. 238 and 255–56. On the social dynamics surrounding debt among individuals in modern Europe, cf. Fontaine 2008, esp. pp. 70–72.

100. Millett 1991.

101. Harris 2005, p. 7,

102. Ibid., p. 15, who gives, in the Greek world, some examples of IOU's being exchanged like money, pp. 8–9, and of purchases on credit, p. 16.

103. Millett 1991, pp. 188–206, without specificying the physical forms these loans might have taken.

104. Harris 2005, pp. 8–17, 24.

105. "Dans les fermes des Pays-Bas, les propriétaires des fermes et les paysans qui travaillent pour eux échangent sans cesse des services réciproques. Très peu d'argent circule mais tout s'inscrit dans les livres et une ou deux fois l'an, le fermier et ses journaliers font compte ensemble et les salaires dus sont compensés contre les denrées et les services fournis." Fontaine 2008, p. 68.

106. Harris 2005, p. 9.

107. Picard 1994, pp. 41–42.

of cities like Aradus were significantly monetized. In the second century, the numerous series struck by the city[108] supplied the local market, notably that of the Peraea, but also beyond that. For example, Epiphaneia, which struck only a little coinage, has produced a not insignificant number of Aradian coins. The same holds true for Ras Ibn Hani and Posideion-Ras el-Bassit. Aradian bronzes are also found in more distant sites like Djebel Khalid, Dura Europos, and caravan way stations around Nabataea (Map 29).[109] The number of series, volume of production—only partially capable of estimation in view of the poor die frequency indices—and diffusion warrant the supposition that Aradian bronze was abundant in the second century and the first half of the first. It was able to function well as a means of payment for no small part of transactions under a tetradrachm, and perhaps also for larger transactions.

Silver coinage appears indispensable for only certain types of exchange: generally intermediate in value (except when it is a question of paying an indemnity to the Romans), often official (royal taxes; payment of certain categories of services: soldiers, artists). But the fact of its being the metal *par excellence* in hoards highlights its privileged place versus bronze and gold. Yet it is appropriate to view this dominant role of silver in hoarding with a skeptical eye. Gold is stunningly absent from hoards, and not just in Hellenistic Syria. Baslez showed, more than 25 years ago, that this metal was present in descriptions of payments in the Classical period, much more so than coin finds would lead one to think.[110] Rich Athenians saved gold in their treasure chests. I will give just one example. Lysias in 404 BC, seeking to get a price for his survival at the hands of Peison, opens the casket (*tēn kibōton*) in which he held his cash reserves.[111] The sum is striking since Lysias kept at home three talents of silver (form not identified), 400 electrum cyzicenes, 100 darics, and four silver cups (*phialai*).[112] Buried in Syria this treasure would have ranked second in value after the colossal find of Saida (**93**). The Roman world also provides explicit written data on the manner of preserving riches in the home. Andreau has pointed out a series of citations that mention chests, strong boxes, cupboards sometimes reinforced with metal (*armaria*), and, especially, the existence among the wealthiest of vaults (*horrea*) where the family riches were stored.[113] The Digest, in the same vein, gives clear instructions to the *paterfamilias* who is supposed to separate his gold and silver possessions into two lots: those for daily use and those meant for capital formation. The latter are supposed to be safeguarded in a cupboard called an *argentarium*. The cities in the region of Mt. Vesuvius have revealed evidence of this practice in the form of coffers and cupboards that contained coins and manufactured items.[114] They are typical of the most well-off families, other people not appearing to distinguish between everyday items and valuables.

108. Duyrat 2005a, table, p. 293.
109. Graf et al. 2005, pp. 434, 437; Durand 2008, p. 110.
110. Baslez 1989. Lewis 1989 emphasized the importance of Persian gold in relations with the Greek world.
111. Lysias 12.10.
112. *Lysias* 12.11: τρία τάλαντα ἀργυρίου καὶ τετρακοσίους κυζικηνοὺς καὶ ἑκατὸν δαρεικοὺς καὶ φιάλας ἀργυρᾶς τέτταρας. "three talents of silver, four hundred cyzicenes, a hundred darics and four silver bowls."
113. Andreau 2008, pp. 214–15.
114. Ibid., pp. 223–24, citing three examples.

Gold was not meant, therefore, to rest idle in the ground but to circulate, provide easily available cash, and, if need arose, to be transported elsewhere in the face of imminent danger. This does not mean that it was not hoarded, just not in the ground.[115] This attitude would explain its quasi-absence from hoards, despite its being well-attested in written sources and studies of production.[116] The absence of coins of high value from our documentation perhaps also explains another phenomenon. Philistine mints took up again the type of the owl facing, wings spread, struck on Athenian decadrachms.[117] The latter are very rare in Syria in hoards (**7** and **13**, in fragmentary form).[118] But perhaps they were not so rare in the actual circulation as opposed to the frozen circulation the buried hoards reveal to us. This might explain why this characteristic type was copied on fractions.

Neither did the silver of the wealthy rest in the ground: it was lent at interest, in small sums or large investments. The fortune of the father of Demosthenes illustrates this practice.[119] It consisted of 50 artisan slaves and raw material for his two workshops (iron, ivory, wood, copper, nutgall); a family residence valued at 3,000 drachmas, with its furnishings; the *kosmos* of Demosthenes' mother; and, especially, money mostly lent at interest. A talent of silver is thus loaned at one drachm per mina (12%), in tranches of 200 to 300 drachms.[120] Additionally, there are 70 minas in a bottomry loan with Xouthos, 2,400 drachms with the banker Pasion, 600 drachms with Pylades, another 1,600 tied up with Demomeles, and "only" 80 minas of silver (2,000 tetradrachms) at home in a chest comparable, one imagines, to that of Lysias. None of this was kept in the ground.

The non-hoarding of certain coinage in the ground may partly explain the problem Athenian owls in the Athenian Empire pose: very few of its hoards have revealed tetradrachms of the imperial city. Recently Flament and Konuk have proposed two contrasting explanations. The first has emphasized the phenomenon of reverse flow to Athens, notably as tribute payment, which would have sent back the owls to their source.[121] Konuk, on the other hand, has suggested that the owls never found a place in the cities of Asia Minor belonging to the Empire, since the cities needed fractions instead, and suffered sizeable levies in silver via the tribute.[122] These two hypotheses are not mutually exclusive, and the two phenomena must probably have interacted such that owls ended up so poorly represented in hoards. Bearing in mind that cer-

115. Unlike Thrace, for example, which has produced a very large number of gold hoards.

116. In Syria, especially in the time of Alexander and the Successors, and again under Demetrius I and the Ptolemies in Syria and Phoenicia.

117. Gitler, Tal 2006, pp. 380–81, Ascalon mint.

118. With the exception of large hoards of decadrachms in the Taurus region, several hundred kilometers distant from the southern Levant, see hoards A and B, pp. 309–310.

119. Demosthenes, *Against Aphobos* 1.9–11.

120. This dispersal of some capital in small loans provides an ancient echo for a practice attested in modern Europe that allowed the wealthy to extend their social influence and establish their political power. Fontaine 2008, pp. 69–70, gives some suggestive examples from the Alps and England.

121. Flament 2007, p. 46, and Flament 2011.

122. Konuk 2011.

tain currencies are less likely to be buried in the ground than others, and the flow of silver to the center of the Achaemenid Empire described above, the eclipse of owls may have been almost total; but this does not mean that they did not circulate in Asia Minor.

Hoards, therefore, do not necessarily reflect the reality of monetary circulation, much less of transactions. Some transactions were concluded without coins, from habit or because struck silver was scarce. The proportion of non-monetized exchanges varies from one region to another. I have shown elsewhere that the Syria that used coinage in fact corresponds to a large strip running north-south between the Mediterranean and, in the east, a line stretching from Aleppo to the Dead Sea by way of the Beqaa Valley.[123] It is difficult to define the role of coinage more precisely, but better-documented periods can provide some examples of this disparity in use within the same society. In an article depicting the monetary map of France at the end of the *Ancien Régime*, Dermigny showed that some regions used money only rarely. The mints put into circulation principally gold and copper. There are the "regions of the louis and of the penny—and they are similarly contrasting societies. But, in the zone poor in gold, where silver therefore prevails, some southern areas are starved for small change."[124] In the same kingdom and during the same time, monetary usage therefore differs from one region to the next. Meuvret has highlighted certain traits in currency use in modern France: in his opinion, retail sales or certain services were concluded in cash, "but the amount of each transaction was extremely small ... So small change is what the populace used in its daily transactions."[125] And to cite a 1638 manuscript from the Cour des Comptes, stating that even in Paris "the lesser populace is only paid in such coins."[126] Examination of the uses of coinage in Lower Normandy in the modern period led Jambu to a noticeably different conclusion: the lower orders might sometimes possess gold coins, at the time of a payment, for example, or they might succeed in amassing no mean sums of silver from their work, even if these examples are not what is commonly found among the most modest.[127] Among the wealthy, cash is not so abundant in estate inventories, the use of credit being widespread. Meuvret emphasizes for the sixteenth and seventeenth centuries "the place of pure barter transactions." A barter transaction is understood here as exchanging one sort of merchandise for another upon evaluating their relative worth in coinage. The intrusion of coinage is a purely accounting phenomenon; coinage itself does not appear physically in any of the transactions cited as examples.[128] Jambu confirms the varying use of coinage according to circumstances: exchanges in kind, self-sufficiency, re-employing of used objects restored to good condition, extensive use of credit among merchants like the baker

123. Duyrat 2004.

124. "régions du louis et de la piécette – et de même contrastées au point de vue social. – Mais, dans la zone pauvre en or, où donc prédomine l'argent, certains secteurs méridionaux sont affamés de petite monnaie." Dermigny 1955, p. 484.

125. "mais le montant de chaque opération était extrêmement faible. [...] c'était donc de la menue monnaie qu'utilisait la population dans ses transactions habituelles." Meuvret 1947, p. 21.

126. "le menu peuple n'est payé qu'en de telles espèces." Ibid., p. 21, n. 1.

127. Jambu 2013, pp. 236–40.

128. Meuvret 1947, p. 22, n. 1.

Table 9.11. Plated coins in hoards

No.	Findspot	No. *IGCH* or *CH*	Date of Burial	Plated Coins
17	Massyaf	*IGCH* 1483 = *CH* 8.587 = *CH* 9.362	425–420/425–400	Athens: 1 dr. plated? (1.52 g)
37	Al Mina	*IGCH* 1488 = *CH* 8.587 = *CH* 9.397	375	Athens and imitations: 3 tetr. Sidon: 1 sixteenth-shekel
40	Beach south of Beirut	*IGCH* 1500 = *CH* 8.587 = *CH* 9.404	368–333	Tyre: 1 AR
50	Samaria	*CH* 8.587 = *CH* 9.413	345 or 355	Aradus: 1 fraction (<1 g) Sidon: 1 sixteenth; 1 frag. of a shekel
52	Sebastiye	*CH* 7.40	340	Samaria: 2 obols
69	Byblos	*IGCH* 1496 = *CH* 8.587 = *CH* 9.435 = Noe 175	333	217 AR, some not plated but not identified
77	Nablus	*IGCH* 1504 = *CH* 9.440	333/2	Tyre: 1 twenty-fourth
80	Abu Shusheh, Judaea (called Gezer Hoard)	*IGCH* 1507 = *CH* 8.587 = *CH* 9.434 = Noe 429	333–320	Sidon: 1 sixteenth Tyre: 1 AR
101	Lebanon	*CH* 8.207	315	Alexander III: 1 tetr. Babylon
114	Samaria	*CH* 10.237	End 4th cent.	Athens: 1 frags. of tetr.
120	Aleppo	*CH* 8.231	c. 300	Alexander III: 2 tetr. of the first Seleucids
188	Lebanon	*CH* 9.510	165	Aradus: 2 dr. Ephesus: 1 dr.
191	Qal'at el-Moudiq	*CH* 10.298	165	Seleucus I: 1 tetr. Susa
247	Lebanon	*CH* 9.532	133	Aradus: 2 dr.
258	Golan	*IGCH* 1600 = *CH* 1.75	128/7–126/5 (autonomy of Tyre)	Antiochus VII and Demetrius II (2): 7 plated tetr. Tyre
316	Seleuceia Pieria	*IGCH* 1573	76/5?	Philip I Philadelphus: Antioch 4 tetr. in bronze (cores without silver plating?)
353	Kırıkhan	*CH* 9.579	38/7	Ariarathus IV of Cappadocia: 1 dr. Ariarathus VI: 1 dr. Ariobarzanes I: 2 dr.

Table 9.12. Plated coins in excavations

Site	Plated Coins
Dura Europos	Alexander III: 1 tetr. mint uncert.
Jablah, necropolis of al-Jbeibat	Alexander III: 1 dr. Magnesia?
Jebel Khalid	Aradus: 2 tetr.
Jerusalem, City of David	Tyre: 1 imitation of shekel (126/5 BC)
Seleuceia Pieria, 1932–1939	Alexander III: 1 dr. mint uncert.
Tel Anafa	Seleucid uncert.: 1 tetr.

whom one pays only at a due date.[129] Such practices limit the use of struck coin; they must have been current already in antiquity. These contrasts between the use of small change and credit by different socio-economic groups also obtained in classical Athens, as noted above. These observations are probably valid for Hellenistic Syria as well.

2.3.2. Confronting Demand?

According to place and context, silver coinage does not cover all exchanges. The same probably holds for bronze, but in proportions we cannot possibly assess. So it happens that, despite the normal ability to make do without coins, there still ended up being a shortage. That is probably one of the major reasons for the appearance of quality imitations: they do not seek to deceive the user about the coin's worth[130] but to replace one kind of hard to find coin with a copy of the same value, and sometimes of quite good manufacture. Four prototypes led to imitations: Athenian tetradrachms, Alexanders, tetradrachms of Antiochus VII and those of Philip I Philadelphus. In the case of Athenian tetradrachms, I have already expressed my reluctance to characterize as imitations the fractions from the southern Levant that replicate their types. The fractions could not replace them in circulation; they simply used types with which users were comfortable. As for true owl imitations, obvious ones are not that numerous, and those that are very well made are the subject of an interminable debate on their number and origin. Alexanders especially became the object of barbarian imitations and are rare in Syria (**95**, **100**, **103**, **107**?). On the other hand, the imitations of Antiochus VII were so credible that for a long time they were attributed to the mint of Antioch when they actually came from Cappadocian mints.[131] Imitations of tetradrachms of Philip I Philadelphus are essentially later than the period under study here (**335**, **345**). It seems therefore that imitations play only a relatively modest

129. Jambu 2013, p. 234.

130. Unlike the counterfeit coin against which cities defended themselves with severe sanctions to deter counterfeiters. The death penalty could be required, as the law of Dyme (*SIG*³ 530, Melville Jones 1993, no. 534) or an analogy in Demosthenes, *Against Leptines* 167, show.

131. Lorber, Houghton 2006. Hoover, in Houghton, Lorber, Hoover 2008, 2, pp. 266–71, shows that the largest proportion of imitations of Seleucid silver coins comes from the eastern regions of the empire.

role in the monetary circulation of Hellenistic Syria, or else that they were of such quality that they have not been identified.

The temptation to attribute all "deviant" coinage to a situation of scarcity of currency is obviously attractive. Plated coins—lead core covered with silver overlay—would be one indication (Tables 9.11–12). They appear in 17 hoards, and in eight cases the coins pre-date Alexander (Table 9.11). The practice is therefore old.[132] More surprising, it sometimes involves quite small coins, like the twenty-fourth of a shekel in the Nablus Hoard (*IGCH* 1507, **77**) or the Aradian fraction of less than a gram in the Samaria Hoard (*CH* 9.413, **50**). The profit for the counterfeiter was minimal while the technical difficulty was probably rather great. So the hypothesis of fraudulent manufacture must be discarded. In view of these examples, Meshorer and Qedar suggested that the plated fractions resulted from marginal adjustments that the mint master must have needed when, at the end of his silver reserve and not having reached the number of coins expected, he would himself have produced these plated coins to achieve his quota.[133]

The two plated Aradian tetradrachms found at Jebel Khalid are particularly interesting:[134] no trace of surface silver remains, but the obverse is still clearly legible and the city's official obverse dies are very easily recognizable. Die D89 is well represented between local years 196 (64/3 BC) and 199 (61/0 BC); D91 was used only in 196 (64/3 BC).[135] Some other plated specimens struck with die D92 date from 196 (64/3 BC). That year witnessed an increase in tetradrachm production with the placing into service of seven dies. This should probably be connected to Pompey's Syrian campaign because a similar increase is observable at Laodiceia ad Mare.[136] This is not a unique case in the history of Aradus: between 198/7 and 184/3 BC, six tetradrachms with types of Alexander are also plated.[137] In two cases (nos. 1331, 1349) only the plated coin attests to the obverse dies, but in the other four, as with the Tyche/Nike tetradrachms, some apparently unplated coins were struck with the same obverse. This could be a case of official mint productions.[138] A more thorough analysis of the apparently genuine silver coins would be helpful. In 2010, when the Ptolemaic collection in the Cabinet des Médailles in Paris underwent LA-ICP-MS analysis,[139] Olivier was able to show that a tetradrachm, seemingly genuine silver, was in fact a plated coin whose silver surface was intact.[140] This leads one to believe that unidentified plated coins are more numerous, perhaps, than one thought.

132. This was known for the Greek world thanks to a juicy anecdote in Herodotus 3.56, on Polycrates of Samos.

133. Meshorer, Qedar 1991, p. 67. Sheridan 1971 points out that a Tyrian coin in a hoard found on the Beirut beach (**40**) is plated (no. 11). He adds that "it is probable that the plating was done in an official mint, inasmuch as it does not seem practical to counterfeit such small pieces profitably" (p. 1128). The British Museum possesses several of these plated coins.

134. I want to thank Oliver Hoover for having sent me pictures of these coins in his safekeeping.

135. Duyrat 2005a, pp. 98–103.

136. Callataÿ 1997a, p. 384; Duyrat 2005a, pp. 281–83.

137. Duyrat 2005a, nos. 1306, 1319, 1331, 1345, 1346, 1349.

138. Hoover, in Houghton, Lorber, Hoover 2008, 2, pp. 243–44, also points out some plated Seleucid coins apparently issued from official mints.

139. These analyses were conducted at the Centre E. Babelon (IRAMAT, CNRS Orléans, UMR 5060). On the method LA-ICP-MS, cf. Gratuze, Blet-Lemarquand, Barrandon 2004.

140. Paris, Bibliothèque nationale de France, Fonds général 180, in Olivier, forthcoming.

Hoover offers three hypotheses to explain the striking of plated coins with official Seleucid dies: 1) a temporary crisis that drove the authorities to this expedient; 2) the theft of dies; 3) production by magistrates and/or corrupt workmen for their own gain. The last has support, because the story about Diogenes the Cynic in Diogenes Laertius (6.2.20–21) famously confirms it.[141] Stahl's study of the Venetian mint in the Middle Ages offers some parallels. In 1322, an employee of the mint stole some apparently unengraved dies; in 1395, five mint employees were caught making counterfeit coinage with dies and flans stolen from the mint;[142] in May, 1324, one last case concerns the discovery at a mint employee's home of dies and punches that would have allowed the manufacture of counterfeit Venetian coins from a clandestine workshop in Ravenna.[143] Antiquity can provide similar instances. Yet in my opinion one ought not to dismiss too quickly a technical explanation, the lack of bullion. This need not have been tied to a grave crisis. As Meshorer and Qedar suggested, there may simply have been a problem with the amount of metal entrusted to the mint master, who adjusted his order in this way. The practice could be tolerated, if limited. In the case of Alexanders and autonomous Aradian tetradrachms, production underwent changes that involved tensions in mint supply. This did not represent a crisis so much as a temporary breakdown in metal supply, a problem of adjustment of metal intake compared with expected outcomes. Theft or illegal activity by workers and magistrates may explain exceptional issues of plated coins, but excavations and hoards reveal a practice that, while not very frequent, was not uncommon either. Hoover even suggests that there may have been, at certain periods, official recognition of this plated currency. He also gives some examples of previously plated coins that subsequently circulated as bronzes.[144] Plated coins may therefore have been manufactured to adjust production or as coins of necessity.[145]

If there was a serious lack of silver currency, one probably has to conclude that non-coinage means of payment moderated it. Stepping up bronze production may have played such a role, along side other, more traditional methods.

3. BRONZE COINS AND MONETIZATION

The presence of silver and bronze fractions, the absence of cut coins or other objects in precious metal, and the existence of countermarks are all signs of a developed use of denominated coinage. In Hellenistic Syria, the very feeble production of fractions, including royal production, might then run counter to the idea of an important monetization of transactions. A conjecture of Picard, however, explains this scarcity in a way more favorable to monetized exchanges: "When making a payment, the payer able to employ both bronze coins unusable outside the city and silver coins with a value recognized everywhere was surely better advised to choose the

141. Hoover, in Houghton, Lorber, Hoover 2008, 2, pp. 244–45.
142. Stahl 2000, p. 237.
143. Ibid., p. 238.
144. Hoover in Houghton, Lorber, Hoover, 2008, 2, pp. 245–46.
145. Apart from Hasmonean coins (excavations from the Jewish Quarter in Jerusalem), a few lead issues are known. One specimen from the Coele Syria Hoard (**323**) bears types related to Ptolemaic types. Hoover 2008 suggests seeing here an issue of necessity produced during Ptolemy X's campaign against Damascus in 103–101 BC.

former, which must have logically led to a holding back of silver coins and thus a depreciation of bronze coins.... That bronze drove out silver is a fact on Thasos and in a number of cities, but not all, with the steady elimination of silver coins under a tetradrachm."[146] This observation corresponds well to the Syrian situation, especially from the second century, when bronze currency develops in an important way. Any overall quantification of this alloy is not conceivable at present, in the absence of die studies. When these do exist, we have seen that the ratios of observed specimens to dies are quite low, something true, in fact, for the majority of the bronze series classified by dies.[147] These results have two chief causes. The first is that a pair of dies striking bronze is used up more rapidly than a pair of silver dies. The alloy is clearly less malleable than the pure metal, especially if the former is of good quality, without too much lead.[148] Accordingly, the original number of dies used to strike a quantity, x, of bronze coins will necessarily be much higher than the original number of dies used to strike the same quantity of silver. This partially explains the very low die frequency indices for bronze. This appraisal of the situation is not without hope, however. Decades of excavations by the French School at Athens on the site of Thasos have managed to collect 2,230 coins struck from 144 obverse dies, or an average of 13 specimens per die.[149] This exceptionally high figure suggests that almost all the dies are known. But Thasos remains an unusual case. In all, the quality of our bronze database is proportionally rather lower than that for silver. The ancients carefully preserved coins in precious metal, rarely losing them and burying them together, often in protective containers. Moderns have collected them passionately, intent on large quantities for their coin displays. In contrast, bronze coins, being less valuable, were much less hoarded in antiquity. The vast majority of them come to us through archaeological digs, in the form of isolated finds. These coins were therefore not particularly protected and are often very worn. Their dispersion makes one legitimately think that a large portion were destroyed or have eluded us. Butcher recalls how on different occasions the low number of small diameter bronzes has elicited comment. The systematic use of sieves by the excavators of the souks of Beirut have provided highly suggestive results: "about 48% of the coins found on BEY 006 and 045 were 12 mm or less in diameter.[150] ... A large proportion of these were recorded during sieving."[151] These small diameter bronzes were dated mostly from

146. Picard 1994, p. 41. "Dès lors que pour effectuer un paiement, le payeur pouvait utiliser soit des espèces en bronze inutilisables hors de la cité, soit des espèces en argent qui avaient partout une certaine valeur, il était assurément plus avisé de choisir la première solution, ce qui devait amener logiquement une rétention des pièces en argent, et donc une dépréciation des pièces en bronze. [...] Que le bronze ait chassé l'argent se constate, à Thasos et dans bien des cités, mais pas dans toutes, par l'élimination progressive des espèces d'argent inférieures au tétradrachme."

147. Callataÿ 1997b, pp. 309–23.

148. Faucher 2013 offers an in-depth study of bronze coinage and its characteristics, based on investigation of the Ptolemaic mint at Alexandria.

149. Picard 2015.

150. Fragments with diameters impossible to determine have not been taken into account.

151. Butcher 2001–2002, p. 25. Reece points out that 25% of the coins on the site of Uley in Great Britain were found through sieving. He is of the opinion that "for the coins, in both the casual (metal-detector) and complete (sieving) methods of recovery, the results do not change the balance between the periods of coins found" (Reece 1996, p. 342) on sites overall. This statement would probably merit discussion. One must remember especially that the smallest denominations typically escape the excavator's notice and are found thanks to sieving. Our knowledge of the place of coinage in daily transactions would undoubtedly change with a one-quarter increase in the volume of bronzes found in excavations, a quarter essentially composed of very small fractions.

the late Roman Empire, but all periods were represented. An incomplete harvesting is usual, and to this we must add the fact that these coins are little collected, even if enlightened amateurs have favored them. This weak interest is being reversed more and more, but still not enough to alter the state of affairs. The consequences for our ability to evaluate the monetization of Hellenistic Syria are important: we lack an appreciable percentage of the bronze currency, silver fractions are rare, probably driven out by abundant bronze more than by the poor monetization of transactions, and we can really only be confident about silver.

So we have to assume that bronze coinage was much more plentiful than our present information entitles us to say. Usage was probably also rather elastic. In his particularly painstaking work on the coins from the Beirut souks, Butcher emphasizes the relativity in the value of bronze: "coin finds provide a window onto extinct social relations. To study excavation finds is to attempt to understand the social life of a particular and rather peculiar class of commodity: small change. … Like other commodities the circulation of coinage in pre-modern cultures was dependent on a variety of constraints which do not fit into the neo-classical mould, with its dismissal of state and society and emphasis on individual rational choice and maximizing efficiency. This is not to say that coins circulated in an environment devoid of rationalizing tendencies and that patterns are never formed by the aggregate choices of rational individuals, but it is an attempt to acknowledge that values are generated by social contexts which cannot be characterized as wholly rational."[152] Butcher judges that the functions "means of exchange" and "storing value" were not applied to the same coins: "it is essential that a store of value maintain its worth over a long period of time and perhaps over long distances, whereas this is not essential to the medium of exchange," even if the two functions are not completely separate.[153] This has an influence on the nature of coins lost and hence found in excavations. It also has a bearing on the way in which the Syrians of the Hellenistic period accepted this currency or not.

Use of the coinage sometimes seems to have been of rather long duration. This longevity has been observed in other societies in other times, where the duration of circulation is easily calculated. Jambu gives a few illustrative examples for Lower Normandy in the sixteenth and seventeenth centuries: the hoards or patrimonies studied have revealed coins struck between 85 and 230 years earlier.[154] This phenomenon affects all metals, but gold coins hold the endurance record, with *agnels d'or* struck starting in 1311 under Philip IV the Handsome still circulating in the 1540s. But it also holds for coppers: "In purses, this small coinage useful for everyday expenses might have been mixed in with coins a century or two old."[155]

The same phenomenon is attested in ancient Syria, although we cannot always date it as precisely. For silver, the intrinsic value and maintenance of the Attic and Ptolemaic standards for

152. Butcher 2001–2002, p. 21.
153. Ibid.
154. Jambu 2013, pp. 345–46.
155. "Dans les bourses, cette petite monnaie utile aux dépenses quotidiennes pouvait être mêlée à des pièces vieilles d'un à deux siècles." Ibid., p. 345.

several centuries permit it. Bronze coinage is largely fiduciary, its worth essentially dependent on the users' confidence and consent. Butcher elaborates on this point: "It appears from the evidence of hoard material that old coins could sometimes return to circulation after a period of obsolescence, particularly in periods when users were not looking very carefully at the coins they used (as seems to have been the case in the fifth century AD), but in such cases the coins were usually chosen for their size and shape and general physical resemblance to current issues. As far as the state was concerned these old coins may not have been legal tender, but if the coinage in circulation at a certain date was not particularly carefully regulated, such abuses to the system may have been tolerated in low-level exchanges between individuals (what we might term the private pay community). Thus one could posit a tension between the desire of states to regulate the coinage in circulation, and the desire of communities to have currency to supply their needs."[156] These coins may have been old or "irregular," including moulded coins or imitations. In such cases, private individuals used them with each other, but not for payments to the state, like taxes. Butcher cites a very clear example of latter-day use of bronze coins in the Roman Empire, from c. AD 218 to c. AD 318, which clean stratigraphy and firmly dated ceramic material well document.[157] The Beirut souk excavations lead one to think that in several periods some clearly earlier currency continued to circulate: Julio-Claudian bronze after AD 100, issues of the years AD 330–347 occasionally down to the sixth century. Excavations as well as hoards show this.[158]

This adaptability in the use of bronze is also attested in the Hellenistic period. Parallel circulation of the royal coinage and civic issues beginning in the second century probably encouraged it. Even earlier, bronzes of Alexander are found on rather numerous sites (about a third of those in the catalogue), although in very small amounts. Likewise, the royal Seleucid coinage circulates everywhere. The bronzes of Antiochus III are much better represented than those of other monarchs since they were certainly struck in sizeable quantities and because Antiochus' reign was long. On sites without a mint, the royal coinage is usually in the majority. As Butcher stresses, "the relationship between the royal bronze coinages and these civic issues is poorly understood." At the present time, it has not received a specialized study.

Were foreign bronzes systematically rejected in transactions of a given city or was there a margin of tolerance? This question does not arise for royal Seleucid coins. At Beirut, they represent more than 55% of the Hellenistic finds made in excavations (of which nearly 55% are of Antiochus III), whereas coins of foreign cities constitute only 9.6 %. The plentiful presence of foreign bronze coins in cities that struck little or no coinage has been clearly established for Greece: Callataÿ has gathered the results of 16 archaeological publications, the results of which have revealed from a third to more than 91% foreign coins. In eight cases, they amount to more

156. Butcher 2001–2002, p. 24.
157. Ibid., pp. 75–76.
158. Ibid., pp. 114–15.

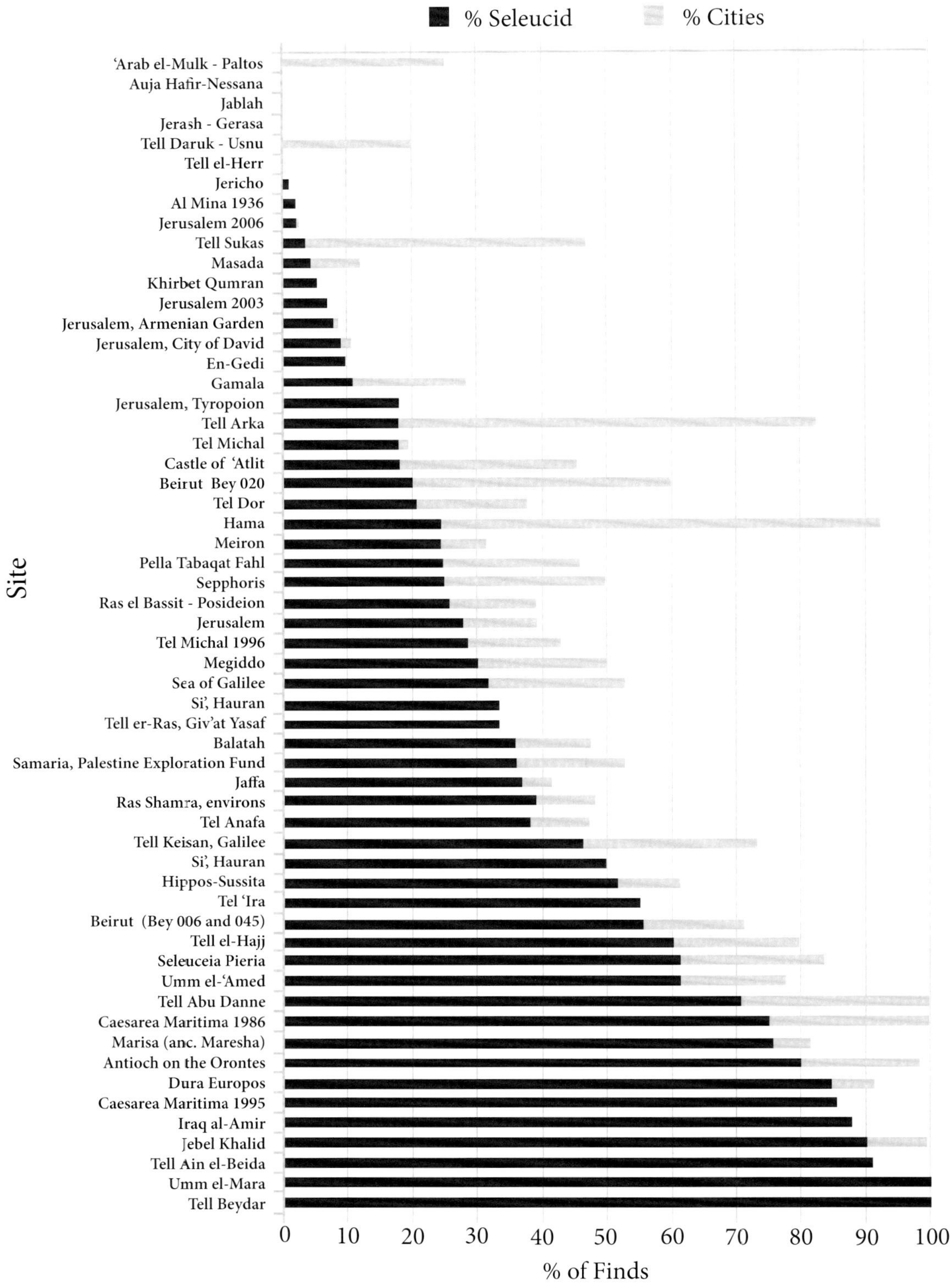

Figure 9.9. Proportion of royal Seleucid coins and civic issues (local and foreign mints) in excavations.

than 50% of the finds.[159] One can only conclude that they were accepted in local exchanges. It remains to establish what proportion coins from neighboring mints represent and to what extent they were officially or tacitly accepted in exchanges, among individuals. This acceptance of coins that were not legal tender prefigures certain practices in modern France, where withdrawn coins continued in use and are found even in the inventories of notaries. Scarcity of coin led users to brave the prohibitions.[160] Withdrawn coins constituted the core of the metallic stock that the Caen mint struck in early-modern times, and so that mint's exchange ledgers list the melting down in 1726 of quarter écus made in 1578 and withdrawn from circulation in 1679.[161] Another, even more telling, example is that mediaeval and modern tokens could circulate as coinage among private individuals despite official warnings.[162] This sort of situation existed in antiquity. Legislative attempts against these practices, epigraphically attested, are probably the clearest sign. The law of Olbia, c. 360, requires "that all sales and all purchases be concluded in the city's coinage, with Olbiopolitan bronze and silver"(πρὸς τὸν χαλκὸν καὶ τὸ ἀργύριο[ν] τὸ Ὀλβιοπολιτικόν, ll. 15–16),[163] that is, with legal tender local coinage. The mere fact that the government of Olbia felt the need to promulgate such a law underlines the common use of other coins than the city's, in silver as well as bronze. The same text in another place mentions this explicitly since, in the absence of local issues of gold coins, Cyzicene electrum received official status (ll. 23–26). Stated penalties are severe: the lawbreaker would suffer loss of the amount transacted in foreign coinage.

Figure 9.9 shows that, save for some cases involving small sites with few coins, the Seleucid royal coinage is always more important by far than that of civic mints. It must have circulated unimpeded, which would explain its omnipresence in varying amounts depending on the history of the sites, but almost always in top position. This phenomenon is increased, in proportions impossible to measure until close analysis of excavation results occurs, by the fact that civic issues from sites mostly date from the first century, while Seleucid coins are mostly second-century (and from the third century in northern Syria).[164]

It is understandable that the royal Seleucid coinage was accepted everywhere; but civic currencies also had the ability to travel. Phoenician bronzes overstruck by Tigranes are an interesting case. Tigranes of Armenia ruled over Syria and conducted military campaigns there from 83–69 BC. It remains difficult to identify the mints where he struck coins, but there is general agreement that his tetradrachms came principally from Antioch and, in far smaller amounts, from Damascus. The mints that issued bronzes are much more difficult to identify, and debate remains ongoing. One particular phenomenon interests us here: 10–15% of these coins were

159. Callataÿ 2006b, pp. 184–85.
160. Jambu 2013, pp. 347, 380–83.
161. Ibid., p. 186.
162. Illustrative examples in Sargent, Velde 2002, pp. 216–18.
163. Dubois 1996, no. 14, pp. 30–31; P. Gauthier in the "Bulletin épigraphique" of *REG* 111 (1997), pp. 553–54, no. 420.
164. The date of these bronzes is, moreover, not always well established, much less their time in circulation.

Table 9.13. Bronzes of Aradus and Marathus in excavations (Map 29 and Map 37)[165]

Site	Aradus	Marathus
'Arab el-Mulk - Paltos	1	
Beirut Bey 020	1	
Gamala	1	1
Jebel Khalid	1	
Umm el-'Amed	1	
Ras Shamra, environs	1	
Seleuceia Pieria 1932–1939	1	
Tell Ain el-Beida	1	
Tell Daruk - Usnu	1	
Tell el-Hajj	1	
Tel Anafa	2	
Tell Sukas	3	2
Antioch on the Orontes, 1932–1939	6	1
Ras el Bassit – Posideion	6	
Beirut (Bey 006 and 045)	8	2
Dura Europos	13	
Tell Arka, 1974–1980	16	3
Hama	24	4
Al Mina, 1936	30 to 40 frags.?	
Ras Ibn Hani[165]	53+?	5
Total	**88**	**13**

poorly overstuck on mostly Phoenician bronzes, among which a large number come from Aradus. In 2005, I conjectured that the stock of coins overstruck by Tigranes resulted from a capture made in the Aradian hinterland, the only place where such a quantity of this city's bronze coins could be found. Since the non-Aradian coins came mostly from neighboring mints (Orontes Valley, northern Syria), and very few from the south, I concluded that the non-Aradian bronzes might nonetheless have come from that Aradian hinterland, representatives of the natural penetration of coins occasioned by commercial coin movements and movements of people. Such a variety of bronze on one and the same site has numerous parallels. Some other, better-

165. According to partial results published in Augé 2000, cf. supra, pp. 356–57.

documented examples show a certain porousness in monetary systems. Thus, in France of the Ancien Régime, Meuvret observes that:

> among imported precious metals, coins of different countries appeared, as well as ingots and jewelry too. People were not always in a hurry to transform everything into French coins. This was a reaction to French taxes, because a rather high seigniorage was added to the cost of coining, not to mention the "*traite foraine*" tax. Moreover, mint masters were sometimes of modest means and did not have extensive credit. They often lacked raw materials, as the frequent and lengthy closings of many mints show. Hence the maintenance in circulation of numerous foreign coins, some of which were tolerated and attained legal status. The most famous of all was the "*pistole*", which became a commonplace term, in standard French, to designate "gold coin."[166]

The situation in ancient Syria may have been quite different; but the fiduciary character of bronze coinage, the easy acceptance of currencies of neighboring cities, and probably the fact that here, too, coinage always failed to satisfy demand surely aided in the acceptance of foreign bronzes in circulation. A remark of Noe underlines the regressive porousness of monetary systems: "For commercial transactions bronze coins are acceptable only within the area in which the badge of the issuer is recognized and honored. They might be rejected by a rival state or an enemy. Bronze coins would have passed freely within the city of issue, less freely among its nearby friendly neighbors and seldom or not at all beyond these limits."[167]

One example of the distant circulation of civic bronzes may profitably be elaborated upon. Bronze coins of Aradus and, to a lesser degree, its neighbor Marathus are attested on several southern sites (Table 9.13). Butcher also singles out an Aradian coin in Jerusalem.[168] Five sites have revealed more than ten Aradian coins. Al Mina stopped being densely occupied c. 300 BC, although Hellenistic coins are still found there.[169] This port at the mouth of the Orontes probably became depopulated (either by Seleucus I or natural attrition) after the creation of the large port of Seleuceia a little to the north. The heavy representation of silver and bronze Aradian fractions from the Persian period far surpasses other civic coinages and underlines the privileged relations that the Aradian port had with that of Al Mina at the end of the fourth centu-

166. "parmi les métaux précieux importé, figuraient des monnaies de divers pays, des lingots mais aussi des bijoux. Or on ne se pressait pas toujours de transformer le tout en monnaies françaises. On reculait souvent devant les taxes, car, au prix du monnayage, s'ajoutait un seigneuriage assez élevé sans compter le droit de traite foraine. D'autre part les maîtres des monnaies étaient parfois de fortune médiocre et ne disposaient pas d'un grand crédit. Ils manquaient souvent de matières comme l'attestent les fermetures fréquentes et prolongées de beaucoup d'hôtels. De là le maintien, dans la circulation, de nombreuses pièces étrangères dont certaines, tolérées, recevaient un cours officiel. La plus célèbre de toutes fut la 'pistole', devenue le terme usuel, dans la langue classique, pour désigner la monnaie d'or." Meuvret 1947, p. 23. The "*traite foraine*" tax was a royal tax on the movements of goods between two regions of the kingdom, including bullion or foreign coins. Jambu 2013, pp. 332–45, devotes an entire chapter to "The Invasion of Foreign Coins" in Lower Normandy during the modern period.

167. Noe 1949, p. 241.

168. Butcher 2001–2002, p. 54.

169. Callot 2002.

ry.[170] At Epiphaneia/Hama, Aradian coins (24 bronzes and five tetradrachms in hoard **325**) and those from the Peraea (Marathus, 4) rival the issues of Apamea, located nearby in the Orontes Valley. The same situation obtains at Ras Ibn Hani. Here, too, the Aradian bronzes (about 50) and those from the Peraea (10)[171] vastly outnumber the other contemporary civic coinages. In these three cases, the cities did not have mints with wide reach, and so one has to wonder if the civic authorities did not accept the abundant Aradian production officially. Elsewhere, Aradian coins are not so numerous. But it is remarkable that they are found on no fewer than five sites between Aradian territory and the Sea of Galilee. Since these bronzes are later than 200 BC and the reconquest of Ptolemaic Syria and Phoenicia by Antiochus III, they demonstrate the permeability of this border after Ptolemaic domination ceased. The southern frontier, therefore, is no longer defined by the closed monetary zone connected with the Ptolemaic standard but rather by Aradus' sphere of activity. One must also note that the excavations of the souks of Beirut have revealed a not insignificant number of coins from the Aradian region: eight from Aradus, two from Marathus, representing the highest number after the bronzes of Berytus itself (18). Here, again, relations among large coastal ports stand out. Completing this picture are the discoveries by excavators of Jordanian sites who report the unexpected presence of Aradian coins on caravan routes to the south.[172]

So the circulation of Hellenistic civic coins gives different results from that of royal bronzes (Alexandrine, Seleucid, Ptolemaic, Hasmonean). The last are the most plentiful, as we saw earlier. Their royal pedigree endowed them with possibilities for circulation that transcended the issuing mint and the reach of the state. Dispersion maps of civic bronzes actually eliminate a large number of sites that only, or almost only revealed royal coinage (Fig. 9.9). Study of the mints most featured in excavations produces an instructive map. To the south of the Aradian domain are clearly the mints of Sidon (Map 30), Tyre (Map 28), and Ake-Ptolemais (Map 31), all well represented in the area between the Mediterranean and the right bank of the Jordan. Ascalon, on the other hand, only supports its own hinterland (Map 33). These regional circulation maps tally with those of silver autonomous issues produced by the same mints. To the north of the Aradian Peraea, however, the civic coins of Antioch and Seleuceia are most in evidence. Those of Antioch are also found on certain southern sites, having probably followed the circulation routes of royal issues struck by this mint until the end of the second century (Map 27).[173]

4. CONCLUSION

From the fifth to the first century BC, the role of coinage evolved greatly in Syria. Marginal and foreign at first, it became a local production of Phoenician and southern Levantine mints,

170. One need not see here, it seems to me, a sign of Al Mina's belonging to the Aradian Peraea, *pace* Elayi 1987, pp. 262–63.

171. Two of Gabala, three of Carne, five of Marathus.

172. Graf et al. 2005; Durand 2008, vol. I, pp. 208–209.

173. Syon 2015 was published too late to be included in this book.

sharply divided into large, indeed very large denominations and tiny fractions in silver, at a time when the Greek world adopted bronze. The Macedonian Conquest imposed the dominance of large silver denominations exclusively, and bronze only appears later, in the second century, initially more through royal than civic issues. During the same period, silver flows, originally directed towards the heartland of the Achaemenid Empire, underwent a brutal change in course with Alexander the Great's conquest. Masses of silver coined by the Macedonian and his immediate successors in eastern mints are hoarded west of them in a general movement of sizeable proportions still to be quantified. This westward flow reverses in the third and second centuries. But the appearance of local standards and the increasing scarcity of Alexanders dilute the phenomenon and regionalize it.

Hoards and excavation coins do not reflect the entire range of Syrians' wealth in the Hellenistic Age but probably a large median segment, which one should resist making into the "middle class" in the absence of socio-economic data. The under representation of gold is typical of hoarding practices in the region, which preferred silver and burial of intermediate amounts in the ground. Coinage did not cover all transactions, since it was never struck in sufficient quantities. That is why hoards and excavation coins show great adaptability in the use of coinage, which complemented other means of payment and wealth accumulation, although about these we are poorly informed. In conclusion, this adaptability must be kept in mind, it seems to me, when I cite this remark of Hoover: "because of the token nature of the [bronze] coinage, it is far from certain that the official reckoning of eight chalkoi to the obol was always enforceable everywhere and at all times. It would not be surprising if old bronzes and issues of usurpers were accepted only at reduced face value on the marketplace, or if during the period of Seleucid hegemony in western Asia Minor, Seleucid bronze coins passed in some of the cities accustomed to the Aeginetic system at twelve to the obol."[174] This adaptability in the use of coinage, it seems to me, may derive at least partially from the persistence of other means of payment throughout antiquity, coinage being only one among them. The fiduciary character of bronze gave it a greater advantage in adaptability, so long as users had confidence. Butcher's observations on the "double value" of coinage, depending on whether transactions occurred under official oversight or took place among private individuals, share the same perspective.

174. Hoover in Houghton, Lorber, Hoover 2008, 2, p. 51.

General Conclusion

The coins at the core of this book are, first and foremost, objects lost by their owners, with all the chance characteristics that such an origin entails. Nevertheless, taken as a whole and submitted to critical inquiry, they form a *corpus* of sources still in its early stages of development. The two catalogues that are the book's foundation rest on two contrasting actions: the amassing of riches (in the case of hoards), and the chance loss of coins, often of little value, in the case of isolated finds. Hoards come about only because some individuals were able to accumulate coinage that exceeded their other assets, which traditionally consisted of land, a workshop, tools, raw materials, or able-bodied slaves. In short, they had more than a subsistence level of production. The isolated coins found in excavations are, by contrast, the result of negligence: they went astray, and their owners did not think them worth looking for intently. The parable of the lost coin in St. Luke's Gospel (15.8–9) depicts what differentiates hoarded coins and those lost in isolation: "What woman having ten pieces of silver, if she lose one piece, doth not light a candle, and sweep the house, and seek diligently till she find it? And when she hath found it, she calleth her friends and her neighbors together, saying, Rejoice with me, for I have found the piece which I had lost."[1] This woman's attitude is a literary archetype that accords with the available data. The ten coins of silver could form a hoard, and one of them justifies a long search, which would not happen with a bronze piece.

By bringing together 360 hoards with the coins from 58 excavated sites, we may gain access to all levels of coin use, ranging from the accumulation of wealth, with hoards containing gold and silver, down to the contents of a modest purse, with small collections of bronze. The latter, like bronzes found in excavations, provide a window onto the daily use of currency. Combined with gold and silver hoards, they provide data for local, regional, or international circulation, depending on the case. But this material does not permit investigation of the question of monetary circulation, because it is not a snapshot of this; as always in ancient history, the evidence

1. King James Version. "Ἢ τίς γυνὴ δραχμὰς ἔχουσα δέκα, ἐὰν ἀπολέσῃ δραχμὴν μίαν, οὐχὶ ἅπτει λύχνον καὶ σαροῖ τὴν οἰκίαν καὶ ζητεῖ ἐπιμελῶς ἕως ὅτου εὕρῃ; καὶ εὑροῦσα συγκαλεῖται τὰς φίλας καὶ τάς γείτονας λέγουσα· Συγχάρητέ μοι, ὅτι εὗρον τὴν δραχμὴν ἣν ἀπωλεσα."

that survives suggests only one piece of the reality, reshaped by the accident of transmission. Moreover, the absence of standardization in excavation publications makes comparative work particularly difficult. A few suggestions are therefore made in the section devoted to excavations for improving their format.

I have devoted a chapter to assessing the assembled material. Numerous external factors, indeed, shape the knowledge that can be gleaned. Hoards, or 85% of them, come from the coin trade and often have to be reconstituted. Studying the dates when they appear on the market makes patent the influence of wars in the twentieth century on coin sales. The importance of archaeology for nations in search of a national identity has also had consequences for the treatment of numismatic material. Once a hoard's own internal history and reconstitution are settled, the most thorny problem remains its dating, which is generally established by the date of its most recent coins and parallels with similar hoards. After these tasks are finished, there is a great temptation to identify the motives that brought the hoard about and to draw from this a general profile. This effort, however, quickly reaches its limits, given that the immediate conditions leading to the deposit remain unknown and the elements of the last owner's personal history remain absolutely inaccessible. When the daunting task of reconstitution is over, historical study can begin. The heart of this book is the Hellenistic period, but understanding developments requires taking into account monetary circulation from the Achaemenid period. This is the topic of one chapter, which brings out the use of *Hacksilber* in tandem with foreign, especially Athenian coins, and coins from local mints that from the mid-fifth century struck their own types or imitations of Athenian tetradrachms. The fourth century is characterized by widespread use of silver fractions, sometimes tiny, which were chiefly issued by Phoenician and southern Levantine mints.

The Macedonian Conquest and the Wars of the Successors brought significant changes to the monetary landscape. Production of coins with the types of Alexander, mostly tetradrachms, swept away all other coinages from hoards starting c. 325 BC. The bulk of issues, in fact, date from the Wars of the Successors, the intensity of which meant that their owners never recovered numerous hoards, thus leading to an increase in our available data. Production of gold coins with the types of Alexander is also a peculiar feature of this period, since gold was never a monetary metal in Syria prior to this time, and remained a prerogative of royal coinage thereafter. Commonly accepted coins *par excellence*, Alexanders travelled far from their regions of production for the next two centuries.

In comparison, wars seem to affect the monetary production of the third century less, notwithstanding the five Syrian conflicts running through it. The partition of the region between the Seleucids in the north and the Ptolemies in the south led to the development of two completely different monetary profiles. In the north, the Attic standard enabled a circulation open to other regions of the Greek world sharing this system. Seleucid coins are especially abundant as bronzes, on the different archaeological sites studied. Silver coinage in hoards initially consists of fourth-century Alexanders. Between 246 and 219 BC, a large Ptolemaic enclave was established around Seleuceia and Ras Ibn Hani following the brilliant campaign of Ptolemy III in 246 BC. Written sources only describe this occupation in broad strokes and do not permit us to discern its distinctive features. The presence of Ptolemaic bronzes on several sites around Seleuceia helps to sharpen this picture. In the south, Ptolemaic Syria and Phoenicia entered into the closed monetary system Ptolemy Soter established in all his dominions, for silver as well as bronze. These practices did not change after the region's conquest by Antiochus III at the time of the Fifth Syrian War. The Ptolemaic standard was maintained for silver, and the border with the Attic standard zone remained closed; but quantities of bronze issues of Antiochus III appear on all the archaeological sites.

The second century marks a turning point in the region's history. Reunited under Seleucid dominance, it experienced a significant increase in the production of royal coinage, propelled by the fratricidal wars dividing the dynasty and probably also by the steady disappearance of fourth-century Alexanders that had been used until then despite their worn state. The persistence of the Attic standard in the northern zone facilitated the arrival of Alexanders struck by the cities of Asia Minor and then of civic wreathed tetradrachms with the same provenance, according to a recent reinterpretation of the chronology. The reign of Alexander I Balas is another turning point. During the second half of the second century, the royal coinage takes pride of place in hoarding, and so probably in the available currency, including in Coele Syria and Phoenicia where the mints began to strike coinage in the name of the Seleucid king but on the Ptolemaic standard. Between 152/1 and 138/7 BC, Aradus and its Peraea, soon to be followed by Tripolis and Laodiceia ad Mare, adopted a local standard that isolated the region monetarily. This development, at a time when the royal coinage became everywhere dominant, marks an important change in monetary practices in the region: the start of the dismantling of the Attic standard. During the final years of the century, other cities seized their autonomy and began to strike their own silver coinage. The Attic standard still used by the Seleucids was debased and approached the lighter standards of Aradus or the Ptolemies. Considerable growth in the production of bronze coins accompanied the Hasmonean dynasty's expansion, especially under Alexander Jannaeus. The splitting of monetary circulation therefore characterizes the first century. The Attic standard progressively crumbled to the profit of regional systems. The principal cause for this was historical: the Seleucid dynasty's weakening encouraged local autonomy and the emergence of autonomous coinages, notably in Coele Syria and Phoenicia. But there was also a technical reason: Alexanders almost disappeared from circulation. Those of the fourth century were too worn; those of the second are less numerous in hoards as early as the 150s BC. Wreathed tetradrachms briefly replaced them. Seleucid mints issued much more of this currency, but was it sufficient in a world where the use of coinage was probably expanding? Aradus' move to its own standard is very symptomatic: these coins circulated only in the city's sphere of influence, despite the wreath decorating their reverse. Perhaps what one should see here is a concern to retain silver currency within the region, at a time when Macedonia and the Attalid kingdom also passed to regional standards that prevented their silver coinage from traveling far.[2] In such a context, explanations privileging civic prestige and pride, with cities able to place their own type on their own coins, seem rather secondary.

The number of coins gathered for writing this work, the literary tropes surrounding the image of the hoard, the present role of currency in the economy all quite naturally lead us to investigate our sources for what they tell us concerning the wealth of those who owned these coins. Archaeologists often disregard containers; based on inventoried data, these turn out to be, with rare exceptions, objects of everyday life. In most cases, a ceramic pot was chosen, or a piece of cloth, now disintegrated. The contents of hoards, overwhelmingly and in all periods, belong to an intermediate category, between 11 and 50 silver coins. Hoards tell us far less about the wealthiest and the less well-off. It appears, judging by both written and physical evidence, that the rich did not usually bury their fortunes in the ground but kept them in strongboxes.

Following these observations, the last chapter tries to define the role of coinage in the economic practices of the region and to situate Syria in the overall environment of precious metal flows. Hoarding essentially involves the large silver denominations, and that includes the Persian period when, however, small fractions also occupy a significant place. Gold remains the exception, no matter the period. Bronze appears in the fourth century and expands noticeably in the second, and especially the first, thanks to production by the Hasmonean kings. That explains the over-representation of this alloy in the southern Levant in the first century BC. Thus silver has a dominant position in hoarding from the start, with concurrent use of *Hacksilber* and struck coin under the Achaemenids. Hoards are also a reliable indicator of silver flows in the Attic standard area over the long term because we know the mints of origin, the time of striking, and the date and place of burial. At first the movement generally was from the Mediterranean towards the heart of the Persian Empire, where the price of silver and the Achaemenid taxation system immobilized sizeable metal reserves. This tendency reversed with the Macedonian Conquest and the Wars of the Successors. Following soldiers who were returning west, where the price of silver was probably higher, plentiful eastern issues in the name of Alexander were hoarded on the Mediterranean seaboard. These general tendencies tapered off in the second and first centuries BC as metal flows became regionalized with the appearance of reduced standards. Despite the amounts produced, coined silver never covered the totality of exchanges. Plated coins and especially imitations probably partially complemented monetary circulation. The role of gold is difficult to assess, for a large part of our information has been lost because the biggest fortunes were not hoarded in the ground. Bronze coinage, too, is probably underestimated. Less of a collectors' item, less studied, in circulation sometimes long after its issue, and used more readily than coins in precious metal, bronze travelled over greater distances than is generally believed. Practices observable in Syria have parallels in other pre-industrial societies

2. All else being equal, one might see here a type of monetary localism aimed at avoiding a dearth of coinage. Modern examples cited by Blanc are closely connected to economies whose rates of monetization are very high, and we probably should not push the parallel too much further, but it does seem that the protection mechanism here is the same as that evident in the creation of parallel local coinages in the modern period in situations where official coinage was markedly wanting. Blanc 2000, pp. 187–88, among others.

that allow us to make a better assessment of how coinage performed in exchanges and in the broader society as well (recourse to debt, social dimension of coinage, etc.).

This work aimed first of all at being methodological, and a few paths for research emerge from this approach. In order to extract the most information possible from hoards and excavation coins, as we have seen, a chronological and geographical approach was required. It permits us to distinguish developments and regional characteristics, as well as to trace their borders with some precision. It seems imperative to me that no material be ignored. Le Rider's selection of some well-known hoards to study circulation in the Seleucid Empire, or Newell's particularly painstaking reconstitution of the Demanhur Hoard undoubtedly permitted valuable documentation of certain aspects of monetary circulation, but they also created a skewed picture inapplicable to the entirety of our sources.[3] It is preferable to rely on the best known hoards while still placing them within the mass of those we know less well, and with the additional help of excavation coins to obtain an overall picture least removed from the original situation.

Chapter Two provided an opportunity to propose some rules for publications of excavation coins to follow. Broadly speaking, the study of these coins justifies observations of a more general sort. For example, during the third and second centuries BC, the concentration of Seleucid bronze coins is especially important in the royal capitals (Antioch, Seleuceia), strategic cities (Dura Europos, Jebel Khalid), and, after 200 BC, the ports and major sites seized from the Ptolemies in the southern Levant (Beirut, Caesarea, Marisa). The presence of the royal administration and garrisons certainly played a role in this influx of Seleucid bronze. Standardizing excavation coin publications, which would allow the aggregating of large quantities of data, would surely prove to be a serious historical contribution.

Hoard studies are much more standardized ever since Newell laid the groundwork with the Demanhur Hoard. Yet some useful pieces of information are often missing. A good hoard study agrees with a die study that quite often reaches no conclusion because the specimens come from a sampling of the general circulation. But some cases still have the capacity to surprise (**22**). The deliberate study of parts of hoards leaves me very perplexed. Van Alfen engaged in such an exercise when he interested himself only in the owls from the hoards found in Iraq and Syria.[4] These partial approaches risk losing a sense of the material's context, even though context is essential in defining the place of each hoard in a given period.

Can one distinguish any "monetary profiles" by periods and regions? This question immediately raises another: such profiles apart, is it possible to locate and date the hoards that come to us by and large without archaeological context? "Yes" is the decided response to both questions. The chronological and geographical parameters of this book follow, in fact, evolutions in the profiles of monetary circulation. But I have not attempted to systematize them, by giving them a name, for example. That would have risked rigidifying analysis and making it an overly systematic tool for interpreting the material. As often happens in numismatics, each new object

3. Le Rider 1986b; Newell 1923a.
4. Van Alfen 2000; 2002a.

of investigation—hoard or isolated coins—must involve putting back on the table all the data and taking account of the fact that exceptions are often the rule and the rule the exception. In sum, it is therefore difficult to prescribe a systematic protocol for hoard study, and it is probably undesirable to try to create an interpretative matrix that would necessarily be reductionist. To the well-established technical aspect (identification of specimens, dating, denominations, die study, etc.) must be added adaptations often resulting from the ingeniousness of the researcher and his knowledge of the place and period being studied.

Numismatics, for several decades now, has entered the age of statistics. Numerical precision here, as always in ancient history, is very relative. The study of incomplete collections and their dating, always susceptible to revision, calls for prudence. The mapping of hoards reinforces the feeling of precision in organizing our data. It is absolutely necessary to remember that hoard geography is only a very partial reflection of circulation. It illustrates the concentration of activity in the coastal region and the Beqaa-Jordan-Dead Sea circulation strip. But wars and past and present instability also strongly affect it, as do other, even less tangible motives tied up with the individual destinies of the owners and their families. One additional factor is impossible to estimate: the movements of the earth that, with no human intervention, can make an object disappear from the place where it was preserved.

These different conclusions, as interesting as they may be, are not unexpected. Some other pieces of information drawn from the data are less commonplace. Indeed, it seemed to me, as I studied the material, that certain coins were not hoarded in proportion to their production and circulation. I have, briefly, elaborated on the example of gold and of Athenian owls in the Athenian Empire. It would certainly be necessary to delve further into this point that would allow us to explain the gap between the written evidence, which testifies to the abundance of both currencies, and the latter's comparatively modest presence in hoards. Flexibility in the use of coinage, it seems to me, must also be emphasized. Coinage circulates for a long time, silver as well as bronze,[5] and can see its value modified in accordance with need: circulation of cores of plated coins, circulation of foreign bronze, etc. The so-called "*Lex* Louis Robert" that says that bronze coinage does not circulate far from its origin, except, almost inadvertently, in the purses of travellers, has to be refined. Bronze coinage travels extensively in the territory of the issuing state and its neighboring cities when they do not issue any or only a little of their own coinage. Thus the notion of the legality of the *nomisma* is utterly relative. Individuals might accept it, even as the state refuses it, or it may lose its value but be accepted all the same outside the issuing authority's territory. These observations require us to show a great deal of versatility and prudence in interpreting especially what is found in excavations.

Close examination of the broad movements of silver has also highlighted the variety of reasons for these flows: the local price of silver and the proximity of mining resources[6] must be added to military troop movements, fiscal needs, especially of kingdoms, and the hoarding and

5. But not gold. Cf. Touratsoglou 1998.
6. Kroll 2011.

non-hoarding practices of certain coins in the ground. In a context of strong silver flow, closed monetary systems may be seen as a way of countering the forceful current and of benefiting from returns on seigniorage on overvalued coinage.

The investigation of wealth accumulation and monetary circulation through hoards and excavation coins therefore opens some new perspectives. If their further development requires rather weighty treatment, they are no less usable for that, especially thanks to abundant publications and the computer tools that have arisen in recent years. The volume I close here is only an exploratory introduction to what this material allows us to hope for.

Appendix 1

Containers

No.	Place of Burial	No. *IGCH* or *CH*	Containers
1	Ras Shamra	*IGCH* 1478 = Noe 851	Pot
11	Byblus	*CH* 8.587 = *CH* 9.356	Bronze box in shape of an anepigraphic Egyptian cartouche
22	Ascalon	*CH* 8.587 = *CH* 9.369	Linen sack
33	Al Mina	*IGCH* 1486 = *CH* 8.587 = *CH* 9.395 = Noe 39	Silver container 6.7 cm high and 2.5 cm in diameter, with a lid and rings for hanging
36	Al Mina	*IGCH* 1487 = *CH* 8.587 = *CH* 9.396	"Vase of plain drab clay, type L3, ht. 0,15 m"
50	Samaria	*CH* 8.587 = *CH* 9.413	Terracotta pyxis of local manufacture
55	Tell Abu Hawam	*IGCH* 1502 = *CH* 8.587 = *CH* 9.426 = Noe 1039	Near fragments of an earthen jug that still bore traces of silver oxidation
66	Aradian Peraea	*CH* 8.587 = *CH* 9.368	Pot
69	Byblos	*IGCH* 1496 = *CH* 8.587 = *CH* 9.435 = Noe 175	Small jug of local type, 22 cm high
93	Saida	*IGCH* 1508 = *CH* 8.190 = Noe 881, 882, 884	Lead vases
105	Tel Tsippor	*IGCH* 1514	Jug with a hole pierced in its side
107	Byblos	*IGCH* 1515 = *CH* 8.587 = *CH* 9.436	Bronze vase
130	Unknown findspot	*CH* 9.485	Pot
131	Sikka	*CH* 8.279	Pot
142	Beth-Shan	*IGCH* 1585 = Noe 148	Pot
145	Tell Sukas	*IGCH* 1528	Bottom of a jug
158	Tel Michal	*CH* 7.85 = *CH* 8.307 = *CH* 9.498	Pot
161	Homs	*IGCH* 1532 = Noe 488	Vase
166	Oylum Höyüğü	*CH* 9.501	Jug
169	Balatah	*IGCH* 1588	"Jug [...] clogged with a plug of earth"
184	Latakia	*IGCH* 1544 = Noe 603	Urn
272	Antakya	*IGCH* 1565	Pot
279	Bassit	*CH* 8.476 = 10.326	In a sheet of lead
285	Maresha	*CH* 9.544	Jug
294	Ascalon	*CH* 9.548	Supposedly in a purse
296	Jericho	*IGCH* 1607	Pot

No.	Place of Burial	No. *IGCH* or *CH*	Containers
298	Megadim		In a Rhodian amphora
322	Samaria	*IGCH* 1614 = *CH* 7.110 = Noe 901	In a rag
323	Coele Syria ?	*CH* 10.349	Container apparently of organic material, perhaps leather
357	Khirbet Qumran	?	Pots

Appendix 2

Conditions of Discovery of the Kırıkhan Hoard (**231**).

CH 10.310

E-MAIL FROM EDOARDO LEVANTE TO ARTHUR HOUGHTON, MARCH 3, 2003

Subject: Kırıkhan

Dear Arthur,

Here below is what I remember after almost thirty years on the discovery of the famous "Kırıkhan hoard" as it was narrated to me by a high official of Kırıkhan at the time and by some other people who saw the hoard that same night before its dispersion who also said it consisted of about 3000+ big and small coins (4AR and drachms).

In 1974 (I don't remember the exact date), a shepherd was relaxing near a small rivulet in the vicinity of Baghras village (district of Kırıkhan) and watching his herd drinking water. The river sides consisted of a very friable chromium ore (serpentine) very common in the area. At one point he was attracted by some kind of shining tiny objects falling in the water from the river side where the animals were grazing.

Looking more closely, he understood that these were unknown foreign silver coins keeping falling from the rivulet side. He filled his pockets but this was not enough so he tied his baggy trousers (sharwal) on the ankles and he also filled his trousers with coins! Not knowing what to do, he went back to his village, walking in a rather uncomfortable way and started to loose coins from the hastily attached ankles! In a moment all the village was aware of the story and started to follow him and grab fallen coins!

Villagers gathered in the shepherd's hut, pretended a share and promised to keep the whole matter secret. As expected, the matter was immediately made known in the whole area and that same night people arrived from Kırıkhan and Antakya for advise and make buying offers. Useless to say that nobody in the village was aware of the importance and value of the hoard which was subsequently called "Kırıkhan hoard." It would have more appropriately been called "Baghras hoard."

A big part was sold that night to various people (antiquarian intermediaries and one not specified dentist called the "Agha" (the Boss)).

Next morning the Security raided the village but nothing was found. A subsequent raid in Harbiye (Daphne) at an antiquarian home where about sixty 4Ar were found and later on put on display in the Antakya museum.

A couple of weeks later the shepherd was found killed near the river and two other small buyers stabbed in Kırıkhan. Investigation did not clarify the puzzle.

I hope you will be interested by the rememberances [*sic*] which look more like a detective book than a numismatic adventure!

....

Concordance[1]

1. Rejected hoards are in gray.

IGCH	CH	Duyrat 2016	Elayi, Elayi 1993a	Seyrig 1973	Kadman 1967	Schlum-berger 1953	Noe 1937	Place of burial	Date of discovery
1478		**1**				21	851	Ras Shamra	April 1936
1479		**4**				19	605	Jablah	1929
1480		**5**				15	55	Region of Seleuceia	Before 1898
1481	8.587 = 9.357	**12**	17					Northern Syria	1953
1482	9.355	**13**	53					Region of Bostra, "Jordan" or "Jordanian" Hoard	1967
1483	8.587 = 9.362	**17**	54					Massyaf, "Lebanon" or "Syrian" Hoard	1961
1484		**2**				8		Marash	1898
1485		**32**	57					Syria	1932
1486	8.587 = 9.395	**33**	6			22	39	Al Mina	1936
1487	8.587 = 9.396	**36**	40			23		Al Mina	1936
1488	8.587 = 9.397	**37**	41			24		Al Mina	1936
1489	8.587 = 9.366 = 10.216	**18**	21			16	134	Beithir	1901
1490	8.587 = 9.360	**20**	55			14	28	Aleppo	Before 1866
1491	8.587 = 9.398	**35**	44					Phoenicia or Palestine	
1492	8.587 = 9.400	**38**	27					Palestine?	1943
1493	8.587 = 9.425	**53**	24					Qasr Naba	Between 1929 and 1967

IGCH	CH	Duyrat 2016	Elayi, Elayi 1993a	Seyrig 1973	Kadman 1967	Schlum-berger 1953	Noe 1937	Place of burial	Date of discovery
1494	8.587 = 9.414	**79**	5				605a	Latakia	1936
1495	8.587 = 9.427	**56**	3					Vicinity of Tripoli	1937
1496	8.587 = 9.435	**69**	9				175	Byblos	1931
1497	8.587 = 9.443 = 10.257	**74**	16					Phoenicia	1946 or before
1498	8.587 = 9.442	**73**	28					Palestine	1963
1499	8.587 = 9.419	**49**	20					Tell el-Mellaha	c. 1886
1500	8.587 = 9.404	**40**	43					Beach south of Beirut	Autumn, 1966
1501	9.382	**84**	33		4			Tell el-Fukhar	1962
1502	8.587 = 9.426	**55**	35		3		1039	Tell Abu Hawam	August 15, 1930
1503	8.587 = 9.451	**87**	48					Wadi Daliyeh	1962
1504	9.440	**77**	51					Nablus	1968
1505		**25**						Phoenicia or Palestine	1965 or before
1506	8.587 = 9.445	**85**	23			20	846	Qasr Naba	1902
1507	8.587 = 9.434	**80**	47		1	17	429	Abu Shusheh, the "Gezer" Hoard	1930
1508	8.190	**93**					881, 882, 884	Saida	1829, 1852, 1863
1509	8.587 = 9.461	**97**	34					Region of Akko?	1966
1510	8.587 = 9.462	**99**	26					Khirbet el-Kerak	1936

IGCH	CH	Duyrat 2016	Elayi, Elayi 1993a	Seyrig 1973	Kadman 1967	Schlum-berger 1953	Noe 1937	Place of burial	Date of discovery
1511		**100**						Sfire	1932
1512		**104**						Baalbek	1885
1513		**103**						Phoenicia	1968 or before
1514		**105**			6			Tel Tsippor	1960
1515	8.587 = 9.436	**107**	42					Byblos	1931
1516		**108**					29	Aleppo	1892?
1517	8.587 = 9.455	**92**	22			18	512	Jdita, near ancient Chalcis	1894
1518		**116**					133	Beirut	1900
1519		**119**						Beirut	1964
1520		**117**						Galilee, near Tarshiha	1964
1521		**118**						Saida	Before 1954
1522		**121**						Syria?	1964
1523		**127**						Latakia	1940
1524		**123**						Aleppo	1933
1525		**129**						Syria?	1966
1526		**138**						Seleuceia Pieria	1932–1939
1527		**143**						Syria?	Before 1917
1528		**145**						Tell Sukas	1958
1529		**148**					487	Homs	1927
1530	1.75	**154**		2				Tartus, Northern Phoenicia	1940
1531		**149**						Syria?	1962
1532		**161**					488	Homs	1934
1533	1.75	**160**		3				Syria	January, 1960
1534		**140**						Bab	1944
1535		**162**						Syria	1959

IGCH	CH	Duyrat 2016	Elayi, Elayi 1993a	Seyrig 1973	Kadman 1967	Schlumberger 1953	Noe 1937	Place of burial	Date of discovery
1536		**172**		6				Latakia	1946
1537		**171**		7				Kosseir	1949
1538		**173**		5				Dniye	1952
1539		**170**					30	Aleppo	1896
1540		**194**						Syria	
1541		**176**		10				Baiyada	1949
1542	9.528	**242**		13			24	Ain Tab	1920–1921
1543		**167**						Idlib	1959
1544		**184**		11			603	Latakia	1759
1545		**187**					650	Amrith	1893–1894
1546	1.75	**189**		12			31	Aleppo?	1931
1547	1.75	**190**		14				Khan Cheikhoun or Gaziantep	1940
1548		**199**					1033	Northern Syria	1912
1549		**249**						Syria?	Before 1964
1550	1.75	**211**		22				El-Aweiniye	1941
1551		**206**						Syria?	1937
1552	1.75 = 9.513	**201**		17				‘Arab el-Mulk	1940
1553		**207**						Antakya	1959
1554		**215**						Syria?	Before 1917
1555		**224**						Northern Syria	1906
1556	1.75	**217**		20			475	Northern Syria, “Caiffa Hoard.”	c. 1905
1557	1.75	**225**		21				Teffaha	1954
1558		**238**						Antakya	1962
1559	1.75	**209**		18				Akkar	1956
1560	1.75	**210**		19				Ghonsle	1955

IGCH	CH	Duyrat 2016	Elayi, Elayi 1993a	Seyrig 1973	Kadman 1967	Schlumberger 1953	Noe 1937	Place of burial	Date of discovery
1561	1.75	**208**		16				Latakia	1950
1562	1.75	**235**		25				Aleppo?	Before 1930
1563	1.75	**256**		27				Latakia	1948
1564		**270**						Antakya?	1963
1565		**272**						Antakya	1932–1939
1566		**283**						Amrith	1947
1567	1.75	**214**						Baarin	1955
1568	1.75	**288**		30				Kessab	1952
1569		**295**					543	"Kefir"	1910
1570		**304**						Antakya	Before 1960
1571		**305**						Kessab	1947
1572		**308**		31				Yahmour	1956
1573		**316**						Seleuceia Pieria	1932–1939
1574		**313**		33				Tartus	1968
1575	1.75	**315**		32				Aleppo	1940
1576		**325**						Hama	1937
1577		**329**						Syria	1968
1578	1.75	**335**		35				Aleppo	1950
1579		**341**						Syria	1951
1580		**337**						Hama	1937
1581	3.78	**347**					604, 871	Syria (Latakia) or Northern Phoenicia (Arwad)	1922
1582		**348**		36				Tartus	1952
1583	1.75 = 10.348	**314**		37				Akkar	1951
1584		**125**			10			Balatah	1956
1585		**142**			9		148	Beth-Shan	1921–1923
1586	1.75	**144**		40				Saida	1949
1587		**165**						Idna	1967
1588		**169**			7			Balatah	1960

IGCH	CH	Duyrat 2016	Elayi, Elayi 1993a	Seyrig 1973	Kadman 1967	Schlumberger 1953	Noe 1937	Place of burial	Date of discovery
1589	1.75	**157**		41				Damour	1949
1590		**185**						Kishon River	1958
1591		**220**		42				Tyre	1955
1592		**216**						Madaba, Jordan	1919
1593		**232**		24				Ras Baalbek	1957
1594		**239**					883	Saida	1862 or 1863
1595		**240**						Palestine	Before 1945
1596	10.309	**230**					1143	Tyre	1935
1597		**255**						Khan el-Abde	1938
1598		**261**						Tyre	1966
1599		**262**						Phoenicia	1966
1600	1.75	**258**		44				Golan	1932
1601	8.587 = 9.539	**267**	50		15		727	Nablus	1891
1602	1.75	**266**		45				Capernaum	1957
1603		**264**						Bethlehem	1971
1604	1.75	**276**		46				Thalalaia	1952
1605	3.63 = 8.477	**281**						Haifa, Israel	1969
1606		**287**						Palestine	1970
1607		**296**						Jericho	1965–1966
1608		**297**						Hebron	1967
1609	9.550	**292**						Rafah	Summer 1968
1610		**310**						Palestine	Before 1941
1611		**312**			20			Jaffa	September, 1949
1612		**321**			21			El-Jib	1956
1613		**300**						Golan	1940
1614	7.110	**322**			11		901	Samaria	1910

IGCH	CH	Duyrat 2016	Elayi, Elayi 1993a	Seyrig 1973	Kadman 1967	Schlumberger 1953	Noe 1937	Place of burial	Date of discovery
1615		**327**						Tiberias, Galilee	1967
1616		**331**						Ascalon	1927
1617		**334**			14			Palestine	1942
1618		**332**					725	Nahr Ibrahim	1874
1619		**301**					1130	Tripoli	1884–1885
1620		**302**						Damascus	1940
1621	1.75	**336**		47				Beirut	1950
1622		**344**			8		879	Safed	Before 1877
1623		**342**			18		714	Mt. Ophel, Jerusalem	1926
1624		**346**			19			Beth Sahur	1946
1625		**350**						Jerusalem, Temple Mount	1968
1626		**351**						Palestine	1942
1627		**343**						Gaza Region	1940
1628		**355**						Jerusalem, Mt. Scopus	1944
1629		**359**			12			Nablus	1935–1936
1630		**290**			13		788	Palestine	1930
1631		**293**						Kurnub	1966
1770		**212**					354	Dura Europus	1934
1773	1.75	**198**						Tell Kotchek	1952
	1.14 = 8.587 = 9.363	**15**	29					Northern Syria	1974
	1.74	**152**						Asia Minor or Northern Syria	1970
	1.75	**328**						Mardine?	1952
	1.77	**183**						Syria	Before 1960

IGCH	CH	Duyrat 2016	Elayi, Elayi 1993a	Seyrig 1973	Kadman 1967	Schlum-berger 1953	Noe 1937	Place of burial	Date of discovery
	1.79	**200**						Phoenicia	1971
	1.82	**205**						Northern Syria	1974
	1.86	**229**						Cheikh Miskin	1967
	1.87A = 2.90 = 10.310	**231**						Kırıkhan	1972
	1.103	**339**						Syria	1970–1971
	2.39 = 8.587 = 9.406	**41**	25					Lebanon	1970
	2.54	**106**						Byblos	1971
	2.69	**136**						Nuba, Hebron	1975
	2.81 = 10.289	**174**						Syria, perhaps the Aradian Peraea	1971
	2.83	**180**						Syria	1971
	2.95	213						Akken	1974–1975
	2.121	**320**						Damascus	1968
	2.128	**349**						Jericho	1973
	2.129	**358**						Near East	1974
	3.24	**102**						Hammaman	1912 or before
	3.59 = 9.529	**221**						Dura	1976
	3.60 = 4.64	**234**						Southeast-ern Turkey	1976
	3.61	**251**						Hebron	1976
	4.40	**139**						Region of Hebron	1977
	4.55	**197**						Near East	1977
	4.58	**195**						Southern Palestine	1977

IGCH	CH	Duyrat 2016	Elayi, Elayi 1993a	Seyrig 1973	Kadman 1967	Schlum-berger 1953	Noe 1937	Place of burial	Date of discovery
	4.60	**204**						Lebanon	
	4.65	**269**						Israel	1977
	4.69	**307**						Gaza Strip	1977
	5.26	**96**						Near East	1978
	5.35	**137**						Near East	1978?
	6.4 = 8.45	**8**						Antilebanon	1978
	6.5	**6**						Latakia	1979
	6.37 = 7.98 = 8.433 = 9.511	**193**						Maʿaret en-Numan	1980
	6.39	**282**						Lebanon or Syria	1979
	6.50 = 8.531	**340**						Syria	
	6.52	**356**						Syria	1978
	7.12	**7**						Syria	1978–1979
	7.16	**9**						Near East	1980
	7.28	**24**						Near East	1966
	7.40	**52**						Sebastiye	May, 1970
	7.66	**128**						Near East	1981
	7.77	**141**						Amman	1979
	7.85 = 8.307 = 9.498	**158**						Tel Michal	1977
	7.100	**203**						Near East	1965–1966
	7.109	**236**						Hebron	1979
	7.111	**268**						Hebron	1980
	8.29	**3**						Vicinity of Gaza	1983
	8.59	**14**						Ramallah	
	8.81 = 8.587 = 9.368	**66**	1					South of the Aradian Peraea	September, 1983

IGCH	CH	Duyrat 2016	Elayi, Elayi 1993a	Seyrig 1973	Kadman 1967	Schlum-berger 1953	Noe 1937	Place of burial	Date of discovery
	8.98	**39**						Saida	1983
	8.118	**47**						Beirut	1983 or before
	8.120	**44**						Byblos	1986
	8.123 and 8.587 = 9.386	**31**	2					Region of Arwad	1983
	8.126	**46**						Near East	1951
	8.129	**48**						Unknown Findspot	Before 1993
	8.143 = 9.422	51						Lebanon? Dinar Hoard?	1985
	8.144	**34**						Al Mina?	1986–1987
	8.149	**62**						Northern Galilee	1983
	8.150? = 9.468	**98**						Region of Hebron or Gaza	Before 1987
	8.152	**57**						Eastern Turkey or Syria	
	8.154	**63**						Phoenicia	1985
	8.156	**64**						Phoenicia	1988
	8.158	**76**	56					Syria, 100 km east of Aleppo	1989
	8.172	**90**						Lebanon	1985
	8.185 = 9.465	**95**						Syria or Lebanon	Before 1991
	8.189 = 9.460	**94**						Near East	1993
	8.199	**45**						Near East	1985
	8.207	**101**						Lebanon	1987
	8.215	**109**						Jericho	1991

IGCH	CH	Duyrat 2016	Elayi, Elayi 1993a	Seyrig 1973	Kadman 1967	Schlum-berger 1953	Noe 1937	Place of burial	Date of discovery
	8.216	**110**						Near East	
	8.220	**111**						Ascalon	1990
	8.231	**120**						Aleppo (ancient Beroea)	1983
	8.250 = 10.263	**122**						Region of Antakya	1992
	8.255	**124**						Near East	1983?
	8.279	**131**						Sikka	1990
	8.290 = 9.491	**360**						Northern Syria	
	8.304	**156**						Region of Hebron	1991
	8.306 = 8.311 = 8.344	**168**						Syria	Before 1981
	8.319	**151**						Northeast Syria	
	8.320	**150**						Jordan	1987
	8.323	**153**						Syria	1985
	8.332	**159**						Lebanon	1983
	8.339	**164**						Syria	Before 1991
	8.360	**163**						Citadel of Afamya	May, 1986
	8.412	**182**						Jericho (?)	1991
	8.432	**192**						Near Bethlehem	1984
	8.434	**196**						Syria	1990
	8.456	**223**						Syria	1984
	8.458	**219**						Sea of Galilee	
	8.459	**222**						Lebanon	1985?
	8.462	**237**						Syria	1989
	8.463	**233**						Hauran (?)	1979 or 1980

IGCH	CH	Duyrat 2016	Elayi, Elayi 1993a	Seyrig 1973	Kadman 1967	Schlumberger 1953	Noe 1937	Place of burial	Date of discovery
	8.464	**246**						Ramallah Region	Early 1992
	8.465	**248**						Unknown Findspot	
	8.467 = 9.526	**227**						Unknown Findspot	1986
	8.468	**271**						Unknown Findspot	
	8.469	**263**						South of Jerusalem	Early 1991
	8.470	**274**						Vicinity of Gaza	1983
	8.471 = 10.322	**277**						Tartus	1987
	8.472	**278**						Waqqas	1982
	8.476 = 10.326	**279**						Bassit, Syria	1978
	8.479	**280**						Baalbek Area?	1979
	8.511	**311**						Lebanon	1987
	8.515	**309**						Kamishliyye	1980
	8.522	**326**						Israel	Before 1992
	8.527	**333**						Lebanon	1984
	8.587 = 9.346	**10**	52					Moshav Dalton	1971
	8.587 = 9.356	**11**	10					Byblos	1933–1938
	8.587 = 9.367	**19**	31					Near East	1984
	8.587 = 9.369	**22**	45					Ascalon	1989
	8.587 = 9.372	**23**	19					Beirut	1982–1983

IGCH	CH	Duyrat 2016	Elayi, Elayi 1993a	Seyrig 1973	Kadman 1967	Schlum-berger 1953	Noe 1937	Place of burial	Date of discovery
	8.587 = 9.373	**28**	13					Byblos	March, 1983
	8.587 = 9.374	**29**	14					Byblos	1984–1985
	8.587 = 9.383	**30**	32					Unknown Findspot	1985–1986
	8.587 = 9.399	**27**	7					Unknown Findspot	1983
	8.587 = 9.405	**42**	4					Jablah	1983
	8.587 = 9.413	**50**	49					Samaria	Before 1990
	8.587 = 9.428	**58**	38					Damascus	February, 1959
	8.587 = 9.429	**59**	36					Vicinity of Gaza	1985–1990
	8.587 = 9.430	**60**	18					Saida	1959
	8.587 = 9.431	**61**	39					Unknown Findspot	1987
	8.587 = 9.433	**67**	37					Safed	1965
	8.587 = 9.437	**70**	11					Byblos	1933–1938
	8.587 = 9.438	**71**	12					Byblos	1957
	8.587 = 9.439	**72**	15					Byblos	1988
	8.587 = 9.444	**75**	8					Unknown Findspot	1988
	8.587 = 9.448	**89**	46					Vicinity of Gaza	1975
	8.587 = 9.449	**88**						Syria	1988

IGCH	CH	Duyrat 2016	Elayi, Elayi 1993a	Seyrig 1973	Kadman 1967	Schlum-berger 1953	Noe 1937	Place of burial	Date of discovery
	8.587 = 9.449	**260**	58					Syria	1988
	9.416	**43**						Unknown Findspot, southern Asia Minor probably	1984–1985
	9.432 = 10.243	**65**						Near East, Jbeil?	1992
	9.441	**78**						Nablus	Before 1890
	9.446	**86**						Aradus	1999
	9.453	**113**						Region of Nablus? Gaza?	Before 1970
	9.456	**83**						Near East	1992
	9.457	**115**						Unknown Findspot	1996
	9.483	**126**						Phoenicia	1997
	9.484	**132**						Region of Hebron	1999
	9.485	**130**						Unknown Findspot	Before 1991
	9.488	**134**						Unknown Findspot	Before 1985
	9.489	**135**						Hüseyinli	1986
	9.497 = 10.268	**147**						ʻIraq al-Amir	1993
	9.501	**166**						Oylum Höyüğü	1989
	9.507	**181**						Lebanon	1989
	9.510	**188**						Lebanon	1997
	9.517	**253**						Eastern Anatolia?	Before 1991
	9.527 = 10.308	**228**						Gaziantep	1994

IGCH	CH	Duyrat 2016	Elayi, Elayi 1993a	Seyrig 1973	Kadman 1967	Schlum-berger 1953	Noe 1937	Place of burial	Date of discovery
	9.531	**218**						Yatta	1978
	9.532	**247**						Lebanon	1997
	9.533	**254**						Tyre	1987
	9.534	**257**						Samaria	1999
	9.541	**179**						Unknown Findspot	Before 1980
	9.544	**285**						Maresha	Summer, 1989
	9.545	**286**						Homs	1987
	9.546	**291**						Israel	1997
	9.548	**294**						Ascalon	1988
	9.579	**353**						Kırıkhan	Before 1994
	10.218 = 10.219	**21**						Phoenicia	1998
	10.224	**112**						Ramallah	
	10.226	**26**						Tel Michal	1996
	10.237	**114**						Samaria	
	10.244	**68**						Near East	Before 2006 (c. 1986?)
	10.253	**54**						Near East	
	10.256	**91**						Tel Michal	1977–1980
	10.295	**177**						Beqaa Valley	1995
	10.297	**186**						Unknown Findspot	2004
	10.298	**191**						Qalʿat el-Moudiq	Before 1996
	10.301	**202**						Unknown Findspot, "Demetrius I Hoard"	2003
	10.311	**243**						Unknown Findspot	Before 1997

IGCH	CH	Duyrat 2016	Elayi, Elayi 1993a	Seyrig 1973	Kadman 1967	Schlumberger 1953	Noe 1937	Place of burial	Date of discovery
	10.312	**241**						Region of Hama	2001
	10.313	**244**						Vicinity of Saida (?)	1993
	10.314	**252**						Syria	1997
	10.315	**265**						Beth Ummar	2001
	10.318	**273**						Coastal Syria or Northern Lebanon	2000
	10.319	**275**						Northern Israel	2002
	10.337	**303**						North-Central Syria	2004
	10.345	**317**						Syria	Early 1980
	10.346	**318**						Unknown Findspot	1991
	10.347	**319**						Unknown Findspot	2003
	10.349	**323**						Coele Syria?	c. 1988
	10.350	**330**						Unknown Findspot	2007
	10.358	**345**						Syria	1991
	10.361	**354**						ʻEin Feshkha	2001
		16						Region of Jbeil?	
		81						Tel Gamma	1970
		82						Near Jerusalem	Before 1982
		133						Unknown Findspot	Before 1982
		146						Tel Michal	1977–1980
		155						Tel Michal	1977–1980

IGCH	CH	Duyrat 2016	Elayi, Elayi 1993a	Seyrig 1973	Kadman 1967	Schlum-berger 1953	Noe 1937	Place of burial	Date of discovery
		175						Jablah, Msaitbe	2005
		178						Tel Michal	1977–1980
		226						Region of Hebron	April, 2004
		245						Near Antioch	
		250						Syria or Southern Anatolia	1999
		259						Region of Hebron	July, 2004
		284						Amrith	1955
		289						Samaria Region	Before 1991
		298						Megadim	1962
		299						Megadim	1983
		306						Phoenicia	2011?
		324						Coast of Mt. Carmel	1994
		338						Unknown Findspot (Aradian Peraea?)	Before 1994
		352						Jerusalem, Jewish Quarter	
		357						Khirbet Qumran	March 21, 1955

Abbreviations

KINGS NAMES

AI	Antiochus I
AII	Antiochus II
AIII	Antiochus III
AIV	Antiochus IV
AV	Antiochus V
AVI	Antiochus VI
AVII	Antiochus VII
AVIII	Antiochus VIII
AVIII (1)	Antiochus VIII (first reign)
AVIII (2)	Antiochus VIII (second reign)
AVIII (3)	Antiochus VIII (third reign)
AVIII (4)	Antiochus VIII (fourth reign)
AVIII&Cleo	Antiochus VIII and Cleopatra
AIX	Antiochus IX
AIX (4)	Antiochus IX (fourth reign)
AX	Antiochus X
AXI	Antiochus XI
AXII	Antiochus XII
AXIII	Antiochus XIII
AHierax	Antiochus Hierax
A son of SIV	Antiochus son of Seleucus IV
AlexI	Alexander I Balas
AlexII	Alexander II Zebinas
DI	Demetrius I
DII (1)	Demetrius II (first reign)
DII (2)	Demetrius II (second reign)
DIII	Demetrius III
PI	Ptolemy I
PII	Ptolemy II
PIII	Ptolemy III
PIV	Ptolemy IV
PV	Ptolemy V
PVI	Ptolemy VI
PVIII	Ptolemy VIII

PP	Philip Philadelphus	SIII	Seleucus III
SI	Seleucus I	SIV	Seleucus IV
SII	Seleucus II	SVI	Seleucus VI

STATISTICS

n	number of coins collected
d	number of obverse dies observed
n/d	number of coins per die

BIBLIOGRAPHY

AJC Meshorer, Y. *Ancient Jewish Coinage*, vol. I: *Persian Period through Hasmonaeans*, New York, 1982.

ANS NNM American Numismatic Society. Numismatic Notes and Monographs.

BMC British Museum Catalogue.

BnF Bibliothèque nationale de France.

CH 1 Price, M. J. (ed.). *Coin Hoards* 1, London, 1975.

CH 2 Price, M. J. (ed.). *Coin Hoards* 2, London, 1976.

CH 3 Price, M. J. (ed.). *Coin Hoards* 3, London, 1977.

CH 4 Price, M. J. (ed.). *Coin Hoards* 4, London, 1978.

CH 5 Price, M. J. (ed.). *Coin Hoards* 5, London, 1980.

CH 6 Price, M. J. (ed.). *Coin Hoards* 6, London, 1981.

CH 7 Price, M. J. (ed.). *Coin Hoards* 7, London, 1985.

CH 8 Wartenberg, U., M. J. Price, and K. A. McGregor (eds.). *Coin Hoards* 8, London, 1994.

CH 9 Meadows, A. and U. Wartenberg (eds.). *Coin Hoards* 9, London, 2002.

CH 10 Hoover, O., A. Meadows, and U. Wartenberg (eds.). *Coin Hoards* 10, New York, 2010.

ESM Newell, E. T. *The Coinage of the Eastern Seleucid Mints from Seleucus I to Antiochus III*, New York, 1938.

IGCH Thompson, M., O. Mørkholm, and C. M. Kraay. *An Inventory of Greek Coin Hoards*, New York, 1973.

SC1, 1 Houghton, A. and C. Lorber. *Seleucid Coins. A Comprehensive Catalogue. With Metrological Tables by Brian Kritt. Part I. Seleucus I through Antiochus III*, vol. I. *Introduction, Maps, and Catalogue*, New York/Lancaster/London, 2002.

SC1, 2 Houghton, A. and C. Lorber. *Seleucid Coins. A Comprehensive Catalogue. With Metrological Tables by Brian Kritt., Part I. Seleucus I through Antiochus III*, vol. II. *Appendices, Indices, and Plates*, New York/Lancaster/London, 2002.

SC2, 1 Houghton A., C. Lorber, and O. Hoover. *Seleucid Coins. A Comprehensive Catalogue. Part II. Seleucus IV through Antiochus XIII*. Vol. I. *Introduction, Maps, and Catalogue*, Lancaster/London, 2008.

SC2, 2 Houghton, A., C. Lorber, and O. Hoover. *Seleucid Coins. A Comprehensive Catalogue. Part II. Seleucus IV through Antiochus XIII*, Vol. II. *Appendices, Indices, and Plates*, Lancaster/London, 2008.

RPC 1 Burnett, A., M. Amandry, and P. Ripollès, *Roman Provincial Coinage* I, London/Paris, 1998.

SNG *Sylloge Nummorum Graecorum.*

Sv. Svoronos, J.-N. *Τα νομίσματα του κράτους των Πτολεμαίων*, 4 vols., Athens, 1904–1908.

WDSP Gropp, D. M. *Wadi Daliyeh I. The Samaria Papyri from Wadi Daliyeh*, Oxford, 2001.

WSM Newell, E. T. *The Coinage of the Western Seleucid Mints from Seleucus I to Antiochus III*, New York, 1941.

Bibliography

Anonymous. 1899. "Marash. Athenian Coins", *American Journal of Archaeology*, p. 251.

_______. 1900. "Münzfunde", *Blätter für Münzfreunde* 8/9, p. 137.

_______. 1969. *Annual Report of the American Numismatic Society for the Period Ending September* 30, New York.

_______. 1975. "A Hoard of Test-cut Athenian Tetradrachms", *Journal of Numismatic Fine Arts* 4, p. 30.

Abou Diwan, G. 2010. *Sidon de l'inauguration du monnayage municipal à la colonie sévérienne. Approche historique et monétaire (169/8 av. J.-C. - 235 ap. J.-C.)*, 2 vol., unpublished thesis, Université Paris I, 13 mars 2010.

Abou Diwan, G., W. Khalil, and M. Khreich. 2006. "Problèmes et entraves de l'historien au Proche-Orient: l'exemple du Liban", *Réflexions croisées sur le 'métier' d'historien du Proche-Orient antique, Actes de la table ronde de l'Institut catholique de Paris, 5 novembre 2004. Transeuphratène* 31, pp. 115–116.

Agut-Labordère, D. 2014. "L'orge et l'argent. Les usages monétaires à 'Ayn Manâwir à l'époque perse", *Annales. Histoire, Sciences sociales* 69/1 (janvier-mars), pp. 75–90.

Alfaro Asins, C., C. Marcos Alonso, P. Otero Morán, P. Grañeda Miñon (eds.). 2009. *Diccionario de Numismática*, Madrid.

Amandry, M. (ed.). 2001. *Dictionnaire de numismatique*, Paris.

Amandry, M. and D. Bateson. 2009. "Introduction générale," in M. Amandry and D. Bateson (eds.) *A Survey of Numismatic Research 2002–2009*. Glasgow, pp. x–xii.

Anderson, L. and P. Van Alfen. 2008. "A Fourth Century BCE Hoard from the Near East", *American Journal of Numismatics* 20, pp. 155–198, pls. 47–58.

Andreau, J. 2008. "The Use and Survival of Coins and of Gold and Silver in the Vesuvian Cities," in W. V. Harris (ed.) *The Monetary System of the Greeks and the Romans*. Oxford, pp. 208–225.

Ariel, D. T. 1986. "The Coins," in L. I. Levine and L. I. Netzer (eds.) *Excavations at Caesarea Maritima, 1975, 1976, 1979. Final Report, Qedem* 21. Jerusalem, pp. 137–148.

_______. 1999. In A. Gorzalczany and Y. Rand (eds.) "Tel Michal," *Hadashot Arkheologiyot - Excavations and Surveys in Israel* 109, pp. 49–50.

_______. 2000. "Coins from the Synagogue at Korazim," in Z. Yeivin, *The Synagogue at Korazim: the 1962-1964, 1980-1987 Excavations*. Jerusalem, pp. 33–49.

_______. 2002. "Israel law regarding antiquities," *Conseil International de Numismatique. Compte Rendu* 49, pp. 63–64 = "Israel law regarding antiquities," *Conseil International de Numismatique. Compte Rendu* 45 (1999), pp. 76–77.

_______. 2006a. "Coins from Tel Mikhal (Tel Michal)," *'Atiqot* 52, pp. 71–88.

_______. 2006b. "The Coins," in H. Geva (ed.) *Jewish Quarter Excavations in the Old City of Jerusalem Conducted by Nahman Avigad, 1969-1982. Vol. III. Area E and Other Studies, Final Report*. Jerusalem, pp. 192–217.

_______. 2007. "Coins of En-Gedi," in E. Stern (ed.) *En-Gedi Excavations, 1. Conducted by B. Mazar and I. Dunayevsky. Final Report (1961–1965)*. Jerusalem, pp. 423–427.

Arslan, M. and M. J. Price. 1994. "A Hoard from the Durmaz Collection from the Region of Antakya," *CH* 8, pp. 80–81, pls. 30,37–31,1.

Aubin, G. 2007. "Les trésors (monétaires) antiques: le mot, les choses et les chercheurs," in F. Baratte, M. Joly, and J.-C. Béal (eds.) *Autour du trésor de Mâcon. Luxe et quotidien en Gaule romaine*. Mâcon, pp. 51–73.

_______. 2012. "The Law and Practice Regarding Coin Finds. La législation française sur les trouvailles monétaires," *Conseil International de Numismatique. Compte Rendu* 59, pp. 18–26.

Augé, C. 1985. "Les monnaies de la fouille de Si' et la circulation monétaire antique dans le Hauran," in J.-M. Dentzer (ed.) *Hauran I. Recherches archéologiques sur la Syrie du Sud à l'époque hellénistique et romaine*, I, BAH 124. Beirut, pp. 205–218.

_______. 1987. "La réutilisation des monnaies de bronze à l'époque impériale: quelques exemples proche-orientaux," in G. Depeyrot, T. Hackens, and G. Moucharte (eds.) *Rythmes de la production monétaire de l'Antiquité à nos jours*. Louvain-la-Neuve, pp. 227–235.

_______. 2000. "Les monnaies de Ras Ibn Hani, près de Lattaquié et les guerres de Syrie," *Revue Numismatique*, pp. 59–69.

_______. 2001. "Note sur le trésor de monnaies ptolémaïques de 'Iraq al-Amir (Jordanie)," *Annual of the Department of Antiquities of Jordan* 45, pp. 483–485.

_______. 2003. "Les monnaies de Si' 8," in J. Dentzer-Feydy, J.-M. Dentzer, and P.-M. Blanc (eds.) *Hauran II. Les installations de Si' 8: du sanctuaire à l'établissement viticole*, I. Beirut, pp. 230–266.

Augé, C., A. Davesne, and R. Ergeç. 1994. "Le début des tétradrachmes d'Athènes du 'nouveau style': un trésor trouvé près de Gaziantep en 1994," *Anatolia Antiqua* 5, p. 44–82.

Avigad, N. 1983. *Discovering Jerusalem*, Jerusalem.

Babelon, E. 1901–1907. *Traité des monnaies grecques et romaines*. Paris.

Badawi, M. 2009. *Jablé (Syrie) et son territoire à l'époque hellénistique et romaine: développement urbain et culture matérielle*, 2 vol., thèse inédite, Université Paris I, 28 mars 2009.

Balmuth, M. S. and C. M. Thompson. 2000. "*Hacksilber*: Recent Approaches to the Study of Hoards of Uncoined Silver. Laboratory Analyses and Geographical Distribution," in B. Kluge and B. Weisser (eds.), *XII. internationaler numismatischer Kongress, Berlin 1997. Akten* I. Berlin, pp. 159–169.

Barag, D. 1991. "Jewish Coins in Hellenistic and Roman Time," in T. Hackens *et al.* (eds.) *A Survey of Numismatic Research, 1985–1990*, I. Brussels, pp. 106–108.

_______. 1994–1999. "The Coinage of Yehud and the Ptolemies," *Israel Numismatic Journal* 13, pp. 27–38.

_______. 2007–2008. "Ptolemaic Silver Currency of Cyprus in Seleucid Phoenicia and Coele Syria," *Israel Numismatic Journal* 16, pp. 28–56.

Baramki, J. 1945. "Coin Hoards from Palestine II," *Quarterly of the Department of Antiquities in Palestine* 11, pp. 86–90.

Barkay, R. 1992–1993. "The Marisa Hoard of Seleucid Tetradrachms minted in Ascalon," *Israel Numismatic Journal* 12, pp. 21–26, pls. 3–5.

_______. 2003–2006. "Undated Coins from Hellenistic Marisa," *Israel Numismatic Journal* 15, pp. 48–55.

Baslez, M.-F. 1989. "La circulation et le rôle des dariques en Grèce d'Europe à la fin du Ve et au IVe s.: apport des inscriptions phéniciennes et grecques," *Revue des Etudes Anciennes*, pp. 237–246.

Bellinger, A. R. 1949. *The Excavations at Dura-Europos conducted by Yale University and the French Academy of Inscriptions and Letters, Final Report, VI, The Coins*. New Haven.

_______. 1950–1951. "An Alexander Hoard from Byblos," *Berytus* 10, pp. 37–49.

_______. 1962. "Coins," in H. D. Colt (ed.) *Excavations at Nessana (Auja Hafir, Palestine)* I. London, pp. 70–75.

Bercé, Y.-M. 2004. *A la découverte des trésors cachés du XVIe siècle à nos jours*. Paris.

Berman, A. 2003. "Hippos-Sussita 4th season (July 2003). The Coins Find Catalogue," in A. Segal *et al.* (eds.) *Hippos-Sussita. Fourth Season of Excavations (June–July 2003)*. Haifa, pp. 89–101.

_______. 2004. "The Coins Find Catalogue - Hippos-Sussita 5th season (2004)," in A. Segal *et al.* (eds.), *Hippos-Sussita. Fifth Season of Excavations (September–October 2004) and Summary of all Five Seasons (2000–2004)*. Haifa, pp. 123–134.

_______. 2005. "The Coins Catalogue - Hippos-Sussita 6th season (2005)," in A. Segal *et al.* (eds.) *Hippos-Sussita. Sixth Season of Excavations (July 2005)*. Haifa, pp. 108–112.

_______. 2006. "The Coins Catalogue - Hippos-Sussita 7th season (2006)," in A. Segal *et al.* (eds.) *Hippos-Sussita. Seventh Season of Excavations (July 2006)*. Haifa, pp. 144–153.

_______. 2007. A., "The Coins Catalogue - 8th season (2007)," in A. Segal *et al.* (eds.) *Hippos-Sussita. Eighth Season of Excavations (July 2007)*. Haifa, pp. 155–171.

_______. 2008. "Hippos-Sussita - 9th season (2008) - Coins Catalogue," in A. Segal *et al.* (eds.) *Hippos-Sussita. Ninth Season of Excavations (June–July 2008)*. Haifa, pp. 143–162.

_______. 2009. "Hippos-Sussita - 10th season (2009) - Coins Catalogue," in A. Segal *et al.* (eds.) *Hippos-Sussita. Tenth Season of Excavations (July and September 2009)*. Haifa, pp. 157–172.

_______. 2010. "Hippos-Sussita - 11th season (2010) - Coins Catalogue," in A. Segal *et al.* (eds.) *Hippos-Sussita. Eleventh Season of Excavations (July 2010).* Haifa, pp. 153–169.

_______. 2013. "The Coin Finds of Hippos-Sussita," in A. Segal *et al.* (eds.) *Hippos-Sussita of the Decapolis. The First Twelve Seasons of Excavations. 2000–2011*, Vol. I. Haifa, pp. 279–301.

Berman, A. and D. T. Berman. 1999. "Coins from Excavations at Giv'at Yasaf, Tell er-Ras," *'Atiqot* 37, pp. 23–24.

Betlyon, J. W. 1976. "A New Chronology for the Pre-Alexandrine Coinage of Sidon," *American Numismatic Society. Museum Notes* 21, pp. 11–35, pls. II–IV.

Bijovsky, G. 2004. "A Hoard of Coins of Mattathias Antigonus from 'Ein Feshkha," *Israel Exploration Journal* 54/1, pp. 75–76.

_______. 2007. "The Coins," in Y. Hirschfeld (ed.) *En-Gedi Excavations, 2. Final Report (1996–2002).* Jerusalem, pp. 157–233.

_______. 2009. "The Levant," in M. Amandry and D. Bateson (eds.) *A Survey of Numismatic Research, 2002–2007.* Glasgow, pp. 90–103.

Blanc, J. 2000. *Les monnaies parallèles. Unité et diversité du fait monétaire.* Paris.

Blanchet, A. 1900. *Les trésors de monnaies romaines et les invasions germaniques en Gaule.* Paris.

_______. 1907. "Chronique," *Revue Numismatique*, pp. 111–121.

_______. 1936. "Les rapports entre les dépôts monétaires et les événements militaires, politiques et économiques," *Revue Numismatique*, pp. 1–70.

Bland, R. 1995. "The Law of 'Treasure trove' in England and Wales," *Commission Internationale de Numismatique. Compte rendu* 42, pp. 62–74.

Bodenstedt, F. 1981. *Die Elektronmünzen von Phokaia und Mytilene.* Tübingen.

Boehringer, C. 1972. *Zur Chronologie mittelhellenistischer Münzserien, 220–160 v. Chr.* Berlin.

Bordreuil, P. and E. Gubel (eds.). 1990. "Bulletin d'Antiquités archéologiques du Levant inédites ou méconnues VI," *Syria* 67, pp. 483–520.

Borghesi, B. 1862–1864. *Œuvres complètes.* T. 1–2, *Œuvres numismatiques.* Paris.

_______. 1868–1872. *Œuvres complètes.* T. 6–8, *Lettres.* Paris.

Bounni, A., J. Lagarce, E. Lagarce, and N. Saliby. 1978. "Rapport préliminaire sur la deuxième campagne de fouilles (1976) à Ras Ibn Hani (Syrie)," *Syria* 55, pp. 233–301.

Brandis, J. 1886. *Das Münz-, Mass- und Gewichtswesen in Vorderasien bis auf Alexander den Grossen.* Berlin.

Bresson, A. 2002. "L'inscription agoranomique du Pirée et le contrôle des prix de détail en Grèce ancienne," in *La cité marchande.* Bordeaux, pp. 151–182.

_______. 2008. *L'économie de la Grèce des cités. I. Les structures de la production. II. Les espaces de l'échange.* Paris.

_______. Forthcoming. "Coins and trade in Hellenistic Asia Minor: the Pamphylian hub" in B. Woytek (ed.), *Infrastructure and Distribution in Ancient Economies. The Flow of Money, Goods and Services.* Vienna.

Brett, A. B. 1945. "Seleucid Coins of Ake-Ptolemais in Phoenicia, Seleucos IV to Tryphon," *American Numismatic Society. Museum Notes* 1, pp. 27–28.

Briant, P. 1996. *Histoire de l'Empire perse, de Cyrus à Alexandre*. Paris.

Briend, J. and J.-B. Humbert (eds.). 1980. *Tell Keisan (1971–1976), un cité phénicienne en Galilée*. Paris.

Burnett, A. 2000. "The Scheme for Recording Portable Antiquities in Britain: Progress Report," *Commission Internationale de Numismatique. Compte rendu* 47, pp. 78–85.

_______. 2002. "Syrian Coinage and Romanisation from Pompey to Domitian," in C. Augé and F. Duyrat (eds.) *Les monnayages syriens. Quel apport pour l'histoire du Proche-Orient hellénistique et romain ? Actes de la table ronde de Damas, 10–11 novembre 1999*. Beirut, pp. 115–122.

Butcher, K. 1996. "Bey 006. The Coins – Preliminary Report," *BAAL. Bulletin d'Archéologie et d'Architecture Libanaises* 1, pp. 207–211.

_______. 2001–2002. *Small Change in Ancient Beirut: the Coin Finds from Bey 006 and Bey 045. Persian, Hellenistic, Roman and Byzantine Periods. Archaeology of the Beirut Souks: AUB and ACRE Excavations in Beirut, 1994–1996. Berytus*, pp. 45–46.

_______. 2002. "Circulation of bronze coinage in the Orontes valley in the late Hellenistic and early Roman periods," in C. Augé and F. Duyrat (eds.) *Les monnayages syriens. Quel apport pour l'histoire du Proche-Orient hellénistique et romain ? Damas, 10–11 novembre 1999*. Beirut, pp. 145–152.

Buttrey, T. V. 1982. "Pharaonic Imitations of Athenian tetradrachms," *Actes du congrès international de numismatique, Berne 1979*, I, Berne, pp. 137–140.

Buxton, R. F. 2009. "The Northern Syria 2007 Hoard of Athenian Owls from the Near East: Behavioral Aspects," *American Journal of Numismatics* 21, pp. 1–27, pls. 1–3.

Cahill, N. 2002. *Household and City Organization at Olynthus*. New Haven.

Cahn, H. A. 1970. *Knidos. Die Münzen des sechsten und des fünften Jahrhunderts v. Chr.* Berlin.

Callataÿ, F. (de). 1989. "Les trésors achéménides et les monnayages d'Alexandre: espèces immobilisées et espèces circulantes ?" *L'or perse et l'histoire grecque. Revue des études anciennes* 91/1–2, pp. 259–274.

_______. 1993. "Les tétradrachmes hellénistiques de Tripolis," *Numismatica e Antichità Classiche* 22, pp. 111–123.

_______. 1994. "Réflexions sur les ateliers d'Asie Mineure d'Alexandre le Grand," *Trésors et circulation monétaire en Anatolie antique*, Paris, pp. 19–35.

_______. 1996. "Quelques estimations relatives au nombre de monnaies grecques: les collections publiques et privées, le commerce et les trésors," *Revue belge de numismatique* 143, pp. 21–94.

_______. 1997a. *L'histoire des guerres mithridatiques vue par les monnaies*. Louvain-la-Neuve.

_______. 1997b. *Recueil quantitatif des émissions monétaires hellénistiques*. Wetteren.

_______. 1999. "Fiscalité et monnayage dans l'œuvre de Georges Le Rider," in M. Amandry and S. Hurter (eds.) *Travaux de numismatique grecque offerts à G. Le Rider*. London, pp. 109–121.

_______. 2002. "La production des tétradrachmes civiques de la Cilicie jusqu'à la Palestine à la fin du IIe siècle et dans la première moitié du Ier siècle avant J.-C. (Elaiussa Sébastè, Aigeai, Séleucie-de-Piérie, Laodicée, Arados, Tripolis, Sidon, Tyr, Ascalon)," in C. Augé and F. Duyrat (eds.) *Les monnayages syriens. Quel apport pour l'histoire du Proche-Orient hellénistique et romain ? Actes de la table ronde de Damas, 10–11 novembre 1999*. Beirut, pp. 71–89.

_______. 2003. Compte rendu de M. Pfisterer, *Ein Silberschatz vom Schwarzen Meer. Beobartungen zum Geldumlauf im Achaimenidenreich*, Paris, 2000, in *Revue belge de numismatique* 149, pp. 267–272.

_______. 2004. "La richesse des rois séleucides et le problème de la taxation en nature," in V. Chankowski and F. Duyrat (eds.) *Le roi et l'économie. Autonomies locales et structures royales dans l'économie de l'empire séleucide. Topoi*, Supplement 6, pp. 23–47.

_______. 2005. "L'instauration par Ptolémée Ier Sôter d'une économie monétaire fermée et la question de l'approvisionnement intentionnel en numéraire," in F. Duyrat and O. Picard (eds.) *L'exception égyptienne ? Production et échanges monétaires en Egypte hellénistique et romaine. Actes du colloque d'Alexandrie, 13–15 avril 2002*, Etudes alexandrines 10, IFAO. Cairo, pp. 117–134.

_______. 2006a. "Réflexions quantitatives sur l'or et l'argent non monnayés à l'époque hellénistique (pompes, triomphes, réquisitions, fortunes des temples, orfèvrerie et masses métalliques disponibles)," *Approches de l'économie hellénistique*, Saint-Bertrand-de-Comminges, pp. 37–84.

_______. 2006b. "Greek Coins from Archaeological Excavations: a Conspectus and a Call for Chronological Tables," in P. Van Alfen (ed.), *Agoranomia: Studies in Money and Exchange Presented to John H. Kroll*. New York, pp. 177–200.

_______. 2006c. Compte rendu de Gitler, Tal 2006, *Israel Numismatic Research* 1, pp. 167–169.

_______. 2010. "Le comte de Caylus et l'étude des monnaies antiques," *Comptes rendus de l'Académie des Inscriptions et Belles Lettres* (juillet–octobre), pp. 1329–1364.

_______. 2012. "Les statères de Pergame et les réquisitions d'Alexandre le Grand: l'apport d'un nouveau trésor ('Statères de Pergame 2004')," *Revue Numismatique*, pp. 179–196.

_______. 2013. "The coinages of the Attalids and their neighbours: a quantified overview," in P. Thonemann (ed.) *Attalid Asia Minor. Money, International Relations, and the State*, Oxford, pp. 207–244.

Callataÿ, F. (de), G. Depeyrot, and L. Villaronga. 1993. *L'argent monnayé d'Alexandre le Grand à Auguste*. Brussels. 1993.

Callot, O. 2002. "Les monnaies des environs de Ras Shamra," in C. Augé and F. Duyrat (eds.) *Les monnayages syriens. Quel apport pour l'histoire du Proche-Orient hellénistique et romain ? Actes de la table ronde de Damas, 10–11 novembre 1999*. Beirut, pp. 93–103.

Campbell, E. F. 1960. "Excavations at Shechem, 1960," *The Biblical Archaeologist* 23/4, pp. 102–110.

Capdetrey, L. 2007. *Le pouvoir séleucide. Territoire, administration, finances d'un royaume hellénistique (312–129 avant J.-C.)*. Rennes.

Carcassonne, C. and A. Davesne. 1987. "Le trésor de Gülnar: considérations sur le rythme de la production monétaire au IIIe s. av. J.-C.," in G. Depeyrot, T. Hackens, and G. Moucharte (eds.) *Rythmes de la production monétaire de l'Antiquité à nos jours*. Louvain-la-Neuve, pp. 21–29.

Carradice, I. 1987. "The 'Regal' Coinage of the Persian Empire," in I. Carradice (ed.) *Coinage and Administration in the Athenian and Persian Empires*. Oxford, pp. 73–95, pls. X–XV.

_______. 1994. "The Coins," in K. J. H. Vriezen (ed.), *Die Ausgrabungen unter der Erlöserkirche im Muristan, Jerusalem (1970–1974)*. Wiesbaden, pp. 311–330.

_______. 1998. "The Dinar hoard of Persian sigloi," in R. Ashton and S. Hurter (eds.) *Studies in Greek Numismatics in Memory of M. J. Price*. London, pp. 65–81, pls. 17–20.

Carrez-Maratray, J.-Y. 2007. "Les monnaies," D. Valbelle (dir.) *Tell el-Herr, les niveaux hellénistiques et du Haut-Empire*, Paris, pp. 226–235.

Casana, J. 2007. "Structural Transformations in Settlement Systems of the Northern Levant," *American Journal of Archaeology* 111/2 (April), pp. 195–221.

_______. 2015. "Satellite Imagery-Based Analysis of Archaeological Looting in Syria", *Near Eastern Archaeology, Special Issue: The Cultural Heritage Crisis in the Middle East* 78/3 (September), pp. 142–152.

Casey, E. J. and R. Reece (eds.). 1974. *Coins and the Archaeologist*, British Archaeological Report 4. London.

Chankowski, V. Forthcoming. *Parasites du dieu. Pratiques financières et vie économique dans la Délos hellénistique*.

Chéhab, M. 1977. *Monnaies gréco-romaines et phéniciennes du Musée national, Beyrouth, Liban*. Paris.

Chryssanthaki, K. 2005. "Les monnaies lagides en Egée," in F. Duyrat and O. Picard (eds.) *L'exception égyptienne ? Production et échanges monétaires en Egypte hellénistique et romaine*. Cairo, pp. 159–175.

Clarke, G. W. and H. Jackson. 2002–2003. "Jebel Khalid on the Euphrates: an Overview," *Annales archéologiques arabes syriennes* 45–46, pp. 189–206.

Comstock, M. and C. Vermeule. 1964. *Greek Coins, 1950 to 1963, Boston Museum of Fine Arts*. Boston.

Connor, M. and D. D. Scott. 1998. "Metal Detector Use in Archaeology: an Introduction," *Historical Archaeology* 32–4, pp. 76–85.

Courbin, P. 1953. "Recherches archéologiques dans la région de Marathus. Note préliminaire," *Annales archéologiques arabes syriennes*, pp. 165–170.

_______. 1986. "Bassit," *Syria* 63, pp. 175–220.

_______. 1989. "Bassit," *Contribution française à l'archéologie syrienne 1969–1989*, Damascus, pp. 102–106.

Crawford, M. H. 1990. "From Borghesi to Mommsen: the Creation of an Exact Science," in M. H. Crawford, C. R. Ligota, and J. B. Trapp (eds.) *Medals and Coins from Budé to Mommsen*. London, pp. 125–132.

Cross, F. M. 1963. "The Discovery of the Samaria Papyri," *The Biblical Archaeologist* 26/4, pp. 110–121.

Crowfoot, J. W. and G. M. Fitzgerald. 1927. *Excavations in the Tyropoeon Valley, Palestine Exploration Fund Annual*. Jerusalem.

Curiel, R. and D. Schlumberger. 1953. *Trésors monétaires d'Afghanistan*. Paris.

Daremberg, C. and Saglio, E. (eds.). 1877–1919. *Dictionnaire des Antiquités grecques et romaines*. Paris.

Daux, G. 1954. "Décret de Sigée trouvé en Corse," *Bulletin de correspondance hellénique* 80, pp. 53–56.

Davesne, A. 1999. "La seconde guerre de Syrie (*ca.* 261–255 avant J.-C.) et les témoignages numismatiques," in M. Amandry and S. Hurter (eds.), *Travaux de numismatique grecque offerts à G. Le Rider*. London, pp. 123–134.

Davesne, A. and A. Lemaire. 1996. "Trésors hellénistiques du Proche-Orient," *Revue Numismatique*, pp. 51–76.

Davesne, A. and G. Le Rider. 1989. *Le trésor de Meydancıkkale, Cilicie Trachée*, 1980, 2 vols. Paris.

Davesne, A. and V. Yenisoğanci. 1992. "Les Ptolémées en Séleucide: le trésor d'Hüseyinli," *Revue Numismatique*, pp. 23–36.

Davies, J. K. 1971. *Athenian Propertied Families, 600–300* BC. Oxford.

Dembski, G. 2001. "Münzfunde und Münzsammlungen – die gesetzlichen Bestimmungen in Österreich", *Commission Internationale de Numismatique. Compte rendu* 48, pp. 66–68.

Dentzer J.-M., F. Villeneuve, and F. Larché. 1982. "Iraq el-Amir: Excavations at the Monumental Gateway," in *Studies in the History and Archaeology of Jordan* I, Amman, pp. 201–207.

Dermigny L. 1955. "La France à la fin de l'Ancien régime: une carte monétaire," *Annales E.S.C.* 10/4, pp. 480–493.

DeRose Evans, J. 1995. "Ancient Coins from the Drew Institute of Archaeological Research Excavations of Caesarea Maritima, 1971–1984," *The Biblical Archaeologist* 58/3, pp. 156–166.

Desneux, J. 1949. "Les tétradrachmes d'Akanthos", *Revue belge de numismatique* 95, pp. 5–122.

Destrooper-Georgiades, A. 1987. "La Phénicie et Chypre à l'époque achéménide: témoignages numismatiques," *Studia Phoenicia* V, Leuven, p. 351 and n. 48.

Deutsch, R. 1994–1999. "Five Unrecorded 'Yehud' Silver Coins," *Israel Numismatic Journal* 13, pp. 25–26.

Donceel, R. 2007. "Canatha de la Décapole de Syrie. Contribution à l'établissement du catalogue des monnaies et à l'examen des types," in G. Moucharte *et al.* (eds.), *Liber Amicorum Tony Hackens*, Louvain-la-Neuve, pp. 229–266.

Doumergue, C. 2008. *Les mines antiques. La production des métaux aux époques grecque et romaine*. Paris.

Doyen, J.-M. 1987a. *Les monnaies du Tell Abou Danné et d'Oumm el-Marra (campagnes 1976–1985). Aspects de la circulation monétaire en Syrie du Nord sous les Séleucides*. Brussels.

________. 1987b. *Musées de Charleville-Mézières. Catalogue des monnaies antiques, monnaies du monde celtique et des cités grecques*. Paris. (*non vidi*)

Draganov, D. 1993. *The Coinage of Cabyle*. Sofia.

________. 1994. "Cabyle in the mid-third century BC according to numismatic data", in D. Draganov (ed.), *Studies on settlement life in ancient Thrace : proceedings of the IIIrd International Symposium "Cabyle," 17–21 May 1993*. Jambol, pp. 277–282.

Droulers, F. 1980. *Les trésors de monnaies royales de Louis XIII à Louis XVI découverts en France et dans le monde depuis le XIXe siècle*. Paris.

Dubois, L. 1996. *Inscriptions grecques dialectales d'Olbia du Pont*. Geneva.

Dunand, M. 1939. *Fouilles de Byblos* I, *1926–1932*. Paris.

_______. 1958. *Fouilles de Byblos* II, *1933–1938*. Paris.

Durand, C. 2008. *Le rôle des Nabatéens dans le commerce oriental et méditerranéen de l'époque hellénistique aux campagnes de Trajan (IVe s. av. J.-C. – IIe s. ap. J.-C.). Etude historique et archéologique*. Unpublished thesis, Université Lyon II, 29 nov. 2008.

Durand, X. 2003. *Des Grecs en Palestine au IIIe siècle avant J.-C. Le dossier syrien des archives de Zénon de Caunos (261–252)*. Paris.

Dušek, J. 2007. *Les manuscrits araméens du Wadi Daliyeh et la Samarie vers 450–332 av. J.-C.* Leiden.

Duyrat, F. 2002a. "Les ateliers monétaires de Phénicie du Nord à l'époque hellénistique," in Chr. Augé and F. Duyrat (eds.) *Les monnayages syriens. Quel apport pour l'histoire du Proche-Orient hellénistique et romain ? Actes de la table ronde de Damas, 10–11 novembre 1999*. Beirut, pp. 21–70.

_______. 2002b. Compte rendu de G. Le Rider, *Antioche de Syrie sous les Séleucides. Corpus des monnaies d'or et d'argent. I. De Séleucos I à Antiochos V,* c. *300–161*, Paris, 1999 in *Revue Numismatique* 158, pp. 408–417.

_______. 2003. "La politique monétaire d'Arados: les alexandres (IVe-IIe siècles avant notre ère)," *La Syrie hellénistique. Colloque de Tours, 6–8 octobre 2000, Topoi*, Supplement 4, pp. 25–48.

_______. 2004. "La circulation monétaire dans l'Orient séleucide (Syrie, Phénicie, Mésopotamie, Iran)," in V. Chankowski and F. Duyrat (eds.) *Le roi et l'économie. Autonomies locales et structures royales dans l'économie de l'empire séleucide. Topoi*, Supplement 6, pp. 381–424.

_______. 2005a. *Arados hellénistique. Étude historique et monétaire*. Beirut.

_______. 2005b. "Le trésor de Damanhour (*IGCH* 1664) et la circulation monétaire en Egypte hellénistique", in F. Duyrat and O. Picard (eds.) *L'exception égyptienne ? Production et échanges monétaires en Egypte hellénistique et romaine. Actes du colloque d'Alexandrie, 13–15 avril 2002,* Etudes alexandrines 10, IFAO. Cairo, pp. 17–51.

_______. 2008. "Bibliographie numismatique de la Syrie III. Périodes achéménide, hellénistique, romaine et byzantine (2000–2005)," *Syria* 85, pp. 347–376.

_______. 2011a. "Guerre et thésaurisation en Syrie hellénistique, IVe – Ier s. av. J.-C.," in Th. Faucher, O. Picard, and M.-C. Marcellesi (eds.) *Nomisma. La circulation monétaire dans le monde grec antique, Actes du colloque international, Athènes, 14–17 avril 2010, BCH Supplement* 53, pp. 417–431.

_______. 2011b. "La conquête macédonienne: monnaie et mutations politiques en Transeuphratène occidentale," *Transeuphratène* 40, pp. 61–81.

_______. 2012. "Tigrane en Syrie. Un roi sans images," in A. Suspène and F. Duyrat (eds.) *Le* Charaktèr *du Prince. Expressions monétaires du pouvoir en temps de troubles, Cahiers d'histoire ancienne* 49, pp. 167–209. http://etudesanciennes.revues.org/491.

_______. 2013. "La frontière entre les possessions lagides et séleucides en Syrie," in G. Gorre and P. Kossmann (eds.) *Espace et territoire de l'Egypte gréco-romaine*. Geneva, pp. 1–25.

_______. 2014. "Circulation of Coins and Economic History in Hellenistic Syria, 6th–1st century BC," in B. Van der Spek (ed.) *The Efficiency of Markets in Pre-Industrial Societies: the Case of Babylonia (c. 400–60 BC) in Comparative Perspective*, pp. 363–395.

_______. Forthcoming. "Phoenician Alexanders," in S. Kremydi and M.-C. Marcellesi (eds.) *Les alexandres après Alexandre: histoire d'une monnaie commune, colloque international d'Athènes*, 23–24 mai 2014.

Duyrat, F. and J. Olivier. 2010. "Deux politiques de l'or. Séleucides et Lagides au IIIe s. av. J.-C.," in *Regards croisés en numismatique. Journées scientifiques en hommage aux travaux de Jean-Noël Barrandon, Orléans, 12 décembre 2008, Revue Numismatique*, pp. 71–93.

Eckhel, J. H. 1792. *Doctrina numorum veterum conscripta*. Vienna.

Elayi, J. 1987. "Al Mina sur l'Oronte à l'époque perse," in E. Lipinski (ed.) *Phoenicia and the East Mediterranean in the First Millenium BC, Studia Phoenicia V*. Leuven, pp. 249–266.

_______. 1992. "Le phénomène monétaire dans les cités phéniciennes à l'époque perse," *Numismatique et histoire économique phéniciennes et puniques*, Studia Phoenicia 9, Louvain-la-Neuve, pp. 21–31.

_______. 1999. "Un trésor de tétradrachmes aux types d'Alexandre trouvé dans la Beqa'," in M. Amandry and S. Hurter (eds.) *Travaux de numismatique grecque offerts à G. Le Rider*. London, pp. 135–138, pl. 11.

_______. 2006. "An Updated Chronology of the Reigns of Phoenician Kings during the Persian Period (539–333 BCE)," *Transeuphratène* 32, pp. 11–43.

_______. 2008. "On Dating the Reigns of Phoenician Kings in the Persian Period," in C. Sagona (ed.), *Beyond the Homeland: Markers in Phoenician Chronology*. Leuven, pp. 97–112.

Elayi, J. and A.-G. Elayi. 1986. "A Treasure of Coins from Arwad," *The Journal of the Ancient Near Eastern Society* 18, pp. 3–24, pls. I–VI.

_______. 1990. "Trésor d'époque perse de la région d'Arwad," *Revue Numismatique*, pp. 7–16, pls. 1–2.

_______. 1991a. "Un trésor de monnaies séleucides de la trouée de Homs," in R. Martini and N. Vismara (eds.), *Ermanno A. Arslan Studia Dicata*, Glaux. Milan, 157–162, pls. xxxviii–xxxix.

_______. 1991b. "Les monnaies de Tyr au dauphin et à la rosette," *Annotazioni numismatiche* 3, pp. 38–42.

_______. 1993a. *Trésors de monnaies phéniciennes et circulation monétaire (V–IVe s. av. J.-C.)*. Paris.

_______. 1993b. "Nouveau trésor de monnaies de Byblos (1992)", *Revue belge de numismatique* 139, pp. 17–30, pls. I–IV.

_______. 1994. "Un nouveau trésor de tétradrachmes athéniens," *Revue Numismatique*, pp. 26–33, pls. 1–3.

_______. 1996. "Nouveaux trésors de monnaies phéniciennes (*CH* VIII)," *Transeuphratène* 11, pp. 95–114.

_______. 1998. "Une série de petits bronzes d'Alexandre frappés à Tyr," *Revue Numismatique*, pp. 107–117.

_______. 1999. "Nouveau trésor de monnaies aradiennes, athéniennes et / ou pseudo-athéniennes," *Transeuphratène* 18 (1999), pp. 75–84.

_______. 2001. "Un nouveau trésor de tétradrachmes d'Alexandre II Zébina," *Annotazioni numismatiche* 43, pp. 999–1004.

_______. 2002. "Un trésor de monnaies séleucides de la région de Hama," *Revue Numismatique*, pp. 93–102, pls. V–VIII.

_______. 2003a. "Quelques compléments à l'étude du trésor sidonien de Beithir TXXI," *Bulletin de la société française de numismatique* 58/2 (2003), pp. 33–35.

_______. 2003b. "Nouveaux trésors de monnaies phéniciennes (*CH* IX)," *Transeuphratène* 26, pp. 105–117.

_______. 2004a. "Un nouveau trésor de monnaies séleucides de la région d'Apamée de Syrie," *Bulletin du Cercle d'études numismatiques* 41/2 (mai-août), pp. 43–62.

_______. 2004b. *Le monnayage de la cité phénicienne de Sidon à l'époque perse (Ve–IVe s. av. J.-C.)*, *Transeuphratène* Supplement no. 11. Paris.

_______. 2009a. "Nouveau trésor de Byblos d'après les archives de H. Seyrig (TLXXXIII)", *Transeuphratène* 38, pp. 65–76.

_______. 2009b. *The Coinage of the Phoenician City of Tyre in the Persian Period (5th–4th century BCE)*. Leuven.

Elayi, J. and A. Lemaire. 2009. "Le trésor de Byblos TIX," *Transeuphratène* 38, pp. 77–98, pls. IX–XI.

Faucher, T. 2013. *Frapper monnaie. La fabrication de la monnaie de bronze à Alexandrie sous les Ptolémées*. Alexandria.

Faucher, T., F. Téreygeol, L. Brousseau, and A. Arles. 2009. "A la recherche des ateliers monétaires grecs: l'apport de l'expérimentation," *Revue Numismatique*, pp. 43–80.

Feugère, M. and M. Py. 2011. *Dictionnaire des monnaies découvertes en Gaule méditerranéenne (530–27 av. notre ère)*. Paris.

Feyel, C. 2006. *Les artisans dans les sanctuaires grecs aux époques hellénistique et classique à travers la documentation financière en Grèce*. Paris.

Feyel, M. 1936. "Nouvelles inscriptions d'Akraiphia," *Bulletin de correspondance hellénique* 60, pp. 11–36.

Fischer, T. 1968. "Zwei Münzschätze aus der Zeit des Seleukiden Demetrios II. vergraben um 126/5 (?) v. Chr.," *Schweizer Münzblätter* 18/70 (May), pp. 51–52.

Fischer-Bossert, W. 2008. *The Athenian Decadrachm*. ANS NNM 168. New York.

Fitzgerald, G. M. 1931. *Beth-Shan Excavations 1921–1923. The Arab and Byzantine Levels*. Philadelphia.

Flament, C. 2000. "Les imitations de monnaies athéniennes retrouvées en Cilicie et en Syrie du Nord," *Revue des Archéologues et des Historiens d'Art de Louvain* 33, pp. 184–185.

_______. 2003. "Imitations athéniennes ou monnaies authentiques ? Nouvelles considérations sur quelques chouettes athéniennes habituellement identifiées comme imitations," *Revue belge de numismatique* 149, pp. 1–10.

_______. 2005. "Un trésor de tétradrachmes athéniens dispersés suivi de considérations relatives au classement, à la frappe et à l'attribution des chouettes à des ateliers étrangers," *Revue belge de numismatique* 151, pp. 29–38.

_______. 2007. *Le monnayage en argent d'Athènes de l'époque archaïque à l'époque hellénistique (c. 450 – c. 40 av. J.-C.)*. Louvain-la-Neuve.

_______. 2011. "Faut-il suivre les chouettes ? Réflexions sur la monnaie comme indicateur d'échanges à partir du cas athénien d'époque classique", in Th. Faucher, M.-C. Marcellesi, and O. Picard (eds.) *Nomisma. La circulation monétaire dans le monde grec antique, Athènes, 14–17 avril 2010, BCH Supplement* 53, 39–51.

Fontaine, L. 2008. *L'économie morale. Pauvreté, crédit et confiance dans l'Europe préindustrielle*. Paris.

Fontanille, J.-P. 2007. "Two Unrecorded Hasmonean Coins," *Israel Numismatic Research* 2, pp. 89–92.

Fried, S. 1987. "The Decadrachm Hoard: an Introduction," I. Carradice (ed.) *Coinage and Administration in the Athenian and Persian Empires*, Oxford, pp. 1–10, pls. I–V.

Galili, E. and J. Sharvit. 1999. "Haifa, Underwater Surveys", *Hadashot Arkheologiot. Excavations and Surveys in Israel,* 110, p. 17.

Gândilă, A. 2009. "Early Byzantine Coin Circulation in the Eastern Provinces," *American Journal of Numismatics* 21, p. 151–226.

Gauthier, P. 1985. *Les cités grecques et leurs bienfaiteurs, BCH Supplement* 12. Athens.

Geva, H. 2000. "General Introduction to the Excavations in the Jewish Quarter," in H. Geva (ed.) *Jewish Quarter Excavations in the Old City of Jerusalem Conducted by Nahman Avigad, 1969–1982. Vol. I. Architecture and Stratigraphy: Areas A, W and X2. Final Report*. Jerusalem, pp. 1–30.

Giard, J.-B. 1979. "Préface," *Trésors monétaires* 1. Paris, pp. 7–10.

Gill, D. 2015. "Context Matters: From Palmyra to Mayfair: the Movement of Antiquities from Syria and Northern Iraq," *Journal of Art Crime* 13, pp. 73–80.

Gitin, S. and A. Golani. 2001. "The Tel Miqne-Ekron Silver Hoards: the Assyrian and Phoenician Connections," in M. S. Balmuth (ed.) *Hacksilber to Coinage: New Insights into the Monetary History of the Near East and Greece*. New York, pp. 27–48.

Gitler, H. 1990. "The Coins," in S. Wachsmann (ed.) *The Excavations of an Ancient Boat in the Sea of Galilee (Lake Kinneret), 'Atiqot* 19, pp. 101–106.

_______. 1996a. "New Fourth-Century BC Coins from Ascalon," *Numismatic Chronicle* 156, pp. 1–9, pls. 1–4.

_______. 1996b. "A Comparative Study of Numismatic Evidence from Excavations in Jerusalem," *Liber Annuus* 46, pp. 317–362.

_______. 1997. "The Levant," in C. Morrisson and B. Kluge (eds.) *A Survey of Numismatic Research, 1990–1995*, Berlin, pp. 101–113.

———. 2000. "Achaemenid Motifs in the Coinage of Ashdod, Ascalon and Gaza from the Fourth-Century BC," *Transeuphratène. Actes du IVe colloque international: la Transeuphratène à l'époque perse. Économie, commerce et monnaie. Institut Catholique de Paris, 20–22 novembre 1997*. II 20, pp. 73–87.

———. 2003a. "The Coins," in H. Geva (ed.) *Jewish Quarter Excavations in the Old City of Jerusalem Conducted by Nahman Avigad, 1969–1982. Vol. II. The Finds from Areas A, W and X-2, Final Report*. Jerusalem, pp. 453–492.

———. 2003b. "The Levant," in C. Alfaro and A. Burnett (eds.) *A Survey of Numismatic Research, 1996–2001*. Madrid, pp. 151–175.

———. 2006a. "A Hoard of Persian Yehud Coins from the Environs of Ramallah," *Numisma* 250, pp. 319–324.

———. 2006b. "A *Hacksilber* and Cut Athenian Tetradrachm Hoard from the Environs of Samaria: Late Fourth Century BCE," *Israel Numismatic Research* 1, pp. 5–14, pls. 1–2.

Gitler, H. and Y. Kahanov. 2002. "The Ascalon 1988 Hoard (*CH* 9.548). A Periplous to Ascalon in the Late Hellenistic Period?" in A. Meadows and U. Wartenberg (eds.) *Coin Hoards 9*. London, pp. 259–268, pl. 53.

Gitler, H. and C. C. Lorber. 2000–2002. "Small Silver Coins of Ptolemy I," *Israel Numismatic Journal* 14, pp. 34–42.

———. 2006. "A New Chronology for the Ptolemaic Yehud Coinage," *American Journal of Numismatics* 18, pp. 1–41, no. 5.

Gitler, H., M. Ponting, and O. Tal. 2009. "Athenian Tetradrachms from Tel Mikhal (Israel): a Metallurgical Perspective," *American Journal of Numismatics* 21, pp. 29–49.

Gitler, H. and O. Tal. 2006. *The Coinage of Philistia of the Fifth and Fourth Centuries BC: a Study of the Earliest Coins of Palestine*. Milan.

Gitler, H., O. Tal, and P. van Alfen. 2007. "Silver Dome-Shaped Coins from the Persian Period Southern Palestine," *Israel Numismatic Research* 2, pp. 47–62.

Gitler, H. and D. Weisburd. 2005. "Coin Finds from Villages in Palestine during the Late Roman and Byzantine Periods (A.D. 383–696/7): a Quantitative Examination of Monetary Distributions," in J. Lefort, C. Morrisson, and J.-P. Sodini (eds.) *Les villages dans l'Empire byzantin (IVe–XVe siècle)*. Paris, pp. 539–552.

Golenko, V. G. 1993. "Notes on the Coinage of the Early Seleucid State, I," *Mesopotamia* 28, pp. 71–167.

Gondonneau, A. 2001. *Développement et application des techniques ICP-MS et LA-ICP-MS à la caractérisation de l'or: circulation monétaire entre Orient et Occident dans l'Antiquité et au Moyen Age*, Unpublished thesis, Université d'Orléans, 2001.

Graf, D. F., L.-A. Bedal, S. G. Schmid, and S. E. Sidebotham. 2005. "The Hellenistic Petra Project: Excavations in the Civic Center, Preliminary Report of the First Season, 2004," *Annual of the Department of Antiquities of Jordan* 49, pp. 417–441.

Grandjean, C. 2006. "Histoire économique et monétarisation de la Grèce à l'époque hellénistique," in *Approches de l'économie hellénistique*. Saint-Bertrand-de-Comminges, pp. 195–214.

Gratuze, B., M. Blet-Lemarquand, and J.-N. Barrandon. 2004. "Caractérisation des alliages monétaires à base d'or par LA-ICP-MS," *Bulletin de la Société française de numismatique* 59/6, (June), pp. 163–169.

Grierson, P. 1976. *Monnaies et monnayages. Introduction à la numismatique*. Paris.

Gropp, D. M. 2001. *Wadi Daliyeh I. The Samaria Papyri from Wadi Daliyeh*. Oxford.

Guerra, M.-F. and A. Gondonneau. 2000. "Les statères au type d'Alexandre: apport analytique," *Bulletin de la Société française de numismatique* 55/6 (June), pp. 97–101.

Hakimian, S. 1987. "Une archéologie parallèle: les découvertes clandestines et fortuites au Liban," *Berytus* 35, pp. 199–209.

Hamburger, L. 1892. "Die Silber-Münzprägungen während des letzten Aufstandes der Israeliten gegen Rom," *Zeitschrift für Numismatik*, pp. 241–348.

Hamilton, R. W. 1933. "Tell Abu Hawam," *Quarterly of the Department of Antiquities in Palestine* 3, pp. 74–80.

_______. 1934. "Excavations at Tell Abu Hawam,"*Quarterly of the Department of Antiquities in Palestine* 4, pp. 1–69.

Harris, W. V. 2005. "A Revisionist View of Roman Money," *Journal of Roman Studies* 95, pp. 1–24.

Hazzard, R. A. 1975. "The Tyre Hoard of 1955: *IGCH* 1591," *Cornucopiae* 3/4, pp. 57–63.

Hendin, D. 2000–2002. "A Bar Kokhba Lamp Hoard Collection," *Israel Numismatic Journal* 14, pp. 180–184.

_______. 2010. *Guide to Biblical Coins*. New York.

Hersh, C. A. 1998a. "The Phoenicia 1997 Hoard of Alexander-type Tetradrachms," *American Journal of Numismatics* 10, pp. 37–40.

_______. 1998b. "Tyrus Rediviva Reconsidered", *American Journal of Numismatics* 10, pp. 41–59, pls. 6–9.

Hersh, C. A. and H. A. Troxell. 1993–1994. "A 1993 Hoard of Alexander Drachms from the Near East," *American Journal of Numismatics* 5–6, pp. 13–43.

Hill, G. F. 1910. *Catalogue of the Greek Coins in the British Museum. Phoenicia*. London.

_______. 1925. "Greek Coins Acquired by the British Museum in 1924," *Numismatic Chronicle* 1925, pp. 14–17, nos. 45–48.

_______. 1936. *Treasure Trove in Law and Practice, from the Earliest Time to the Present Day*. Oxford.

_______. 1938. "The Shekels of the First Revolt of the Jews," *Quarterly of the Department of Antiquities in Palestine* 6, pp. 78–83.

Hirschfeld, Y. 2004. *Qumran in Context. Reassessing the Archaological Evidence*. Peabody, Mass.

Holleaux, M. 1952. "Le papyrus de Gourob," *Etudes d'épigraphie et d'histoire grecque* vol. 3. Paris, pp. 281–310.

Holt, W. C. and N. L. Wright. 2010. "A New Seleucid Bronze Coin and Dura Hoard 13 Revisited,"*Israel Numismatic Research* 5, pp. 59–66.

Hoover, O. D. 2006. "A Reassessment of Nabatean Lead Coinage in Light of New Discoveries," *Numismatic Chronicle* 166, pp. 105–119.

_______. 2008. "Ptolemaic Lead Coinage in Coele Syria (103–101 BCE)," *Israel Numismatic Research* 3, pp. 81–85.

_______. 2010. "Northern Israel Hoard, 2002 (*CH* 10.319)," *Coin Hoards* 10. New York, pp. 227–241.

Hoover, O. D. and D. MacDonald. 1999–2000. "Syrian Imitations of New Style Tetradrachms struck over Myrina," *Berytus* 44, pp. 109–117.

Houghton, A. 1991. "The Antioch Project," in W. E. Metcalf (ed.) *Mnemata. Papers in Memory of N.M. Waggoner*. New York, pp. 73–97.

_______. 2002. "The Production of Money by Mints of the Seleucid Core," in C. Augé and F. Duyrat (eds.) *Les monnayages syriens. Quel apport pour l'histoire du Proche-Orient hellénistique et romain ? Actes de la table ronde de Damas, 10–11 novembre 1999*, pp. 5–20. Beirut, pp. 5-19.

_______. 2003–2006. "Some Observations on Coordinated Bronze Currency Systems in Seleucid Syria," *Israel Numismatic Journal* 15, pp. 35–47.

Houghton, A. and C. C. Lorber. 2000–2002. "Antiochus III in Coele Syria and Phoenicia," *Israel Numismatic Journal* 14, pp. 44–58.

_______. 2002. *Seleucid Coins. A Comprehensive Catalogue. With Metrological Tables by Brian Kritt. Part I. Seleucus I through Antiochus III, vol. I. Introduction, Maps and Catalogue, vol. II. Appendices, Indices, and Plates*. New York.

Houghton, A., C. C. Lorber, and O. D. Hoover. 2008. *Seleucid Coins. A Comprehensive Catalogue. Part II. Seleucus IV through Antiochus XIII. Vol. I. Introduction, maps, and catalogue. Vol. II. Appendices, Indices, and Plates*. Lancaster.

Houghton, A., A. Spaer, and C. C. Lorber. 1998. *Sylloge Nummorum Graecorum. Israel I. The Arnold Spaer Collection of Seleucid Coins*. Jerusalem.

Howgego, C. 1995. *Ancient History from Coins*. London.

Huber, C. W. 1867. "Zur alten Numismatik Aegyptens II," *Wiener numismatische Monatshefte*, pp. 1–30.

Humbert, J.-B. (dir.) 2000. *Gaza méditerranéenne. Histoire et archéologie en Palestine*. Paris.

Humbert, J.-B., A. Chambon, and S. Pfann. 2003. *The Excavations of Khirbet Qumran and Ein Feshkha. Synthesis of Roland de Vaux Field Notes*. Fribourg.

Humbert, J.-B., A. Chambon, and R. de Vaux. 1994. *Fouilles de Khirbet Qumran et de Ain Feschkha*, I. Göttingen.

Hurter, S. and E. Paszthory. 1984. "Archaischer Silberfund aus dem Antilibanon", in A. Houghton, S. Hurter, P. Erhart Mottahedeh, and J. Ayer Scott (eds.) *Festschrift für Leo Mildenberg*. Wetteren, pp. 111–125, pls. 14–17.

Huth, M. 1998. "The 'Folded Flan' Coinage of Eastern Arabia: Some Preliminary Comments," *Arabian Archaeology and Epigraphy*, pp. 273–277.

_______. 1999. "An Important Hoard of Early South Arabian Coins from the Kingdom of Qataban," *Schweizerische numismatische Rundschau* 78, pp. 37–45.

Huth, M. and S. Qedar. 1999. "A Coin from North Arabia with an Aramaic Inscription and Related Coins of the Incense Road," *Numismatic Chronicle* 159, pp. 295–298.

Huth, M. and P. van Alfen. 2010. "Introduction," in M. Huth and P. van Alfen (eds.) *Coinage of the Caravan Kingdoms – Studies in the Monetization of Ancient Arabia*. New York, pp. 1–25.

Iossif, P. P. 2011a. "Seleucid Religion through Coins: is it Possible to Quantify 'Iconography' and 'Religion'?" in F. de Callataÿ (ed.), *Quantifying Monetary Supplies in Greco-Roman Times*, Pragmateia 19. Bari, pp. 213–249.

_______. 2011b. "Quantifying Greek Hoards," *Numismatic Chronicle* 171, pp. 435–455.

Iossif, P. P. and C. C. Lorber. 2007. "Marduk and the Lion," in G. Moucharte, M. B. Borba Florenzano et al., (eds.) *Liber Amicorum Tony Hackens*. Louvain-la-Neuve, pp. 345–363.

Jambu, J. 2013. *Tant d'or que d'argent. La monnaie en Basse-Normandie à l'époque moderne (XVIe-XVIIIe siècles)*. Paris.

_______. 2015. "Les monnaies créées par DAESH, soit-disant Etat islamique", *Bulletin de la Société française de numismatique* 70/10 (December), pp. 291-298.

Jenkins, G. K. 1959. "Recent Acquisitions of Greek Coins by the British Museum," *Numismatic Chronicle*, pp. 23–45.

_______. 1967. "The Monetary System in the Early Hellenistic Period with Special Regard to the Economic Policy of the Ptolemaic Kings," in A. Kindler (ed.) *International Numismatic Convention, Jerusalem, 27–31 December 1963. The Patterns of Monetary Development in Phoenicia and Palestine in Antiquity*. Tel Aviv, pp. 53–74.

Joannès, F. 1994. "Métaux précieux et moyens de paiement en Babylonie achéménide et hellénistique," *Transeuphratène* 8, pp. 137–144.

Johnston, A. and T. V. Buttrey. 1981. "Numismatic Site Find Procedures," in T. V. Buttrey, A. Johnston, K. M. MacKenzie, and M. L. Bates, *Greek, Roman, and Islamic Coins from Sardis*. Cambridge, pp. xiv–xvii.

Jursa, M. 2010. *Aspects of the Economic History of Babylonia in the First Millennium BC. Economic Geography, Economic Mentalities, Agriculture, the Use of Money and the Problem of Economic Growth*. Munster.

Kadman, L. 1967. "The Monetary Development of Palestine in the Light of Coin Hoards," in A. Kindler (ed.) *International Numismatic Convention, Jerusalem, 27–31 December 1963. The Patterns of Monetary Development in Phoenicia and Palestine in Antiquity*. Tel Aviv, pp. 311–322.

Kagan, J. H. 1987. "The Decadrachm Hoard: Chronology and Consequences," in I. Carradice (ed.) *Coinage and Administration in the Athenian and Persian Empires*. Oxford, pp. 21–28.

Keen, P. 2016. "The Iraq al-Amir Hoard, 1993 (*CH* IX.497; *CH* X, 268)," in T. Faucher, A. Meadows and C. C. Lorber (eds.) *Egyptian Hoards I, Ptolemaic Hoards*. Cairo, pp. 77–134.

Kindler, A. 1954. "The Jaffa Hoard of Alexander Jannaeus' Coins," *Israel Exploration Journal* 4, pp. 170–185 (= *Recent Studies and Discoveries on Ancient Jewish and Syrian Coins*, Jerusalem, 1954, pp. 34–49, *non vidi*).

_______. 1967. "The Mint of Tyre - The Major Source of Silver Coin in Ancient Palestine," *Eretz Israel* 8, pp. 318–324, pl. 46.5 (in Hebrew with English abstract, p. 79).

_______. 1978. "A Ptolemaic Coin Hoard from Tel Michal," *Journal of the Tel Aviv University Institute of Archaeology* 5, pp. 159–169.

_______. 1989. "Numismatic Report," in Z. Herzog *et al.* (eds.) *Excavations at Tel Michal, Israel.* Tel Aviv, pp. 320–329 and 443.

_______. 1999. "The Numismatic Finds," in I. Beit-Arieh (ed.) *Tel 'Ira. A Strongold in the Biblical Neguev*, Jerusalem, pp. 438–441.

Kinns, P. 1990. "Two Eighteenth Century Studies of Greek Coin Hoards: Bayer and Pellerin," in M. H. Crawford, C. R. Ligota, and J. B. Trapp (eds.) *Medals and Coins from Budé to Mommsen.* London, pp. 101–114.

_______. 1999. "The Attic Weight Drachms of Ephesus: a Preliminary Study in the Light of Recent Hoards," *Numismatic Chronicle* 159, pp. 47–97.

Kirkman, J. S. 1957. "The Evidence of the Coins," in J. W. Crowfoot, G. M. Crowfoot, K. M. Kenyon (eds.) *Samaria Sebaste III: The Objects from Samaria.* London, pp. 43–70.

Kleeberg, J. M. 2006. "Treasure Trove Law in the United States," *Conseil international de numismatique. Compte rendu* 53, pp. 13–26.

_______. 2007. "United States Laws Concerning Historic Shipwrecks," *Conseil international de numismatique. Compte rendu* 54, pp. 13–29.

_______. 2009. *Numismatic Finds of the Americas.* New York.

_______. 2010. "United States Laws Concerning the Trade in Cultural Property," *Conseil international de numismatique. Compte rendu* 57, pp. 11–32.

Kletter, R. and A. De Groot. 2007. "The Iron Age Hoard of '*Hacksilber*' from En-Gedi," in Y. Hirschfeld (ed.) *En-Gedi Excavations, 2. Final Report (1996–2002).* Jerusalem, pp. 367–375.

Konuk, K. 2011. "Des chouettes en Asie Mineure: quelques pistes de réflexion," in Th. Faucher, M.-C. Marcellesi, and O. Picard (eds.) *Nomisma. La circulation monétaire dans le monde grec antique, Athènes, 14–17 avril 2010, BCH Supplement* 53, pp. 53–66.

Kraay, C. M. 1956. "The Archaic Owls of Athens: Classification and Chronology," *Numismatic Chronicle* (1956), pp. 43–68.

_______. 1964a. "The Melos Hoard of 1907 Re-examined," *Numismatic Chronicle*, pp. 1–20.

_______. 1964b. "Hoards, Small Change and the Origin of Coinage," *Journal of Hellenic Studies* 84, pp. 76–91.

_______. 1978. "Some Notes on the Abu Shusheh Hoard," *Israel Exploration Journal* 28, pp. 190–192, pls. 29–30.

_______. 1985. "Near East, 1980," *Coin Hoards* 7. London, pp. 38–39.

Kraay, C. M. and P. R. S. Moorey. 1968. "Two Fifth Century Hoards from the Near East," *Revue Numismatique*, pp. 181–235, pls. 19–28.

Kritt, B. 1997. *The Early Seleucid Mint of Susa*. Lancaster.

Kroll, J. H. 1993. *The Greek Coins. The Athenian Agora*, vol. 26. Princeton.

_______. 2011. "Minting for Export: Athens, Aegina, and Others," in Th. Faucher, O. Picard, and M.-C. Marcellesi (eds.) *Nomisma. La circulation monétaire dans le monde grec antique, Actes du colloque international, Athènes, 14–17 avril 2010, BCH Supplement* 53, pp. 27–38.

Kushnir-Stein, A. and H. Gitler. 1999. "On Some Inscribed Lead Weights from Palestine," *Numismatica e Antichità Classiche* 28, pp. 221–234.

Lambert, C. 1927. "A Hoard of Jewish Bronze Coins from Ophel," *Palestine Exploration Quarterly*, pp. 184–188 *(non vidi)*.

_______. 1931. "A Hoard of Phoenician Coins," *Quarterly of the Department of Antiquities in Palestine* 1, pp. 10–20, pl. 19.

_______. 1932. "Egypto-Arabian, Phoenician, and Other Coins of the Fourth Century BC Found in Palestine," *Quarterly of the Department of Antiquities in Palestine* 2, pp. 1–10, 2 pls.

Lapp, P. W. and N. L. Lapp. 1974. *Discoveries in the Wâdi ed-Dâliyeh*, Annual of the American Schools of Oriental Research 41. Cambridge (Mass.).

Launey, M. 1950. *Recherches sur les armées hellénistiques*, 2 vols. Paris.

Lemaire, A. 1976. "Le monnayage de Tyr et celui dit d'Akko dans la deuxième moitié du IVe siècle av. J.-C.," *Revue Numismatique*, pp. 11–24.

_______. 1990. "Les trésors d'Abu Shusheh et le monnayage d'Ashdod avant Alexandre," *Revue Numismatique*, pp. 257–263.

_______. 1991. "Le monnayage phénicien," in T. Hackens *et al.* (eds.) *A Survey of Numismatic Research 1985–1990*. Brussels, pp. 96–101.

Le Rider, G. 1961. "Monnaies grecques acquises par le Cabinet des Médailles en 1959," *Revue numismatique*, pp. 7–26.

_______. 1963. *Deux trésors de monnaies grecques de la Propontide (IVe s. av. J.-C.)*. Paris.

_______. 1965. *Suse sous les Séleucides et les Parthes*. Paris.

_______. 1975. "Contremarques et surfrappes dans l'Antiquité grecque," *Numismatique antique. Problèmes et méthodes*. Nancy, pp. 27–56.

_______. 1977. *Le monnayage d'or et d'argent de Philippe II frappé en Macédoine de 359 à 294*. Paris.

_______. 1983. "Un trésor de Bassit (1978)," *Bulletin de correspondance hellénique* 107, pp. 451–456.

_______. 1984. "Un trésor de monnaies Séleucides trouvé dans le Hauran en 1979 ou 1980: Antiochos VI à Ptolemais," in A. Houghton, S. Hurter, P. Erhart Mottahedeh, and J. Ayer Scott (eds.) *Festschrift für Leo Mildenberg*. Wetteren, pp. 165–169, pl. 25.

_______. 1986a. "L'atelier de Posidéion et les monnaies de la fouille de Bassit," *Bulletin de correspondance hellénique* 110, pp. 393–408.

_______. 1986b. "Les alexandres d'argent en Asie Mineure et dans l'Orient séleucide au IIIe siècle avant J.-C. Remarques sur le système monétaire des Séleucides et des Ptolémées," *Journal des Savants* (janvier–septembre), pp. 5–51.

_______. 1989a. Compte rendu de J.-M. Doyen, *Les monnaies du Tell Abou Danné et d'Oumm el-Marra (campagnes 1976–1985). Aspects de la circulation monétaire en Syrie du Nord sous les Séleucides*, Bruxelles, 1987, in *Revue Numismatique*, pp. 362–363.

_______. 1989b. "A propos d'un passage des *Poroi* de Xénophon: la question du change et les monnaies incuses d'Italie du Sud," in G. Le Rider, K. Jenkins, N. Waggoner, and U. Westermark (eds.) *Kraay-Mørkholm Essays. Numismatic Studies in Memory of C. M. Kraay and O. Mørkholm*. Louvain, pp. 159–170.

_______. 1991. "Éphèse et Arados au IIe siècle avant notre ère," *Numismatica e antichità classiche* 20, pp. 193–212.

_______. 1992a. "Séleucos IV à Ptolémaïs. Le trésor du Liban 1989," *Revue Numismatique*, pp. 37–45.

_______. 1992b. Compte rendu de M.J. Price *The Coinage in the Name of Alexander the Great and Philip Arrhideus*, London, 1991, *Revue Suisse de Numismatique* 71, pp. 214–225.

_______. 1995. "La politique monétaire des Séleucides en Cœlé-Syrie et en Phénicie après 200. Réflexion sur les monnaies d'argent lagides et sur les monnaies d'argent séleucides à l'aigle," *Bulletin de correspondance hellénique* 119/1, pp. 391–404.

_______. 1997. "Cléomène de Naucratis," *Bulletin de correspondance hellénique* 121/1, pp. 71–93.

_______. 1998a. "Alexander in Asia Minor," in A. Burnett, U. Wartenberg, and R. Witschonke (eds.) *Coins of Macedonia and Rome: Essays in Honour of C. Hersh*, London, pp. 49–57.

_______. 1998b. "Un trésor de monnaies d'argent trouvé en Syrie en 1971 (*CH* II 81)," *Hommage à Ernest Will. Syria* 75, pp. 89–96.

_______. 1999a. *Antioche de Syrie sous les Séleucides. Corpus des monnaies d'or et d'argent I. De Séleucos I à Antiochos V (*c. *301–161)*, Mémoires de l'Académie des Inscriptions et Belles-Lettres 19. Paris.

_______. 1999b. "Sur un aspect du comportement monétaire des villes libres d'Asie Mineure occidentales au IIe siècle: leurs émissions de tétradrachmes de poids attique frappées entre 188 et c. 144", in A. Bresson, and R. Descat (eds.) *Les cités d'Asie Mineure occidentale au IIe siècle av. J.-C.* Bordeaux, pp. 37–63.

_______. 2001a. *La naissance de la monnaie. Pratiques monétaires de l'Orient ancien*. Paris.

_______. 2001b. "Un essai de réforme monétaire sous Antiochos IV?" in R. Frei-Stolba and K. Gex (eds.) *Recherches récentes sur le monde hellénistique*. Lausanne, pp. 269–280.

_______. 2003. *Alexandre le Grand. Monnaie, finances et politique*. Paris.

_______. 2007. *Alexander the Great. Coinage, Finances, and Policy*, translated by W. E. Higgins. Philadelphia.

Le Rider, G. and F. de Callataÿ. 2006. *Les Séleucides et les Ptolémées. L'héritage monétaire et financier d'Alexandre le Grand*. Paris.

Lewis, D. M. 1962. "The Chronology of the Athenian New Style Coinage," *Numismatic Chronicle*, pp. 275–300.

_______. 1989. "Persian Gold in Greek International Relations," *Revue des études anciennes*, pp. 227–234.

Lewis, S. S. 1876. "Shekel of the Year Five," *Numismatic Chronicle*, p. 322.

Lönnqvist, K. 2007. *The Report of the Amman Lots of the Qumran Silver Coin Hoards. New Chronological Aspects of the Silver Coin Hoard Evidence from Khirbet Qumran at the Dead Sea*. Amman.

Lönnqvist, K. and M. Lönnqvist. 2002. *Archaeology of the Hidden Qumran. The New Paradigm*. Helsinki.

_______. 2006. "The Numismatic Chronology of Qumran: Fact and Fiction," *Numismatic Chronicle* 166, pp. 121–166.

Lorber, C. C. 2002. "The Tyre, 1987 Hoard of Seleucid Silver (*CH* 9.533)," in A. Meadows, U. Wartenberg (eds.), *Coin Hoards* 9, London, pp. 253–255.

_______. 2007. "The Ptolemaic Era Coinage Revisited," *Numismatic Chronicle* 167, pp. 105–117.

_______. 2007–2008. "Ptolemaic Bronze Coinage of Tyre," *Israel Numismatic Journal* 16, pp. 11–27.

_______. 2010. "Commerce ('Demetrius I' hoard), 2003 (*CH* 10.301)," *Coin Hoards* 10. New York, pp. 153–172.

_______. 2016. "The Aleppo Hoard, 1893 (*IGCH* 1516)," in T. Faucher, A. Meadows, and C. C. Lorber (eds.) *Egyptian Hoards I, Ptolemaic Hoards*. Cairo, pp. 41–48.

_______. Forthcoming. *Coinage of the Ptolemaic Empire* 1.

Lorber, C. C. and A. Houghton. 2006. "Cappadocian Tetradrachms in the Name of Antiochus VII," *Numismatic Chronicle* 166, pp. 49–98.

Lund, J. 1986. *Sukas VIII. The Habitation Quarters*. Copenhagen.

_______. 1990. "The Northern Coastline of Syria in the Persian Period. A Survey of the Archaeological Evidence," *Transeuphratène* 2, pp. 13–36.

_______. 1993. "The Archaeological Evidence for the Transition from the Persian Period to the Hellenistic Age in Northwestern Syria," *Transeuphratène* 6, pp. 27–45.

Madden, F. W. 1903. *Coins of the Jews*. London.

Magen, Y. 2008. *Mount Gerizim Excavations, II. A Temple City*. Jerusalem.

Malkov, A. V. 2005. "The Russian Law on Import and Export of Old Coins by Individuals," *Commission Internationale de Numismatique. Compte rendu* 52, pp. 13–14.

Marcellesi, M.-C. 2000. "Commerce, monnaies locales et monnaies communes dans les États hellénistiques," *Revue des Etudes Grecques* 113, pp. 326–358.

_______. 2012a. *Pergame, de la fin du Ve au début du Ier siècle avant J.-C. Pratiques monétaires et histoire*. Pise-Rome.

_______. 2012b. "Les monnaies grecques et provinciales romaines," in O. Picard *et al.* 2012, pp. 171–197.

Marot, T. 1998. *Las monedas del Macellum de Gerasa (Ŷaraš, Jordania). Aproximación a la circulación monetaria en la provincia de Arabia*. Madrid.

Mattingly, H. B. 1989. "The Jordan Hoard (*IGCH* 1482) and Kimon's Last Campaign," in I. Carradice (ed.) *Proceedings of the 10th International Congress of Numismatics, London, September 1986*. Wetteren, pp. 59–64.

_______. 1990. "The Beginning of the Athenian New Style Silver Coinage," *Numismatic Chronicle*, pp. 67–78.

_______. 1993. "The Ma'aret en-Numan Hoard, 1980," in M. Price, A. Burnett, and R. Bland (eds.) *Essays in Honour of R. Carson and K. Jenkins*, London, pp. 69–86.

_______. 1994. "A New Light on the Early Silver Coinage of Teos," *Revue Suisse de Numismatique* 73 (1994), p. 8.

Meadows, A. R. 2006a. "Coin hoards 2005 - More from the 'Phoenicia' Hoard (*IGCH* 1497)," *Numismatic Chronicle* 166 (2006), pp. 381–382, pls. 72–73.

_______. 2006b. "Amyntas, Side and the Pamphylian Plain," in P. Van Alfen (ed.) *Agoranomia: Studies in Money and Exchange Presented to John H. Kroll*. New York, pp. 151–176.

_______. 2009. "The Eras of Pamphylia and the Seleucid Invasions of Asia Minor," *American Journal of Numismatics* 21, pp. 51–88.

_______. 2010. "Beth Ummar, Israel, 2001 (*CH* 10.315)," *Coin Hoards* 10. New York, pp. 225–226.

_______. 2011. "The Chian Revolution: Changing Patterns of Hoarding in 4th-century BC Western Asia Minor," in Th. Faucher, O. Picard, and M.-C. Marcellesi (eds.) *Nomisma. La circulation monétaire dans le monde grec antique, Actes du colloque international, Athènes, 14–17 avril 2010, BCH Supplement* 53, pp. 273–295.

_______. 2013. "The Closed Currency System of the Attalid Kingdom," in P. Thonemann (ed.) *Attalid Asia Minor. Money, International Relations, and the State*. Oxford, pp. 149–205.

_______. 2014. "The Spread of Coins in the Hellenistic World," in P. Bernholz and R. Vaubel (eds.) *Explaining Monetary and Financial Innovation. A Historical Analysis. Financial and Monetary Policy Studies* 39. Heidelberg, pp. 169–195.

_______. 2016a. "The 'Syria' 1981 Hoard (*CH* 7.90; 8.306; 8.311; 8.344)," in T. Faucher, A. Meadows, and C. C. Lorber (eds.) *Egyptian Hoards I, Ptolemaic Hoards*. Cairo, pp. 151–195.

_______. 2016b. "Hebron Area, 1979 (*CH* 7.109), Hebron, 1980 (*CH* 7.111), Yatta 1978–9 (*CH* 9.531) and Yatta, 1981," in T. Faucher, A. Meadows, and C. C. Lorber (eds.) *Egyptian Hoards I, Ptolemaic Hoards*. Cairo, pp. 143–147.

_______. 2016c. "Jordan 1987 (*CH* 8.320)," in T. Faucher, A. Meadows, and C. C. Lorber (eds.) *Egyptian Hoards I, Ptolemaic Hoards*. Cairo, pp. 196–197.

_______. 2016d. "Bethlehem area, 1984 (*CH* 8.432)," in T. Faucher, A. Meadows, and C. C. Lorber (eds.) *Egyptian Hoards I, Ptolemaic Hoards*. Cairo, p. 225.

_______. 2016e. "Southern Palestine, 1977 (*CH* 4.58)," in T. Faucher, A. Meadows, and C. C. Lorber (eds.) *Egyptian Hoards I, Ptolemaic Hoards*. Cairo, p. 224.

_______. 2016f. "Gaza Strip, 1977 (*CH* 4.69)," in T. Faucher, A. Meadows, and C. C. Lorber (eds.) *Egyptian Hoards I, Ptolemaic Hoards*. Cairo, pp. 235–236.

Meadows, A. R. and A. Houghton. 2010. "The Gaziantep hoard, 1994 (*CH* 9.527; 10.308)," *Coin Hoards* 10. New York, pp. 173–223.

Meir, C. 2000. "The Historical Evidence of the Ancient City of Jaffa," in B. Kluge, B. Weisser (eds.) *XII. internationaler numismatischer Kongress, Berlin 1997. Akten* I. Berlin, pp. 123–130.

Melville Jones, J. 1993. *Testimonia Numaria. Greek and Latin Texts concerning Ancient Greek Coinage.* Vol. I: *Texts and Translations.* London.

_______. 1998. *A Dictionary of Ancient Greek Coins.* London.

Meshorer, Y. 1967. *Jewish Coins at the Second Temple Period.* Tel Aviv.

_______. 1976. "The En-Gedi Hoard," in H. A. Cahn and G. Le Rider (eds.) *Proceedings of the 8th International Congress of Numismatics, New York – Washington, September 1973.* Paris, pp. 111–112.

_______. 1975. *Nabataean Coins.* Jerusalem.

_______. 1982. *Ancient Jewish Coinage,* vol. I: *Persian Period through Hasmonaeans.* New York.

_______. 1986. "Judaea, Samaria, and Galilee," in M. Price *et al.* (eds.) *A Survey of Numismatic Research 1978–1984.* London, pp. 201–203.

_______. 1989. "The Coins of Masada," in Y. Yadin, J. Naveh, and Y. Meshorer (eds.) *Masada I. 1989: The Yigael Yadin Excavations 1963–1965, Final Reports: The Aramaic and Hebrew Ostraca and Jar Inscriptions. The Coins of Masada,* Jerusalem, pp. 69–132, pls. 61–81.

_______. 1994. "Coins 1968–1986," in S. C. Herbert (ed.), *Tel Anafa I, i. Final Report on Ten Years of Excavations at a Hellenistic and Roman Settlement in Northern Israël. Journal of Roman Archaeology* Supplementary Series 10. Ann Arbor, pp. 241–260.

_______. 1995. "Coins from Areas A and C," in E. Stern (ed.) *Excavations at Dor, Final Reports, Areas A and C: the Finds.* Qedem Reports 2. Jerusalem, pp. 461–472.

_______. 1998. *Ancient Means of Exchange, Weights and Coins,* The Reuben and Edith Hecht Museum Collection, A. Haïfa.

_______. 2001. *A Treasury of Jewish Coins. From the Persian Period to Bar Kokhba.* New York.

_______. 2003–2006. "The Coins from Qumran," *Israel Numismatic Journal* 1, pp. 19–23.

_______. 2004. "The Coins," in E. Netzer and R. Laureys-Chachy (eds.) *Hasmonean and Herodian Palaces at Jericho: Final Reports of the 1973–1987 Excavations. II. Stratigraphy and Architecture.* Jerusalem, pp. 289–312.

_______. 2007. "Appendix 6: the En-Gedi Hoard," in E. Stern (ed.), *En-Gedi Excavations, 1. Conducted by B. Mazar and I. Dunayevsky. Final Report (1961–1965).* Jerusalem, pp. 411–421.

Meshorer, Y. and S. Qedar. 1991. *The Coinage of Samaria in the Fourth Century BC.* Jerusalem.

_______. 1999. *Samarian Coinage.* Jerusalem.

Metcalf, D. M., R. Kool, and A. Berman. 1999. "Coins from the excavations at 'Atlit, Pilgrims' castle and its faubourg," *'Atiqot* 37, pp. 89–164.

Metcalf, W. E. 1994. "A Late Second Century Hoard of Posthumous Alexanders," *Revue Suisse de Numismatique* 73, pp. 19–53, pls. 1–3.

_______. 1998. "The Ain Tab Hoard (*IGCH* 1542)," in A. Burnett, U. Wartenberg, and R. Witschonke (eds.) *Coins of Macedonia and Rome: Essays in Honour of C. Hersh.* London, pp. 59–66.

Meuvret, J. 1947. "Circulation monétaire et utilisation de la monnaie dans la France des XVIe et XVIIe siècles," *Etudes d'histoire moderne et contemporaine* 1, pp. 15–28.

Meyers, E. M., J. F. Strange, C. L. Meyers *et al.* 1981. *Excavations in Ancient Meiron, Upper Galilee, Israël 1971–72, 1974–75, 1977*. Cambridge (Mass.).

Migeotte, L. 1984. *L'emprunt public dans les cités grecques*. Paris.

Mildenberg, L. 1991. "Palästina in der persischen Zeit," in T. Hackens *et al.* (eds.), *A Survey of Numismatic Research 1985–1990*. Brussels, pp. 102–105.

_______. 1993. "Über das Münzwesen im Reich der Achämeniden," *Archäologische Mitteilungen aus Iran* 26, pp. 55–79.

_______. 1995. "Bes on Philisto-Arabian Coins," *Transeuphratène. Actes de la table ronde: la Transeuphratène et l'Égypte à l'époque perse. Institut Protestant de Théologie de Paris. 10–11 mai 1993*, pp. 63–65.

_______. 1997. "On the Imagery of the Philisto-Arabian Coinage. A Preview," *Transeuphratène. Actes du IIIe colloque international: la Transeuphratène à l'époque perse. Contacts et échanges culturels. Institut Catholique de Paris. 21–23 avril 1994*. II 13, pp. 9–16.

_______. 1998. *Vestigia Leonis. Studien zur antiken Numismatik Israels, Palästinas und der östlichen Mittelmeerwelt*, U. Hübner and E. A. Knauf (eds.). Fribourg.

Miles, G. C. (ed.). 1985. "The coins from the Armenian Garden," in A. D. Tushingham, *Excavations in Jerusalem, 1961–1967*, vol. 1, Royal Ontario Museum. Toronto, pp. 156–177.

Millettt, P. 1991. *Lending and Borrowing in Ancient Athens*. Cambridge.

Misch-Brandl, O. and E. Galili. 1985. "Finds from the Hellenistic Period," in *From the Depths of the Sea: Cargoes and Ancient Wrecks from the Carmel Coast*, Israel Museum catalogue no. 263. Jerusalem, pp. 12–13.

Moesgaard, J. K. 1998. "The Law and Practice Concerning Coin Finds in Denmark," *Commission Internationale de Numismatique. Compte Rendu* 46, pp. 74–80.

Monerie, J. 2013. *Aspects de l'économie de la Babylonie aux époques hellénistique et parthe (IVe s. av. J.-C. – Ier s. av. J.-C.* Unpublished thesis, Université Paris I, 7 décembre 2013.

Mørkholm, O. 1967. "The Monetary System of the Seleucid Kings until 129 BC," in A. Kindler (ed.) *International Numismatic Convention, Jerusalem, 27–31 December 1963. The Patterns of Monetary Development in Phoenicia and Palestine in Antiquity*. Tel Aviv, pp. 75–86.

_______. 1975–1976. "The Ptolemaic 'Coins of Uncertain Era'," *Nordisk Numismatik Årsskrift*, pp. 23–58.

_______. 1979. "Greece to India," in R. Carson *et al.* (eds.) *A Survey of Numismatic Research 1972–1977*. Bern, pp. 60–97.

_______. 1980. "A Group of Ptolemaic Coins from Phoenicia and Palestine," *Israel Numismatic Journal* 4, pp. 4–7, pls. 1–2.

_______. 1982a. "The Attic Coin Standard in the Levant during the Hellenistic Period," in S. Scheers (ed.) *Studia Paulo Naster Oblata. I. Numismatica antiqua*. Louvain, pp. 139–149.

_______. 1982b. "Some Reflexions on the Production and Use of Coinage in Ancient Greece," *Historia* 31, pp. 301–305.

_______. 1983. "The Autonomous Tetradrachms of Laodicea ad Mare," *American Numismatic Society. Museum Notes* 28, pp. 89–107.

Morrisson, C., V. Popovic, V. Ivanisevic (eds.). 2006. *Les trésors monétaires des Balkans et d'Asie Mineure (491–717)*, Paris.

Müller, L. 1855. *Numismatique d'Alexandre le Grand*. Copenhagen.

Munro-Hay, S. 1996. "Coins of Ancient South Arabia, II," *Numismatic Chronicle* 156, pp. 33–47.

_______. 2003. *Coinage of Arabia Felix. The Pre-Islamic Coinage of the Yemen*. Milan.

Naster, P. 1967. "Le développement des monnayages phéniciens avant Alexandre," in A. Kindler (ed.), *International Numismatic Convention, Jerusalem, 27–31 December 1963. The Patterns of Monetary Development in Phoenicia and Palestine in Antiquity*. Tel Aviv, pp. 3–24.

_______. 1987. "Trésors de monnaies de Byblos du IVe s. av. J.-C. trouvés à Byblos," in T. Hackens and G. Moucharte (eds.) *Numismatique et histoire économique phéniciennes et puniques*, Studia Phoenicia 9. Louvain, pp. 41–50.

Nercessian, Y. T. 2006. *Silver Coinage of the Artaxiad Dynasty of Armenia*. Los Angeles.

Netzer, E. 1973. "Jericho," *Israel Exploration Journal* 23, p. 260.

_______. 1974. *Qadmoniot* 7/1–2 (1974), p. 31.

Newell, E. T. 1912. *Reattributions of Certain Tetradrachms of Alexander the Great*. New York.

_______. 1916. *The Dated Alexander Coinage of Sidon and Ake*. New Haven, pp. 57–60.

_______. 1923a. *Alexander Hoards, Demanhur, 1905*. ANS NNM 19. New York.

_______. 1923b. *Tyrus Rediviva*. New York.

_______. 1926. *Some Unpublished Coins of Eastern Dynasts*. ANS NNM 30. New York.

_______. 1927. *The Coinages of Demetrius Poliorcetes*. London.

_______. 1936. *The Seleucid Coinage of Tyre*, ANS NNM 73. New York, pp. 22–26.

_______. 1938a. *The Coinage of the Eastern Seleucid Mints from Seleucus I to Antiochus III*. New York.

_______. 1938b. *Miscellanea Numismatica: Cyrene to India*, ANS NNM 82. New York.

_______. 1939. "The Coins," in R. S. Lamon and G. M. Shipton (eds.) *Megiddo I. Seasons of 1925–1934, Strata I–V*. Chicago, pp. 196–212.

_______. 1941. *The Coinage of the Western Seleucid Mints from Seleucus I to Antiochus III*. New York.

Nicolet-Pierre, H. 1973. "Monnaies grecques trouvées en Afghanistan," *Revue Numismatique*, pp. 35–42.

_______. 1999. "Argent et or frappés en Babylonie entre 331 et 311 ou de Mazdai à Séleucos," in M. Amandry and S. Hurter (eds.) *Travaux de numismatique grecque offerts à G. Le Rider*. London, pp. 285–305.

Nicolet-Pierre, H. and M. Amandry. 1994. "Un nouveau trésor de monnaies pseudo-athéniennes venu d'Afghanistan (1990)," *Revue Numismatique*, pp. 34–54.

Nixon, C. E. V. 2002. "The Coins," in G.W. Clarke, *et al.*, *Jebel Khalid on the Euphrates: Report on Excavations 1986–1996, Volume 1, Mediterranean Archaology* Suppl. 5. Sydney, pp. 291–335.

Noe, S. P. 1925. *A Bibliography of Greek Coin Hoards*. New York.

_______. 1937. *A Bibliography of Greek Coin Hoards*. New York (2nd edition).

_______. 1949. "Hoard Evidence and its Importance,"*Hesperia* Supplement 8, pp. 235–242.

Oldenburg, E. and J. Rohweder. 1981. *The Excavations at Tall Daruk (Usnu ?) and 'Arab el-Mulk (Paltos).* Copenhagen.

Olivier, J. 2006. *Le monnayage d'or lagide.* Unpublished master thesis, Université d'Orléans.

_______. 2016. "Syrie 1989 (*CH* 8.462): deux trésors en un?" in T. Faucher, A. Meadows, and C. C. Lorber (eds.) *Egyptian Hoards I, Ptolemaic Hoards.* Cairo, pp. 136–140.

_______. Forthcoming. *Archè et chrèmata en Egypte au IIe s. avant J.-C. (204–81 av. J.-C.). Etude de numismatique et d'histoire,* Etudes Alexandrines. Alexandria.

Olivier, J. and A. R. Meadows. 2016. "Jericho Area, c. 1991 (*CH* 8.412)," in T. Faucher, A. Meadows, and C. C. Lorber (eds.) *Egyptian Hoards I, Ptolemaic Hoards.* Cairo, pp. 198–203.

Olivier, J. and Ch. Parisot-Sillon. 2013. "Les monnayages aux types de Cléopâtre et Antoine. Premiers résultats et perspectives," *Bulletin de la Société française de numismatique* 68/9, pp. 256–268.

Orrieux, Cl. 1983. *Les papyrus de Zénon: l'horizon d'un Grec en Égypte au IIIe siècle avant J.-C.* Paris.

Özgen, E. and A. Davesne. 1994. "Le trésor de Oylum Höyüğü," in M. Amandry and G. Le Rider, *Trésors et circulation monétaire en Anatolie antique.* Paris, pp. 45–49, pls. III–VIII.

Parker, A. J. 1992. *Ancient Shipwrecks of the Mediterranean and the Roman Provinces,* BAR International Series 580. Oxford.

Paunov, E. I. and I. S. Prokopov. 2002. *An Inventory of Roman Republican Coin Hoards and Coins from Bulgaria.* Milan.

Pellerin, J. 1763. *Mélange de diverses médailles de peuples et de villes qui n'ont point encore été publiées ou qui sont peu connues,* Vol. 2. Paris.

_______. 1765. *Mélange de diverses médailles pour servir de supplément aux recueils des médailles de rois et de villes qui ont été imprimés en 1762 et 1763,* Vol. 1. Paris.

Perring, D. 1997–1998. "Excavations in the Souks of Beirut: an Introduction to the Work of the Anglo-Lebanese Team and Summary Report," *Berytus* 43, pp. 9–34.

Petit, H. and J. Meissonnier. 1996. "L'archéologie dans la législation française," *Commission Internationale de Numismatique. Compte Rendu* 43, pp. 87–101.

Pfeiffer-Taş, Ş. 2012. "The Law and Practice Regarding Coin Finds. Protection of Cultural Heritage in Turkey," *Conseil International de Numismatique. Compte Rendu* 59, pp. 11–17.

Pfisterer, M. 2000. *Ein Silberschatz vom Schwarzen Meer. Beobachtungen zum Geldumlauf im Achaimenidenreich.* Paris.

Picard, O. 1994. "Monnaies et commerce à Thasos," *Economie antique. Les échanges dans l'Antiquité: le rôle de l'Etat, Entretiens d'archéologie et d'histoire* 1, Saint-Bertrand-de-Comminges, pp. 31–45.

_______. 1996. "Monnaie ὁλοσχερής, monnaie de poids réduit, *apousia* en Eubée, à Délos et ailleurs," *Charaktēr: aphierōma stē Mantō Oikonomidou,* Athens, pp. 243–250.

_______. 2005. "L'apport des monnaies des fouilles d'Alexandrie," in F. Duyrat and O. Picard (eds.) *L'exception égyptienne ? Production et échanges monétaires en Egypte hellénistique et romaine. Actes du colloque d'Alexandrie, 13–15 avril 2002,* Etudes alexandrines 10, IFAO. Cairo, pp. 81–90.

_______. 2008. "Les tétradrachmes à types thasiens et les guerres thraces au début du Ier siècle avant notre ère," *Comptes Rendus de l'Académie des Inscriptions* (April), pp. 465–493.

_______. 2015. "Corpus et classement des émissions: les bronzes hellénistiques de Thasos," in U. Wartenberg and M. Amandry (eds.), *ΚΑΙΡΟΣ: Contributions to Numismatics in Honor of Basil Demetriadi*. New York, pp. 153–165.

Picard, O., *et al.* 2012. *Les monnaies des fouilles du Centre d'études alexandrines. Les monnayages de bronze à Alexandrie de la conquête d'Alexandre à l'Egypte moderne*. Paris.

Ploug, G. (ed.). 1985. *Hama, fouilles et recherches de la fondation Carlsberg, 1931–1938, III.1, The Graeco-Roman Town*. Copenhagen.

Price, M. J. 1979. "On Attributing Alexanders – Some Cautionary Tales," in O. Mørkholm and N. M. Waggoner (eds.) *Greek Numismatics and Archaeology. Essays in Honor of Margaret Thompson*. Wetteren, pp. 241–250.

_______. 1990. "A Hoard of Tetradrachms from Jericho," *Israel Numismatic Journal* 11, pp. 24–25, pl. 4.

_______. 1991a. *The Coinage in the Name of Alexander the Great and Philip Arrhidaeus*. London.

_______. 1991b. "Circulation at Babylon in 323 BC," in W. E. Metcalf (ed.) *Mnemata. Papers in Memory of N.M. Waggoner*. New York, pp. 63–72.

_______. 1993. "More from Memphis and the Syria Hoard," in M. J. Price, A. Burnett, and R. Bland (eds.) *Essays in Honour of Robert Carson and Kenneth Jenkins*. London, pp. 31–35, pls. 9–10.

Pritchard, J. M. 1962. *Gibeon, Where the Sun Stood Still*. Princeton.

Prokopov, I. S. 2006. *Die Silberprägung der Insel Thasos und die Tetradrachmen des "thasischen Typs" vom 2.–1. Jahrhundert v. Chr*. Berlin.

Psoma, S. 2013. "War or Trade? Attic-Weight tetradrachms from Second Century BC Attalid Asia Minor in Seleukid Syria after the Peace of Apameia and their Historical Context," in P. Thonemann (ed.) *Attalid Asia Minor. Money, International Relations, and the State*. Oxford, pp. 265–300.

Rahmani, L. Y. 1966. "A Hoard of Alexander Coins from Tel Tsippor," *Schweizer Münzblätter* 16/64 (November), pp. 129–145.

_______. 1971. "Silver Coins of the IVth century BC from Tel Gamma," *Israel Exploration Journal* 21, pp. 158–160.

Raymaekers, P. and J.-M. Doyen. 2002. "Un lot de monnaies hellénistiques, romaines et byzantines en provenance de Tell Ain El-Beida, et de ses environs immédiats (Syrie du Nord)," *Bulletin du cercle d'études numismatiques* 39/1 (January–April), pp. 181–183.

Raynor, J., Y. Meshorer, and R. S. Hanson. 1988. *The Coins of Ancient Meiron*. Winona Lake (Ind.).

Reade, J. 1986. "A Hoard of Silver Currency from Achaemenid Babylon," *Iran* 24, pp. 79–88.

Reece, R. 1987. "Coin Finds and Coin Production," in G. Depeyrot, T. Hackens, and G. Moucharte (eds.) *Rythmes de la production monétaire de l'Antiquité à nos jours*. Louvain-la-Neuve, pp. 335–341.

_______. 1996. "The Interpretation of Site Finds – a Review," in C. E. King, and D. G. Wigg (eds.) *Coin Finds and Coin Use in the Roman World. The Thirteenth Oxford Symposium on Coinage and Monetary History, March 25th – 27th, 1993*. Berlin, pp. 341–355.

Regling, K. 1928. "Hellenistische Münzschatz aus Babylon," *Zeitschrift für Numismatik*, pp. 92–132.

_______. 1931a. "Die griechische Goldschatz von Prinkipo," *Zeitschrift für Numismatik* 41, pp. 1–46.

_______. 1931b. "Review of Lambert 1931," *Zeitschrift für Numismatik*, p. 137.

Reichhardt, H. C. 1876. "Miscellen. Münzen aradischer Tetradrachmen," *Numismatische Zeitschrift*, p. 385.

Reisner, G. A., C. S. Fisher, and D. G. Lyon. 1924. *Harvard Excavations at Samaria 1908–1910*. Cambridge.

Rey-Coquais, J.-P. 1978. "Inscription grecque découverte à Ras Ibn Hani: stèle de mercenaires lagides sur la côte syrienne," *Syria* 55, pp. 313–325.

Riis, P. J. 1958–1959. "L'activité de la mission archéologique danoise sur la côte phénicienne en 1958," *Annales archéologiques arabes syriennes* 8–9, pp. 107–132.

_______. 1979. *Sukas VI. The Graeco-Phoenician Cemetery and Sanctuary at the Southern Harbour*. Copenhagen.

Ringel, J. 1974. "Un trésor de tétradrachmes séleucides retirés de la mer à Haïfa (Israël)," *Revue Numismatique*, pp. 42–48, pl. 2.

Robert, L. 1951a. *Etudes de numismatique grecque*. Paris.

_______. 1951b. "Les drachmes du Stéphanéphore à Athènes," *Etudes de numismatique grecque*, Paris, pp. 105–135.

_______. 1966. *Monnaies antiques en Troade*. Paris.

_______. 1977. "Monnaies hellénistiques, l'argent d'Athènes stéphanéphore," *Revue Numismatique*, pp. 34–45.

Robinson, E. S. G. 1937. "Coins from the Excavations at Al-Mina (1936)," *Numismatic Chronicle*, pp. 182–196.

Rochman-Halperin, A. 1999. "Excavations at Giv'at Yasaf (Tell er-Ras), 1984–1985," *'Atiqot* 37, pp. 83–123 (Hebrew) and pp. 172–173 (English summary).

Roma Valdés, A. 2001. "La ley y la realidad en la protección del patrimonio arqueológico español," *Commission Internationale de Numismatique. Compte rendu* 48, pp. 69–79.

Ronde, A. 2002. "Etude sommaire de trois 'trésors' proche-orientaux de provenance incertaine," *Bulletin de la Société française de numismatique* 57/4 (avril), pp. 57–62.

_______. 2003. "Compléments et rectificatifs à l'article du Bulletin d'avril 2002 sur trois trésors proche-orientaux," *Bulletin de la Société française de numismatique* 58/4 (avril), p. 64.

Ronen, Y. 1998. "The Weight Standards of the Judaean Coinage in the Late Persian and Early Ptolemaic Period," *Near Eastern Archaeology* 61/2 (June), pp. 122–126.

Rostovtzeff, M. I. 1939. "Some Remarks on the Monetary and Commercial Policy of the Seleucids and Attalids," in W. M. Calder and J. Keil (eds.) *Anatolian Studies Presented to William Hepburn Buckler*. Manchester, pp. 277–298.

Rotroff, S. I. 1997. "Coins and Stratigraphy," in K. A. Sheedy and C. Papageorgiadou-Bani (eds.) *Numismatic Archaeology, Archaeological Numismatics. Proceedings of an International Conference Held to Honour Dr. Mando Oeconomides in Athens, 1995*. Oxford, pp. 189–198.

Rouvier, J. 1896. "Une métropole phénicienne oubliée. Laodicée, métropole de Canaan," *Revue Numismatique*, pp. 377–396.

_______. 1898. "L'ère de Marathus de Phénicie," *Journal Asiatique* (novembre–décembre), pp. 361–406.

_______. 1899. "L'ère d'Alexandre le Grand en Phénicie aux IVe et IIIe siècles avant J.-C.," *Revue des études grecques* 12, pp. 362–381.

_______. 1900. "Le monnayage alexandrin d'Arados," *Revue Numismatique*, pp. 36–151.

_______. 1901. "Note sur une trouvaille de doubles statères des rois phéniciens de Sidon," *Bulletin archéologique du comité des travaux historiques et scientifiques*, pp. 371–373.

_______. 1902. "Les rois phéniciens de Sidon d'après leurs monnaies sous la dynastie achéménide," *Revue Numismatique*, pp. 243–260.

Ruhlmann, A. 1933. "Le bracelet-bourse romain de Volubilis (Maroc)," *Revue Numismatique*, pp. 51–59.

Salviat, F. and C. Vatin. 1971. *Inscriptions de Grèce centrale*. Paris.

Saraç, L. and A. Davesne. 1994. "Un lot de drachmes cappadociennes à Kırıkhan (Hatay)," in M. Amandry and G. Le Rider (eds.) *Trésors et circulation monétaire en Anatolie antique*. Paris, pp. 61–64, pl. IX.

Sargent, T. J. and F. R. Velde. 2002. *The Big Problem of Small Change*. Princeton.

Sarmant, T. 1994. *Le cabinet des médailles de la Bibliothèque nationale, 1661–1848*. Geneva.

_______. 2003. *La république des médailles. Numismates et collections numismatiques à Paris du Grand Siècle au Siècle des Lumières*. Paris.

Sartre, M. 2001. *D'Alexandre à Zénobie. Histoire du Levant antique, IVe s. av. J.-C. – IIIe s. ap. J.-C.* Paris.

Saulcy, F. (de). 1874–1877. "Note sur quelques monnaies inédites d'Ascalon," *Revue Numismatique*, pp. 124–135.

Saville, A. 2008. "The Treasure Trove System in Scotland – An Update," *Commission Internationale de Numismatique. Compte Rendu* 55, pp. 13–17.

Sawaya, Z. 1997. "BEY 020: the Coins," in U. Finkbeiner and H. Sader, "Bey 020. Preliminary report of the excavations 1995," *BAAL. Bulletin d'Archéologie et d'Architecture Libanaises* 2, pp. 150–156.

Schaeffer, C. F. A. 1939. "Une trouvaille de monnaies archaïques grecques à Ras Shamra," in *Mélanges syriens offerts à M. René Dussaud*, Paris, pp. 461–487.

Scheers, S. 2000. "Seleucid Coins from Tell Beydar 1994," in K. Van Lerberghe and G. Voegt (eds.) *Tell Beydar, Environmental and Technical Studies, Subartu* VI, Turnhout, pp. 135–137.

Schlumberger, D. 1953. *L'argent grec dans l'empire achéménide*. Paris.

Schwabacher, W. 1963. "An Unrecorded Alexander Hoard from Baalbek," *Nordisk Numismatik Årsskrift*, pp. 5–12.

Sellers, O. R. 1962. "Coins of the 1960 Excavations at Shechem," *The Biblical Archaeologist* 25/3, pp. 87–96, figs. 10–12.

Seyrig, H. 1950. *Notes on Syrian Coins,* ANS NNM 119. New York.

_______. 1951. "Antiquités syriennes 51. Tessère relative à l'asylie de Tyr", *Syria* 28, pp. 225–228.

_______. 1958a. "Monnaies grecques des fouilles de Doura et d'Antioche," *Revue Numismatique*, pp. 175–176.

_______. 1958b. "Antiquités syriennes 67. Monnaies contremarquées en Syrie," *Syria* 35, pp. 187–197.

_______. 1962. "Monnaies," in M. Dunand and R. Duru, *Oumm el-'Amed*. Paris, pp. 227–231.

_______. 1964. "Monnaies hellénistiques 12. Questions aradiennes," *Revue Numismatique*, pp. 7–67.

_______. 1973. *Trésors monétaires séleucides II. Trésors du Levant anciens et nouveaux*. Paris.

Shachar, I. 2004. "The Historical and Numismatic Significance of Alexander Jannaeus' Later Coinage as Found in Archaeological Excavations," *Palestine Exploration Quarterly* 136, pp. 5–33.

Sharabani, M. 1980. "Monnaies de Qumran au Musée Rockefeller de Jérusalem," *Revue Biblique* 87, pp. 274–284, pls. III–IV.

Sharp, S. 1865. "Find of Coins near Sidon," *Numismatic Chronicle*, pp. 179–180.

_______. 1870. "The Treasure-Trove at Sidon," *American Journal of Numismatics* 4, pp. 76–78.

Sheedy, K., R. Carson, and A. Walmsley. 2001. *Pella in Jordan 1979–1990. The Coins*. Sydney.

Sheedy, K. A. and C. Papageorgiadou-Bani (eds.). 1997. *Numismatic Archaeology, Archaeological Numismatics. Proceedings of an International Conference Held to Honour Dr. Mando Oeconomides in Athens, 1995*. Oxford.

Sheridan, A. 1995. "'Treasure Trove' Law in Scotland," *Commission Internationale de Numismatique. Compte Rendu* 42, pp. 56–61.

Sheridan, W. W. 1971. "From Cyzicus to Tyre: Numismatic Evidence of an Ancient Ship's Trip, *circa* 400 BC," *The Numismatist* (August), pp. 1127–1133, pl. p. 1129.

Shiloh, Y. and D. T. Ariel (eds.). 1990. "Coins, Flans, and Moulds," *Excavations at the City of David 1978–1985. 2. Imported Stamped Amphora, Handles, Coins, Worked Bone and Ivory, and Glass.* Jerusalem, pp. 99–118.

Six, J. P. 1886. "L'ère de Tripolis," *Annuaire de la société française de numismatique et d'archéologie* 10, pp. 229–234.

_______. 1890. "Monnaies grecques inédites et incertaines," *Numismatic Chronicle*, pp. 185–259, pl. XVII, 19.

Spaer, A. 1965–1966. "A Hoard of Alexander Tetradrachms from Galilee," *Israel Numismatic Journal* 3, pp. 1–7, pls. I–III.

_______. 1970. "A Hoard from Jericho," *Numismatic Chronicle*, pp. 23–28.

_______. 1978. "Le trésor séleucide de la mer de Haïfa: complément," *Revue Numismatique* 20, pp. 43–45, pls. 1–2.

_______. 1980. "More about Jeroboam," *Israel Numismatic Journal* 4, pp. 2–3, pl. 1.

_______. 1984. "Ascalon: from Royal Mint to Autonomy," in A. Houghton, S. Hurter, P. Erhart Mottahedeh, and J. Ayer Scott (eds.) *Festschrift für Leo Mildenberg*. Wetteren, pp. 229–239, pls. 35–37.

_______. 1989. "More on the 'Ptolemaic' Coins of Arados," in G. Le Rider, K. Jenkins, N. Waggoner, and U. Westermark (eds.) *Kraay-Mørkholm Essays. Numismatic Studies in Memory of C. M. Kraay and O. Mørkholm*. Louvain, pp. 67–273, pl. 62.

_______. 1998. "Two Hoards of Minor Silver," in A. Burnett, U. Wartenberg, and R. Witschonke (eds.) *Coins of Macedonia and Rome: Essays in Honour of C. Hersh*, London, pp. 104–107, pls. 6–7.

Spijkerman, A. 1961. "Trésor de sicles juifs trouvé au Mont des Oliviers à Jérusalem," *Schweizer Münzblätter* 11, pp. 25–32.

Stager, L. E. 1991. "Why were Hundreds of Dogs Buried at Ashkelon?" *Biblical Archaeology Review* 17/3, pp. 27–42.

Stahl, A. M. 2000. *Zecca. The Mint of Venice in the Middle Ages*. Baltimore.

Starcky, J. 1972. "Arca du Liban," *Cahiers de l'Oronte* 10, pp. 103–117.

Starr, C. G. 1970. *Athenian Coinage, 480–449 BC*. Oxford.

Steinhauer, G. 1994. "Inscription agoranomique du Pirée," *Bulletin de Correspondance Hellénique* 118/1, pp. 51–68.

Stern, E. 1968. "The Dating of Stratum II at Tell Abu Hawam," *Israel Exploration Journal* 18, pp. 213–219.

_______. 2007. "The History of En-Gedi in the Light of the Excavations: Summary and Conclusions," Y. Hirschfeld (ed.), *En-Gedi Excavations, 2. Final Report (1996–2002)*. Jerusalem, pp. 361–365.

Stern, E. (ed.). 1992. *The New Encyclopedia of Excavations in the Holy Land*, Jerusalem.

_______. 1995. *Excavations at Dor, final report. IA. Areas A and C: Introduction and Stratigraphy*. Jerusalem.

Strange, T. F., T. R. W. Longstaff, and D. Groh. 2006. *Excavations at Sepphoris*. Vol. I. Leiden.

Stucky, R. A. 1972. "Die Münzen," in C. Krause et al. (eds.) *Tel el Hajj in Syrien. Ersten vorlaüfiger Bericht. Grabungskampagne 1971*. Bern, pp. 35–39.

_______. 1983. "Fundmünzen," *Ras Shamra. Leukos Limen, die nach-ugaritische Besiedlung von Ras Shamra*, BAH 110. Paris, pp. 29–54.

Stucky, R. A. and S. Zellweger. 1974. "Die Münzen," C. Krause et al. (eds.) *Tel el Hajj in Syrien. Zweiter vorlaüfiger Bericht. Grabungskampagne 1972*. Bern, pp. 59–65.

Sukenik, E. L. 1947. "A Hoard of Coins of John Hyrcanus," *Jewish Quarterly Review* 27, pp. 281–282. (*non vidi*).

Svoronos, J.-N. 1904–1908. *Τα νομίσματα του κράτους των Πτολεμαίων* 4 vols. Athens.

Syon, D. 1992–1993. "The Coins from Gamala—Interim report," *Israel Numismatic Journal* 12, pp. 34–55.

_______. 2000–2002. "A Hoard of Byzantine Solidi from Hurvat Kab," *Israel Numismatic Journal* 14, pp. 211–223.

_______. 2015. *Small Change in Hellenistic-Roman Galilee. The Evidence from Numismatic Finds as a Tool for Historical Reconstruction*. Jerusalem.

Syon, D., C. Lorber, and E. Galili. 2013. "Underwater Ptolemaic Coin Hoards from Megadim," *'Atiqot* 74, pp. 1–8.

Tabet, N. 1990. in Bordreuil P., Gubel E. (eds.) "Bulletin d'antiquités archéologiques du Levant inédites ou méconnues V", *Syria* 67, pp. 483–520.

Thalmann, J.-P. 1978. "Tell Arqa (Liban nord), campagnes I–III (1972–1974). Chantier I. Rapport préliminaire. Introduction d'Ernest Will," *Syria* 55, pp. 1–151.

_______. 1990. "Tell Arqa de la conquête assyrienne à l'époque perse," *Transeuphratène* 2, pp. 51–58.

Thompson, C. M. 2003. "Sealed Silver in Iron Age Cisjordan and the 'Invention' of Coinage," *Oxford Journal of Archaeology*, pp. 67–107.

Thompson, M. 1961. *The New Style Coinage of Athens*, 2 vols. New York.

_______. 1962. "Athens Again," *Numismatic Chronicle* (1962), pp. 301–333.

_______. 1983. *Alexander's Drachm Mints. I: Sardes and Miletus*. New York.

_______. 1984. "Paying the Mercenaries," in A. Houghton, S. Hurter, P. Erhart Mottahedeh, and J. Ayer Scott (eds.) *Festschrift für Leo Mildenberg*, Wetteren, pp. 241–247.

_______. 1986. "The Armenak Hoard (*IGCH* 1423)," *American Numismatic Society. Museum Notes* 31, pp. 63–106.

_______. 1991. *Alexander's Drachm Mints. II: Lampsacus and Abydus*, New York.

Thompson, M. and A. R. Bellinger. 1955. "Greek Coins in the Yale Collection, IV: A Hoard of Alexander Drachms," *Yale Classical Studies* 14, pp. 3–45.

Thompson, M., O. Mørkholm, and C. M. Kraay. 1973. *An Inventory of Greek Coin Hoards*. New York.

Thomsen, R. 1986. "The Graeco-Roman Coins," in R. Thomsen, A. Papanicolaou-Christensen, and G. Ploug (eds.) *Hama, fouilles et recherches de la fondation Carlsberg, 1931–1938, III.3, The Graeco-Roman Objects of Clay, the Coins and the Necropolis*. Copenhagen, pp. 59–69.

Thomsen, R. A. Papanicolaou-Christensen, and G. Ploug. 1986. *Hama, fouilles et recherches de la fondation Carlsberg, 1931–1938, III.3, The Graeco-Roman Objects of Clay, the Coins and the Necropolis*. Copenhagen.

Thonemann, P. (ed.). 2013. *Attalid Asia Minor. Money, International Relations, and the State*. Oxford.

Touratsoglou, Y. 1998. "Back to the Future. Alexander the Great's Silver and Gold in the Balkans: the Hoard Evidence," in A. Burnett, U. Wartenberg, and R. Witschonke (eds.) *Coins of Macedonian and Rome. Essays in Honour of Charles Hersh*. London, pp. 71–102.

Tourneur, V. 1906. "La trouvaille de Caiffa," *Gazette Numismatique de Bruxelles* 11/1 (October), p. 18.

Tréheux, J. 1992. "L'unité de pesée et l'unité de compte des hiéropes à Délos," in T. Linders and B. Abroth (eds.), *Economics of Cult in the Ancient Greek World*, Uppsala, pp. 21–24.

Troxell, H. A. 1997. *Studies in the Macedonian Coinage of Alexander the Great*. New York.

Troxell, H. A. and I. H. Kagan. 1989. "Cilicians and their Neighbours in Miniature," in G. Le Rider, K. Jenkins, N. Waggoner, and U. Westermark (eds.) *Kraay-Mørkholm Essays. Numismatic Studies in Memory of C.M. Kraay and O. Mørkholm*. Louvain, pp. 275–290, pls. 63–64.

Troxell, H. A. and W. F. Spengler. 1969. "Greek Coin Hoard from Afghanistan", *American Numismatic Society. Museum Notes* 15, pp. 1–19.

Valter, S. 2002. *La construction nationale syrienne. Légitimation de la nature communautaire du pouvoir par le discours historique*. Paris.

van Alfen, P. 2000. "The 'Owls' from the 1973 Iraq Hoard," *American Journal of Numismatics* 12, pp. 9–58.

_______. 2002. "The "Owls" from the 1989 Syria Hoard, with a Review of pre-Macedonian Coinage in Egypt," *American Journal of Numismatics* 14, pp. 1–58.

_______. 2004–2005a. "Herodotus' 'Aryandic' Silver and Bullion Use in Persian-Period Egypt," *American Journal of Numismatics* 16–17, pp. 7–46, pls. 2–5.

_______. 2004–2005b. "A New Athenian 'Owl' and Bullion Hoard from the Near East," *American Journal of Numismatics* 16–17, pp. 47–62, pls. 6–16.

_______. 2005. "Problems in Ancient Imitative and Counterfeit Coinage," *Making, Moving and Managing: the New World of Ancient Economies, 323–31 BC*. Oxford, pp. 322–354.

_______. 2011. "Mechanisms for the Imitation of Athenian Coinage: Dekeleia and Mercenaries Reconsidered," *Revue Belge de Numismatique*, pp. 55–93.

_______. 2012. "Xenophon *Poroi* 3.2 and Athenian 'owls' in Aegean-Near Eastern Long Distance Trade," in M. Asolati and G. Gorini, *I ritrovamenti monetali e i processi storico-economici nel mondo antico*. Padoue, pp. 11–32.

Van Heesch, J. 1996. "Belgian Laws Regarding Coin Finds," *Commission Internationale de Numismatique. Compte rendu* 43, pp. 82–86.

Vatin, C. 1966. "Un tarif de poissons à Delphes," *Bulletin de correspondance hellénique* 90/1, pp. 274–280.

Vaux, R. (de). 1953. "Fouilles de Khirbet Qumrân. Rapport préliminaire," *Revue biblique* 60, pp. 93–94.

_______. 1954. "Fouilles de Khirbet Qumrân. Rapport préliminaire sur la deuxième campagne," *Revue biblique* 61, pp. 229–231.

_______. 1956. "Fouilles de Khirbet Qumrân. Rapport préliminaire sur les 3e, 4e et 5e campagnes," *Revue biblique* 63, pp. 565–569.

_______. 1959. *L'archéologie des manuscrits de la Mer Morte*. Oxford.

_______. 1973. *Archaeology and the Dead Sea Scrolls*. London.

_______. 1994. *Fouilles de Khirbet Qumran et de Ain Feshkha, Album de photographies. Répertoire du fonds photographique. Synthèse des notes de chantier du Père Roland de Vaux*, I. J.-B. Humbert and A. Chambon (eds.). Göttingen.

Vaux, R. (de), F. Rohrhirsch, and B. Hofmeir. 1996. *Die Ausgrabungen von Qumran und En Feschcha. Die Grabungstagebücher*. Göttingen.

Velde, F. R. 2013. "On the Evolution of Specie: Circulation and Weight Loss in 18th and 19th Century Coinage," *Revue Numismatique*, pp. 605–650.

Veyne, P. 1996. *Comment on écrit l'histoire*. Paris (first edition: 1971).

Visonà, P. 1998. "A Hoard of 4th Century Athenian Tetradrachms from Nablus," *Numismatica e Antichità Classiche* 27, pp. 141–149, pls. 1–2.

Von Kaenel, H.-M. and F. Kemmers (eds.). 2009. *Coins in Context I: New Perspectives for the Interpretation of Coin Finds. Studien zu Fundmünzen der Antike* (SFMA 23). Mayence.

Waage, D. B. 1952. *Antioch on the Orontes, IV 2, Greek, Roman, Byzantine and Crusaders' Coins*. Princeton.

Waddington, W. H. 1865. "Trouvailles de Saida et de Marmara," *Revue Numismatique*, pp. 3–28, pls. 1–2 = *Mélanges de numismatique*, Paris, 1867, pp. 33–60.

Waddington, W. H., E. Babelon, and Th. Reinach. 1904. *Recueil général des monnaies grecques d'Asie* Mineure, 4 fascicules. Paris, 1904–1912.

Waggoner, N. M. 1979. "Tetradrachms from Babylon," in O. Mørkholm and N. M. Waggoner (eds.) *Greek Numismatics and Archaeology. Essays in Honor of Margaret Thompson*. Wetteren, pp. 269–280.

Walker, A. S. 1997. "Excavation Coins: the Use and Misuse of Numismatic Evidence in Archaeology," in K. A. Sheedy and C. Papageorgiadou-Bani (eds.) *Numismatic Archaeology, Archaeological Numismatics. Proceedings of an International Conference Held to Honour Dr. Mando Oeconomides in Athens, 1995*. Oxford, pp. 17–26.

Wartenberg, U. 1998. "Eastern Imitations of Athenian Tetradrachms," *Numismatic Chronicle* 158, p. 51.

Weckbecker, C. 1865. "Fund von Alexandre-Stateren zu Saida 1863", *Wiener numismatische Monatshefte*, pp. 5–11.

Wenning, R. 1991. "Die nabatäische Münzprägung," in T. Hackens et al. (eds.) *A Survey of Numismatic Research 1985–1990*. Brussels, pp. 108–110.

Westermark, U. 1961. *Das Bildnis des Philetairos von Pergamon. Corpus der Münzprägung*. Stockholm.

_______. 1979–1980. "Notes on the Saida Hoard (*IGCH* 1508)," *Nordisk Numismatik Årsskrift* (1979/1980), pp. 22–35, pl. 3.

Woolley, C. L. 1938a. "Excavations at al Mina, Sueidia I. The Archaeological Report," *Journal of Hellenic Studies* 58, pp. 1–30.

_______. 1938b. "The Excavations at al Mina, Sueidia II," *Journal of Hellenic Studies* 58, pp. 133–170.

_______. 1953. *A Forgotten Kingdom*. London.

Wright, G. E. et al. 1957. "Shechem, the 'Navel of the Land'," *The Biblical Archaeologist* 20/1, pp. 2–32.

Wright, N. L. 2010. "A Late Seleukid Bronze Hoard, c. 1988 (*CH* 10.349)," *Coin Hoards* 10, pp. 245–264. New York.

Wroth, W. 1895. "Greek Coins Acquired by the British Museum in 1894," *Numismatic Chronicle*, pp. 89–103.

Yadin, Y., J. Naveh, and Y. Meshorer. 1989. *Masada I. 1989: The Yigael Yadin Excavations 1963–1965, Final Reports: The Aramaic and Hebrew Ostraca and Jar Inscriptions. The Coins of Masada.* Jerusalem.

Maps

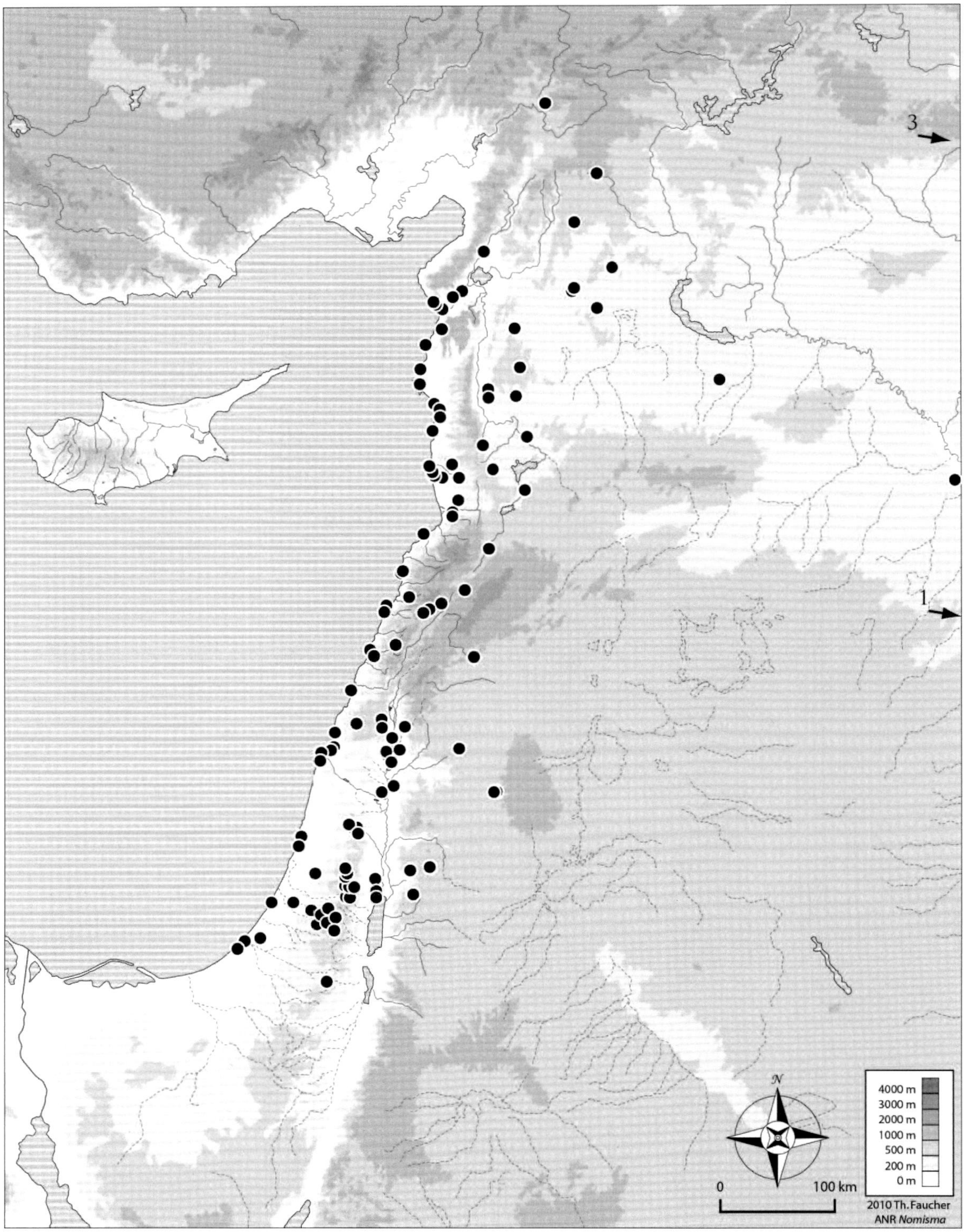
3
1
N
4000 m
3000 m
2000 m
1000 m
500 m
200 m
0 m
0
100 km
2010 Th. Faucher
ANR Nomisma

Map 1. Hoards.

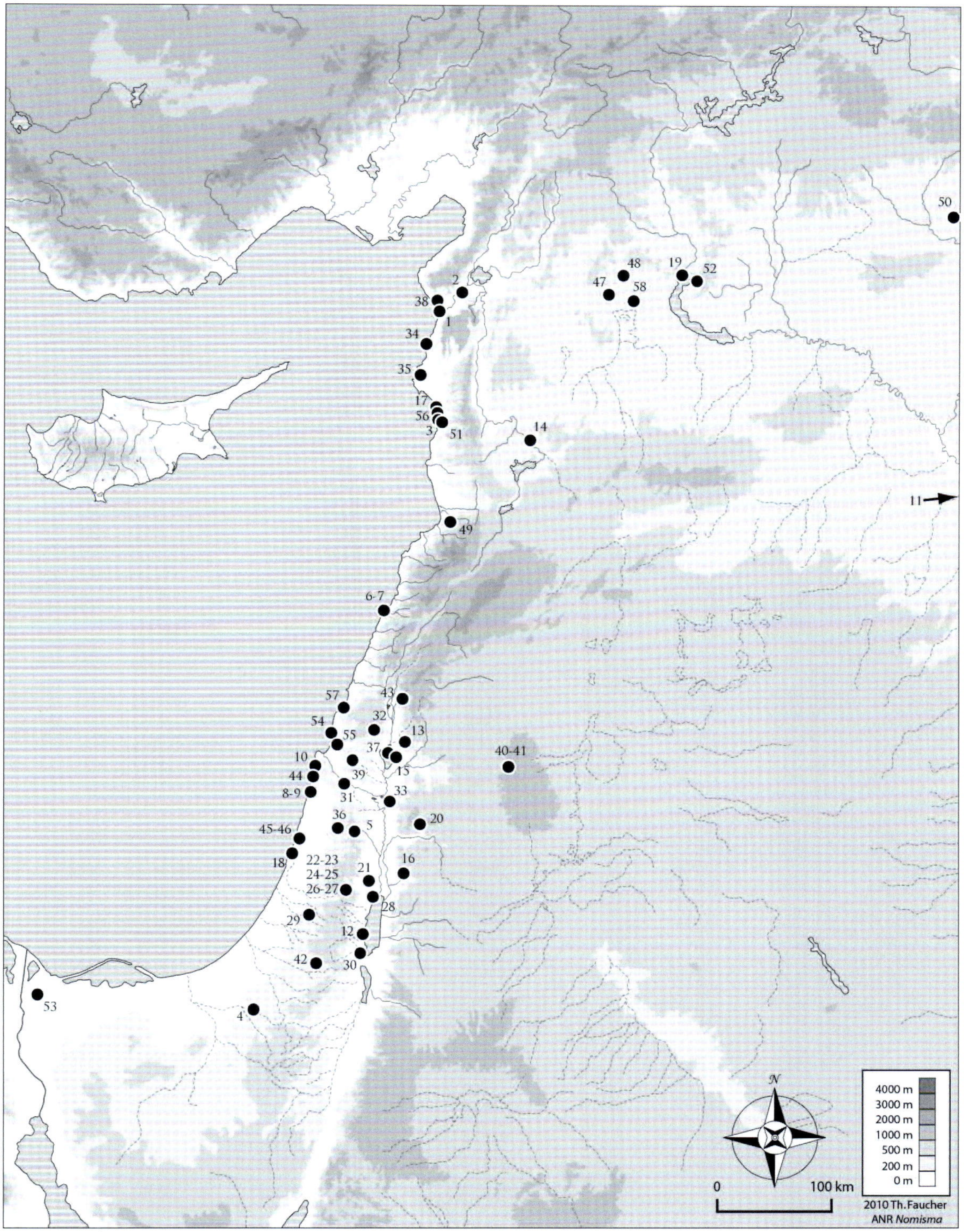

Map 2. Archaeological sites.

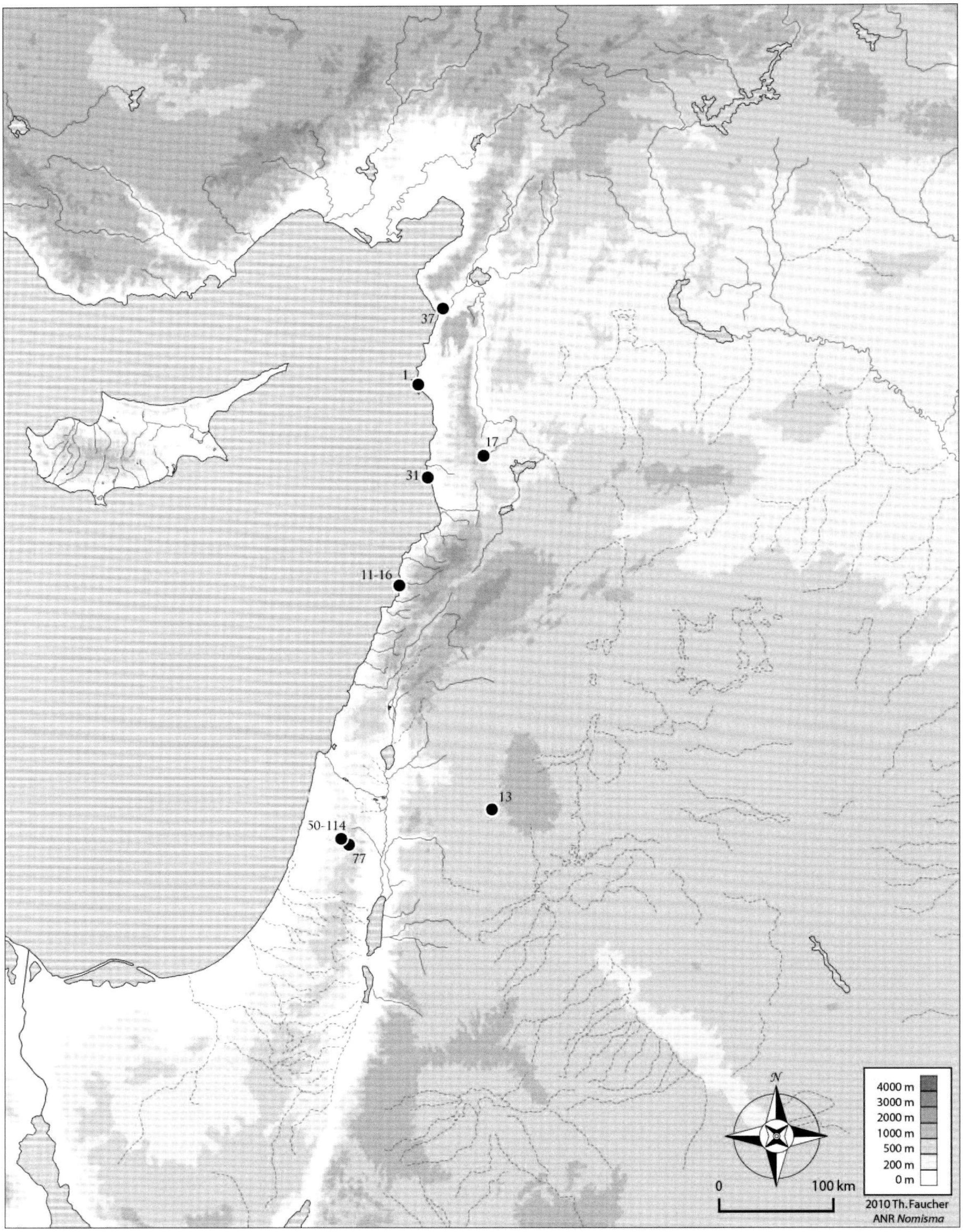

Map 3. *Hacksilber*.

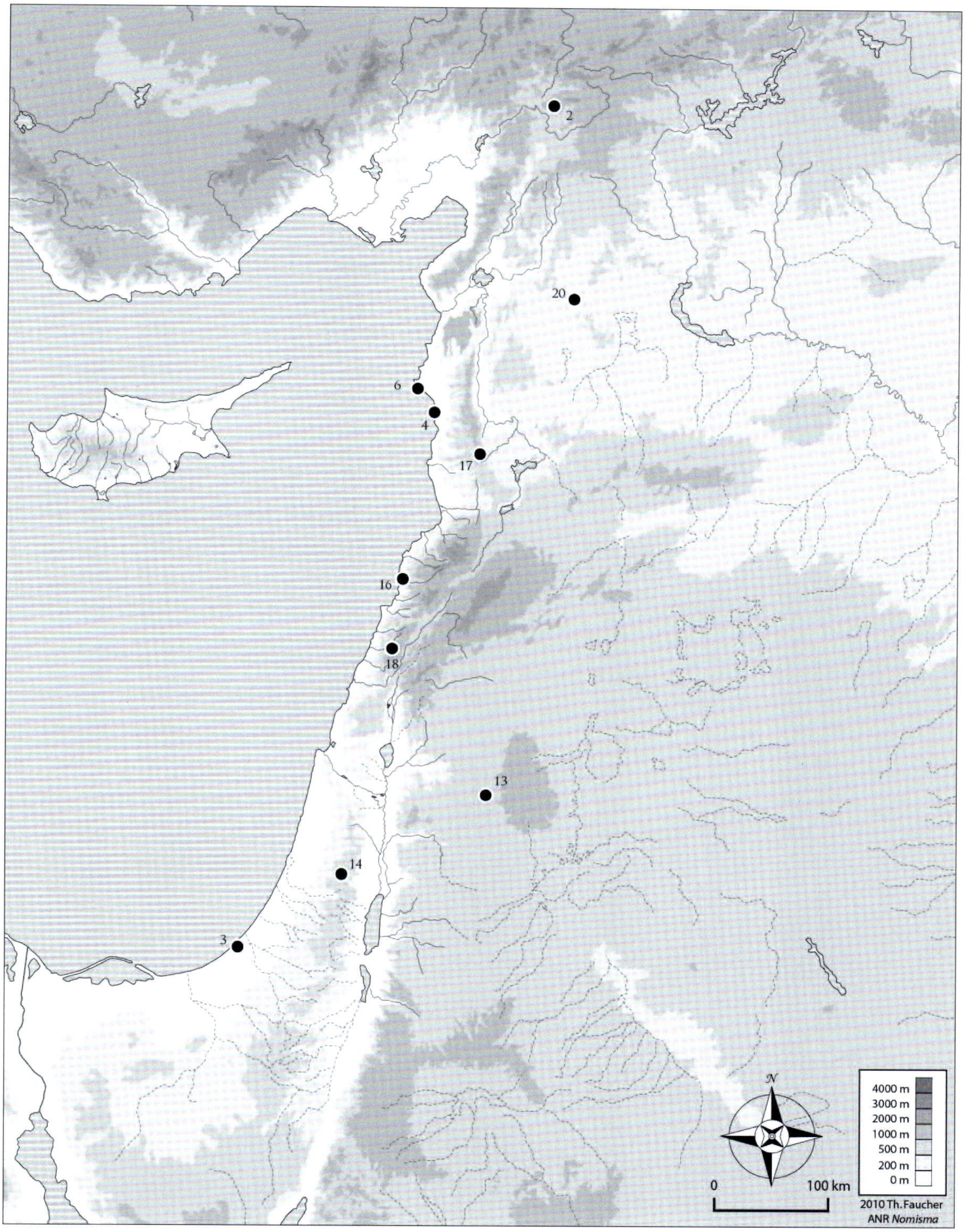

Map 4. Fifth-century Athens.

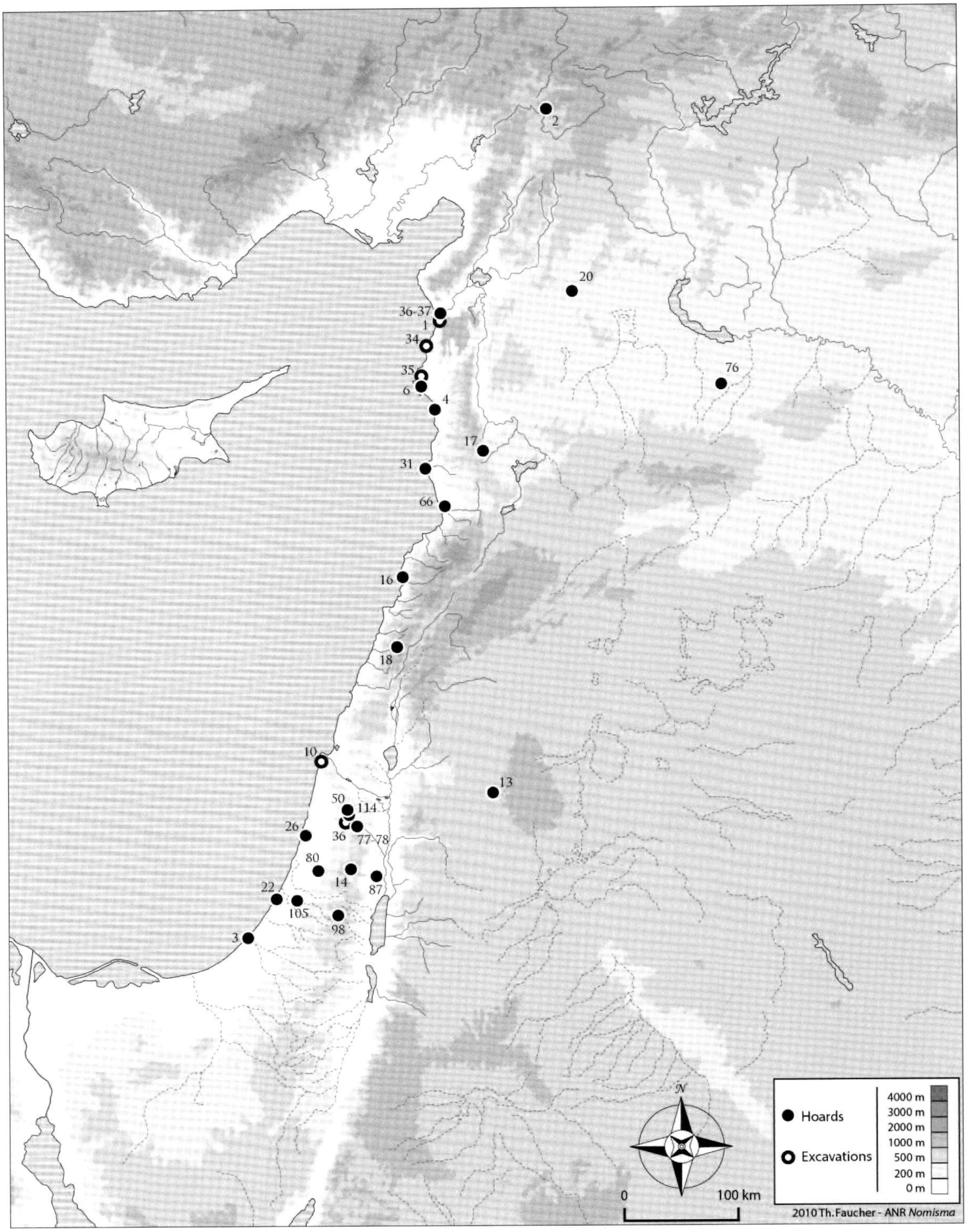

Map 5. Athens: all denominations.

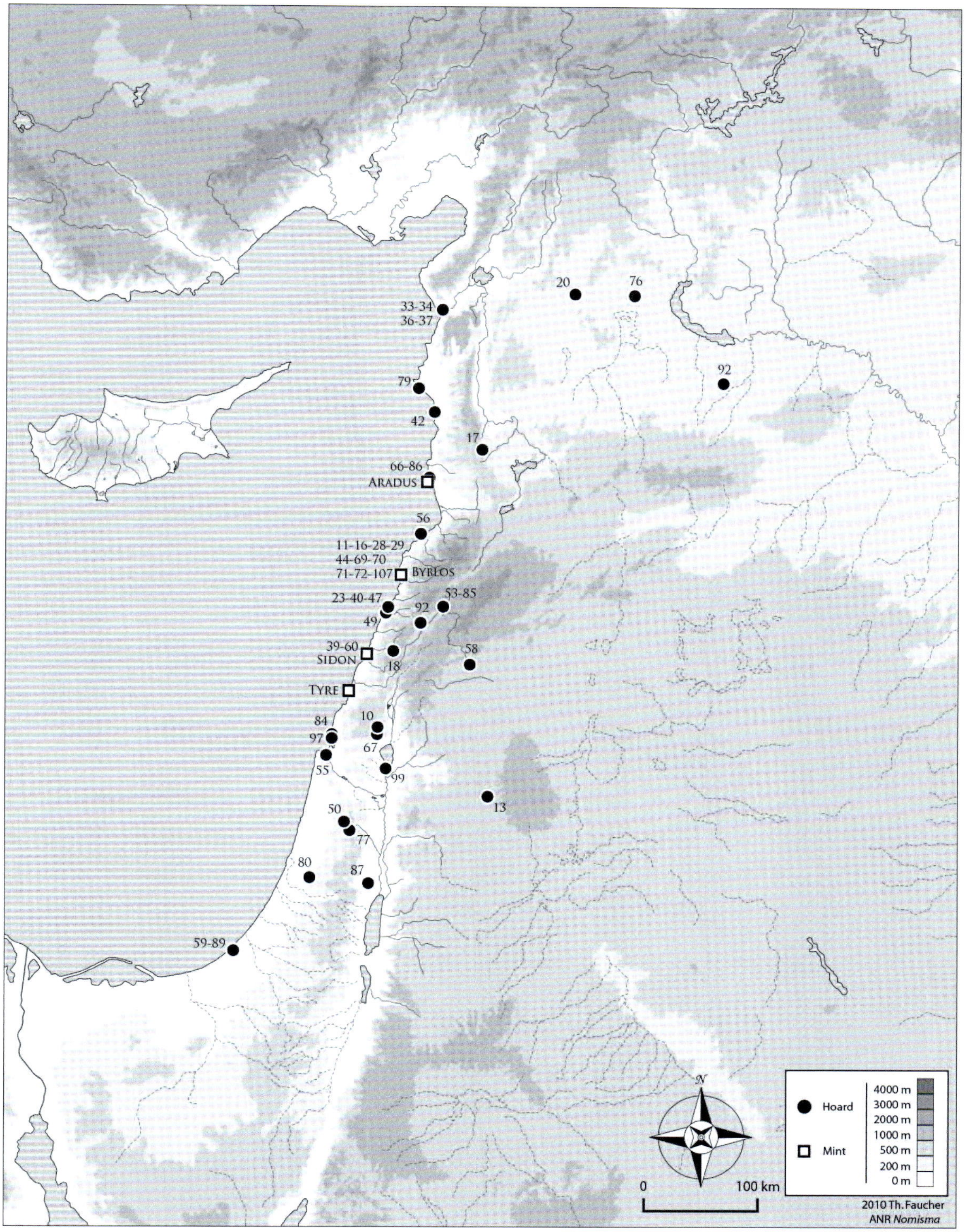

Map 6. Phoenician mints of the fifth and fourth centuries.

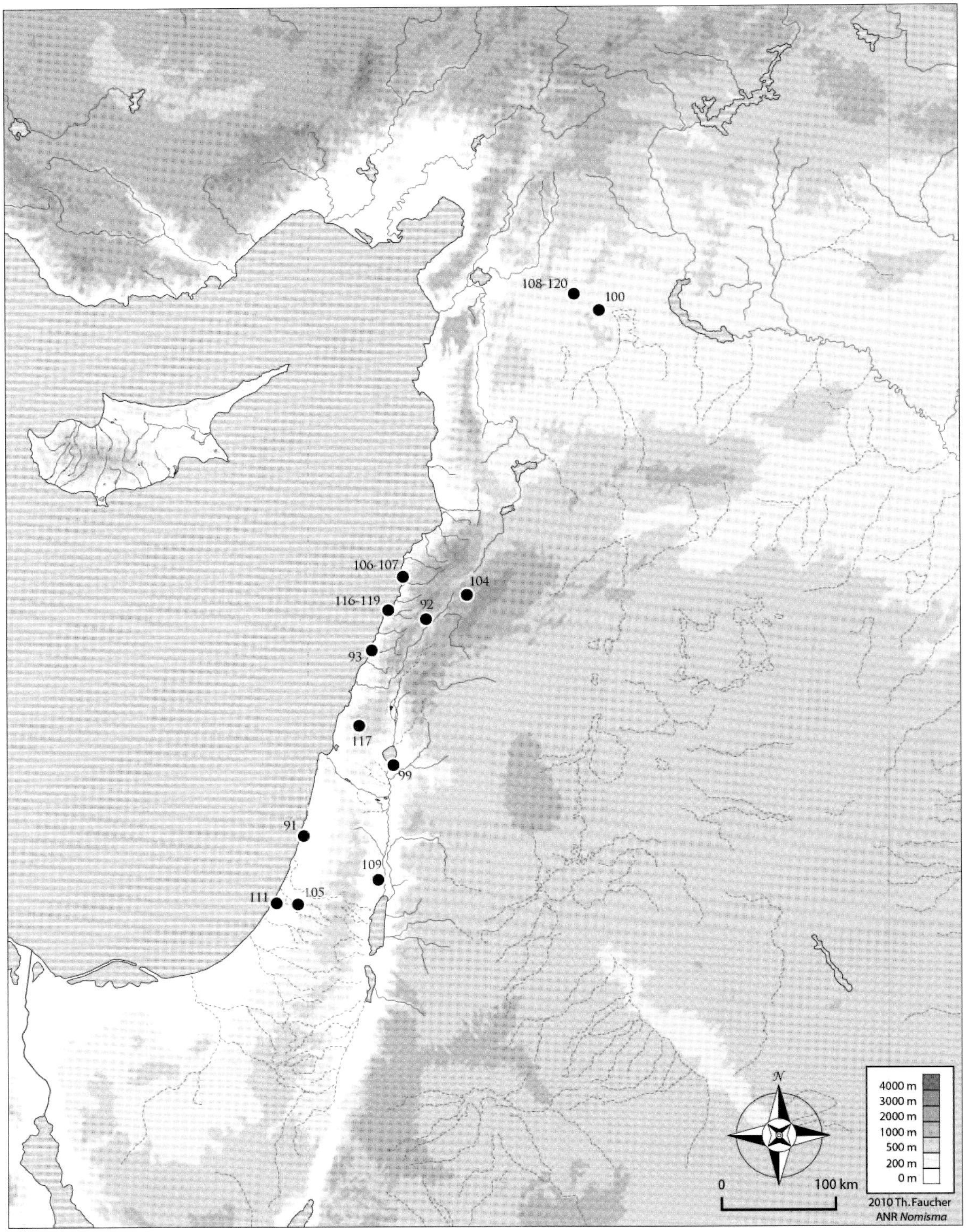

Map 7. Alexanders: 325–300 BC.

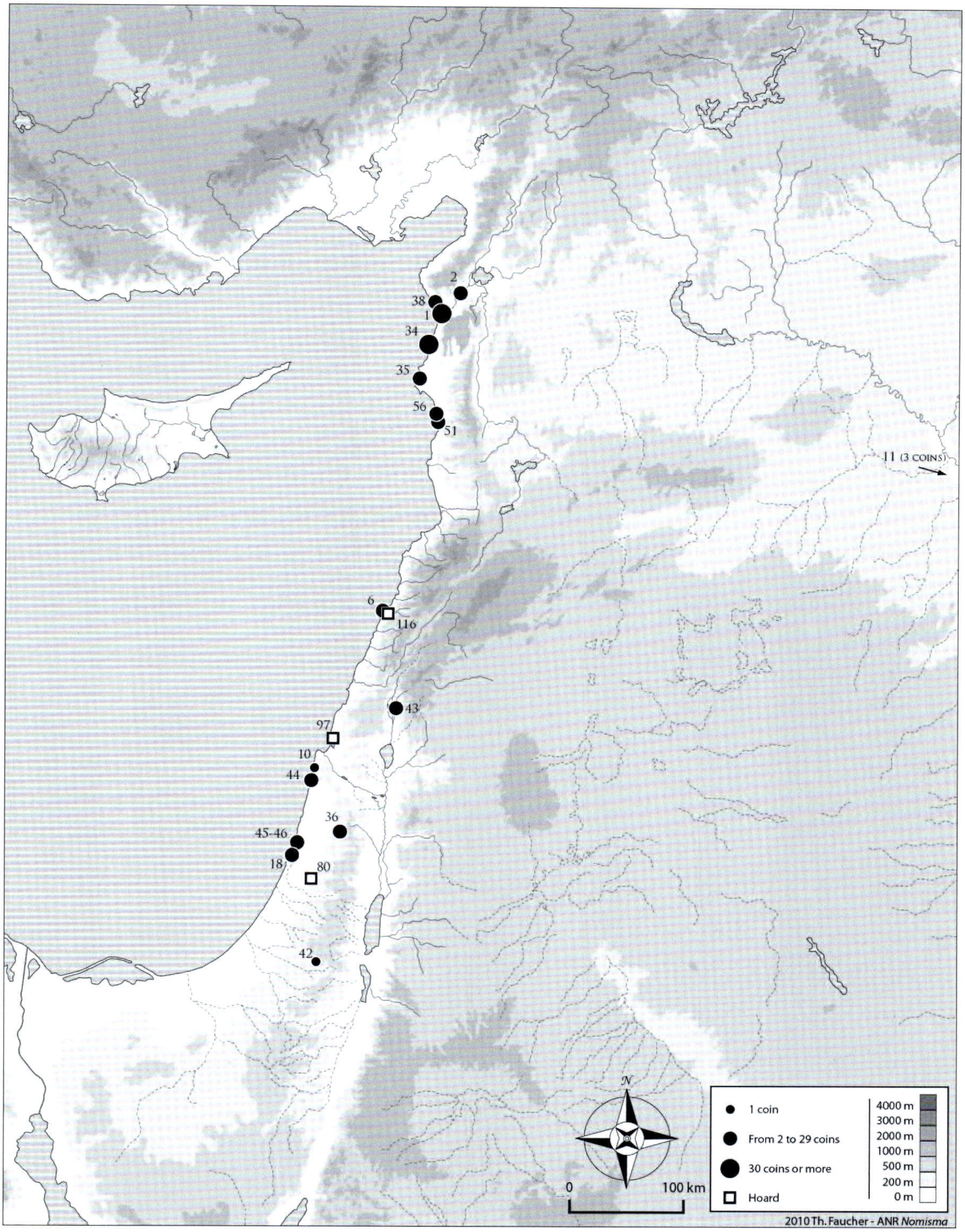

Map 8. Alexanders: bronze.

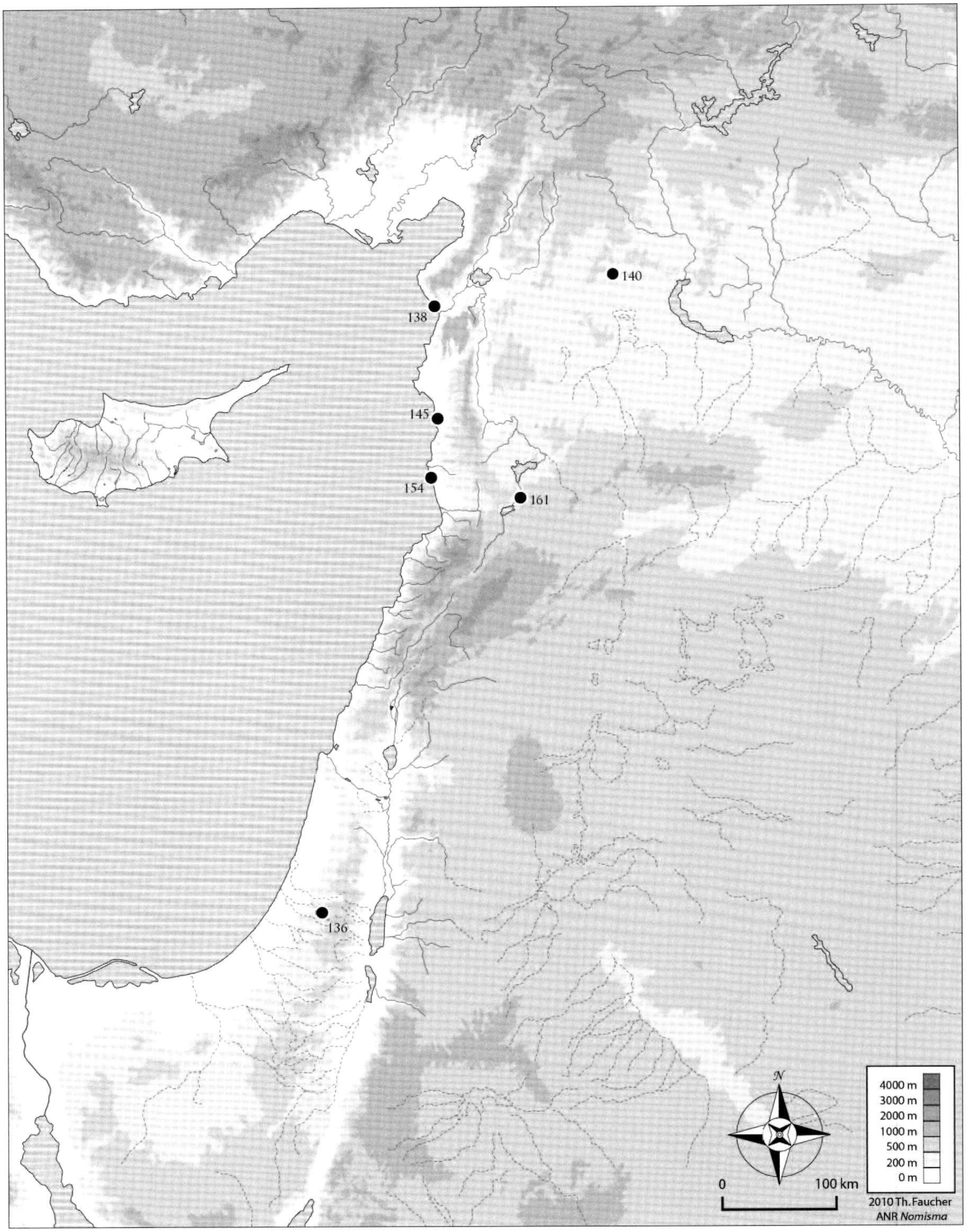

Map 9. Alexanders: third century.

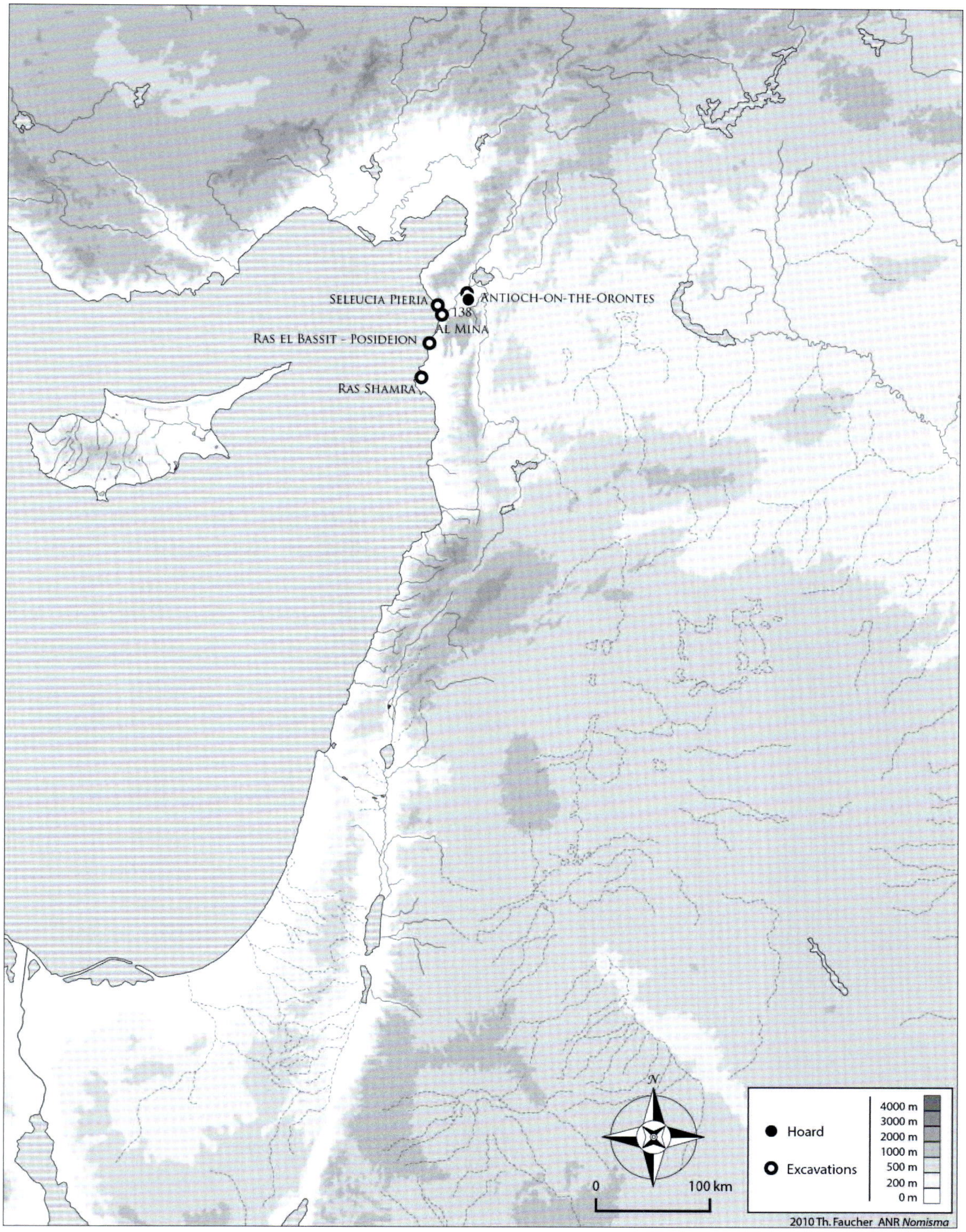

Map 10. Ptolemaic enclave.

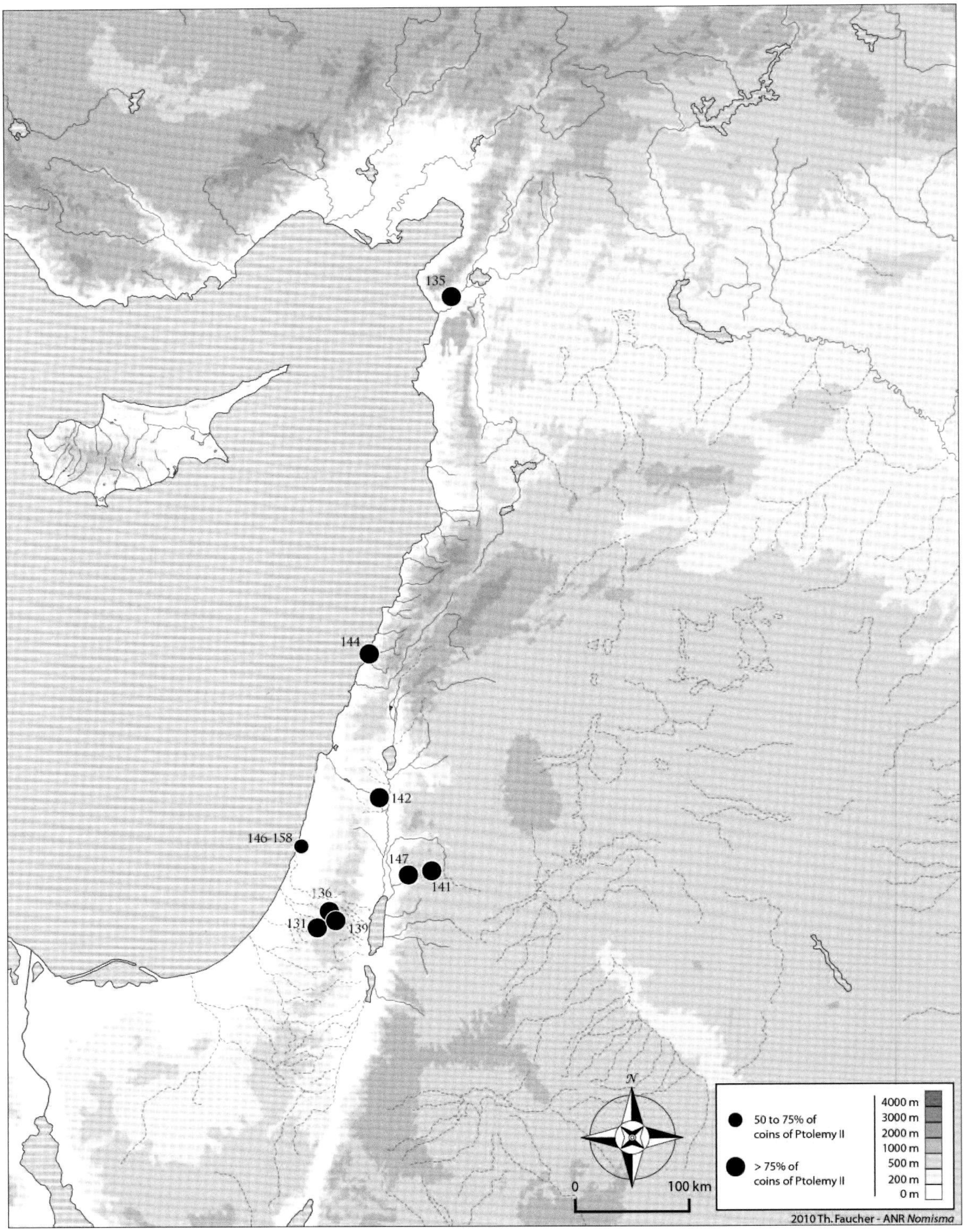

Map 11. Percentage of coins of Ptolemy II in hoards of the third century BC.

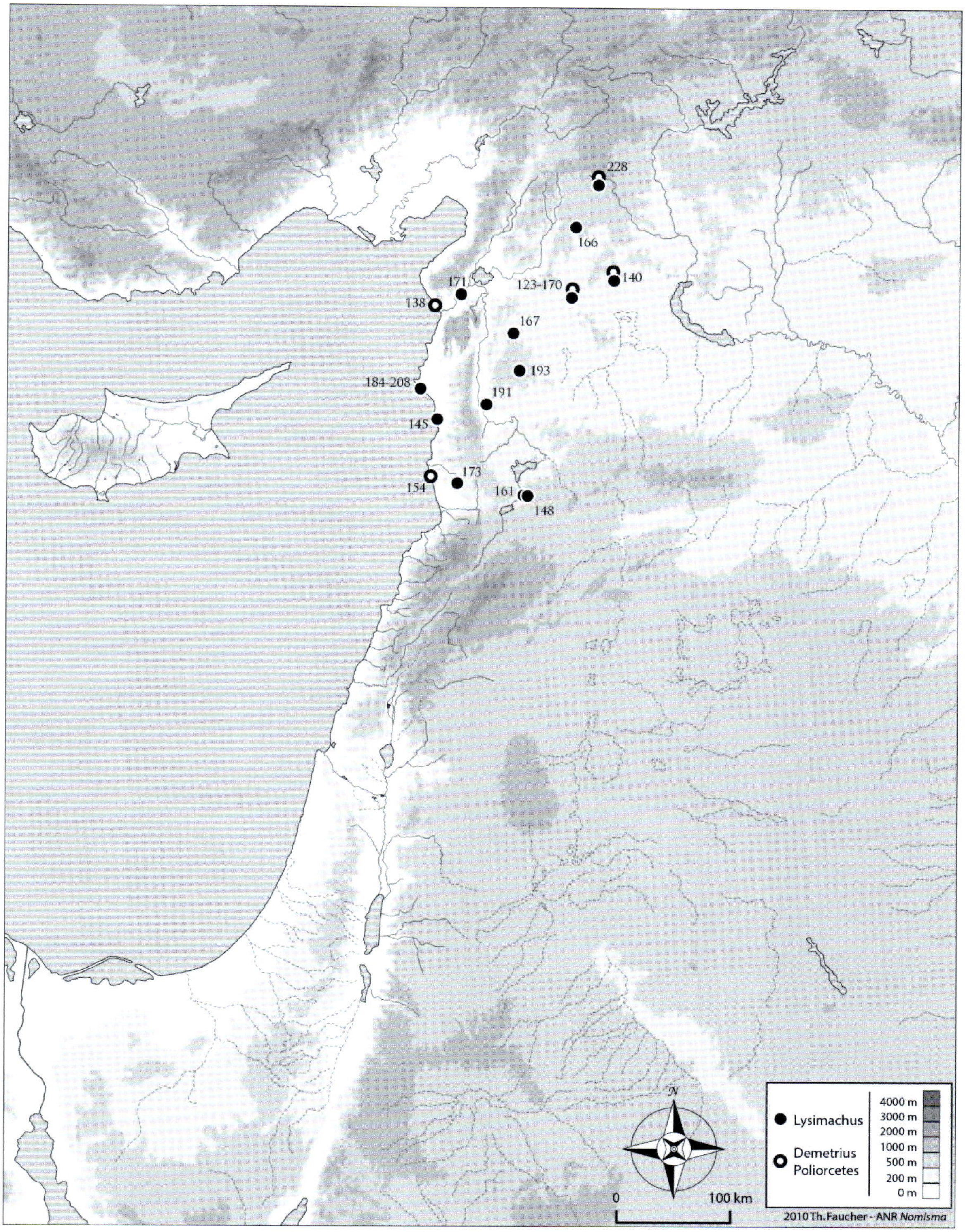

Map 12. Lysimachus and Demetrius Poliorcetes.

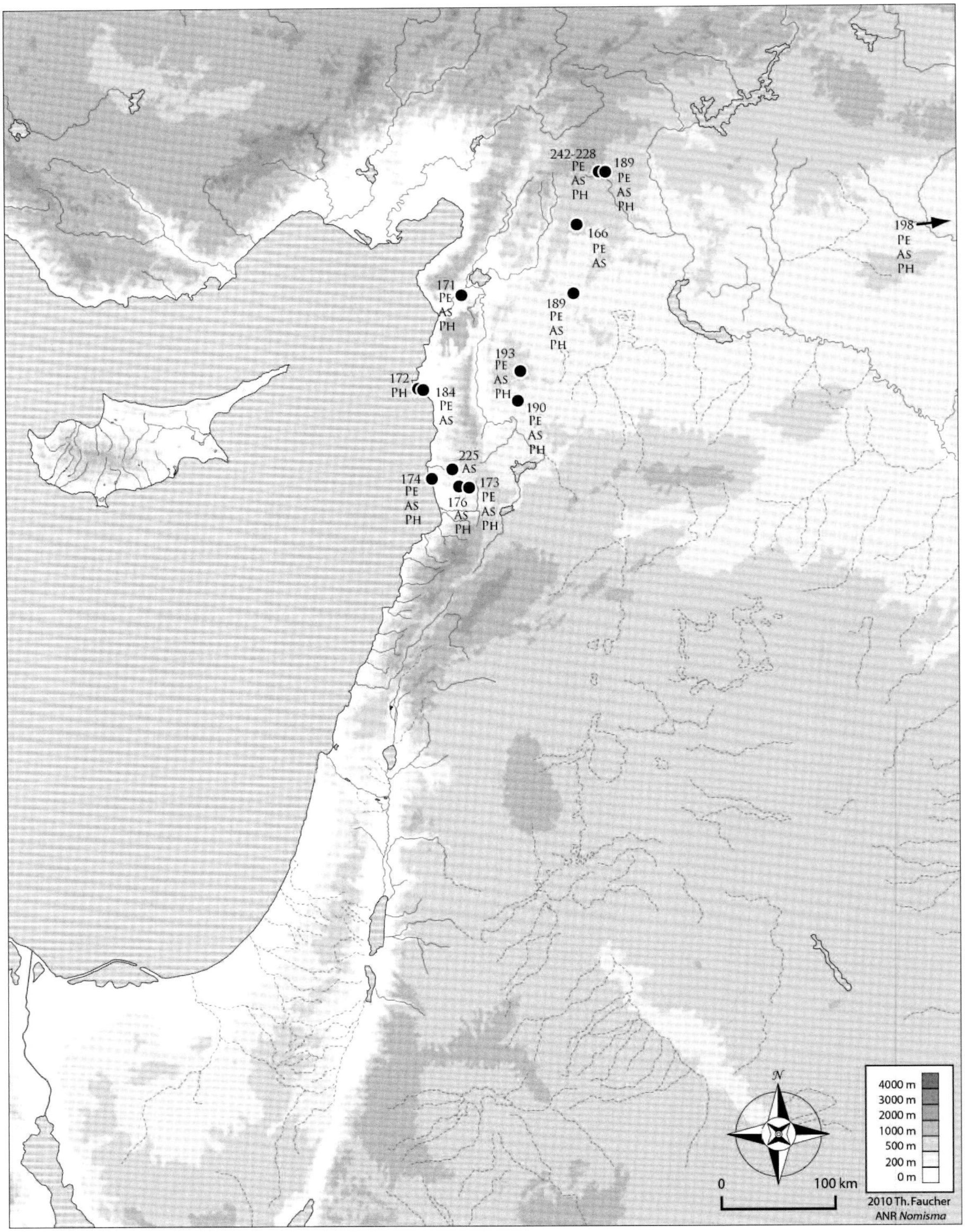

Map 13. Alexanders of Perge, Aspendus, and Phaselis.

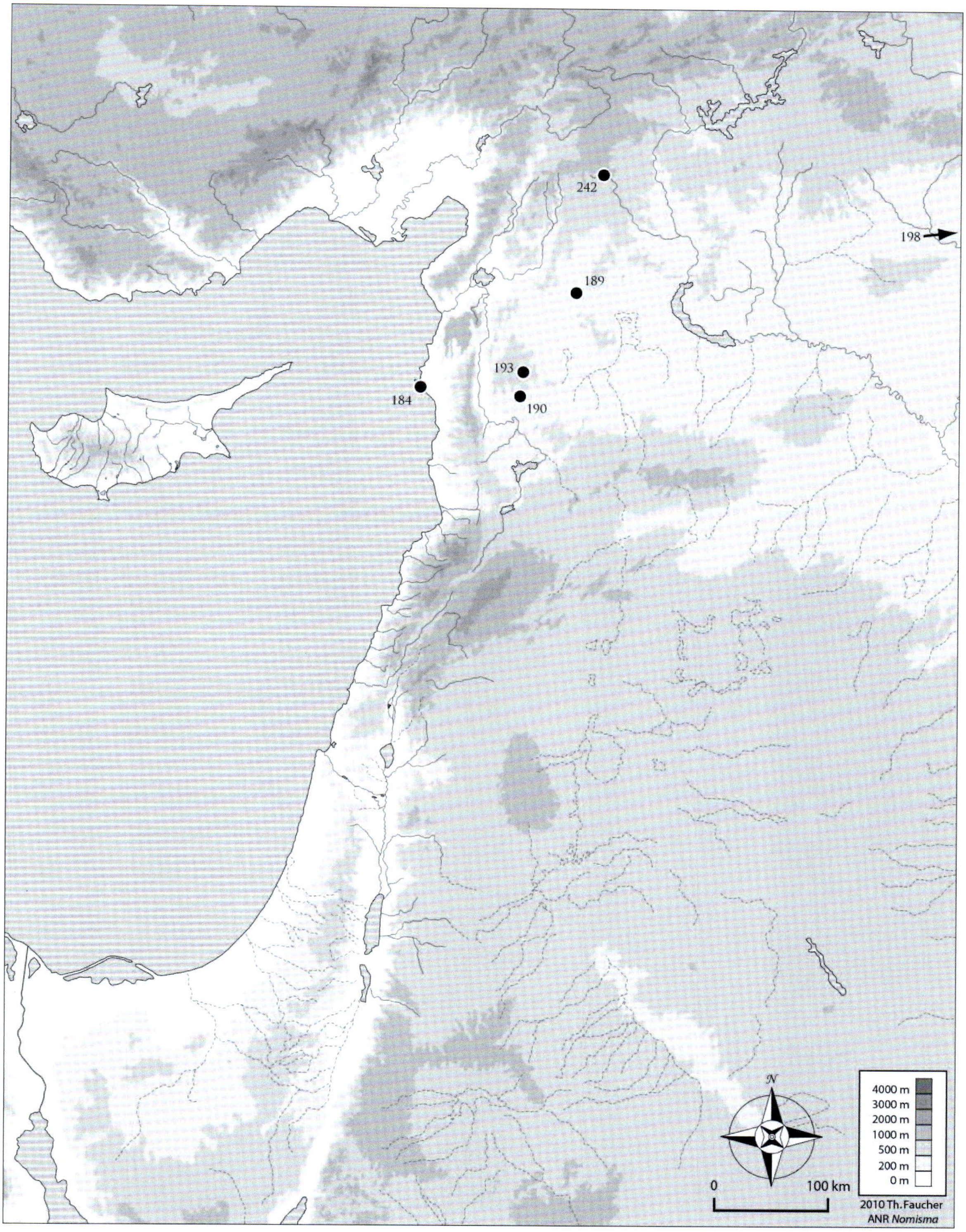

Map 14. Alexanders with countermarks.

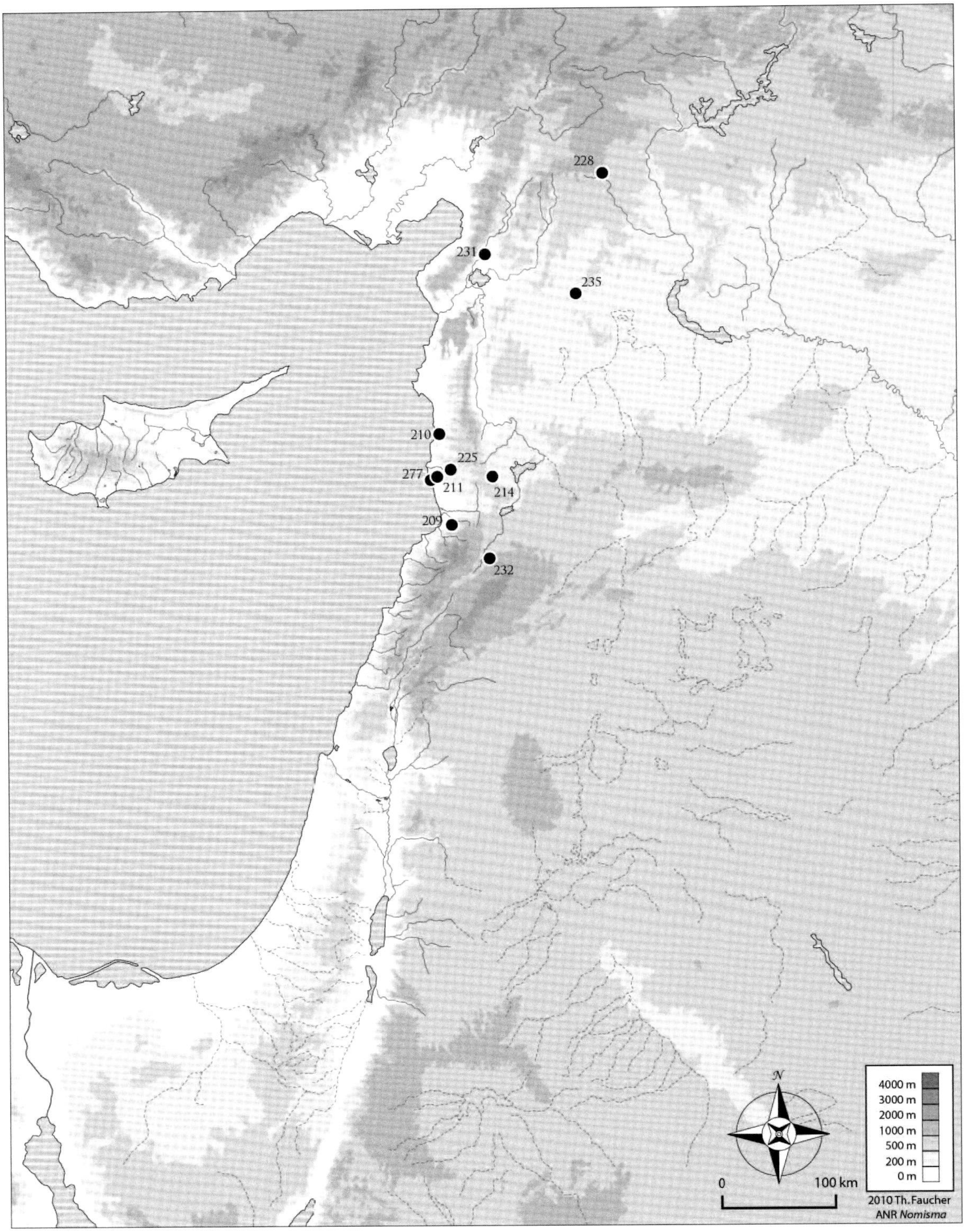

Map 15. Wreathed tetradrachms.

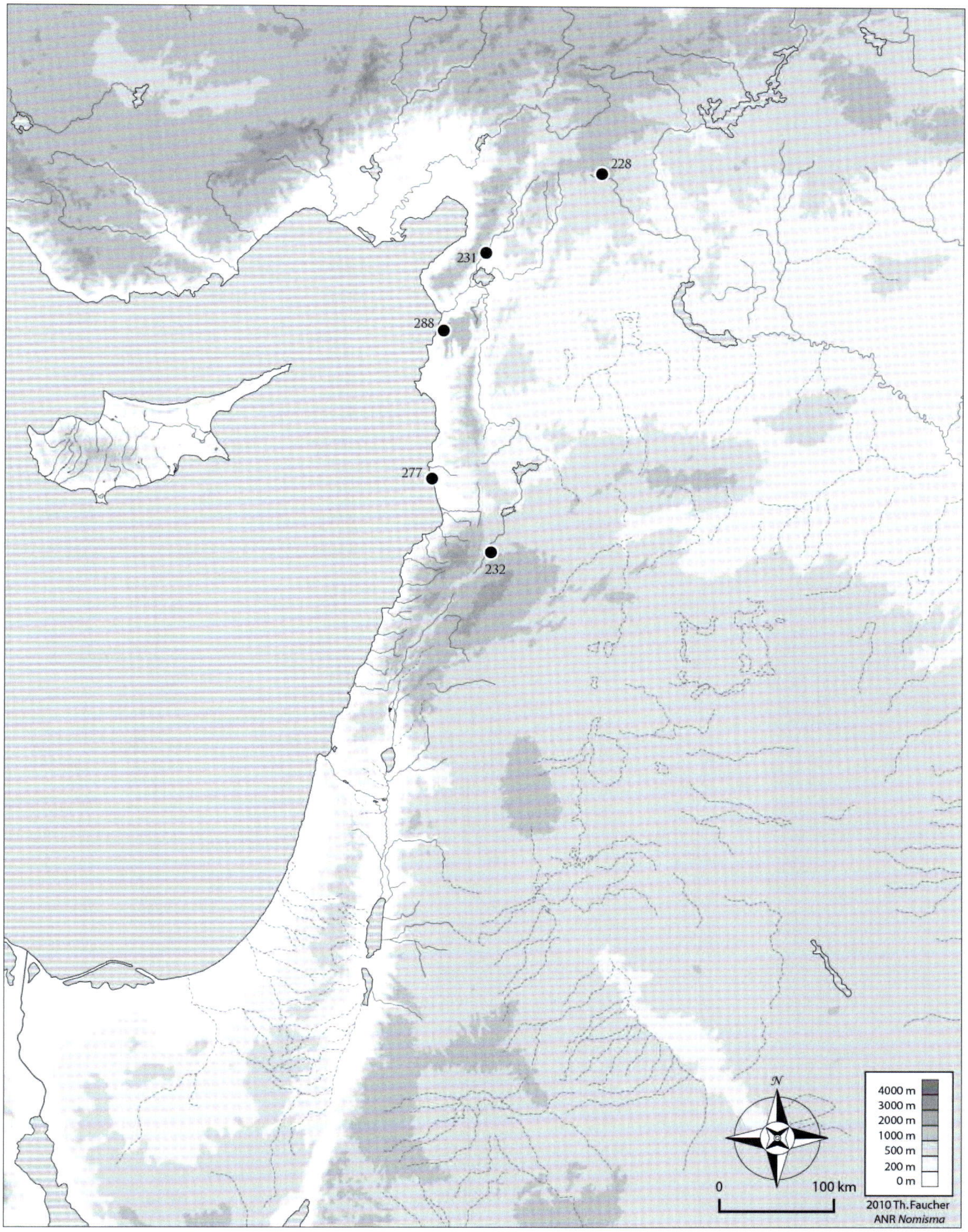

Map 16. New Style tetradrachms.

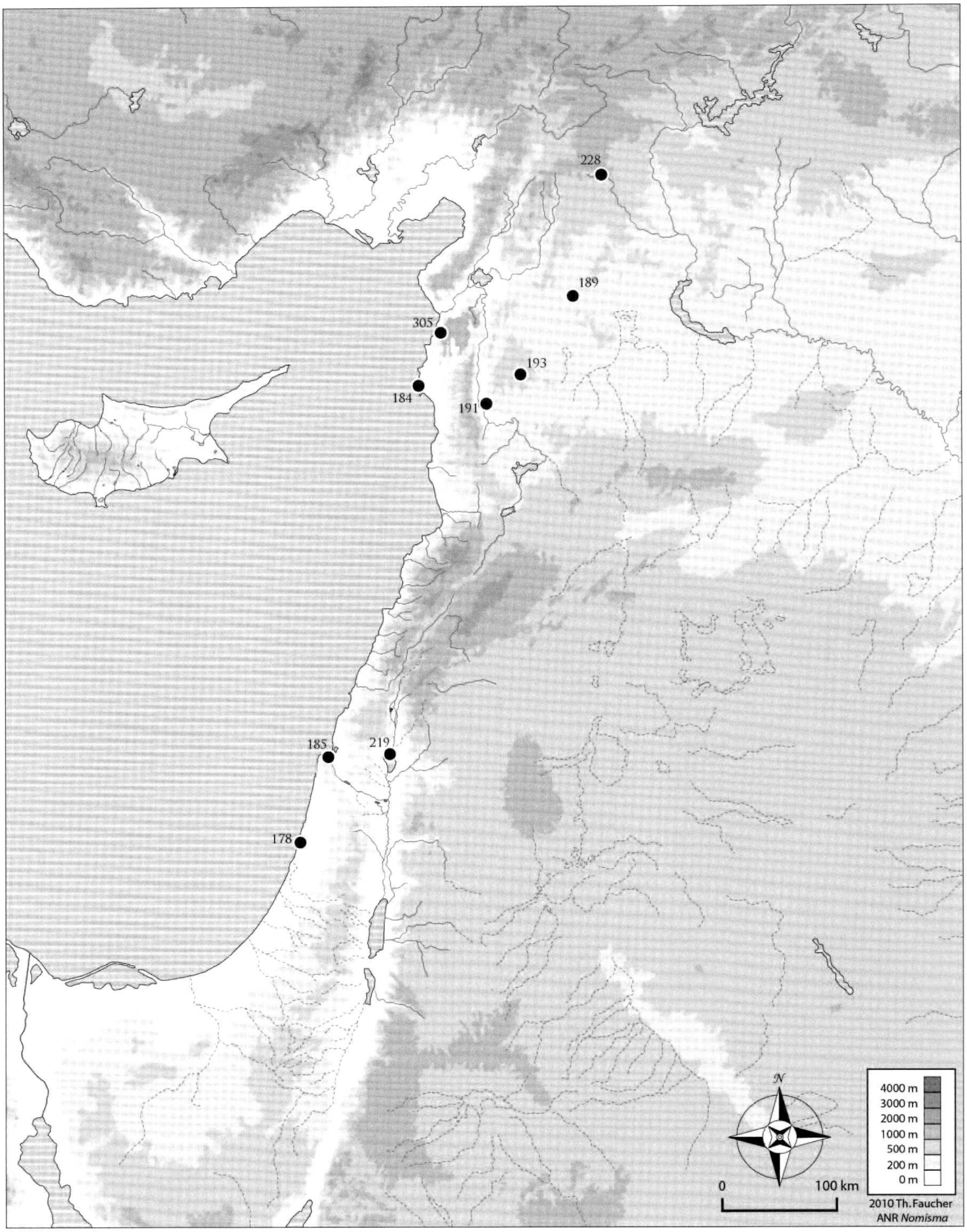

Map 17. Antiochus IV.

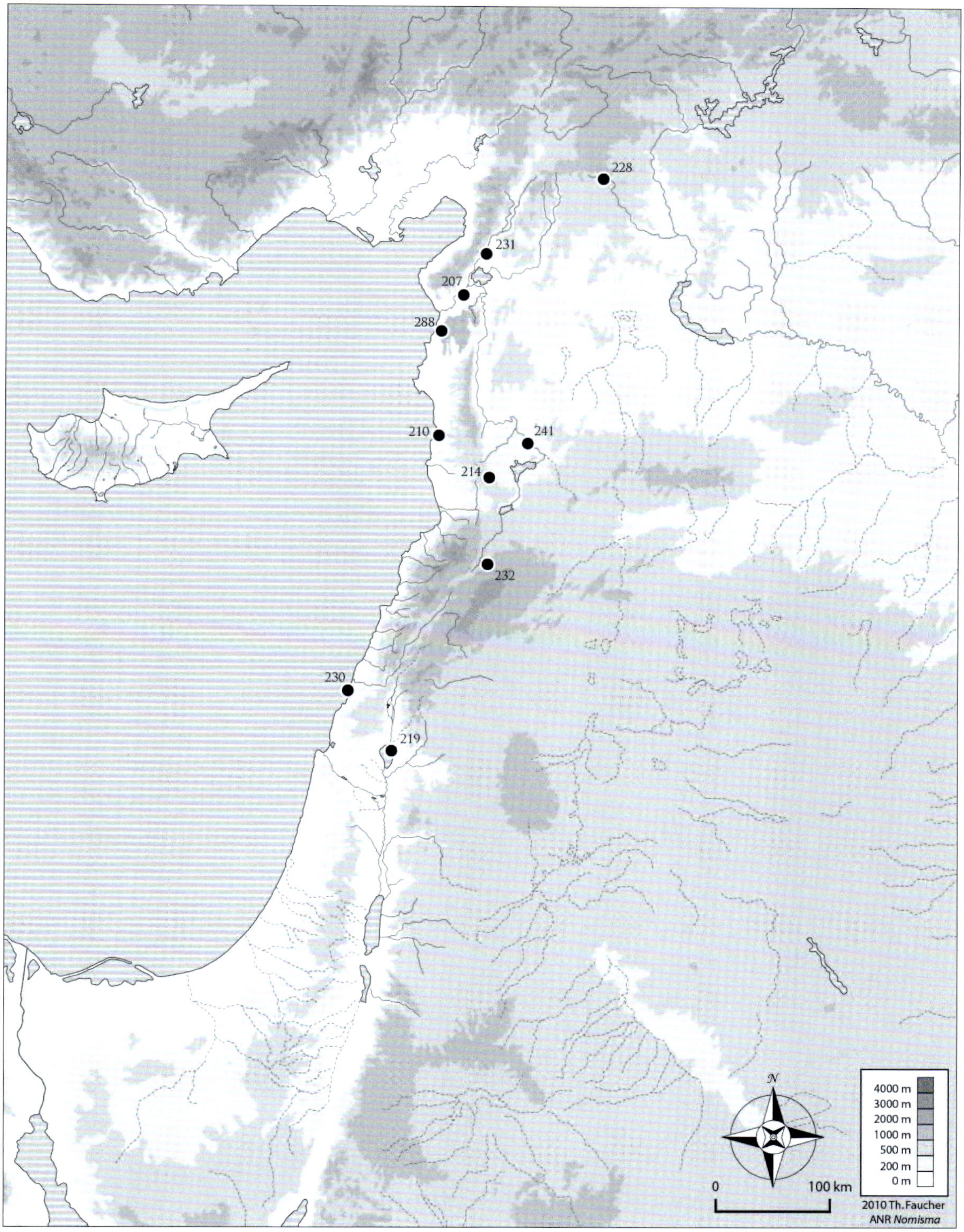

Map 18. Demetrius I.

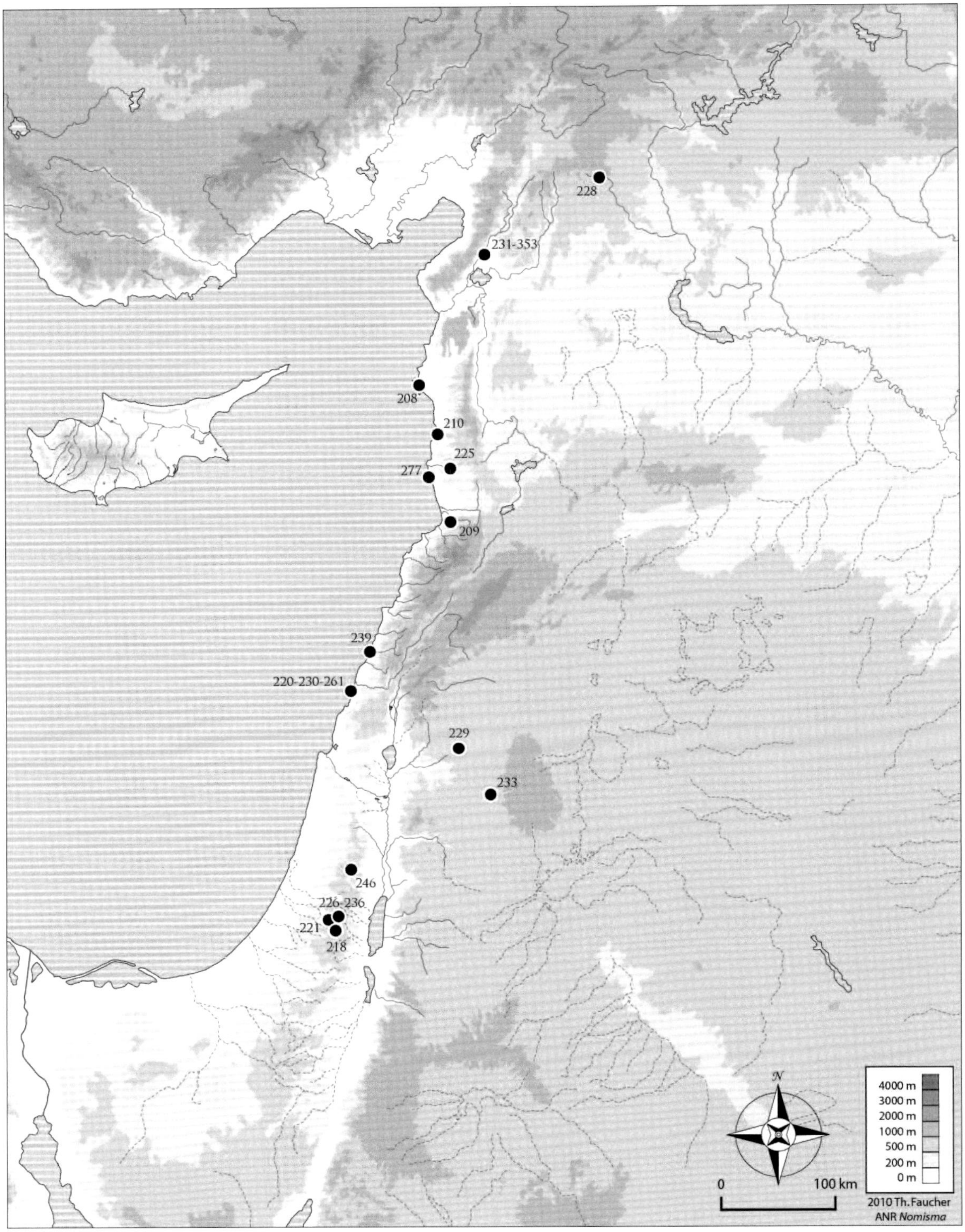

Map 19. Alexander I Balas.

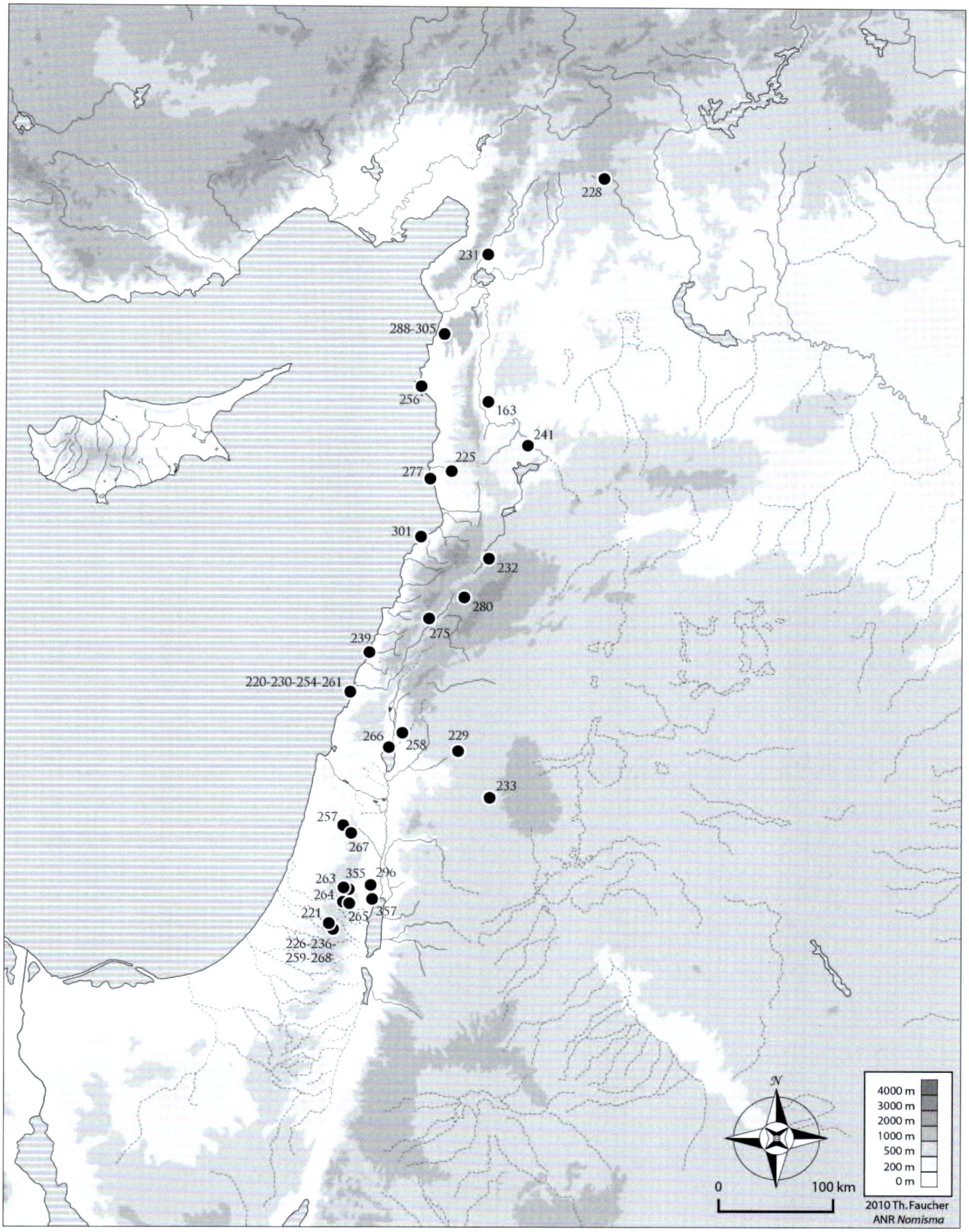

Map 20. Demetrius II.

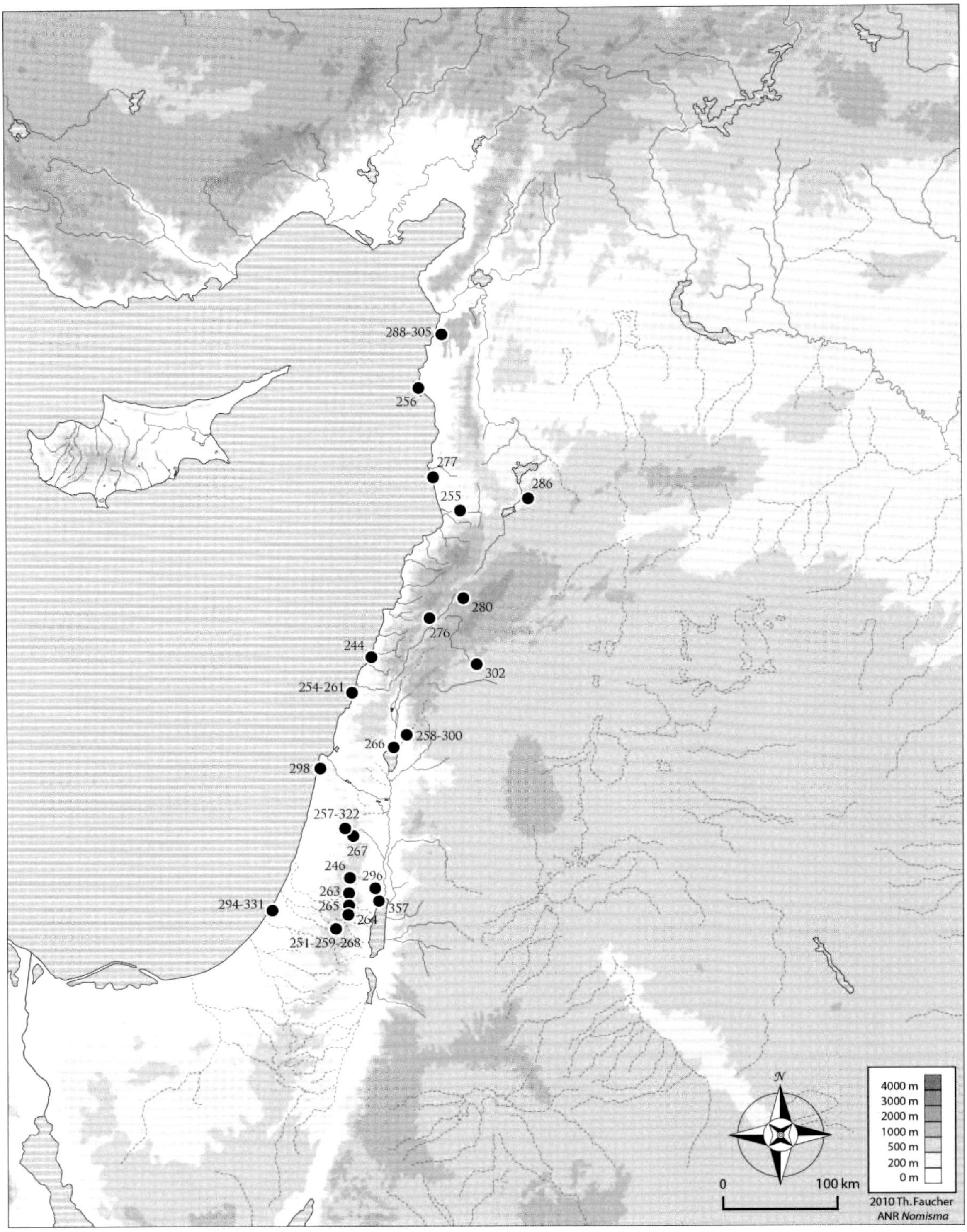

Map 21. Antiochus VII.

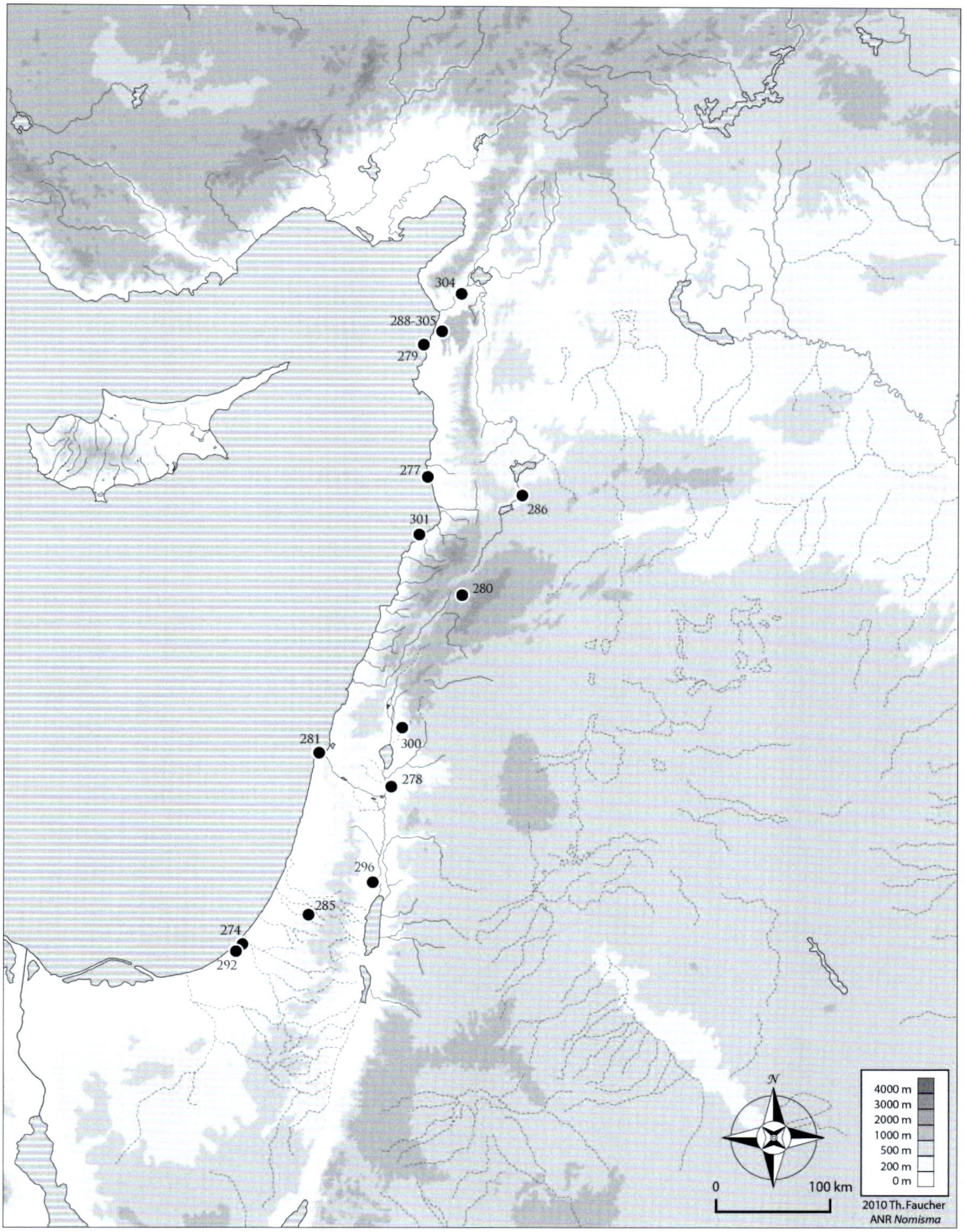

Map 22. Antiochus VIII.

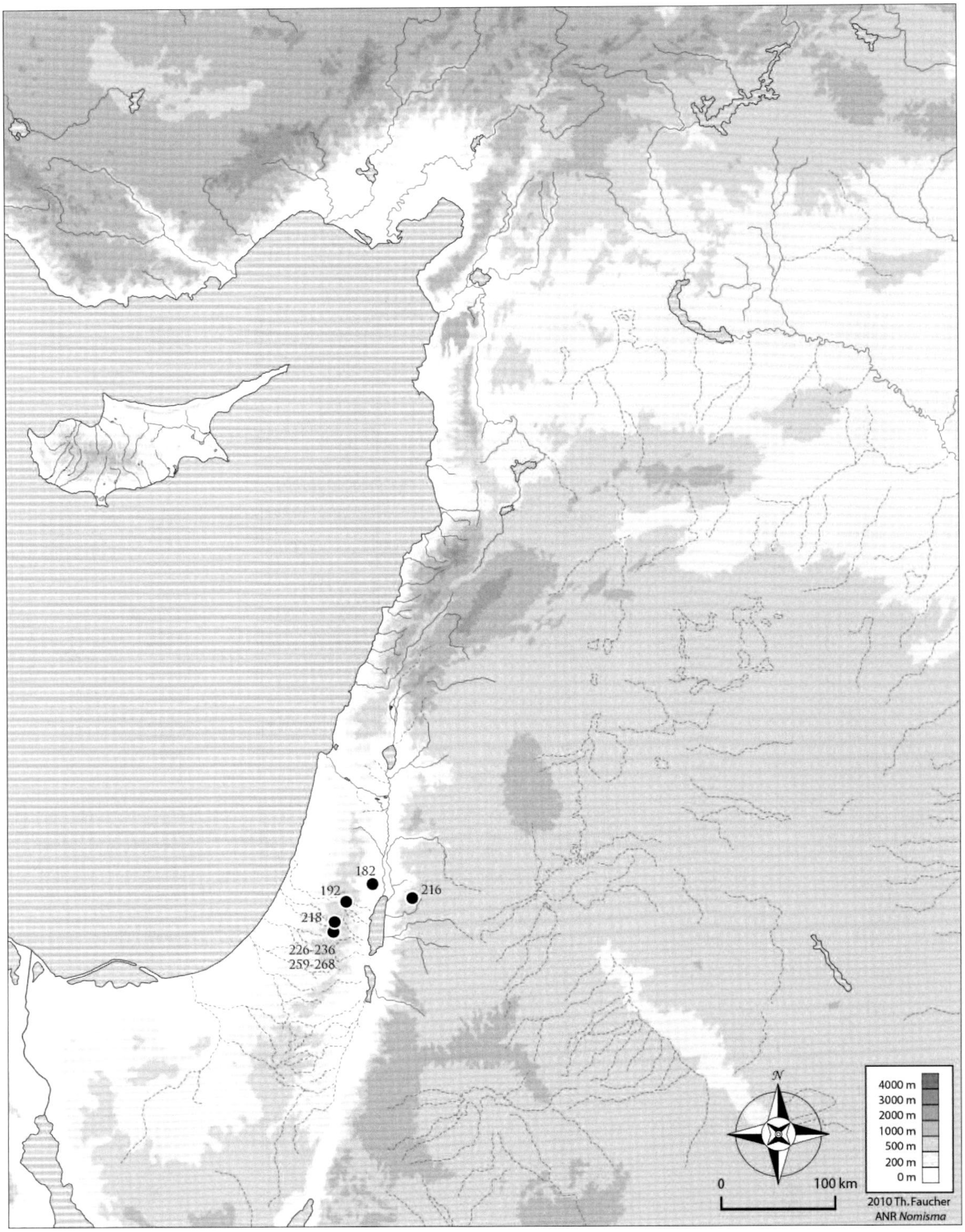

Map 23. Ptolemy VI.

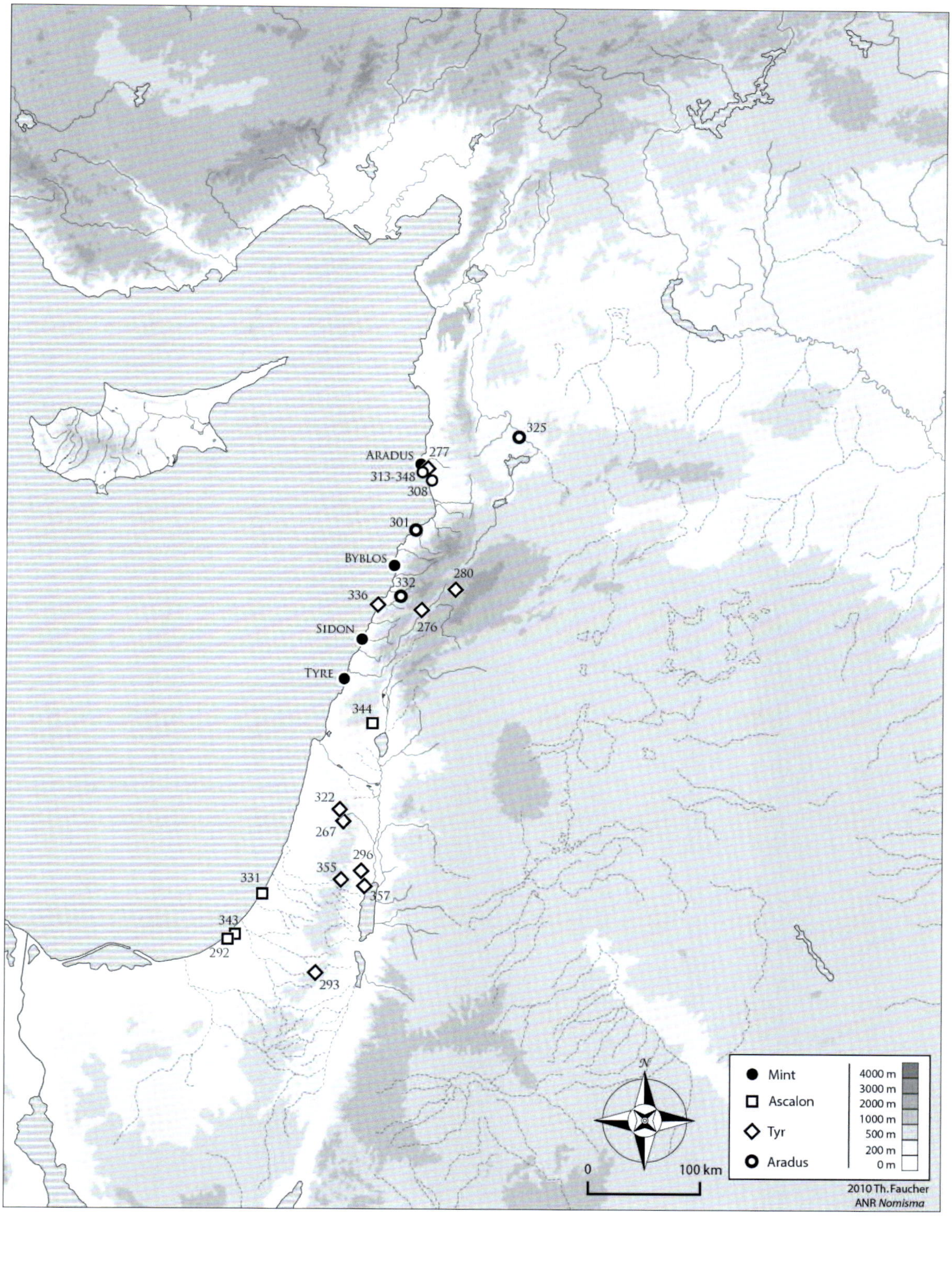

Map 24. Aradus, Tyre, and Ascalon, autonomous silver.

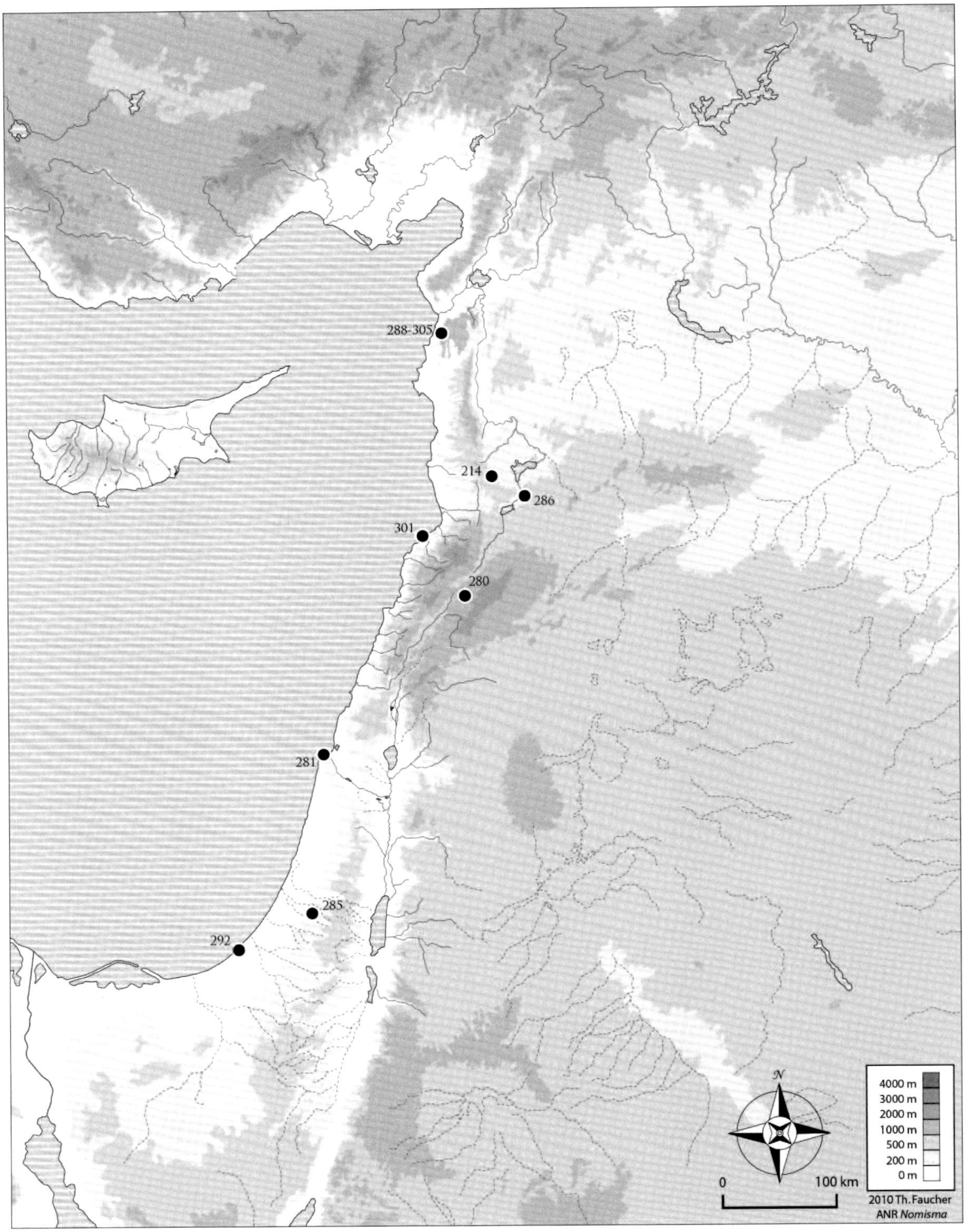

Map 25. Antiochus IX.

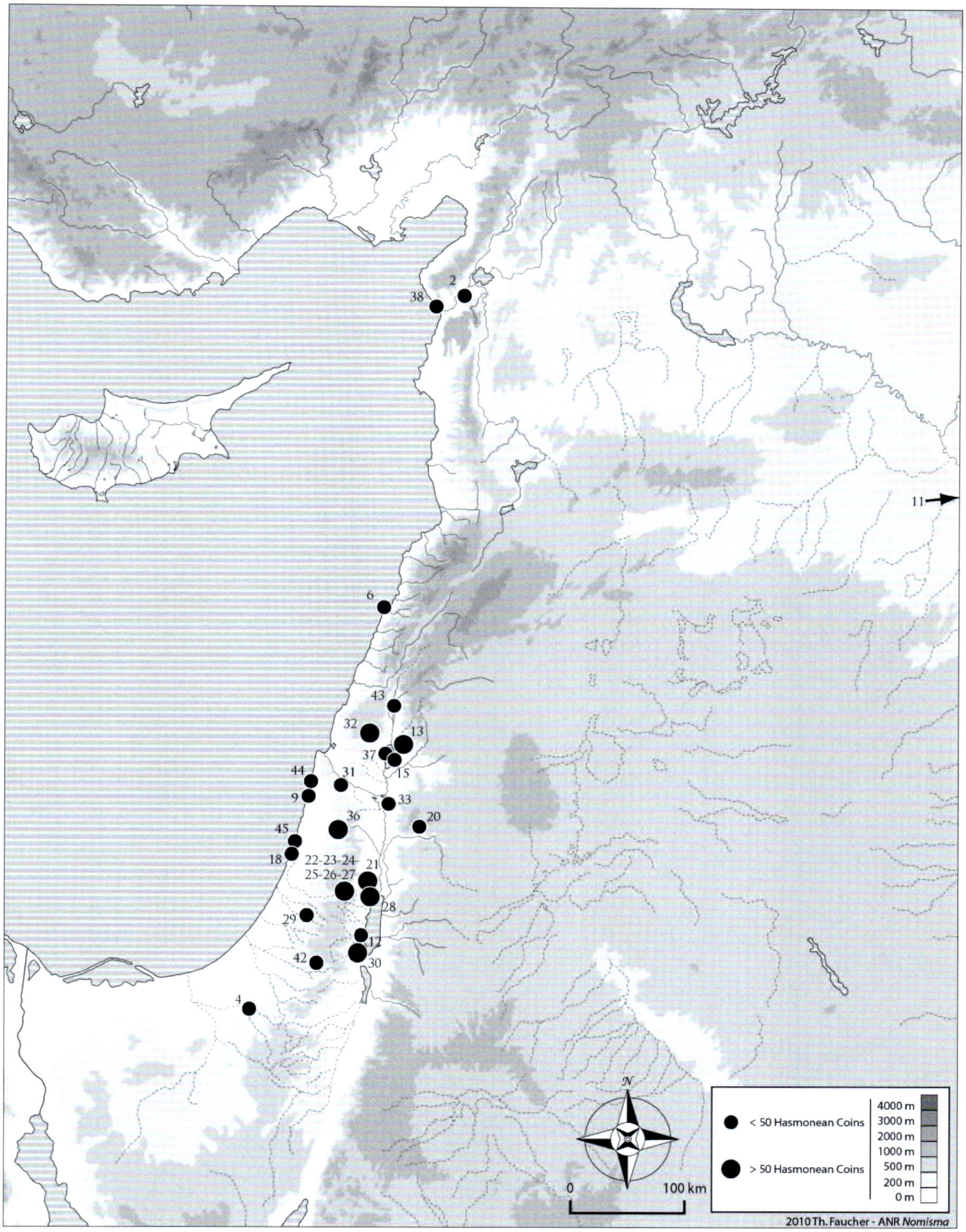

Map 26. Hasmonean coins in excavations.

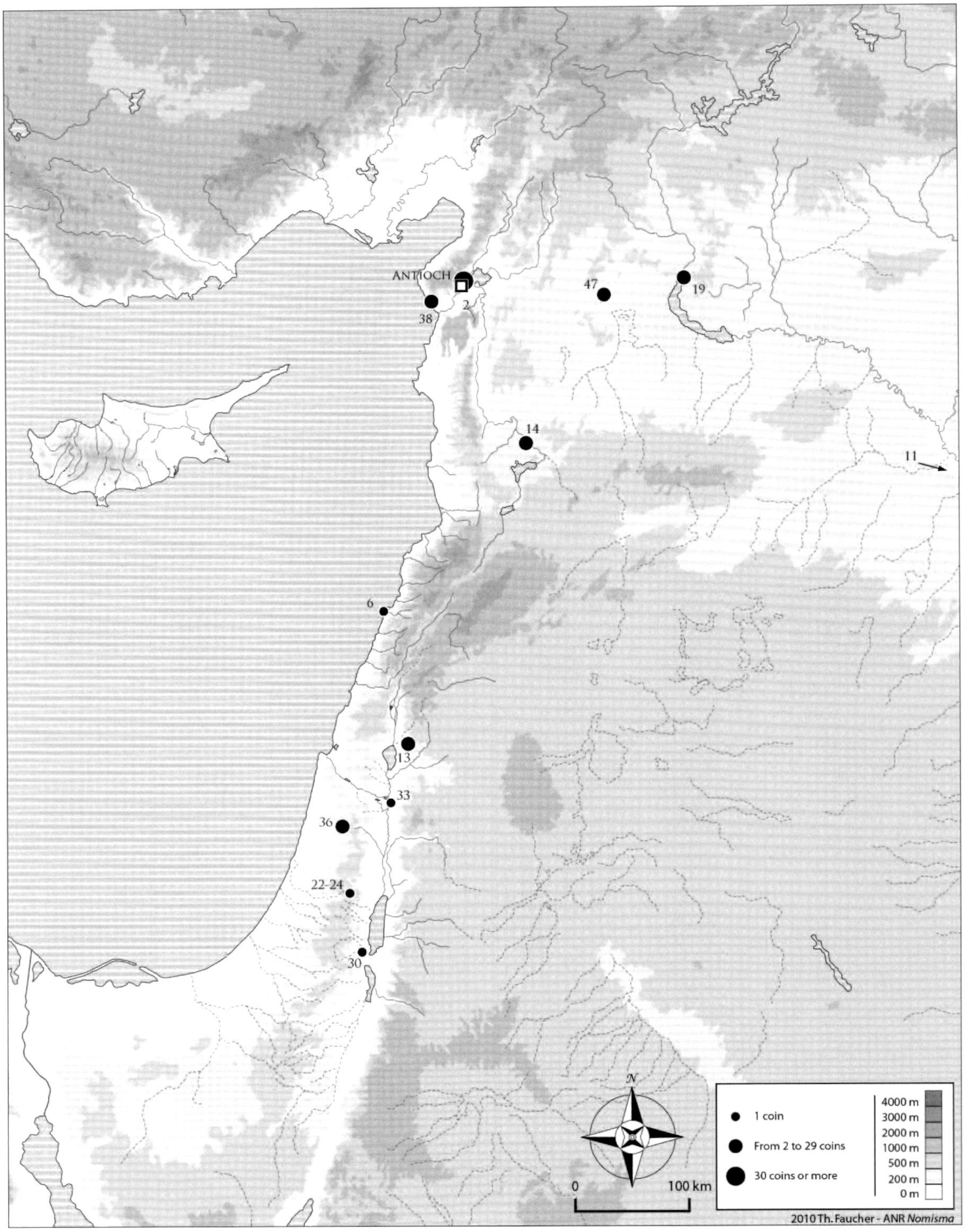

Map 27. Civic coins of Antioch in excavations.

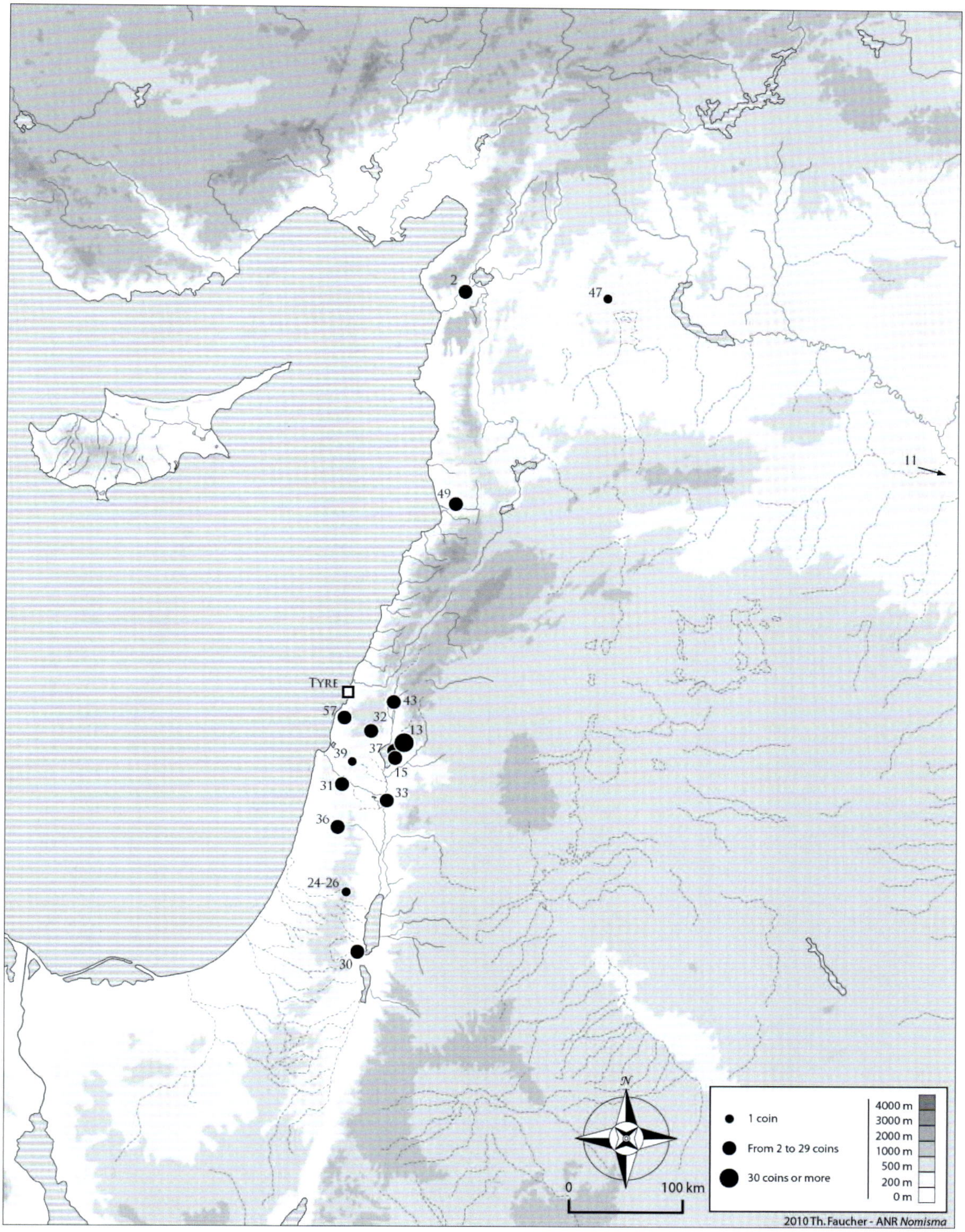

Map 28. Civic coins of Tyre in excavations.

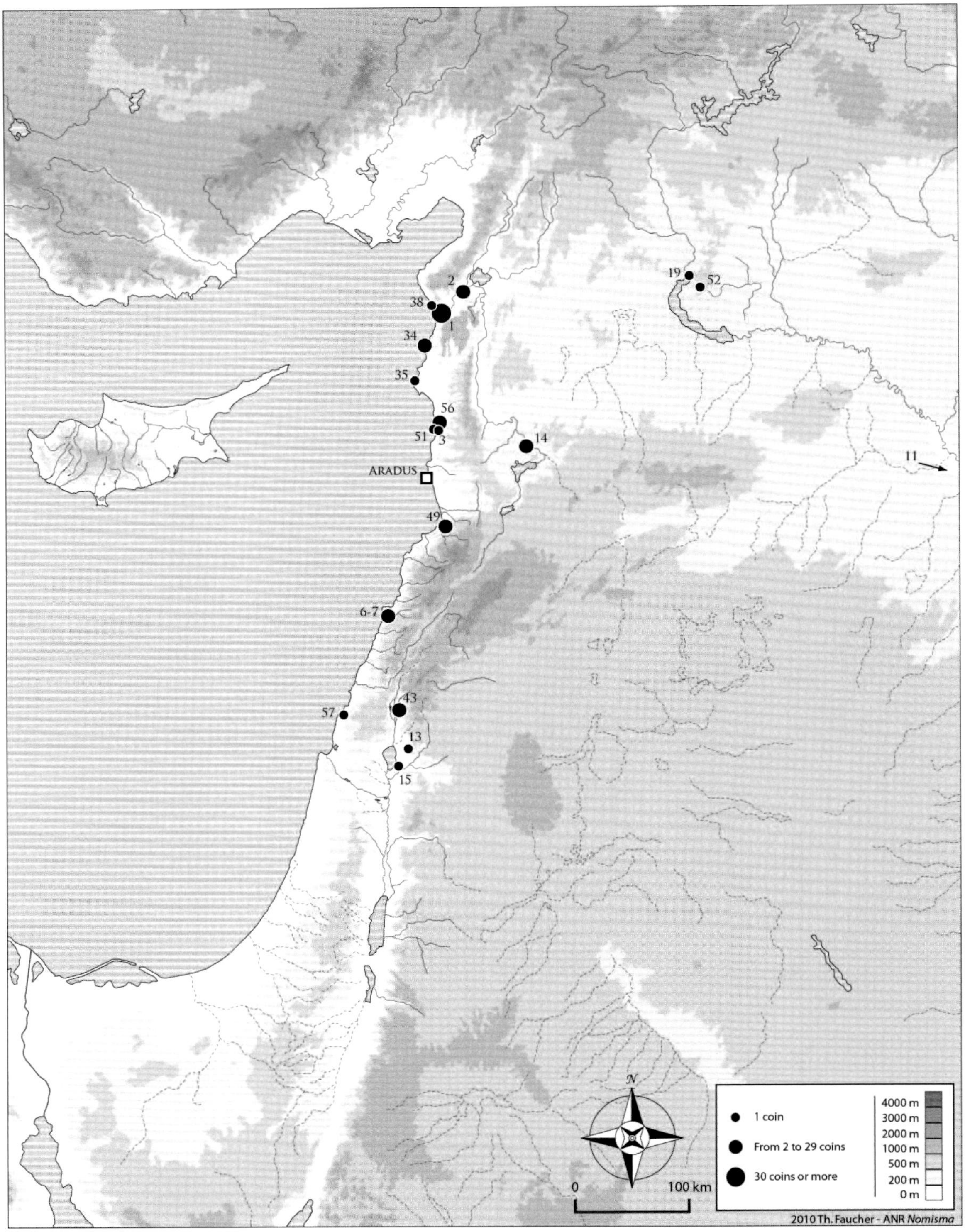

Map 29. Civic coins of Aradus in excavations.

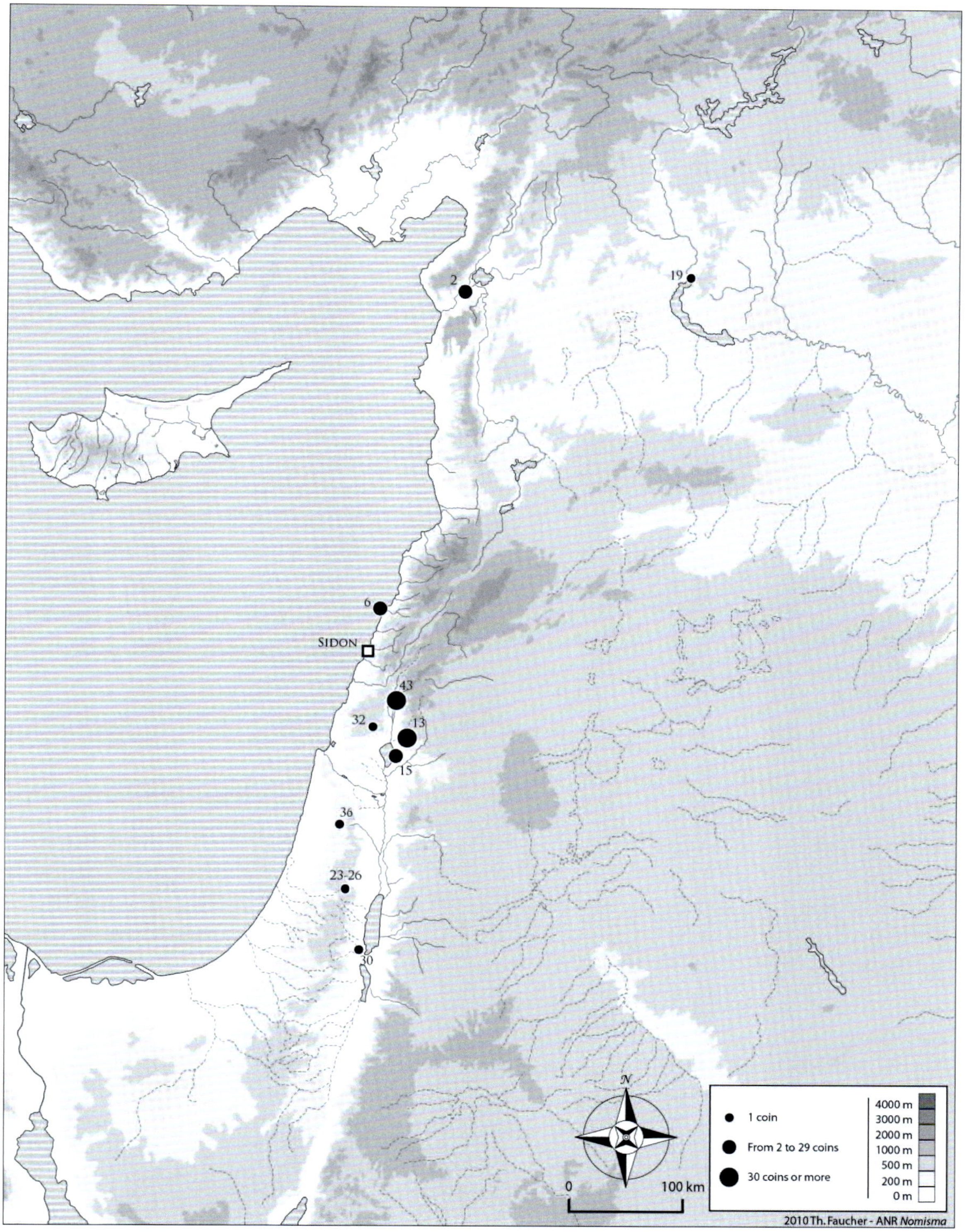

Map 30. Civic coins of Sidon in excavations.

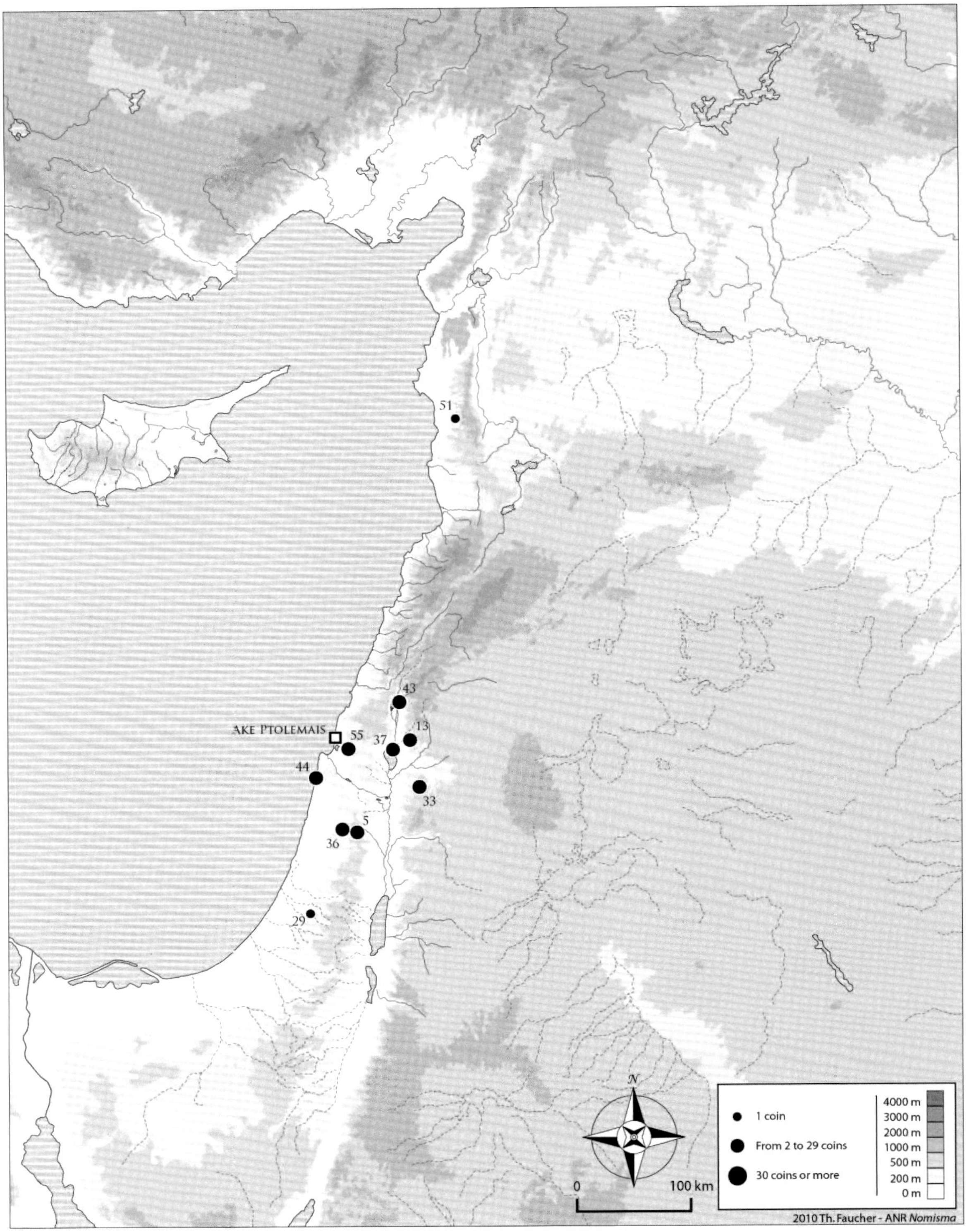

Map 31. Civic coins of Ake Ptolemais in excavations.

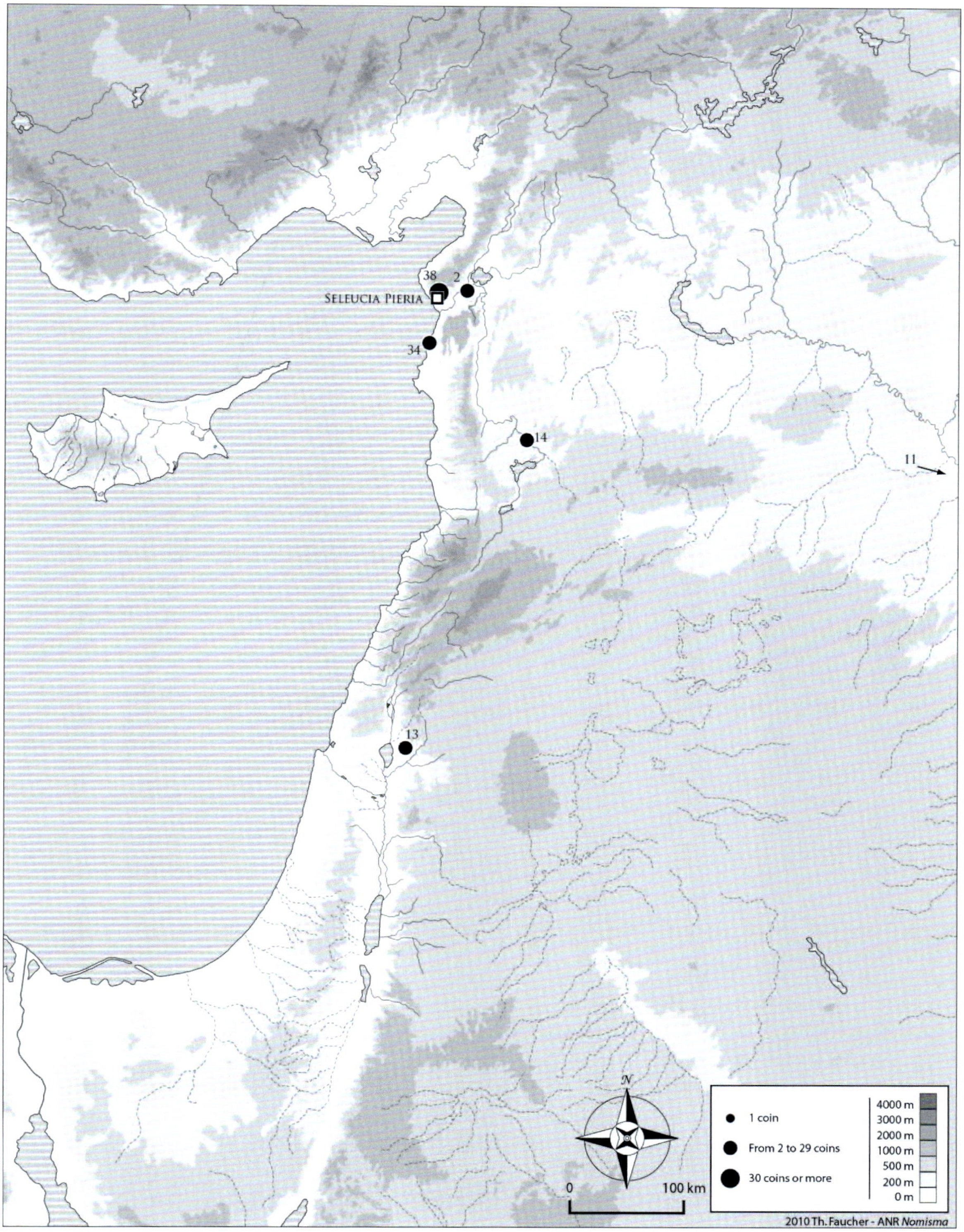

Map 32. Civic coins of Seleuceia Pieria in excavations.

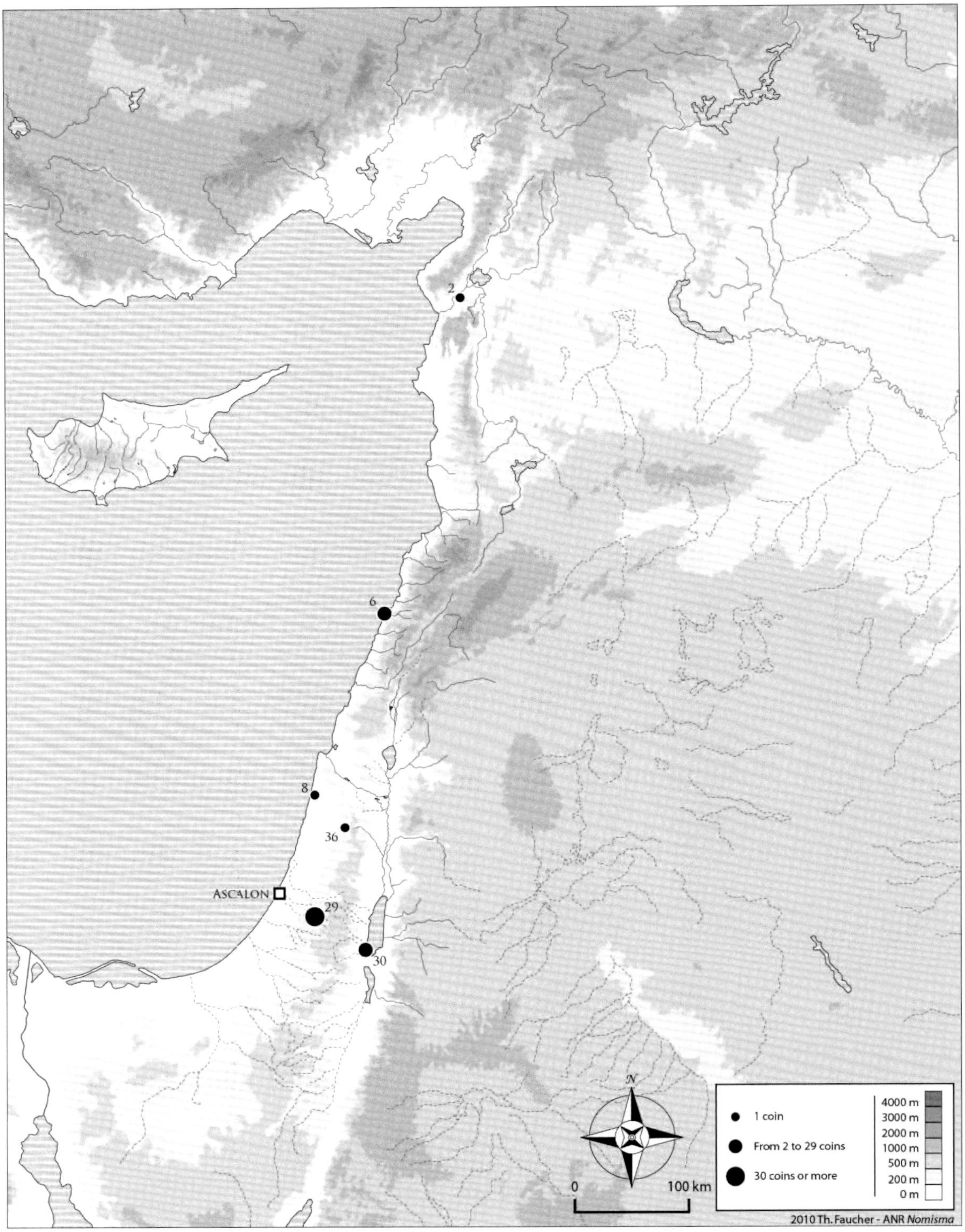

Map 33. Civic coins of Ascalon in excavations.

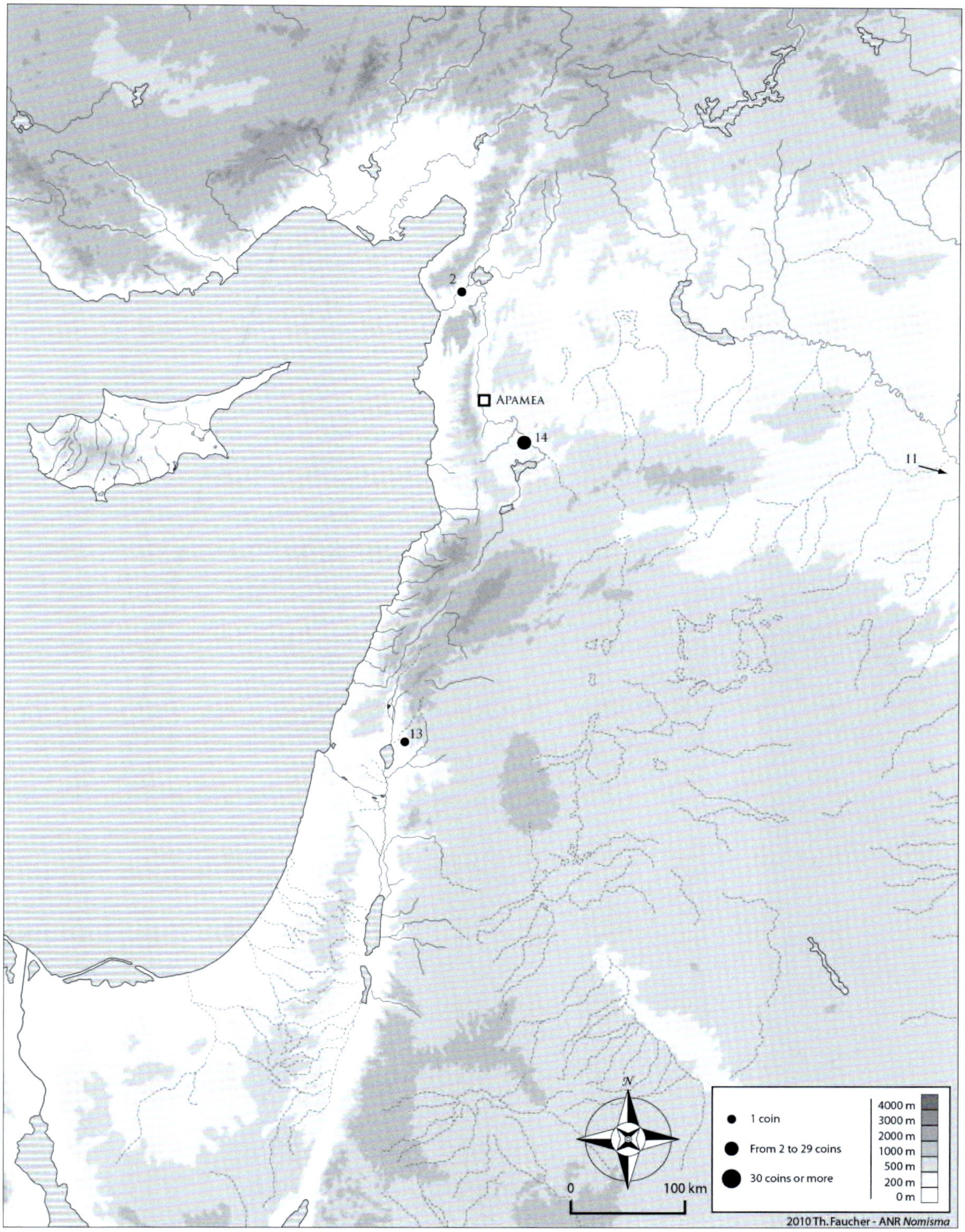

Map 34. Civic coins of Apamea in excavations.

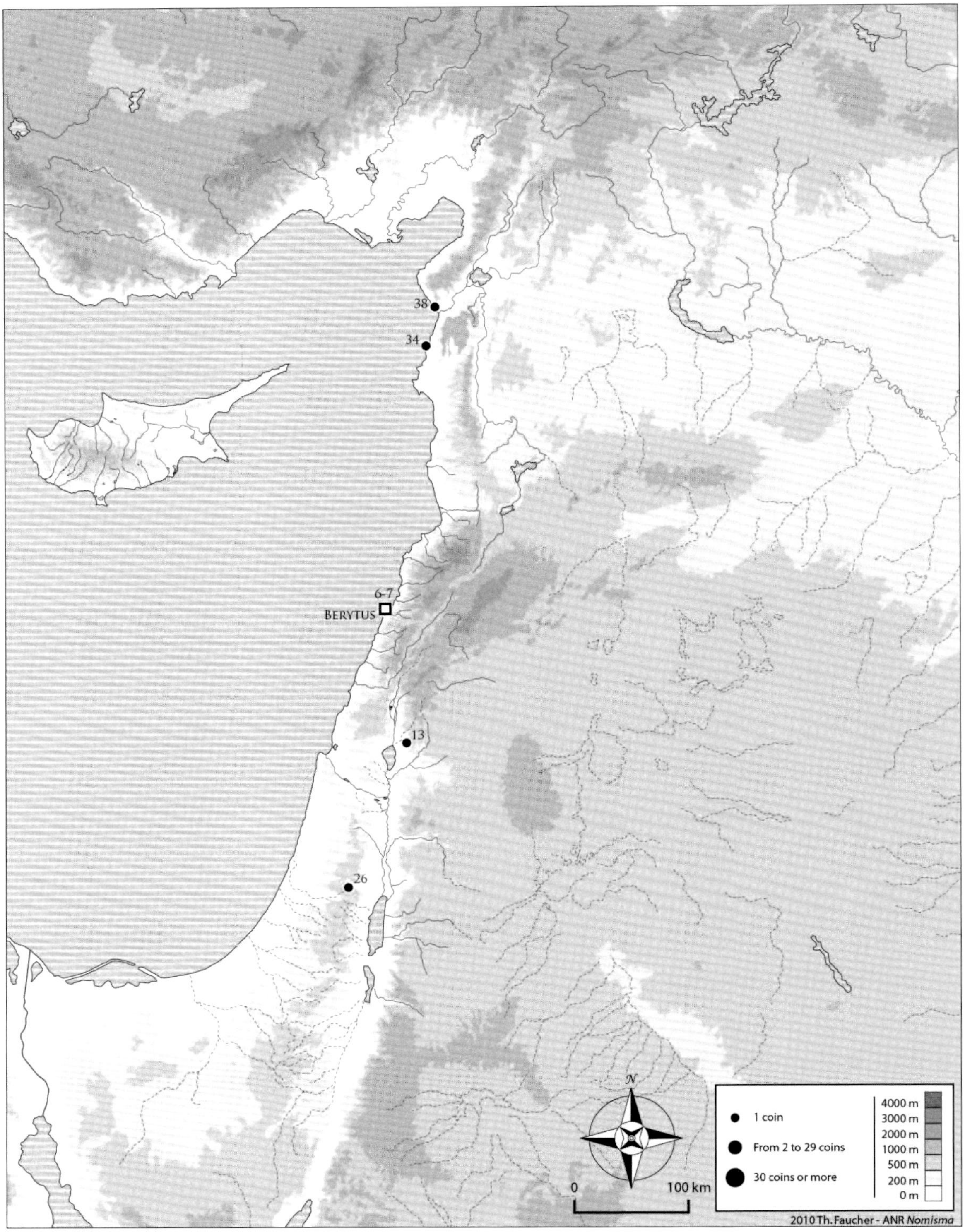

Map 35. Civic coins of Berytus in excavations.

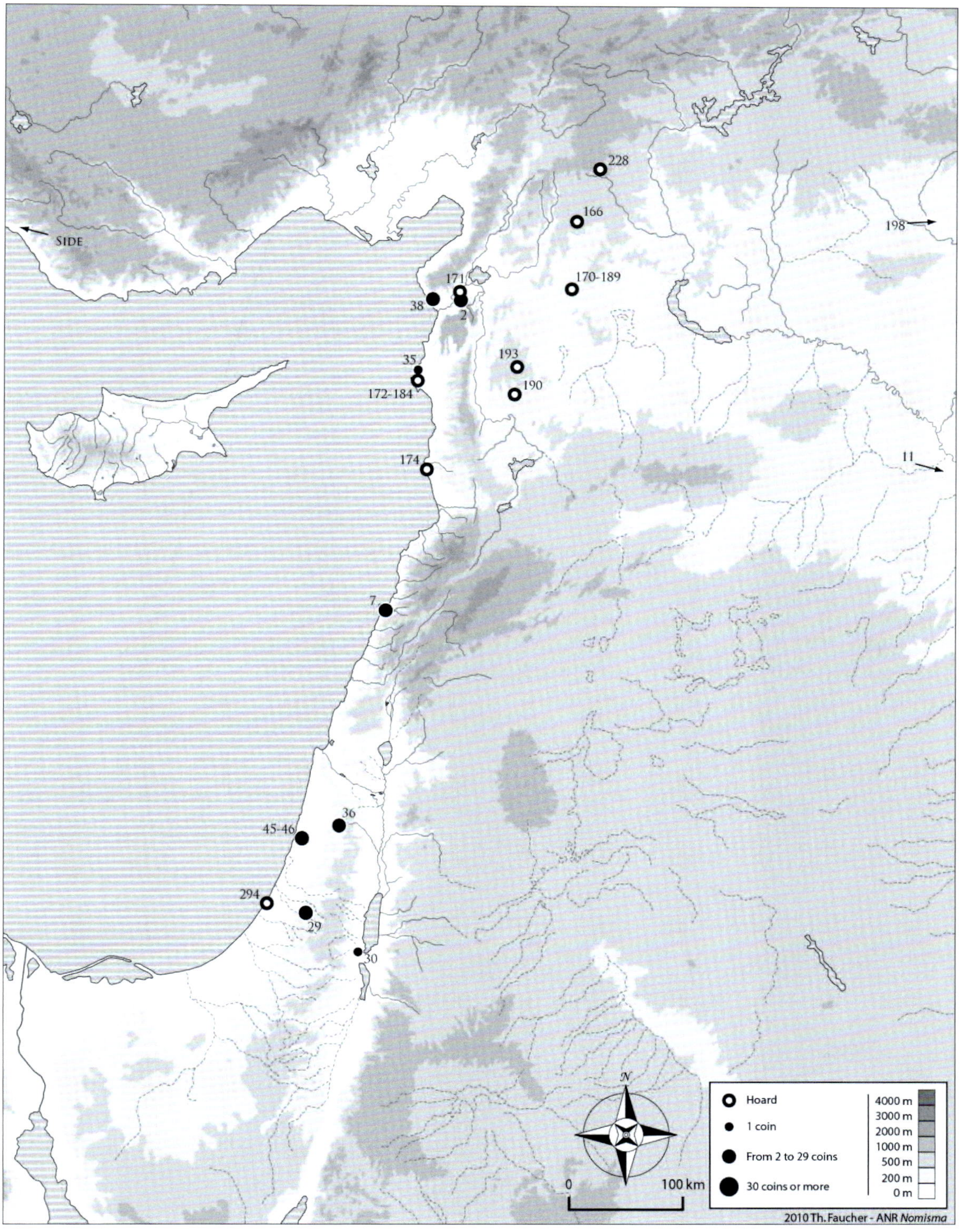

Map 36. Civic coins of Side in excavations.

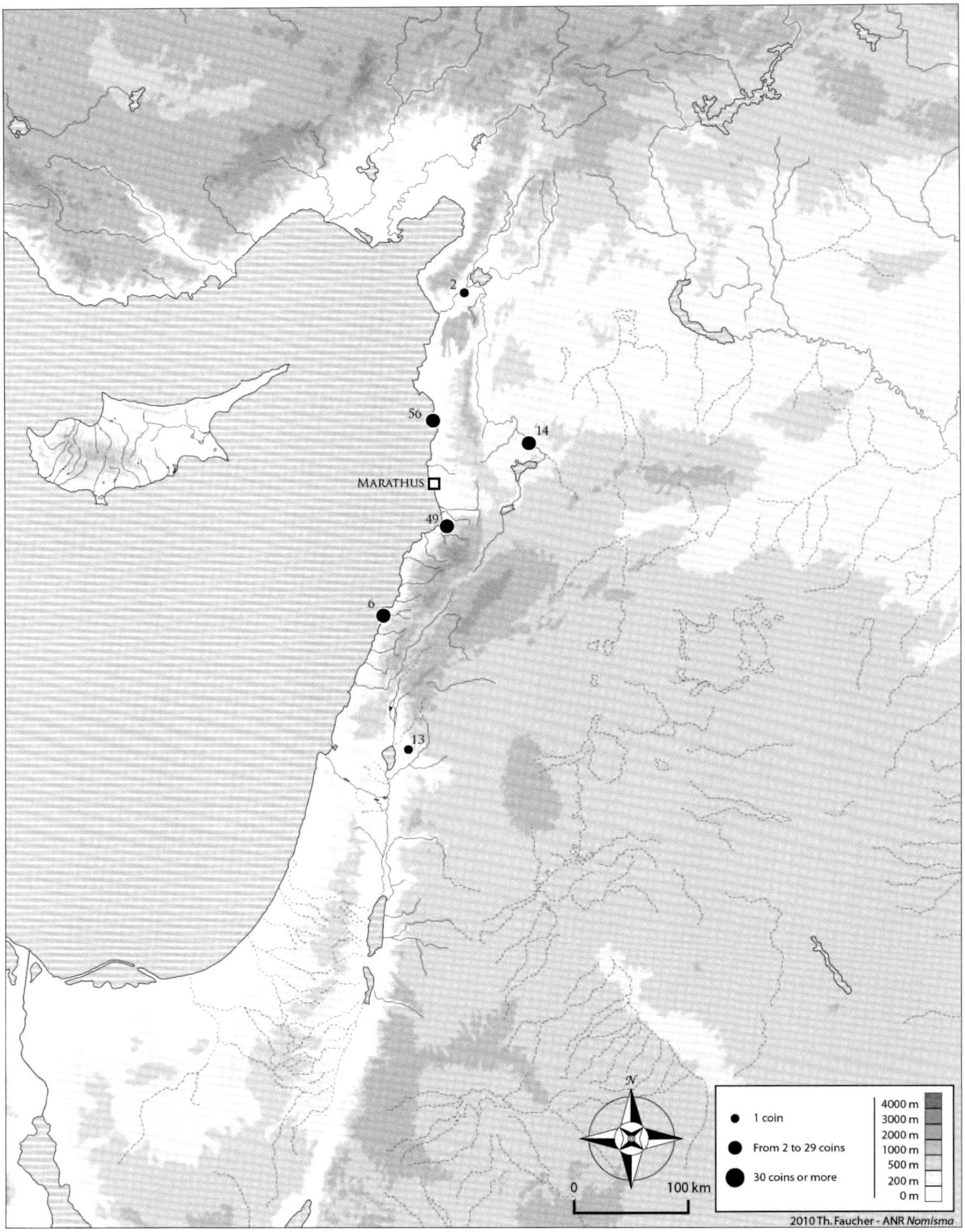

Map 37. Civic coins of Marathus in excavations.

Index